WHAT THEY SAID ABOUT

PART ONE OF
THE WAR OF THE YORKSHIRE GURKHAS

BAPTISM OF FIRE

The 5th Green Howards at the Battle of St Julien, during the Second Battle of Ypres, April 1915

These Territorials landed in France less than a week before the gas attack on 22nd April; and the immediacy of that experience, and subsequent ones, is brought to life by the quotations from the diary of the author's grandfather. Other personal accounts and contemporary sources are also used to make this a very readable account. Well-produced and illustrated (with some useful maps and many photographs of the men) this book is excellent value and does the 'Yorkshire Gurkhas' much credit.

Ann Clayton (Editor of 'Stand To!' - The Journal of the Western Front Association) - Liverpool

I read 'Baptism of Fire' within days of receiving it. It really is excellent and I must congratulate you. I do very much like the balance you have achieved in your historical narrative of the events of the 5th Battalion in the first part, and in the personal accounts in 'in their own write'. It works very well. I look forward to reading 'Bombardment!'

Major Philip Banbury - York

The book contains a lot of previously unpublished information, including first-hand accounts of the horrors of war, which will commend it to members of the regiment (past and present), students of military history and collectors of medals to the regiment.

Ian Hall - (reviewer with Coin & Medal News) - London

I bought a copy of 'Baptism of Fire' and wanted you to know how much I enjoyed it. I look forward to reading the rest in the series.

Steve Metcalfe - Northallerton

I admire people who tackle local or unit history. I read much of 'Baptism of Fire' and enjoyed it. It is through work like this, set in a wider and balanced context, that a real sense of a community's or unit's war effort can be appreciated. Well done.

Dr Peter Liddle - Leeds

I have just read 'Baptism of Fire' and would like to congratulate you on its publication and to say how much I enjoyed it. There is one line which sums up for me the fact these were ordinary Yorkshire lads, no different from us today. The line is in the letter from Corporal Thomas Little on page 83 which describes the horrors he has come across, but who still tells his family, 'The most needed thing we've wanted is a good drink of tea.' My wife would tell you that when abroad I become quite painful with my complaints that nowhere outside Yorkshire can one get a decent cup of tea. Well done. I look forward to your next publication.

Michael Parkin - Scarborough

I hope your book 'Baptism of Fire' is a success as you have obviously put a lot of research and effort into its production.

David Cox - Beverley

I would like to say how much I enjoyed 'Baptism of Fire'. I found it a remarkable 'read'. I think the fact I found it so enjoyable is that it takes me back to the days when my father related his horrors of trench warfare (he served with the 5th East Yorkshires). Please keep me informed of all future works.

David Martin - Driffield

I have just read 'Baptism of Fire' and think it is an exceptional piece of research. The extracts from your grandfather's diaries and the letters of brother Territorial soldiers serving with him tell an engrossing tale of those 'Saturday Night Soldiers'. To have included so much additional information, letters, poems and photos must have been a mammoth undertaking. I hope everyone else will be as impressed as I was. Every success with your future books.

Major D. Whitehead - Bridlington

Your book 'Baptism of Fire' is a credit to you.

Richard Hall - Redcar

I have just read 'Baptism of Fire' and consider it a well-written and well-presented book which I would have no hesitation in recommending to anyone. I look forward to the publication of the remainder of the series.

Tom Heron - Newcastle-upon-Tyne

I have just finished 'Baptism of Fire' and thoroughly enjoyed it. As a Green Howard and medal collector the references will certainly come in useful. I am looking forward to the next instalment of the 5th Territorial Battalion at war.

Kevin Morris - Middlesbrough

The book 'Baptism of Fire' comes alive through the words of the soldiers themselves, with letters, poems, photographs and memories from all over the region, including individual biographical details. I have to say that our battlefield tours will now be better informed, and I can use the examples to add a personal touch to my teaching. I recommend this book to all those who want to find ways of adding a 'local', and at times, very personal dimension to their teaching of the First World War.

Keith Melville (Head of History, Scalby School) - Scarborough

I recently received your book on the Yorkshire Gurkhas, I must say it was well laid out and very well documented - the last remark was made by an officer of the Royal Scots Greys whom I met on a pilgrimage to my late uncle's war grave. In fact your book brought about the pilgrimage as I followed up the story of my uncle who appears in it. Thanks for the 'push' your book gave me and I am certainly awaiting the next one on the bombardment.

Pete Johnson - Kirby-in-Ashfield

Through a gripping narrative, based on official records of the battle, supported by personal letters, diaries, poems and archive photographs, Mark tells how these young men faced their baptism of fire with extreme courage; how they fought for seven days on a diet of bully beef and biscuits, sipping water from the puddles in the bottom of their hastily constructed trenches. He tells how they faced barrage after barrage of German artillery fire which not only destroyed but also prevented their resupply. It was the 5th Green Howards' first action and they suffered terribly. Yet they advanced to fill the gap and support the Canadians, and together they stopped a full-scale German breakthrough and sealed the broken front line. It was this first action which earned the 5th Green Howards the nickname the 'Yorkshire Gurkhas' - a mark of respect from their front-line colleagues. I highly commend this work to Green Howards, students of military history and the people of Yorkshire and the north-east.

Major J. Roger Chapman - The Green Howards Regimental Museum, Richmond

BOMBARDMENT!

THE DAY THE EAST COAST BLED

Also available from Great Northern Publishing:

NON-FICTION: Non-Fiction/Military History/The Great War:

Baptism of Fire
Part One of the War of the Yorkshire Gurkhas
by Mark Marsay
ISBN: 0 9535204 0 4

Published April 2000 from Great Northern Publishing:

NON-FICTION: Non-Fiction/Military History/The Great War:

The Bairnsfather Omnibus
Bullets & Billets and From Mud To Mufti
by Captain Bruce Bairnsfather
ISBN: 0 9535204 2 0

Forthcoming Works from Great Northern Publishing:

FICTION:

Fiction/Adult Humour:
Hazardous to Health - An Obadiah Jones Novel
Under Surveillance - An Obadiah Jones Novel
A Bridge Too Far - An Obadiah Jones Novel
An Alien Affair

Science Fiction/Adult Humour:
Beyond The Void - An Erasmus Novel
The Love Colony - An Erasmus Novel
Howling At The Moon - An Erasmus Novel
Montana Springs

Western/Adult Humour:
Bitter Creek

Adult Fiction:
Dark Passions - Anthology
My Soul To Keep - Anthology
Intimate Strangers

Fantasy Humour:
Poddrantallingtondibble - In Search of Odenhall
Poddrantallingtondibble - Homeward Bound
Granny Capstick

Fantasy:
The Book Of Dale

Fiction/Childrens:
Teddy Buttons
A Time To Wish

BOMBARDMENT!

THE DAY THE EAST COAST BLED

Accounts of the German Naval Raids
on Scarborough and Whitby
on Wednesday, 16th December 1914

~

(with details of the raid on the Hartlepools)

~

and the German Submarine Attack on Scarborough
on Tuesday, 4th September 1917

MARK MARSAY

GREAT NORTHERN PUBLISHING

BOMBARDMENT!
The Day The East Coast Bled

Part Two of the War of the Yorkshire Gurkhas

ISBN: 0 9535204 1 2

~

Cover illustration 'Remember Scarborough' by Edith Kemp-Welch, 1914
Reproduced courtesy of Scarborough Borough Council.

~

~

~

First published by Great Northern Publishing 1999.

GREAT NORTHERN PUBLISHING
PO Box 202
Scarborough
North Yorkshire
YO11 3GE

Printed and bound by
Redwood Books
Trowbridge
Wiltshire

My great-grandparents, Alfred and Diana Stevenson,
with my grandfather Jim, pictured on his first leave from the
Western Front, at 2 Salisbury Street, Scarborough.

Contents

Maps

A Personal Message from Sir Jimmy Savile

Henry Ford, the great American car maker, once said, "History is bunk!"

Well, he may have made a revolutionary car, but his statement was simply 'bunk', because history is both instructive and entertaining.

This book, 'Bombardment! The Day The East Coast Bled', will, I feel sure, prove fascinating not only for the people of Scarborough, Whitby and Hartlepool but for people of all ages too. The older folk will no doubt *feel* the narrative and remember times gone by, or the tales told to them by their parents, aunts and uncles; whilst the youngsters who read it will, I hope, think of it not as something dry and dusty which happened a long time ago, but perhaps see it as something to which they can relate, such as a video game - *only acted out for real!*

Well done Mark - I am still trying to remember where I was on Wednesday, 16th December 1914!

Sir Jimmy Savile Kt., OBE., KCSG
Leeds
December 1999

Preface by Austin Mitchell

As a trained historian who has written history books, had a ring-side seat on history for three decades, and who has made both radio and television programmes about historical episodes, I can testify that nothing brings the past alive quite so well as television reconstructions. By combining eye-witness testimony with photographic and film evidence, all linked with a proper and, hopefully, accurate historical commentary, television has an incomparable power to recreate events. That was what a Yorkshire Television team, of which I was a part, did with the German shelling of Scarborough a quarter of a century ago. That film, based on David Mould's passionate interest, was a great event for me. It still lives on vividly in my memory now that I have become a blur on the collective subconscious.

It was also a film which, sadly, probably would not be made now, particularly by a regional programme, in these 'dumbed down' days. Back then however, it recreated a major, and for Yorkshire, a shocking event. Even better, it also provided a trigger, bringing lots more information and reminiscences flooding in. This led in time to David Mould's monograph (the book with the red cover), and now, nearly a quarter of a century later, to Mark's fascinating study of this major event in the history of Scarborough, Yorkshire and, indeed, the country.

Before Scarborough was shelled five months into the war to end all wars, Jingoism prevailed. Large numbers of troops had been sent to France to block the German onslaught. Yet the hard realities of war had not come over the seas to our island home front. Indeed there had been much talk of early victory, and a war over by Christmas. Yet just a few days before that the shock of war suddenly penetrated the peaceful everyday existence of Scarborough, Whitby and Hartlepool. The shelling stirred the country and shattered the complacency of an Admiralty which had too easily assumed that British naval might was impregnable, and less explicitly, that the coast further south, always better protected, even though it was less vulnerable, was more worthwhile defending than a rugged Yorkshire coast so much nearer the German naval bases.

Scarborough, like truth, was an early victim of that terrible war. As Europe settled down to a long trench siege which was to go on to 1918, this onslaught on our Yorkshire coast and its towns was distorted by both sides. The Germans portrayed it as a near triumph, inflicting great damage on us, our Navy and our morale, whilst their fleet had escaped scot-free. The British, rather more shamefacedly (for the great British Navy had been caught napping) portrayed it as an unimportant pin-prick, a picture a little difficult to reconcile with the other propaganda view of brutal Hunnish might turned against innocent Yorkshire women and children, almost as brutally as it had been against nuns and pregnant women in gallant little Belgium.

The shelling has never really escaped from that propaganda fog. First reports and descriptions were influenced by it. The fascinating descriptions of eye-witnesses were a thousand scattered and partial memories, some more accurate than others. They were not collected together or focused for more than half a century, by which time many had died and some remaining memories had hardened and distorted into a folk memory which, as any historian can testify, can be inaccurate, particularly in details, as well as over-coloured and unconsciously heroic. If only the whole population kept diaries and honestly recorded everything at the time, the historian's job would be so much easier. Just as the television producer's would if we all kept video diaries.

So Mark's task in re-telling the story has been a difficult one. Yet he has done it well and devotedly. For the first time he tells both sides of the story as well as mobilising every contemporary resource, and blending in the folk memory with an accurate and interesting record of the impact of the German shelling and its aftermath. His wonderful collection of photographs helps to bring it alive and his maps put it all in a context that is easy to follow.

This book is a triumph. A major event in Yorkshire's history now emerges from the mists and sea fret, just like the German battleships before Scarborough on that December day in 1914. I am proud to be a part in the crowd spectacular of prefaces and introductions which has assembled to praise it. Indeed, it is nice to be working again with Jimmy Savile and David Mould, as in the good old days, but our purpose now is to sing a combined hymn of praise for the book. It testifies to the way Yorkshire people will feel about Mark's fascinating book: the most complete picture yet, possibly ever, of that dramatic shock.

Austin Mitchell, MP
House of Commons
Westminster
December 1999

Foreword by David Mould

As the newsdesk assistant on Yorkshire Television's *Calendar* news programme in 1974, my first job of the day was to scan the regional newspapers for story ideas. This was how I found it - a short item in the *Yorkshire Post* noting that the 60th anniversary of the German naval bombardments of Scarborough and Whitby was coming up in a week or so. I was intrigued. History had always been my favourite subject. I had studied World War One at school, but no teacher or textbook had ever mentioned these raids. I passed the clipping to the news editor, whose reaction was not encouraging. *"Nowt in it, lad,"* he snorted. *"No one cares about something that happened that long ago. Anyway, it's not a TV story . . . you don't have any pictures."* I deferred to his judgement, but filed away the clipping, determined to investigate further - if only to satisfy my own curiosity.

Two years later, I wangled a film crew for a day to interview three people in Scarborough who remembered the raid. The response to the short feature on *Calendar* was remarkable - a stream of letters and phone calls from viewers who had lived through the raid or whose older relatives had talked about it. Did I know about what happened in Wykeham Street and at the Grand Hotel? Had I heard the story about PC Hunter's miraculous escape? Were the Germans *really* planning to invade?

With viewer interest, I was able to command more resources - a feature film crew, a director and the incomparable Austin Mitchell (then a major *Calendar* presenter, now the Labour MP for Grimsby) as interviewer and narrator. I even found archival footage of the German ships and of a funeral parade through the streets of Scarborough. The fifteen-minute documentary, *'The Day They Shelled Scarborough,'* was shown in 1977 and was repeated twice in the Yorkshire Television viewing region. More phone calls and letters followed - even one from Australia. People sent photographs. Retired naval officers wrote to offer analyses of how the action fitted into the German strategy to engage the British Grand Fleet. I pressed on with my research, eventually producing the forty-eight page illustrated booklet *'Remember Scarborough 1914!'* the following year (1978).

In history, no one has the last word on any subject. There is always more to discover and learn, different ways in which to interpret evidence, new approaches to understanding the past. *'Remember Scarborough 1914!'* (or *'the book with the red cover'* as it has apparently come to be known) was necessarily brief and incomplete. Not even large enough to be a coffee-table book - more of an end-table book, in fact!

Mark's painstaking research offers not only more information than previous accounts, but new ways of interpreting events whose significance stretched far beyond the north-eastern coastal towns and one day in December 1914.

As a social and media historian, what continues to fascinate me most about the raids are not the facts or statistics, but how the events figured - and continue to figure - in the collective and individual consciousness of the past. In terms of military strategy, it was a minor episode, an attempt (perhaps ill-conceived) to draw the British Grand Fleet into a decisive action. The tragedy of the bombardments - for those who lost their lives or whose relatives did - was real and lasting, but in relative terms the human cost was not high; more people died on a quiet day on one section of the Western Front than in these raids. However, the raids shocked a nation which had for so long believed it was an invincible naval power, with a fleet that would protect its shores from invaders. The action, celebrated as a great victory in the German press, gave the Central Powers a fleeting propaganda triumph. The British government, struggling to mobilise the country for what some now realised was going to be a protracted war in Europe, gave it what we now call 'spin', playing heavily on patriotic public reaction in its recruiting drives.

As Mark notes in his introduction, it is impossible to verify and cross-check every contemporary account (though I know he has tried extremely hard to do so). There are just too many variations and conflicting versions. This is the nature and texture of human experience. No two people who experience the same event will recall it the same way; their versions of the past will be shaped by what they saw and felt at the time, who they were then, who they are now, and a host of other social and cultural variables. If we go to past events seeking some definitive version, we are likely to be frustrated and disappointed, because history is by nature messy and incomplete. Social and oral historians such as Paul Thompson in his classic work *'The Voice of the Past'* have argued persuasively that *what actually happened* is maybe not as important as *what people remember*, how they personally reconstruct events to make sense of their lives and the world in which they live. This book is important not only in its attempt to reconstruct the events of the 16th December 1914, and to put them in context, but in showing how the bombardments have found a place in both individual and collective memory.

David H. Mould, Ph.D.,
Professor of Telecommunications
Ohio University, USA
(Former staff journalist with Yorkshire Television's Calendar
and author of 'Remember Scarborough 1914!')
Shade, Ohio
December 1999

Author's Introduction

Those who have read the first volume of *'The War of the Yorkshire Gurkhas'* will know that whilst in the course of preparing a larger work based on the diaries of my grandfather, James Stevenson MM, detailing the story of the 5th Green Howards in the Great War, I have amassed so much material on a number of significant events that it would be impossible to include it all in a single volume. Therefore, as I have an abundance of material relating to the bombardments of Scarborough and Whitby in the early months of the war, I felt I should include it in the series as a book in its own right.

Over the years many 'souvenir' booklets and brochures have appeared featuring photographs alongside a potted, or abridged version of events. Occasionally someone has taken to re-printing a contemporary booklet on the subject (such as those produced by the Scarborough printers E. T. W. Dennis and Sons, and the Whitby printers The Abbey Press - part of Horne & Son Printers and Stationers who were also responsible for the *Whitby Gazette*). To the best of my knowledge no one has ever put together the bombardments of Scarborough, Whitby and Hartlepool in one book, other than in a souvenir photo-booklet.

The most recent account of the Scarborough bombardment has been the forty-eight page booklet by David Mould, (published in 1978) entitled *'Remember Scarborough 1914!'* (and which local people often refer to as 'the book with the red cover'). But, to the best of my knowledge, this is the first time the available material (including a number of David's original correspondences with survivors - for which I am indebted) has been gathered in one place and been written in such a way as to give a chronological feel to those December events. I am indebted too to Scarborough historian Marie Belfitt, for her diligent research into the mystery of Alice Painter; and to author John Ward, for making his material on Hartlepool available to me. I also carry a burden of debt to a number of other individuals who have helped or assisted me in one way or another, and a full 'roll of honour' is given at the back of the book.

With regard to Whitby's bombardment, I am unaware of any previously published work which deals with it in any depth at all. In the case of Hartlepool a number of works have been published and one or two are considered 'authoritative', although, even with the best of intentions, there are discrepancies in these which, although not dealing with Hartlepool in depth, I have attempted to rectify.

My grandfather, who died in May 1996 (aged 101) was the last of the *'original'* 5th Green Howards; those who landed in France in April 1915. The Regiment was officially designated **Alexandra, Princess of Wales's Own Yorkshire Regiment** - or known simply as the Yorkshire Regiment. However, I refer to it as the **Green Howards** (the designation officially approved in 1920) because my grandfather always referred to himself as such - ***"A Green Howard, and proud of it."*** Having got to know men of the Regiment in the course of my research, and counting many among them as friends, I understand a little better what it means to them to be Green Howards, and so use the title in my work as a mark of respect. At the time of the east coast bombardments the majority of the 5th Green Howards were training in Newcastle (a handful were on garrison duties at towns along the east coast - including at least a company at Scarborough), and all were devastated by the news of the German attack on their homes.

Although the narrative and the events described herein do not in any great way involve the Battalion, I have chosen to include it as one of the several planned volumes because it not only involved Scarborians, but had a direct impact on their antipathy towards the Germans; as was shown by the massive influx of recruits in the days and weeks following the bombardment. This is also the reason the Scarborough 'account' takes such precedence. The 5th Green Howards not only went to the Western Front to do their bit for God, King and Country, but went to get their own back on an enemy who had perpetrated such a cowardly attack on the innocents of their home town. It was largely due to the shelling of the town that so many young men from the region joined the 5th Green Howards and fought so ferociously in their first battle at St Julien in April 1915 - where they earned the nickname 'The Yorkshire Gurkhas'. That battle is dealt with in detail in '*Baptism of Fire*', the first book in this series. This account of the bombardment has been written to put that action and their courage, bravery and sense of duty into context.

This work is not an academic tome, but rather the narrative is intended to provide the reader with a guide, a platform, from which to view, in context, the letters and verse of the men and women who are mentioned in its passages, or who underwent that terrible ordeal.

I have endeavoured to provide an accurate chronological account of events in each of the towns. In some instances this has proved difficult because of the conflicting nature of various research materials - but I feel that none of these discrepancies are of a major nature and hope that by combining several accounts I have produced a single 'viable' account. In the various accounts taken from the many witnesses in the aftermath there are also discrepancies, some quite glaring. However, I hold my hands up and beg the reader's indulgence, for it is very difficult, if not wholly impossible at this late stage, to verify every single fact and figure relating to that winter morning's events. For example, many contemporary accounts vary slightly on the exact times the attacks began. At Scarborough some have it as just before eight o'clock, whilst others have it at eight, and others at five past eight. The same is true of Whitby, though an hour later of course. I have opted for the most probable times as being 8.00am at Scarborough and 9.00am at Whitby, as, even if the bombardments did not start bang on the ascribed hour, it is highly likely the Germans, working with typical Teutonic zeal and thoroughness to a pre-defined timetable, had intended them to. In the case of Hartlepool the times are about as precise as it is possible to get because of the military and naval units involved there.

For the purpose of pursuing some form of clarity from the chaos of the various accounts I have assumed (rightly or wrongly - and no doubt 'historians' and 'military experts' will have their own view) that the bombardment of Scarborough fell into two distinct 'phases'; the first, while the German ships steamed southward with their guns in several large volumes of its own, instead of as part of *'The War of the Yorkshire Gurkhas'*. A comprehensive diary of attacks against the British mainland made by German naval and air units is included in the indexes at the end of the book.

With specific regard to the losses to shipping mentioned in the book, I have confined myself to recording just those ships lost directly to mines off this coast between 16th December 1914 and 1st December 1916. Although numerous losses occurred in the North Sea - due to mines, submarines and enemy actions - throughout the war, I did not consider it appropriate to give a comprehensive list of them here. Again, there appear to exist no detailed accounts relating to each and every incident and this has made verification in some cases quite difficult, if not impossible.

Some readers may question the need to have included such items as the Archbishop of York's address at the subsequent memorial service in Scarborough: I included them because I felt they provided an insight into the high patriotic feelings raging at the time, where nothing could cow the nation and where all men were exhorted to take up arms in the 'righteous cause'. Much later in the war, especially after the carnage of the Somme and Passchendaele, many began to question the ethics behind this great crusade, including many of the same 'churchmen' who had at first urged every man to take up arms and go to battle. Many of my own generation and today's youngsters tend to overlook the influence the 'church' had in society in the first half of the 20th century; churchmen, like politicians, were considered by the masses to be their 'betters' and were generally held in high esteem and their words and views given (often wrongly) a great deal of credence and respect. It is no accident that many churchmen were actively involved in recruitment and that the church as a whole upheld the righteousness of the allied cause - even when the high causality lists began appearing in the press.

The many newspaper extracts are also used to highlight the propaganda value of the national and to a lesser extent, the local press, being used in the Great War to its full extent for perhaps the first time in a major conflict. I also believe that all of the material included in this book is necessary and serves to provide the reader with the widest possible historical and personal coverage of the events.

For any errors or omissions I apologise, and if appraised of them will endeavour to correct them in subsequent works. I would also like to apologise for the quality of some of the photographs used, many taken from old newspapers and third or fourth generation copies, but because they are an integral part of the work I felt they should be included nonetheless. I had hoped that my general appeals on the radio and in regional and local papers would have borne fruit in uncovering more 'original' photographs, of which there were literally hundreds, many taken by the numerous local photographers in the towns, especially Scarborough, in 1914, and more personal accounts but alas it was not to be. I would also have liked to have been able to provide fuller biographical details of all those killed, but no relatives contacted me and I have had to assume that either no one is left who remembers anything of note, or that the present descendants of those mentioned have no interest in adding anything to the record of their ancestors. I was also let down over material relating to the later compensation claims, which I had hoped would verify much of the damage caused and the costs incurred. But even with these setbacks I, and those heavily involved with the book, believe this to be the most complete account of the three bombardments to date.

With regard to spellings used throughout the book I have opted to use the most common form of a particular name or place, or the form prevailing and most commonly used at the time of the bombardments. However, in two specific instances it is most important to note where the spellings of the surnames of *Bertha McEntyre* and *Mary Prew* differ with those used by other writers. In each case I have opted for the spelling as used on the birth and death certificates, as opposed to those used in various contemporary newspapers and on the Scarborough War Memorial (McIntyre and Prue). Having consulted with the Imperial War Museum's department for the 'National Inventory of War Memorials', and with the Commonwealth War Graves Commission (with regard to general war memorials) it was brought home to me how often names have appeared incorrectly spelt on local memorials up and down the country, due largely to the way in which they were organised and set up by makeshift committees, who often advertised in the newspapers for names to be sent in and many of whom failed to maintain adequate records of their proceedings. As I was aware of the seventy-six-year-old error regarding Alice Painter's name on the memorial, I felt it wise to opt for the spellings used on 'official' documents.

Since 'Baptism of Fire' was published I have received a large number of letters in praise of it and I would like to sincerely thank everyone who has written for their words of support and encouragement - it is heartening to know one's work is not only read, but strikes a chord with so many readers. I also had a large number of letters whose authors were eagerly awaiting the publication of this second book in the series. The wait has perhaps been a little long, but I hope you will agree the book was worth waiting for and I look forward to hearing from you.

It is largely accidental that the publication of this book coincides with the 85th Anniversary of the bombardments, and the final month of the millennium. But because it does, I hope this account will prove to be the one the folk of Scarborough and Whitby take to heart and keep on their shelves for many years to come. It will be interesting to see if someone comes along and produces a more definitive account for the 100th Anniversary in 2014. Until then, I hope this book will suffice to tell Scarborough and Whitby's story. Were you to ask any person born in the three towns what they believed the most momentous event in that town was in the last century (even, dare one suggest, the last millennium) I have no doubt most would cite the bombardments of 1914.

It is in honour of my Grandfather's service, and for his providing me with the incentive to write about the Great War, that I have dedicated this series of books - 'The War of the Yorkshire Gurkhas' - to his memory. However, I dedicate this particular volume to my great-grandparents, Alfred and Diana Stevenson, who lived through the terrible ordeal of the bombardment at 2 Salisbury Street, Scarborough, and also to the memories of those innocents who died on that devastating December morning eighty-five years ago.

Mark Marsay
Scarborough
December 1999

For the death they dealt in the morning mist,
For the coward blow of the mailed fist,
For the Yorkshire blood set flowing then,
This is the vow sworn by Yorkshire men.

~

For the deaths they dealt in the morning mist,
In an undefended town,
For the sorrows of their sowing,
For the wounds of their bestowing,
For the griefs that pass all showing,
We will hunt the raiders down.

~

We'll pay in full the debts we owe
Though red with blood the rivers flow,
Yet once again our foes shall know
That blow for blow is Britain's way,
And what Britain owes she'll surely pay.

Taken from the poem
'Yorkshire's Reply To The Raid'
by J. T. Mullett.

Scarborough

An Account of the German Naval Raid on Scarborough on Wednesday, 16th December 1914

In those balmy summer days of 1914, under clear blue skies on beaches basking in bright sunlight, few Scarborough folk could have predicted war by the beginning of August. Once war came it would envelop the world, dragging the youth of nations to fight and die on battlefields filled with horror and carnage a long way from home.

How many, even when the war was a reality, could have foreseen Scarborough's hapless part in the greater conflict? How many could have hazarded a guess at the level of the town's sacrifice? Or the sacrifices of her neighbours along the east coast?

On 4th August 1914, with Germany having failed to provide assurances over the neutrality of Belgium, Britain declared war. On 6th August a group of prominent local shopkeepers - among them John Watson Rowntree & Sons, J. L. Hopwood, Wallis & Blakeley and William C. Land & Company - issued the following open letter to the good folk of Scarborough:

> *We wish to assure our friends that during the war we shall endeavour to carry on our businesses in every respect as hitherto.*
>
> *We shall try to reserve our stocks entirely for our own customers, and only make such increased charges as are consistent with advancing markets. All orders will, of course, be subject to our having the goods on hand, and must be limited to moderate quantities.*
>
> *The poorer section of the people cannot afford to lay in large stores of goods, and in their interests, as well as those of the community in general, we would respectfully urge our friends to refrain from any attempt to buy in excessive quantities, and thus avoid the raising of prices to an unnecessary and unreasonable figure.*
>
> *To discourage the giving of orders in excess of normal requirements, our deliveries will be regulated by the supplies we have on hand, and goods will be*

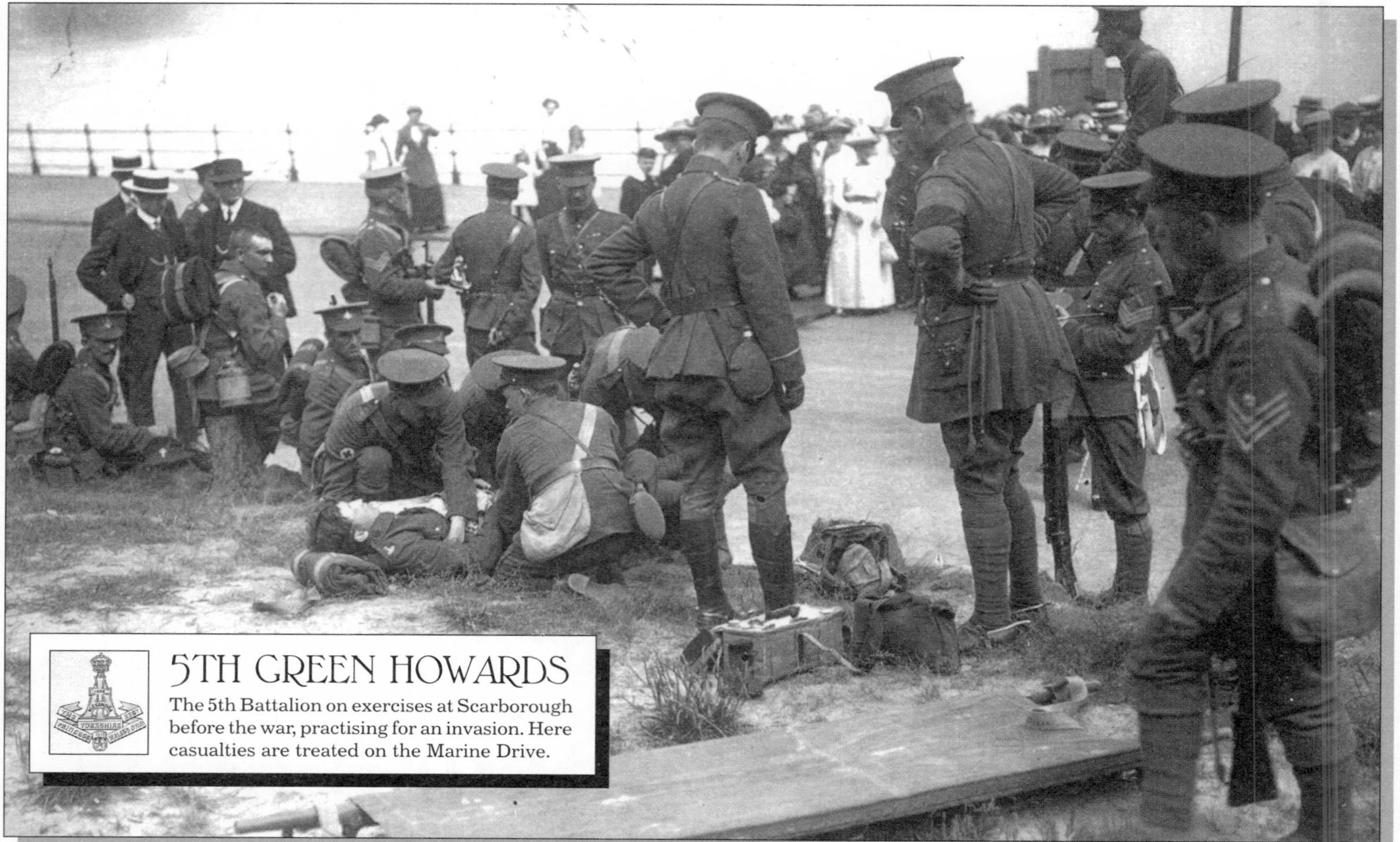

5TH GREEN HOWARDS

The 5th Battalion on exercises at Scarborough before the war, practising for an invasion. Here casualties are treated on the Marine Drive.

booked out at the current price at the time of delivery, not of order given. The financial crisis arising from the war compels us to consider carefully not only the general question of credit to all our customers, but our own position and credit as buyers on terms of cash against delivery.

Under these circumstances, and to enable us to constantly and evenly replenish stocks, we respectfully ask such of our friends as are in a position to do so to send us cash or cheques on receipt of accounts, as a steady influx of cash, with a steady replenishment of goods, will help us to keep things as near a normal level as possible - which is absolutely essential in all interests.

Panic, we should endeavour to minimise, as the hoarding of food creates exorbitant prices in times of stress; it should be the endeavour of everyone to avert this.

Respectfully asking for your hearty co-operation and support in our endeavours to continue our business at normal and reasonable prices.

And many people, in those early days, no doubt believed that that - a tightening of belts - would probably be the extent of the town's involvement in a fracas that most thought would be done and dusted by Christmas. True, some of her sons were already with the forces, and more were joining the colours, eager to join the British Expeditionary Force (BEF), commanded by Sir John French - *before it was too late.*

Yes, the sons of Scarborough had and would go to war, to those far-flung battlefields, there to do their duty to their King; fight, and in many cases, die for their country. But that was a sacrifice to be reckoned with, a believed known quantity - for who could have envisaged the terrible carnage as the war ground on on the Western Front, the Somme and Passchendaele, and further afield in the Dardanelles, at Suvla Bay and Gallipoli. The sacrifice that no one had foreseen was that which was to be made by the innocents of the town, for within a few short months Scarborough (along with Whitby and Hartlepool) would be horribly and tragically drawn into the conflict in a way that few other British towns would ever be.

Those first few heady months of the war had seen the BEF land in France with high hopes of putting a stop to the steamroller-like German advance; high hopes that were quickly dashed by an enemy superior in both number and the equipment and means with which to wage a modern war. At home, volunteers, part of the first 100,000, rushed to enlist and swelled the ranks of the regular Army and the Territorial Forces, bringing them up to fighting strength should they be called upon. The early days of training for these fresh-faced recruits took place in their local towns, the places of their enlistment. Daily they were mustered, paraded and marched to and fro in quiet fields and streets; parades and drills, drills and parades. This was the nearest the war had come to many townsfolk.

Within a matter of weeks those first volunteers had travelled to join their regiments and battalions, some still in training, while others were shipped off to the front to make good the heavier than expected losses. Those earmarked for the Territorial Forces thought they may never see action at the front; while others believed they were destined for garrison duties in Egypt, South Africa or India, where they would free the regular troops for war service; and yet others openly stated the war would be over by the time they had finished mucking about with all this training nonsense - *'Give us rifles and let us at the Hun!'* was their cry. But the war went on and they saw little of it.

5TH GREEN HOWARDS

1: Marching through Scarborough. 2: At a pre-war summer camp.
3: Marching along the Marine Drive before the war.
4: New recruits going through their paces on the Athletic Ground.

The situation across the channel was bleak to say the least. The BEF had all but been routed at Mons. Then, elements of the Force, commanded by General Sir Smith-Dorien, had rallied and fought the Germans to a brief standstill at Le Cateau; thus allowing the bulk of the beleaguered British forces to withdraw without being encircled, something which had been seriously threatened.

At home the volunteers continued to walk into their local recruitment offices, and the folk of the nation went about their business as usual.

The battle of the Marne saw the BEF rally before the constant German onslaught and push them back for five consecutive days and nights. The nation read of this sterling advance by their lads in both local and national papers and rejoiced. Soon it would all be over, with the Germans put in their place and the lads in khaki home for Christmas. However, the battle of the Aisne saw the Germans hold their ground and the BEF's remarkable advance was brought to a shuddering halt. At home it was reported as a hiccup, a temporary blip in an otherwise successful offensive - which would continue in a matter of days. But the advance, once halted never began again. Instead there followed the battles of La Bassée, Messines and Armentières, and still there was no substantive breakthrough.

The first battle of Ypres, in Flanders - consisting of several battles at Langemarck, Gheluvelt and Nonne Bosschen - proved indecisive, and left the British seriously weakened and vulnerable against an enemy well supplied and well dug-in.

Back home in Yorkshire, the devastating news of the decimation of the 2nd Green Howards, after their heroic stand at the Menin Cross Roads, during the Battle for Gheluvelt, was reported and hit home - hard. From a strength of over a thousand men the Battalion had been reduced to just three hundred. The 5th Green Howards - Scarborough's 'local' battalion, filled with local men - a Territorial unit which had volunteered for overseas service, now knew something of what they were to face when they finally arrived in France. Meanwhile, replacements were hastily gathered and rushed out to fill the gaps left by the fallen British troops.

It was obvious to everyone now that the war would last longer than most had predicted, and with this realisation the attitudes of the soldiers in the line - including those from Scarborough - hardened towards those who refused to enlist:

Just a few lines to let you know I'm all right and in the best of health, up to the present. I've got everything a soldier requires, and anything else I want I'll send for. Many thanks for the 'Pictorial' and 'Evening News'. They're very interesting to read in the gun-pits.

You say you had a letter from Joe [brother] stating he was in the coast battle. How he lets you know is marvellous! His officers can't read his letters or else you'd never get them! I thought once I was going to come across him, but we moved away; but I heard he was all right.

I see John [brother] every other day. He's in our column. He was made Bombardier the other day.

As regards rough times, we're all having our share, but the way in which things are being done now is easy. I could stick this for months. We only do one day out of three in the gun-pits, and we've plenty of clothes to keep out the cold; and food - why, we've tons! In fact it's better than manoeuvres.

A certain number of officers are getting 10 days' leave and it's under consideration for Staff-Sergeants and Sergeants too. So I think things are as well

FRANZ VON HIPPER

Admiral Franz von Hipper (1863 to 1932) was the commander of the German High Seas Fleet Battle-cruisers in 1914. He led the attacks against the north-east coast on 16th December 1914, using *HIMS Seydlitz* as his flagship. The Group was nicknamed 'Hipper's Babykillers' by the British press. He succeeded Scheer as commander of the German High Seas Fleet in August 1918. Hipper's plan to attack the British Grand Fleet with the entire German Fleet was seen as suicidal and led to the Kiel Mutiny in November 1918. He presided over the German Fleet's surrender in 1918, before his retirement from active service.

1

2

ALFRED VON TIRPITZ

Admiral Alfred von Tirpitz (1849-1930) was the Prussian naval minister from 1897. By 1914, having lost the arms race to the Royal Navy, he was pessimistic about the German Navy's chances when war broke out. He was an advocate for unrestricted submarine warfare. However, he resigned in March 1916 over continued restrictions on the use of U-boats.

3

FRIEDRICH VON INGENOHL

Admiral Friedrich von Ingenohl (1857-1933) was head of the German High Seas Fleet in 1913. As an Admiral in the Great War he suffered reverses at Heligoland and elsewhere in 1914. He was removed from command in 1915. Succeeded by Admiral Hipper.

as can be expected, considering we're fighting the biggest military country in the world.

You talk about conscription. I only wish it would become law so as to move a few of those fainthearted ones out of it - I think it's disgraceful for young healthy men to be hanging about their mothers' apron strings and the country hard up for men. I'd be ashamed to walk the streets of England nowadays without a rifle and a bandoleer. Girls are just as capable of clerking and serving behind the counter as a man.

Do they realise the vacant places in the trenches and how much harder it is for their own flesh and blood to fight an enemy three or four times their number?

No, I suppose all they think about is dressing up and seeing their best girl!

But I can assure you that 'Kitchener of Khartoum' [Lord Kitchener, the Secretary of State for War] will have no humbug. If he wants men he'll get them one way or another. If it comes to conscription they should make them wear a badge, so we can tell a conscript from a good-hearted volunteer.

But I trust that the young men of England, especially Scarborians, will rally to the undefeated Flag, and help keep it flying for the freedom of our beloved King and country. Put this in the paper for them to read, and if they shirk from the call after this they should be kicked out of the country as undesirables. We in the gun-pits and trenches are sick of reading about the sloppy and childish excuses some make when asked why they don't enlist. You can put all the excuses together and make them into one; 'Health and strength good, but heart in the wrong place.'
[Sergeant William Jennings, Royal Field Artillery, writing home.]

Only the onset of a terrible winter slowed the frantic pace of those first few months of war, as the heavy rain left the low-lying Flanders plains one vast sea of mud. On the Western Front nothing moved, neither side made gains; a stalemate ensued, and with it the misery and blight of the trenches had begun.

From the Western Front to the Home Front

The war looked set to drag on into the New Year, past the Christmas end that many had first espoused, when suddenly the carnage and blood of the battlefields was transferred from the Western Front to the home front, as undefended towns on the north-east coast were subjected to an horrific attack from the sea by the German Navy.

Ingenohl's Plan ~ The Sea War

On 16th November 1914, the German Admiral, Friedrich von Ingenohl, had submitted a plan for a raid on Britain's north-east coast. The plan called for the bombardment of a small number of coastal towns which it was hoped would not only raise the morale of the German Fleet, but might also provoke a portion of the British Grand Fleet into action - an action the Germans were determined to win and thereby seriously reduce the strength of the British Fleet.

The plan's lesser aims were to tie down a portion of the British Fleet, disproportionate to the German raiding group; to inflict damage on a number of British ports and their industrial resources and infrastructure; and to bring home to the British people Germany's capacity to wage war against their homeland. However, what with bad weather and the need to wait for the *Von der Tann* to undergo necessary mechanical repairs, the month came and went.

HIMS VON DER TANN
Kapitän zur See Hahn

FLAGSHIP
Rear-Admiral Tapken

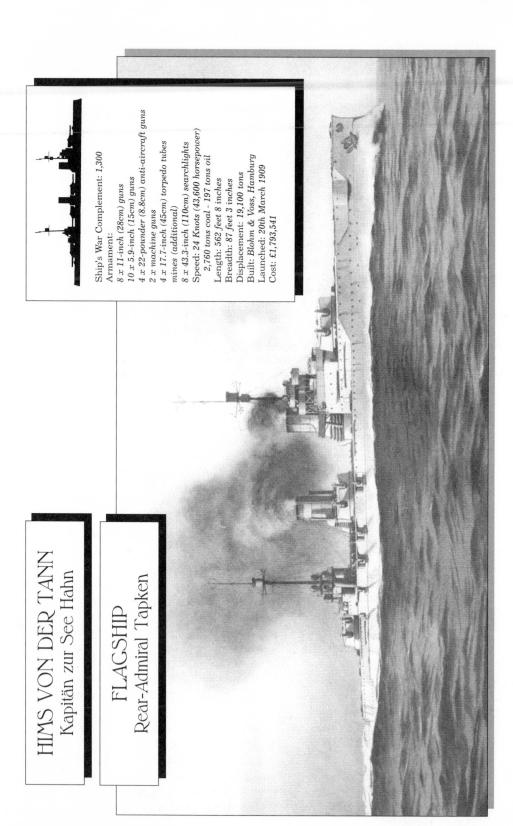

Ship's War Complement: *1,300*
Armament:
8 x 11-inch (28cm) guns
10 x 5.9-inch (15cm) guns
4 x 22-pounder (8.8cm) anti-aircraft guns
2 x machine guns
4 x 17.7-inch (45cm) torpedo tubes
mines (additional)
8 x 43.3-inch (110cm) searchlights
Speed: *24 Knots (43,600 horsepower)*
2,760 tons coal - 197 tons oil
Length: *562 feet 8 inches*
Breadth: *87 feet 3 inches*
Displacement: *19,100 tons*
Built: *Blohm & Voss, Hamburg*
Launched: *20th March 1909*
Cost: *£1,793,541*

Since the success of the Royal Navy's actions in the Heligoland Bight on 28th August, when the Germans had lost the three cruisers *Köln*, *Mainz* and *Ariadne* and a destroyer and had three more cruisers damaged, the German Navy had responded with the sinking of the British cruisers *Aboukir*, *Hogue* and *Cressy* by the submarine *U9*. On 27th October the brand-new British dreadnought *Audacious* was mined and sunk off Northern Ireland. This was followed on 1st November by the destruction of two out of four ships in Admiral Cradock's squadron, which was patrolling off the South American coast. The ships had been caught by Vice-Admiral von Spee's Pacific cruiser squadron at night, silhouetted against the sky by a rising moon. In what was to become known as the Battle of Coronel (off the coast of Chile) the Germans sank Cradock's flagship, *Good Hope*, and the *Monmouth*, and damaged the *Glasgow* - however she managed to escape, as did the *Otranto*. Nevertheless the German Navy's high command was jubilant - until the British decided to exact revenge with the destruction of Admiral von Spee's squadron. This engagement finally took place off the Falkland Islands on 8th December when the German cruisers *Scharnhorst* and *Gneisenau*, and the light cruisers *Nürnberg* and *Leipzig* were sunk. The morale of the German Navy took a nosedive, and now, more than ever, the proposed raids on the English east coast were considered vitally important to German interests.

Another possible reason for the raids was that Kitchener had raised his 'first hundred thousand' and there were genuine fears among the German High Command of what such a force, thrown into the fray on the Western Front, might accomplish. At the time there were rumours of a German invasion of England and the threat was not taken lightly. The Germans may well have hoped to create a public outcry, following the raids, for Kitchener's New Army to be kept in England and used for home defence.

Three days after Admiral von Ingenohl's plan was submitted to the Kaiser he approved it and almost a month later than intended, in mid-December, the entire focus of the war shifted suddenly and dramatically as death and destruction, mayhem and madness, visited the slumbering towns of the north-east coast.

North Sea Minefields

Extensive mining by both the British and German Navies had resulted in massive minefields some thirty miles off England's north-east coast. The British Admiralty had declared two major danger areas for shipping, one extending from the Farne Islands to the Tees, the other from Flamborough Head to the Humber. Diagrams and charts had been issued to the British Merchant Fleet using the area, but at least one set of these is thought to have fallen into the hands of the German Navy when the *SS Glitra* was sunk off the Norwegian coast by the submarine *U17* (Britain's first U-boat victim) on 20th October. Coupled to this was the extensive knowledge of the area of the submarine commander, Captain Wegener of *U27*, chosen to lead the enemy battle group to their targets after a period of heavy reconnaissance in the area. Wegener had correctly reported weak coastal defences and the virtual non-existence of covering British minefields. Travelling with the battle group was one of Wegener's most trusted men, Oberleutnant Ahlefeld. Between them, and with the aid of the captured British maps, they would lead the scouting group safely through the minefields.

THE BOMBARDMENT!

It was with horror that Scarborough, undefended by so much as a single shore battery, awoke on the morning of Wednesday, 16th December 1914; the entire populace startled

HIMS DERFFLINGER
Kapitän zur See von Reuter

Ship's War Complement: *1,400*
Armament:
8 x 12-inch (30.5cm) guns
(90 rounds per gun - 720 rounds)
14 x 5.9-inch (15cm) guns
(160 rounds per gun - 2240 rounds)
8 x 22-pounder (8.8cm) anti-aircraft guns
2 x machine guns
4 x 19.7-inch (50cm) torpedo tubes
(16 torpedoes)
8 x 43.3-inch (110cm) searchlights
Speed: *26.5 Knots (63,000 horsepower)*
4,625 tons coal - 984 tons oil
Length: *689 feet 0 inches*
Breadth: *95 feet 2 inches*
Displacement: *26,180 tons*
Built: *Blohm & Voss, Hamburg*
Launched: *1st July 1913*
Cost: *£2,233,364*

into wakefulness by a sudden and unexpected cacophony of noise - the bombardment levelled on it by two German warships.

Earlier that morning the enemy battle-cruisers *Derfflinger* and *Von der Tann*, and the triple-funnelled light cruiser *Kolberg*, had peeled off from Admiral Hipper's First Scouting Group (comprising five battle-cruisers, with supporting light cruisers and destroyers) under the command of Rear-Admiral Tapken, and had crept up to the north-east coast during the dark early hours. As dawn approached, the trio of vessels remained cloaked from detection by a hell-sent rolling bank of early morning mist - typical to this coast.

Further north at Hartlepool, three more battleships, the *Blücher*, *Seydlitz* and *Moltke*, from the same German group and under Hipper's personal command, mirrored the actions of their counterparts off Scarborough.

Like harbingers of doom the three battleships, hulking masses of cold grey steel silhouetted against the grey of the early morning mist, steamed southward, a mile off shore and parallel to it. As the bow of the leading vessel pierced the cloak of invisibility unwittingly supplied by mother nature, its Captain raised his field-glasses and surveyed the scenic tranquillity of the town's dual bays.

On the dew-damp cliffs north of the town, at Hayburn Wyke, the attention of three workmen engaged on repairing a cottage - Tom Nellist and brothers, David and Thomas Coultas - was caught by the movement of the three warships; two extraordinarily large vessels and one much smaller. The men were struck by the closeness of the vessels to the shore. As the light increased the ships were seen to move away southward towards the town, the smaller one leading the way. The speed of the ships gradually increased and with it the smoke from their funnels changed from grey to black, a dense, heavy cloud left in their wake.

Nothing stood between the enemy and the coast, not even so much as a fishing coble with a pistol on board.

As the *Kolberg* steamed on ahead, towards Filey and Flamborough Head to lay a deadly carpet of mines for any Royal Navy vessel which might come in pursuit, aboard the *Von der Tann* Captain Hahn, satisfied all was well, lowered his field-glasses, turned slightly, received a curt nod from Rear-Admiral Tapken and barked an order to his battle-ready gun crews:

"FEUER GEBEN!"

The giant 11-inch naval guns opened fire with a thunderous broadside, swiftly echoed by her 5.9-inch guns.

Several hundred yards away Captain von Reuter, on the bridge of the *Derfflinger*, gave the same order and her 12-inch gun barrels erupted in gouts of angry crimson flame, quickly followed by a succession of salvos from her 5.9-inch guns.

The time was eight o'clock, and all the fury of hell had been loosed on the gently slumbering 'Queen of the Yorkshire Coast'.

The Enemy's First Pass ~ Southward

Those townsfolk already awake, at breakfast or dressing, rushed to their windows and doors believing the worst thunderstorm in living memory was being visited on the town. Those in bed started into wakefulness and stumbled to their windows to discover the cause of the unbelievable noise. In streets and lanes folk going about their normal daily routine stopped where they were, rooted to the spot, as shells whistled and whined overhead. Horses, harnessed into drays, whinnied and shied nervously, nostrils flared,

HIMS KOLBERG
Fregattenkapitän Widenmann

Ship's War Complement: *440*
Armament (1914):
12 x 4.1-inch guns
1 x 7-pounder gun
2 x machine guns
2 x 17.7-inch torpedo tubes
120 mines
4 x 43.3-inch (110cm) searchlights
Speed: *25 Knots (19,600 horsepower)*
890 tons coal - oil (not listed)
Length: *426 feet 6 inches*
Breadth: *45 feet 11 inches*
Displacement: *4,280 tons*
Built: *Schichau Works, Danzig*
Launched: *14th November 1908*
Cost: *£380,868*

The GREAT WAR

SUBSCRIPTION

PUBLISHED BI-MONTHLY

£20 per annum UK ~ £30 per annum Overseas

I would like to subscribe to ***The Great War*** magazine. The current subscription year includes the six issues from issue 15, September 2004, to Issue 20, July 2005. Full details of how to obtain back issues, binders and the Special Edition will also be sent with your first issue. *Please complete and return this form.*

Name:..

Address:..

....

..........................County or Country:..........................

Post Code:..........................Tel:..........................

Payment method: cheque - postal order - credit/debit card (please circle)

Amount: £20 UK - £30 Overseas (please circle)

Sample copy: £5 UK - £9 Overseas (please circle)

Mastercard - Visa - Delta - Switch (please circle) **receipt will be sent with magazine*

Card Number:..

Valid from:..................Expires:..................Issue Number (Switch only):..................

Your name as it appears on the card:..

You can subscribe by cheque (made payable to 'Great Northern Publishing' and paid in British Pounds Sterling) or postal order, credit or debit card (Mastercard - Visa - Delta - Switch) or cash by completing the form above (please enclose with payment and send to the address below), or by phoning 01723 581329 and asking to subscribe to ***'The Great War'***. Subscriptions can also be arranged on-line from our website (address below). Simply complete the on-line secure order form stating 'GW-Subs'.

GREAT NORTHERN PUBLISHING

The award winning home of quality publishing in Yorkshire

PO Box 202, Scarborough, North Yorkshire, YO11 3GE. United Kingdom.
Telephone and Fax: 01723 581329
E-mail: books@greatnorthernpublishing.co.uk
www.greatnorthernpublishing.co.uk

ears pricked back, their eyes wide with fear and mounting panic as the first shells smashed into buildings and roads, belching smoke, flames and debris high into the air.

There followed but a brief moment of silence, a lull, a pause after the first round of shells, while the enemy reloaded their great naval guns. Then the air was again hot with whistling, exploding shells, flying shell fragments and shrapnel. The town was filled with the cacophony of bursting shells, falling masonry, breaking glass, splintering wood and shattering slates.

Bathers Run for Cover

A group of local men, in the habit of bathing in the South Bay close to the Spa, were frightened out of their wits as the sudden and unexpected barrage began. Within moments of the first shots being fired they had swum to shore, grabbed up their towels and discarded clothing and raced headlong for what they perceived to be the shelter afforded by the sea wall and those buildings nearest the sea front.

Mr Gibson, one of the handful of gentlemen bathers, sought refuge behind a nearby wall and watched in abject horror as shells ploughed into the general areas of The Crescent, Falconer's Road and York Place. An employee of the local Tramway Company, Gibson later gave evidence at the inquests into the deaths of the innocents, in which he claimed to have seen three cruisers steaming parallel to the South Bay firing broadsides into the town.

Captain Mosey Counts One Hundred Shells

Meanwhile the town's boating and bathing inspector, Captain William Mosey, who had been on Foreshore Road above the Aquarium Top when the bombardment opened, had judiciously retired to the Receiving House, perceiving himself safe there. Captain Mosey also gave evidence at the later inquests and described for a rapt audience the view he had whilst the shells whistled continuously overhead; he estimated the number of shells to be close on a hundred.

Mosey saw two warships, one of which he declared big enough to be of the 'Dreadnought' class, creep round the Marine Drive from the north, pass the castle headland and steam level with the South Bay. He judged the pair to be some two and a half miles out to sea, and it was not until they began firing that he had thought anything wrong, or out of the ordinary. The sound of the bombardment was quite terrible and Mosey believed there to be a third vessel also engaged in shelling the town which he assumed to be somewhere off the North Bay and out of his sight.

It is probable that Mosey had confused the ships in his haste to take cover and had seen the *Kolberg*, steaming ahead of the *Derfflinger*, sailing southward and had assumed it too was shelling the town. It is possible she fired a broadside in passing, but there are no contemporary accounts of 4.1-inch shells having been found in the town following the bombardment, and as this was her main armament it is extremely doubtful that she was engaged. The shells Mosey had witnessed were more likely to have come from the *Von der Tann*, which was out of his line of sight and about to steam around the castle headland from the direction of the North Bay.

Having used up his reservoir of courage, Captain Mosey prostrated himself on the floor of the Receiving House and waited for the bombardment to end, fully expecting the place to be blown to pieces at any moment. When the shelling finally ended he rose and watched the ships head out to sea and steam off in a northerly direction towards Whitby, further along the coast.

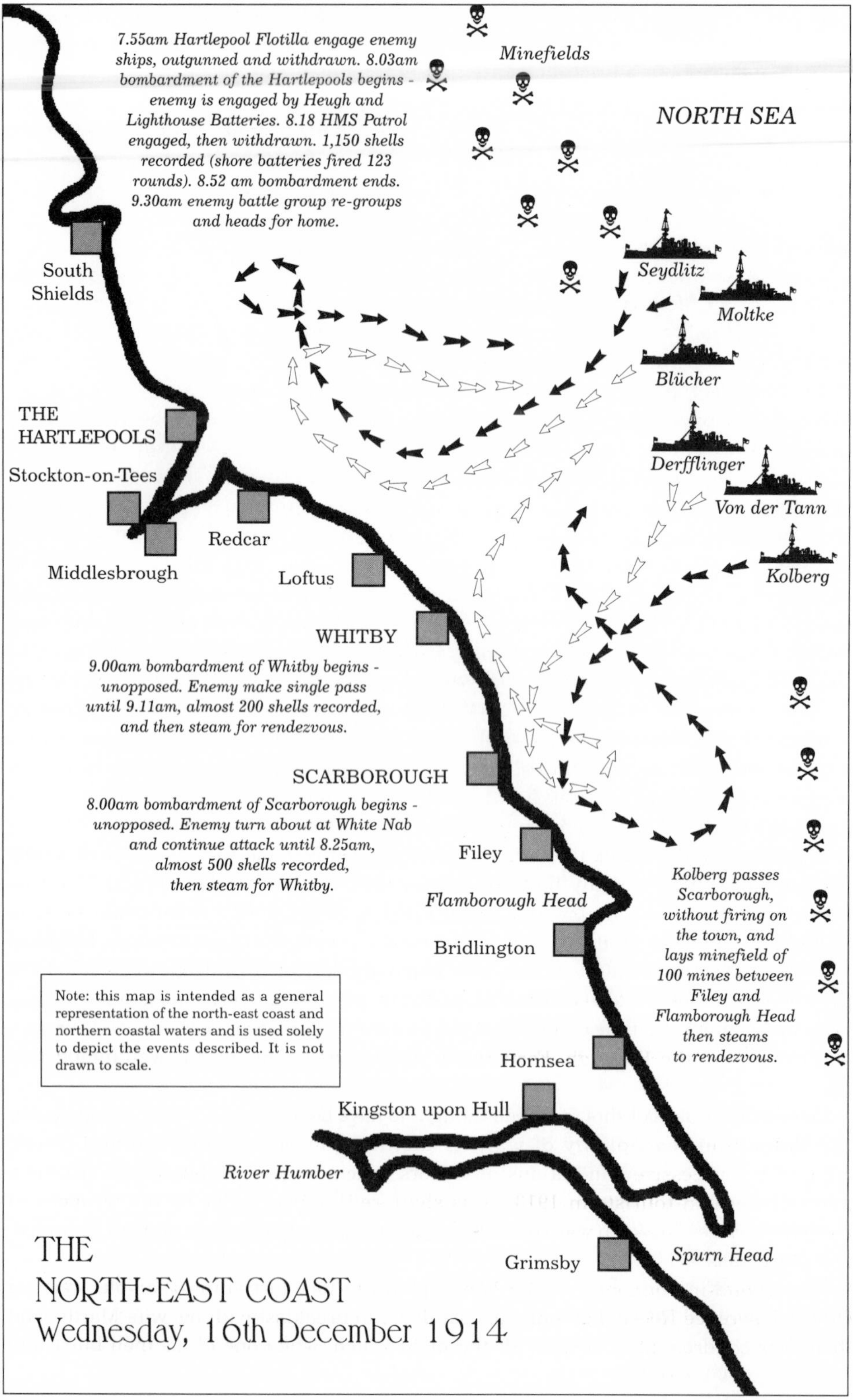
7.55am Hartlepool Flotilla engage enemy ships, outgunned and withdrawn. 8.03am bombardment of the Hartlepools begins - enemy is engaged by Heugh and Lighthouse Batteries. 8.18 HMS Patrol engaged, then withdrawn. 1,150 shells recorded (shore batteries fired 123 rounds). 8.52 am bombardment ends. 9.30am enemy battle group re-groups and heads for home.
Minefields
NORTH SEA
South Shields
Seydlitz
Moltke
Blücher
Derfflinger
Von der Tann
Kolberg
THE HARTLEPOOLS
Stockton-on-Tees
Redcar
Middlesbrough
Loftus
WHITBY
9.00am bombardment of Whitby begins - unopposed. Enemy make single pass until 9.11am, almost 200 shells recorded, and then steam for rendezvous.
SCARBOROUGH
8.00am bombardment of Scarborough begins - unopposed. Enemy turn about at White Nab and continue attack until 8.25am, almost 500 shells recorded, then steam for Whitby.
Filey
Flamborough Head
Bridlington
Kolberg passes Scarborough, without firing on the town, and lays minefield of 100 mines between Filey and Flamborough Head then steams to rendezvous.
Note: this map is intended as a general representation of the north-east coast and northern coastal waters and is used solely to depict the events described. It is not drawn to scale.
Hornsea
Kingston upon Hull
River Humber
Grimsby
Spurn Head
THE NORTH-EAST COAST
Wednesday, 16th December 1914

Incredibly, many of the townsfolk and tradesmen went about their normal duties, seemingly oblivious to the shelling, intent instead on completing their usual tasks rather than discarding everything and seeking shelter - for some it would cost them their lives. The reason for this apparent calm would later be ascribed to the totally unexpected nature of the attack. Many folk believed it to be part of some previously arranged naval exercise about which they had not been informed. Indeed, so unexpected was the attack that boats from the town's fishing fleet, at sea and unable to put into harbour because of the low tide, actually thought the vessels were British warships, and it was only when they turned their guns on the undefended town that they realised what was happening. Equally incredibly, the fishermen were not targeted and returned to the sanctuary of the harbour unscathed.

The Castle, Barracks and War Signal Station

The first fusillade of shells was aimed at the War Signal Station sited on Castle Hill in the still and silent grounds of the town's old castle; a high and conspicuous landmark situated on the promontory separating the North and South Bays; a landmark visible for many miles in all directions - especially from the sea. The withering storm of high explosive and shrapnel shells burst against the ten-feet thick castle walls, crashed through the ruined keep and exploded against the empty yeomanry barracks alongside it.

The 'old' barracks had been built in 1746 to accommodate some 120 men, with a small portion of the building being devoted to officers' quarters. Not since 1878 had it been occupied by regular troops, and indeed, the roof had been in need of work a few years earlier, while the sanitary arrangements left much to be desired and were not up to 'modern' standards. The building, nestled snugly against the south-east wall of the castle near the Queen's Tower, was totally devastated. The whole roof was smashed in, exposing beams, joists and laths to the open air. Almost the entire upper two storeys were levelled, the major portion of the debris crashing into the ground-floor rooms. Of the two tall chimneys, one set at either end of the long building, only one remained intact, the other reduced to a heap of rubble.

At the time of the attack the barracks were unoccupied and were being used simply for storage. But the enemy had not known that, for they had been acting on the assumption that the infantry and Royal Field Artillery units, which could be seen training in the castle grounds daily, were actually encamped there. If troops had been stationed there heaven alone knows how much greater the final death toll would have been. Furthermore, it had even been suggested by the town's civic leaders, in the months prior to the attack, that the empty barracks be used to house the poor and needy women and children of the Borough. Fortunately, nothing had come of this well-intentioned plan.

The castle, its days of shot and shell thought to have been long since over, resounded to the thunderous cacophony of war, its picturesque beauty and tranquil peace, enjoyed by successive generations of visitors - including a well-publicised visit by a party of German tourists in 1913 - was shattered, rent asunder by the weapons of modern warfare. The keep was struck twice, but no great damage was done to its twelve-feet thick walls.

The second-in-command at the War Signal Station, forty-nine-year-old Warrant Officer Lawrence Reeve, had only just sat down to breakfast with his wife Martha and their four children, after coming off the night watch, when one of his men burst into his house unannounced.

The 'Old Barracks'
were all but demolished

The old beacon was blown off the castle walls
and ended up embedded in the castle dykes

St Thomas's school on Longwestgate had many of its
windows broken by shrapnel and remained closed for the day

Three trawlers and several yawls, moored in
the harbour, were slightly damaged

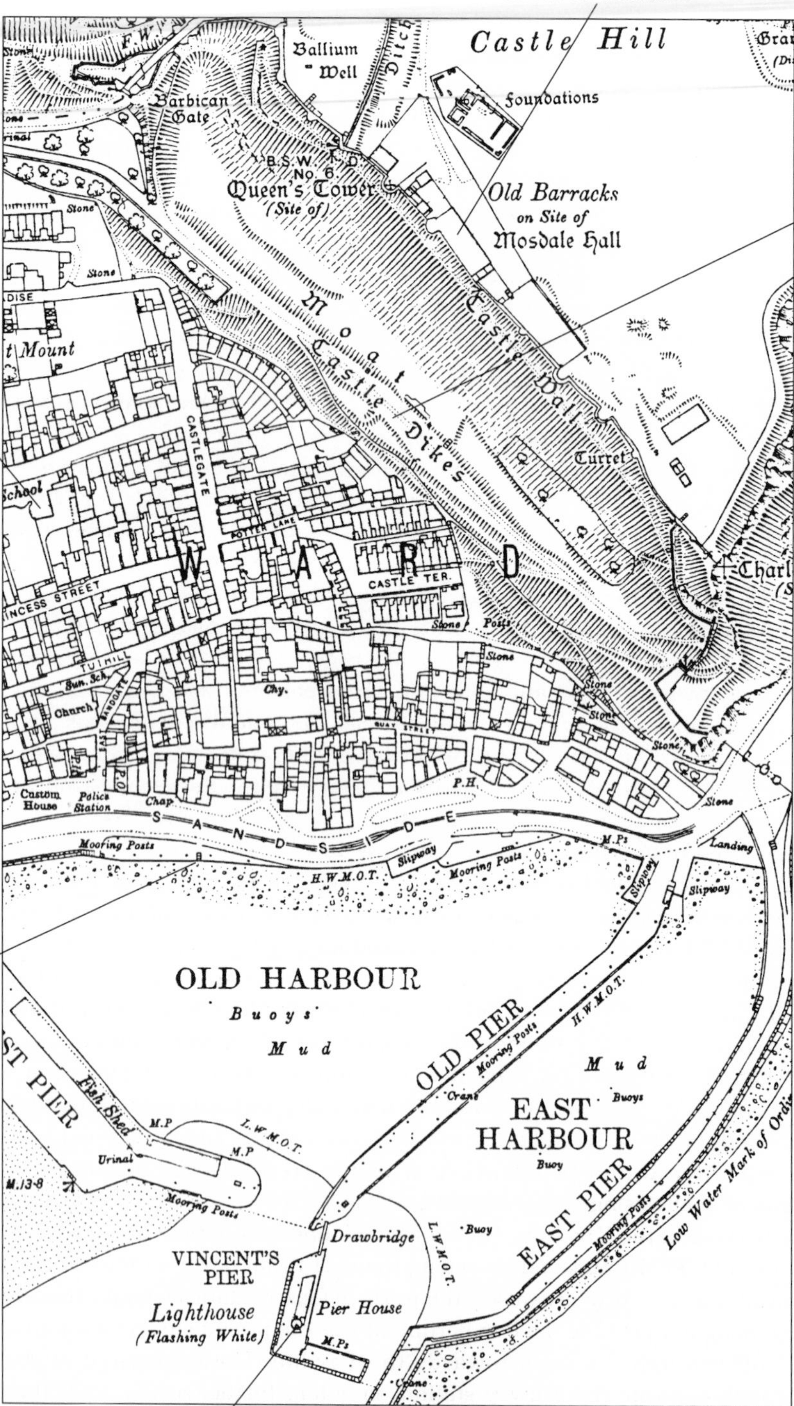

The lighthouse
was the final casualty

"There are some strange ships in sight, but we can't make out what they are . . ." he cried, his sentence cut short by the howling of shells. Together the men raced back up the hill from the Coastguard Station and Admiralty houses, opposite St Mary's Church, through the castle gates and headlong for the War Signal Station through the hail of shells falling on the castle.

Meanwhile, James Walsh, who had only moments earlier left the War Signal Station to stretch his legs and get a breath of fresh air at the end of his shift, dashed back inside, told Harry Holden to get the other men together and sent PC Harry Hunter to call out the Hussars billeted in cottages nearby. He then grabbed up the telephone and called the Wireless Station, situated behind Falsgrave Park, determined to appraise the Admiralty of what was happening.

"Some strange ships are approaching from the north. I cannot make out what they are. They don't answer my signals." Walsh's voice suddenly rose in strangulated terror, "They're Germans! They're firing on us . . ."

The line suddenly went dead. A single shell had scored a direct hit and severed the line.

With Holden and Hunter back, Walsh decided the Station was unsafe and grabbing up papers, charts and code books, the three of them flung themselves down the steps into the arched vault of the nearby Lady's Well. An instant later a shell struck the small War Signal Station, blowing it to bits.

Face red with excitement, Robert Barnes, Walsh's relief, who had been casually walking up to the station when the shelling started, threw himself into the shelter of the Lady's Well to join the others.

"There's going to be a landing . . . get rid of the papers!"

Walsh, determined the papers should not fall into enemy hands, took up a can of paraffin, stored in the vault for safe-keeping, and doused them before Barnes put a match to the lot. Flaming, the code books, charts and papers were heaved down into the darkness of the depths of the Lady's Well.

Just then Reeve and his colleague stumbled down the steps to join them, and there they all stayed while the heavy fusillade continued overhead.

Another shell blew the old beacon away and took a chunk out of the wall upon which it had stood. The brazier, which had been used hundreds of years ago to warn ships of danger along the coast, and the people of the town of imminent danger, was later found battered and bent, partly embedded halfway down the steep slopes of one of the castle's dykes. The castle's grounds - broad expanses of grassland, the resting place for many weary townsfolk after a hard week's toil; where picnics had been enjoyed beneath open blue skies in the lea of ancient walls with a breathtaking view of the coastline and the town's twin bays and where town shows and events had been staged - were left littered and pockmarked with fist-sized chunks of masonry, jagged fragments of shell-casing and shrapnel bullets.

Trooper Davis of the Yorkshire Hussars, which unit was stationed in the town, having been roused by PC Hunter and on seeing the shells rain down on the castle, gathered his comrades and swiftly organised them for defensive duties, should the need arise (for they thought it possible the bombardment was the prelude to an invasion) and then hurried off through the town towards the Pavilion Hotel, situated at the top of Westborough opposite the railway station, to obtain further orders from the officers billeted there. Meanwhile, across the town, other men of the Hussars were hastily despatched to man the trenches in St Nicholas Cliff Gardens, and a machine-gun

THE CASTLE

1: The castle walls from the ballium on the west side of the keep.
2: The castle walls around the ballium.
3: The 'old' barracks.
4: Residence on the left of the entrance to the Castle Yard, behind the Guard Room, previously the home of the Chief Gunner.

section, among which was Trooper Stanley Cunningham who had been out on patrol and thought the shelling was part of a naval exercise, was sent post-haste to the West Pier with orders not to open fire unless a landing was attempted.

Warriner and Mason Raise the Flag

With the ships steaming at a leisurely pace along the South Bay the shelling moved on, over the castle with its shattered walls, the bombardment extending into the town.

At last, the men taking refuge in the Lady's Well were able to emerge to view the destruction about them. PC Hunter hurried to retrieve his cape which, after his rather damp night shift, he had left on some nearby railings to dry out, only to discover it now torn to shreds by shrapnel from the shells which had exploded over the castle. The image of the Constable and his tattered cape was captured on film and the photographs of him with it (some reproduced as souvenir postcards) remain one of the most abiding images of the bombardment.

Special Constable Robert Warriner of the Municipal Police was ordered to the War Signal Station post-haste to discover exactly what damage had been done there. On arrival Warriner was joined by Leading Boatman George Mason of the Coastguard and together they hurried through the debris-strewn castle grounds to the remains of the War Signal Station. There, at their feet, among the wreckage and debris lay the splintered flagpole, the Union Flag still attached. Determined that the nation's flag be kept flying during the atrocity being perpetrated by the enemy, the two men sought to secure it to a nearby telephone pole - which, by some miracle, had remained intact. Once the task was complete and the flag was once more hoisted into the breeze, Warriner turned to his comrade. "Are we downhearted?" he asked.

"No!" replied Mason emphatically.

Custodian's Donkey Mortally Wounded

In 1911 Albert Pickup had taken up the duties of the Custodian of Scarborough Castle and he and his wife, Emily, and their family had moved into the custodian's quarters next to the castle. Never in their wildest dreams could they have imagined what befell them that terrible morning as the shells whistled overhead and crashed into the castle's ancient walls. Thirteen-year-old Mildred Pickup was so terrified she fled the house and ran through the street in her nightgown, only to be taken up and hurried to safety by some members of the Red Cross who were staying near the castle at the time. Though no one in the family was hurt, their donkey, Topsy, was hit and so badly injured the poor creature later had to be destroyed.

The Foreshore

The Royal Northern Sea Bathing Infirmary and Convalescent Home on the Foreshore, housing wounded British and Belgian soldiers, was damaged as a shell travelled the entire length of an upstairs ward doing minor damage, but injuring no one. Further along, a shell hit the Olympia Picture Palace buildings and fragments of shell rained over the cloth roof inside the building, puncturing holes in it and damaging the café. The day's planned performances were cancelled due to the damage, and scenes along the Foreshore after the bombardment were chaotic as literally hundreds of local people passed along the sea front to view the extent of the damage.

A shell went clear through Vose and Company's confectionery shop, at 13a Foreshore Road, hit a back window, went through the casing, through a wall and into the staithes

1

2

3

FORESHORE ROAD & BLAND'S CLIFF

1: Rose and Violet Jarvis of Neptune House (above Vose's Confectioners).
2: Mrs Hill's, 1 Bath Terrace, Bland's Cliff. 3: The door to Neptune House.

behind the shop. A large piece of the shell was quickly claimed as a souvenir by Victor Walton of Prospect House, at 24 Foreshore Road.

At *Neptune House*, at 2 Neptune Terrace, 13 Foreshore Road (the rooms above Vose's confectionery shop), a shell struck the pavement outside, ricocheted upwards and through the front window, crashed through two walls and an eight-inch wooden lintel above the back door, sped across a six-foot wide passageway and burst into an unoccupied cottage, striking the ceiling and then the floor before exiting back into the street and onto the pavement. Fortunately Rose Jarvis, and her daughter Violet (both in bed at the time of the incident) escaped, barefoot, shaken, but unhurt. The pair, terrified out of their wits, made straight for the homes of relatives deeper in the town. On their return to the devastated house following the bombardment, Rose Jarvis discovered her false teeth were missing, believed stolen, and later included them on her claim for compensation!

Nearby, the roof of printer Martyn King's house, *Hope Cottage*, at 32 Foreshore Road, was badly damaged. So too was the roof of Catlin's Arcadia on South Foreshore Road, which was hit by a shell, while a huge gaping hole was punched through the side of the Grand Picture House also on Foreshore Road, causing extensive damage and shattering the glass roof.

Bland's Cliff and Eastborough

The Bell Hotel on Bland's Cliff, owned by Byron Atkinson, was struck by a shell which entered the upper storey and laid waste four entire bedrooms, while the blast from the explosion not only blew out the hotel's windows but those of jet dealer, Thomas Hawxwell's shop next door; the flying debris causing much damage to his stock.

At 59 Eastborough, the home and grocery business of Alice Hastie took a direct hit which partially demolished the side of the building facing the sea, breaking many of its windows. Though the damage was serious and the building badly damaged, no one was hurt. The roof of Mrs Winn's house, at 71 Eastborough, was also badly damaged and all the windows facing the sea were shattered. At Henry Burrows' home next door, at 73 Eastborough, the damage was worse, with the chimney stack being blown away completely and the outer wall of the upper storey being blown in. The bay windows were shattered and much of the furniture was damaged.

King Street

The offices of the Kingscliffe Holiday Camp at 13 King Street were so seriously damaged that anyone entering them afterwards put their life at risk. The part of the premises closest to the King Street steps, leading down onto Foreshore Road, had been hit by a shell which blew a hole in the wall and destroyed several rooms inside. Another shell hit the steps at the front of the premises leading down into the basement. Twenty-nine-year-old Herbert Greenwood was actually standing on the steps unlocking the door at the time and was hit. The blast broke both his legs as the shell sped through into the basement below. Despite the severity of his injuries and obvious pain, Greenwood managed to crawl into the basement, for what little safety it now offered from the bombardment raging outside. Another shell struck the premises' dining-hall, but did minor damage. After the raid spoons from the building, bent into peculiar shapes, were found scattered over a wide area of King Street.

Havoc was also caused by a shell which struck the upper offices of the Health Office on King Street, whilst at 25a King Street, Joe Dobson's roof was smashed in and

The 'Royal Suite' at the Royal Hotel was badly damaged

A shell crashed through into the empty Council Chamber of the Town Hall

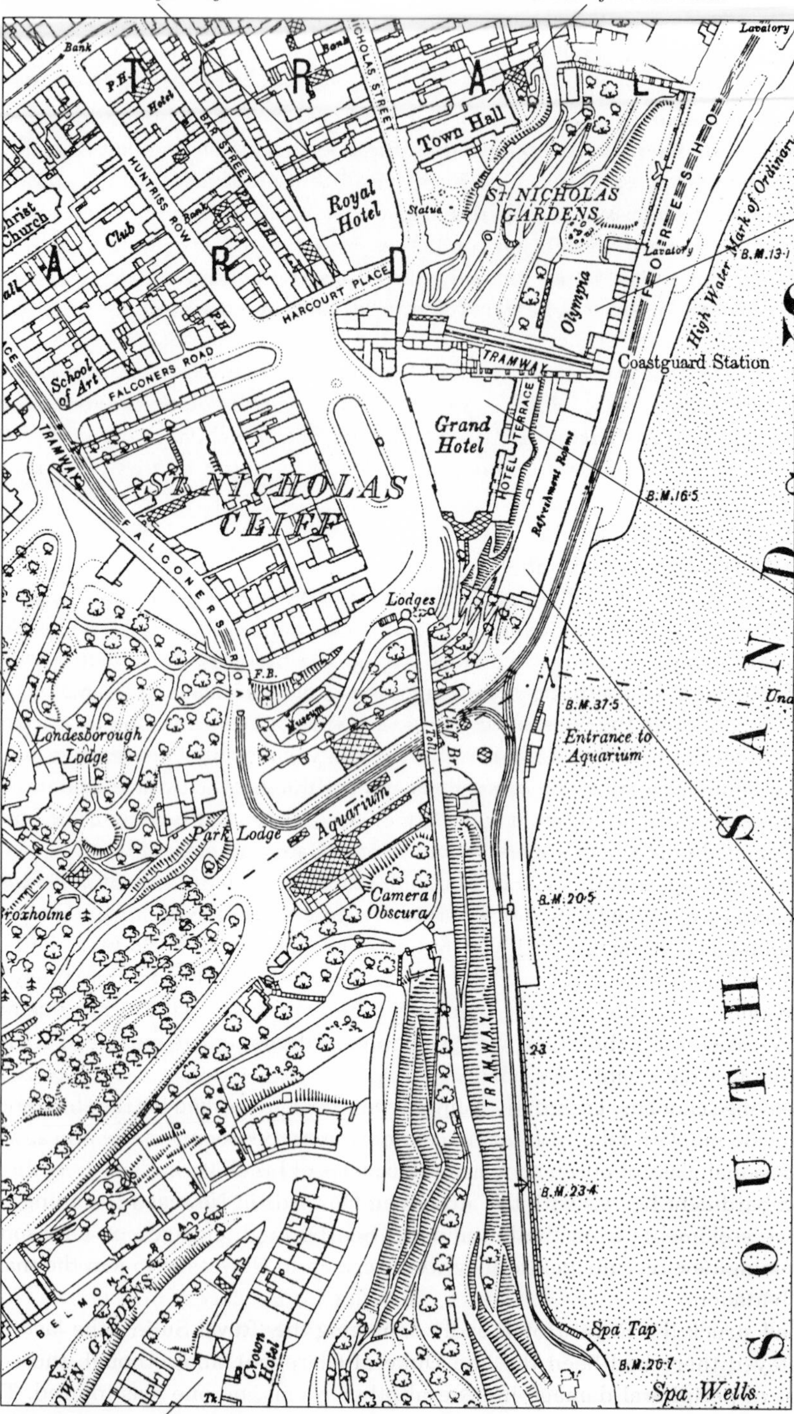

The Olympia Picture Palace was damaged and performances were suspended for the day

The Grand Hotel, whose huge size made it an easy target

The Grand Hotel's Picture House and Restaurant suffered badly

The Scarborough residence of Lord Londesborough, Londesborough Lodge, emerged unscathed

A shell crashed through the roof of the Crown Garage, but no one was hurt damage done to the upper rooms. The roof and upper storey of the Red Cross Headquarters were also severely damaged. A piece of shell was later found embedded in the outer wall of the Waterworks offices situated at the end of King Street.

Falconer's Road, York Place and Huntriss Row

On Falconer's Road Mrs Coleman, of 13 York Place, had a narrow escape. She was in the street when shells began bursting all around her, and immediately cried out for someone to help her get home to her invalid father. A gentleman passer-by escorted her through the passageway behind York Place and no sooner had the pair reached the other side than a shell hit a house and showered the spot where she had been standing moments earlier with huge chunks of masonry and debris. York Place itself felt the full force of the nearby blasts on The Crescent with thirteen out of twenty-one houses having their windows broken.

At the Constitutional Club on Huntriss Row a shell exploded close by and sent a shell splinter through the roof, breaking a number of ceiling lights. Another fragment from the same shell struck the corner window facing the sea in the club's reading-room, shattering it.

The South Cliff ~ St Nicholas Cliff and St Nicholas Street

Leaving the castle in their wake, the German ships levelled with the town's South Bay, their guns finding easy targets in the heavily built-up and well-populated area overlooking the Foreshore.

The Gentleman's Club at 9 St Nicholas Cliff was pierced by a shell which swept through the steward's sitting-room, doing considerable damage, and crashed through the interior wall into the main bedroom but did not explode. The club steward, Clifford Rowden, and his wife, had only a few moments earlier left the room. On his way to shave in another room at the moment of impact, Rowden, closest to the impact, was lucky to escape without injury. It was claimed an expensive telescope in the path of the shell remained unharmed while all about it was chaos and mayhem.

The luxury department store of Marshall and Snelgrove at 4-11 St Nicholas Street was blasted by a shell which ploughed into the store's workrooms situated at the rear of the building, facing the sea, and blew out an entire interior wall. Had the shell struck a few minutes later the workroom would have been crowded with more than thirty women, all bent on tasks at their sewing machines (the main core of the firm's business was drapery). Although the store was extensively damaged, it mattered little when compared to what might have been.

On leaving school my grandfather, Jim Stevenson, had worked for the store and would often regale me with tales of freezing cold dormitory bedrooms in the attics, with only the occasional glass of porter to warm the cockles of his shivering heart. At the time of the bombardment he was with the 5th Green Howards in Newcastle, training - though there were elements from the battalion in Scarborough engaged on garrison duties and training new recruits before they were sent on to Newcastle to join the main body of the battalion.

A shell struck the Royal Hotel, badly damaging the 'Royal Suite', (the last 'royal' to have stayed there had been the late Duke of Clarence), and although there was an amount of peripheral damage in several other rooms, no one was injured. That the town was in its 'off season' was a major reason there were not more casualties. Over one hundred and sixty windows in the hotel were broken or damaged by shrapnel shells

THE GRAND HOTEL

The Grand Hotel, brainchild of a group of businessmen whose aim was to build a magnificent hotel which would attract an affluent clientèle, has dominated the town's South Bay since it was completed in 1867 - when full board cost ten shillings per day, breakfast three shillings and dinner five shillings. However, there were fears in 1865 that it would not be completed, when work was suspended due to a lack of finances. In 1866 work recommenced and the building became the first ever Grand Hotel and the largest brick-built building in Europe. It had taken over six million bricks to complete the 'themed' hotel, based on time; with its four towers denoting the seasons, its twelve floors the months, its 52 chimneys the weeks and its 365 rooms the days of the year. Winston Churchill, Gracie Fields, James Herriott and the Beatles have all stayed there.

1: The Grand Hotel facing the South Bay. 2&3: Exterior damage.

exploding outside. The hotel's only guests at the time, a bank manager and his wife, escaped shaken but unhurt. The shrapnel also took out the windows of Wherritt's Tobacconists, at 2 Royal Hotel Shops, and damaged the stock.

A moment later a shell smashed its way through the wall of the Town Hall, situated on the opposite side of St Nicholas Street to the Royal Hotel (the side of the road nearest the sea), and crashed through into the unoccupied Council Chamber leaving a gaping hole in its wake.

A pair of houses on St Nicholas Cliff, numbers 16 and 17, were each struck by single shells. The inhabitant of number 16, William Slack managed to escape uninjured, while next door the house was empty and the shell which struck it passed through and ploughed into Mr Ashley's Spa Boarding House on St Nicholas Parade behind it, destroying a number of rooms.

A shell struck Mac's Café, at 36 St Nicholas Cliff, and ploughed through the roof and into the upper storey, demolishing it. Nearby, the roof of Kate Hoare's home at 34 St Nicholas Cliff and that of Tugwell's Hairdresser's at number 35 were also damaged by the same blast.

Grand Damage at The Grand Hotel

The imposing façade of the majestic Grand Hotel, with its commanding position overlooking the South Bay, proved an easy, almost too inviting target for the hard-working enemy gunners. The £250,000 hotel was struck by a hail of shells, some thirty-five in total. The roof and attic windows were badly damaged, while several rooms facing the sea, always the most popular with guests, were blown apart. The interior of the hotel's majestic sea-view restaurant was left shattered and splintered as if by a whirlwind. A reporter from the *Daily Mirror* later entered the ruined restaurant and reported that the only thing left in one piece was a decanter of wine. No doubt in the cause of journalism, the brave fellow tasted it to make sure it was still palatable!

Guests and staff alike hurried from the building into the street only narrowly to escape injury there from falling masonry and flying glass. At the time of the enemy raid the hotel was reported to have only two guests (the holiday season long gone and the expected Christmas influx having not yet arrived), and both escaped unhurt. A narrow escape was also made by an Austrian member of staff, a waiter with a nasty habit of 'sleeping in'. The man was on a final warning from the hotel's manager, Robert Beaumont, and had been ordered out of his bed and to work by eight o'clock - or else! Only moments later a shell had crashed through into his bedroom, shattering furniture and lacerating the walls with shrapnel. It was later reported that the only thing left upright in the room was the head of the bedstead.

The total cost of the damage to the hotel, restaurant and picture house was later put at around £13,000.

Marine Parade ~ Artist's Narrow Escape

On Marine Parade, situated at the side of the Grand Hotel, a flat and studio belonging to Chalmers-Park (an artist from Leeds) was badly damaged - both by falling brick and masonry from the hotel, which demolished a major portion of the flat, and by the shrapnel from the shells exploding above. It was the artist's habit, on rising, to partake of a cup of coffee whilst enjoying the extensive and panoramic view from his studio windows, which overlooked the South Bay and the castle headland. Here he would gather his inspiration for his forthcoming day of artistic endeavour. However, on this

The Pavilion Hotel served as the Headquarters for Colonel Smithson of the Yorkshire Hussars

Thirteen out of twenty-one houses on York Place had their windows broken

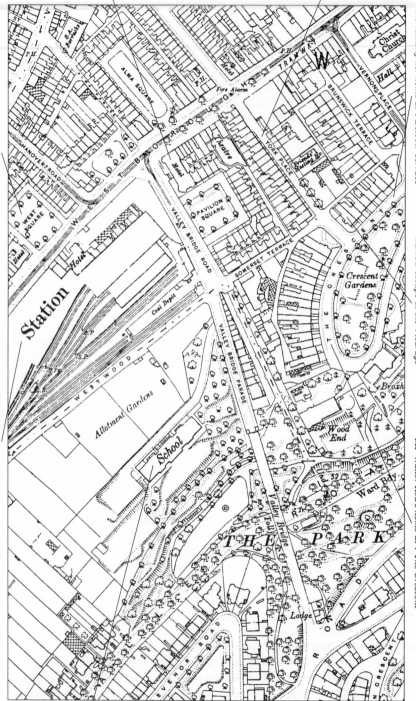

On West Square numbers 18 and 20 were badly damaged by the same shell, which also broke the windows in seven other houses in the square

The Station was littered with debris, but not seriously damaged

Invalid Mrs Keble had to be carried out of the ruins of her home at 6 Belvoir Terrace

The Reverend Cecil Cooper had a narrow escape at the Vicarage

A shell punched a hole through the wall of Liberal MP Walter Rea's home at 7 The Crescent

The Municipal School (later Westwood) escaped with only superficial damage particular morning, his calm and tranquil habit was rudely interrupted by the appearance of a battleship firing shells at the castle. It was some moments before it dawned on the poor bemused fellow that this was an enemy bombardment and not a naval exercise, and without a second thought for his breakfast, prepared and ready on the table in front of him, he made good his escape. No sooner had he left the premises than a huge piece of moulded cornice, blown from the roof of the Grand Hotel, struck his own roof and ploughed through it into the rooms below causing much damage; strangely, some twenty-five cases of stuffed birds remained wholly intact, whilst all around them everything else was shattered and broken. Thinking himself extremely lucky the artist made his way on to St Nicholas Cliff and there narrowly escaped being buried under an avalanche of masonry and debris which showered down from a building which had just been hit.

The Crescent ~ MP's House Hit

A number of shells narrowly missed Londesborough Lodge, but one of them came down instead on the home of the town's Liberal MP, Walter Rea, at 7 The Crescent. The MP was not at home at the time, but his poor wife and two housemaids were. Luckily Mrs Rea had, only a split second earlier, left the sitting-room to give instructions to one of the maids when a shell smashed into the room and exploded against the far wall. The furniture was smashed to smithereens, yet the clock on the mantelpiece remained intact, as did a set of china, earlier moved from its usual cabinet to the top of a piano prior to its being cleaned.

The shell which hit the Rea's home exploded against the wall adjoining the neighbouring terraced house, 8 The Crescent, the home of the Micklethwaites. There Mr and Mrs Micklethwaite had earlier been alarmed by the first sounds of the bombardment and, on witnessing the shells pouring into the town, had prudently removed themselves to the lower part of their home and hidden in the cellar, thus escaping injury altogether. A number of other houses in the terrace had their windows (those facing seaward) broken by shrapnel as the bombardment continued.

At Wood End, the home of Sir George Sitwell, a shell crashed through the front door and shrapnel bullets from others exploding in The Crescent smashed many of the windows. Sir George, dressing when the bombardment began, hurried to his wife, who refused to change her habit of remaining in bed to read the morning newspapers. Unable to convince her, Sir George took the rest of the household into the cellar, bar a footman, a Swiss national who was determined to watch the shelling from the roof of the house. The following day Lady Sitwell joined a packed train to London to see her eldest son, Osbert before he went off to France with his regiment. With her she took a fragment of shell which she gave him for luck. Whether it was due to the piece of shell or not, Osbert survived and twelve years later, thinly disguising Scarborough as the fictional 'Newborough', described the events in the town leading up to the attack in his novel 'Before the Bombardment'.

Belvoir Terrace ~ Mrs Keble Carried to Safety ~ Somerset Terrace

At 6 Belvoir Terrace (which runs on from The Crescent), three of the third-floor bedrooms and a part of the lower drawing-room were destroyed as shells blew a gaping hole in the front of the house - the explosion shattering the windows of the houses on either side of it. A young woman, Mrs Keble, an invalid, was bodily carried by the force of the explosion into the adjoining room and was badly injured. Hearing her screams,

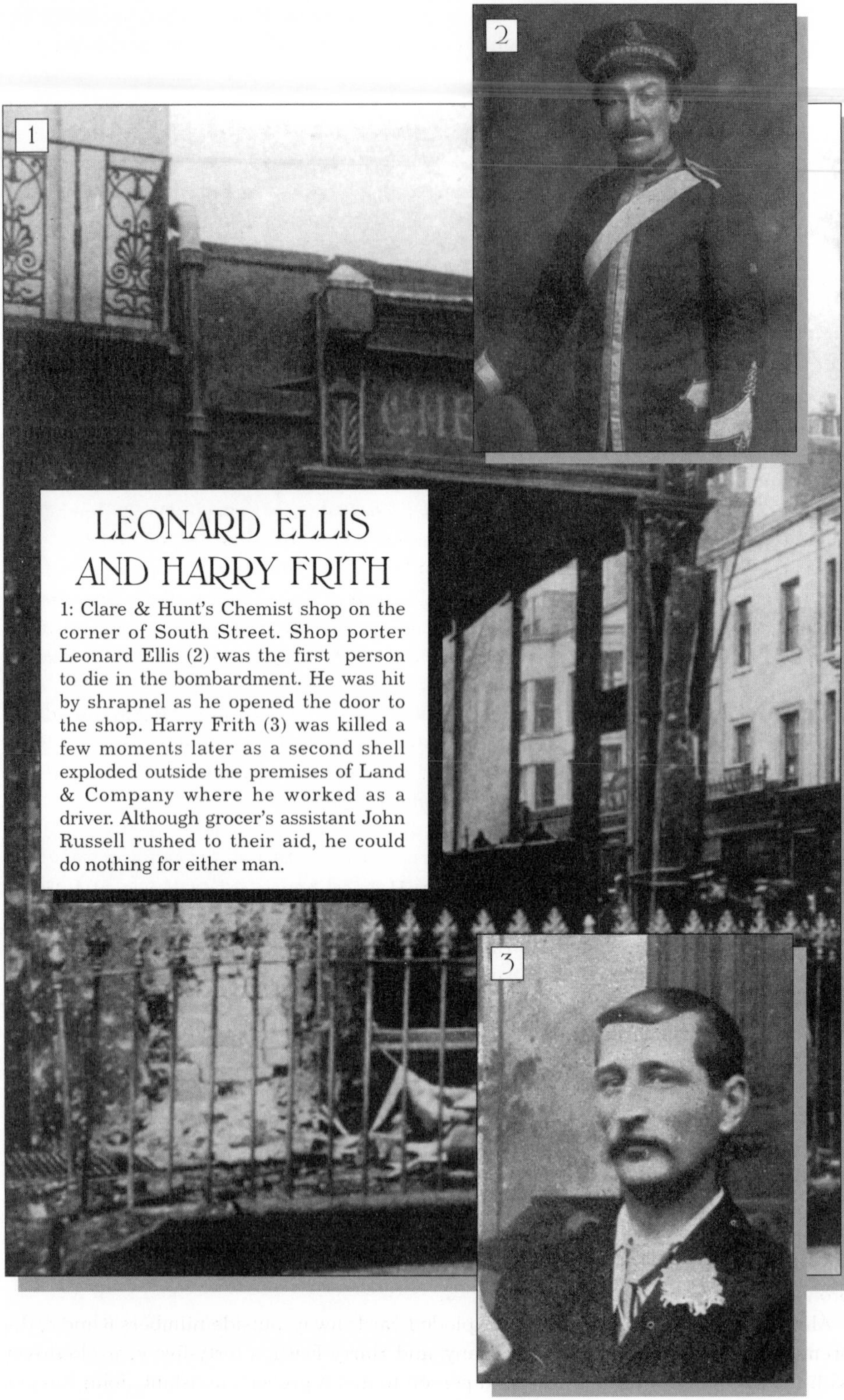

LEONARD ELLIS AND HARRY FRITH

1: Clare & Hunt's Chemist shop on the corner of South Street. Shop porter Leonard Ellis (2) was the first person to die in the bombardment. He was hit by shrapnel as he opened the door to the shop. Harry Frith (3) was killed a few moments later as a second shell exploded outside the premises of Land & Company where he worked as a driver. Although grocer's assistant John Russell rushed to their aid, he could do nothing for either man.

rescuers ran to her aid through a yard now strewn with books and oddments blown outward from the bedroom by the blast. On reaching the young woman the rescuers had to break down a door to get to her before finally being able to carry her to safety.

The roof of the Vicarage, home of Reverend Cecil Cooper, was blown in by a shell which entered the bathroom where he was shaving. Despite it exploding, he escaped serious injury.

The roof of the house belonging to Edward Barnett on the corner of Somerset Terrace (number 5), facing The Crescent was hit and badly damaged.

The Spa

The beach area and sea wall in front of the Spa were gouged by shells which fell short of their target, while splinters, fragments and shrapnel bullets peppered the building breaking many of its windows. Above the ornate building the South Cliff Gardens too were struck and dug up by a cluster of shells which again missed the Spa buildings.

Ramshill Road Area ~ Archdeacon Continues with Communion

A shell crashed into the tower of the South Cliff Wesleyan Church, while two more struck the imposing church of St Martin's-On-The-Hill, off Ramshill Road. One hit the roof and crashed through it, creating an immense hole; the other struck the east wall, knocking an amount of stonework from it. Inside the building, consecrated in 1863, Archdeacon Charles Mackarness was celebrating Holy Communion. Despite the commotion outside and the damage within, he quietly informed his obviously terrified congregation that they were as safe there as anywhere else and calmly went on with the service.

A stray piece of shell broke a window of St Martin's Vicarage on St Martin's Road and embedded itself in a bookcase, destroying the books on it, while at St Martin's Villa, also on St Martin's Road, and the home of Miss Geldard, fragments of a shell broke several windows. No one was injured in either incident.

Albion Road and Crown Crescent

Chunks of flying shell holed the roof of Mrs Holmes' house, *Albert House*, at 1 Albion Road, situated just off the Esplanade. All the windows were shattered and the back of the building was scarred by shell fragments and shrapnel. Further along, the windows of number 6, the home of Mrs Watson, were broken by the same blast.

At nearby 4 Crown Crescent, the home of Bertha Gregory was badly damaged and her bedroom and its accumulated furniture was decimated by a direct hit.

South Street ~ The First Fatalities ~ Alfred Street

On South Street, part of Clare and Hunt's Chemist shop at number 2 was demolished as a shell burst on the road outside the premises digging out a large crater. It was here that the life of the bombardment's first victim was claimed, for the shop's porter, forty-nine-year-old widower Leonard Ellis, was killed by the explosion of the shrapnel shell as he opened the door to the shop. The entire contents of the shop were blown up and mixed with the debris of masonry, brick and glass which littered the street around Ellis's prone and badly lacerated form.

Almost immediately another shell exploded yards away, outside numbers 6 and 8, the premises of William C. Land & Company, and Harry Frith, a forty-five-year-old driver with the company, became the second person to die. A grocer's assistant, John Russell,

SOUTH STREET

1: The corner of South Street.
2: Charles Smith outside the shattered windows of his shop poses with a lump of shell.
3: Clare & Hunt's Chemist shop.

on his way to work, rushed to the aid of the stricken men, but could do nothing for either one, both of them having died instantly.

Across South Street several shops including Charles Smith's Antique and Silversmith Dealers at number 4 and the flat over the premises, were badly damaged.

The Montpellier Boarding House on Alfred Street was practically demolished by a direct hit. However, the only people in the place at the time were the caretakers and they managed to escape from the ruins relatively unharmed. Adjoining Clare and Hunt's Chemist shop, a branch office of the London and Joint Stock Bank Limited at 2 Alfred Street had all its windows blown out, whilst the blast from the Montpellier Boarding House shell shattered the windows of Charles Emerson's Boarding House at 5 and 6 Alfred Street and the windows of the empty number 7. The house of Cab Proprietor Richard Sigsworth, at 8 Alfred Street, was hit and damaged and the windows broken, whilst on the opposite side of the street the former Sarony photographic studio also suffered broken windows from the blast.

Valley Road and Royal Crescent Lane

A shrapnel shell burst over the imposing grandeur of the Municipal School in the Valley (later Westwood School and the Theatre in the Round), its hail of deadly bullets falling in the playground. A number of pupils had already arrived at the school from outlying areas and it was with great presence of mind that the caretaker, Francis Ogle, gathered them together and shepherded them into the school's cellars out of harm's way. No one was hurt and no serious damage was done.

Elsewhere on Valley Road, Colonel Tatham's home, *The Priory*, had its windows broken, whilst at *Normanhurst*, the home of Mrs Rines, the roof was badly damaged when a shell blew off a large number of slates.

At the stables on Royal Crescent Lane, owned by Mr Jackson of 76a Falsgrave Road, the entire roof was blown off from the blast of a nearby explosion. There were no reports of any injuries.

Cromwell Road, Cromwell Terrace, Grosvenor Crescent, Westbourne Grove and Carlton Terrace

In the next street, Cromwell Road, a house was struck and one of its upper floor bedrooms was simply blown to bits. Another house in Cromwell Terrace was damaged and the stables at the rear of the property were demolished. The house of J. Kitson, at 10 Grosvenor Crescent, was also damaged.

As shells rained down, several houses on Westbourne Grove were hit. At the homes of Mr Gibson, number 26, and solicitor Percival Medley, number 28, the roofs and chimney stacks were struck and damaged, while the rear of Mrs Davey's house, number 27, and that of the Headmaster of the Art School at the Municipal School, Albert Strange, number 29, both suffered severe damage and broken windows.

At the Westlands School on Westbourne Grove, where the pupils were at breakfast, the noise of the bombardment was put down to thunder until one little Belgian girl, who had been through the horrors of shelling in Belgium, cried out, "No! It is cannon!"

A moment later a portion of shell smashed into the upper part of the building, shattering the windows, destroying desks and blackboards. The Headmistress, Miss Wood, ordered everyone to the school's cellars where they remained until the shelling ceased. The entire school was then paraded, the roll called and then they were all marched briskly to Seamer station where they entrained en bloc for the safety of York.

PRINCE OF WALES HOTEL

The hotel at 30-31 Prince of Wales Terrace
was owned by Henry Furniss.

Further along the street a young man named Dent emerged unscathed when his house was struck by a shell and partly demolished. The roof and three upper rooms were destroyed by a shell which also shattered the windows of grocer John Shaw's house at 7 Carlton Terrace.

The Esplanade Area ~ Belmont Road, Esplanade, Prince of Wales Terrace and Esplanade Gardens

In the Esplanade area (which road runs along parallel to the cliff-top of the South Bay) a whole series of shells fell causing much destruction and mayhem.

The Esplanade Boarding Establishment, owned by Councillor Frank White, on Belmont Road, was hit and damage done to several of its rooms. Miss Beardsley's house at 17 Esplanade was damaged when a shell blasted through the wall leaving a scorch mark in its wake burnt into the fancy gilded wallpaper. At number 18, Albert Gilbank's balcony was damaged by the same shell which hit number 19, home of the antique dealer Maria Inskip, where all the windows were broken. At the photographer's, Brigham's, at number 20, a shell pierced the outside wall and entered the house doing a great deal of internal damage. At number 21 a shell went through the front of invalid Elizabeth Bromet's house, narrowly missing her for she had been unable to leave the room to seek shelter elsewhere. Another shell ploughed through number 22, builder John Jaram's house, and number 23, the home of Miss Barker, doing considerable damage to both; the blast from the shell being responsible for shattering the windows of a further five houses in the row. A further shell struck the cornice at the top of William Fletcher's house at 29 Esplanade, changed direction and ploughed through the roof into the upper storey. As the shelling continued more and more properties along the length of the Esplanade were damaged.

The frontage of Henry Furniss's imposing Prince of Wales Hotel at 30 and 31 Prince of Wales Terrace, overlooking the South Bay, suffered greatly when a shell exploded in the street in front of it, peppering the stonework and windows with shrapnel bullets and causing an estimated £4,000 worth of damage. Stone coping and pallisading at the front of the building was blown off, while a portion of the shell buried itself deep into the hotel's foundations. At the back of the premises one of its many chimney stacks was so severely battered by shell fragments it was in danger of collapse onto any unfortunate passer-by at any moment.

Also on Prince of Wales Terrace, the Red Lea Boarding House, owned by the Ridley sisters, was hit. A shell caught the outer mullion of a top-floor bay window before entering the building and doing immense damage to a number of rooms inside. Indeed, the shell hit the building with such force that all the bay windows below the one struck were so thrown out of alignment they had to be pulled down and rebuilt. Next door, at number 6, the home of Mr Arnott, all the windows were shattered by the force of the Red Lea blast, whilst twenty-two-year-old Marjorie Sawdon, from Cottingham, staying at number 14, was badly wounded in the neck and arm and was taken to hospital for treatment. At 32 Prince of Wales Terrace, the roof of *Rothsay House*, belonging to Mrs Taylor, was damaged. At the home of Miss Barlow, at 26 Esplanade Gardens (a road running off the Esplanade), the entire middle floor of the house was demolished by a direct hit. Despite these varying degrees of damage however, no one was killed, though a number of people were injured, among them nineteen-year-old Richard Mason of 19 Esplanade Gardens who was wounded in both legs. Indeed so severe were his injuries that he was taken to hospital and there had one of his legs amputated.

The Esplanade, high over the South Bay was particularly badly hit, with many properties damaged

At St Martin's, Archdeacon Mackarness continued with Holy Communion despite two shells hitting the church

The bombardment's first two victims, Leonard Ellis and Harry Frith, were killed on South Street

The Spa escaped unscathed, though the gardens behind it were littered with shells, debris and craters

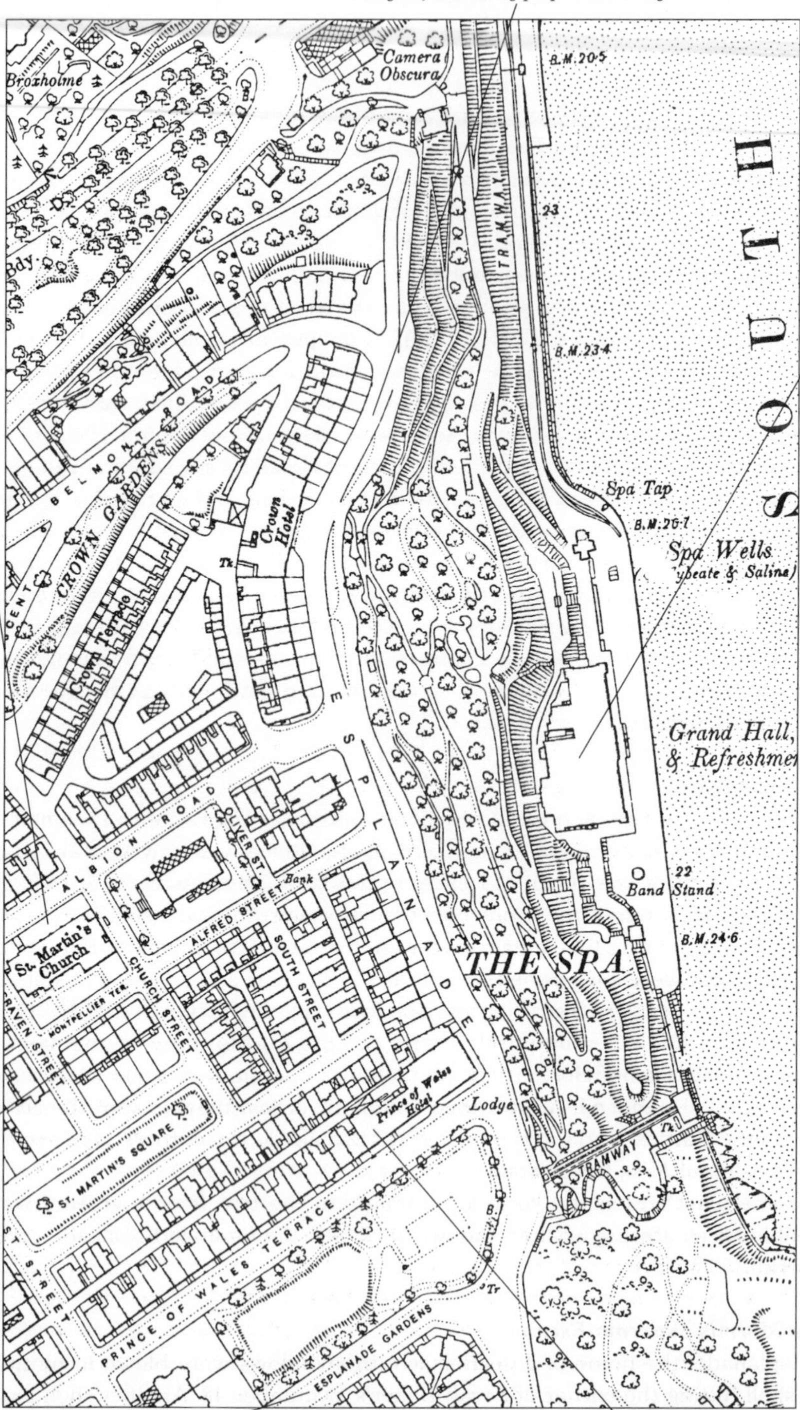

At 19 Esplanade Gardens Richard Mason was so severely wounded he needed a leg amputating

Henry Furniss's Prince of Wales Hotel suffered over £4,000 worth of damage

The Granville Private Hotel Fatality

Further along the Esplanade a gaping hole was ripped in the roof of the house sited at the corner of the Esplanade and Esplanade Gardens. The windows of Miss Cook's rooms, and of the rest of the *Tower House* at 32 Esplanade, were broken by shrapnel bullets from a shell which burst in front of them. The Granville Private Hotel, at 36-37 Esplanade, owned by Mr Truefitt, also had its windows broken. Worse, however, was yet to come for at 38 Esplanade, John and Alice Duffield, believing there was a lull in the shelling, had come out of their house only to be accosted by a neighbour shouting that her house was on fire and could one of them phone the fire station for help. Dutifully John Duffield undertook the task and ran for the nearby Granville Private Hotel, itself damaged seconds before, where he knew there to be a phone. A moment later the apparent lull in the firing came to an end as more shells crashed into the town. Fearing for her husband's safety, Alice Duffield left her home and made a dash for the Granville. As she set foot upon the first step on the flight up to the main entrance, where her husband was standing framed in the doorway crying for her to go back, a shrapnel shell exploded almost on top of her and both were wounded, she fatally so. Despite swift assistance from the Granville nothing could be done for her and she died soon after from her injuries; for days afterwards her innocent blood stained the steps and pavement as a reminder of the horrific event.

At 34 Esplanade, situated between Esplanade Gardens and Esplanade Road, the Cecil Boarding House, belonging to the Harrowby sisters, was hit and a large hole punched in it. The same explosion broke many of its windows. Another shell came close to hitting the South Cliff Tramway, with its carriages partially filled with people, but struck a wall instead - partly demolishing it - veered off and ploughed a deep furrow in the nearby Belvedere Gardens.

Visitors Lose Legs

All the while, the houses and buildings along the Esplanade continued to come under the aim of the enemy gunners. At numbers 39 and 41, both owned by Mary Atkinson, considerable damage was done, especially to the latter which was the Parade Private House. Here a shell burst inside one of the main rooms, the blast smashing a piano to matchwood and injuring two female visitors to the town. The pair, Mrs Bell-Irving and Miss Bertha Lee, were each severely wounded in the legs and required hospitalisation and extensive surgery for their injuries. The following day (Thursday, 17th December) Mrs Bell-Irving had a leg amputated, and despite efforts to avoid the same thing happening to her friend, Bertha Lee, she too was operated on again (Saturday, 19th December) and also lost a leg. After their traumatic ordeal the pair were sent from the hospital to the Barnes Nursing Home at 47-49 Esplanade Road, there to recover under the supervision of Miss Greenwood.

The same blast which did so much damage to the two female visitors was also responsible for shattering all the windows of *Kilburn House* at 40 Esplanade, the home of Miss Hill.

Minnie Merrils' Narrow Escape

At 47 Esplanade, the home of José Reixach, the windows were blown in by the blast from a shell hitting the corner of Sarah Baker's at number 48. Another shell ploughed into the front of the Astoria Boarding House at numbers 51-56. A large house occupying the corner site where Belvedere Road enters the Esplanade was literally blown to

SOUTH CLIFF

1: London & Joint Stock Bank, 2 Alfred Street. 2: Esplanade Gardens. 3: Belvedere, Esplanade. 4: Astoria Boarding House, 51-56 Esplanade. 5: South Cliff Wesleyan Church . 6: Brigham's Photographers, 20 Esplanade.

kingdom come by a shell which scored a direct hit. The mammoth blast from this explosion shattered the windows of houses hundreds of yards away along the Esplanade. At number 66, where the local Justice of the Peace, Mr Beeforth, resided (having recently moved from the larger house down the road - which had just been hit) a shell crashed through the roof, ploughed through two floors and came to rest in the dining-room on the ground floor. With most of its awesome power spent, a maid in the room, Minnie Merrils, was able to escape with only minor cuts and bruises. It was a narrow escape and she was lucky enough to live to tell the tale.

South Cliff, West Street and the Filey Road Area

A shell went through the roof of Mr Fisher's house at 34 West Street and did some considerable damage inside, where it blew out the windows and wounded passer-by Betsy Bradley in the head and upper body. She was taken to hospital for treatment and later released.

At Scarborough College, on Filey Road, the youngsters in the prep school had been dressing when the bombardment began. One or two of the smaller ones began to cry, thinking it was thunder. However, the headmaster of the prep school, Lawrence Armstrong, told them the truth, that the town was being bombarded by German warships in the bay, as he strode through the dormitories exhorting them to finish dressing and go to their breakfasts. The news of the shelling brought fresh tears to many a young face, though there were others amongst them who crowded the seaward windows to watch the huge ships pound the town. To their horrified fascination the boys witnessed a shell blow the garden shed of the Scarborough Convalescent Home for Children - on the opposite side of Filey Road, the side nearest the sea - to bits, parts of the shell damaging a brick wall and breaking the Home's windows. Another shell ploughed into the earth bank in front of the College, breaking several of its own windows.

By now most of the older boys had been escorted by their headmaster, Percy Armstong, (the elder of the two Armstrong brothers) across the golf links to the dubious shelter of Oliver's Mount - one of the most dangerous places on the south side of the town as a large number of shells crashed into its wooded hillsides - whilst the younger boys went down to breakfast. By the time they had finished eating the shelling was over and the older boys returned. Although subdued, things continued as normal at the college throughout the day, including the prep school's end-of-term Christmas party that evening. However, with many pupils unsettled by the German attack and parents wanting their children sent home, the college brought forward its end of term by several days and closed the following day, 17th December.

With fears of another attack in everyone's minds the college's governors took the drastic step of removing the entire school to the Park Hotel in Keswick, Cumbria, and it was here that the majority of the pupils returned in the New Year. The college eventually returned to Scarborough in 1916.

Within minutes of the deaths of Leonard Ellis and Harry Frith on South Street, and Alice Duffield at the Granville Boarding House, the shelling was to claim two more victims some several hundred yards further south in the area of Filey Road, the main coastal road leading into the town from the direction of Filey, Bridlington and Hull.

The Deaths at Dunollie

At *Dunollie* - one of the largest and most imposing houses in the town, situated at 31

1

2

ALFRED BEAL

The last thing local postman Alfred Beal (1) saw before he died was the front door (2) of *Dunollie* (3) as he walked up the drive to deliver the morning's mail.

3

Filey Road - the first of three shrapnel shells exploded above the broad porch at the front of the house.

Local postman, Alfred Beal, on his way up to the house to deliver the morning mail, was blown from his feet and killed instantly by the blast. Inside, the maid, Margaret Briggs, in the library off the main hall, died an horrific death as the second and third shells exploded.

The owner of the house, John Turner (a former sheriff of the county), having been awakened by the noise of the explosion, rushed downstairs in his dressing-gown and slippers to discover the hallway full of dense smoke and debris. Shocked and confused he called out for Margaret, his maid of ten years, three times. Receiving no reply to his calls he began feeling his way, with outstretched hands, to the front of the house. Just as he reached the front door another shell crashed into the house, flew over his shoulder and exploded against a pair of doors at the far end of the hallway - the ones he had only moments before negotiated his way through. Greatly concerned for the welfare of the missing maid, Turner staggered from the devastated hall and into the library, the nearest room to hand. There he discovered the lifeless body of twenty-nine-year-old Margaret Briggs sprawled face down across a couch. He called her name, all the while struggling to reach her through the debris of scattered books, many embedded with shrapnel, splintered wood and shattered glass. On reaching her he shook her softly, and then more vigorously when she failed to respond; but she was dead. Gently turning her over, Turner was sickened to discover the poor woman's stomach laid open, cleanly, as if by a knife, the wound evidently made by a fragment from one of the many shells to have fallen on the house. On further investigation of her numerous injuries, both her legs were found to have been broken, as if by a blow from some heavy object. At the later inquest into her death, John Turner stated that three shells had landed at the front of the house, and some thirteen to the rear of it.

Some minutes later a local policeman, PC Robert Shepherd, having rushed to the scene, discovered the crumpled body of forty-one-year-old Alfred Beal in the drive leading up to the house. The postman's body was some twenty yards from the porch and it was believed it had been thrown a good portion of that distance by the blast of the first explosion. Alfred Beal's injuries extended from his left shoulder to the lower portion of his body. Close by lay his postal cap and delivery bag; the letters from which, many torn and tattered by the explosion, were scattered over the drive and gardens along with great chunks of masonry from the partially demolished front portico and two of its eight stone columns which were felled by the blast.

Mount Lea

Of the many shells which fell on Filey Road and struck the wooded hillsides of Oliver's Mount, several shells crashed into the Sanderson home *Mount Lea*, at number 44. Mrs Sanderson, feeding the family's dog in the greenhouse when the shelling started, saw a shell crash through into the drawing-room, devastating it, followed by another which devastated the kitchen. Immediately the family made for the coal cellar and hid just as another shell crashed into the maid's bedroom upstairs. Fearing for his family, Mr Sanderson, who had already left to catch the 8.30am train, rushed back to the devastated house. At first he could see no one and called out, his voice frantic with worry. Gradually his wife and children emerged, blackened, from the coal cellar, unharmed. Leaving the family together in a huddle to survey the ruins of their home, Mr Sanderson sped off to the Crown Garage on Ramshill where he kept his car.

Esplanade Road, where Dr Thornley's chauffeur, Fred Smith, carried another man to safety even though wounded himself

The home of Kathleen Walker at 14 Lonsdale Road was practically demolished by a direct hit

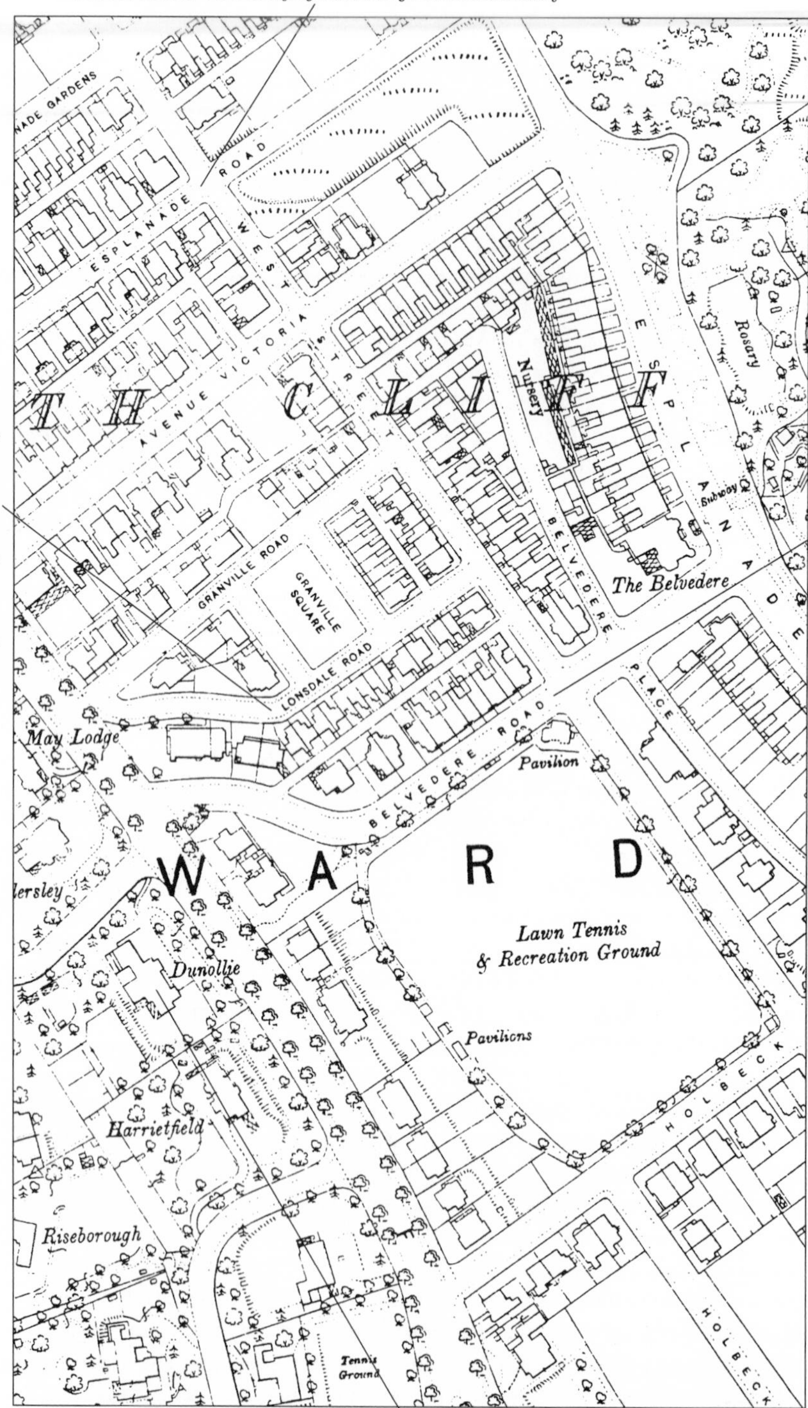

Selina Tindall's maid, Edith Crosby, was killed by a dud shell which crashed through 1 Belvedere Road and ploughed on through the house next door before coming to rest in the garden

Dunollie, 31 Filey Road, the home of John Turner where postman Alfred Beal and maid Margaret Briggs were killed by three of the sixteen shells which fell on and around the house

He almost didn't make it back to his family, for a shell burst through the roof of the garage as he reached it. Nevertheless, despite the damage, he managed to get the car out and, returning for his family and the dog, fled the town for Pickering by way of Seamer Road, passing crowds of others doing likewise, on foot, by horse, wagon and cart.

Belvedere Road and Lonsdale Road ~ Dud Shell Slays Maid

On Belvedere Road - which connects Filey Road with the Esplanade - extensive damage and another death were caused by a shell which failed to explode. The shell entered a house on the Esplanade, facing the sea, passed straight through it from front to back, crashed through a brick garden wall, sped across the road and smashed through the home of Selina Tindall at 1 Belvedere Road, killing her maid, thirty-nine-year-old Edith Crosby, as it went. The shell sped on and ploughed through Miss Blackburn's house next door (number 2) before landing harmlessly and spent in the garden.

A street away from the fatality at Belvedere Road, another shell from the cluster that fell in this area scored a direct hit on 14 Lonsdale Road, doing it considerable damage. Half of the roof and upper two storeys were demolished, leaving the chimney stack precariously perched on the remaining piece of roof. The house, the home of Kathleen Walker, was unoccupied at the time for she was away. The houses on either side also sustained damage from the blast, though again, no one was hurt. Had the shell fallen on the house next door (number 13) it would have claimed many casualties, for there, at *Lawnside*, the entire Railton family were at home and so had a remarkably lucky escape, though the house did suffer some damage.

Filey Road ~ Queen Margaret's School Evacuated

Towards the Ramshill Road end of Filey Road more houses were damaged, as was Queen Margaret's Hall (now Queen Margaret's Nursing Home) at number 19. The imposing building had started life in the late 1800s as the Orelton Boys School, before becoming part of the residential buildings of Queen Margaret's School. At the outbreak of war the pupils were moved out and the building was earmarked for use as a temporary hospital. The same blast shattered all the windows at 6 Filey Road, the shop premises of Whitfield and Son Chemists.

On Queen Margaret's Road (then little more than a cart-track), which runs off Filey Road, around Oliver's Mount and down to the Mere and Seamer Road, the girls of Queen Margaret's School - amongst them the sixteen-year-old Winifred Holtby - were at breakfast when the bombardment began. At the sound of the first loud bang it was assumed by those at breakfast that someone had fallen over upstairs in one of the rooms above them. However, it swiftly became apparent that the thunderous roars they were listening to were being made by large guns. With the girls sitting in terrified silence the headmistress, Miss Fowler, gathered her mistresses and took command of the situation, ordering everyone to the cloakroom.

"Put on your long coats, tammies and thick boots; we're going for a walk into the country till it is over," she told them.

The girls, escorted by the mistresses, trooped out of the school and along Queen Margaret's Road in the direction of the Mere. All about them shells whistled and exploded. Many too close for comfort.

"RUN!" bellowed Miss Fowler suddenly, and the girls, needing no second bidding, ran for all they were worth. One girl caught her foot and sprawled headlong on the

A number of houses on Westbourne Grove suffered damage to roofs, chimneys and windows

The girls of Queen Margaret's School were evacuated to Seamer, via the Mere road. Among them was Winifred Holtby who would later write a dramatic account of the bombardment

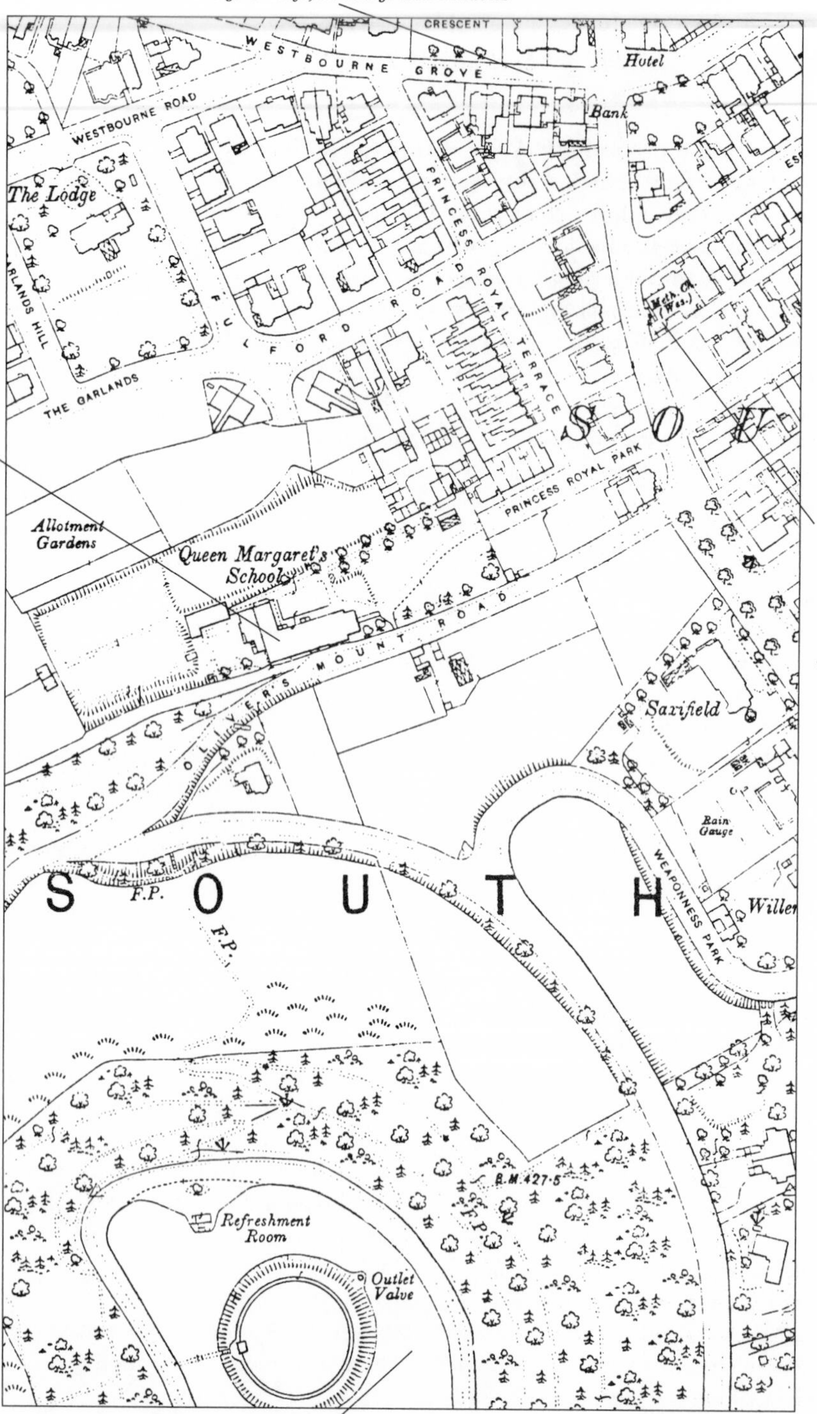

The tower of the South Cliff Wesleyan Church on Ramshill Road was struck and damaged

A whole clutch of shells fell on and around Oliver's Mount (later the site for the town's war memorial)

muddy track, but was quickly helped to her feet by others who urged her on as the crowd headed down the hill towards the Mere. Down Queen Margaret's Road they ran, and had almost reached the railway level-crossing (where now stands a bridge) when a shell struck the ground fifty yards ahead of them, sending up a huge shower of mud and stones. Across the road a house was hit by a shell and demolished, an angry red spurt of flame shooting briefly into the air to the terrified astonishment of the onlookers.

"BACK! BACK!" cried Miss Fowler, still in the lead. The girls turned about and headed off down the path which skirted the Mere, then simply carried on across the rough ground, across mud littered with broken bottles, crockery and refuse until they could get across the railway line and up onto Seamer Road (now the A64). Here they joined the throng of refugees streaming out of the town towards Seamer via the main road (what is now Stoney Haggs Rise). Amidst all the confusion and panic a group of girls found themselves caring for four small children, barely clothed, who had become separated from their mother. At the top of the hill the children's mother, frantically searching, welcomed them with open arms. The girls of Queen Margaret's did not stop moving until they were within sight of the village of Seamer, and there they gratefully sank to the ground, exhausted.

Following the bombardment the school (as with so many others) was moved to the safer environs of the Palace Hotel, Pitlochry in Perthshire, well out of the reach of the guns of German warships.

Enemy's Second Pass ~ Northward

As the *Derfflinger* and the *Von der Tann* levelled with White Nab (close to Cornelian Bay), they veered away, turned and began to retrace their steps, all the while maintaining their rate of fire. Meanwhile the *Kolberg* continued south-east, laying a screen of over a hundred mines to parry any attempt by the Humber and Harwich Royal Naval flotillas to intervene, should they try. The concentration of mines laid by the *Kolberg* was heavy to say the least, and many of the mines being discovered in recent years (including the one in the Imperial War Museum) come from the 'Kolberg minefield'. These mines, together with the British and German minefields already laid off the north-east coast from the Tyne to the Humber, were to continue to claim many more victims long after the raid was over.

At Cayton Bay, the Yorkshire Hussars guarding the Scarborough Waterworks Pumping Station were on alert. At the sound of the first salvo the order to 'Stand To' had been given. However, the NCOs, enjoying their 'billet' breakfast in the home of the pumping station manager, George Sewell, were ordered by Mrs Sewell to sit back down and finish eating it before it went cold! As the men eventually left the house to make their way to the trenches and machine-gun nests dug into the cliffs above the pumping station they watched two of the German battleships turn about and loose a salvo of about twenty rounds in the general direction of the Waterworks Pumping Station (most of these overshot and landed beyond Cayton village) whilst the third, described as 'having three funnels' continued on its course. Immediately it was assumed by the Hussars there would be a landing on the beach at Cayton Bay and the Corporal in charge decided to move the Sewell family into Cayton village out of harm's way.

Whilst the Hussars manned their trenches and machine-gun pits, Scarborough's usually placid and peaceful streets, its tree-lined avenues and leafy lanes, had become places of terror, injury and death. Each battleship now altered the elevation of its guns and deliberately targeted different areas of the town. The bombardment suffered so far

SEAMER ROAD

1&2: The Scarborough Brick and Tile Company's brickworks tower, Barry's Lane, off Seamer Road. 3: John White, wounded on Seamer Road. 4: Fred Linn's *Inkerman Villa*, 25 Seamer Road.

was as nothing compared to the hail of shells that now fell. Steel, shell, high explosive and shrapnel rained down from the skies over the most populated parts of the town, and there was practically no escaping it as the place was swept from sandy coast to borough boundary by withering fusillade after withering fusillade.

Death and destruction was visited on Scarborough with all the ferocity of hell, the dogs of war let loose to run rampant through her desperate streets. The formerly grey, early morning sky was lit up with huge flashes from the naval guns and an eerie crimson glow could be seen all over the town. Now there was no order or pattern to the shelling; it became totally random and indiscriminate and the whole town lay at the gunners' mercy - though not a jot was shown.

Had the local populace stayed within their homes it is possible fewer would have suffered injury. As it was, frightened, bewildered and anxious to be away from the shelling, hundreds dashed into the streets where they were caught by flying shrapnel, glass and falling building debris.

The Seamer Road Area

In the Seamer Road district of the town (now the main A64 road into Scarborough from Malton and York) the raised elevation of the enemy guns served up more misery and mayhem in what were then the quieter suburbs of the town, on the borough boundary.

Crowds of 'refugees' left their homes and made for the open country, heading as far out as the village of Seamer. An old woman, an invalid, was transported there on a chair carried by three other elderly ladies; cars were kept busy ferrying people from the mayhem in Scarborough, depositing them in Seamer, before turning around and starting back for more. However, the village itself was not out of range of the enemy's guns, for men working close to the lime kilns had watched shells raining down into nearby 'planting' at Claude Norton's recently built Irton Manor House.

Later in the morning the police in Seamer received a telegram telling them all was once again 'safe' in Scarborough, and that the refugees should now return to their homes, but via the footpaths, as there would be artillery on the roads.

The Gas Works, Harcourt Avenue, Asquith Avenue and Milton Avenue

Further along Seamer Road, roughly opposite the football ground, a large shell fragment narrowly missed the gas works foreman, Mr Atkinson, of 2 Gas House Cottages. One of the gas holders was holed and some of the gas escaped, but failed to ignite. There was no more damage.

Another shell took away the entire crown off the tall Scarborough Brick and Tile Company's tower, whilst a number of shells exploded in the nearby quarry. A team of five later repaired the damage to the tower.

On Harcourt Avenue, leading off Asquith Avenue (in which a horse already lay dead) and running parallel to Seamer Road, major damage was caused by a shell which hit Ellen Johnson's house at number 3, blowing in the roof and windows. The blast from the explosion had an enormous effect on the surrounding streets. On Harcourt Avenue itself the majority of the properties, some seventeen in number, had their windows smashed. In nearby Asquith Avenue, running off Seamer Road, ten houses suffered broken windows. Three houses on Milton Avenue, situated behind Harcourt Avenue, also suffered broken windows and one of them had severely splintered woodwork about the window frames as a result of the shrapnel.

The premises of the Electric Supply Works situated at the top of Beaconsfield Street where Private Bowman of the 5th Green Howards was seriously wounded

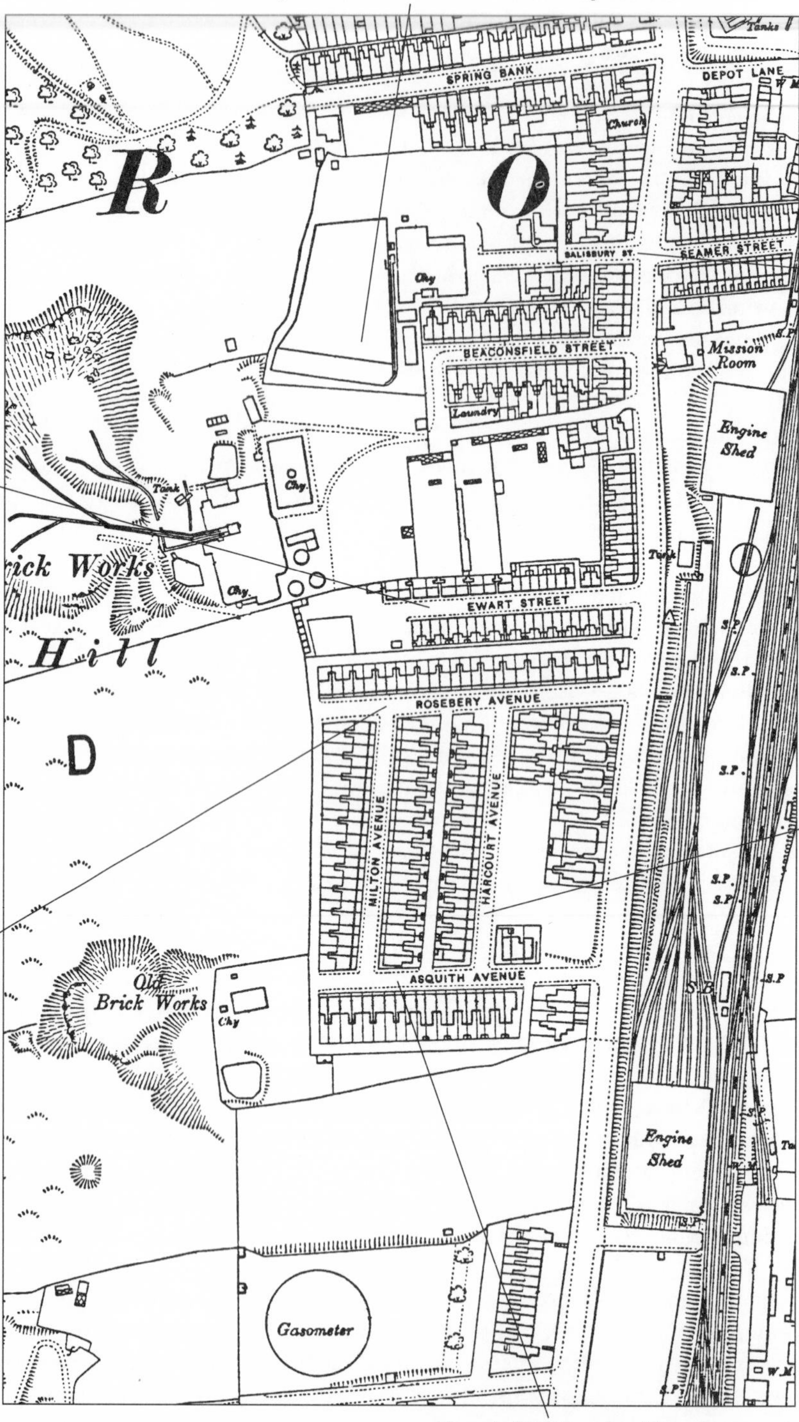

The home of Alfred and Diana Stevenson at 2 Salisbury Street had all its windows broken by a nearby blast

The blast from the shell which hit Robert Stead's house broke the windows of seven houses on nearby Ewart Street

The home of Ellen Johnson at 3 Harcourt Avenue was seriously damaged by a direct hit

At 7 Rosebery Avenue, Robert Stead's home was seriously damaged

The only fatality on Asquith Avenue was a milkman's horse

Rosebery Avenue, Ewart Street, Beaconsfield Street and Salisbury Street ~ Private Bowman Gravely Wounded

The path of damage continued on Rosebery Avenue when a shell struck number 7, blasting its way into one of Robert Stead's upper-floor bedrooms and blowing out all the windows in the house. The blast shattered the windows of five houses close by, and on Ewart Street, the road running parallel to Rosebery Avenue, seven more houses had their windows broken by the same blast.

Outside the Electric Supply Works (the power station and one of the only 'genuine targets' in the town) situated at the top of Beaconsfield Street, a shrapnel shell exploded, seriously wounding Private Bowman of the 5th Green Howards, the sentry who was on guard duty outside the premises. Despite having both legs shattered by the blast, Private Bowman managed to pull himself along a passageway to reach his stunned comrades. It is said the first thing he asked for was a cigarette. Bowman was rushed to the hospital in the basement of Westborough Wesleyan Chapel.

Though the Electric Supply Works was relatively unscathed, thirteen houses in the street were not so fortunate and had their windows blown out. The same blast from the explosion also blew out the windows in three houses in adjoining Salisbury Street and the spent shell tore off painter Arthur Metcalfe's chimney stack at number 3 on its way down.

The Borough Laundry building on Beaconsfield Street had its elevator housing roof blown clean off by the same blast which injured Private Bowman.

Spring Bank and West Bank

In the next street, Spring Bank, another shell exploded outside number 7, Mrs Cameron's, causing severe damage to the frontages of a whole row of houses. The front downstairs rooms of the house were blown in and the furniture decimated, while all the windows, both front and back were blown out. At 8 Spring Bank an elderly lady, seventy-four-year-old Mrs Heald, was struck on the head by flying debris from the blast and collapsed, stunned, sustaining more cuts and bruises. In the road a broken water pipe quickly filled the hole made by the shell. In all some seventeen houses on the street suffered damage, mainly to windows, with minor damage inside where numerous ornaments and bric-a-brac fell and were broken. At the back of Spring Bank all the rear windows of 6 West Bank, the home of Mrs Stobart, were broken by the blast.

Seamer Road and Highfield

Several shells landed along the length of Seamer Road. At number 17 the greenhouses and cold-frames of gardener Christopher Elsdon were demolished, though no one was injured and the house remained intact. Further along at *Inkerman Villa*, 25 Seamer Road, the home of Fred Linn, a shell (having travelled all of two miles) scored a direct hit and all but levelled the house. The entire upper portion was blown away, the ceilings of the ground-floor rooms were caved in and all the windows, those that remained after the initial impact, were broken. The house adjoining it, *Rosevear*, owned by local house agent Mr Wrightson, suffered similar damage from the same shell.

Another shell burst through the upper front bedroom wall of Robert Storry's house, at 41 Seamer Road, creating a large hole and destroying the room's entire contents, before it ploughed through an interior wall to the room beyond where the windows were blown out. The walls of the house were later discovered to have been peppered with bullet holes, indicating that the shell had been filled with shrapnel.

At 51 St John's Road, Lily Bain had a miraculous escape when a shrapnel shell exploded outside her house peppering the room she was in with bullets. She emerged unscathed

Charles Herbert's house at 79 Commercial Street was seriously damaged by a direct hit

Both Bertha McEntyre and baby John Ryalls were killed at 22 Westbourne Park

At 25 Seamer Road, the home of Fred Linn, Inkerman Villa, was almost levelled by a direct hit

Architect and Justice of the Peace, John Hall, was mortally wounded at 28 Westbourne Park and died on the hospital steps

Along the length of the road a large number of windows were damaged by the blasts from various shells, one of which exploded in the front garden of *Luxmount*, the home of Mr McGachen, doing considerable damage. The entire garden was torn up; the boundary wall enclosing it and a nearby culvert were blown to bits and the horse of milkman Edward Leng, who was continuing with his round despite the shelling, was killed outright, though the milk escaped intact. The house itself sustained damage to its frontage as well as suffering the obligatory smashed windows.

Seventy-seven-year-old John White, walking along Seamer Road at the time of the shelling, was wounded in the head, nose and side by shrapnel and flying debris and was taken to hospital for treatment.

The damage on Seamer Road extended as far as Naylor's Coal Yard (now flats) situated at the junction of Seamer Road with Valley Road, and here again, more windows were broken at *Alice House*, coal merchant Alfred Naylor's home.

Further along Seamer Road, nearer the Falsgrave area, the home of the Vicar of St James' Church, Reverend A. Pawson, *Burleigh House* at 1 Highfield, was hit and the roof blown in. As the shell passed through the house it devastated two upper bedrooms and ended up in the drawing-room where a little less damage was done. No one was hurt.

Westbourne Park ~ Three More Victims ~ Youngest Life Claimed

On the opposite side of Seamer Road, on Westbourne Park - a crescent with both ends adjoining Seamer Road - five houses suffered broken windows. At 22 Westbourne Park, the home of engineer Jasper Ryalls, severe damage was done when a shell smashed through the rear part of the roof, destroying an upper bedroom and demolishing an interior wall. Two people were killed in the incident. One, fourteen-month-old John Ryalls, was the youngest person to die during the bombardment, the other was forty-two-year-old Bertha McEntyre, an insurance agent from Sheffield. Bertha had only moments before taken the child from his father, George, in order to try and comfort him, for the noise of the bombardment was upsetting him greatly. The well-intentioned Bertha had taken the child up to her own bedroom at the rear of the house while she dressed and an instant later the shell had struck, killing her outright and fatally wounding the child. Little John Ryalls, his injuries extensive, especially to his head which was laid open exposing the child's brain, died in absolute agony some ten minutes later cradled in the arms of his distraught father. Ironically, had Bertha McEntyre taken the child to his own room, rather than hers, it is possible both would have survived.

Next door, Miss Coates of number 24 had her windows shattered by the same blast.

Further along the street at 28 Westbourne Park, another shell claimed the life of architect and Justice of the Peace, John Hall. The shell crashed through the dining-room window and exploded; the full force of the shrapnel blast directed upward. Sixty-five-year-old John Hall, who was in the room above dressing, was severely injured by the blast as the floor opened up beneath his feet. His injuries were severe, one of his legs was broken in two places, the other had had the flesh and muscle torn from it, one arm was broken in two places and he had a gaping wound in his side which was pouring blood. His daughter Gertrude, who had raced upstairs on hearing his cries and witnessed his plight, dashed into the street and was lucky enough to find Dr Hollings of *Willow Dene*, Stepney Road, hurrying by. There was little the doctor, or anyone else, could do as John Hall's injuries were so severe he required immediate hospitalisation and treatment.

ALL SAINTS' CHURCH

Falsgrave Road. Interior damage.

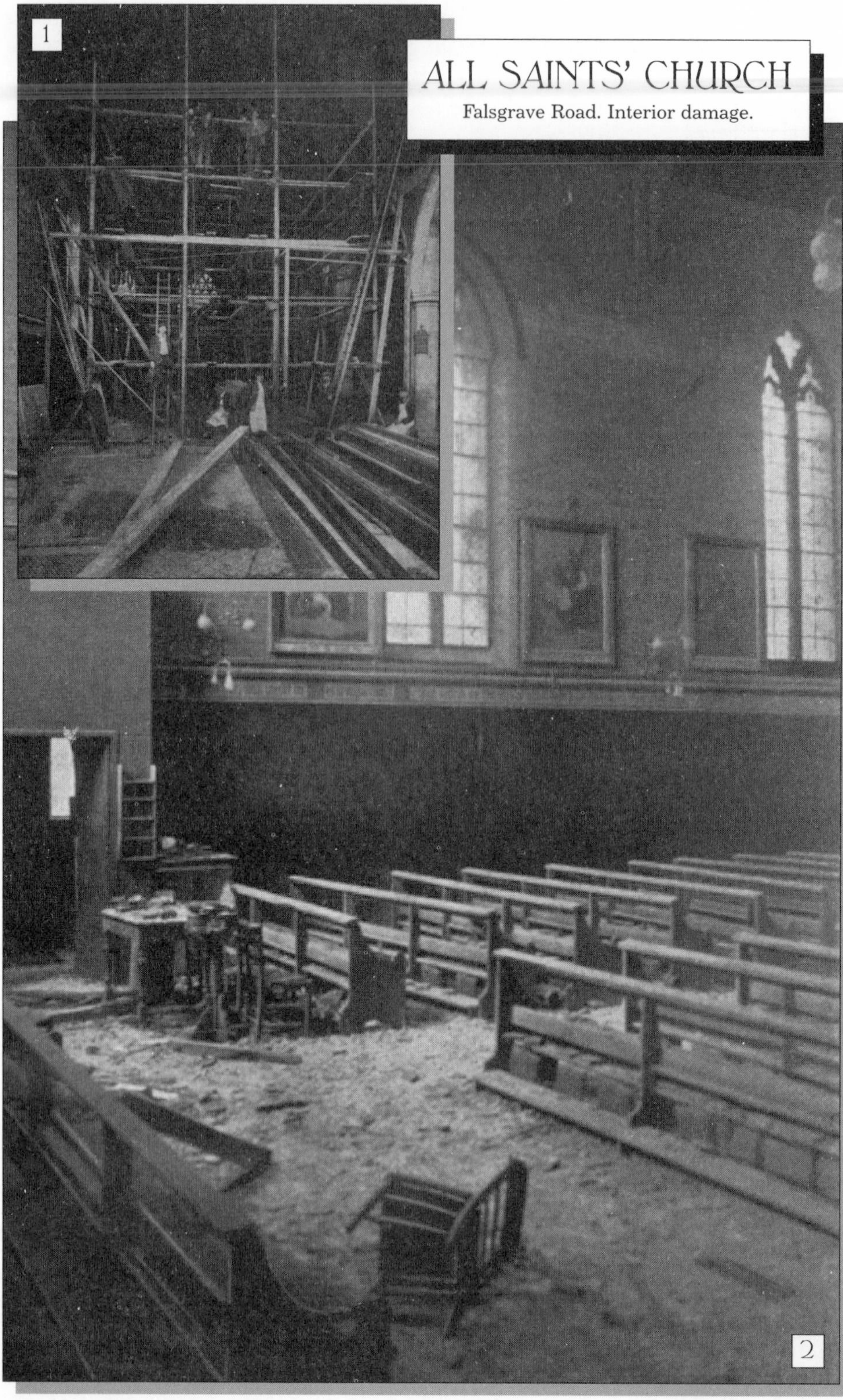

1

2

However, by the time an ambulance had arrived and he had been conveyed to the hospital, he was beyond help and expired on the stretcher on the steps leading up to the main entrance.

Avenue Road, Park Avenue, Londesborough Road, Belgrave Crescent and Belgrave Terrace

The home of Hannah Coates at 16 Avenue Road was severely damaged by an exploding shell and most of its windows were broken as the enemy gunners attempted to knock out the Wireless Station situated behind Falsgrave Park. One house, George Ward's *Coneysthorpe*, at 11 Park Avenue, close to the Wireless Station, was also badly damaged, whilst a second explosion punched a hole in the side of number 10, stripping the roof clean and shattering all the windows. Inside, an elderly lady, Mrs Gibson, wife of Ambrose Gibson, in bed with rheumatism, escaped unharmed, though she was very badly shaken. A stray shell fragment from the explosion struck the front of the Borough Accountant Mr Fawcett's home at number 6, shattering the windows and embedding itself in a window frame.

The rear of 48 Londesborough Road, the home of Mr Daglish, a house agent, was badly damaged, while at 14 Belgrave Crescent, *Belgrave Lodge*, the home of Marie Tonks, had its windows shattered by a nearby blast, which also damaged the front of the Industrial Home for Blind Women at number 13. The roof and upper storey of John Anderson's house, at 2 Belgrave Terrace, was badly damaged, and the furniture inside was wrecked by a direct hit.

Stepney Avenue, Stepney Road and the Falsgrave Road Area

A shell struck 41 Stepney Avenue, the home of Ellen Smith, blowing one of the bedrooms to pieces and shattering all the windows in the house. The sitting-room furniture was destroyed and buried under a mountain of debris from the upper floor. Six houses further along the street had their windows broken by the force of the explosion.

On Stepney Road a shell dived into a field at the entrance to the road and gouged a hole three yards across and several feet deep. Another exploded in the street causing damage to four nearby houses, peppering their garden walls and fronts with shell fragments. The slates were also blown from the roof of Mr Chatwin's home, *Oxenhope*, by the force of the blast. *Myrtle Bank*, home of Captain John Hirst had its windows broken, as were those of Benjamin Hold at *West Leigh*, and Dr Hollings at *Willow Dene* (the doctor who attended John Hall).

The broad Falsgrave Road (then beautifully tree-lined, with trams running its length) joins Seamer Road with Westborough and here more than fourteen residences, along with the Falsgrave Temperance Hall at number 143, suffered from the numerous nearby side-street explosions with many broken windows and sundry minor damage. The road's overhead tramlines were also brought down.

All Saints' Church was struck by a shell which knocked a large hole through the roof at the western end of the building, and also took out much of the glass of the west window. Although little interior damage was done, the windows facing the main road were broken in many places and there were real concerns for the safety of the roof, which it was feared would come down at the first blast from the organ!

At 28 Falsgrave, the home of Captain William Mosey (who was at that moment lying prone on the Receiving House floor), a chimney stack was sent crashing into the road,

BERTHA MCENTYRE AND JOHN RYALLS

Bertha McEntyre with John Ryalls. Both were killed at 22 Westbourne Park.

LILY BAIN

Fourteen-year-old Lily Bain had one of the most miraculous escapes at 51 St John's Road.

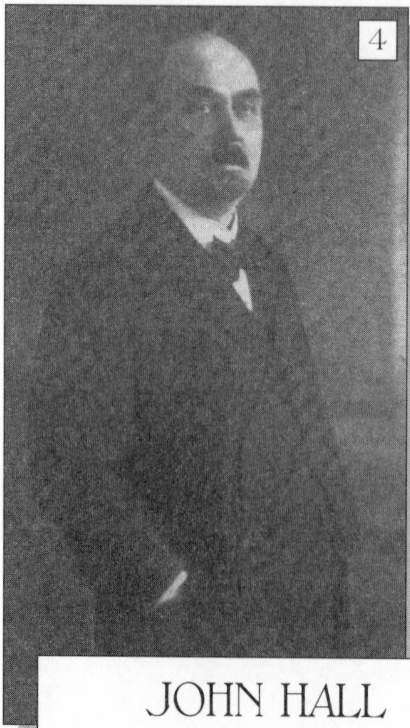

JOHN HALL

Mortally wounded at 28 Westbourne Park.

PARK AVENUE

SPRING BANK

and the roof of number 91, Taylor's Drugstore, was seriously damaged, as was that of number 93, the home of Reginald Hirst (the manager of Taylor's Drugstore next door).

The Death of Ada Crow

At the home of Mary Moorhouse, at 124 Falsgrave Road, the maid, Ada Crow, on hearing the bombardment, had rushed upstairs to her employer's bedroom to tell her not to worry about the noise as it was only the fleet practising offshore. Twenty-eight-year-old Ada had then turned around and rushed back downstairs to begin preparing the breakfast. Moments later a shell exploded inside the house, fatally injuring Ada in the chest just as she reached the bottom of the stairs. Though mortally wounded she managed to stagger upstairs again, where she collapsed in a pool of blood on the landing at the feet of her terror-stricken employer who had got up to see what was happening. Ada died moments later, her hands clasped to the bleeding wound in her chest.

The three terraced homes of Mary Bell at number 132, the wheelwright Walter Harland at number 134, and Miss Marshall at 136 Falsgrave Road all had their windows blown out by the blast from a shrapnel shell which burst in the street outside.

At 147 Falsgrave Road, the home of chemist Mr Eyre, a shell burst and seriously damaged the property, while a little further on at number 163, Harriet Webster was just leaving her home when she was struck and injured on the hand by a flying piece of shell.

St John's Road and St John's Avenue

Off Falsgrave Road, on St John's Road, a shell burst through the roof of number 19 and destroyed a top-floor bedroom; indeed the burst was so powerful it shattered the interior walls and doors of the upper storey of gardener Mr Skelton's home. At *Ebor Villa*, 8 St John's Road, another shell partially demolished fish dealer Henry Walker's roof, took off a chimney stack and did considerable internal damage to the upper floor.

The Remarkable Escape of Little Lily Bain

On St John's Road, number 51 was the recipient of the majority of the contents of a shrapnel shell, and here one of the most remarkable escapes of the whole attack occurred, when fourteen-year-old Lily Bain emerged from the place, unscathed, despite bullets from the exploded shell having decimated most of the house.

Prior to the German attack on the town, Andrew Bain, an engineer's manager, had taken himself off to work as usual, leaving his wife, daughter and baby son in the house. Mrs Bain was in a room at the front of the house with her son when the bombardment began, whilst her daughter was in the dining-room at the rear of the house. Lily, readying herself for school, was seated on a sofa in front of the dining-room window pulling on her boots when the shrapnel shell burst above and behind the house. The blast blew in the window and demolished the back of the building, while bullets rained into the exposed rooms. The vicious hail of shot tore through the curtains, wrenching them from their hangings as the glass from the shattered window sprayed the interior of the dining-room, most of it embedding itself in an unoccupied easy-chair on the opposite side of the room. The boot Lily was about to pull on was wrenched from her hands by the force of the blast and the sofa on which she sat was riddled with bullets. At her side, her leather school satchel was ripped to shreds and every one of the books inside was pierced and holed; even the satchel's steel handle was left mangled and mutilated. By

WIRELESS STATION

Throughout the war the Wireless Station, Scarborough's only genuine 'military' target, was situated behind Falsgrave Park and was under the command of Chief Officer Dean of the Coastguard.

The station was manned twenty-four hours a day, every day of the year and was used to listen to enemy ship-to-ship radio signals which were then used to fix the position of the enemy ships whilst at sea.

1: Chief Officer Dean takes a despatch from attached boy scout Victor Stunnell from the 1st Scarborough Troop. Many of the local scouts received awards for their performance during and after the raid. 2: The Wireless Station Staff: A. Reid (A), B. Geer (B), J. Williams (C), W. Johnstone (D), J. Salmon (E), A. Andrews (F), N. Abrahams (G), C. Keast (H), A. Penticost (I), Chief Officer Arthur Dean (J), Lieutenant E. Hilary Weighill, 5th Green Howards (K), H. Ovenden (L), 'Bob' (M). The civilians pictured worked for 'General Post Office Telephones'.

some strange fluke all the ornaments on the mantelpiece remained undamaged, though a number toppled onto the sofa on which Lily had been seated and where she was now curled into a tight ball praying for her ordeal to end. Across the room, beneath the dining-table, a makeshift kennel for the family's recently arrived puppies, though damaged, had served to protect them from harm. Also unharmed were the Bains's canary and goldfish, likewise housed in the devastated dining-room.

Upstairs, in the bedroom above the dining-room, all was chaos. The windows were gone, the interior walls were partly demolished and the heavy wooden furniture had been strewn about the room as if tossed casually aside by a giant hand. In the corner of the bedroom a large wardrobe had been pierced by a myriad bullets and every garment hanging within had been holed. Similarly, a chest of drawers beneath a dressing-table had been pierced and the clothing inside was left torn and tattered. In the bathroom the toilet cistern had been ripped from the wall and carried off by the blast to shatter against an opposite wall, leaving water spraying from the broken pipes into the rest of the carnage.

Mrs Bain and her baby son had been most fortunate to be in the front of the house when the shell had exploded, but Lily's escape from harm, emerging from the wreckage into the street without so much as a scratch, carrying the family pets, was little short of miraculous.

Nearby, a house had its rear windows smashed from the blast that had caused so much damage, but so little injury. Meanwhile, amid the confusion and mayhem, furniture remover George Harper of 81 St John's Road, was using his vehicles to move refugees out of the surrounding area to Scalby.

Another explosion took off much of Mr Brown's roof at *Franklin Villa*, 6 St John's Avenue, blew out his bathroom and broke most of his windows. The blast from this explosion also broke most of the windows in the *Red House*, situated at the top of Sitwell Street on the site of the former Strawberry Gardens. The *Red House* had been founded by Lady Sitwell for the 'reclaiming and employing of fallen girls'.

The Wireless Station and Falsgrave Farm

It was said that the people in the Falsgrave area flocked from their houses in their hundreds during the bombardment, as mothers with little ones huddled close made for the nearest road away from the devastation being visited upon them. The roads to East Ayton (where many older residents beat a track to John Newton's White Swan Inn on Main Street), Forge Valley, Seamer and Scalby were thronged with folk carrying whatever they had been able to lay their hands on at the time of their flight, many barely clothed in their haste to flee.

The Germans, evidently intent on destroying the town's Wireless Station, sent over a large number of shells, but all, bar one, fell well short. The men on guard duty, and those working at the station, sensing the danger they were in, retired some hundred or so yards to the rear of the station and were safe. Meanwhile, the station's guard dog and mascot 'Bob' - a little wire-haired terrier - had decided to abandon his post too, and he shot off at high speed as fast as his four paws could carry him. He was eventually found on the Racecourse well away from the Wireless Station!

Several men working near the station also had narrow escapes and threw down their tools and fled to safety. One shell dropped a few yards from a residence at the top of Falsgrave Park, one of those nearest to the Wireless Station. All its windows were shattered by the blast. Although the shells ploughed up tons of earth on the hill in front

At 67 Gordon Street Miss Faulder's roof was blown off

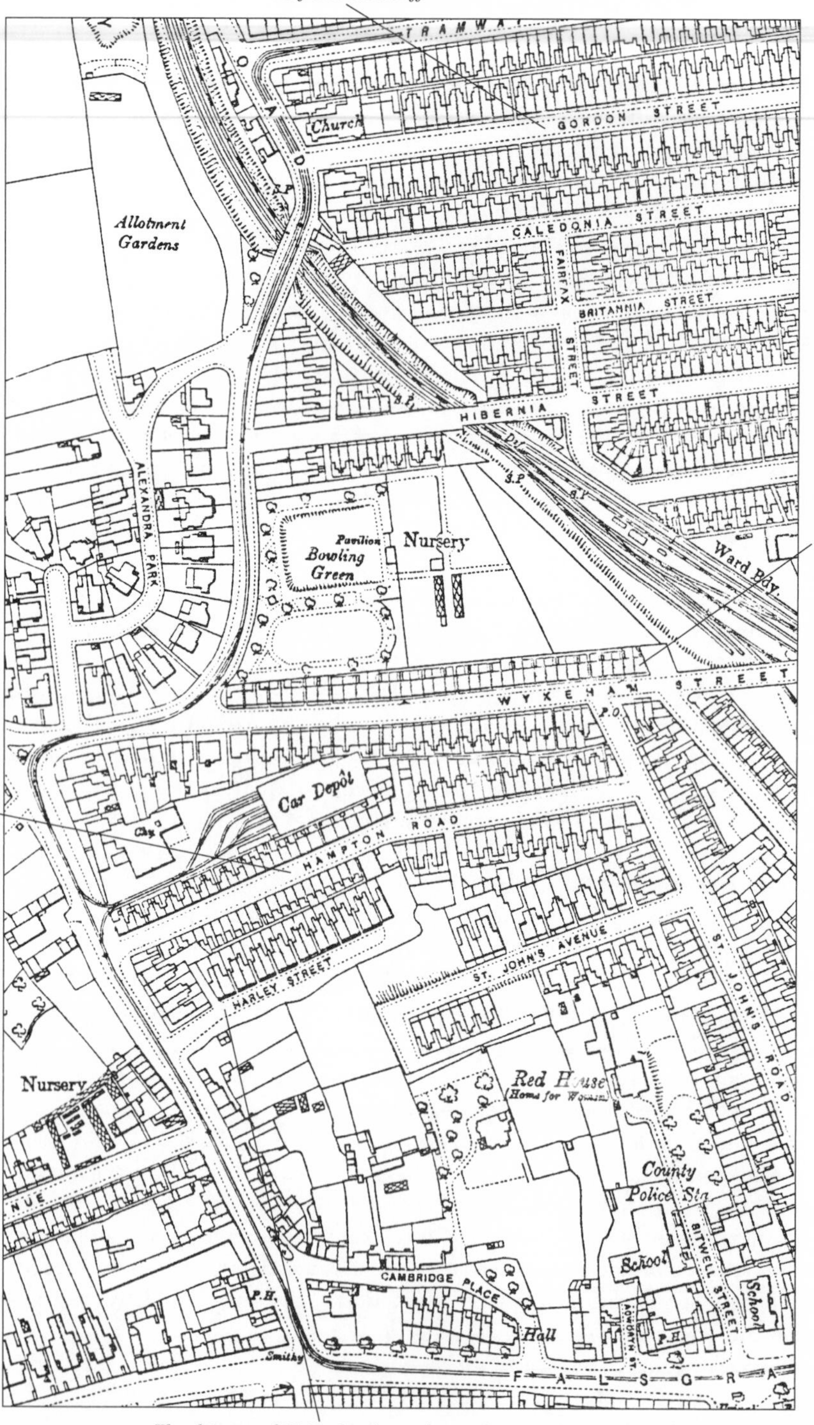

At the Warley home at 71 Hampton Road panic set in when the baby was struck by a stray piece of shell

Christopher Bennett was forced to drag his mother Johanna, brother Albert and the children George Barnes and John Ward from the wreckage of the family home at 2 Wykeham Street when it received a direct hit

The chimney of 35 Harley Street, home of Constance Dobson, was damaged of the station, no damage was done to it, though one shell fell just ten yards from the Wireless Receiving House. Two shells intended for the Wireless Station overshot and hit Falsgrave Farm some three miles from the coast. One of the farm buildings was struck and damaged, while a large crater was gouged in one of the fields.

In truth the Wireless Station could be said to have been a justifiable war-time target, for with it the British could listen to the radio communications of enemy shipping and, quite accurately, fix their positions. Something it appeared they had not done on this occasion!

Commercial Street, Harley Street and Hampton Road

On Commercial Street, which joins Falsgrave Road with Wykeham Street, even more significant damage was done. Number 79, the home of Charles Herbert, received a direct hit and was all but blown to bits. The entire roof was demolished and the outer walls of the house had large holes punched through them. Inside the house considerable damage was done, not only to the furniture, but to many of the interior walls. In the aftermath of the attack, at approximately 3.00pm, searchers from the St John Ambulance Brigade discovered an elderly lady (some reports claimed she was in her 80s, others in her 90s) and her daughter, fifty-five-year-old Jane White, huddled together in the ruins of the house which they had steadfastly refused to leave throughout the bombardment. The daughter, who had been struck in the back by shrapnel, was badly wounded and in need of immediate hospitalisation. Her elderly mother was found to be uninjured, but was suffering from severe shock.

The blast from the shell also did damage to William Webster's home at number 77, where again, the windows were broken and the exterior walls sustained some slight damage. At nearby 81 Commercial Street, William Ramm's home, another shell struck the side of the house, demolishing a large portion of it and collapsing the roof. The combination of the explosion and the weight of the roof and upper storey falling in destroyed much of the interior. Further along at number 99, the home of Mr Davison was also hit and damaged. All these houses and that at number 68, the home of William Clubley, were so severely damaged as to be rendered practically uninhabitable by the damage to their upper storeys.

At 35 Harley Street the chimney of Constance Dobson was damaged.

A street away, at 71 Hampton Road, a piece of shrapnel crashed through the window of the Warley home and struck a seven-month-old baby girl, the youngest of the six children in the house, all of whom were sat at their breakfast of porridge, and all of whom were terrified out of their wits. Mrs Warley was distraught, paralysed with fear, and it was only the return of her husband which brought her back to her senses. Bundling the baby into the pram, the Warleys gathered their youngsters around them and left the house for the sanctuary of Scalby. En route they joined the crowds already on the move into the countryside. As they reached the road (now known as Coldyhill Lane) someone told them of a nearby doctor named Tenison and they sought his help with the baby. Once the child was bandaged and quietened the Warleys again took up their flight and were taken in by the Huggan family at *Crimbles Court*, Scalby. Later in the day Dr Tenison made his car available to them and the Warleys returned home in some style and comfort.

The Wykeham Street Massacre

Four members of the Bennett family died when their house at 2 Wykeham Street

2 WYKEHAM STREET

1: The interior damage. 2&3: Damage to the side elevation of the house where the shell burst through and killed four people. 4: Exterior damage viewed from the bridge.

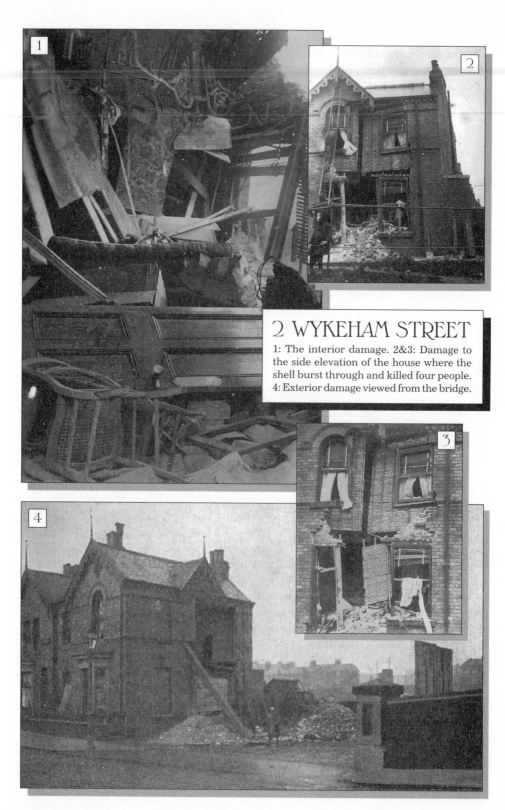

received a direct hit; three others escaped with minor injuries and shock. Among the survivors was twenty-five-year-old Christopher Bennett, one of a small band of heroes that day - as deserving of a medal as any soldier serving in France.

I'd been getting out of bed and was beginning to dress when the shot came crashing in. It hit the house fully, and I fell through the bedroom floor into the kitchen. Everything fell on top of us. Father, mother and the children were downstairs in the kitchen, and Albert called out to me, "Come on lad, let's away downstairs. It's the Germans. Come and look after mother."

But before I'd time to get downstairs it had all happened. It was a long time before I realised anything, or where I was. I was practically buried in stuff. When I could look around me I'd only a shirt and one slipper on. I had to butt in and do the best I could. If I asked one I asked a dozen, but could not get a soul to help me. There wasn't one who would come, bar two or three Territorials [5th Green Howards]. They got Albert out and took him to hospital. They were good chaps, and I shan't forget them.

I found mother and the children in one corner. Albert was with them. They were all crowded together, buried beneath it all. Mother was on a chair nursing the children - she'd lost her hand. Father was in the kitchen covered with debris but somehow he pulled himself out. They hadn't been downstairs seven minutes before it happened.

I don't remember much about what happened after that - it was too terrible - but father and I got the others out as best we could. We moved mother into the yard, with little Jack and little George - but it was too late. Mother wasn't dead when we pulled her out, but she was gone by the time we got her into the yard. I carried little George into the next house, but he died as I put him down. I'd been to see about Mrs Edmond before that. She was sat on the bedside, and I told her, "Sit there till I come back. I'll get mother and the children out, they're worse than you."

She did what I asked, and after moving mother and the children I helped her into the next house. She was uninjured, with the exception of shock, of course.

As soon as I got out into the yard I asked some men to go for a doctor. But he never came.

The ambulancemen came, but it was too late by then. Albert was terribly injured and died about twenty minutes to five in the afternoon. Father was cut badly about the head, neck and thigh. He was bathed and bandaged by PC Taylor and the ambulancemen, and went to hospital, but he didn't stop there. There was only me and my poor father for it and he stuck it like a gentleman.

Having acted without thought for his own safety Christopher, who had suffered with wounds to his legs, was rightly hailed a hero.

At the beginning of the bombardment there had been seven people in the Bennett house; Mr Bennett, Johanna Bennett, his wife, Christopher Bennett, Albert Bennett of the Royal Field Artillery, John Ward (the Bennett's grandson), George Barnes and Mrs Edmond. Four of them died directly from the shell that flattened the house; Johanna (aged 58), Albert (aged 22), George (aged 5) and John (aged 9). A pet dog and caged birds also died in the blast and the family's cat had disappeared. However, a few days later, while workers sifted through the debris and the wreckage the black cat was

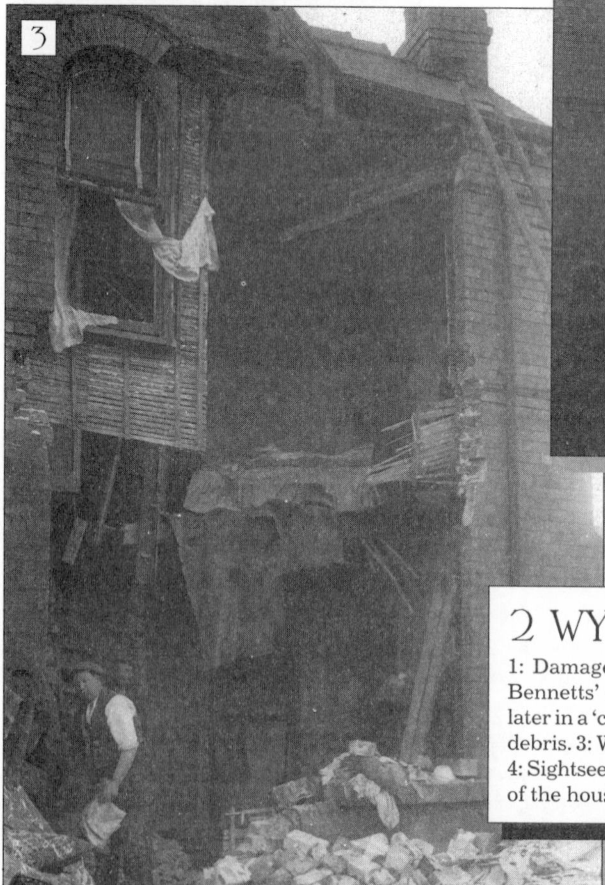

2 WYKEHAM STREET

1: Damage to the side elevation. 2: The Bennetts' cat was discovered a few days later in a 'copper' by workmen clearing the debris. 3: Workmen begin clearing the site. 4: Sightseers stand and gaze at the remains of the house.

discovered hiding in the family's copper, and although its fur was singed it appeared none the worse for its ordeal and one assumes eight of its nine lives were still intact.

A 'copper' was a boiler used for washing clothes. It was cylindrical, stood on short legs and was loaded from the top. A fire was lit in the bottom, where there was also a tap for draining the water. Originally made of copper (hence the name) many were in fact made of other metal.

The house next door to the Bennett family's, (number 4), occupied by Mrs Steele, was fortunate indeed for it only suffered a couple of broken windows.

I was standing at the corner of St John's Road and saw it all. The shell came flying straight over the railway bridge - it smashed a lot of windows in Gladstone Road School - and went clean through Mrs Bennett's house. The place was blown up and things went flying in all directions. A lot of it was carried into my house on the other side of the road. My windows were smashed and afterwards I found glass and brickwork littered all over the place.

One remarkable thing was that my husband's waistcoat was hanging in the passage and a piece of brick had found its way into the pocket!

Just before it all happened I saw Mr Bennett.

"For God's sake," I cried, "get up!"

And with that it was all done. I shut our door and ran. I had just come downstairs and something hit me on the leg, a bit of brick also striking my little boy who was standing at the end of the bridge with his father.

How I dressed I don't know, and we are lucky to be alive. We were the only three who saw what happened across the road. Everybody else was running.

I saw Christopher Bennett drop through the top bedroom into the kitchen. He had only his shirt and a sock on, and - would you believe it - people were laughing at him, and not a man would go up and help him. He dropped through the bedroom as he was in the act of putting his trousers on and I never stopped to see what happened after that for I ran to Klondyke. But when we came back we found him, and that little man is a hero. All Christopher thought about was his poor mother and the others. With only his shirt and a sock on he got them out all by himself and there was not a soul to help him. It was a sight I shall never forget so long as I live.

Albert Bennett, who died in the hospital, was riddled with bullets. He seems to have been doing something by the fireside and was petrified on the spot. Mrs Bennett was killed, and also the two children who were found clasped round her knees. Poor little George was nearly blown to pieces, and Mrs Bennett was terribly mutilated.

The most remarkable thing about it all was the escape of Mrs Edmond, who was unhurt, despite the fact that she was in bed upstairs close to Christopher's room. She has been an invalid for two years, but when my husband and son got up to help her she got up and walked away!

But the thing I shall always remember is Christopher, he is a hero, a hero indeed!

Annie Agar of 1 Wykeham Street, who lived opposite the unfortunate Bennett family, gave the above account of the terrible incident. Her husband John and son Charlie also had narrow escapes from the explosion of the same shell, though their home suffered

A shell smashed straight through St Columba's Church on Columbus Ravine

Both Mrs Ingham and her housekeeper, Miss Clarke, were buried beneath the remains of 26 Mayville Avenue

Alice Painter of 53 Moorland Road committed suicide on 14th December and her name was added to the War Memorial by mistake

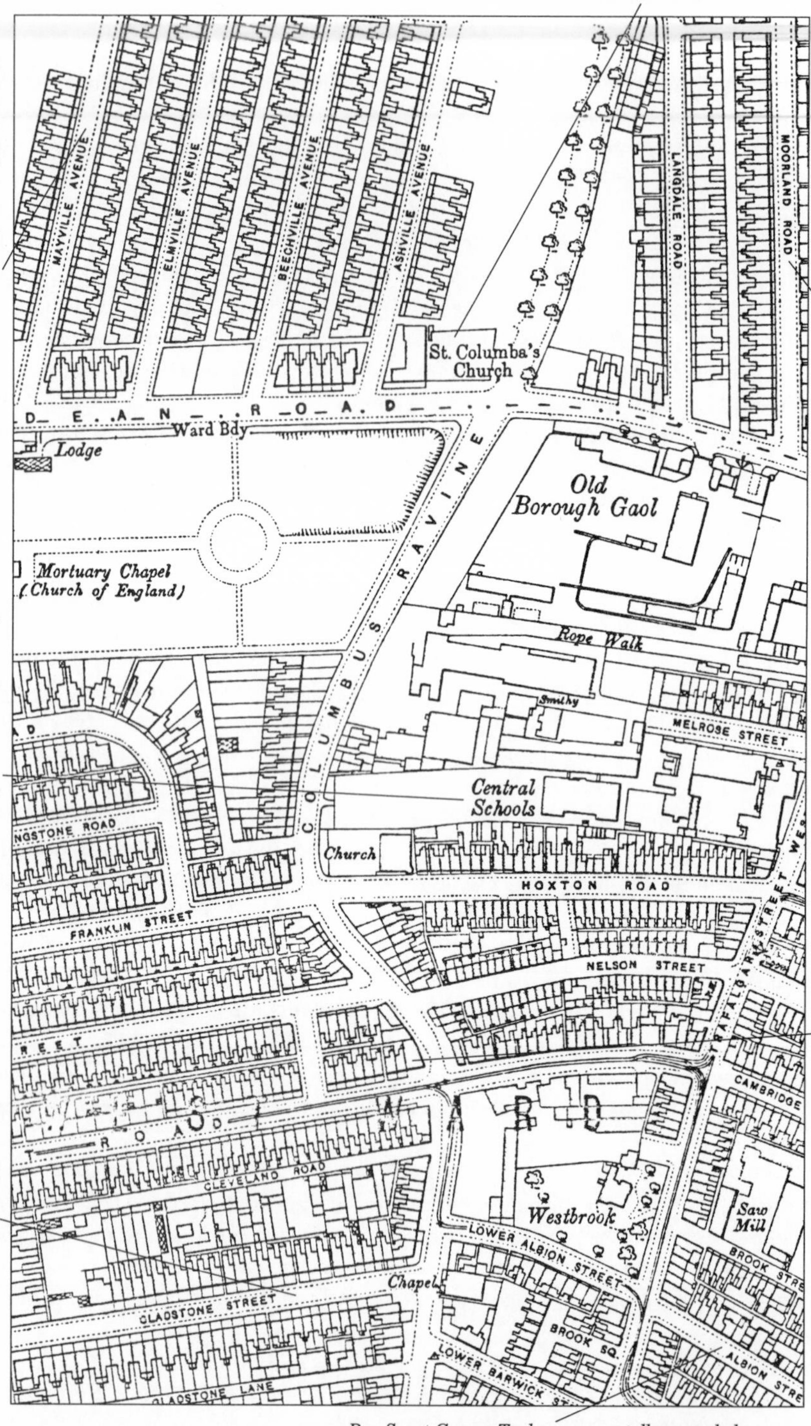

The Central School was slightly damaged and remained closed for the rest of the day

Emily Merryweather was mortally wounded outside her shop at 43 Prospect Road whilst helping friends to shelter

At 39 Gladstone Street, George Usher was wounded by a stray piece of shell

Boy Scout George Taylor was mortally wounded on Albion Street (now Northway) on the way to a friend's house far less, as did the house adjoining it, number 3, the home of Thomas Rawding, a military storekeeper. Annie Agar assisted Mrs Rawding and her two small children - clad only in their night-clothes - to leave, and they took refuge in the outskirts of the town. And although John Agar and his son, Charlie, had been nearly blinded by the debris flying from the Bennett home, the boy was only concerned with the fate of his little Pomeranian terrier and would not leave for safety until they had rescued it.

One of the worst aspects of the tragedy at the Bennett house was the lack of help offered by passers-by, including soldiers, despite Christopher Bennett's pleas for help. More than one contemporary eye-witness account remarks how the poor lad was left to save what was left of his family by himself as people ignored his cries and passed him by, no doubt intent on their own salvation.

Alice Flees Naked

Also on Wykeham Street, at number 56, John Crooks had all his rear windows smashed in and the copper blown out by a nearby explosion. He also lost his daughter for a time. Little Alice Crooks had rushed headlong into the street, naked as the day she was born, on the first shots being fired and had disappeared into the milling crowds of people dashing hither and thither. She was eventually discovered in Scalby village at *Crimbles Court*, the home of Halliday Huggan, where she had been taken via a cart with a group of other local children, a large overcoat wrapped around her to cover her nakedness and to keep her warm. Once in Scalby the children were plied with liberal amounts of steaming hot soup.

Local postman, John T. Harland, of 47 Wykeham Street was injured, with cuts and bruises, when his house was hit and sustained damage. He was escorted to hospital by friends for treatment.

At 58 Wykeham Street, the home of baker George Douthwaite, the chimney stacks were knocked off, the roof holed and bedroom ceilings cracked, while the pantry and coalhouse were wrecked by a shell which narrowly missed ploughing directly into his house. Next door, at number 60, all the windows of coal porter John W. Harland were broken by the blast.

Alexandra Park and the Prospect Road Area

An unoccupied, newly built house on Alexandra Park had a portion of the roof blown in by a flying lump of shell.

Serious damage was done on Bow Street where the entire roofs of two houses were stripped bare and the windows shattered. At the end of Bow Street, (then opposite Merryweather's shop on Prospect Road), the plate glass window of Marriner's fruit and vegetable shop was shattered.

Prospect Road ~ Another Female Fatality

Along the length of Prospect Road many of the houses had their windows smashed, while Richard Tindall's roof at number 25 was badly damaged, along with the roof of his neighbour Fred Watson at number 27, whose chimney stack was knocked clean off.

Thirty-year-old Mrs Emily Merryweather, the proprietor of the general store at 43 Prospect Road on the corner with Columbus Ravine, was struck on the lower left side of her body by shrapnel from a shell which exploded against the pillar of the doorway to the shop; into which she was ushering friends to the shelter of the cellar. Though initially only thinking herself wounded, by the time she could be taken to a nearby

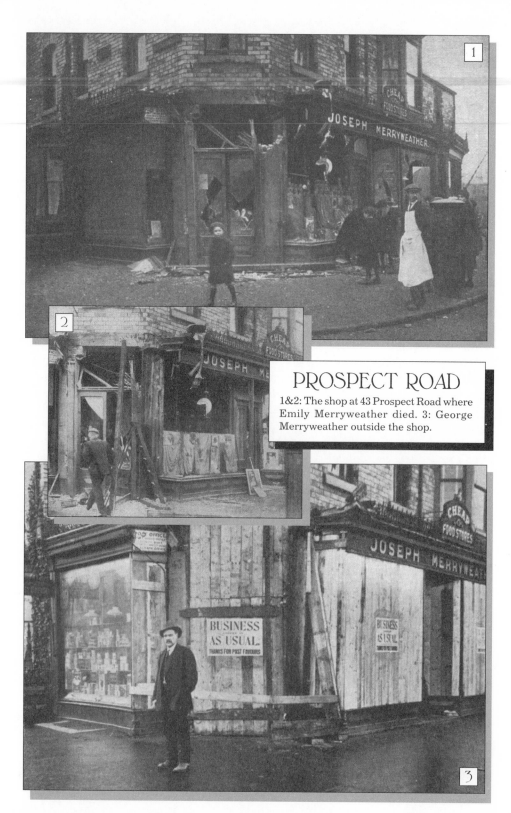

1

2

3

PROSPECT ROAD

1&2: The shop at 43 Prospect Road where Emily Merryweather died. 3: George Merryweather outside the shop.

doctor she had died. That such an act of kindness should result in her death was unbelievable. Her husband, George, was buried beneath debris caused by the same incident but survived.

On the opposite side of the road the off-licence at 42 Prospect Road, belonging to Mr Thomas Laughton, and occupied by Mr Bean, was struck by splinters from the shell that had mortally wounded Emily Merryweather. Next door, number 44, the home of chemist William Halmpshaw had all the street-facing windows blown in from the same blast and fragments of shell embedded themselves in the walls. At the next house along, that of Frederick Shields, at 46 Prospect Road, severe damage was done when what was believed to be a shell (though it could have been a large fragment from one) crashed through the gateway and on through the wall and into the sitting-room. All the windows here and further along the street were broken by the impact.

At the home of greengrocer Edwin Smith, 109 Prospect Road, a piece of lead piping was driven through the kitchen window by the blast of a shrapnel shell and did some small damage inside, whilst outside, the back of the house was peppered with bits of shell casing and shrapnel. Further along the road outside 153 Prospect Road, the home of Mrs McCallough, twenty-five-year-old Thomas Place was wounded in the left thigh by a splinter of shell casing and required hospital treatment.

Gordon Street and Ramsey Street

The home of the Robinson family at 65 Gordon Street had its roof severely damaged, the chimney stack knocked clean off, windows shattered and the furniture in the upper rooms destroyed. Needless to say, the family fled to take shelter elsewhere. The houses next door both suffered similar damage. At 67 Gordon Street part of Miss Faulder's roof was blown off, while Alfred Coates' house at 69 Gordon Street was badly damaged and his windows were broken.

In the small concrete yard of 36 Ramsey Street, Welshman Llewelyn Hughes and his little five-year-old son Robert watched in fascinated horror as a shell careered off the corner of an outhouse at the rear of 52 Ramsey Street, shattered Mrs Feetenby's windows, peppered Henry Nettleton's house at number 53 with shrapnel, smashing his windows and damaging furniture inside the house, before it ploughed through the rear kitchen wall of 54 Ramsey Street, the home of Mary Brown, whose pantry and coalhouse were devastated. In a remarkable incident, the shell passed between Mary Brown, in the wash-house, and her daughter in the kitchen and both escaped without serious injury.

With the damage done to Ramsey Street the Drake family at number 44 finally sat down to their breakfasts. Despite worrying about his wife Mabel and their three boys, Frankie, Geoff and Walter, schoolteacher Frank Drake nevertheless went off to school, determined the day should continue as normal. However, despite his optimism, very few children turned up for school that morning.

Murchison Street ~ Mary Horsley Wounded

A number of houses on Murchison Street had their roofs blown off and a large number of windows in the street were broken. At 10 Murchison Street the twenty-one-year-old daughter of Thomas Horsley, Mary, was injured in the leg and arm and was taken to hospital for treatment.

At number 61, vanman Henry Greenlay's chimney stack was blown off and the roof stripped bare. Henry, fearing the worst, gathered his family and took them to nearby

EASTBOROUGH

1: Looking up Eastborough, the main road into the centre of the town from the Foreshore, towards a substantial barricade of sandbags.
2: Damage to grocer Alice Hastie's shop and house at 59 Eastborough. The house was badly damaged.
3: Looking down Eastborough from the other side of the barricade.

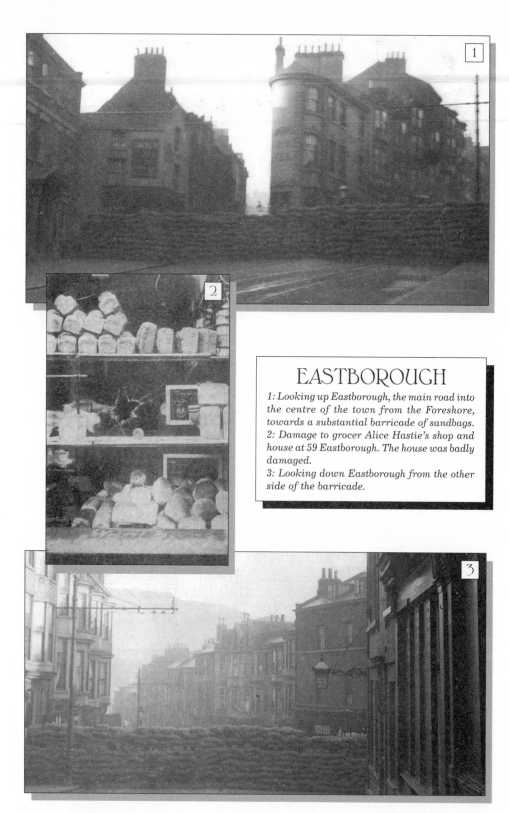

Snainton for safety. At both number 63, Henry Milnthorpe's, and number 65, John Thrustle's, the houses were damaged and the windows broken.

The fanlight and windows of Mrs Stringer's grocer's shop at 74 Murchison Street were broken and the shop interior was damaged when a shell splinter flew through the shop and impaled a canister full of tea against the furthest wall.

Raleigh Street, Garfield Road and Livingstone Road

The front room of the Misses Devall at 16 Raleigh Street was completely wrecked by a shell which was reported to have passed over Gladstone Road and crashed directly into the front of their house. The front room and its furniture were wrecked and the windows at the front of the house were wrecked, but no one was hurt. At the corner of Raleigh Street and Prospect Road (number 31) a shell splinter smashed the plate glass window of Czarena Smith's confectionery shop and another embedded itself in the doorway.

At the Garfield Road entrance to the Manor Road Cemetery (then called the New Cemetery) a branch was severed from a tree and several headstones chipped and damaged by flying shell fragments. Bricks were also knocked out of the boundary wall by a shell which was thought to have struck a tree, fragments from which were later collected from within a thirty-yard radius. However, a youth living in Livingstone Road, close by, later claimed to have seen the shell fall in the cemetery just twenty yards from him. He further claimed that on bursting, the shell had smashed several gravestones and brought down a large thirty-foot tree.

Meanwhile an unexploded shell embedded itself in the wall at the rear of 19 Livingstone Road, the home of joiner John Hord.

The Westborough Area ~ Commercial Traveller's Narrow Escape

The premises of Rowntree and Sons at 20-21 Westborough were peppered with shrapnel and a number of windows were broken. At number 53, Henry Watson's, the building was struck several times by shell fragments, but no great damage was done. Further along the street the top floor of John Dickinson's Carlton Hotel, at 99 Westborough, was severely damaged, whilst the photographic premises of local printer E. T. W. Dennis were severely damaged, and much of the stock ruined.

The railway station, now the focus for crowds of locals trying to flee the carnage, was peppered with shrapnel from nearby blasts and a number of windows were broken, though no one was reported injured. Further along, at the junction of Westover Road and Londesborough Road, the railway excursion station (situated behind Falsgrave Road) was also damaged by flying shrapnel. Though no one was reported hurt, a shunting engine was overturned by a nearby blast.

At Matson's Temperance Hotel and Boarding House one man had a near miraculous escape from almost certain death. The gentleman, a commercial traveller, had spent the night there, and on being rudely awakened by the sounds of the first part of the bombardment had risen, dressed and packed his bags at breakneck speed. Grabbing his coat and hat, he had just lurched out of room five onto the landing and pulled the door shut behind him when a shell burst through the wall into the room blowing everything in it to kingdom come.

What was left of the shell finally came to rest in the remains of the chimney-breast, amid a devastated pile of bricks and mortar which had a moment earlier constituted the traveller's room. No record is left as to whether he fled the scene of destruction to

EASTBOROUGH

Prepared for an invasion.

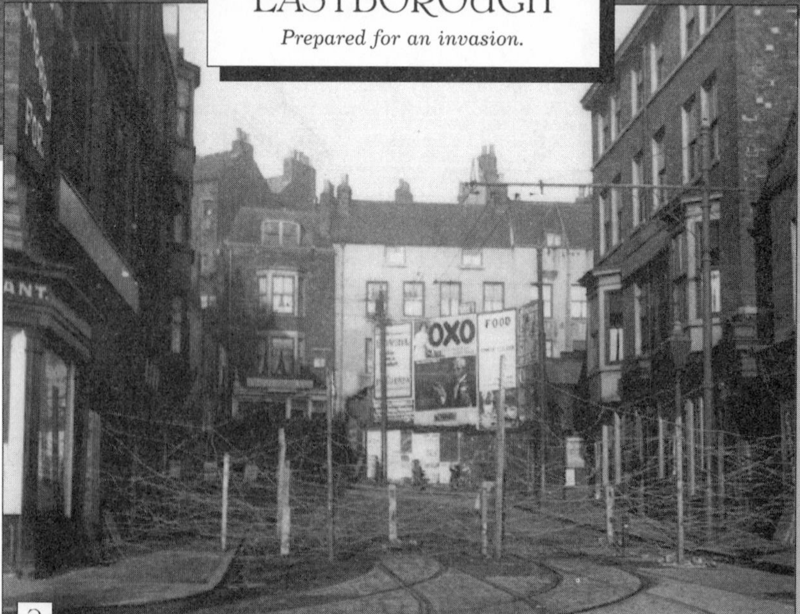

seek shelter and swift passage from the town, or whether he stayed to pay his bill and continue to ply his trade.

Almost in the dead centre of the town, the Balmoral Hotel at 119 Westborough was hit and suffered some damage and broken windows.

Alma Square, West Square and Hanover Road

Shrapnel from a shell exploding nearby put twelve distinct holes in the roof of Mr Pearce, at 10 Alma Square, peppered the facade and shattered all of his windows. Another shell smashed into the empty Alma Square Boarding House close by doing severe damage.

The windows of at least seven houses on West Square (including Mrs Shepherdson's at number 12) were smashed when a shell blew away the entire roof of number 18, the home of Mr Smith, and shattered all his windows. Although the family was downstairs at the time, no one was hurt. At 20 West Square the same blast destroyed a bedroom on the third floor of Mrs Foster's home.

The blast from the explosion at the Matson's Temperance Hotel and Boarding House on Westborough shattered the shop windows of chemists Hunt and Ruff at 81 Westborough, and those of the Waverley Temperance Hotel at 9 Westfield Terrace (close to West Square). It also badly injured the head bookkeeper of the Scarborough Electric Supply Company, Arthur Wood, who lived at 7 Hanover Road. Both Arthur and his twelve-year-old son, Clifford, were wounded in the head by flying glass and shrapnel. After emergency treatment in hospital the Wood family (mother, father and son) boarded a train and fled the town for the capital. On arrival at King's Cross later in the day, they were pounced on by waiting journalists eager for news from war-torn Scarborough. With bloodstained bandages about their heads, Arthur and Clifford Wood were ideal fodder for the men from the press.

York Place, Albemarle Crescent, Bedford Street and Aberdeen Walk

A cap from a shell struck the window of the west transept of Albemarle Baptist Church on Albemarle Crescent, and went on to chip the moulding from the wall behind the pulpit - luckily no one was in it at the time. A piece of shell came through the roof of David Gough's home at 38 Albemarle Crescent and did some minor damage. However, had it been a couple of minutes later his son, Stackwell Gough, would have been lifting down his coat from the peg ready to depart for work. As it was, the shell fragment tore through the coat and cut through the sovereign case in the pocket.

At 39 Albemarle Crescent, the home of Mrs Briggs, the roof was severely damaged and the rooms on the top storey were wrecked. The Lightfoot family home, at number 40, had its roof struck and all four rooms on the upper storey wrecked. Every window in the house was shattered with the sole exception of the bedroom where Mrs Lightfoot and her daughter were when the bombardment started. Further along at William Craven's, number 45, a number of rooms were badly damaged, while numbers 46, Mrs Powell's, and 47 Mrs Stephenson's, had all their windows broken and suffered lesser, miscellaneous damage.

At 13a Bedford Street, *Wilton House*, the home of Mrs Randall, was practically destroyed as the roof was blown off and several bedrooms demolished. Mrs Randall's son narrowly escaped being injured, or worse, having left his bedroom a moment earlier.

Round the corner, at 47 Aberdeen Walk, the home of William Ellis was severely damaged by a lump of shrapnel.

KING STREET

The Headquarters of the Red Cross.

YORK PLACE

The chimney stack was blown off George Astrom's house, number 14.

Victoria Road

Victoria Road, one of the town's main thoroughfares, saw the most recorded damage of any street in Scarborough. Damage was both extensive and wide-ranging, with the majority of properties along its length, and on the many roads leading off it, damaged in some form or another (most having their windows broken). Hardly any building escaped the effects of the litter of shrapnel shells which burst in this area, and glass from the many shattered shopfronts littered the pavements and roads for days.

A shell entered the premises of Petch's joinery shop at the top end of Victoria Road through an exterior wall and exploded inside, blowing off the roof and doing great damage to the wood and tools within; while at number 43, the home of Richard Cliffe, a large portion of the roof was torn away and severe damage was done to the window supports and surrounds.

At number 69, George Scales, a wounded merchant seaman at home recovering from a forty-foot fall down a ship's hold in Montreal, Canada, during which he sustained two fractured ribs and a dislocated spine, had the narrowest of escapes when a shell hit the house. The roof was torn apart and the upper floor of the house was all but demolished, with every window in the premises being blown out. A stray fragment of shell tore through George's topcoat and shirt as he hurried downstairs to escape, grazing the flesh of his arm but doing him no other injury. Below, the living quarters of his mother Alice's Boot and Shoe shop also sustained damage, but she and her other son, Robert, managed to escape without injury. Later, the chimneys of the house were found to be so choked with debris from the explosion that the unfortunate Scales were unable, for several days, to light so much as a small fire to keep themselves warm. The same shell caused damage to the premises of hay, straw and corn dealers Bielby & Company at 71 Victoria Road, where the roof was demolished. Luckily there was no one there at the time. The building was also the home of Robert Bielby, who lived above the shop and many of his windows were broken by the blast.

The lower rooms, furniture and windows of Miss Baynes at 85 Victoria Road were damaged by an explosion directly outside. The chimneys, roof and upper floor of John Foreman's bakers and confectioners shop, at 98 Victoria Road, were struck and totally destroyed, and all the windows were smashed. John Foreman later estimated the damage at £100. The same explosion damaged the top and second storeys of number 100, Fred Normanton's hairdressers and newsagents shop, and shattered the windows. Nearby, the windows of Wilson's butchers, 102 Victoria Road, and Frank Abbey's fruit shop, number 104, were all broken by the blast and flying shrapnel.

The house of Mr Arnold, a music teacher, at 118 Victoria Road, was struck by a shell and severely damaged. The roof of the Misses Eamans' Boot, Shoe & Hosiery Stores, at 160 Victoria Road, was struck and holed and the furniture in the upper rooms badly damaged. Numerous windows in the property were broken by the blast.

Further along the road windows were smashed and broken, and at 182 Victoria Road, confectioner Robert Wells's premises, an upper room was totally destroyed by a direct hit. The remainder of the buildings on Victoria Road between Albion Street (now Northway) and Barwick Street had their front-facing windows smashed, along with a row of four houses at the Victoria Road end of Tindall Street. The road, one of Scarborough's busiest, was left devastated like no other.

Norwood Street ~ Two More Wounded

The roof of Mr Wittup's at 19 Norwood Street was struck, causing damage to the

Francis Trousdale's home at 6 Gladstone Lane was almost entirely demolished by a direct hit

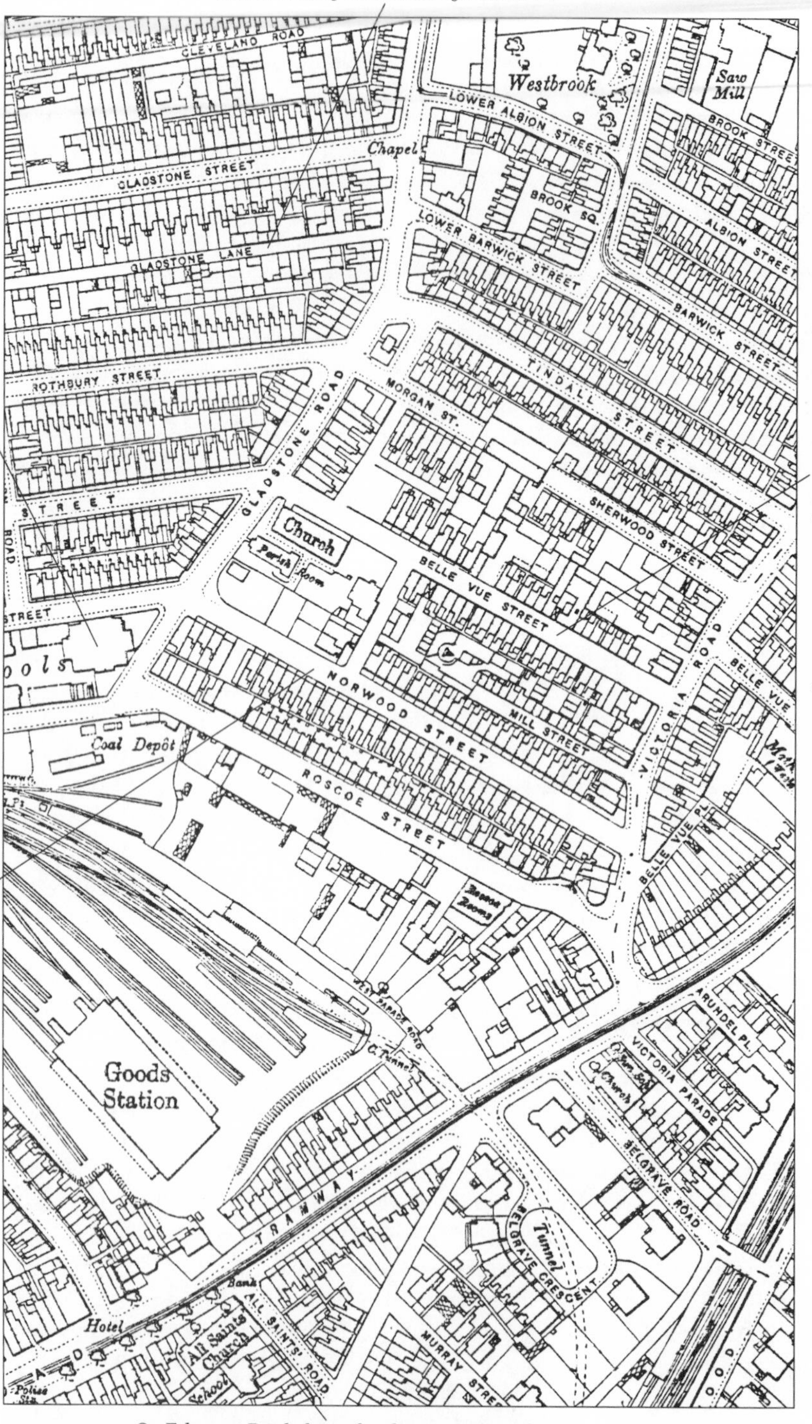

Gladstone Road School was badly damaged and stayed closed until after Christmas

At 31 Norwood Street Mrs Bethel Sharp and her daughter Millie were wounded

On Belle Vue Street, Albert Webb and Sarah Petch were both wounded, John Wood 'died' three times but survived, Harry Harland was mortally wounded and Mary Prew was killed

On Falsgrave Road, the roof and west window of All Saints' Church were damaged bedrooms and shattering the windows, whilst at number 31, forty-two-year-old Mrs Bethel Sharp was wounded in the back and face and taken to the hospital for treatment, as was her fourteen-year-old daughter Millie (a fifth-form pupil at the Municipal School) who suffered a broken arm and various other injuries. The rear of Charles Taylor's house, number 36, was also hit, and when the occupants emerged from hiding in an upper bedroom they found the landing and staircase had been destroyed leaving them high and dry. Further along, at 43 Norwood Street, George Coe had part of his roof blown away and damage done to a window support.

Belle Vue Street ~ Boy Dies Three Times

On Belle Vue Street eleven-year-old John Wood, of number 4, was injured on his way to school when a shrapnel shell burst in the street. A piece of shrapnel hit the schoolboy's head and literally threw him twenty yards along the road. People rushed from their doorsteps, where they had been listening to the bombardment, to his side. Local PC Harold Nalton, quickly at the boy's side, attended to the stricken youngster as he was rushed to the hospital where, on three separate occasions doctors gave the lad up for dead. Miraculously he confounded them each time, pulled through and survived.

Belle Vue Street ~ Webb and Petch Wounded

Also injured on Belle Vue Street were twenty-eight-year-old Albert Webb, who was wounded in the thigh, leg and wrist by shrapnel and was taken to hospital for treatment, and Sarah Petch (of 6 Belle Vue Street), who, whilst standing in her doorway wondering at the commotion, was struck in the side by a shell fragment. She was attended to at home, the severe wound requiring several stitches.

Belle Vue Street ~ Harry Harland Fatally Wounded

On that fateful morning shoemaker Harry Harland had bidden farewell to his wife, Selina, and their four children at 8 Belle Vue Street and left for work as usual at 7.45am for the short walk from his home to Coe's Boot and Shoe Repairers at 78 Victoria Road (on the corner of Alma Parade) where he was employed. He arrived just before eight o'clock and a few minutes later, with shells screaming into the town, was running for home, leaving his employer to defend his own property against the hordes of bayonet-wielding German troops he and countless others believed would shortly be rampaging through Scarborough's devastated streets. Harry ran for home to try and protect his family and arrived back on Belle Vue Street as it was being subjected to a deadly hail of shell and shrapnel. Bursting into the kitchen he shouted to Selina and the children, "Grab your coats . . . we'll go to Scalby and escape the Germans."

As with thousands of other Scarborough residents, the family fled their home in panic, but they had barely gone twenty yards before a shell exploded over a nearby house and shrapnel peppered the street. Harry suddenly collapsed to his knees, a gaping wound in his back gushing blood beneath his left shoulder blade. "I'm dying," he cried, sinking forward onto the road surrounded by his terror-stricken family, "It's hit my heart!"

In desperation Selina Harland cast about for help. At the end of Belle Vue Street, on Gladstone Road she spied an abandoned handcart and with a determination borne of despair she managed to get Harry onto it and manhandled him to Wykeham Street, and the home of his father, George, at number 52. Dr Henry Maingay was urgently summoned from his surgery at 33 Queen Street and on seeing Harry at once ordered him transported to the Westborough Wesleyan Chapel hospital, staffed by the

GENERAL DAMAGE

1&2: The roof of a house on Belle Vue Street. 3: Sarah Petch was wounded at 6 Belle Vue Street and required stitches. 4: Interior damage at 118 Victoria Road, the home of music teacher Mr Arnold.

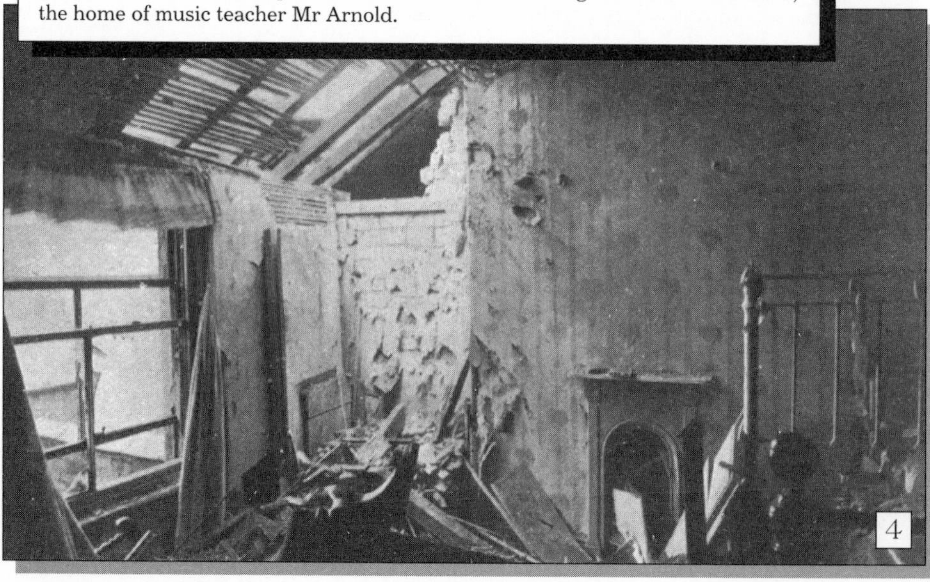

Red Cross and St John Ambulance Brigade. There he would remain for ten long days, fighting for life, a fight he would eventually lose.

Belle Vue Street ~ Mary Prew Killed

Indeed, by the time the dust finally settled on Belle Vue Street there was hardly a window left intact, and another innocent victim, the elderly Mary Prew, lay dead amid the ruins. Mary, of 17a Belle Vue Street, had been walking along the street when a shell exploded outside the shop at number 1, blowing her off her feet and carrying her a distance of several yards. John Wilson, the owner of the shop, who had seen the incident, rushed to her aid, but she was already dead when he reached her. Scooping her up, he desperately cradled her limp and lifeless body in his arms, the blood running from her open mouth to stain his coat.

Further down the road, a shell struck the chimney stack of builder Robert Hunter's house, at 14 Belle Vue Street, and blew it off, carrying most of the roof away with it. It was this blast which shattered the windows of most of the houses in the street. The vicarage and church of St Saviour's at the corner of Belle Vue Street and Gladstone Road were also damaged, though not severely.

The New Co-Op Building Hit

At another corner site, this one at the entrance to Belle Vue Street, at 176 Victoria Road, the new Co-operative Stores Boot Shop, sited alongside their existing property, had been nearing completion. Now, a shell which had already caused major havoc and damage in the nearby streets of Hanover Road and West Square, ploughed into the upper storey of the new building and ripped it apart, sending a huge shower of masonry, wood and bricks flying into the street. The Co-op's shop next door was left without windows from the same blast.

Fred Eden, a joiner working on the new building, had stepped outside a moment earlier, thinking the noise was a naval exercise and hoping to get a look. Instead he was blown across the road by the force of the blast that rocked the building. Somehow he managed to stagger away, but collapsed in the road. With people fearing for their lives running past him it was the action of Lance-Corporal Bob Thompson which probably saved his life. Thompson hunkered down over the unconscious man and tended to a severe neck wound before checking for further injuries. He discovered an artery in Eden's foot had been severed and bound it as tightly as he could before ensuring the injured man was taken to the hospital. Thanks to his prompt action the foot was saved and did not have to be amputated as was at first feared. However, thirty-three-year-old Eden, who had planned to enlist after work that day, was kept in hospital for ten weeks and when he eventually presented himself for army service was classed as C3 and assigned to non-combatant duties because the damage to his foot meant he couldn't march. In 1915 he received a lump sum of £50 in compensation for his injuries.

It was also this same blast which all but ripped off the roof and blew out the windows of the Eamans' Boot, Shoe and Hosiery Stores at 160 Victoria Road and the windows of local dressmaker Mrs Moore at number 162, where a large amount of furniture was damaged.

Sherwood Street ~ Breakfast Saves Cammish and Lickiss ~ Mr Newby Partially Blinded

On Sherwood Street, off Victoria Road, two shells demolished the roof of the

GENERAL DAMAGE

1: Rowntree's shop on the corner of Westborough and Vernon Road. 2: The Co-op building on the corner of Victoria Road and Belle Vue Street where joiner Fred Eden was wounded. 3: Numbers 80 to 90 Victoria Road.

warehouse of Morland's Builders' and Plumbers' Merchants and ploughed into the showrooms below causing extensive damage. Here two warehousemen, Samuel Cammish and Thomas Lickiss, had a narrow escape when a beam, over a foot thick, was sliced in two by one of the shells and the whole upper floor gave way and tumbled into the lower portion of the premises, the two men only moments before having left to partake of their breakfasts! The warehouse and its entire, rather expensive stock, was reduced to a smouldering pile of rubble and ruin. Yards away the roof of number 21, the home of John Dearden (Builders' Merchant), was also hit and holed.

At the far end of Sherwood Street, furthest from Victoria Road, a large house, *Avondale*, number 33, took on the appearance of a brick pin-cushion with a host of embedded shell splinters sticking from its façade. The tenant of *Avondale*, Mr Newby, had just opened his front door when one of the shells exploded in the street, a fragment from which struck him in the left eye, partially blinding him. However, despite his injury he considered himself a fortunate man, for a much larger and certainly lethal piece of the same shell had missed him by a mere inch and embedded itself in the wide wooden door frame. The same shell, on its way down, took off the roof of the house opposite *Avondale*, number 24, belonging to John Crawford, reducing the furniture in the upper rooms to matchwood. Close by at number 28, the house and workshop of Robert Turner was badly damaged and his tools were widely scattered by the blast.

The damage from the three shells in Sherwood Street - caused mainly to windows - extended to no less than eighteen houses, practically the entire street. The shops, with their larger display windows, suffered particularly badly.

Tindall Street and Another Death on Albion Street

On Tindall Street, also off Victoria Road, some eighteen houses suffered broken windows due to the blasts from the numerous shells falling in the vicinity. Among them were the homes of Mr Bentley at number 3, Charles Turner at number 35 and John Jarrett at number 38 all of which also had the majority of the slates blown from their roofs, while the roof and windows of tripe-dresser, Mrs Lord, at 31 Albion Street (now Northway) were also damaged. It was this shell blast which fatally wounded local boy scout George Taylor.

Fifteen-year-old George had left his home at 45 North Street whilst the bombardment was in progress, despite his father John's attempts to stop him, to fetch the local newspaper (the *Scarborough Pictorial* - published weekly on a Wednesday) which was running a story and photograph of him. Having collected the paper he had been hurrying along Albion Street on the way to a chum's house, when he was struck in the back by a piece of shell. James Normandale, who had been working in Castle House's garage close by, looked up as George cried out in pain, saw the boy stagger and fall, and rushed to his aid. When he reached him the boy was still alive, though struggling to breathe. Carefully, James slid his arms under the boy and carried him into a nearby house where a doctor was at once sent for. James then searched the boy's pockets for some sign of his identity and discovered the newspaper and a postcard. With George growing weaker by the second, James then rushed through the town to the boy's home to acquaint his mother and father with his fate, but by the time he returned with the boy's frantic parents, George had died from his injuries.

Brook Street, Hoxton Road and Trafalgar Street West

At 2 Brook Street, the home of painter Mr Binney was severely damaged when the

1

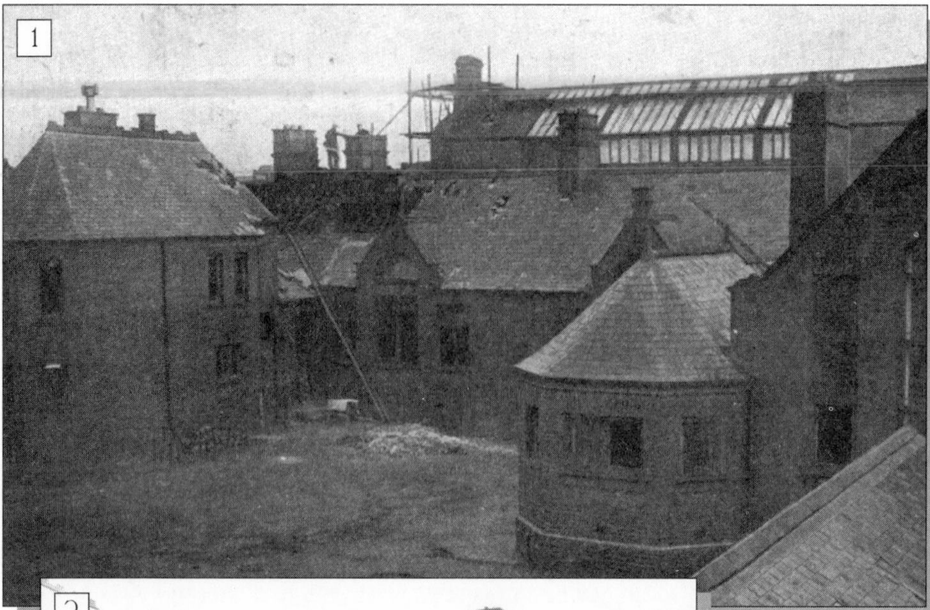

2

GLADSTONE ROAD

1&2: The roof of Gladstone Road School was severely damaged.
3: Workmen begin much-needed repairs. The school remained closed until 6th January 1915.

3

roof was hit. A top bedroom was totally wrecked, while in the lower part of the house the scullery and two interior doors were damaged. All the windows were smashed.

On Hoxton Road, William Reed's chimney at number 52 was struck and damaged along with the front door, whilst his windows were broken. At both 54 Hoxton Road, the home of William Cammish, and 56a Hoxton Road, the home of Mr Mawman, the roofs were badly damaged by the blast at number 52.

Behind Hoxton Road on Trafalgar Street West, the Central School was hit and some damage done, but the school did not close, even though few children turned up for lessons that day.

Gladstone Road, Holborn Terrace, Roscoe Street, Gladstone Lane and Gladstone Street

Running almost parallel with the top end of Victoria Road and connected to it by several smaller streets is Gladstone Road, and here a shell burst at the rear of the Cleveland Farmers' Dairy Company (81 Norwood Street), opposite the Gladstone Road School, breaking most of the windows. A passer-by, a builder named Alex Bell, of nearby Gladstone Street had a miraculous escape from injury when a massive wooden splinter, blown upward by the explosion, came down within inches of him. At the junction of Gladstone Road and Roscoe Street, the same blast wrecked the stables of a local cabman, Walter Dove of 39 Roscoe Street, killing one of the horses inside and damaging the cab. Across the road the blast also damaged the roof and windows of the railway goods shed.

At 8.25 precisely a shell scored a direct hit on Gladstone Road School's main hall where the caretaker, Mr Crawford had shortly before taken a number of children (among them Catherine Watson of Knapton who had arrived early) to the cellar for safety. The blast stopped the school clock and thus the precise time of the strike was fixed. Miss Gertrude Horsley, Mistress of the Girls' School recorded the following in her school diary:

> *Wednesday, December 16th 1914*
> *German raid on Scarborough, Whitby and Hartlepool. Fortunately it occurred before school assembled. It commenced at 8.00am and lasted about 40 minutes, and it was estimated that about 500 shells were fired. Great damage was done to the town, seventeen people were killed and many injured.*
>
> *The school hall was badly damaged - a five-inch cap of a shell was found inside. The hall clock stopped at 8.25am and one cannot feel too thankful that the children had not assembled in the hall for prayers. A classroom adjoining the hall (number 4) was badly damaged.*
>
> *Two country children were in the hall when the bombardment commenced, but Mr Crawford, the caretaker, took them down into the cellar and they were safe.*
>
> *I came to school immediately the firing ceased and was relieved to find no one had suffered bodily injury. No school until the New Year. We were due to close on Friday, 18th December, but it would be impossible to resume work under the circumstances.*

The school actually re-opened on Tuesday, 5th January 1915, and one of its classes had to be accommodated in the kitchen. On that first day back after the bombardment there were just 319 pupils present out of a total of 450. It was recorded in the school

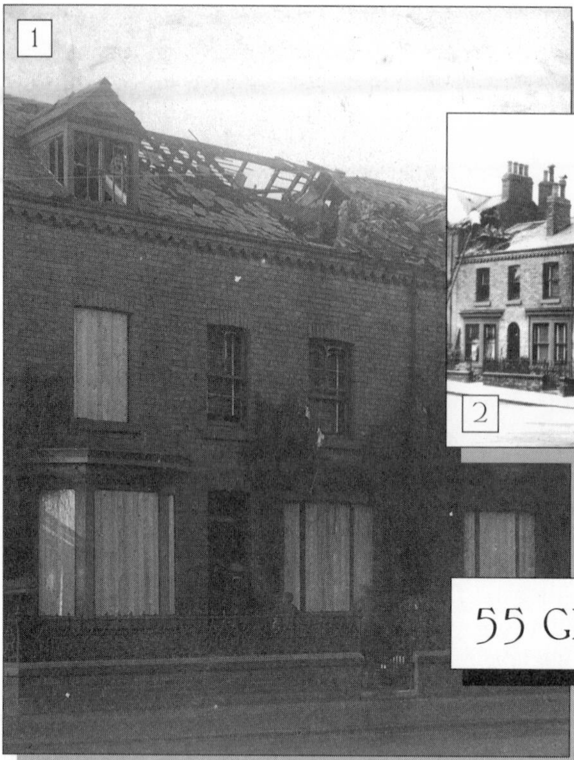

55 GLADSTONE ROAD

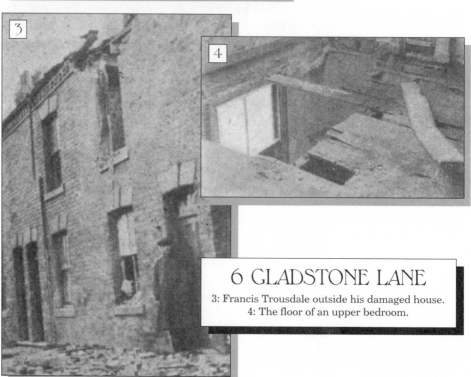

6 GLADSTONE LANE

3: Francis Trousdale outside his damaged house.
4: The floor of an upper bedroom.

diary that a great number of the children were out of town, and some had left the district altogether.

At 3 Gladstone Road, the roof of Mr Pickup's tinware shop (whose home was above it) was stripped right off and the upper rooms suffered severe damage, whilst at 7 Gladstone Road the upper storey of Hunter's Flour and Corn Dealers was also damaged.

Further along, at number 36, the home of Mrs Pickering (alone in the house at the time) was severely damaged when a shell took off the entire roof and decimated the upper floor which hung down into the devastated lower rooms.

[Several addresses on Gladstone Road are actually given as Holborn Terrace, which is correct, as the terrace forms part of Gladstone Road. For instance, number 53 is correctly written as 53 Holborn Terrace, Gladstone Road. However, to avoid confusion I have simplified the matter by giving the addresses as Gladstone Road as the local paper did at the time.]

The roofs of 53 Gladstone Road, belonging to Elizabeth Hinchey, and number 55 belonging to the Hydes, were struck by consecutive shells and badly damaged. The rear dormer window and the roof of an upstairs bedroom were stripped away, the fireplace blown out and the room below gutted. The pillow on the bed in the upstairs bedroom was riddled with shrapnel, and although almost everything was destroyed a clock, a recent present, which had stood on the now destroyed mantelshelf, was later discovered under the rubble unscathed; while a leather brush case was found firmly embedded in the window sill, forced there by the blast. A single pane of glass was all that remained intact of all the windows in the house. At the very moment the shell struck the roof, the occupants were making a dash for safety following the shell falling next door. Five of them, Frederick and Mrs Hyde, Miss Hyde, Miss White and Miss Wade escaped unharmed, while a chap named Derwent (who hailed from Bradford) had his overcoat sleeve torn at the shoulder, elbow and cuff by a fragment of the shell. Frederick, a reporter with the Scarborough Evening News, escorted them all to a nearby rail tunnel for shelter. Later they joined the throng heading for Seamer, where friends welcomed them in and gave them food and shelter.

The blast caused damage to the roof of 57 Gladstone Road, Rose Ash's house, and fearing for their lives, the family attempted to flee the town, only to be turned back at the Mere on Seamer Road by soldiers. Ronald Ash, youngest son of the Ashes, had only a few minutes earlier had a narrow escape at the home of his aunt, Mrs Pickering at nearby number 36. He had been visiting her earlier that morning, but had left to get ready for school, thus escaping the direct hit which all but levelled the house. That he survived the damage to his own home too is quite remarkable. Later that afternoon the Ash family managed to board a train for York where they stayed with relatives until the panic had subsided.

Some damage was also done to the interior of the Primitive Methodist Chapel on Gladstone Road when a large shell fragment crashed through the roof. Ninety-year-old Mrs Laycock had to be helped away from 67 Gladstone Road when it was hit, and she later went by train to York and to safety.

The home of Francis Trousdale at 6 Gladstone Lane was almost entirely destroyed by the blast from a single shell which fell on it.

George Usher, of 39 Gladstone Street, was wounded when a stray fragment of shell-casing crashed through his gate and into his house to embed itself in his lip (it was later removed). George, a grocer by trade, having recovered somewhat from the massive shock, later found his clothing torn and his overcoat 'perforated' with bullet holes.

The Goods Station behind Falsgrave Road (now a supermarket) was slightly damaged

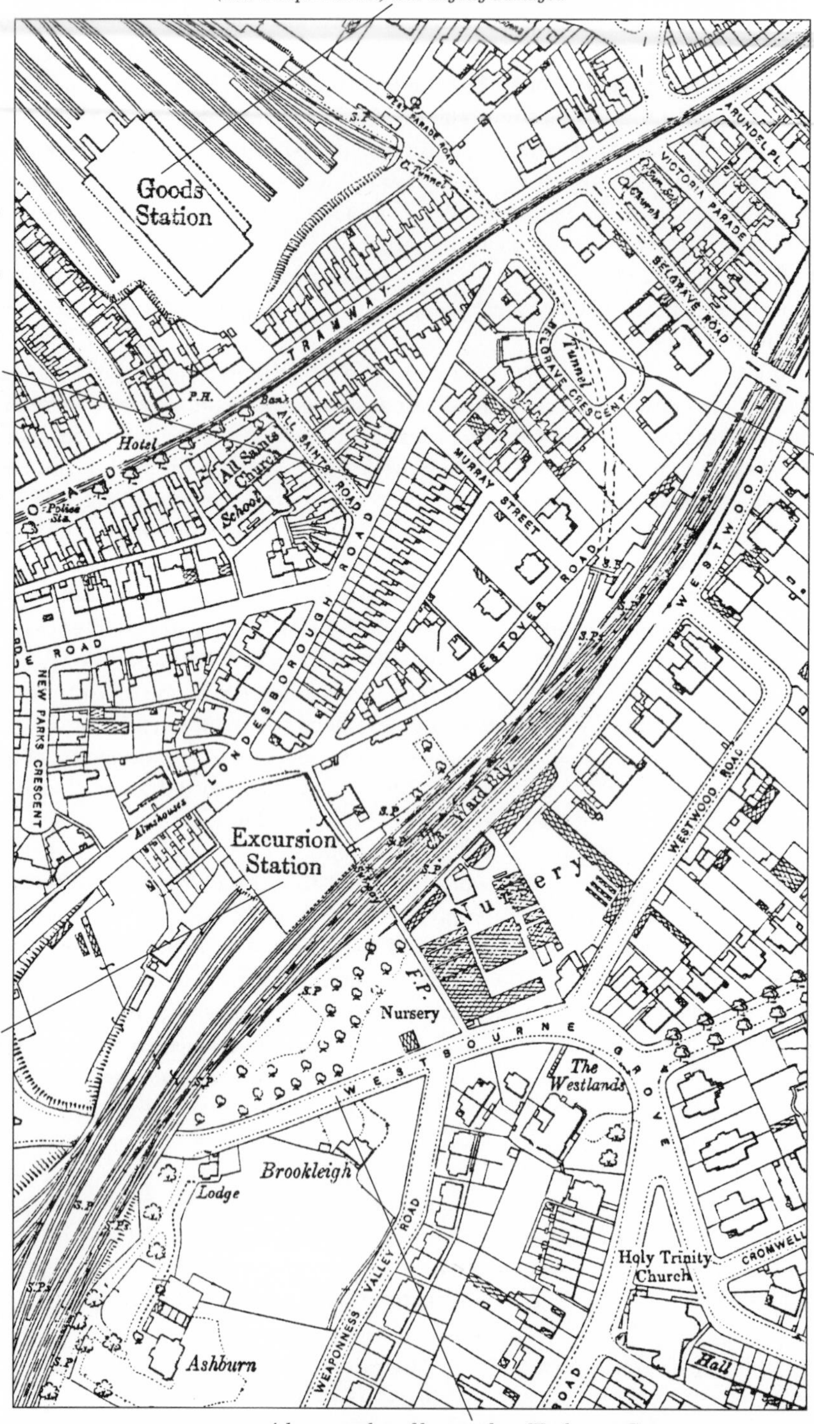

The rear of 48 Londesborough Road, the home of Mr Daglish, was seriously damaged

The Excursion Station, thronged with people trying to flee, escaped relatively unscathed

On Belgrave Crescent the home of Marie Tonks, Belgrave Lodge, and the Industrial Home for Blind Women both suffered broken windows from a nearby blast

A large number of houses along Westbourne Grove suffered damage to roofs, chimneys and windows

A number of windows and some woodwork were also damaged by the shell which burst near his home. However, his neighbours were not quite so fortunate. At number 40 Mrs Askham's chimney stack was struck and damaged, the slates were shattered and knocked from the roof, the guttering was broken and the fireplace was blown out. At number 41, the home of Edgar Bootland, a hole was made in an interior wall and damage done to the room from a piece of shell which came through one of the shattered windows, whilst at number 42, all the windows in the house and greenhouse belonging to Thomas Luccock were broken.

Many people fleeing the Gladstone Road area did so by way of the railway line towards Whitby. But this route was no safer than any other.

Wooler Street and the Goods Yard

On Wooler Street, which runs off Gladstone Road, Rowntree's Furniture Warehouse was damaged, and many of its windows were broken by the shell which took off a large portion of the roof of Gladstone Road School.

Candler Street, Rothbury Street and Seaton Terrace

Houses on Candler Street were hit and sustained varying degrees of damage. At number 1, the home of Mr Wood, and number 3, the home of Jane Kirby, both roofs were damaged and the windows smashed, while at Thomas Haram's, at 5 Candler Street, the end wall, under the eaves, was badly damaged.

On Rothbury Street number 24, the home of Alfred Brown, was badly damaged and the rear of number 34, belonging to Georgina Brown, was blown in and all but demolished.

At 45 Seaton Terrace (part of Hibernia Street) the home of Mrs Brand was damaged by parts of the shell which fell in nearby Rothbury Street.

Castle Road, Clifton Street, Wrea Street and Rutland Terrace

A shell exploded on Castle Road and smashed a large number of windows. At number 43 the son of William Temple, ten-year-old John, was injured in the arm by flying glass and taken to hospital for treatment.

The large plate glass windows in the ground and first floors of Edward Newham's Criterion Hotel, at 49 Castle Road, were shattered by a bursting shrapnel shell, whilst the bedrooms, windows and skylights at the top of the building were smashed in as the roof crashed in onto them, the gable end of an adjoining building having been struck, toppled over and fallen through it. Another piece of shell struck the hotel's roof and did yet more damage.

At the home of Miss Robinson, at 54 Castle Road, a shell passed straight through a bedroom, with predictable results, but no one was reported hurt. Riding's Fried Fish Shop, at 72 Castle Road, had its chimney blown away, the roof damaged and its windows broken. The flat above the shop was badly damaged. A little further on at 74, 76 and 78 Castle Road, the dentist Mr Grierson's house, dental treatment rooms and workshop were hit and although the house escaped the worst, some severe damage was done to the workshop and his equipment.

Off Castle Road, at 6 Clifton Street, builder Mr Smelt was wounded in the head and wrist and taken to hospital for treatment.

The roof of 7 Wrea Street was severely damaged and Francis Hudson and his wife, in their bedroom at the time, had a very narrow escape as the ceiling collapsed on them.

GENERAL DAMAGE

1&3: Damage to the glass roof of the Floral Hall.
2: Workhouse Master John Dyde (A) and local electrician Mr Whitehouse (B) with one of the shells which hit the Workhouse on Dean Road.
4: The interior of 26 Mayville Avenue where Miss Clarke and Mrs Ingham were both buried under debris, seriously injured and hospitalised.
5: The interior of postman Mr Southwick's (C) home at 164 Queen's Parade, North Marine Road.

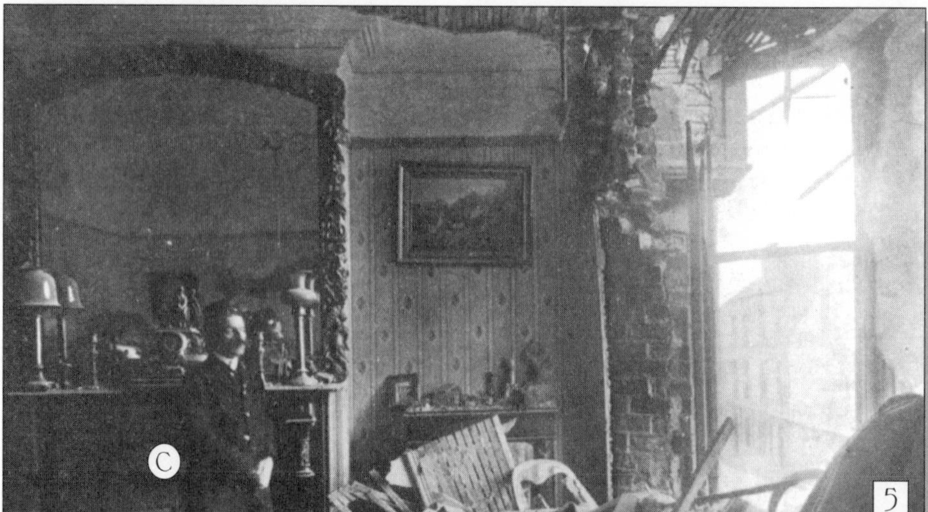

At 35 Rutland Terrace, Miss Snowden's bedroom was wrecked and a number of windows were broken by a shell which came through the wall.

The roof of St Mary's, the Borough's Parish Church, nestled beneath the shadow of the castle walls, was struck and damaged.

Mayville Avenue ~ Ladies Buried Alive

Among the few houses hit or damaged in the Dean Road area was 26 Mayville Avenue, where the elderly Mrs Ingham and her housekeeper, Miss Clarke (from Manchester), both in bed at the time, were buried beneath debris as the house was all but flattened by a direct hit. The property was reduced to a smouldering ruin, with only the outer walls, and a small portion of the roof left standing. Everything in the house was destroyed. Fearing for the ladies' lives, neighbours solicited the help of some nearby workmen and a way was forced through to them. The pair were in a pitiable state. The explosion had caused them numerous injuries and they were both in a serious condition. They were removed to a nearby house before being conveyed to hospital for treatment.

In the adjoining house, at 24 Mayville Avenue, Mary Cooper and her daughter suffered slightly in comparison. Their windows were smashed and a number of holes were punched through the outer walls by the shell which devastated Mrs Ingham's. This pair of ladies escaped unharmed, but shaken. No other houses in the street were touched.

Beechville Avenue and Columbus Ravine

At 36 Beechville Avenue, the home of Albert Bower, the windows were shattered by shrapnel from the Mayville Avenue shell two streets away.

At the junction of Dean Road and Columbus Ravine, the imposing St Columba's Church was hit by a shell which smashed through a window on the Columbus Ravine side of the building, flew through the church scattering chairs in its wake, and demolished a portion of the far wall, behind which runs Ashville Avenue. The altar and chancel were reported to have suffered no damage whatsoever. Afterwards the congregation were thankful the bombardment had taken place on a Wednesday morning, instead of a Thursday, when the church was often filled with early-morning worshippers.

Dean Road ~ The Workhouse Shell

At the Workhouse on Dean Road (now the site of St Mary's Hospital), a shell struck the building, bursting through the roof of the dormitory in the Albert Hall where one of the men, busy making beds, was almost buried alive by the debris. The shell crashed through into the room below, narrowly missing the men at their breakfasts. Another man, kneeling by the fire, stoking it, had a narrow escape as the shell missed his head by less than ten inches and buried itself in the fireplace.

Although the Workhouse Master, John Dyde, rushed to the scene from his home nearby, there was nothing he could do but order the men to begin to tidy up. The pieces of shell were later gathered and fitted together by Mr Whitehouse (a local electrician). The reconstructed shell was twenty-two inches long - without the nose-cone - and measured almost six inches round. The pieces weighed eighty-three pounds, and it was estimated that the original shell had been one hundred pounds.

At 7 Wrea Street the roof was so badly damaged it brought the bedroom ceiling down on top of Mr and Mrs Hudson

Local builder Mr Smelt of 6 Clifton Street was wounded in the head and wrist

The pieces of the shell that struck the workhouse (later St Mary's Hospital) on Dean Road were put back together and put on show

Albemarle Baptist Church, on Albemarle Crescent, was slightly damaged when a shell-cap entered it

North Street, North Place, Oxford Street and Sussex Street

The premises of furniture dealers the Summers Brothers, at 15 North Street, were hit by a shell which largely destroyed the roof and damaged much of the furniture. The home of painter and decorator Thomas Dent, at 15a, was damaged by the same shell. Further along, at number 76, the back of John Devlin's house was severely damaged by the shell which struck number 77, the home of the Bissett family. The family had a very narrow escape when their house received a direct hit; three bedrooms were wrecked and the sitting-room ceiling and furniture was damaged, but they managed to escape the devastation unharmed.

On North Place, just off North Street, at the Rutland Rooms, the chimney and room of the Mothers' Union Office was damaged.

At 7 Oxford Street a fragment of shell smashed through John and Elizabeth Dixon's front room window and embedded itself in the chiffonier. No other damage was done.

And on nearby Sussex Street a shell struck the 'pattern chamber' of Brogden and Wilson's Scarborough Ironworks and smashed all the moulds kept there, scattering the pieces widely.

St Thomas Walk and St Thomas Street

The roof of 2 St Thomas Walk, home of Alfred Gowan, was smashed in completely. Alfred was in Sawdon at the time, and fortunately for Mrs Gowan, she was next door administering to her sick mother-in-law. Furniture in the house was damaged and a hole was knocked through the wall. At tailor Thomas Swift's house, number 4, the chimneys and roof were badly damaged and a piece of shell smashed through a window. Likewise at Mrs Simpson's properties, numbers 10 and 11, the chimneys and roofs were severely damaged.

The roof of 25 St Thomas Street, belonging to Mr Richardson, was damaged and all the windows were smashed.

At the fish and chip shop at 61 St Thomas Street, the baby of the Crosby family, Clifford, had a near miraculous escape, for when the bombardment had started his mother, Margaret Crosby had taken the 16-month-old infant from his cradle in the rooms above the shop - which were the Crosby family's home - to the ground floor. Only minutes later an entire nose-cone from a shell crashed through the roof and ceiling of the child's bedroom and landed in the centre of the now empty, but still warm cradle. The infant's crying had, without doubt, saved his young life. The day should have been a happy one, for it was father John Crosby's 51st birthday - although he was out working on the trams as a conductor at the time of the incident, a position forced on him by the shortage of potatoes for his fish and chip shop - but for the Crosbys and their children, Doris, Bernard and Clifford, the day was the most terrifying of their lives:

> *I shall never forget that dreadful day. I was seven years old and it was my father's 51st birthday. Our breakfast was ready at about eight o'clock when there was an awful noise which sounded like claps of thunder. The tea got cold, bewildered relations and strangers began to arrive, but nobody had any idea what was happening. The strangers were not fully dressed - they thought they would be safer with us as my mother and father were good people.*
>
> *My youngest brother, Clifford, should have been asleep in his cradle, but before the noise began he had decided to cry and we were all together. Later we saw in the middle of the pillow in his cradle a round, heavy piece of metal*

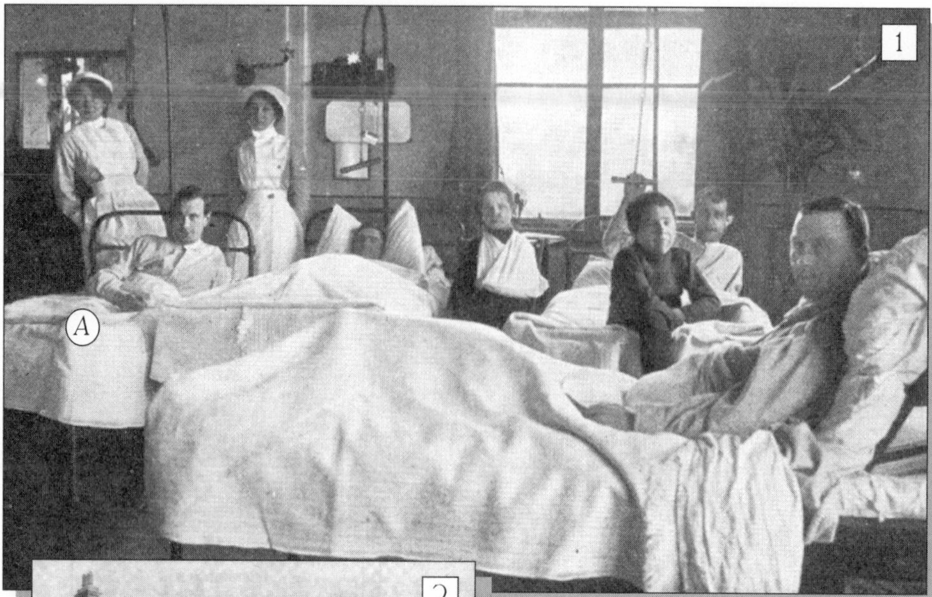

THE HOSPITAL

1&3: Wounded from the bombardment. Joiner Fred Eden (A) was wounded outside the new Co-op building and it ruined his chances of joining up. 2: A view of the Hospital at Friar's Entry.

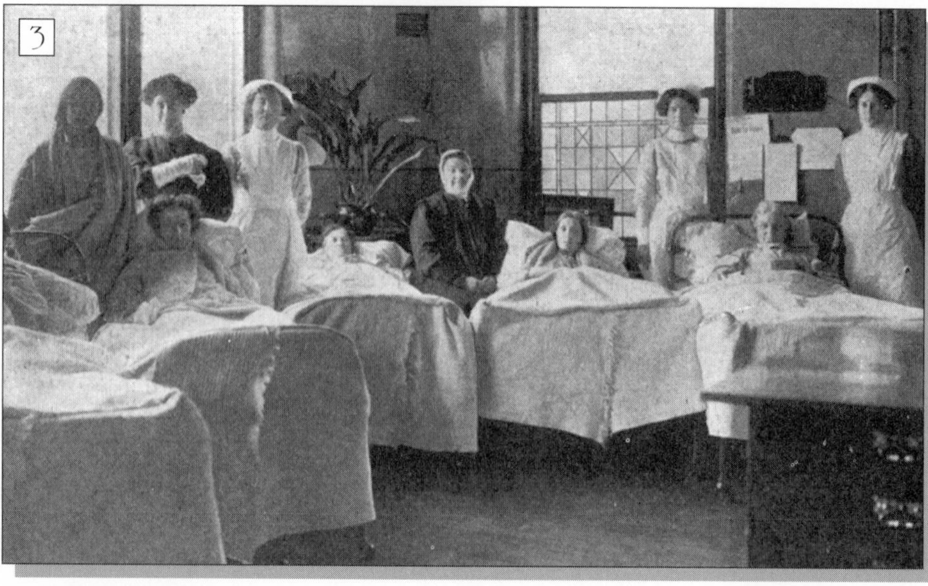

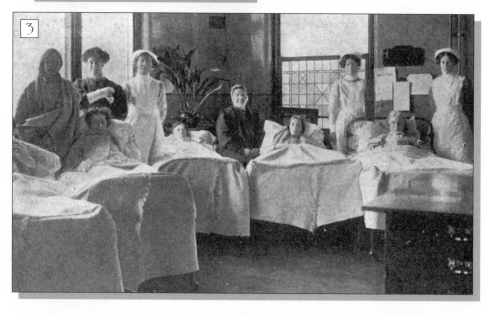

(approximately two pounds) and a hole in the ceiling. My father was told it was the cap of a shell that had spun off the shell that demolished a house in St Thomas Walk [Alfred Gowan's].

The time for school was long since past by the time the noise had ceased, and our helper, Annie, was told to take me to see if the school was open. Central School was open, but there were not many children or teachers there. We were told not to return in the afternoon.

So recalled Doris Crosby many years later. By a strange coincidence, some forty years later, after moving to Cornwall, she made a friend of a girl who had been a pupil at Queen Margaret's School at the time of the bombardment. The pair had much to talk about.

Elders Street, Queen Street, Cross Street and Albert Row

At 9 Elders Street, the home of John Hornsey, the chimney stack was blown off, part of the roof was damaged, and the windows were broken. The roof of the Wesleyan Chapel on Queen Street was hit and a hole punched through close to the organ. Although the roof was holed and a number of roof beams hung down there was no other damage.

Twenty-eight pieces of shell did an estimated £20 to £30 worth of damage at Hooker's Fancy Warehouse at 7-11 Market Hall on Cross Street where the fragments broke signs and shutters, glass, jewellery and an assortment of fancy goods.

Off New Queen Street, on Albert Row, the walls, railings and windows of John Carter's house at number 4 and Mary Temple's at number 5, were damaged by flying shrapnel from the same blast.

Friar's Entry, The Hospital, Auborough Street and Taylor's Yard

The hospital, on Friar's Entry, ministering to the ever growing band of wounded, was itself hit by a shell which knocked the gable end off and then rebounded across the street and through the wooden door of the premises of Mr Chapman, a joiner and undertaker, at 19 Auborough Street. Many windows along the street were shattered by the blast. Close by, at the home of George and Sarah Stevenson at 1 Taylor's Yard (Friar's Entry), shrapnel broke windows at the back of the house.

During the bombardment, and throughout the rest of the day, injured people were brought or sent to the local hospital on Friar's Entry, among them two from the same street, though injured in different parts of the town. The first was a thirteen-year-old boy called William Reynolds, of 5 The Bolts, Sandside. William had been close to Queen Margaret's School at the time a shell had exploded, had been hit by flying shrapnel and had two toes torn off. The second was a young woman, twenty-six-year-old Maggie Sellers, of 26 The Bolts, Sandside, who had been struck in the thigh by shell splinters near her home.

For fifteen-year-old Nancy Louth, of 14 Friar's Gardens, the ordeal of the bombardment had to take second place to her commitment to her patients, for Nancy had been on the top floor of the hospital's nurses' home when shrapnel struck the roof and burst through the fireplace in the Kendall Ward, covering her in plaster, soot and debris.

I was working at the Scarborough Hospital on the morning of the bombardment. At the time I was nearly 16 and was on the top floor of the nurses' home in

Dr Henry Maingay of 33 Queen Street was kept busy tending the wounded

The roof of Wilton House, 13a Bedford Street, home of Mrs Randall, was blown off

The Hospital on Friar's Entry was hit but not seriously damaged

At 9 Elders Street, John Hornsey's chimney was blown off and his roof badly damaged

The home of William Ellis at 47 Aberdeen Walk was damaged by shrapnel

Auborough Street when the shrapnel of the first shell fired at the castle walls hit the roof. I was covered in plaster.

I flew down the stairs into the main hospital where we were called to move all the children into the women's ward. A nurse and I were taking a woman with a broken leg down from Kendall Ward when the fireplace blew in around us and we were smothered with soot and brick dust. We had some wounded Belgian soldiers on the upper floor and they were telling us to get everyone down to the bottom floor.

We were all busy moving patients and the main hospital entrance was full of people bringing in the wounded, and the small lift was working overtime. In all the confusion people were filling the entrance thinking it was safe to come inside, but the wounded were - well, it was awful to see.

Earlier we had to get the isolation wards ready and erect all the beds and make them up. Matron wasn't with us because she'd gone to St Malo in France to nurse the wounded. So it fell to all of us to do what we could.

All of us were shaking like leaves all the time the guns were firing and Scarborough itself looked like a ball of fire. I should never have noticed it, but a doctor and I had to go upstairs to the X-ray room for something and he drew my attention to the sky. Just at that moment there was a lull in the firing and then suddenly it all started again and as I came out of the X-ray room the cupboard where 'Tommy' the skeleton was housed suddenly flew open and there he was . . . shaking. That did it for me and I flew!

Existing patients, including three Belgian soldiers and a member of the Yorkshire Hussars (injured prior to the bombardment) were moved to *Wydale Hall* at Snainton, owned by Harry Illingworth, to make room for the wounded and injured streaming in from the shelling.

Those convalescing at the hospital were quickly gathered together and sent home to free up the much-needed beds. Meanwhile, local people helped clear the debris in the hospital.

Other wounded and injured were taken to the Westborough Wesleyan Chapel, the basement of which had been taken over for the war and was being used as the 2nd Military Naval Base Hospital serving the north-east's military camps. Here the local Red Cross and St John Ambulance Brigade volunteers worked on a rota system to staff the hospital and care for the patients, which included several injured children and the badly wounded Private Bowman of the 5th Green Howards.

Longwestgate

The Reverend Ellis, curate of St Thomas's Church was injured by a piece of shell when he rushed out of the vicarage into Longwestgate to urge a number of women and children to come inside for shelter. His wounds were treated in the nearby home of Dr Maingay and he was later taken to the nursing home belonging to Nurse Robson on Westborough to recuperate.

Also wounded on Longwestgate, at Clarkson's Buildings, was fifty-two-year-old Mary Cammish who was caught in the neck by flying shrapnel. She was taken to hospital for treatment.

St Thomas's School was struck by shrapnel and a number of windows were broken. The school remained closed for the rest of the day.

In the North Bay, Clarence Gardens were left pockmarked with shells

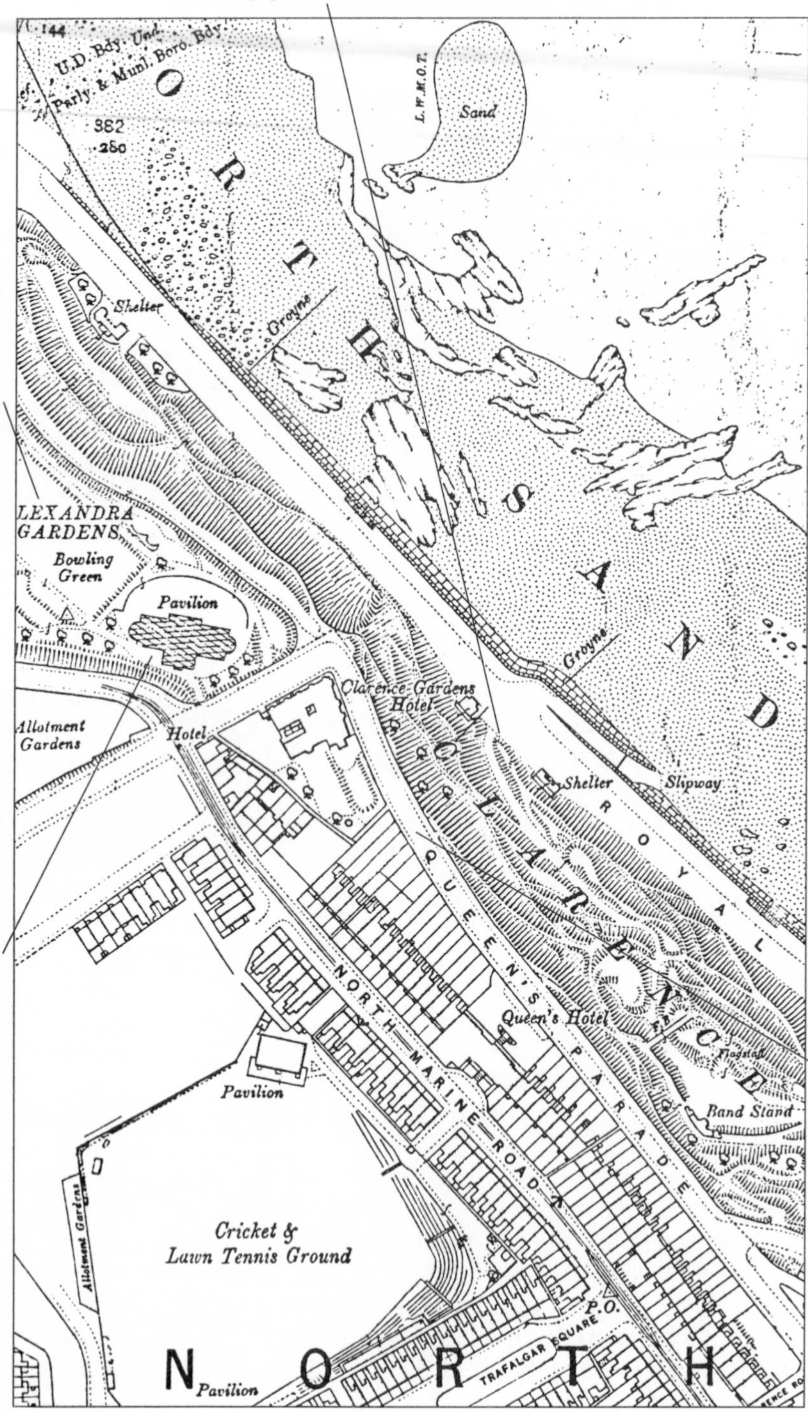

The Alexandra Gardens were ploughed up by shells and shrapnel

The splendid glass canopy of the Floral Hall, recently refurbished, was shattered by sharpnel

When postman Mr Southwick returned home to 164 Queen's Parade (North Marine Road) he found a scene of total devastation awaiting him

Atlas Place and Trafalgar Square

With shrapnel flying left, right and centre, twenty-two-year-old Lily Crosby was badly wounded in the face and shoulder at 10 Atlas Place and required immediate hospital treatment.

At 38 Trafalgar Square Miss Scott's house was badly damaged by a shell which exploded nearby. The home of Mrs Andrews at 40 Trafalgar Square received a direct hit and half of the house was demolished in one instant. Close by, at number 42, the home of Detective-Inspector George Nawton was badly damaged from the same blast.

Victoria Park, The Floral Hall, North Marine Road and Queen's Parade

In the Victoria Park area a shell fell straight into the Peasholm Park boating lake, throwing up a huge wall of water and mud and scattering the ducks, but doing no real damage.

The Floral Hall, close to Queen's Parade on the north side, remained relatively unscathed, although vibrations from nearby explosions, and flying shrapnel did some damage to the glass in the roof of its 'pleasure palace' which fronted out over the North Bay. Close by, the Alexandra Gardens were ploughed up by a handful of shells.

On North Marine Road, five houses were severely damaged. The chimney and roof of Mrs Harrison's house, at 97 North Marine Road, were damaged and her windows broken by the shell which struck next door. The home of PC Robert Roper, at 99 Queen's Parade (North Marine Road), had a hole punched clean through its chimney stack and a number of its windows broken, whilst at 164 Queen's Parade (North Marine Road) local postman, Mr Southwick, returned home after the bombardment to find a scene of total devastation awaiting him, his front-facing bedrooms and second-floor drawing-room having been blown to pieces. At John Wallis's home, at 166 Queen's Parade (North Marine Road), his daughter had a very narrow escape, for only a moment before a shell burst through the window and caused chaos in the room, the young woman had been standing at it, her face pressed against the glass, watching the enemy ships firing from the North Bay. However, despite being blown right across the room by the blast she emerged unscathed apart from some minor cuts and bruises. The same could not be said for the room, which was beyond help.

The north side of the town suffered little in comparison to the centre and south side; however, shells tore up asphalt paving in parts of Clarence Gardens. The Borough park-keepers and gardeners had gone to a lot of effort to maintain the gardens, and even threatened fines for those who abused them:

> *The public are requested to keep to the footpaths. Any person who shall allow any dog, or other animal in his charge to enter upon any of the flower beds in these grounds is liable to pay a penalty not exceeding £5.*

Now much of the gardens were scarred and pitted with shells and shrapnel.

Again on Queen's Parade, *Gresham House*, the home of the Crosslands was hit. The Crosslands had watched the German ships manoeuvre through the early morning mist and begin their bombardment of the town. Although using binoculars and later claiming that the ships were so close to shore that he could see the sailors going about their business on deck, Mr Crossland claimed he was unaware the ships were German and of the danger the town was in, even when the guns began firing; he believed them to be British vessels which were simply signalling to each other - mistaking the flashes

THE LIGHTHOUSE

The damage made the structure *'distinctly unsafe'* and work began on pulling it down three days later. Plans were put in hand by the Harbour Commissioners for the lighthouse to be rebuilt after the war. The pier, dating back to 1732, escaped relatively unscathed. The lighthouse had stood since 1801, its six tallow candles serving to warn of the dangers off the coast until 1844 when gas light had been introduced. It was 1931 before a new tower was built, paid for with money raised by the Townsmen's Association.

1&2: Work begins to dismantle the lighthouse.
3: The dismantled lighthouse pictured in early 1915.

from their gun muzzles for flashlights. However, Mr Crossland was rudely appraised of the truth of the matter when a shell smashed through the roof of his home and into an upstairs bedroom, leaving everything in it destroyed. Household articles and clothing were strewn all over the place, while shrapnel holes were punctured through several walls.

Burniston Road and The Barracks

At the barracks on Burniston Road a single shell landed close by, but did little damage apart from chipping some brickwork. Several more shells fell in the fields between the barracks and town. The alarm had been raised with the firing of the first shell and the men there, the 14th King's Hussars, had been mustered, armed and given twenty rounds of ammunition each and sent to man the trenches and emplacements along the cliff top behind the officers' mess. Quite what they could have done with their rifles against the might of the battleships is unclear, but it was widely felt by many at the time that the attack could well presage an enemy invasion. The soldiers prepared to meet the enemy with fixed bayonets. If they came ashore they would feel the sharp stab of cold British steel. As they watched and listened, having been ordered not to return fire for fear of giving away their location, shells sped overhead into the Peasholm and Northstead Manor area. But now the enemy ships were almost finished with their gory work and were already plotting a course for Whitby, further up the coast. As the attack faded, a number of shells ploughed into the grounds of the North Cliff Golf Club, one of them creating a huge hole in Burniston Road.

The Lighthouse ~ The Final Casualty

The Germans' parting shot, fired as they steamed away from the scene of their crime towards the fishing port of Whitby further up the coast, punched a gaping hole in the side of the town's lighthouse situated on Vincent's Pier in the harbour in the South Bay. The Harbour-Master, Cass Smith, later claimed the shell had struck the lighthouse and ricocheted off to hit the corner of the Grand Hotel. As the shell went clean through the lighthouse from one side to the other, it is more likely the projectile simply blew its way clean through the tower and continued on its way until it struck the hotel.

The damage caused by the shell was considered by experts to be so bad as to make the entire structure *'distinctly unsafe'* and work on pulling the lighthouse down began three days later (Saturday, 19th December) whilst plans were put in hand by the Harbour Commissioners for it to be rebuilt after the war.

The pier on which the lighthouse stood, dating back to 1732, escaped relatively unscathed. The lighthouse had stood sentinel since 1801, its six tallow candles serving to warn sailors of all nations of the hidden dangers off the coast until 1844 when gas light was introduced. Now its light was extinguished and it would not shine again until well after the war. To many, the destruction of one of the town's most familiar landmarks brought to mind the words of the British Foreign Secretary, Sir Edward Grey, spoken in earnest on the eve of war (3rd August 1914), *'The lamps are going out all over Europe; we shall not see them lit again in our lifetime.'*

Prophetic words for Scarborough as it turned out. It would be 1931 before a new tower was built, paid for with money raised by the Townsmen's Association.

The shell also wrecked a bedroom in the adjoining house, where the Harbour-Master lived. Mrs Smith, terrified, rushed from the building with her pet parrot tucked under her arm and ran to shelter in the lee of the pier with some of the local fishermen.

THE LIGHTHOUSE

Vincent's Pier, South Bay.

Three trawlers and several yawls, lying at rest in the harbour, were damaged during the final stages of the bombardment. Two of the trawlers were damaged by the same piece of shell when it crashed straight through the *Volta* and into the *Rameses* alongside her. Both ships were holed above the waterline. However the third vessel, the *Industria*, was struck below the waterline and as the tide came in she began to fill with water. All were later repaired and once more made seaworthy. Had the majority of the town's fleet not been out in the bay awaiting high tide, it is quite possible many more of them would have sustained damage.

The Aftermath

The town's ordeal had lasted for just twenty-five minutes, but by the time the German battleships had left the place was in uproar and panic; some seventeen people lay dead, among them women and children, and more than 80 had been injured. Many more were suffering from shock. When the final death-roll was called the total would number 18.

Although all the routes out of the town were littered with people, the railway station became the obvious focal point for 'escape' and even during the bombardment was quickly thronged with families and individuals hoping to get away from the carnage and into safer territory as the fears of an invasion by German troops escalated. Stories later emerged of people being refused entry to the station without a ticket; of one woman with three small children who was a shilling short of her fare and was refused a ticket until the crowd made up the difference; and of those who had bought third-class tickets, unable to find room in other carriages and who had taken seats in first-class carriages, having to be physically removed by porters and staff before the 8.25am train to Leeds could leave.

Indeed so frightened were many that the Post Office on Aberdeen Walk was crowded with townsfolk desperate to withdraw their life savings before the Germans arrived and looted the place. Many of those at the railway station, waiting for a train *to anywhere* in most cases, stood only in what they had been wearing when the bombardment had begun. Some reports told of a man dressed only in a shirt and carrying a razor, while another told of an old woman in a plum-coloured flannelette night-dress, while yet another told of a man in a top hat with a parrot for a companion!

Trains pulled out of Scarborough carrying refugees bound for Pickering, Malton, York, Leeds and Hull. Some from the town even fled as far as London where a *Daily Sketch* reporter at King's Cross told of a woman from the town with three children in tow who was 'homeless, friendless and with nowhere to go'. The poor woman had grabbed her offspring and fled with a few clothes wrapped in a counterpane to try and locate her husband, a soldier, who was in a London hospital recovering from wounds. Often the trains were flagged down outside the town, on the outskirts, as more refugees, having fled on foot, sought to put a greater distance between themselves and the threatened invasion.

Yet more people fled inland on foot, horseback, cart and car, though it was hardly safer outside the town boundary, for a local policeman found shell fragments in Ayton (west of the town), while a Mr Raw later told the press that three or four shells had fallen in Cayton (to the south of the town). No damage was reported, although one shell had fallen close to the waterworks and two more behind the Wesleyan Chapel on Main Street.

In actual fact there were nine recorded shells in and around Cayton and Osgodby

5TH GREEN HOWARDS

1: On the Marine Drive before the war. 2: New recruits go through their paces on the Athletic Ground. 3: The Battalion at the Athletic Ground. 4: Drilling on the Athletic Ground (now the McCain Stadium).

and what are now the Eastfield (around Pindar School and McCains) and Southwold (Harvest Way) areas - all open fields at the time.

The town's authorities did the best they could, and while members of the police force tried to arrange emergency accommodation in such places as Leeds, an appeal was issued for Scarborians to take in those families whose homes had been damaged or destroyed. Telegrams flooded into the town as relatives from far and wide, on hearing of the bombardment, endeavoured to find out what had become of their loved ones. The situation, though perhaps not panic-ridden, was nonetheless chaotic.

Men from the 5th Green Howards, fresh recruits who had been drilling at the railway station, were issued with white armbands and detailed to assist with the injured and wounded (although many local citizens would have no doubt preferred to have seen them issued with weapons and sent off to stand guard on the beaches). One man, seventeen-year-old Private Herbert Potter, later recalled carrying the wounded and injured from their shattered homes to lay them on the pavements there to wait for an ambulance, *"We tried to comfort them, but everyone was terribly distressed."*

The casualties were ferried to the hospital throughout the rest of the day and most of the evening. *"The saddest sight of all,"* commented Mayor Graham, *"was the little children, those between eight and nine years, who had been injured."*

Once the initial paralysis was over, official bureaucracy swung into gear as local papers were warned by officials not to print any independent accounts of the bombardment - they were to carry the 'official' accounts and 'authorised' statements only. Likewise, the Post Office was obliged to refuse to handle any telegrams describing the bombardment, though one engine driver did manage to get a message through to his wife in York stating, *"Shells falling heavily all around me, but I am alright."*

The use of the telephone was prohibited under the pretext that the lines were needed for the military and civil authorities' use, and the Mayor himself was forced to issue a notice stating, 'I have been asked by many people what they should do in consequence of the bombardment of Scarborough this morning. I have only one piece of advice to give, and that is to keep calm and help others to do the same.'

A New Page in the Town's History

Not since 1066, when the last of the great Vikings, Harald Hardrada and Tostig Godwinson, had come ashore from their longships to sack the town, had Scarborough been attacked. Not since William the Conqueror's successful invasion, also in 1066, had an enemy's attack resulted in such a high loss of life. And not since 1797 had Britain's shores been invaded by a foreign force. On that occasion the invaders had been a small detachment of the 'Black Legion', a French force commanded by the Irish-American William Tate, which had landed at Fishguard in Wales with the intention of raising a rebellion against George III. The invaders mistook the red cloaks of the local women for British redcoats and promptly surrendered.

Indeed, the last time Scarborough had heard the angry retort of naval guns was in September 1779, when American Paul Jones captured two British warships within sight of the town after a fierce engagement.

Wednesday, 16th December 1914 had seen a new and frightening page written in the town's history.

The Official Reports Begin

The first official notice relating to the attacks on Scarborough, Whitby and Hartlepool

Mr Atkinson, the foreman at the gas works, had a narrow escape at his home, 2 Gas House Cottages

The Athletic Ground where the recruits for the Green Howards trained before being shipped out to Darlington and Newcastle

One of the gasometers was holed at the Gas Works, but not ignited

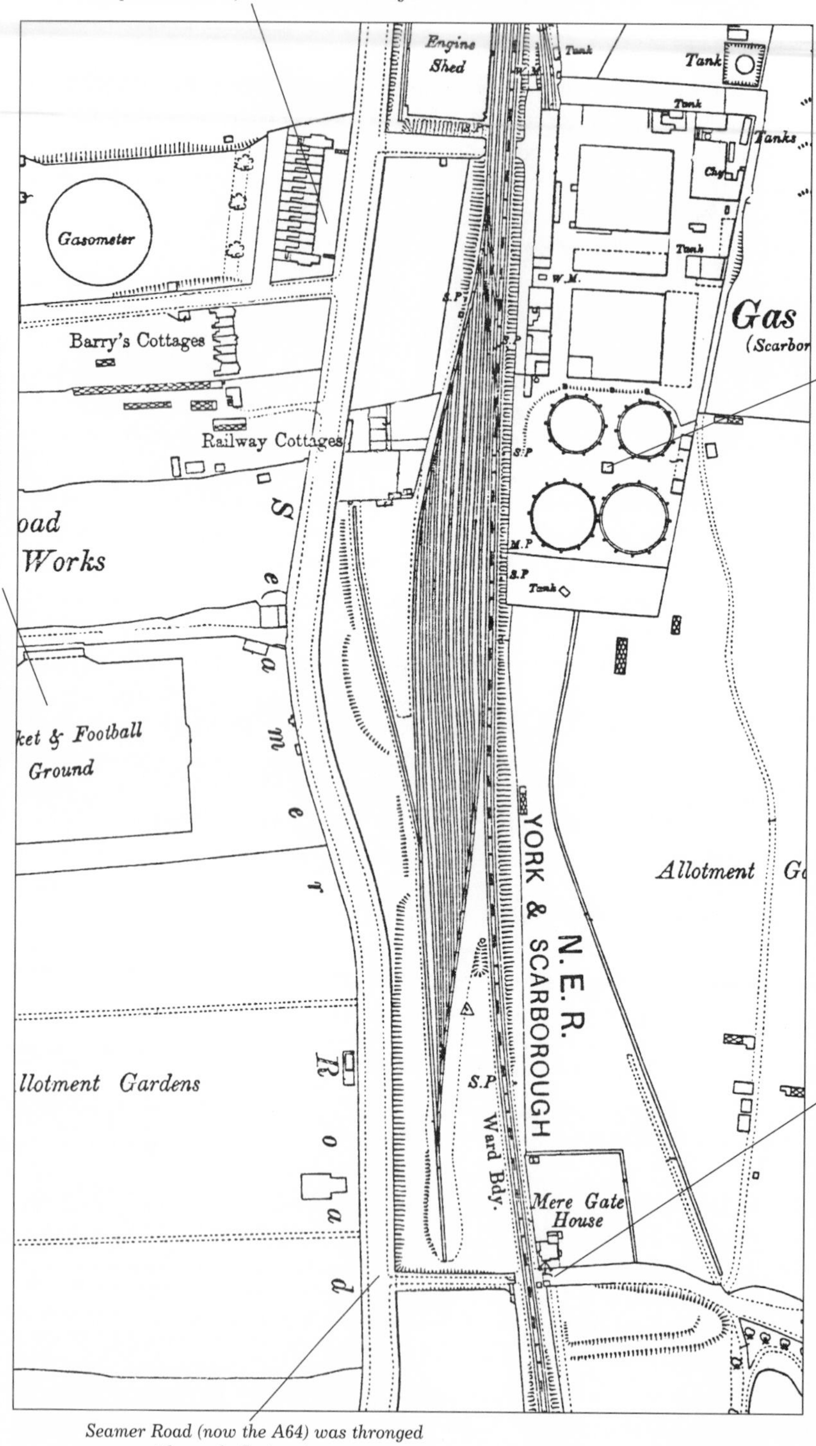

Winifred Holtby and the girls of Queen Margaret's had a narrow escape when a shell landed on the level-crossing fifty yards ahead of them

Seamer Road (now the A64) was thronged with people fleeing the town was made by the Admiralty at 11.25am that same morning (Wednesday, 16th December 1914).

> *German movements of some importance are taking place this morning in the North Sea. Scarborough and Hartlepool have been shelled and our flotillas have at various points been engaged. The situation is developing.*

Thirty-five minutes later the Prime Minister, Herbert Asquith, was appraised of the current situation at a special 'War Council' meeting convened at 10 Downing Street at twelve noon. Present, along with the Prime Minister, were David Lloyd George (Chancellor of the Exchequer), the Marquess of Crewe (Secretary of State for India), Winston Churchill (First Lord of the Admiralty), Lord Fisher (Admiral of the Fleet, First Sea Lord), Sir Edward Grey (Secretary of State for Foreign Affairs), James Balfour (MP), Field Marshal Earl Kitchener (Secretary of State for War), Lieutenant-General Sir James Wolfe Murray (Chief of the Imperial General Staff) and Lieutenant-Colonel Hankey (Secretary).

> *Mr Churchill communicated such information as had come to hand regarding the bombardment and its results. He explained that a division of the First Battle Fleet, a squadron of battle-cruisers with armoured cruisers and light cruisers, had been disposed with the object of intercepting the enemy's retreat and bringing him to action. In addition, part of the Second Battle Fleet had issued from the Forth to cut the enemy off from the north, and a destroyer force, under Commodore Tyrwhitt had sailed from Harwich and should before long establish contact with the division of battleships.*
>
> *In addition, a submarine flotilla was off Terschelling on its way to intercept the enemy on his homeward route, though it was doubtful whether it would arrive in time. These dispositions justified the hope that if the weather should prove favourable the enemy would be intercepted on his return to port. It was believed that the enemy's object in making this raid was mainly as an act of retaliation for his recent defeat in the Falkland Islands; also to re-establish the prestige of the German Navy in Germany and in neutral countries; and possibly to endeavour to influence the dispositions of our fleet and draw them into an area where they would be more accessible to the German submarines.*
>
> *After some discussion, the Prime Minister suggested an adjournment of the discussion on this question until further news was available.*

At 1.35pm the War Office put out the following statement:

> *The Fortress Commander at West Hartlepool reports that German war vessels engaged that fortress between 8.00am and 9.00am this morning. The enemy were driven off. A small German war vessel also opened fire on Scarborough and Whitby.*

The Leeds Rifles

With fears rife across the country of an imminent invasion by the Germans the 8th Battalion, The West Yorkshire Regiment (Territorials), also known as 'The Leeds Rifles', were despatched to defend Scarborough, partly at the insistence of the civil

THE GUNS

The guns shown here represented the infamous 'South Steel Battery'. All of the guns were outdated and useless. 1&3: The gun from the Crimean War beside the Grand Hotel, St Nicholas Cliff. 2: Clarence Gardens. 4: Osborne House. 5: Clarence Gardens' second gun. 6: Holbeck Gardens.

authorities who wanted them in the town as much to defend it as to keep order among the highly agitated populace.

The Leeds Rifles had been formed at Selby on 10th August 1914, as part of the 1st West Riding Brigade, which was part of the 1st West Riding (Territorial) Division. Curiously, a battalion of the West Yorkshires had been in Scarborough during August for an annual summer camp, but when war had come had been pulled out to train and prepare for such duties as their superiors saw fit. Generally, where the Territorials were concerned, this was 'home defence' - although, as with the 5th Green Howards, many Terrier units volunteered for active service overseas and indeed, the Terriers supplied more troops to the fighting fronts than the Regular Army and Kitchener's New Army combined, a fact that is overlooked by many even to this day. In early November 1914 the West Yorkshires had been put on alert and told to be ready to move at a moment's notice. On that occasion they thought they would be heading for Lowestoft on the Norfolk coast. As it transpired they were stood down later in the day, much to the men's chagrin.

At the time of the bombardment the Leeds Rifles, billeted in the dining-room of the Rowntree's chocolate factory in York, were marching to the firing ranges at Strensall. Lieutenant John Gawthorpe was in charge of a group of new recruits training with machine guns when, just after 10.00am, a young motorcycle despatch rider roared up to him with orders to return at once to Rowntree's and to have the Battalion 'stand by'.

The Commanding Officer of the battalion, Lieutenant-Colonel Edward Kitson Clark ordered all available men to be mustered - they numbered some 800. Once assembled in the dining-room they were given a meal of sandwiches and issued extra rations of bread and cheese as well as ammunition. Still there was no hint or clue as to where they were heading. It could have been to the Western Front for all they knew. But they felt ready no matter where they were being sent. Indeed, the entire West Riding Division was 'stood to' as a precautionary measure and the regulars at the Army Depots in York were also told to pack up and be ready to move off. However, despite their eagerness to see action, the Leeds Rifles were thwarted in their attempt to leave York promptly due to North Eastern Railways having to check the line to Scarborough was clear and undamaged, and that there were sufficient trains and carriages for the 800 men they were expected to transport.

At 1.00pm the order to 'move' was given and the battalion was paraded and informed that Scarborough was under attack. The information caused a sensation amongst the men, many of whom could not wait to get into a scrap. In the highest of spirits the battalion marched off to York's railway station with crowds of people lining the streets to see them off. At the station the men were bemused to see hordes of women and children, unkempt and dishevelled milling about, unaware they were witnessing the refugees from the seaside resort they were off to defend.

It was 2.30pm before the first train eased out of York, bound for Scarborough, the troops now knowing where they were going and why. The closer they got to the coast the higher their expectation and excitement. As that first train pulled in to Scarborough just before dusk the Leeds Rifles could clearly see for themselves the signs of the earlier shelling, for the station was littered with broken glass and debris, and a shunting engine had been knocked off its tracks. The station was also still busy with many of Scarborough's worried citizens still trying to flee the place. The Leeds Rifles arrived expecting to face the enemy, having been led to believe the Germans had actually landed troops at Scarborough, but were immediately detailed to clear the

THE CASTLE

1: The Pickup family prepare to defend the Castle after their donkey, Topsy, was badly wounded and had to be put to sleep. Left to right: Hilda, Doris, Albert (Castle Custodian), Alberta, Mildred, Emily (wife).
2: Yorkshire Hussars on the Castle walls.
3: The damaged keep.
4: Another view of the 'old' barracks.

debris-strewn platforms and to tidy up. While this was done the majority of the battalion was called to order and marched briskly through the devastated town to the Foreshore, there to take up positions to thwart any attack the enemy might make. As they marched, the pavements, tarmacadam and cobbles ringing to the steady beat of their boots, locals rushed out of their homes and cheered them as if they had liberated the town from under the noses of the Germans; pies, cakes, buns and coins were pushed gratefully into the bemused hands of the soldiers as they strode jauntily to the beach. At the rear of the column came the battalion's twin Maxim guns; though some of the locals feared they would be of little use against the mighty naval guns which had been levelled on the town. What they would have liked to have seen was the big guns being brought up - but there were none available.

Whilst the men of the Leeds Rifles dug trenches on the beach in front of the battered Grand Hotel, the machine guns were set up at the foot of the Castle Hill. Later, in the gathering dusk, the troops on guard along the Foreshore cheered, along with the assembled crowd of locals (the Foreshore was heaving with locals surveying the damage done that morning), when two British destroyers from the coastal patrol appeared off the South Bay.

The presence of the soldiers had helped to restore some semblance of calm to the town, and as the day drew on men from the battalion who were not required for look-out and guard duties were sent into the town to help with the clean-up operations. That night, those not on duty, slept fitfully aboard the trains which had brought them to the town.

An interesting footnote to the Leeds Rifles' arrival in the town is that in the summer of 1909 the Regiment's 7th Battalion had taken part in a mobilisation exercise at Scarborough, in which they had defended the town against an imaginary sea-borne invader. Needless to say, during the exercise they had successfully repelled the imaginary invaders.

Trawlermen Report Sight of German Squadron

Some six hours after the raids on the north-east coastal towns, local trawlermen witnessed the passage of six German warships, proceeding due east at full speed. It was presumed they were heading for Heligoland (a small North Sea island where the Germans had a naval base). Three of the ships in the squadron were thought to be cruisers, between which signals were being exchanged. Though there were several trawlers in the vicinity, not a single person on board any of them could read the signals, and the warships simply steamed on, ignoring them.

London ~ The Rumours, the Panic and the Truth

By mid-afternoon rumours were rife in London that the Germans had landed on the east coast, and in number. These rumours were quickly dispelled however.

It later transpired that the attacks were not quite as unexpected as had at first been thought, for the intelligence services had alerted the Admiralty to possible enemy fleet action along the North Sea coast. They in turn had sent part of the British Fleet to meet the threat, and in part the Navy had been successful by turning aside a larger German force.

That evening, at 9.20pm, the Admiralty put out the following thoroughly comfortless statement:

The roof of St Mary's Church was damaged

The Kingscliffe Holiday Camp offices at 13 King Street were severely damaged and Albert Greenwood had both his legs broken by the blast, but survived

The Market Hall, on St Helen's Square, was damaged

A shell travelled the length of an entire ward of the Royal Northern Sea Bathing Infirmary but did little damage

The Town Hall on St Nicholas Street was damaged

This morning a German cruiser force made a demonstration upon the Yorkshire coast, in the course of which they shelled Hartlepool, Whitby and Scarborough. A number of their fastest ships were employed for this purpose, and they remained about an hour on the coast.

As soon as the presence of the enemy was reported, a British patrolling squadron endeavoured to cut them off. On being sighted by the British vessels the Germans retired at full speed, and favoured by the mist, succeeded in making good their escape.

The losses on both sides are small, but full reports have not yet been received.

The Admiralty take the opportunity of pointing out that demonstrations of this character against unfortified towns or commercial ports, though not difficult to accomplish, provided that a certain amount of risk is accepted, are devoid of military significance. They may cause some loss of life among the civil populace, and some damage to private property, which is much to be regretted, but they must not in any circumstances be allowed to modify the general naval policy which is being pursued.

Hot on the heels of the Admiralty's statement the War Office responded with its own version of events:

At 8.00am today, three ships were sighted off Hartlepool, and at 8.15am they commenced a bombardment. The ships appeared to be two battle-cruisers and one armoured cruiser. The land batteries replied, and are reported to have hit and damaged the enemy. At 8.50am the firing ceased. None of our guns were touched. One shell fell in the Royal Engineers' lines, and several in the lines of the 18th Service Battalion of the Durham Light Infantry.

The casualties among the troops amounted to 7 killed and 14 wounded. Some damage was done to the town, and the gasworks were set on fire.

During the bombardment, especially in West Hartlepool, the people crowded the streets, and approximately 22 were killed and 50 wounded.

At the same time a battle-cruiser and an armoured cruiser appeared off Scarborough and fired about 50 shots, which caused considerable damage, and 13 casualties are reported.

At Whitby two battle-cruisers fired some shots, doing damage to buildings, and the following casualties are reported, namely, 2 killed and 2 wounded. At all these places there was an entire absence of panic, and the demeanour of the people was everything that could be desired.

The shattered folk of Scarborough were left wringing their hands with impotence and rage, and to rebuild their lives and their town. It was of little comfort to the grieving families, or to the town, to learn later that at Hartlepool the German ships *Seydlitz* (Admiral Hipper's flagship), *Moltke* and *Blücher* had come under fire from the shore batteries and the cruisers stationed there.

Navy Blamed

For a short time the British Navy took the flak of an angry populace and an angry nation who blamed them for failing to prevent the carnage; as it was also perceived to have done on November 3rd, when a German squadron (Von Hipper's First Scouting

NOTICE.

Bombardment of the Hartlepools, Scarborough and Whitby by German Warships.

A Committee having been set up by His Majesty's Government to investigate the damage to persons and property sustained in the recent Bombardment,

Notice is Hereby Given

that all Claims in respect of such damage must be forwarded IN WRITING to me at:

The Bombardment Committee's Office,
Board of Education,
Whitehall,
London, S.W.

not later than SATURDAY, FEBRUARY 6th, 1915, and that such claims will in the first instance be considered in the order in which they are received.

AUBREY T. LAWRENCE,
Secretary to the Committee,

23rd January 1915.

Group comprising the *Seydlitz*, *Moltke*, *Von der Tann* and *Blücher*) had attacked the Norfolk coast and shelled Yarmouth and *HMS Halcyon* - a diversionary ploy to cover the laying of mines, one of which damaged the British submarine *D5*. Obviously this had been a foretaste of things to come.

Sir Walter Runciman, the MP for Hartlepool, demanded in the House of Commons:

> *How does it come to pass that when German vessels did risk coming into the open from their hiding place, they were allowed to come to our shores unobserved, unchallenged and obviously unknown?*
>
> *I think it fair criticism to ask, without casting any reflection on a branch of the national service whose deeds during the present war have thrilled us with pride of race, why it happened that the German ships were first of all allowed to get here without interruption, and secondly, why they were allowed to escape?*
>
> *What has the Intelligence Department to say to this?*
>
> *Were we caught napping?*

Meanwhile, one Samuel Storey, a Commission Agent of 38 Londesborough Road, had this interpretation to make of the Admiralty's official declaration the day after the bombardment:

> *Open towns on the east coast must expect to be bombarded and we cannot help it.*
>
> *Those who are killed must be killed and their relatives who mourn must mourn. We are sorry, but this cannot be prevented.*
>
> *Though we are supposed to command the North Sea, we cannot scatter our big ships about to prevent bombardments, which, though deplorable are devoid of military significance.*
>
> *I think that nothing more calculated to depress and alarm the public - mind you, not a record of facts, but a prophecy of future misfortunes - could be designed by the most irresponsible alarmist.*

Springing sharply to the Navy's defence, *The Times* carried the following rebut to Runciman and the numerous others far and wide demanding answers to the same basic question; "Where was Britain's mighty bloody Navy?"

> *The protection of these shores is not the primary object of the Royal Navy in war. The safeguarding of England - not necessarily little bits of England - is a consequence of military strategy, but not its primary and immediate object.*
>
> *The purpose of the Royal Navy is to engage and destroy the ships of the enemy, and that purpose will be inflexibly pursued in spite of all subtle temptations to abandon it for other objects.*
>
> *Neither raids nor even invasion will deter our fleet from the aim for which it was created, and for which it keeps the seas. A good many people in this country still think of our warships as stationed like a row of sentinels on a line drawn before the German ports. Whatever their occupations may be, it is not that.*
>
> *The possibility of a German raid upon the English coast has always existed since the war began, and will continue to exist so long as a single German warship of great speed remains afloat; but the indignant protests we have received whenever we have pointed these matters out, show that the first*

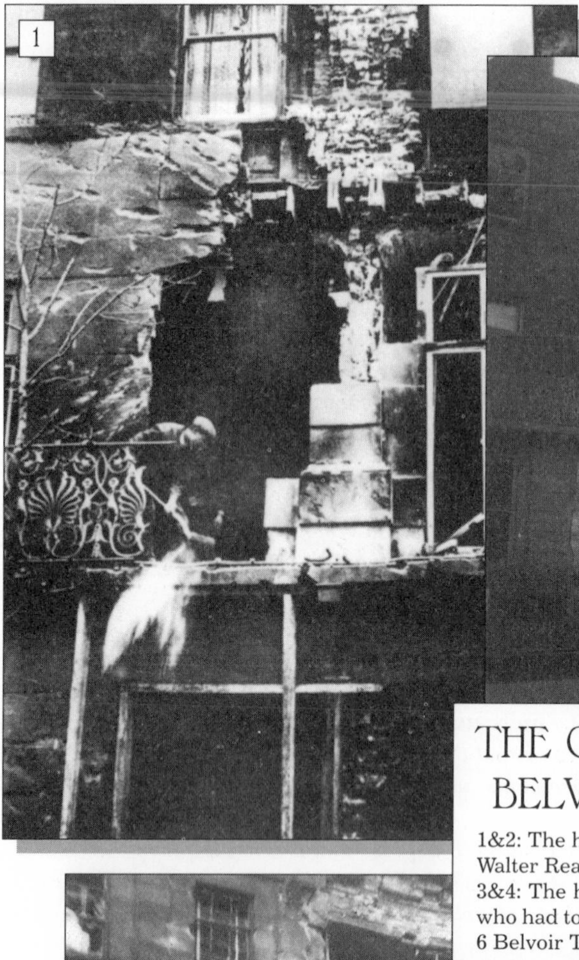

THE CRESCENT AND BELVOIR TERRACE

1&2: The home of the town's Liberal MP, Walter Rea at 7 The Crescent.
3&4: The home of the invalid Mrs Keble who had to be carried out of the debris of 6 Belvoir Terrace.

principles of naval strategy are still imperfectly understood even by this maritime race.

The duty of repelling invasion, should it be attempted, rests upon the manhood of the nation. Perhaps it will now be more clearly discerned. The Royal Navy is doing its work, doing it resolutely and doing it well. It has not failed us yet, and it will not fail us upon that great day for which it longs and waits.

Despite being a great public-relations coup for the Navy, there was much truth in what the newspaper said, even if the people of the north-east coast did not yet want to acknowledge it. The Admiralty had consistently resisted the temptation to split the fleet and station it throughout the North Sea in protection of the coast. Also, every time it put to sea en masse there were the added risks of both mines and enemy submarines whittling away at it. The Admiralty was determined to keep as much of the fleet as possible intact in order that it should be able to fight, and win, any decisive major naval engagement with the enemy's fleet.

Also unknown to the greater populace was the Navy's attempt to trap and engage the German strike force, even before it hit the east coast.

By December 1914 the British held the means to decipher the Germans' three main naval and diplomatic codes. The first of these, the HVB Code (Handelsverkehrsbuch), which was used primarily by merchant ships, small warships, U-boats and Zeppelins, had been obtained on 11th August when the Royal Australian Navy captured the German steamer *Hobart*. The second, the major unit code the SKM (Signalbuch der Kaiserlichen Marine), was handed, partially decoded, to the British by her allies the Russians on 13th October. The Russians had obtained three copies of the code when the German light cruiser *Magdeburg* ran aground on Odensholm Island at the mouth of the Gulf of Finland on 26th August. Although the Russians boarded her it was claimed that several hours later they fished out of the water the body of one of the ship's officers, clasping to his bosom - in arms stiff with rigor mortis - the cipher and signal books of the German Navy. The third, the VB (Verkehrsbuch), used by Berlin and its embassies, consulates and detached warships in foreign waters, was obtained quite by chance by a British trawler. The ship, working off the Dutch coast, brought up a chest in her nets which contained the code and ciphers of the German torpedo-boat *S119*, sunk on 17th October.

Baiting the Trap

By Monday, 14th December 1914, and acting on information from the secret Navy Intelligence Department (set up that same month) known as Room 40, which had collated reports from spies in Germany, submarines patrolling the North Sea and from monitoring the enemy's ship-to-ship wireless transmissions, the Admiralty was now certain an attack was imminent. The Harwich Force was ordered to station itself off Yarmouth on the Norfolk coast, while eight submarines were stationed off Terschelling (one of the West Frisian islands, in the North Sea, off the coast of the Netherlands) to guard against an enemy raid. At the same time, coastal defence forces were put on alert. The following message was sent from the Admiralty to the Commander-in-Chief, Admiral Jellicoe, at 9.30pm on 14th December:

Good information just received shows German First Cruiser Squadron with destroyers leave Jade River on Tuesday morning [15th December] early and return on Wednesday night [16th December]. It is apparent from the information that the battleships are very unlikely to come out. The enemy force will have time to reach our coast.

Send at once, leaving tonight, the Battle-Cruiser Squadron and Light Cruiser Squadron supported by a Battle Squadron, preferably the Second. At daylight on Wednesday morning they should be at some point where they can make sure of intercepting the enemy on his return.

Tyrwhitt, with his light cruisers and destroyers will try and get in touch with the enemy off British coast and shadow him, keeping Admiral informed.

From our information the German First Cruiser Squadron consists of four battle-cruisers and five light cruisers and there will possibly be three flotillas of destroyers.

From this message it is plainly obvious the Admiralty had prior knowledge of the forthcoming attacks to be made on the east coast, even if they didn't know exactly where they were to be made, and, that it was prepared to let those attacks go ahead with the intention of trying to catch the enemy either as it approached or as it sped for home. This was further borne out by the message sent the following day (at 2.05pm on Tuesday, 15th December 1914) by the Admiralty to Commodore Tyrwhitt at Harwich:

There is a good probability of German battle-cruisers, cruisers and destroyers being off our coast tomorrow about daybreak.

One 'M' Class destroyer is to patrol vicinity of North Hinder Lightship from midnight until 9.00am.

A second 'M' Class destroyer is to patrol a line extending 15 miles south magnetic from a position of latitude 53 degrees north, longitude three point five degrees east, from midnight until 9.00am.

The duty of these destroyers is to look out for and report the enemy and trust to their speed to escape.

If the weather is too bad they are return to Harwich. Report their names.

The 1st and 3rd Flotillas with all available light cruisers are to be under way off Yarmouth before daylight tomorrow, ready to move to any place where the enemy may be reported from, whether it is to the northward or southward. Their duty is to get touch with the enemy, follow him and report his position to the Vice-Admiral 2nd Battle Squadron and Vice-Admiral 1st Battle-Cruiser Squadron.

The 2nd Battle Squadron, 1st Battle-Cruiser Squadron, 3rd Cruiser Squadron and Light Cruiser Squadron will be in a position latitude fifty-four point ten degrees north, by longitude three degrees at 7.30am ready to cut off the retreat of the enemy.

Should an engagement result, your flotillas and light cruisers must endeavour to join our Fleet and deal with the enemy destroyers. If the weather is too bad for destroyers, use light cruisers only and send destroyers back.

The east coast was to become the bait in a daring attempt to trap and engage the enemy. None of this was public knowledge at the time and it is no wonder the people of Scarborough, Whitby and Hartlepool felt so aggrieved afterwards. Unaware, however, that the entire German High Seas Fleet was to provide long-range cover for Hipper's raiding group, the Admiralty opted to despatch only a portion of the Grand Fleet's strength in two battle groups. The first group, based at Cromarty, was Vice-Admiral Beatty's First Battle-Cruiser Squadron, comprising *Lion* (his flagship), *New Zealand*, *Tiger* and *Queen Mary*. The second group, based at Scapa, was Vice-Admiral Warrender's Second Battle Squadron, comprising *King George V* (his flagship), *Orion*, *Ajax*, *Centurion*, *Monarch* and *Conqueror*. Supporting cruiser, destroyer and submarine squadrons were also ordered to sea. The British forces consisted of some 28 vessels (six battleships, four fast battle-cruisers, four heavy cruisers, six fast light cruisers and eight submarines). Further to this force, Admiral Jellicoe requested the rest of the British Grand Fleet be brought into action, but this was turned down by the Admiralty, who remained unaware of the entire German High Seas Fleet following in support of Hipper.

The plan now was for Beatty and Warrender's groups to rendezvous off the south-east of Dogger Bank at first light on the morning of 16th December. This position was in an almost direct line between Scarborough (180 miles) and Heligoland (110 miles). In effect, the Admiralty had decided to trade off the east coast in the hope of destroying all or the major part of Hipper's group. This, it firmly believed, was a prize which far outweighed any collateral damage or losses inflicted on the undefended coastal towns.

At 3.00am on the morning of 15th December Hipper's First Scouting Group, comprising *Seydlitz*, *Derfflinger*, *Von der Tann* and *Blücher*, accompanied by light cruisers of the Second Scouting Group and its twin flotillas of torpedo-boats, steamed for a rendezvous with Admiral von Ingenohl's battle squadrons north of Heligoland. During the late evening of 15th December, Hipper's First Scouting Group turned towards the east coast and embarked on its bombardment run. Admiral von Ingenohl's force, deployed in three battle squadrons, steamed in support.

Wednesday, 16th December ~ The Early Hours

In the early hours of 16th December, at 5.15am, Warrender encountered von Ingenohl's screen of destroyers and cruisers and a hard, confused action ensued. The action lasted for some two hours. However, a message had been sent to Admiral von Ingenohl of the engagement from one of the ships engaged and, believing the British ships were part of the advanced screen for the entire British Fleet, and further expecting a massed torpedo-boat attack against his own High Seas Fleet he withdrew his capital ships and steamed for the safety of Cuxhaven at about 6.20am. Both Navies had thus missed the opportunity to do significant damage to the other.

The withdrawal of von Ingenohl's forces left Hipper both isolated and vulnerable to Warrender's force. However Warrender, for the moment, remained unaware of Hipper's position.

With the weather in the North Sea deteriorating Hipper decided to order his escorts, apart from the light cruiser *Kolberg* (heavily laden with mines), to return to the High Seas Fleet. The time was 6.32am.

Now steaming without support, Hipper fixed his position off the north-east coast at 6.40am and then divided his force. The three ships he commanded headed for Hartlepool. The three commanded by Tapken steamed for Scarborough. The scene was now set for the bombardments of the north-east ports.

With the Admiralty believing everything was in readiness and its forces ready, there was nothing to be done but to wait and see what developed. By 8.00am Scarborough and Hartlepool were under attack.

Of that fateful morning Winston Churchill later wrote:

HERBERT ASQUITH

Herbert Henry Asquith (1852-1928). Liberal Prime Minister 1908-1916. After the outbreak of war Asquith headed a Liberal-Conservative coalition 1915-1916. Following disillusion with the war after the failure of the Somme in 1916, the coalition came to an end in December of that year. He was succeeded as Prime Minister by Lloyd George.

WINSTON CHURCHILL

Winston Leonard Spencer Churchill (1874-1965). Served in the army and as a war correspondent during the Second Boer War (1899-1902). Became a Conservative MP in 1900. Joined the Liberals in 1904. First Lord of the Admiralty 1911-1915 after a spell as Home Secretary. Rejoined the army in 1915 and served in France. Minister of Munitions 1917. At the outbreak of World War Two he again became First Lord of the Admiralty. Was Prime Minister of the coalition government of 1940-1945.

All measures having been taken, we awaited during thirty-six hours the events of Wednesday morning with a doubting, but expectant curiosity.

On the morning of December 16th, at about 8.30am, I was in my bath when the door opened and an officer came hurrying in from the War Room with a naval signal which I grasped with dripping hand. 'German battle-cruisers bombarding Hartlepool'. I jumped out of the bath with exclamations. Sympathy for Hartlepool was mingled with 'the anodyne of contemplated retaliation'. Pulling on clothes over a damp body, I ran downstairs to the War Room. The First Sea Lord had just arrived from his house next door. Oliver, who invariably slept in the War Room and hardly ever left it by day, was marking positions on the map. Telegrams from all the naval stations along the coast affected by the attack, and intercepts from our ships in the vicinity speaking to each other, came pouring in two and three to the minute.

Everything was now sent to sea or set in motion. The 3rd Battle Squadron from the Forth was ordered to prevent the enemy escaping to the northward. As a further precaution the Grand Fleet was brought out. Commodore Tyrwhitt and his cruisers and destroyers of the Harwich Striking Force were directed to join Sir George Warrender, who commanded the Second Battle Squadron, and was the senior Admiral with the intercepting force.

By 9.00am, with news of the bombardments having reached them, both Beatty and Warrender's groups were making for the north-east coast in an attempt to intercept Hipper's First Scouting Group which, by 9.30am, had rejoined and was steaming hard for the Heligoland Bight.

At 10.11am Jellicoe, acting on intuition, radioed Warrender that Hipper would probably try to escape through a twenty-mile gap in the Tyne and Humber minefields off Whitby. Meanwhile, he ordered the 3rd Battle Squadron of eight battleships south from the Scottish port of Rosyth with the intention of cutting off any German retreat to the north inside the minefield.

At 11.25am, with the weather having worsened and driving rain cutting visibility to a little under a mile, the cruiser *Southampton*, the most southerly of Beatty's force, sighted a German light cruiser from the force screening Hipper. Five minutes later the *Southampton* and the *Birmingham* had engaged the enemy. However, a badly phrased signal from Beatty's ship led to the two ships breaking off the action.

Hipper's luck was in, and alerted by the engagement he altered course at 11.50am to support his screening ships. By 12.15pm Beatty had thoroughly lost contact with the enemy. Warrender, however, fifteen miles south-east of him, now had the Germans in his sights. Again Hipper changed course and steamed hard for Heligoland, his escape conveniently covered by heavy rain. A final attempt by the British to deploy destroyers and submarines to intercept the bombarding force also failed and thus Hipper made good his escape with the assistance of a combination of typical north sea weather and typical British bad luck. Much to the Admiralty's chagrin.

Admiral Jellicoe later wrote:

The escape of the enemy's force was most disappointing, seeing that our own squadrons were in a very favourable position for intercepting the raiders. Low visibility was the main reason for their escape, but the absence from the battle squadron (through bad weather) of its attached cruisers and a sufficient force of

KING GEORGE V

George V, King of Great Britain and Ireland, Emperor of India (1865-1936). George V came to the throne in 1910 on the death of his father Edward VII. Responsible for exchanging German family names for those with a 'British' connection in 1917; Saxe-Coburg-Gotha became Windsor, Battenberg became Mountbatten and Teck became Cambridge.

DAVID BEATTY

Admiral Sir David Beatty (1871 to 1936). Appointed to command of the Grand Fleet's Battle-Cruiser Squadron in 1913. Took part in battles of Heligoland Bight (28th August 1914), Dogger Bank (24th January 1915) and Jutland (31st May 1916). Succeeded Jellicoe as Commander-in-Chief, 1916, and was promoted over eight more senior admirals. Took the surrender of the German High Seas Fleet at Rosyth in 1918. First Sea Lord 1919-1927.

JOHN JELLICOE

Admiral John Rushworth Jellicoe (1859-1935). Director of Naval Ordnance 1905. Commander of British Grand Fleet 1914-1916. Criticised for being over-cautious at the Battle of Jutland, 31st May 1916, in which the German Navy escaped relatively unscathed. His primary aim was the preservation of the Grand Fleet. After Jutland he was removed from active command and became First Sea Lord. Dismissed by Lloyd George in December 1917. Raised to peerage January 1918. Promoted to Admiral of the Fleet in 1919. Became Governor-General of New Zealand.

destroyers was a contributory cause, as well as the fact of our light cruisers having, by mischance, lost touch with the enemy at 11.50am.

In hindsight, had the entire German High Seas Fleet been able to get within range of the British coast, who knows what the final death toll might have been. As it was, and as bad as it was, the people of the north-east coastal towns had, in all probability, got off lightly thanks to Warrender's dogged pursuit of the enemy fleet.

With the clamour for answers from the Admiralty by the public showing little sign of abating in the days that followed there was little it could do but shutter itself away and wait for the uproar to die down. At this stage in the war the Admiralty could not explain openly to the Great British public that it had had prior warning and how it had come by it, for fear of enlightening the enemy that his codes had been broken. The future of the war, at sea at least, depended on the Admiralty's silence, and this it maintained, stony-faced and resolute. Winston Churchill later commented:

We could not say a word in explanation. We had to bear in silence the censures of our countrymen. We could never admit, for fear of compromising our secret information, where our squadrons were, or how near the German raiding cruisers had been to their destruction.

However, the German raids brought subtle changes to British naval planning. On 21st December the Admiralty ordered Beatty's 1st Battle-Cruiser Squadron and the 1st Light Cruiser Squadron to be based at Rosyth as a precautionary measure against another north-east coast attack.

Scarborough's Mayor Calls for Calm

That evening (16th December), in the *Scarborough Evening News*, the Mayor called for the townsfolk to remain calm and to ignore the many baseless rumours of further shelling and enemy invasions that were being circulated.

False Alarm

The next morning (Thursday, 17th December) there was a general alarm as the men of the Leeds Rifles, on watch in the trenches in front of the damaged Grand Hotel, saw a boat approaching the town. The battalion 'stood to' and orders were barked out for each man to load with five rounds. Bullets clattered into their Lee Enfields as bolts were worked back and forth. Suddenly a group of women and children ran past their positions and on towards the harbour; the vessel had been recognised by the locals as one of the town's fishing boats which had been missing since the bombardment and had been presumed lost by many. The battalion was ordered to stand down.

Later, in a show of strength to any watchers from land or sea, the battalion marched some four miles along the Foreshore, some of the men collecting shell fragments from the Castle Hill as grim souvenirs of their defence of the now quiet seaside town. Much to everyone's surprise, including the men of the Leeds Rifles, the battalion returned to York that afternoon and resumed its normal routine of training for the front.

As a footnote of historical fact, it will no doubt be of interest for readers to learn that the French Croix de Guerre was awarded to every man Jack of the 8th Battalion, West Yorkshire Regiment, The Leeds Rifles, for a daring attack made on the German stronghold of Montagne de Bligny on July 28th 1918 during the Battle of the Marne (Western

1

EDWARD GREY

Sir Edward Grey (1862-1933) was the British Foreign Secretary from 1905 to 1916. Sir Edward is perhaps best known for the most famous quotation of the Great War *"The lamps are going out all over Europe; we shall not see them lit again in our lifetime."* In the case of Scarborough's lighthouse, hit during the bombardment, these words were indeed prophetic. He was excluded from Asquith's war cabinet in November 1915 and was ennobled in July 1916 before being replaced by the former Conservative Prime Minister, Arthur Balfour.

2

CHRISTOPHER GRAHAM

Alderman Christopher Colborne Graham (1857-1943) retired to Scarborough from Hull in 1905 and few people have been more generous to the town. He was Mayor from 1913 to 1919; his daughter Maisie acting as his Mayoress. In 1918 Christopher bought the Paradise estate to prevent it falling into the hands of speculators and gave it to Scarborough. It was used for the Graham Sea Training School from 1918 to 1974. In 1919 both he and his daughter were made Freemen of the Borough. He personally donated £1,000 towards the building of the Scarborough War Memorial (one fifth of the entire cost), and a further £28,000 to the Scarborough General Hospital building fund, behind which he was a major driving force.

Front), when the battalion was outnumbered five to one. The award of the medal to every man in the battalion was an honour only conferred by the French on two other regiments and a battery of the Royal Field Artillery during the whole war.

The Germans Issue a Statement

The official German statement, made in Amsterdam on Thursday, 17th December, made no mention of the helpless victims of their attacks:

> *When approaching the English coast our cruisers were unsuccessfully attacked by four British destroyers in misty weather. One destroyer was sunk and the others disappeared in a badly damaged condition. The batteries at Hartlepool were silenced and the gasworks destroyed. Several detonations were heard and three big fires in the town could be observed from our ships. The coastguard station and waterworks at Scarborough, and the signal station at Whitby were destroyed. Our vessels received some shots from coast batteries, but suffered only slight damage. In another place another British destroyer was sunk.*

The Germans treated the raid with great elation and news of its 'success' gained front-page news status with all their domestic newspapers the day after the attack. The following extract is from that day's *Nürnberger Zeitung*:

> A NEW COURAGEOUS DEED BY OUR NAVAL FORCES.
> BOMBARDING OF ENGLISH RESORTS:
> PANIC IN SCARBOROUGH, HARTLEPOOL AND WHITBY.
>
> *The joy of victory of the English after their success in the Falkland Islands has been short-lived. On Wednesday morning parts of our naval forces appeared off the English east coast and started a surprise cannon attack at the resorts of Scarborough, Hartlepool and Whitby, where a lot of damage was done.*
>
> *This bold stroke by our brave 'Blue Boys' is felt in the whole of Germany as a fantastic revenge for our unavoidable defeat at the Falkland Islands. It is proof that neither the North Sea, which is spiked with English mines, nor the English Navy is able to frighten our fleet.*
>
> *Only a few months have gone by since Winston Churchill spoke those proud words about 'fetching German rats out of their water holes.' Well, the 'rats' have come out when it suits them best. In a short time, we have managed to cause more damage than the English have in the whole sea war, up to now.*
>
> *Not only have they lost materially, more important is their loss of prestige. For centuries their coasts were secured. For decades they could rob and get rich in all corners of the world without being punished. The much smaller German fleet put the glories of England in the shade and keeps the English fleet in their home ports while Churchill tries to comfort the worried British people.*
>
> *It is time that the English rats came out of their holes. Have the German successes at sea really broken the English spirit?*
>
> *Does Great Britain only feel safe from our fleet when it has, as in the Falkland Islands, overwhelmingly superior strength (43 against 5)?*

And from the *Berliner Tageblatt*:

Once more our naval forces, braving the danger of scattered mines in the North Sea have shelled fortified places.

From the *Berliner Neusten Nachrichten:*

This time it is not merely a daring cruiser raid or the mere throwing of a bomb, but a regular bombardment of fortified places. It is further proof of the gallantry of our Navy.

The cold-blooded ruthlessness of the enemy left Scarborians incensed anew. Many must have been the young man, serving with his unit, who, on learning of those terrible events, would have given anything to return home to ensure the safety of his family.

The first we heard of the attacks was of those against Hartlepool. Later on rumours started about attacks on Scarborough and Whitby. People were talking about the Germans invading and putting the town to the torch. Many of us were for starting for home there and then, but our officers and the older men calmed us somewhat. We couldn't help but wonder where our mighty Navy was during the attacks. At one point there was even talk of us having to fight the Germans in our home towns! As it turned out the rumours were far worse than the facts - when we got them. We couldn't wait to get at them I can tell you.

My parents' house had all the windows blown out by a nearby blast, but thankfully they were unhurt - I only learned of it later though. There was a small bit about it in the paper, I still have it somewhere. Uncle George and Aunt Sarah's house was hit too I think, down in the old town at Taylor's Yard - I know the old hospital was hit too.

[2234 Private Jim Stevenson, 5th Green Howards, speaking with the author later in life.]

So it was for my own grandfather, Jim Stevenson, whose home in Salisbury Street had had all its windows blown out by the blast from a shell which fell close by. Despite the damage, his parents, Alf and Diana, emerged unscathed, though badly shaken. Jim and his comrades would have a score to settle once they got face to face with the enemy! As to that cutting from the paper, less than an inch square, Jim kept it with him, inside his wallet until the day he died in 1996 and it was the very first sliver of the jigsaw puzzle of information which would later form the basis for this book.

Magistrates Saddened by Colleague's Death

At the North Riding Police Court on Thursday, 17th December, Mr Robinson, the Chairman, expressed the regret felt by all the magistrates at the loss sustained by the death of John Hall, their colleague. Everyone, he said, knew the death had occurred under sad and tragic circumstances. Mr Hall had regularly attended the Court and the Chairman said his advice had always been much appreciated. The Bench offered their sincere sympathy to Mr Hall's relatives. The Clerk to the Court, Mr Donner, then made the following statement:

It is deplorable that the life of an innocent person should be sacrificed under circumstances of wanton ruthlessness and violation of international law, but it has in no way lessened the confidence which the country feels in the justice of their cause, or of the sure and certain hope of ultimate victory.

So far as Mr Hall is concerned, I can pay recognition to the assiduity with which he performed his duties, and the leniency he extended to those brought before him. Speaking personally, I have always received from him the greatest courtesy and kindness.

On behalf of the North Riding Police Force, PC George Boynton added their expressions of sympathy. And, after a life-long friendship with the deceased, local Justice of the Peace Joshua Rowntree wrote:

May I bear testimony to the unfailing courtesy, diligence and ability which distinguished his life, devoted as it was to various forms of public service, ever most willingly rendered. It seems passing strange that his sad death should be one to be ever associated with this wicked attack upon a town famed everywhere as a beneficial health resort. His whole nature was so emphatically a kindly and conciliatory one amongst us.

References to the death of John Hall had also been made at the Borough Police Court the previous day, on the morning of the bombardment, when Mayor Graham had voiced the deep sympathy felt by all the magistrates and officials of the court towards the family. Mr Black, the magistrate's clerk, observed that Mr Hall had taken a great interest in the work of the court.

Strange and Curious Tales

In the days following the bombardment a number of tales and stories emerged from various townsfolk concerning the sometimes novel situations they found themselves in before, during and after the shelling, and of the unusual incidents which had occurred; including the story of the mysterious stranger and his warning . . .

The Mysterious Warning

During the early afternoon of 15th December 1914, a day like any other, a group of local men had been engaged on road renovations between the nearby villages of Scalby and Burniston, when they were approached by a tall, white-haired, mustachioed man. Unsure of who this fellow was, or might be, the group's foreman, Edward Bell, had stepped up to greet him and bid him good day. The stranger had stopped and gestured with his walking cane towards the sea, which could just be seen from that point on the Burniston Road.

"You will be safe here behind that rise when the Germans come," the man declared with something less than a clear English accent, noting the site of the nearby four-mile road marker by adding, "Ah, I've walked out four miles."

Edward Bell had been taken aback. "The Germans will never come here," he had put in quickly, while gazing out in the general direction in which the stranger had pointed with his stick.

The tall man had then leaned forward and tapped the foreman on the chest with the handle of his cane. "Ah, but they will," he had avowed softly, but with great authority, all the while fixing Bell with a clear, hard stare, "and come quickly too, you'll see, you'll see."

SCARBORIANS DO THEIR BIT

1: All of these local fishermen volunteered for full-time duty aboard minesweepers. 2: The Boy Scouts of Lady Londesborough's Own Troop received badges for their work during and after the bombardment. 3: The ladies of Albemarle Baptist Church, on Albemarle Crescent, knit for the boys at the front. 4: The crew of the local minesweeper (converted from a trawler) the *John Sanderson*. 5: Publican John Newton's White Swan Inn at East Ayton, became a safe haven for many of the older residents fleeing from the bombardment.

And without waiting for a reply, or to discuss the matter further, the stranger had turned about and strode smartly off, retracing his steps back towards Scarborough. More than a little bemused, Edward Bell had then returned to his grinning colleagues and tried to put the incident from his mind. But the events of the following morning (the day of the bombardment) were to make it impossible for him so to do.

Refuge in Cave

Then there was the incident of the manager of the Scarborough Tramways Company, Walter Nicoll, who, along with his entire family and a group of friends had left their homes in Manor Road and sought refuge inside a 'cave' constructed entirely from piles of tram-tracks in the company's yard on Scalby Road.

Naval Engagement

Further south, along the coast at the fishing port of Bridlington, it transpired that during the bombardment of Scarborough many local townsfolk had hastened down to the harbour, sea front and pier to watch what they believed to be a naval engagement in the region of Filey (situated on the coast between Scarborough and Bridlington). The sound of the guns was clear and the reverberations from them was said to have rattled many a window in the town. Yet it was to be more than an hour before those eagerly looking out to sea, in the hope of glimpsing some impressive action, learned the truth of the noise they had heard.

Guns Heard at Malton, Rillington and Hovingham

Although more than twenty miles away, on the road to York, the bombardment could also be heard in Malton, where it was claimed the constant booming was accompanied by the rattling of doors and windows in the town. Indeed large numbers of refugees, fleeing the shelling in Scarborough, arrived at Malton via the train and were helped by Mrs Stephenson (wife of the station-master), before being taken on to the Parish Hall, where a number of local ladies, under the direction of Mrs Russell (wife of the Council Chairman) took care of them and sought out quarters in the town.

A farmer from the village of Rillington claimed later in the morning that the bombardment had also been heard clearly in his home village (also on the Scarborough to York road and more than eighteen miles away).

The rumble of the mighty German naval guns was heard at *Hovingham Hall* too, the home of Sir William Worsley (former commanding officer of the 2nd Battalion North Yorkshire Rifles Volunteers, a forerunner of the Green Howards).

Sir William - whose eldest son, also William Worsley, had fought with the 2nd Green Howards at the famous defence of the Menin Cross Roads in October 1914, and who had subsequently been taken prisoner - visited Scarborough later in the afternoon and was of the opinion that perhaps some 200 shells had fallen on the town.

> *Scarborough seemed to be little altered from the ordinary, and there was no sign of panic. The people seemed to be going about just as usual. The shops were of course shut, as Wednesday is the weekly half-holiday, but an officer assured me that everything was calm again.*
>
> *It is despicable that the Germans should make such an attack upon an undefended town.*

LITTLE 'BOB'

Scruffy little wire-haired terrier Bob was the Wireless Station's mascot and unofficial guard dog. When the shelling began he was off like a rocket, to the safety of the Racecourse! Here he is pictured going through his paces in 1914.

Politics Be Blowed

An officer of a Territorial unit was reputed to have come across a workman with a basket of tools slung carelessly over his shoulder as he hurried through the streets to the sea front.

"This kind of thing would never have happened if we'd had a Conservative government in power!" the workman had declared.

The bewildered officer was too struck to think of a suitable retort.

"I didn't want to hear about governments," he later stated, "there was too much high explosive shell bursting in the vicinity for one to stand and thrash out political arguments just there and then!"

Proven Right

One local citizen told of rushing into his garage to tell his driver, an elderly man, to get the car ready at once in order to take the family away from the shelling to safety. He had reputedly entered to find the old chap sat quietly polishing a bit of brass with a look of smug satisfaction on his face.

"Ah! Master George," he declared proudly, "they've come! I always said they'd come . . . and they've come!"

Invalid Cured

One of the most remarkable recoveries reported after the bombardment was that of Mrs Edmond of 2 Wykeham Street - the home of the Bennett family, which suffered a direct hit and several tragic deaths. The lady had been an invalid for some two years, confined to her bed, and yet after the shell struck she emerged unscathed from the wreckage and simply walked away.

To Arms

It was reported that one elderly lady, living on South Cliff, had been so incensed by the bombardment that she had grabbed up a rifle and hurried down to the sea front to take pot shots at the enemy.

Mr Dove's Horses

On Roscoe Street, where the local cabman Walter Dove had a stables in which was housed his cab and horses, it was considered exceedingly strange that despite the devastation wrought by the shell, which scored a direct hit on the stables, only one of the horses inside was killed. The other, by all accounts, emerged from the stall beside it completely unscathed and unharmed. On the wall beside the lucky horse, on the opposite side of it to its dead companion, hung the shredded and tattered remains of its large leather and brass harness. The fortunate animal had had a narrow escape indeed, and one that everyone was at a loss to explain away.

Not Without the Christmas Pudding

In another incident a lady, when ordered to leave her home and flee to safety, had looked around about her to see which of her possessions she should strive to save by taking it with her. In the end she settled on a Christmas pudding, which she seized up, tucked under her arm and fled to safety with.

This story, or versions of it, crops up time and again in contemporary accounts from the three towns which were victims that day.

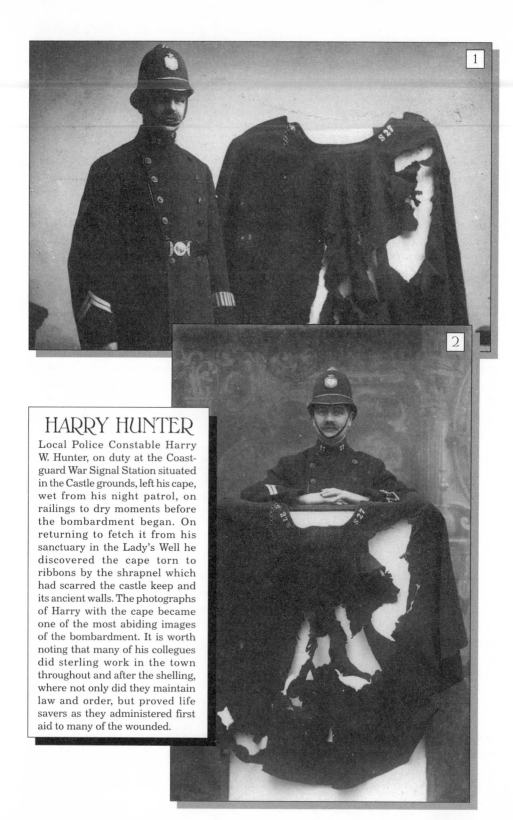

HARRY HUNTER

Local Police Constable Harry W. Hunter, on duty at the Coastguard War Signal Station situated in the Castle grounds, left his cape, wet from his night patrol, on railings to dry moments before the bombardment began. On returning to fetch it from his sanctuary in the Lady's Well he discovered the cape torn to ribbons by the shrapnel which had scarred the castle keep and its ancient walls. The photographs of Harry with the cape became one of the most abiding images of the bombardment. It is worth noting that many of his collegues did sterling work in the town throughout and after the shelling, where not only did they maintain law and order, but proved life savers as they administered first aid to many of the wounded.

Search for Women in Night-Clothes!

An unusual incident was reported in the press the following day of two ladies suffering from pneumonia who had run into the streets at the height of the bombardment dressed only in their night-clothes and had not been seen since. An appeal went out that if found they should be escorted to the Waifs and Strays Home on Belgrave Crescent. Nothing further was reported so one assumes they were successfully caught and 'incarcerated'!

Children Hide Under Bench

Another of the reported stories was that of an unnamed schoolgirl, who, with a group of friends was in the St Nicholas Gardens at the time of the bombardment. Whilst the other children had raced for cover beneath a nearby park bench, the little girl had apparently fallen to her knees, closed her eyes, bowed her head, clasped her hands together and prayed to God to save her mother and father.

This done she uttered, "Amen" and crawled to join her comrades beneath the wooden bench.

The Fall of 'Imperial Germany'

But by far the strangest recorded incident (and the one most often quoted) was the fall of *'Imperial Germany'* - the only book to topple from the shelves of Dalton's Bookshop at 69a Newborough during the whole of the bombardment.

Fred Smith's Bravery

After the bombardment, stories emerged of individual acts of bravery. One such was the tale of Fred Smith, the chauffeur to Dr Thornley of 35 Esplanade Road, who, on hearing a cry, rushed outside to the aid of a fellow chauffeur who had been wounded in the leg, and carried him several hundred yards under fire to a nearby doctor's surgery. On their way the wounded man was hit a couple of times more by fragments of flying shell. On finding no one at the surgery, Fred left the wounded man and went off to fetch an ambulance. Having ensured the other man was safely aboard he then transported Mrs Thornley and her children to Leeds, despite being injured himself, in the car he had been preparing in the garage when the raid began.

After the furore of the bombardment had died down Fred joined the Royal Flying Corps and was sent to France to do his bit.

Bridlington Removes her Guns

It was reported in the *Whitby Gazette* that, shortly after the bombardments, Bridlington Town Council decided to remove three useless old cannons from the sea-front area, in order to give the Germans no reason to fire on the town!

Messages from Far and Wide

As news of the German atrocity perpetrated against the defenceless citizens of Scarborough spread throughout the country and around the globe, messages of condolence and sympathy flooded in from all quarters, as did condemnation of the enemy's heinous act.

The first messages to arrive were by telephone and telegram, of which there were a number from various other towns and organisations around the country:

YORKSHIRE HUSSARS

1: Guard duty. 2&8: Drilling on the South Bay beach. 3,4,5&6: The trenches in and around the town. 7: Officers playing polo on the beach.

Reported your town bombarded. Pray accept the kindly sympathy of Margate. Trust no lives lost. I tender my regard in view of mutual position.
The Mayor of Margate.

Please accept York's sincere sympathies for the grievous loss of life at Scarborough today, and serious damage which your beautiful town, so well known to York citizens, has suffered.
The Lord Mayor of York

Deeply regret Scarborough's experience and extend Bridlington's sympathy to all who have suffered.
The Mayor of Bridlington.

The Chairman and members of the Orsett Rural District Council, now in meeting assembled, herewith desire to express to yourself and citizens their heartfelt sympathy at loss of life and damage occasioned by yesterday's visit from our inveterate foes.
Blair Williams (Chairman) and James Beck of Orsett Rural District Council, Essex.

At a meeting of the Chamber of Commerce a vote of condolence and sympathy was passed with the inhabitants of Scarborough in their terrible suffering caused by the bombardment of the town by German warships.
The Cardiff Chamber of Commerce.

The Board of Management of the National Order of Free Gardeners Friendly Society, wish to convey to you and the people of Scarborough their great sympathy in the sad circumstances brought about by the inhuman attack made upon your unprotected town by the German Fleet.
The Secretary of the National Order of Free Gardeners Friendly Society, Sandbach.

Eastbourne, in common with every part of the British Empire, sincerely sympathises with you and inhabitants in the grievous loss you have suffered by the recent outrageous German bombardment.
The Mayor of Eastbourne.

Torquay sincerely sympathises with your inhabitants on lost life, injury and damaged property recently caused by German utter disregard of international law.
The Mayor of Torquay.

From the Front

To the Mayor came a letter from a group of local men serving at the front with the 56th Company of the Army Service Corps. The letter was dated the day after the bombardment, Thursday, 17th December, was addressed to the '*Mayor and inhabitants of Scarborough*', and was signed by eight men:

It is with great regret we have heard of the awful outrage committed on Scarborough, and the loss of life of non-combatants. We wish you to extend our warm sympathy to all those who have suffered in any way.

R. O. Vasey, C. L. Marson, J. Crabtree, F. Heeley, E. T. White, J. W. Rines, G. F. Turner and J. Hornby.

From the HQ of the 4th Cavalry Brigade

On Friday, 18th December, two days after the bombardment, a letter was received by the Mayor of Scarborough from Captain, the Honourable George Monckton-Arundell, who was serving on the Headquarters Staff of the 4th Cavalry Brigade:

Dear Mr Mayor,

News has only just reached me of the damage done to Scarborough by the attack from the German cruisers. Words fail me to express to you on behalf of the Borough, my sincere sympathy with all who have suffered. I deplore the heavy loss of life, and should be very grateful if you would express to the relatives of those killed and wounded my heartfelt sympathy.

Minute details have not reached me as to the loss inflicted on the buildings of the town, but I feel sure that it will bring home to everyone, not only in Scarborough, but in Yorkshire as well, the urgent need of every able-bodied man, who has not already done so, to join some branch of His Majesty's forces.

I feel sure that the spirit of patriotism which all Englishmen feel will enable those who have suffered to make still greater efforts to bring this war to a successful issue.

Again assuring you how deeply I feel with those who have suffered from this outrage.

Fears Allayed Over Gas Works

Following the minor damage to one of the gas holders at the gas works on Seamer Road an engineer (from the Hartlepool gas works where a fire was started during the bombardment) was quick to allay the fears of worried residents living in the immediate vicinity over the possible explosion of the gas holders:

You can't possibly have an explosion of gas unless you have a mixture of four of air and one of gas. The escaping gas from the holes made by shellfire in a gasometer may get alight, as it did in Hartlepool, but, provided the mechanism is in order and the holder goes down steadily as the gas escapes, it is impossible for the gas inside the holder to explode. That fact ought to be known generally by the public. It would lessen alarm materially.

The Inquest

The inquest into the deaths of the victims of the German raid, held at the Court House on Castle Road, was officially opened on Friday, 18th December 1914 by the Borough Coroner, George Taylor.

Due to the number of deaths the Coroner decided to divide the inquest into two sections, thus dealing with the dead in groups; those reposing at home (John Ryalls, Emily Merryweather, George Taylor, Ada Crow and Alice Duffield) or at the Hospital (Albert Bennett and John Hall) were to be dealt with first, while the deaths of those at the mortuary on Dean Road (Leonard Ellis, Harry Frith, Alfred Beal, Margaret Briggs, Bertha McEntyre, Johanna Bennett, John Ward, George Barnes, Mary Prew and Edith Crosby) would be addressed later.

The Coroner began proceedings by addressing the jury at length about the despicable way the enemy had conducted its war by bringing it to the innocent and undefended:

> *You have been brought together to inquire into the tragic incidents which occurred in Scarborough on Wednesday, the 16th December.*
>
> *Such a thing has not occurred in this town, so far as we have any information to the contrary, for a thousand years - that is the deaths which occurred by the tragedy enacted through the bombardment of the town by the enemies of the country. Our enemies had thought it proper, in their wisdom and their own interests, for some reason to make an unusual attack which was contrary to the rules of all civilised nations, on a defenceless and helpless community, on a town which was not a fortified place in any shape whatever. We certainly had a few troops here, who might possibly have protected us in some slight way, but we were not a fortified town, and it was quite contrary, according to all the rules of civilised nations, to attack places which were not protected.*
>
> *We have information from the newspapers and from other sources, that our enemies did not confine themselves to this unusual warfare, but had attacked places, and killed people there, which, generally considered, ought not to have been attacked. This war has not, in a great measure, been carried on by our enemies in a way it should have been by a civilised nation.*
>
> *The bombardment which has taken place by the Germans has set aside all the rules generally acknowledged by countries at war. I believe that when we are at war we carry it on as civilised nations should, but in this case the attack on the town was an unjustifiable proceeding in which the lives of innocent people, who could not protect themselves were jeopardised, and, unfortunately, a great many lives have been sacrificed.*
>
> *It will be impossible for you to come to any conclusion as how the enemy might have benefited from the attack. It might be that it was made in order to strike terror into the inhabitants, and possibly that that same terror might not be solely confined to the inhabitants of this place, but that it might affect the community at large. It might also be that the enemy hoped to inspire confidence in their own people by the attack. That, however, is not a way I think other nations would be disposed to agree with, or follow. Indeed, I do not think such people would agree in any way with such an act as committed against this town on the 16th. We were helpless then and we are helpless now.*
>
> *There is no doubt whatever that if the Germans chose to come again we could not help it unless our fleet should be in the fortunate position, at the time, of attacking them! There has been a good deal of talk about the fleet, but you should bear in mind that the fleet had a great deal of work to perform. Its duties were enormous and its responsibilities equally great.*

The inquest was then adjourned while the jury was taken to view the first seven bodies.

THE COASTGUARD WAR SIGNAL STATION

Chief Officer Arthur Dean (A), Boatman James Walsh (B), Warrant Officer Lawrence Reeve (C), Leading Boatman Robert Barnes (D), PC Harry Hunter (E), and Trooper James Eastwood, Yorkshire Hussars (F), Wilfred Durant RNVR (G), Leading Boatman George Mason (H) and Harry Holden RNVR (I).

Chief Officer Dean's Evidence

The inquest was resumed at 11.45am and its first witness was Arthur Dean, the Chief Officer of the Scarborough Coastguard who gave an account of what he had seen.

"How long did the firing last altogether?" asked the Coroner.

"I should say about forty minutes," Dean answered.

"And how many vessels were there?"

"Two large cruisers, and two smaller ones further off."

"Were the two smaller ones in the South Bay?"

"No," answered Dean, shaking his head. "They were outside, covering the larger ships. You had to look hard to see them."

"Did they fire?"

Dean shook his head again, "I did not see them fire."

The Coroner pursued his line of questioning, "So, all the firing you saw was from the larger cruisers in the bay?"

"Yes."

"Were the other ships too far away for you to see?"

The Coastguard Chief thought for a moment before replying, "Yes, there was a very thick mist and it was hazy. It was only at times that you could make the ships out, and sometimes not at all."

"But you could distinguish what they were?"

"Certainly, yes."

"And you consider that they were covering these other two who were firing?"

"Yes," answered Dean, "that is what they were doing."

The Coroner then went on to ask Arthur Dean if he had seen any flags or any other signs of identification on the ships.

"No," Dean answered emphatically. "None."

The Coroner asked again and the reply was the same, though this time Dean added, "One of the ships may have been trying to signal to the other . . . but there was no national ensign."

This was noted and the questions then moved on to the various reports of the distances of the ships as they stood off from the shore. The Coroner quoted a variety of distances ranging from between two to eight miles and these were put to Dean for his comment.

"When they first opened fire," he answered with authority, "they were some 600 yards off the castle head, but by the time they had passed the harbour I should say they were within 500 yards."

"Of what type were the shells?" asked the Coroner.

"All sorts."

"And they simply fired as long as they pleased?"

"Yes, there was nothing to stop them."

"And then they went away?"

"Yes."

"How many shells would you say were fired?" asked the Coroner finally.

"Initially about 50 at the Castle," answered Dean. "Followed by about another two hundred at the town. Then there was a lull as the ships turned and came about, then about another 250. I should say some 500 in all."

"Thank you. I'm glad to hear that from you," commented the Coroner with feeling, "for some have said as few as 50 shells, and anyone could tell there were more than that. You may step down." Dean returned to his seat and the Coroner went on to comment, "The amount of shells fired on the town goes to show the ruthlessness of the enemy. The general public should be made aware of this so they might get some idea of what war is like. Quite possibly this raid may stir up the public and so let them know the type of danger we are all in."

John Hall

The death of John Hall was then looked into, and his daughter, Gertrude, took the stand to confirm she had identified the body of the deceased as that of her father and also to confirm his profession as that of architect.

"He was also a Justice of the Peace?" asked the Coroner.

"Yes," replied Miss Hall.

"For the Borough or the County?"

"Both." She was then asked to describe the scene that day and what had happened. "Besides father, my mother and I were in the house. At about 8.15am a shell hit the house and came clean through the dining-room window."

"Where were you all at the time?"

"Mother and I were downstairs, and father was upstairs, when we . . . that is I, heard the crash. Father was in the room above the dining-room and he called for us to come to him. I found him on the floor, wounded."

"Can you tell us, briefly, the nature of his injuries?" asked the Coroner.

"One of his legs was broken in two places, and the other had the flesh torn off it. One arm was also broken in two places and he had a wound in his side."

"Was he conscious?"

"Yes," she answered.

"Did he say anything to you?"

"He said he was killed."

"And what was the condition of the room . . . the room your father was in?"

"The shell had burst in the room below and gone through the ceiling . . . making two large holes in the floor of that room. We called for Dr Hollings who was passing by in the street outside, and on his advice father was taken to the hospital. He died shortly after arriving there."

"What was his age?"

"Sixty-five." Miss Hall was then asked to step down.

The Coroner told the jury that that was all the evidence he proposed to call. He told them the bombardment was the obvious cause of Mr Hall's death and they would find that the deceased had been killed by the enemy's attack on the 16th.

"I suppose we cannot say it was murder?" asked Mr Yeoman, the jury foreman (who himself lived on Westbourne Park where John Hall had been killed).

"Where there is a verdict of murder," explained the Coroner, "I am obliged to bind someone over to be prosecuted. I cannot do that in this case, and such a verdict would only serve to make a farce of these proceedings. When persons are killed in war it is not always necessary for inquests to be held on combatants. I have conferred with the Coroner's Society as to cases of deaths concerning non-combatants and I believe the verdict in such cases should be as I have already suggested to you."

"But it was a murderous attack which caused these deaths!" exclaimed Mr Yeoman forcefully. "A murderous attack on an unfortified town and all the world should know it."

Nevertheless, the jury returned the verdict the Coroner had suggested, and in all the cases the verdict was to be the same.

John Ryalls

The case of the child, John Shields Ryalls, was taken next, and his father, unemployed George Ryalls, said the house was struck by a shell which ploughed through the roof at the back and entered the child's bedroom. Though fourteen-month-old John Ryalls was injured on the head and body, he survived for about ten minutes after the incident. As a rule, George Ryalls said, the child did not sleep in that particular room, but on being distressed at the loud noise of the bombardment, he had been taken from his father by Miss Bertha McEntyre (an insurance agent from Sheffield) and taken to her room in order to pacify him while she dressed. Moments later the shell had hit the room and both had been killed.

Emily Merryweather

The case of thirty-year-old Mrs Emily Lois Merryweather followed. Evidence was given by the deceased's husband, George Merryweather, who confirmed they lived in the house next to the shop on the corner of Prospect Road and Columbus Ravine. At the time of the incident Mr Merryweather had been unlocking the shop door ready to start the day's business. His wife, on hearing the commotion outside, had gone out into the street with the idea of offering shelter in the shop's cellar to some friends living a few doors away. Moments later she had returned with her friends and was standing in the shop doorway when a shell struck the main pillar of the door and shrapnel from it struck her. Mrs Merryweather had fallen to the ground crying that she was wounded. The other women standing near the door were unharmed. By the time a vehicle had been fetched and the stricken woman had been conveyed to nearby Dr Wilkinson (head of the local St John Ambulance Brigade) she had died.

Ada Crow

In the case of Ada Crow, the body was identified by her mother, Mercy Crow of 37 Harcourt Avenue. Mrs Crow confirmed that Ada had been in service at 124 Falsgrave Road, which is where she died, and that she was twenty-eight years old.

Ada's employer, Mary Moorhouse, was then called to give an account of events. On that morning Ada had gone upstairs to her employer's bedroom to ask if she had heard the guns, and to tell her not to be alarmed as it was likely only the fleet practising offshore. She then went back downstairs and two or three minutes later there was a resounding crash as a shell hit the house. Mary Moorhouse had dashed from her bed and onto the landing where she found Ada collapsed at her feet; she had been struck at the bottom of the stairs but had managed to stagger up to the landing. She had a large and severe wound to her chest and died shortly after.

It was revealed at the inquest that Ada's fiancé, Sergeant Sturdy, of the Indian Army (Meirut Division), had arrived in the town on the afternoon of the 16th December to be greeted with the sad news of her death. The couple had not seen each other for eight and a half years, and the outbreak of war had prevented them from getting married earlier in the year. Sergeant Sturdy had been taken ill on his way to the Front and had been sent to a base hospital. From there he had been granted a few days' leave and although sent a telegram telling him of Ada's death, he had already left to return home and so never received it. When given the news on his arrival in Scarborough he was

1

2

EMILY MERRYWEATHER

George Merryweather's wife Emily (1) died shortly after being struck down by shrapnel from the shell which exploded in the doorway of the couple's shop at 43 Prospect Road (2). Emily had been ushering friends and neighbours into the shop's cellar for safety.

greatly overcome. By a strange twist of fate Ada was eventually laid to rest on the day the pair were to have been married, Saturday, 19th December.

The court was then adjourned for lunch. The time was 2.25pm.

Albert Bennett

Just over an hour later, at 3.30pm, the inquest resumed with the case of Albert Featherstone Bennett. The deceased's brother, John Bennett, identified the body and confirmed that Albert was 22 and a Territorial in the Royal Field Artillery. Prior to joining up he had been a railway porter. He was, at the time of his death, billeted at home. The deceased's other brother, Christopher Bennett (a stonemason, residing at Norwood Street since the bombardment), then took the stand and gave an account of the events of the 16th December. He said he had been in bed when his brother, Albert, had run into the room and asked him to 'go and see after mother'. Albert had then turned and rushed back downstairs just as a shell struck the house. Christopher had fallen through the floor to the room below, the house having collapsed about his ears. He immediately set about the debris to find his mother and other family members. He discovered Albert in the fireplace, buried in debris; he was still alive but seriously injured. Help was called for and Albert was transported to the hospital where he died from his injuries at 4.20pm.

Alice Duffield

The case of fifty-six-year-old Alice Duffield followed. Her sister, Miss Bramfitt, identified the body and gave an account of what had happened. John Duffield (Alice's husband) had gone out during a lull in the shelling to try and find a phone from which to call the Fire Station as a nearby house was on fire. Mrs Duffield had then gone out onto the footpath after her husband just as the lull ended and the shelling began again in earnest. Mrs Duffield was struck by a shell at the foot of her next-door neighbour's house (Mr Truefitt). Although not stated, it was assumed she was killed instantly.

George Taylor

The final case to be heard in the afternoon session was that of the young scout, George Harold Taylor - a fourth-form pupil at the Municipal School. Severely wounded in the back by a piece of shell whilst on his way to a friend's house on Albion Street, he had fallen to the ground. Working nearby was James Normandale who saw the boy fall and rushed to his aid. The boy was carried to a nearby house and a doctor was called. However, by the time a doctor and the boy's parents had arrived, he had died.

The inquest's afternoon session ended at 4.40pm.

Johanna Bennett, John Ward and George Barnes

The inquest resumed in the evening with the case of Johanna Bennett. Her sons, John and Christopher, were called to the stand again to give an account of their mother's death. The story of the shell hitting the family home was retold. Mrs Bennett had been found buried beneath the rubble in the kitchen with the two children, John Ward and George Barnes; one had had his head blown off and the other had been disembowelled.

Bertha McEntyre

The case of Bertha McEntyre was heard next, with George Ryalls repeating what he had earlier said regarding the death of his son. There was little else he could add.

SOUTH CLIFF

1: A house in Westwood. 2: Fred Smith was injured on Esplanade Road whilst helping a severely wounded man to safety. 3: A dud shell in the garden of Miss Blackburn, 2 Belvedere Road.

Margaret Briggs

Following this was the case of Margaret Briggs, who had died at *Dunollie*, 31 Filey Road. Thomas Briggs of Sherwood Street identified the body and confirmed that Miss Briggs had been born in Huddersfield in 1884, was single, a domestic servant at the house where she had died, and was thirty years of age. John Turner, Miss Briggs' employer, then gave an account of her death and concluded, "I am of the opinion that it is not safe for any womenfolk to remain in Scarborough."

"I am sorry to hear that opinion expressed," replied the Coroner, "And though I do not altogether agree, I must confess to having sent my typist away for her own safety."

The fatalities on South Street were then dealt with.

Harry Frith

In the case of Harry Frith, John Foreman confirmed he had been a driver with Land and Company, and that he was 45 years old. A description of Frith's death was then given by grocer's assistant John Russell, of Tindall Street. John had been at work in the grocer's shop when he heard a loud crash as a shell hit the street outside. He dashed to the front of the shop and saw two bodies nearby, amid the devastation; one of them was Harry Frith, the other was Leonard Ellis who was lying in the doorway of Clare and Hunt's chemist shop.

Leonard Ellis

John Russell's account was accepted as the evidence in this case too, and Alice McKinley (the deceased's sister-in-law) identified the body for the inquest. Leonard Ellis had been a widower and had two children aged 18 and 16 respectively. Forty-nine-year-old Ellis had been a porter at Clare and Hunt's chemist shop, and a drummer with the local Salvation Army Band.

Edith Crosby

The death of Edith Crosby was dealt with next. Thomas Lightfoot identified his half-cousin for the inquest and confirmed her age as 39, and her address as 1 Belvedere Road. PC Robert Shepherd then took the stand and said that he had removed the body of the deceased to the mortuary at about 10.30pm on the evening of the 16th December. He also added that he had discovered an unexploded shell in Belvedere Road - which measured 18 inches in length and 6 inches in width - and had taken it to the police station. It was his opinion that the shell was the one which had killed Miss Crosby.

Mary Prew

In the case of Mary Prew, Thomas Buckle from Halifax who, at the time of the bombardment resided at the same address, identified her for the inquest and confirmed her age as being 65 years. A fellow resident and shopkeeper of 1 Belle Vue Street, John Wilson, then gave an account of Mary's death. He said he had seen Mrs Prew standing in front of his shop window when a shell burst close by and knocked her off her feet. He immediately rushed to her aid, but found her dead, with blood coming from her mouth.

Alfred Beal

Late into the evening the final case, that of Alfred Beal, the postman, was heard. The body was identified by James Beal, a joiner. PC Robert Shepherd was then called upon again, as it had been he who had found the body some twenty yards from the doorway of *Dunollie* - where the body of Margaret Briggs was also discovered - his sack and letters scattered everywhere. PC Shepherd confirmed that Alfred Beal was already dead when he reached him and described his injuries.

Close of Inquest

With the inquest drawing to its close the same verdict 'death by fire from enemy vessels' was returned in each and every case. The jury had wanted to return a verdict of 'Wilful Murder' against the Germans, but as previously explained to them by the Coroner, this was impossible to do, although it did not stop the phrase being emblazoned across every newspaper in the land.

Mr Yeoman, the jury foreman, expressed the view that PC Shepherd's evidence had been of great assistance. The Coroner agreed and stated that other officers had also acted in a manner worthy of the police force. The foreman finally expressed, on behalf of the full jury, their sympathy for the relatives of the deceased in what he described as 'this murderous business'.

The Coroner said he appreciated the expression of such sympathy, and went on to say that it had been a sad thing and showed the misfortune which might very well have happened to any one of them. They could only express their thankfulness that they were not amongst the unfortunate victims.

The inquiry, which had lasted all day and most of the night finally closed a few minutes short of 10.00pm.

Harry Harland ~ The Final Fatality

By the end of the year another name, the eighteenth, had been added to the list of Scarborough's dead. On the morning of the 16th December, shoemaker Harry Harland had been seriously injured on Belle Vue Street whilst trying to flee the town with his family. Barely had the family left their home than Harry had crumpled to the ground, mortally wounded. In desperation, his wife Selina had got him onto a handcart and taken him to his father's home on Wykeham Street. From here Harry had been taken to the Westborough Wesleyan Chapel hospital, staffed by the Red Cross and St John Ambulance Brigade on the orders of Dr Maingay.

Despite treatment, Harry remained gravely ill for ten long days and finally succumbed to his injuries at 11.00pm, late in the evening of Boxing Day, 26th December. An inquest was held two days later (28th December) and the jury delivered the verdict that Harry had died 'due to injuries sustained in the bombardment'. He was buried in the New Cemetery on Manor Road the following day.

Thus he became the eighteenth and final Scarborough victim of the *Derfflinger* and the *Von der Tann*.

The Mystery of Alice Painter

In 1923, when the Scarborough War Memorial (paid for by public subscription) was unveiled, the name of Alice Painter had been added to the list of the dead. No contemporary records mention her even being injured, let alone dying from the bombardment. One explanation proposed was that she had died of consumption and that her name had been added to the fallen by mistake. The truth is that the sixty-four-year-old widow died, bitterly lonely and depressed, on Monday, 14th December.

Alice, of 53 Moorland Road, had lived alone with Yorky, her faithful Yorkshire Terrier, since the death of her husband James in 1903. Considered to be something of a recluse,

Alice seldom ventured out and was in the habit of having her groceries and meagre provisions delivered to her home by the local shopkeepers (not an altogether uncommon practice at the time). At about 3.30pm on that Monday afternoon local baker, James Milnthorpe, out on deliveries from William Clarkson's bakers and confectioners at 13 Murchison Street, called at Alice's home expecting to find in the porch her order and payment as usual. However, what he actually found was a warning note from Alice, 'Please turn off the gas. Don't strike a match. Hope I shall be dead'.

Loath to enter the house and fearing for Alice's safety, James ran hell for leather to the Central Police Station on St Thomas Street, the note still clutched in his hand. On arrival he blurted out the contents of the note to PC Albert Oldroyd, the Coroner's Officer, and together they hurried back to the silent house on Moorland Road.

PC Oldroyd gained entry to the house via an unlatched window at the rear. On entering he was assailed by the stench of gas and immediately made for the main to turn off the supply. After a thorough search he discovered Alice's frail form lying prone across a bed in an upstairs room. Her loyal companion and faithful dog, asphyxiated, lay dead beneath it.

The Borough Police Surgeon, Dr James Hutton, was called from his home at 11 Albemarle Crescent, and on examining Alice declared she had died from gas poisoning and had, in all probability, been dead for some twelve hours or so (this would put her death at about 3.30am on 14th December). The note found by James Milnthorpe clearly indicated suicide, but added to this were a number of sealed and private letters she had written, addressed to the Borough Coroner.

The inquest into Alice Painter's death was set for the evening of the following day, 15th December, the day on which a notice of her suicide appeared in the local paper. The inquest was to follow hard on the heels of the inquests into the deaths of two fishermen whose bodies had been discovered at the foot of Holbeck Cliffs on the 12th December. The men, local fisherman Frank Anderson of 3 Burr Bank (East Sandgate), and Colin Harding of Bridlington, had been lost from the fishing coble the *Grace Darling* almost a month earlier, on 10th November. However, the inquests proved much lengthier than the Coroner had anticipated and did not close until 10.30pm. There was no alternative but to reschedule Alice's inquest for the following morning, Wednesday 16th December.

Fate then took a hand in affairs, and events on that Wednesday morning prevented many people, including the Coroner, from going about their planned and prescribed business. Again, Alice's inquest was postponed. By mid-morning on Thursday, 17th December, the Coroner finally found time to deal with the death of Alice Painter, albeit briefly. The jury found that she had died from 'suicide, while temporarily insane'. She was buried the same day, alongside her husband in the New Cemetery on Manor Road.

Given that a committee was set up to organise the War Memorial and the names on it, I find it hard to comprehend how this mistake was made, and impossible to understand why it has never been rectified. Indeed, any records there were relating to the memorial appear to have 'disappeared'. As much as one can sympathise with Alice's obvious loneliness and distress, it is my opinion her name should not be on the War Memorial alongside those who died in the service of their country, or as innocents in the actions of the country's enemies. Eighty-five years on, it is time for someone at the Town Hall to act decisively and correct this grave error so it does not persist into the next millennium and thus continue the seventy-six years of shame brought on the town by its officials and mandarins who have, to date, refused to rectify the mistake.

The War Memorial and the Omission of Margaret Briggs

The names of all of the above deceased appear on the Scarborough War Memorial, bar that of thirty-year-old Margaret Briggs, killed at *Dunollie*. The presumption for this is that she was not a local girl, having been born in Huddersfield (and buried in Barnsley). However, at the inquest she was identified by one Thomas Briggs, whose address was given as Sherwood Street, and it is therefore possible she had family in the town. This leads me to believe she should have been included on the War Memorial, and certainly had a more worthy claim to be so than did Alice Painter. Indeed, the name of Bertha McEntyre (from Sheffield) on the memorial disproves my earlier suggestion, and lends weight to the argument that it is time to add the name of Margaret Briggs to those of the other civilians killed during the bombardment. [It is worthy of note that a number of the men listed on the memorial were not born in, or from Scarborough.]

Avenge Scarborough

On the same day as the inquest (Friday, 18th December) the National Recruiting Department issued the following statement from its headquarters:

> AVENGE SCARBOROUGH! UP AND AT 'EM NOW!
>
> *The wholesale murder of innocent women and children demands vengeance. Men of England, the innocent victims of German brutality call upon you to avenge them. Show the German barbarians that Britain's shores cannot be bombarded with impunity. Duty calls you now. Go today to the nearest recruiting depot and offer your services for your King, home and country.*

Reports from all over the country showed that the German raid on the east coast towns had given great impetus to recruitment, and the above statement was quickly followed with lurid recruiting posters plastered over every city, town and village in the country. One of the most famous posters was that painted by Edith Kemp-Welch (and featured on the cover of this book) of Britannia exhorting the men of Britain to 'Enlist Now' and avenge Scarborough, which can be seen in flames in the background. The original painting was donated to the town almost a year later on the 13th December 1915 and now hangs in the Town Hall.

The *Daily Mirror* informed von Tirpitz on the 18th December:

> *Many thanks von Tirpitz; you bagged some eighty-odd civilians, a church and two ruins; we get about two new army corps in response to your call. Was it worth it?*

On the same day the *Daily Sketch* declared:

> *Wanted - a thousand men for every shell dropped. The immediate result would thus be five new army corps for active service. Every brick displaced in Hartlepool or Scarborough must count one man more to Sir John French's force, one rifle more to Britain's power to defeat the foe. Don't talk about what ought to be done; prepare yourself to take a hand in doing it.*

Indeed, recruitment, especially in the north-east, rocketed and many young men flocked to join the colours quite simply looking for revenge for the coastal

RECRUITING POSTERS

1&3: Two of the many posters which appeared all over the country immediately after the bombardment exhorting men to enlist and avenge the fallen. The army recruiting halls all over the land swelled with the influx of new recruits. In response to the raid the Daily Mirror snorted with derision, *'Many thanks von Tirpitz, you bagged some eighty-odd civilians, a church and two ruins, we get two new army corps. Was it worth it?'*

2: The most famous recruiting poster of the Great War.

MEN OF YORKSHIRE
JOIN THE
NEW ARMY
And help to Avenge the Murder of innocent Women and Children in Scarborough, Hartlepool & Whitby.
Shew the Enemy that Yorkshire will exact a full penalty for this COWARDLY SLAUGHTER.
ENLIST TO-DAY
Recruiting Office:
ST. NICHOLAS STREET, SCA

1

BRITONS
"WANTS
YOU"
JOIN YOUR COUNTRY'S ARMY!
GOD SAVE THE KING

2

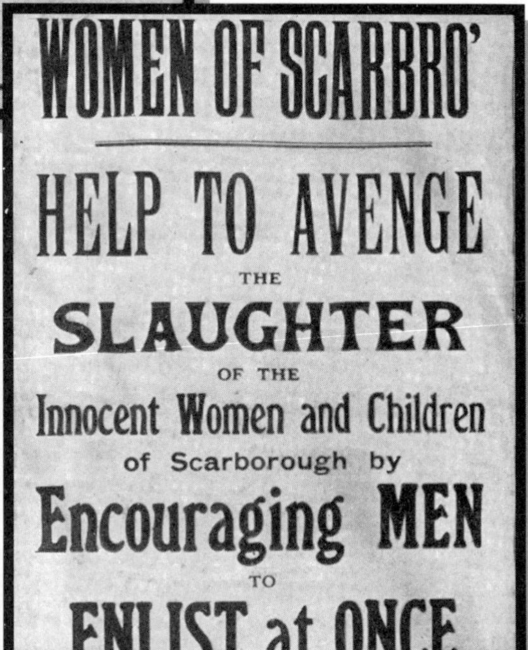
WOMEN OF SCARBRO'
HELP TO AVENGE
THE
SLAUGHTER
OF THE
Innocent Women and Children
of Scarborough by
Encouraging MEN
TO
ENLIST at ONCE
Recruiting Office, St. Nicholas Hall, Scarborough

3

bombardments. Even in London and the towns of the south, recruitment was reported to be significantly up following the bombardments.

A Message from The King

Messages too continued to flow into the town in the wake of the bombardment and its aftermath. A week after the attack King George V sent a personal message to the people of the town. It was relayed via the Lord Lieutenant, Sir Hugh Bell, who telephoned the message to the police station, from where the senior officer delivered it on to the town's Aldermen, Councillors and townsfolk:

> *The people of Scarborough and Whitby have been much in my thoughts during the past week, and I deeply sympathise with the bereaved families in their distress. Please let me know as to the condition of the wounded. I trust they may have a speedy recovery.*

The Mayor of Scarborough replied with:

> *May it please your Majesty,*
> *Sir Hugh Bell, Lord-Lieutenant of the North Riding of the County of York, has communicated to me your Majesty's gracious message of sympathy with the bereaved families in Scarborough in their distress consequent upon the recent bombardment of this town by part of the enemy's fleet, and I humbly beg that your Majesty will accept the thanks of the people of Scarborough for such message, which will be greatly appreciated.*

On Saturday, 19th December the Institute of Certified Grocers sent the following letter, expressing their sympathy, to its local members:

> *On behalf of the Institute, permit us to express our most sincere sympathy with yourself and your fellow citizens in the recent infamous outrage committed on your town by our ruthless and unscrupulous enemy.*
>
> *That it caused you distress of mind is only natural. We trust however, that no personal injury was inflicted on yourself or on any of your immediate friends: and we also trust that your property was undamaged.*
>
> *Feeling that you have suffered in the common cause, we beg of you, as representing the foully injured among our brother and sister Britons in your town, to accept our heartfelt sympathy.*
>
> *We can assure you that the late happening can have but one effect, viz: to stiffen the national resolve to see the war through to a victorious conclusion.*

The following replies were returned. Sadly, only the first is attributable. It was written by grocer Jack Taylor of Westborough:

> *I write to thank you, as the representatives of the Institute, for your kind message of sympathy. Fortunately, neither the houses, nor businesses of any of my partners or relatives have been touched; but I am sorry I cannot say the same of friends, two of whom are killed and two wounded, whilst the houses of several are shattered. I was sitting at breakfast during most of the bombardment and had*

not at all realised the extent of the damage that was being done, but a shell hitting an adjoining house made us seek safer quarters.

*

Accept my best thanks for your sympathetic letter of the 19th December. We have not suffered in any way materially, but some of our friends were removed in a painful and tragic manner, and many others have suffered injury to their property. It was an unforgettable experience, especially to the female members of our families.

*

Please accept my sincere thanks for your kind sympathy. I am glad to say we received no damage whatever either to person or property, if I may except the lead of our cornice above the shop, which was turned up by a flying splinter of shell. After seeing five shells burst within 100 yards of our house, two women and a little girl were struck and badly injured within ten yards of the shop door, and after receiving first aid from my wife and a doctor who was fortunately passing, we got them to the hospital. As you may think, trade was not brisk during the bombardment, but one of my customers, having fallen short of bacon for breakfast, came in for a pound in slices during the height of the affair. I have never cut bacon under more irritating circumstances. 'Business as usual' is all very well, but there are limits! Yorkshire people are not reputed cowards, and the behaviour of the great majority of the people, including, or I may say, especially, women and children, was beyond praise.

*

It is exceedingly kind of you to send me such a warm, sympathetic letter. It is very sad that such a terrible episode should occur in the 20th century of the Christian era. Reckless firing resulting in much destruction of property is bad, but what is so much more sad is the loss of life and serious injury to men, women and little children. For those acts it behoves us to remember the highest standard of Christian manhood and suppress the spirit of revenge. All this brings the horrors of war very close to home. When will the nations learn the utter futility of the present system, a survival of barbarism that must be replaced by strong and close international relations in place of bolstering up an idea of a 'Balance of Power', which has proved such a ghastly failure.

From the First Lord of the Admiralty

In a lengthy letter to the Mayor, on Sunday, 20th December, the First Lord of the Admiralty, Winston Churchill, expressed his sympathies and those of the Navy as well as castigating the enemy for their crime:

My Dear Mayor,
I send you a message of sympathy, not only on my own account but on behalf of the Navy, for the loss that Scarborough has sustained. We mourn with you the peaceful inhabitants who have been killed or maimed, and particularly the women and children. We admire the dignity and fortitude with which Scarborough, Whitby and the Hartlepools have confronted this outrage. We share your disappointment that the miscreants escaped unpunished. We await with patience the opportunity that will surely come. But viewed in its larger aspect, the incident is one of the most instructive and most encouraging that has ever happened in the

war. Nothing proves more plainly the effectiveness of British naval pressure than the frenzy of hatred aroused against us in the breasts of the enemy. This hatred has already passed the frontiers of reason. It clouds their vision, it darkens their councils, it convulses their movements. We see a nation of military calculators throwing calculations to the winds, of strategists who have lost their sense of proportion, of schemers who have ceased to balance loss and gain.

Practically the whole fast cruiser force of the German Navy, including many great ships vital to their fleet and utterly irreplaceable, has been risked for the passing pleasure of killing as many English people as possible, irrespective of sex, age or condition, in the limit of time available. To this act of military and political folly they were impelled by a violence, or feeling, which could find no other vent. It is very satisfactory, and should confirm us in our course. Their hate is the measure of their fear. Its senseless expression is a proof of their impotence and the seal of their dishonour. Whatever feats of arms the German Navy may hereafter perform, the stigma of the 'baby killers' of Scarborough will brand its officers and men while sailors sail the sea, believe me dear Mr Mayor.

The Mayor replied the following day:

Dear Sir,
On behalf of the inhabitants of Scarborough I have to thank you for the kind messages of sympathy conveyed in your letter and which will be greatly appreciated. It is evident that the enemy did not dare to face our fleet, and so attacked this undefended town. In this way Scarborough has taken her part in the great struggle that is now proceeding.

Whilst we deplore the loss of life and property, mourn for our dead and sympathise with our wounded, we are, nevertheless, as fully determined as ever that the war must be fought to a successful finish.

Our surprise at the attack was the greater as we were led to believe from the conduct of the plucky commander of the 'Emden' that German sailors understood something about the glorious old traditions of the sea. It is evident from our experience of Wednesday that this is not so. Some newcomers into honourable professions first learn the tricks and lastly the traditions. As their commanders get older in the service, they will find that an Iron Cross pinned on their chest even by King Herod, will not shield them from the shafts of shame and dishonour.

Again I thank you for your letter.

From the Prime Minister
Following an approach from Scarborough's Member of Parliament to the Government for compensation for losses and damage caused by the enemy raid on the town, the Prime Minister, Herbert Asquith (himself the son of a Yorkshireman), responded on Tuesday, 22nd December with an offer of assistance:

My Dear Rea,
In reply to your letter of yesterday, I have to say that the Government have resolved to provide relief from Imperial funds in respect of damage to persons and property sustained in the recent bombardment of the towns of Scarborough, Whitby and the Hartlepools. The scope and measure of such relief, and the

machinery for ascertaining and administering it, are matters which are receiving careful consideration. I need not assure you of my deep personal sympathy with your constituents who have been made the victims of this barbarous outrage.

However, that fine promise of compensation and the administration of it was to prove a constant source of disagreement between the Government's mandarins in Whitehall and the Scarborough Borough Council during and throughout 1915. And as if that was not bad enough, local property insurance rates more than quadrupled following the bombardment as Scarborough, Whitby, Hartlepool and the other coastal towns became 'high risk' areas.

From Aldershot

Even Scarborians serving in the forces spared the time to pen short letters home, as with this from Company-Sergeant-Major Mundy of the 8th Battalion Green Howards, at that time based in Aldershot:

Just a few lines from the Scarborough men serving the flag. We send our deepest sympathy to the inhabitants of the old town who have lost children, relatives and friends through the dastardly attack made by the cruel Germans, and if the opportunity comes you can rely on us to avenge the deed which has gone to the bottom of our hearts.

Similarly, in an act of fraternal brotherhood, the National Chamber of Trade sent a letter of sympathy to the town's Drapers and Allied Trades.

From the British Press

Without exception, every newspaper in the country condemned the brutal attack of the enemy on the defenceless coastal resorts. Some writers asked questions of various people and institutions. A writer in the *Sunday Chronicle* wished to put a question to the Kaiser:

I wonder if the German Emperor, when he launched his ships of war against defenceless Scarborough, remembered that Lord and Lady Londesborough have a residence there? The last time his Majesty was in England he was the guest of this Peer and Peeress at their town house in Regent's Park. The garden party that was given there in his honour was almost the last occasion on which Field-Marshal Kitchener met his Imperial Majesty. Where will they meet next? Will it be at Potsdam?

At the time, Lord Londesborough had residences in Lincoln, Market Weighton, Scarborough, Epsom and Mayfair. His Lordship's Scarborough home was Londesborough Lodge situtated on The Crescent and which escaped any real damage.

Meanwhile another reporter, this time writing in the *Daily Telegraph*, looked for answers a little closer to home:

There is no mystery about the position of our seaside resorts, but why, it has to be asked, did no one tell the nation that in the case of war, places like Scarborough,

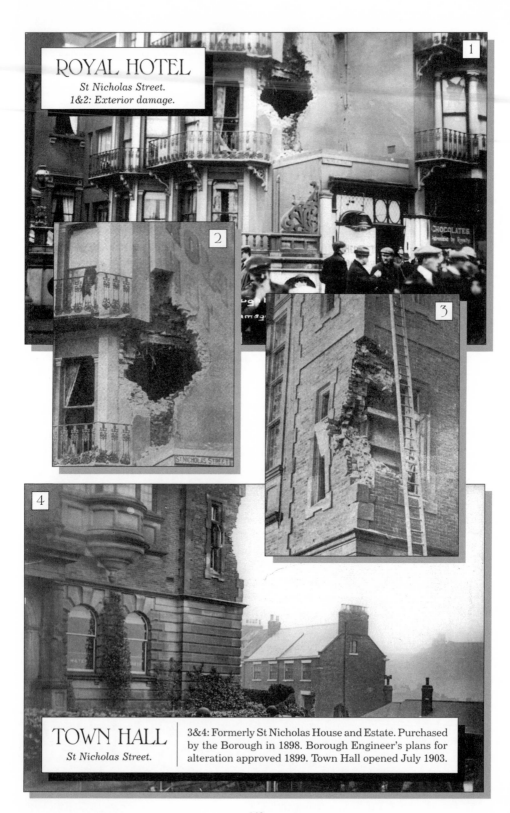

ROYAL HOTEL

St Nicholas Street.
1&2: Exterior damage.

TOWN HALL

St Nicholas Street.

3&4: Formerly St Nicholas House and Estate. Purchased by the Borough in 1898. Borough Engineer's plans for alteration approved 1899. Town Hall opened July 1903.

Whitby, Cromer, and a score and more of other towns, such as Brighton and Eastbourne might be bombarded; surely they ought to have had fortifications, since the Navy can give no absolute guarantee of safety. What is the answer?

Before the present war such towns could not be bombarded; all the nations, great and small, had met together and decided that any Navy which committed such an act would outrage the law of humanity, and, inferentially, make all humanity its enemy. There seems to have been some idea that any Power which misbehaved itself would be punished by the other countries whose signatures had been put to the agreement. We are learning many things in these days, and among them is the fact that, so far as belligerents like Germany are concerned, Hague Conventions are of no validity; they are brushed aside by necessity. Nor is this all.

We are learning that Germany can commit such acts without suffering reprisals from her partners, for all the neutral nations were involved in the act of framing the convention against the bombardment of 'open towns'. They have all been outraged; we have to mourn the dead and maimed, but they equally, with us, have suffered in one respect - this law has gone.

However, even if those elements of the Royal Garrison Artillery (Territorials), which had previously been quartered in the town, had still been stationed there, and had also been in a position to have fired upon the enemy ships, it is doubtful they could have prevented the majority of the bombardment taking place - the horrific situation at Hartlepool was ample proof of that. Scarborough had originally been a Royal Artillery Depot and as such had had a battery of guns positioned at the castle foot on the Marine Drive. However, the battery had been removed when, under the Haldane Army Reforms, the town was changed from an artillery depot to a cavalry one.

The special correspondent of *The Times* made the following report to his readers:

The shells which shattered the buildings of Scarborough have made no impression on the spirits of the people. Nothing could be more praiseworthy than the manner in which the town passed through its ordeal and returned to its normal life. The people of Yorkshire are proverbially hard to impress, and the stranger who came to Scarborough in ignorance would have nothing but the broken buildings to tell him that this quiet seaside town had been subject to an experience unknown to an English town for more than a hundred years.

Even the Admiralty announcement that such incidents will not affect the naval policy has evoked practically no criticism. Scarborough accepts its risks. It is also able to be amused at the description 'fortified town' which the Germans have applied to it, and a local wag has affixed to the brick wall of his humble dwelling-place a notice: 'Please don't touch the fortifications - fragile'. Today business is as usual, except the business of the builder and the glazier is much brisker, for in almost every street in certain quarters, the windows have been shattered.

Waxing lyrical, Wells Brex, writing in the *Daily Mail*, wondered if the Germans had made a mistake in attacking Scarborough:

Think a moment of Scarborough. Not Scarborough in its recent hibernation -

grey sky, grey sea, grey old town with a sleepless eye cocked at that newly portentous North Sea - but the Scarborough known to the English holidaymaker. Up north they call it 'the Queen of Watering Places'; we, down south, who knew it and loved it, felt no jealousy of the title. 'There's nowt like Scarborough' is the proud Yorkshire claim, and who will dispute it?

Just as Yorkshire, with the Yorkshire qualities, is perhaps the most typically 'English' of all counties, so is Scarborough perhaps the most 'English' of all seaside towns. For all its summer loveliness it has a bluff look, a grey look, a northern austerity. The Castle Rock rears like a bastion of England, the tight little harbour is no haven for pleasure steamers, but a running shelter for hard fishermen. Handsome spa gardens, winding walks, wind-blown music, and the cliff promenade, where the north country paraded at its loveliest and best - they all made the beautiful picture, but still they seemed exotic to us lovers of Scarborough. Our best Scarborough was in the saffron and pearl of September - hours before the fashion's breakfast, when all the brown cobles went stealing out to sea and scarves of grey mist still clung to the dear grey town. A kindly town and broad, slow-spoken, kindly people.

Did the Huns think the bandstand a fortress cupola? Or the Spa sea wall, whose only December tenantry are a drift of wind-borne leaves and spray-borne seaweed, a fortress parapet?

Meanwhile the *Daily Sketch* announced boldly:

German Kultur means shells on churches.

And went on to declare:

Our fleet can be trusted to avenge this unscrupulous act of German savagery in due time and with full effect.

A *Daily Mirror* headline cried:

GERMAN GHOULS GLOATING OVER MURDER OF ENGLISH SCHOOLBOYS.

We know now that the Germans cannot resist hitting out wildly at anybody near them, if they happen to have been opposed and defeated. They murdered Belgian civilians because Belgium opposed and delayed them. Gradually the whole world sees and realises the true colour and quality of German civilisation.

On the Wednesday following the bombardment (23rd December), the town's own local weekly paper, the *Scarborough Pictorial*, carried the following editorial comment:

Wednesday, December 16th, 1914, will go down in history as the day on which Scarborough underwent its baptism of fire, thus signalling England's first direct experience of the greatest war of all time. Almost on the stroke of eight, a terrific explosion gave the first intimation that powerful vessels of the German Fleet, creeping up through the mists of the morning, had singled out the Queen of Watering Places, a defenceless town, for a merciless bombardment. It was peculiarly in keeping with German 'Kultur' that a beautiful seaside resort should be their first choice for sacrifice on the altar of frightfulness. All those who lived through those terrible thirty-five minutes, exposed to a veritable hail of death and destruction - a coastguard, whose opinion may be taken as absolutely reliable, says at least five hundred shells shattered over the town - will carry the memory of them to their graves.

It would be idle to profess that the inhabitants underwent such a terrifying ordeal with anything like equanimity. At the same time, it must be placed on record that the behaviour of the population was admirable throughout. The first thoughts of the men, with a few unworthy exceptions, were for the women and the little ones, and everything possible was done, in trying circumstances, to secure for them a place of safety.

Little need be said of the wholesale demolition of property which was crowded into that dreadful half-hour. The description and pictures in this issue, which speak louder than can columns of words, tell their own terrible tale. We could have accepted all this with some degree of resignation. It is not the loss of worldly goods which has cast a gloom over the town. They can all be replaced in time. But the innocent little ones, their mothers, and other women, honoured citizens and workers of the town, whose lives were ruthlessly taken, cry out to the nation and humanity to be avenged. The sympathy of every heart goes out to the bereaved ones. Their loss has been swift and tragic, and words of comfort and consolation seem so poorly inadequate.

But in the end it may be something to know that theirs, the greatest sacrifice, has not been in vain. Scarborough has been bombarded, with cruel consequences. When the day of reckoning comes, what Scarborough and its people suffered must not be allowed to be forgotten.

The final sentiment, though admirable in the last few days of 1914, was made before the overwhelming losses suffered by the British and her allies at the Somme and Passchendaele were inflicted on the nation. By the time the war ended, Scarborough's twenty-five minutes of terror and carnage was a mere drop in the ocean of blood and sacrifice that had swept the battlefields of Northern France, Belgium, Italy and the Dardenelles, and would only be remembered, by the country, as a small paragraph, a mere footnote, in the history of the war. Though Scarborians, it has to be said, would never forget.

Meanwhile the *Eastbourne Gazette* exhorted northerners to support Scarborough in its hour of need by visiting the resort to extend a helping hand, while at the same time calling for financial support for the town - perhaps with an eye to what might be their own fate if the Germans began making a habit of assaulting seaside towns along the British coast:

In Sir Walter Scott's most famous poem we are assured that 'Yorkshiremen are stern of mood'. As that description still holds good whenever they are put to the test, they may be relied upon to do their full share in avenging a cruel and purposeless crime which has caused the deaths of women and children and unarmed men. The most practical way in which Yorkshiremen and others in the north can show their sympathy with Scarborough is by visiting the town and making a stay there in order - if need be - to extend a helping hand to those who have lost their homes, their means of livelihood, their all. In such cases nothing can possibly equal direct and personal action. It will be the duty of the local authorities to approach the Government at once with a request for a special grant to make good the damage to property and to compensate the inhabitants for personal losses.

The bombardment was brought about not by any local circumstances, but by the war, for which the nation as a whole is responsible.

No town in the kingdom is entirely exempt from danger, and hence it is to be in the interests of all that the needs of Scarborough should receive the fullest attention at the earliest possible moment. Apart from its beauty, antiquity and historic interest, the town has many claims upon the consideration and goodwill of the English people.

From the American Press

Various prominent Americans (the USA was still neutral at this stage) and their newspapers were fervent in their condemnation of what they saw as German brutality. In an article entitled 'Crime against Civilisation' the *New York Tribune* declared to its readers:

Germany has set a vicious and dangerous precedent, just as in disregarding important provisions of the code of war on land in Belgium. In wantonly killing non-combatants, women and children among them, in undefended British coastal towns, Germany cannot escape responsibility for having taken the first step from recognised practice, in restoring barbarity, which the world had hoped to see eliminated from the practice of war.

The *New York Times* claimed that the ruthless bombardment of unfortified towns and the utterly useless massacre of non-combatants had not only shocked the people of other nations, but had aroused the whole world. The *New York World* published a cartoon entitled 'Aroused at Last' which depicted the British Lion standing defiantly astride the beach of Scarborough, despite an arrow sticking into its side bearing the words 'North Sea raid'.

The danger has been brought home in the most effective way and the new knowledge of this danger ought to be worth a million recruits to Kitchener's Army. It may be doubted if those recruits could have been obtained in any other way. In the long run, Great Britain stands to gain infinitely more in this daring raid by the German cruisers than the Germans themselves can hope to do.

Meanwhile the *New York Sun* had a drawing of Uncle Sam sternly facing the figure of a strutting Prussian - the latter inscribed with the motto 'Might is right', while Uncle Sam commented, 'I don't believe it, but still, if this is war then assassination is no crime'. Further, the *New York Sun* added:

The raid upon the Yorkshire coast has an unpleasant significance for the English, since their Navy, which is their chief bulwark, can neither keep the North Sea clear, nor prevent attacks. The patrol is inadequate and Germany has demonstrated its ability to come out of its hole.

OLYMPIA PICTURE PALACE

Foreshore Road. 1 & 3: The veranda. 2: The operating box.

The *Evening Mail* followed in the *Sun's* footsteps, stating in its editorial that the Germans had dealt their cause a staggering blow:

> *The bombardment of the East Coast was not a brilliant exploit, but plain, brutal murder. If this is war, then assassination is no crime. Belgium cost Germany dearly, and lost it many friends. The Belgian invasion however, had a defence, the bombardment none.*

And in an effusive outpouring in the *London Daily Chronicle*, the American writer R. W. Kauffmann, stated:

> *For thirty minutes. During that period - and it seemed as many hours - the black boats that had come from the sea spat fire and flung twelve-inch shells into Scarborough; the old town had heard nothing like it since its castle was twice beleaguered during the Cromwellian Wars. The place shook with the noise, with the banging of the guns, the smashing of masonry, the tinkle of glass, the collapse of house-fronts, the shrieks of women and children. It was all darkness and howling horror.*
>
> *Then, as suddenly as it had begun, the firing ceased. A streak of light appeared in the sky to the south-east. Before it the mist retreated, and the black-nosed boats disappeared. The bombardment was over. Instantly, under heavens rapidly brightening to the deepest blue, the entire appearance of the town changed. Policemen came from nowhere. A rapidly devised, but thoroughly efficient order manifested itself; the crowds that swarmed into the streets were being quietly marshalled toward the hospitals, and through many a street were moving little processions of ambulancemen and boy scouts bearing stretchers on which lay figures swathed in bloody bandages, the faces ashen, the eyes glazed . . .*
>
> *You would have thought that the remedy for the effects of the bombardment was a part of the daily routine of the British municipal authority. I tramped about amid the crunching glass and cracked slates. I saw all the horrors and all the grotesque devilries of the cannonade. Nearly everybody accepted the situation with a calm that was amazing to my American consciousness.*
>
> *It made a mere American remember the Scarborough warning, 'A word and a blow, but the blow first.' The town that can have made such a phrase current knows how to accept that phrase if made a reality and used against it.*

What They had to Say in Germany

While the whole world joined in the condemnation of the German nation, the Germans themselves were proving to be rather jubilant about the whole affair, certainly expressing no remorse whatever. In their newspapers and journals prominent officials, statesmen and citizens lauded the 'bravery' of their fine seamen, praising their 'gallantry' in reducing to rubble the British north-east towns. Scarborough was described as a town with a six-gun redoubt [the long obsolete 'South Steel Battery'] - a redoubt which had not replied to the German cannonade because, they claimed, the British gunners had fled at the first sight of the enemy ships!

Rear-Admiral Schlieper claimed that the attacks were in part an act of revenge for the German defeat off the Falkland Islands:

The news of the successful attack by our cruisers on the two fortified English ports, Scarborough and Hartlepool, will have come as a blessing to all Germans after the tidings of the Falklands battle. Not that this success can be regarded as compensation for that great sacrifice - no; but there will be a feeling of daring, the determination and the 'will to win' which prevails on board our ships cannot be affected or diminished by a 'Falkland' day. The word reprisal naturally represents a great incitement, and helps considerably to bring about a good result.

The moral impression of this attack on English strategists will certainly not be small. These are the invisible fruits of such naval operations. They do not appear in the form of this-or-that many dead and wounded, but in the shape of other measures and omissions which are favourable to us, for the effect upon the morale of British naval commanders will be great, with the result that there will be measures taken, or measures neglected, to the future advantage of Germany.

No less important - and this we must not underestimate - is the refreshing effect of such a success on the spirits of our boys in blue, who, although they are certainly on board modern ships, which are fitted with steam heating, and are much more comfortable than their comrades in the trenches, are still not altogether on a bed of roses. We shall not exaggerate the importance of this fine cruiser raid, but we want to give our heroes a 'Bravo!' and wish them further success.

The German newspapers regarded the raid as a naval operation of great importance, which they believed would, in some mysterious, unspecified way, considerably affect the whole course of the war, especially at sea. Indeed, one Captain Perseus (no doubt a nautical nom de plume), the best known German naval correspondent writing for the *Berliner Tageblatt*, even went on to describe for his readers just how important Scarborough was:

Scarborough is the most important harbour on the entire east coast of England between the Thames and the Humber. It is defended by strong batteries. Its trade thrives in times of peace and wheat is exported. We will hope that several such cargoes now rest at the bottom of the sea.

One cannot help but be impressed by the correspondent's sheer *ignorance* of his topic, for had he but deigned to glance at an atlas and encyclopaedia he would not only have discovered the exact whereabouts of the town, but perhaps something of its nature too. And this despite his having been afforded the courtesy, before the war, of a tour of British naval facilities! As to his wish that cargoes went to the sea bed, he would be sadly disappointed to learn that only three vessels were holed, and those not seriously.

In Copenhagen the Germans eagerly spread the notion that the effect of the bombardment was all but indescribable, everything they could have hoped for. Indeed they told everyone that not only were the English terrified all over the country, but they were trembling more than ever at the thought of a German invasion, and did not trust their own Navy, or those in control of it, to defend them.

Meanwhile Count Reventlow, writing for the *Deutsche Tageszeitung* went on to explore, in his own Teutonic fashion, the psychological impact caused by the attack:

The news has created a sensation throughout the world. We do not think of drawing the inference that a German attack on, and destruction of, two English destroyers possesses some considerable military importance - but it would be wrong if people in Germany were to suppose that. The enormous sensation excited everywhere by the raid is of all the greater psychological interest because it indicates the superstitious respect which Great Britain was able to procure for herself prior to it, for the destruction, or even bombardment, of a British warship was regarded as something unheard of, but the ideas of throwing shells, real shells, which destroy and kill, at the coastworks of Great Britain - that is a crime against the majesty of British supremacy such as no enemy of Great Britain has ever ventured upon. Great Britain can only be defeated by ruthless naval warfare, for she is fighting a war of annihilation against the German Empire and the German people, who are not disposed to reply to such a war with a polite bow.

Quite possibly Count Reventlow's piece of rhetoric was intended to inspire his readers against the supposed ideals of the British and their belief in themselves and contempt for others (especially the Germans), but perhaps goes to say more about the German psyche at that point in the war than that of the British. The overwhelming view of the Germans and their press was that the rest of the non-English world would greet with satisfaction the fact that the great British Navy could be shaken to its scuppers and the arrogant and superior British people humbled on their own shores. The *Cologne Gazette* commented:

We think we may say that - the English part of the world apart - people everywhere will have heard with satisfaction of this second punishment of the great sea robber who oppresses the whole world. The punishment has been inflicted with England's own particular weapon, and inflicted in England's very own country, on the soil of the arrogant island upon which John Bull believes himself to be secure and safe from such punishment.

The *Tägliche Rundschau* added:

Will the overwhelming effect upon English nerves be diminished by the fact that it is from a German source that the people of London hear the painful news of the destruction of two destroyers and of serious injury to a third? Already the European echo of the thunder of the German guns on the English coast rings unpleasantly in English ears. What will it be like when the world learns the news kept back by the English Admiralty of the complete success of the German blow?

The world will learn with new astonishment that England is able to make the North Sea a field of death and destruction for all neutral shipping and even for its own shipping, but that it was not able to make the North Sea unsafe for the German Navy.

Rear Admiral von Kirchoff, expounding on the raid in the *Nürnberger Kurier*, had no doubt it would affect and even change British naval policy:

Apart from the material damage we have inflicted - mainly on the civilian population - which has already caused great horror, we have also won a more important moral victory. It will force the English Admiralty to send out their ships to attack their bold opponents. Now people in England will shout out, 'Where are our big fast battleships? Should they not be kept in our home waters rather than be sent out to Cape Horn?'

The Germans' ally, Austria-Hungary also had its voice to add in the pages of the *Vienna Extrablatt*:

The German fleet has again proved that they are more courageous than their opponents. England's presumption to rule the ocean is getting more ridiculous every day. This is one of our best victories so far.

And so it went on, for in the enemy's eyes the raids had not only been well planned and executed, but had hit strategic military targets with exemplary results. Part of a report in the *Nürnberger Kurier* read:

Despite the dangers of the North Sea and the dominance which the English have there, the fact that the Germans have managed to get as far as the English east coast renews our admiration for the heroic fleet. The English fleet has not dared to attack our coast and has hidden her ships. Only through the completely worthless attack on the Belgian coast is it known that the British have a big fleet!

In the face of mounting world opinion against Germany for what was seen as a direct and blatant breach of the Hague Convention which claimed *'The bombardment by naval forces of undefended ports, towns, villages, dwellings or buildings is forbidden'*, the *Nürnberger Zeitung* decried British attempts to clarify the position of the undefended seaside towns:

You have to know the English affection for Scarborough to understand how painful the attack was for them. The English Admiralty is obviously trying to play down the success of the attack. But it has no right to make false statements. How dare it say that Scarborough and Hartlepool were unfortified. It is well known that they are naval bases.

And went on to describe the scene during the attack:

It was a dark morning. One of those winter days before Christmas. The inhabitants were sitting down to breakfast. Children were on their way to school. Then, in the grey morning mist appeared the outlines of battleships which the inhabitants thought were English. Suddenly, flashes! Thousands streamed out into the streets and ran inland. You could see mothers with screaming children in their arms. A lot of them escaped to trains that were standing ready.

The newspaper then included two supposedly 'independent' telegram accounts of the attack, the first made from Rotterdam:

The bombardment caused great panic. The people stormed the station where packed trains stood ready to set off to Hull. There were incredible scenes of wildly screaming people defending their places and holding on to the carriage steps and the roofs of the wagons.

The second telegram account came from Amsterdam:

The attack must have come as a complete surprise for the English. Their patrols must have failed otherwise it would not have been possible for the German fleet to have bombarded two such important places as Scarborough and Hartlepool. The attack comes at a very bad time for the English, as some of their best ships are in the Atlantic after the battle near the Falklands. Scarborough is the most popular seaside resort in Northern England.

No doubt the Kaiser was already well pleased - what with the reports in the German press - when, on 23rd December, he visited the German Headquarters at Charleville and received Admiral von Pohls' glowing report of the north-east coast raids.

Churches Unite in Prayer and Condemnation

The Saturday after the bombardment (19th December) a special memorial service was held at St Mary's Parish Church, itself struck during the bombardment, at noon. It was the first time in Scarborough's living memory that both Anglican and Free Churchmen had taken part in a united service. Attending in their official capacity were the Mayor and members of the Corporation. The greatest proportion of the town's shops and stores closed between 11.45am and 1.15pm to allow employees and owners alike to attend the service.

The solemn service began with Beethoven's Funeral March, played on the organ by Mr England. This was followed by the processional hymn 'Rock of Ages', which in turn was followed by the 90th Psalm 'The Prayer of Moses, the Man of God'. The Lesson (1 Corinthians, Chapter 15, 20th verse to the end) was read by the Reverend Lockley. After the hymn 'They Whose Course on Earth is O'er' the Archbishop of York, the Most Reverend Cosmo Gordon Lang, addressed the congregation at length:

The terrible and memorable experience through which, dear people of Scarborough, you have passed this week, draws all our hearts together, and indeed, draws the heart of the whole people of this realm to you. It is fitting that you should wish to bring that common heart of solemn grief and sympathy and trust into this building whither for so many generations your fathers here have brought their cares, their distress, their faith and their prayers to the one abiding Father of us all.

Fitting too, I think it is, that before we fall to our prayers, some voice should try to give unity of direction, and of expression to this unity of emotion which binds us all together. Let me have the privilege of expressing that voice, as one who has given to him the special care of the souls of the people - as at all times, so especially at these times of solemn experience - of one who comes to you this morning from the ancient capital of our country and the central shrine of our northern faith and religion, and whose office is itself a reminder of that strong faith in God which links the experience of all generations in our English history together. Our heart then is filled with grief for those peaceful men and women and innocent children whose lives have been so suddenly and so cruelly taken away. Our heart is full of sympathy with those to whom they were near and dear, and with all, especially the aged people, to whom the terrible event of this week has brought such inevitable anxiety and distress. Our heart is filled with indignation at the cruel onslaught upon the peaceable folk of a defenceless town.

We could well bear with fortitude the dread necessities of war, but this was not necessity, it was a breach of all those restraints which hitherto civilised nations have sought to impose upon the inevitable horrors of war. Deep, therefore, and just is the indignation which fills today this common heart. Grief, then, sympathy, indignation, all of them sincere and overflowing - these are the emotions which bind us together. But they will move us not to more distress or excitement, or alarm, but rather to a more quiet and determined resolution that we, to whom an experience so strange and terrible has come, will not fail our country at this time of need. We shall be only the more eager to prove by our steadiness, our calmness, our determination, that we are ready to meet the calls which at this solemn time, our country makes upon us. These men and women and children, whose loss we are assembled here this morning to mourn, will not have died in vain. Their deaths will be a reminder to all of you here, and to the whole people of this country, of the ruthless ferocity of that war spirit which we, with our Allies, are so sternly and solemnly summoned for the sake of the world's peace to destroy. Their death will have been a fresh vindication of the righteousness of our cause.

It brings to us in this country at a time when perhaps we have some need of it, a quick, vivid sense of the dread realities of war, not in order that they should alarm us, but in order that they should prepare us to steel our hearts for the inevitable sacrifices which a great war demands. I am sure that this death of those who shared the life of this town with you will move, as perhaps nothing else could have moved, the heart of the manhood of this North of England to see that the cause for which they suffer will be the more eagerly, and with more self-denying chivalry, taken up and carried through by the strength of the men who remain. I am convinced your example, dear people - the example, Mr Mayor, of all your town - justifies the conviction that what has happened will only bring into this common heart of ours a more quiet and settled determination that no alarm shall spoil and no danger shall affect our determination, as one people, to see our righteous cause vindicated. There was a force touching and striking in the words with which the familiar lesson you have heard closed; 'Therefore be ye steadfast, immovable.' And if we are to gain that steadfast, immovable strength into which this ready and hearty sympathy of ours will move, if we are to gain that strength whither shall we look to find it? Surely to that trust in God which is the fount of all that is deepest, strongest and most endurable in human life and character. 'God is our refuge and strength, a very present help in trouble'. 'Thou art our refuge from one generation to the next'.

This morning those assembled in this ancient Parish Church, I bid you 'Stay your souls afresh in God'. It is a great strength to remember that behind all this ruthlessness, this ferocity, behind all these unspeakable calamitous horrors of war, there is still the will of truth, justice, of righteousness which is restrained by that mysterious gift of human freedom which sometimes, as now, seems to make such havoc of the Divine purpose. But though restrained, it is not suspended. It will reveal itself in judgement, the time will tarry, but it will surely come. And it

ALL SAINTS' CHURCH

Falsgrave Road.

1

2

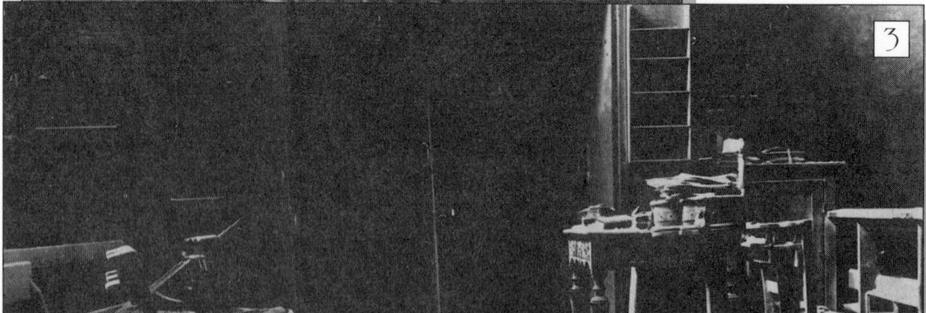

3

is well for us to leave this morning, ourselves, this town, and our country this cause to that supreme power of truth, justice, righteousness, and to beseech Him to judge between us and our enemy.

But lastly we remember that the supreme power is also perfect love. And the love which it is, is not restrained by any sinfulness or pride or false freedom in man. The love of God is not restrained. It has revealed itself in the Cross of Our Lord and Saviour Jesus Christ, suffering for our suffering humanity at its very heart. And therefore I bid you take these lives that have been lost, these men, these women, these innocent children, and commend them today to that unfailing Love, and it will bring to us in the midst of our concern and distress a touch of hope and of peace. When we remember that, we can thus, with fresh confidence, bring those of whom we think, whom we mourn, with whom we sympathise, to that unfailing life which is beyond all human strife, and to that region where beyond these voices there is Peace. And there, in the sure hands of an eternal love we leave them. Wherefore, brethren, I bid you with these thoughts, these prayers, befitting a time so moving and so solemn, to fall to prayer, for which prayers let there be silence, indeed, for a space.

There were several moments of silent prayer before the hymn 'Jesus Lives' was sung. Prayers were then offered by the vicar, and the Nunc Dimittis and the Benediction were followed by the singing of 'God Save the King' and the playing of the 'Dead March'.

The following day, Sunday, 20th December 1914, the churches of the borough were filled with congregations still reeling from the bombardment. At the Parish Church (St Mary's) there was a large contingent of the Yorkshire Hussars, accompanied by their band, and recruits from the Cavalry Depot on Burniston Road. The Vicar's sermon was given over largely to the bombardment:

December the 16th will long be remembered by you and your children. It was a very terrible experience for us all. In the midst of that hazy morning, mercifully before any of the children had gone to school, our town was shelled by the enemy's warships. Death and injury were inflicted on defenceless people and a large proportion of those who suffered were women and children. We have reason, however, to offer up thanks that the results were not far worse. We have to thank God it was not a night raid, with thick darkness prevailing, and the number of casualties has been small considering the population of forty thousand. The church itself bears the mark of an enemy shell, and we should be thankful it has been spared from the worst damage. We, the people of Scarborough, sympathise with our friends at Hartlepool and Whitby. In visiting the injured I have been struck by the delightful quality of courage and self-control in their behaviour. I have seen most of the wounded and the smiles and brave faces of the boys and girls has been one of the brightest features in what has been for us all a tragic occurrence. I have a certain pride and certain satisfaction in that Scarborough has been the first English town to suffer and to receive its baptism of fire, and to have been allowed in a humble way to share in the incidents of war which have befallen our sailors and soldiers. Ours is a righteous cause, but the festival of Christmas will be shorn of much of its secular joy, and Christian Europe never needed so much the spiritual touch of Christmas.

The Muncipal School where the caretaker, Francis Ogle, took the children to safety

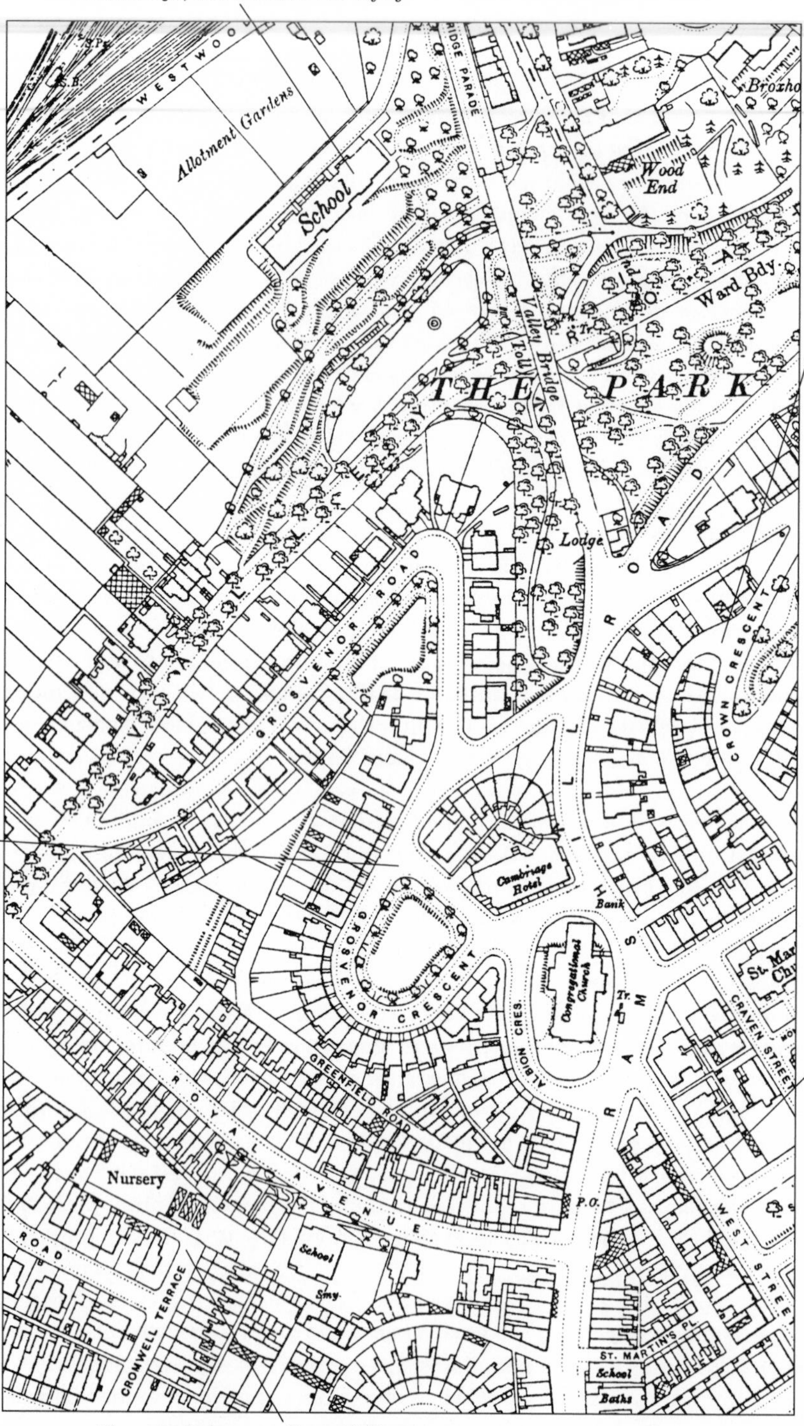

On Crown Crescent Bertha Gregson's property, at number 4, was badly damaged though she was unhurt

The home of J. Kitson, 10 Grosvenor Crescent was badly damaged

Betsy Bradley was badly wounded in the head and body as she walked past Mr Fisher's house at 34 West Street, just as a shell struck it damaging the roof

The rear of a house on Cromwell Terrace was damaged when a shell demolished its stables

At St Martin's Church, Archdeacon Mackarness spoke of the damage that had been done during a service on that Wednesday morning, though, he stressed, the damage had not been as severe as at other places in the town. A substantial amount would be required to effect the necessary repairs, he went on, but he was pleased to say that already five people had made contributions to the repair fund. Archdeacon Mackarness then read a letter to the congregation from the Archbishop of York:

My Dear People,
You have lived through a memorable and terrible experience. Let me send a message of heartfelt sympathy to those whose nearest and dearest have been so suddenly and cruelly killed; to those who have themselves been hurt; to those whose homes have been shattered, and to you whose churches have been damaged. Our hearts burn with just indignation at this wanton onslaught on a practically defenceless town and its peaceable people; at this cruel breach of law by which civilised nations have agreed to restrain the horrors of war.

Let us sternly set ourselves to defeat its object. If the object was to create a general panic and alarm, you who have quietly stayed at home have already proved its banality. If the object was to hinder the discharge of fresh reinforcements to the battle line in France and Flanders, I am sure that the men of our county and our country will make it futile by enlisting in even greater numbers, so that for every man who is sent abroad another will be ready to take his place and defend our land.

The ordeal through which you have passed will not have been suffered in vain, if it brings home to all of us the nature of that ruthless war spirit which we and our lives are called upon for the sake of the world's peace to destroy, and that it leads us with deeper earnestness to turn to God and to commit ourselves and our cause to Him. It was given to you, dear Vicar of St Martin's, and to some of your people to teach us all a lesson which we shall never forget.

I heard with pride and thankfulness of the calmness with which you refused to allow the celebration of the Holy Communion to be interrupted by the noise of the guns or the bursting of the shells. You realise that 'God is in the midst of His Church, therefore shall He not be removed'. And today, in the quiet and ordered worship of the Church you will learn afresh the secret of strength. 'God is our refuge and strength, a very present help in trouble. Thou wilt keep him in perfect peace whose mind is steady in Thee, because he trusteth in Him'.

I send you my sympathy and my blessing. May God bind, strengthen and settle you. Unto His gracious mercy and protection I commit you.

The Pastor of the Claremont United Methodist Free Church, and President of the Free Church Council, Reverend Lockley, took as his text part of the 4th verse of the 103rd Psalm, 'Who redeemeth thy life from destruction'. And then continued in like vein to the town's other churchmen:

We have passed through a stirring and startling week. One in which the unexpected has occurred. In defiance of international law the town has been bombarded, with the subsequent loss of life and the wanton destruction of property. And the chief note of this service should be thankfulness. Yes, it has been a week of danger and destruction, but by God's love most of us are able to meet together. One member of our congregation has lost her life, Mrs Duffield, and our sympathy goes out to her family. Her own church was struck in several places, but the damage, thankfully, was slight. Owing to the bombardment, the sale of work which we have long been preparing for is to be postponed indefinitely. This week too has brought its illusion. The coming of the enemy we know is possible. We were the first town, or one of the first to be shelled, and though there had been losses there had also been gains. For though we are mourning in sympathy, and uniting in suffering, it has broken down the barriers and drawn us closer together; and though the nation is at war, the God of peace remains with us here.

Preaching at the South Cliff Wesleyan Church, Reverend Kirtlan chose as his text 'He hath put down the mighty from their seat. He hath exalted the humble and meek', and from it delivered his sermon:

The text contains a principle in absolute opposition to the law of the world, the natural world, the struggle for existence. Brute force rules the natural world and the battle is to the strong. That was the law of the world until Christ came, and it remains the law of the world where the spirit of Christ is not predominant. This law, the rule of the strong and the tyranny of the strong over the weak has found its latest exposition in the political and religious creed of the 'great Prussian blond savage' who has staked everything on the mailed fist. It has found expression in devastated Belgium, in its blood-stained canals, in its despoiled women and bayoneted children. The law said that what a strong man, armed, had strength enough to grab, that he had a right to grab; what the strong man had strength to do, that he had a right to do. Pity, mercy and consideration for the weak and helpless, these are held to be contemptible qualities.

Christianity itself, in so far as it teaches these qualities and virtues, is a contemptible and infamous religion and was to be swept away into oblivion. Honour, 'scraps of paper', treaties, international law, what he, the enemy, might call the humanities of war, must be relegated to the limbo of forgotten puerilities if they block the way of the strong man armed.

That is the moral significance of the bombing of Scarborough. Scarborough blocked the way to the wireless station, so Scarborough had to be deluged with shot and shell, without warning. Innocent people, their wives and children had to be blasted into eternity. Reason must give place to terror, stark horrible terror, even if there was no profit in blood and devastation. That is the doctrine of Metzoche and Putochke and Bernhardi and the Kaiser William and Admiral von Tirpitz and General von Kluck. But that is not the doctrine of Christmas, or of the babe of Christmas, or of the blessed Virgin Mother. The text I have given contains the new principle by which humanity can also be redeemed 'He hath exalted the humble and meek'.

The Wesleyan Superintendent Minister, Reverend John Gould, preaching at Westborough Wesleyan Chapel, confessed to having prepared his sermon, 'Thou shalt not kill - whosoever hateth his brother is a murderer', well in advance of the bombardment and by strange coincidence found it to be more than apt on that occasion. As he gave his sermon he could not have helped but think of those who had been brought for succour to the basement of his own church, being used as a hospital for the duration of the war:

The gospel of love which is taught from the Christian pulpit has been the cause of the high value we, as a nation, attach to human life. Consequently, the resources of science, medicine, legislation and sanitary reform have all been utilised to prevent and to remedy human suffering and to prolong and benefit human life. No skill, no pains, no outlay or fatigue is spared that can prolong for a single day a human life, however humble that life or obscure. But when a nation puts aside the conditions of the Christian scripture and substitutes for it the gospel of science, philosophy and culture, it is upon a slippery slope down which it rushes with ever-increasing velocity, to the inhuman degradation which is capable of cruelty exceeding the wild outburst of the most ferocious savages of heathenism.

And so it went throughout the town. At the Albemarle Baptist Church, the Pastor, Reverend Burgoyne, expressed deep sympathy with the bereaved, the injured and those who were affected financially by the damage to their homes and businesses. He remarked too on the providential escape of many of the townsfolk due to the high number of shells which had fallen outside the town. The congregation was urged to make Christmas as happy as possible for those about them.

At both the morning and evening services at the Bar Congregational Church, Reverend Middleton expressed sympathy for the relatives of the bereaved and especially those of Harry Frith, who had been a member of the church for many years.

There were losses too in the congregation of Reverend Fawcett, at the Primitive Methodist Chapel on St Sepulchre Street. References were made to the bitter experiences the town had passed through on Wednesday the 16th, and sympathy was expressed for those who had suffered, and especially to the bereaved of Reverend Fawcett's own congregation. Following the usual service, one of thanksgiving was held to enable those 'spared' to express their 'gratitude and mercy'.

Meanwhile, at St Peter's Roman Catholic Church, on Castle Road, Canon O'Connell exhorted his flock to show their gratitude to God:

The attack was totally unexpected and we could not have expected it from a civilised enemy. I scarcely know what to say about it. It is universally acknowledged that it was a wanton and violent outrage against the recognised laws of warfare amongst civilised people. Being at war we expect to suffer in the ordinary way of things. We know that each side will do what it can to beat the other in a fair and clean way. Indeed, we expected to suffer in many ways, to make sacrifices in many ways, personally or otherwise. But all who have any honour at all resent such an outrage as we have had to suffer. Thank God that as far as the Catholics, as a community, are concerned no life has been lost, as far as I know.

But we must not conclude from that that we are perfect, and that God has saved us on account of our goodness, for it did not necessarily follow. Sometimes the purest, the most holy, the most innocent are taken away, and the waster allowed to live for many years. So we should not definitely conclude that because God has spared us that we are therefore good. But no Catholic can deny that the better they are in the sight of God, the more God's protection would be with them.

A great help towards God's protection is the way we live our lives. Let us all try and do the best we can. I offer our condolence and sympathy to the few Catholics, I think there were only three, who were very slightly injured; and I am sure I express the wish of us all when I offer to all the other Christian communities of the town my deep sympathy with the loss they have sustained in their members. To all we offer our condolences. We, as Catholics, having passed through this time of trial unscathed should show our gratitude to God.

Mines Claim More Victims

Having laid mines (in an already heavily mined North Sea) both during and after the bombardment of the north-east ports, to dissuade Royal Naval vessels from giving chase, the German squadrons continued to claim victims long after their grisly work on shore had been done.

The Elterwater and the Princess Olga

At approximately 6.00pm on 16th December, the Tyne collier *Elterwater* was sunk off Flamborough Head. Twelve of the crew were picked up by the steamer *City* and taken to South Shields, but six more were lost.

The steamer *Princess Olga*, on its way between Liverpool and Aberdeen, was struck by a mine some nine miles east of Scarborough at about 7.30pm, again on 16th December, and by 10.00pm had sunk. The crew managed to launch the lifeboats and the chief, second officer and eight of the crew reached Scarborough safely around midnight. The Scarborough lifeboat, the *Queensbury*, put to sea at around 2.45am on Thursday morning (17th December) - after the crew had been noisily rousted from their slumber, nearby local residents fearing the Germans had returned to murder them in their beds - to try and pick up any more survivors. The *Queensbury* remained at sea all night, but returned at 8.10am (18th December) empty handed, with no news of the ship's captain, D. Maclachlan, and remaining eight crewmen. They were eventually brought safely into the town by the *Glen Roon*.

The Orianda and the Passing

The Admiralty had sent minesweepers, many of them converted from trawlers, to check the area for the newly-laid mines. On the morning of Saturday, 19th December the *Orianda*, one of the many ships commissioned by the Royal Navy for such hazardous war work, struck a mine and went down off Scarborough. The crew, bar one man, who was said to be missing, were saved and brought home. The same day another minesweeper (a converted trawler out of Grimsby) struck a mine, and was holed but not sunk. The vessel, minesweeper 58, (its name, the *Passing*, painted over to avoid identification by the enemy) managed to limp back to the safety of the harbour by 6.00pm that evening.

The following day the damaged minesweeper proved the object of much local interest, as sightseers stood and stared in awe at the huge hole in the ship's side. The hole was claimed to be 'big enough to drive a horse and cart through' and on seeing it many wondered how the stricken vessel had managed to make it home without sinking - this was attributed to her modern design and watertight compartments.

The Garmo

At about 10.00am on that same Sunday (20th December) the coastguard was alerted by radio to another vessel, the *Garmo*, an armoured trawler on patrol duty with the minesweepers, which had struck a mine and was in urgent need of assistance about a mile south of Cayton Bay and some two miles from the shore.

The lifeboat put to sea, but found on reaching the area that the *Garmo* had gone down, stern first, and that the survivors had already been picked up by boats from the minesweeper's sister ship and a cargo vessel, the *Hepworth*; which had, rather fortunately, been passing at the time of the distress call. By the time the lifeboat had finished ensuring all the survivors were safe, the prow of the stricken *Garmo*, the only part of it still visible when the lifeboat arrived, slipped beneath the waves.

The second minesweeper took aboard the survivors and took them back to Scarborough, where they were landed at the lighthouse pier and the more seriously injured - Walter Allen, John Wilkinson and John Wood - were transported by car to hospital, while the rest of the crew were taken to the Royal Northern Sea Bathing Infirmary on the Foreshore. The toll from the crew of the minesweeper was one man dead (but brought back) and five men missing. Of those missing, two were later saved, wet and cold, but otherwise unhurt.

The Boston

At 4.00am on Tuesday, 22nd December, a Norwegian cargo ship, the *Boston*, struck a mine three miles east of Scarborough. The *Boston*, out of Bremen, was bound for London with a cargo of wood for papermaking when it struck the mine. The Captain, A. J. Olsen, and his sixteen-man crew were spotted in their lifeboats by a minesweeper which oversaw their safe return to dry land. The ship itself eventually drifted onto Filey Brigg. The *Boston's* two lifeboats brought the survivors ashore at Scarborough and Filey. The nine men landed at Scarborough were put in the care of the Shipwrecked Mariners' Society and lodged with Maria Christian at 21 Sandside, while the Captain, the second mate (suffering from concussion) and eight others were taken off their lifeboat by the Filey lifeboat and landed at Filey. The *Boston's* lifeboat was subsequently brought safely into port by two men from the Filey lifeboat. As at Scarborough, the men were put into the care of the Shipwrecked Mariners' Society and housed at the Foord Hotel. None of the crew - mostly Norwegians or Swedes, with the exception of three Russians - were seriously injured.

The Night Hawk

On Christmas Day, Friday, 25th December, shortly before noon, the Grimsby-based minesweeper *Night Hawk* struck a mine three and a half miles east of Scarborough and the terrific explosion was reported to have sent the vessel to the bottom within ten seconds. It went down with the loss of six lives. The survivors, who had just enough time to leap into the water, and some of whom were said to have been blown off the ship by the force of the explosion, were picked up by lifeboats from the *Night Hawk's* companion vessels.

Of the crew, five men were missing, presumed drowned, while eight were picked up. However the Chief Engineer, Alfred Chappell, died of his injuries before reaching Scarborough. The survivors were landed shortly after 1.00pm and were admitted to the hospital. By later that afternoon they were all reported to be doing well. The body of Chief Engineer Chappell was taken to the mortuary where the Coroner considered whether to hold an inquest, although there were no subsequent reports of one having been conducted.

STANLEY CUNNINGHAM

2565 Trooper Stanley Howard Cunningham, Yorkshire Hussars, was based at Scarborough at the time of bombardment.

Born on 24th May 1898 in Leeds, Stanley was just 16 when he joined up on 9th September 1914, having lied about his age (he gave his birthdate as 1895).

During the bombardment Stanley took a machine-gun section to the lighthouse pier in case of an enemy landing. After the bombardment he was one of those detailed to guard the ruins of the old barracks at the Castle.

He went to France in February 1915 as a Corporal with 'A' Squadron, Yorkshire Hussars, and was gassed on his 17th birthday - the 24th May 1915.

He also served as a Private, with the 9th West Yorkshires (service number: 235960) and with the Machine Gun Corps of the 4th Division (service number: 136466), where he damaged a finger and part of his arm when stopping a runaway limber after the four-horse team had bolted in a service area behind the lines. On the 6th May 1918 he received a severe shrapnel wound to his knee, resulting in a stay in hospital, a nine-inch scar and another change of unit. He then became a Driver with the Royal Air Force (service number: 300999) and was finally demobbed on 24th March 1919.

In May 1921 he married Kate and they had three children, Mavis, Raoul and Adrian. All three served in the armed forces; Mavis with the ATS, Raoul with the Royal Army Service Corps in the Second World War, and Adrian in Malaya (1954-1955) with the 1st West Yorkshires as a machine-gun instructor. During the Second World War Stanley served in the Home Guard and left with the rank of Captain. He died on 9th November 1972, aged 74.

Top right: Stanley in Paris, 1915.

Right: Stanley and Black Bess, 1914.

Below: 'A' Squadron, Scarborough, 1914.

1

2

3

The Eli, the Gallier and the Gem

There were three further casualties to mines on Christmas Day. The first was a Norwegian vessel, the *Eli*, out of Blyth and bound for Rouen carrying a cargo of coal. The ship struck a mine and took about three minutes to sink. The entire crew of fifteen and a pilot managed to make it to the two lifeboats and were saved. At the time a small coasting vessel, the *Alastair*, out of Montrose and bound for London, was in the vicinity and the shipwrecked crew made it to her. The *Alastair* then towed the two lifeboats to Scarborough. Once ashore the survivors were put in the care of the Shipwrecked Mariners' Society and lodged at Mrs Christian's at 21 Sandside.

As the lifeboats of the *Eli* had been making for the *Alastair*, the survivors witnessed a steamer, a little further south of their position, strike a mine. This was later discovered to be a large steamer with forty-five hands aboard, the *Gallier*. Despite striking the mine the vessel did not sink. Half the crew were taken aboard a nearby minesweeper, while the rest remained aboard. Both the Scarborough and Filey lifeboats put out, but the Filey lifeboat returned home at about 8.30pm that night, while the Scarborough lifeboat did not return until 9.00am the following morning - her crew having been supplied with tea by the crew of the damaged vessel. The Scarborough lifeboat lent assistance over a four-day period to the vessel until it was towed safely into the South Bay.

The third casualty of the day was the merchant vessel *Gem*, which struck a mine and went down with the loss of its Master and nine crew members.

The Leersum and the Linaria

On Boxing Day the Scarborough lifeboat, the *Queensbury*, put to sea when the steamer *Leersum* struck a mine and foundered four miles south-east of the town. The ship had been bound for Newcastle from Rotterdam with a general cargo aboard. Seventeen of the nineteen-man crew were saved, the remaining two having been lost when the ship struck the mine. All the men were brought safely back to Scarborough.

The final casualty of 1914 to the Germans' North Sea mines was the merchant vessel *Linaria* which sunk off Filey on Boxing Day, 26th December.

The Banyers, the Elfrida, the Deptford and the Sapphire

However, the end of the year did not bring any relief and come the New Year shipping continued to be lost in the mine-infested waters of the North Sea. The *Banyers*, a trawler commissioned by the Navy, went down on 6th January 1915. The merchant vessel the *Elfrida* struck a mine and followed her a day later (the 7th). There was then a little over a month before the next loss, when another merchant vessel, the *Deptford*, went down on 24th February with the loss of one life. Several days later, on 1st March, the fishing vessel the *Sapphire* was sunk off Filey, again with the loss of one life.

Throughout the rest of the war shipping of all kinds would continue to be claimed and sent to the bottom by the mines strewn like poppy seeds across the vastness of the grey, cold and forbidding waters of the North Sea. It is quite possible that many more vessels than those mentioned here were victims of the mines, but records are incomplete and some are far from precise or accurate on the subject. Indeed many vessels are simply recorded as 'lost - cause unkown'. Suffice to say that eventually the *Kolberg* probably claimed (and continued to, long after the war was over) as many lives with her mines as were lost on that December morning's raids on Scarborough and Whitby by her sister ships the *Derfflinger* and *Von der Tann*.

The Queensbury

Throughout the war the Scarborough lifeboat, the *Queensbury*, and its volunteer crew (and the other lifeboats and crews along the north-east coast) gave sterling service going to the aid of stricken vessels, ships and submarines, many struck by mines or sunk by enemy vessels, often at great risk to their own lives. Many was the sailor, master mariner or sub-mariner who had cause to thank the *Queensbury* in those dangerous years between 1914 and 1918.

This was the third Scarborough lifeboat to carry the name *Queensbury* and she had a proud tradition to uphold, which she did from the moment she arrived on station at Scarborough on 19th February 1902. She was thirty-five feet long and eight foot three inches in width; was a 10-oared self-righter; built at the Thames Ironworks boatyard and cost the princely sum of £729. She gave 16 years of unstinting service before she was withdrawn from service on 2nd August 1918. Whilst the town awaited a new lifeboat (the *Herbert Joy* in 1924) the *Brothers Brickwood* was put on temporary station duty at Scarborough.

Money for the East Coast Towns from HMS Albemarle

On Christmas Eve Mayor Graham wrote to his counterparts at both Whitby and Hartlepool:

> *I have received the following letter from Staff Paymaster Victor O. Padwick of HMS Albemarle dated 21st December:*
>
> *'To the Mayor of Scarborough,*
> *I am requested by the ship's company of this ship to forward to you the sum of fifteen pounds in the hope that it may be of use in relieving distress in Scarborough, Hartlepool and Whitby caused by the recent raid of the enemy.'*
>
> *I therefore have pleasure in enclosing a five pound note (No. 94/A-16,196). I am writing to Staff Paymaster Padwick thanking him for this generous contribution and am sending him a receipt for five pounds retained by myself for Scarborough. Will you kindly send him a receipt for the enclosed five pounds.*

Such a gesture was typical of the generosity of ordinary men and women all over the country, who dug into their meagre pockets to send amounts large and small to the dispossessed, injured and bereaved of the east coast towns - their largesse was an example to the government of the day.

Light Relief

On the night of Saturday, 26th December, Boxing Day, after a trying week, many of the locals, in need of a diversion, packed the Opera House on St Thomas Street for the Christmas Pantomime, 'Little Bo-Peep and Bonnie Boy Blue', and were able, for a short time, to put the horror and terror of the bombardment behind them. At both the Londesborough Theatre and Picture House at 44 Westborough and the Palladium Picture Theatre on Foreshore Road, business was brisk as locals took in the delights and temporary escapism of the films on offer; at the Londesborough it was a war film 'VC', billed as a thrilling story of Kitchener's Army, while at the Palladium it was 'The Tragedy at the Pepper Box Inn'.

BENNETT FAMILY FUNERAL

1: The twin hearses for the two adults who died, Johanna Bennett and Albert Bennett.
2: The cortège pictured in Norwood Street.
3: The open landau bearing the two children, John Ward and George Barnes.

The Funerals

In the wake of the town's ordeal, funerals for the victims were held. Fifteen-year-old George Taylor, killed in Albion Street, was accorded full scouting honours as hundreds of townsfolk, many in tears, followed the hearse bearing his flag-draped coffin to the graveyard.

The bodies of the Bennett 'family', carried in three carriages (a hearse for each adult and an open landau for the two children), were escorted by men from the Royal Field Artillery and the 5th Green Howards; and local dignitaries abounded at the burial of well-respected Justice of the Peace, John Hall, as he was laid to rest in the New Cemetery. The funeral cortège of young boy scout George Taylor was followed by a huge crowd of locals from the boy's home to his final resting place.

> *As I recall, the town was in a sorry state by the time we were allowed some leave and returned, with buildings wrecked and ruined and falling to bits everywhere. Work was still going on to try and get things straight. We helped where we could, but there wasn't a lot left to save. Some people were up in arms about it, but I think most were still too shocked and dazed to comprehend it properly. Men of our Battalion escorted some of the coffins at the funerals . . . we didn't envy them the job, it must have been awful, especially with the children.*
> [2234 Private Jim Stevenson, 5th Green Howards.]

Some small part of the horror of war, and the terrors their lads faced at the front, had been brutally brought home to the people of Scarborough. The enemy's foul deed had, however, done recruitment in the area no harm at all.

In the Bombardment's Wake

In the wake of the bombardment a number of folk departed the town for safer inland habitats. One contemporary report estimated as many as 6,000 had fled, including some who had pledged 'to defend the town to the last' in the shape of some members of the Special Constables and the Athletes' Volunteer Corps. Given that Scarborough had a population of under 38,000, much was made of this 'exodus' in the press, yet when news of it reached those serving at the front it caused little comment; though expressing sympathy for the town's ordeal they were, not unnaturally, more interested in their own affairs. As if to counteract this exodus of locals, sightseers from across the country flooded into the town to see the damage wrought by the Germans for themselves.

The Story of the German Visitors takes on a Fresh Slant

Following the bombardment stories were rife, both in the press and locally, of spies and espionage and in particular of a visit made to the town in August 1913, which became the most suitable target for comment.

A German liner, the *Kronprinzessin Cecilie,* carrying some 250 men and women who had attended the International Medical Congress in London, had chosen to break its journey home at Scarborough and had steamed into the bay, where she had been met by the pleasure paddle-steamer *Cambria*. Greetings were exchanged, chocolates were given to the ladies and a bouquet of flowers was presented on behalf of the Mayor and Mayoress by a German resident of the town, before the guests were brought ashore by the *Cambria*. After being officially received at the Town Hall, the German visitors had been given a guided tour of the castle and its grounds - including the Signal Station - by

THE VISITORS

1: The *Cambria* (front) and *Kronprinzessin Cecilie* (back) alongside each other. 2&3: The visitors on the paddle-steamer *Cambria*.

the Borough Meteorologist Mr Larkin. They then went on to view other sights of interest in the town - such as the coastguard station opposite St Mary's Church and the harbour - where German flags flew prominently from many buildings as a sign of welcome. An evening of entertainment was provided for them at the Spa, where Madame Marge Neisch of the German opera sang.

With the bombardment came a number of stories pointing to the duplicity of this so-called 'friendly' visit in 1913, when the Hun had obviously been getting the 'lie of the land'. On the tour of the castle Mr Larkin had been accompanied by his grandson, who, apparently able to speak fluent German, had overheard one of the visitors say, "The castle could easily be taken if wanted." Later, a local doctor had told Mr Larkin that a number of the visitors had not been medical people at all, for he had spoken to two of them, asking a couple of simple medical questions which they were totally at a loss to answer; thus proving beyond a doubt that they were spies!

Business as Usual

On Wednesday, 30th December, two weeks later, the editorial of the *Scarborough Pictorial* - still full of the horrors of the bombardment - gave some indication of how the town was trying to get back to normal:

> *After the dislocation of business and the drastic interference with the domestic life of the town, no feature is more gratifying to record today, in dealing with the aftermath of the bombardment than the manner in which the people of Scarborough have settled down once again to the daily round, the common task.*
>
> *The poor dupes of the Kaiser and his cohorts, who are regaled with stories in Berlin, and other parts of the Fatherland, of the terror and tremblings of the people on the East Coast, would have been sadly disillusioned could they have taken a tour through the streets of Scarborough during the days of Christmas which have just passed. It seemed hardly believable that, only such a short time before, the men, women and children of the town had gone through the experience of a fortnight ago.*
>
> *It was not that they had forgotten it, nor that any of the horrors had become less real by the passing of the intervening days. The memory of that terrible half-hour is engraved on their soul forever. Merely has it been a wonderful manifestation of the indomitable British bulldog spirit, which proves that German 'frightfulness' will never pay here in this country. We have been made to realise the barbarism and the brutality with which the Germans are pursuing this struggle. The desolated homes and the shattered houses in every part of our town have left no doubt as to the fury and hatred with which they intend to try and subdue us, utterly regardless of the simple principles of humanity. Yes, we understand all that. And our answer is plastered on every shop which the German people have been deluded into believing has been closed and its occupants fled: 'Business as usual'.*
>
> *We do not hesitate to say that the fortitude and calm of the people of Scarborough during the days which have followed Wednesday, December 16th, stands as an example to the nation at large. That is the outstanding fact today. Of other matters dealt with in this issue, which have comprised the succeeding events to the unforgettable day, little need be added here. The greatest gratification has been expressed for the kindly messages from the King and Mr Churchill, and*

other sympathisers in every part of the country. But that which has satisfied the townspeople most of all is the promise of the Prime Minister that all loss, personal and material, will be compensated out of the national coffers. For this prompt and exceedingly favourable pronouncement the warmest thanks are due to the Borough Member, Mr Walter R. Rea, who dealt with the matter in a most businesslike way and pleaded the cause of the suffering town with such gratifying success.

It was also reported at the time that a postcard had been received in the Scottish town of Dunfermline from a seaman aboard one of the destroyers which had engaged the German ships after their bombardment of the east coast towns. On the postcard the seaman claimed that four British destroyers came into contact with the enemy, and had they been able to 'shoot for nuts' they would have sunk the British ships, which were like rowing boats compared to the German cruisers. However, despite the Germans not being able to shoot straight, the seaman's ship had been holed and had returned to harbour for repair!

Bombardment Commemorative Medals

Following the ordeal suffered by the town and its inhabitants, the owners of the local newspaper organised and struck a set of Commemorative Medals - one the size of a sixpence, the other of a half-crown. The smaller of the two was struck in gold, silver, bronze and aluminium, while the larger was struck in silver, bronze and aluminium. The medals were available through local jewellers, stationers and the newspaper's offices and the prices ranged from three pennies up to £1 (one pound). No mention was made as to where the proceeds from the sales of the medals was to go. Six years of research have failed to turn up the sight of a single medal and one wonders how many were struck and how many were actually bought.

The Ruins of Scarborough

Shortly after the bombardment Miss Phylis Sarll, of Mansfield - among a group of British women and children released by the Germans (probably from internment) - returned to her home via Belgium and claimed to have seen many pictures in Germany of the ruins of Scarborough, where not a single house was said to be left standing. The Germans also issued a special commemorative silver medal of the bombardments of the east coast for those actively involved in it. The obverse of the medal was inscribed *'God blesses the United Armies'*, and the reverse, *'Bombardment of Scarborough and Hartlepool through German ships, 16th December, 1914'.*

Fears over Safety of London

Following the attacks on the east coast, and what was regarded by many as the failure of the Navy to defend sovereign soil, other parts of the country began to worry for their safety, asking were they next? In particular the people of London grew uneasy, envisaging Zeppelin bombing raids:

News of the raid by German cruisers against non-combatants and civilians in Scarborough and neighbouring towns on the east coast has revived interest in the problem of defence of London against possible bomb-throwing raids by aeroplanes or Zeppelins.

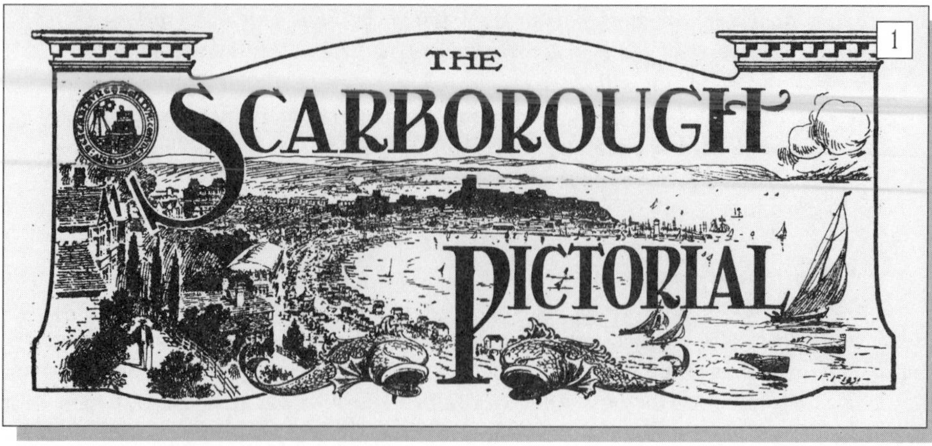

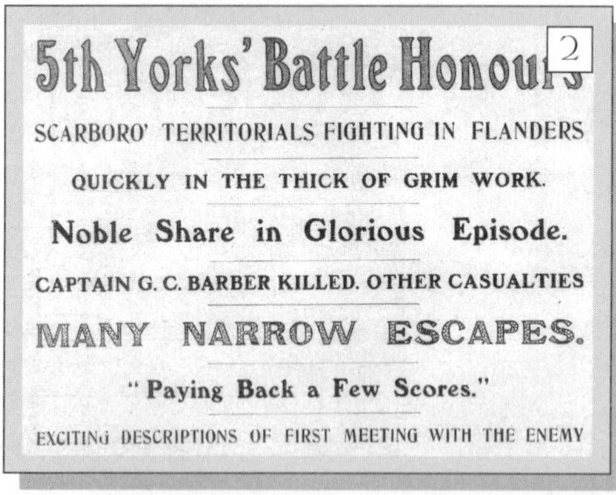
2

5th Yorks' Battle Honours

SCARBORO' TERRITORIALS FIGHTING IN FLANDERS

QUICKLY IN THE THICK OF GRIM WORK.

Noble Share in Glorious Episode.

CAPTAIN G. C. BARBER KILLED. OTHER CASUALTIES

MANY NARROW ESCAPES.

"Paying Back a Few Scores."

EXCITING DESCRIPTIONS OF FIRST MEETING WITH THE ENEMY

SOUVENIRS

1: The header from the Scarborough Pictorial, the weekly newspaper which featured two bombardment specials. 2: The headlines in April 1915, after the 5th Green Howards had taken their revenge. 3: The coins issued by the Scarborough Mercury Company to commemorate the bombardment. 4: Pieces of shell. 5: The medal issued to the German sailors who took part in the bombardments.

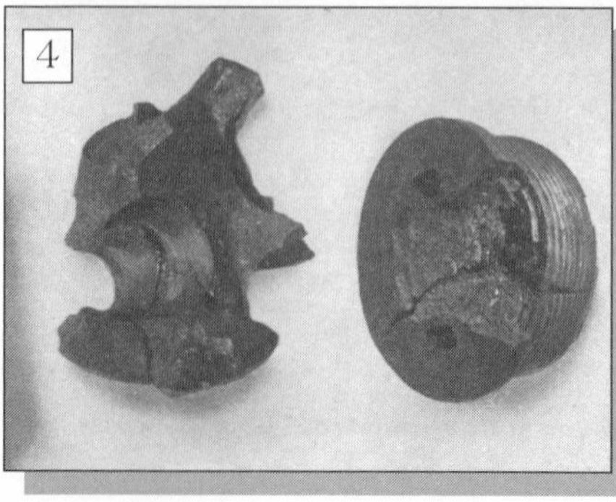

There is little sign of apprehension in any class of people in the metropolis, but the approaching season of the mist and fog might, it is thought, afford the Germans opportunity for an aerial dash upon London.

Every precaution however is being taken in this and other matters of defence by the authorities. With regard to the special constables, Major Wilkinson, who, in co-operation with Colonel Ward, is in charge of the organisation, has informed me that in greater London there are now 23,000 'specials' doing extra police duty by day and night shifts. Many of them are making sacrifices to be able to do their turn in this capacity. No complaints and no withdrawals have been officially notified so far and the health of the men is remarkably good, considering that many of them are on duty for four and eight hours in the night.

In addition to the 23,000 special constables, 8,000 regular employees of important works have been sworn in, who take guard duty by night at the works in which they are employed.

The special constables are receiving a certain amount of drill and instruction in companies, and thus are brought together, and a bond of sympathy is developed among them.

Thus read the editorial in the *Scarborough Evening News*. What was not made clear was just what these special constables were supposed to do to stop the bombing raids of planes and Zeppelins. Nor was it asked why so many able-bodied men could be found for this work and why they had not joined the colours!

However, these proved to be prophetic words indeed, for the first German air-raid occurred against Dover on 24th December 1914, just eight days after Scarborough's ordeal. On this occasion no one was hurt and the only damage was a hole in someone's garden.

The first airship raid occurred on 19th January 1915 over the Norfolk towns of Yarmouth, King's Lynn and Snettisham. This time the damage was more severe. Four people were killed, including two women, while fifteen were wounded, including four women and 2 children. One soldier was also killed. [A full diary of recorded attacks against the British mainland can be found at the back of the book.]

At last it had been brought home to a largely disbelieving nation that no longer was its soil sacrosanct. Not only were its forces fighting and dying on foreign soil, but now the enemy could bring the war to its very doorstep. No one felt safe. There was only one thing the nation could do, rally to the cause and see the war won.

New Year Dawns ~ Schoolgirl's Account Published

On the first day of January 1915, a Friday, the *Bridlington Chronicle* printed an account of the Scarborough raid written by the sixteen-year-old Winifred Holtby, a pupil at Queen Margaret's School. The vivid account created such interest that not only was it syndicated as far away as Australia, but copies of it were printed and sold for the princely sum of threepence by the Holtby family to raise money for the Red Cross (the piece is reproduced in full in 'In their own write').

Emboldened by her success and approbation, Winifred then wrote a long letter to the press exhorting Britain not to adopt a policy of reprisals against Germany after the war - a war she obviously expected them to win. This, however, met with far less approval, although it is perhaps fair to say that living through that terrible ordeal probably set her on the cause for world peace she was to follow rigorously all her life.

BOMBARDMENT BOOKLETS

1: The 1915 booklet produced in paper and hardback by local printers E.T.W. Dennis. This was the first souvenir booklet to be produced. 2: The 1978 booklet written by David Mould (a staff journalist with Yorkshire Television) with its famous 'red cover'. 3,4&5: The advert for, and front and back cover (printed in colour) of the 1915 booklet produced by The Scarborough Mercury Company, featuring 81 photographs. The company also produced two 'bombardment' editions of its weekly newspaper, *The Scarborough Pictorial*.

1

2

3

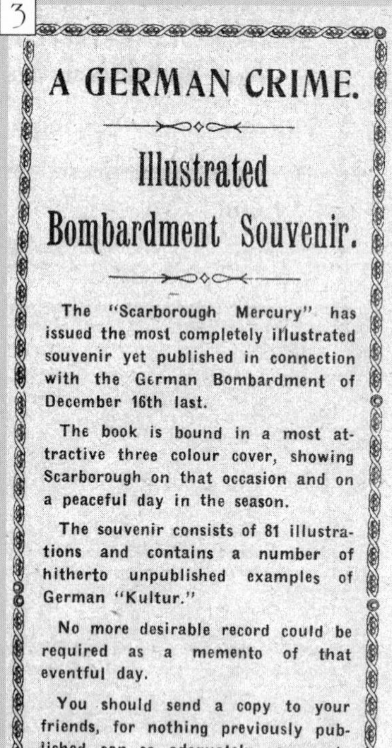

A GERMAN CRIME.

Illustrated

Bombardment Souvenir.

The "Scarborough Mercury" has issued the most completely illustrated souvenir yet published in connection with the German Bombardment of December 16th last.

The book is bound in a most attractive three colour cover, showing Scarborough on that occasion and on a peaceful day in the season.

The souvenir consists of 81 illustrations and contains a number of hitherto unpublished examples of German "Kultur."

No more desirable record could be required as a memento of that eventful day.

You should send a copy to your friends, for nothing previously published can so adequately convey to the mind the extent of the damage done on that morning.

On sale at newsagents and at the "Mercury" Office.

Price: SIXPENCE.
Post Free, Sevenpence.

4

5

Report to Coastal Defence Headquarters

By the start of January the Yorkshire Hussars' Commanding Officer, Colonel Smithson, was able to provide the following report on the raid from his base at the Pavilion Hotel to the Yorkshire Coast Defence Commander based at Hornsea:

I beg to report as follows:

The town was shelled without previous warning on a hazy morning, by four enemy vessels, which commenced firing at 8.06am and ceased firing at 8.35am.

The number of vessels engaged were four, two battle-cruisers and two small cruisers, two in the South Bay and one close in under the north-west corner of the Castle Hill. The fourth vessel stood out to sea, but it is not known whether she actually fired on Scarborough. She had three funnels [the Kolberg] and was supposed to be a battle-cruiser. The others opened fire at under 1000 yards range on the Castle Hill and sea front, steaming between Cayton Bay and Scarborough's North Bay and back.

It is estimated that 500 rounds were fired by the enemy. Notices were printed and circulated in the town immediately, warning people to report the position of any unexploded shells. Eight shells were located and taken over by the Ordnance Department. There is no doubt there are other unexploded shells in the sands and neighbouring fields.

Our force available was as follows:

Cayton Bay: Yorkshire Hussars Reserve - I officer and 10 men.

Scarborough: South Bay and castle dykes - Yorkshire Hussars Reserve - 13 officers, 100 trained men, and 170 recruits (of which 70 had fired as part of a course of musketry).

North Bay: Northern Cavalry Depot - 7 officers and 170 men (mostly recruits).

No rifle was fired in reply.

The military casualties were: 1 driver, Royal Field Artillery (Territorial Force) killed, one man, 5th Yorkshire Regiment (Wireless Guard) dangerously wounded.

Civilians: killed 17, wounded 99, since died 1.

The damage done to public and private property is scattered over the whole town and is considerable. In addition, scattered shells fell in Scalby, Irton, Cumboots, and Seamer (in the latter place not actually in the village).

A map of the Borough is attached showing the approximate position of the shells. The Borough Engineer is compiling a detailed report of the damage to buildings which will be forwarded later.

Of the shells fired at the Grand Hotel, seven fell short in the sands without exploding.

The officer at Cayton Bay reports as follows:

Shortly before 8.00am I saw three German vessels, one with three funnels [the Kolberg], within two-thirds of a mile of the coast. The larger cruiser did not fire, but proceeded east-south-east. One or both of the other cruisers opened fire on the Water Works, shooting about 20 rounds. They then turned and opened broadside fire on Scarborough.

Borough Engineer's Preliminary Report

As mentioned in the preceding report from Colonel Smithson, the Borough Engineer, Harold Smith, and his department were busy throughout the end of December and the

THE YORKSHIRE HUSSARS

Following the Haldane Army Reforms, Scarborough was changed from an artillery depot, to a cavalry depot. At the time of the bombardment troopers from the Yorkshire Hussars were stationed in the town, where they had dug trenches on the cliffs and erected barbed-wire barricades and sandbagged machine-gun nests in the town.

The picture shows the Hussars in 1914.

early days of January collating details of the damage and drawing up a map of the town with the location of the fallen shells marked on it. The map would largely be used to help determine and settle compensation claims. The following is the letter sent by Harold Smith to Colonel Smithson's Adjutant, Captain Pearson, at the Pavilion Hotel:

> *Dear Sir,*
> *Herewith I beg to hand you a copy of the 6-inch map of the town showing approximately the places struck during the bombardment on the 16th December.*
> *As I explained to you this afternoon, the plan is incomplete inasmuch as there are considerable numbers of shells which fell in districts not covered by this plan, and there are still a few places to mark within the borough itself.*
> *I have not yet got a complete tabulated list of the damage done, but the following may be considered as approximately representing the property struck: - 20 public buildings and 180 private buildings.*
> *This number does not take into account the minor damage caused by the bursting shells, such as the breaking of windows, damage to roofs etc. etc., which would swell the total very considerably.*

By the time the 6-inch map was completed, Smith and his team had listed a total of 209 buildings which they claimed had been struck individually by entire shells (the figure did not include any damage done by partial shell fragments or by shrapnel - had it done so the list would have been mammoth). They were further able to break down the figures into confirming 7 churches hit, 10 public buildings and 5 hotels. From the bombardment a total of 489 shells had been accounted for by the engineers, including those which had fallen in parks, fields and on the beach. A further 30 shells had been reported to them but had yet to be investigated and verified.

Harbour Master Requests Defence

On 1st February 1915 the Scarborough Harbour-Master, Walter Cass Smith, wrote the following letter to the Admiralty:

> *I wish to bring before your notice the helplessness of this port should the enemy attempt a landing raid by night.*
> *The port being open to night traffic, our first intimation of the raiders' presence would be learned when the vessel was alongside the pier. It would then be an easy matter to overpower the military guard (two in number) and the three policemen on duty on the pier, and to land and get possession of the town, the streets of which are open to the Harbour.*
> *This helplessness to a night raid has been clearly shown during the last month, when minesweepers of the 'Brighton Queen' class, each capable of carrying a thousand men, have come alongside the pier in the dark and remained several hours lying there, two and three at a time.*

There is no record of a reply. But it was obvious the Admiralty had far more important things on its mind than the defence of an east coast fishing port.

The Compensation Row Rumbles On

As stated earlier, the matter of compensation, though promised by the Prime Minister,

Herbert Asquith, in his letter to the town's MP on 22nd December 1914, continued to provide fuel for dissatisfaction among the people of the town, many of whom had lost loved ones. Indeed, those who had lost a husband or father found themselves without a breadwinner and were soon in desperate straits. The damaged buildings (a number demolished for safety's sake), were simply patched up and made barely habitable as their owners were unwilling to undertake full-scale, long-term repairs until the question of the level of their compensation claims was settled.

To aid in the work of assessing the damage the Borough Engineer went to great lengths to compile a map of the town and district upon which was marked the places the shells had fallen (or at least those that could be confirmed by the greatest proportion of damage done to a street or area).

As part of the administration of the Government money the East Coast Bombardment Committee was formed under the auspices of Lord Parmour and was charged with determining the scale of compensation to be paid and to assess each individual claim. However, bureaucracy was and still is a cumbersome beast, and in the meantime the Mayor of Scarborough launched an emergency fund which attracted generous gifts from across the nation. Regrettably the money did not last long, and by August 1915 the Mayor's fund had been thoroughly exhausted.

The arguments over compensation continued, with the town's mayor writing to his counterpart in Hartlepool to decry the level of compensation being paid out. Some claims, he stated, had been cut by twenty and thirty percent and in some instances by as much as fifty percent. Among the many claims being pursued by the council through the East Coast Bombardment Committee was that of Mrs Selina Harland, widow of Henry Harland of 8 Belle Vue Street, who died from his injuries on 26th December.

Henry had been a shoemaker earning an average of 30 shillings (£1.50) a week; his rent had amounted to 4/6 (four shillings and sixpence - 22½ pence). His widow, with five children to care for, had been in receipt of £1 a week from the Mayor's emergency fund until the money had run out. The East Coast Bombardment Committee, after reviewing her claim, had awarded her a single lump sum of £87/10s (eighty-seven pounds and ten shillings) which was based on Henry's earnings - enough to last about a year.

The continuing controversy over the compensation awards led to angry exchanges between Scarborough Borough Council and the Committee. Scarborough's Town Clerk, Sydney Jones, requested the Mayor meet with the Committee to discuss the mounting list of disputed claims. Meanwhile the town's MP, Walter Rea, tried unsuccessfully to raise the matter in a Commons debate.

Indeed, on Thursday, 7th January, Lord Southwark raised the matter in the House of Lords, reminding their Lordships of the promise made by the Prime Minister to provide relief in respect of the damage to personal property caused by the bombardment of the east coast towns. He wanted to know if all future losses sustained by bombardments would be fully borne by the state. In reply, Lord Beauchamp, for the Government, stated he was unable to say in exactly what way the Government intended to proceed in regard to this matter.

As the year of 1915 dragged on, the East Coast Bombardment Committee remained unmoved by the pleas emanating from Scarborough over the level of compensation being paid and maintained that the awards were both consistent and fair. By September the Committee had completed its work and been wound up. There was to be no more money for Scarborough. The war, too, was dragging on and now all the country's resources and finances were required to keep the war effort going.

1

3

2

4

SCARBOROUGH

1&3: By unnamed British artists. 2: *'Panic at Scarborough'*, by Professor Hoger. 4: One of the postcards from the *Von der Tann* picked up by Reginald Webster in 1918. 5: By Simon Begg, artist for the *Illustrated London News*.

5

The nation's memory of the shelling of Scarborough and the east coast towns was already beginning to fade as the news grew steadily worse from the ravages and horrors of the Western Front into which so many local lads had now been plunged.

Advance Notice

It was also revealed in Parliament during the early days of 1915 that the military authorities had served notices on a number of Scarborough's more influential residents, ordering them to leave the town for their own safety in advance of the bombardment. Twenty-eight people were reported to have left the town as a result. But a telegram from the War Office put paid to any more of the further 414 notices in hand being served for fear of creating a panic among the populace and alerting the enemy to the fact his codes had been broken.

Germans Dismiss Breach of Hague Conference

In the days and weeks following the bombardment the Germans were constantly accused by the British and many other countries of breaching the rules governing warfare as laid out in the Second Hague Conference, in particular as laid down in Convention Nine, the first sentence of which read, 'The bombardment by naval forces of undefended ports, towns, villages, dwellings or buildings is forbidden.'

It was the view of the Germans that every time the British suffered some small setback they hid behind the rules and clauses of international law. In an attempt to stem the tide of protest and in an effort to put its own case for the 'legality' of the raids the German Government printed the following statement in the *Norddeutsche Allegemeine Zeitung* on the 4th January 1915:

> *The bombardment of the three English towns, Hartlepool, Scarborough and Whitby, has been attacked in the English press as a breach of international law. We are accused of having bombarded towns without previous warning and of having created the deaths of many civilians. The accusations are totally unjustified.*
>
> *To begin with, there is no doubt that we were not bound by the conventions of international law when bombarding with naval vessels. The only contract concerning bombardment by naval forces - the 9th Hague Convention of 18th October 1907 - cannot be applied in this war since it had not been ratified by all the belligerents.*
>
> *Moreover, according to Article 8, they do not bind the contracting nations in this war anyway. The clauses of the convention have only to be observed in so far as they correspond with the general law of nations. There is no certainty here whether undefended localities should not be bombarded, and there is the precedent that in the Crimean War, open Russian coastal towns were bombarded by English warships.*
>
> *However, the German Navy adhered strictly to the Hague Convention, for Articles 1 and 2 include bombardment of all defended areas and all military installations in undefended places. This applies to the coastal towns bombarded by our Navy.*
>
> *Hartlepool, according to the official British monthly list, belongs to the 'coast defences', which are manned in peace and war by the British Army. These were the men who shot at the attacking German ships from their batteries.*

LETTERS & POSTERS

1: Although the bombardment was put to use in the army's recruitment drive, it was also used to help sell products, as in this instance for electric light fittings. 2: The handbill put out by the Scarborough Local Emergency Committee, after the bombardment, when fears of another attack and perhaps an invasion were at their height. 3: The letter sent to Scarborough's grocers, via local grocer Jack Taylor, by the Institute of Certified Grocers condeming the shelling of the town by the Germans (*see page 144*).

Remember Scarborough !

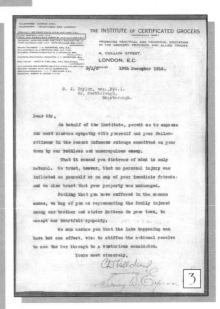

A Photograph of the Fine Art Saloon, Marine Parade, Scarborough, after the German Bombardment, lighted throughout by Corona wire drawn electric lamps. They stood up against the German shells and are still shedding their usual brilliant light over the ruins of the premises. . .

CORONAS DEFEAT THE **GERMANS**

1

PRIVATE AND CONFIDENTIAL.

Scarborough Local Emergency Committee.

To Owners of Motor Cars and Bicycles.

In the event of a hostile landing all Motor Vehicles and Bicycles must be driven away at once, with or without passengers, to the Collecting Area, Hagg House, on the Pickering Road, between Thornton Dale and Pickering.

They may go by the Scalby Road or Lady Edith's Drive through Hackness, Troutsdale, and Snainton, or by Stepney Hill to Ayton, proceeding thence by the Pickering Road.

Spare tyres, spare parts, and Petrol must also be taken away, but if this is impossible, the Petrol must be run off and the Tyres, &c., rendered useless. Motor Cars and Bicycles which cannot be taken away at once must be rendered useless, but only on the distinct order to this effect from the Military Authority or the Chief Constable.

Such Order, which is in readiness, will be sent out to each Owner by a Special Messenger in the event of a landing being actual or imminent.

All enquiries in connection with the above should be addressed to Mr. Councillor White, Tranby House, Westwood, Scarborough.

2

TELEPHONE: AVENUE 2761.
TELEGRAPH: "INCERTIGRO, FEN, LONDON"

THE INSTITUTE OF CERTIFICATED GROCERS
(INCORPORATED 1909.)

PROMOTES PRACTICAL AND TECHNICAL EDUCATION IN THE GROCERY, PROVISION AND ALLIED TRADES.

4, CULLUM STREET,
LONDON, E.C.

B/X/S (DATE) 19th December 1914.

C. J. Taylor, esq., F.G.I.
20, Westborough,
Scarborough.

Dear Sir,

On behalf of the Institute, permit us to express our most sincere sympathy with yourself and your fellow-citizens in the recent infamous outrage committed on your town by our ruthless and unscrupulous enemy.

That it caused you distress of mind is only natural. We trust, however, that no personal injury was inflicted on yourself or on any of your immediate friends: and we also trust that your property was undamaged.

Feeling that you have suffered in the common cause, we beg of you as representing the foully injured among our brother and sister Britons in your town, to accept our heartfelt sympathy.

We can assure you that the late happening can have but one effect, viz: to stiffen the national resolve to see the War through to a victorious conclusion.

Yours most sincerely,

3

Scarborough is not recorded in the British Army list as a fortified coastal place, but on the northern side of the town one can see from seaward a fortification protected by trenches and barbed-wire with a battery of six quick-firing 6-inch guns. Next to Scarborough Castle there are barracks, and in the southern district of the town there is an officially registered wireless station.

According to the official monthly British Navy list, Whitby has a coastguard station, manned in peace and war by Marines. The German forces have bombarded only this station, which is admitted by the British side.

While it is to be regretted that the German attack caused the deaths of civilians, it must be emphasised that these attacks were within the permitted conduct as limited by the law of nations.

The arguments would continue to rage, but the damage had been done and the bombardments of the 16th December were to prove to be only the beginning in a long and deliberate campaign by German naval and air forces to subject mainland Britain to some small part of the war raging across France and Belgium.

Whose Shells?

Four months after the bombardment of the town shells were still being found and laid claim to, despite the need for them to be disposed of properly.

In connection with the recent bombardment of Scarborough, six shells which did not explode have been recovered and emptied of their explosive matter and are now in the possession of the Corporation of Scarborough. The Council have had claims from individuals for shells which fell upon their property and they have appointed a Committee to enquire into these claims.

I am not aware whether enemy shells are, or are not considered the property of the Crown, but in the circumstances I propose, with the sanction of the Army Council, to allow the Corporation of Scarborough to deal with and dispose of the shells in question as they think best.

The above letter, dated 17th April 1915, was addressed to the War Office and was sent by the Commander-in-Chief of the Northern Command based at York. For years afterwards shells, nose-cones and fragments would continue to turn up, often changing hands for a tidy sum. Despite this, very few pieces actually survive to the present day - many having been swallowed up by the war effort in the Second World War, when many locals hoped their fragment of shell would be turned into a bullet or bomb bound for the Fatherland from whence it came.

SCARBOROUGH

IN THEIR OWN WRITE
PERSONAL ACCOUNTS OF THE GERMAN NAVAL RAID ON SCARBOROUGH ON WEDNESDAY, 16TH DECEMBER 1914

The following extracts from letters and verse were written largely by the men and women of Scarborough. A few were printed in the local papers at the time and were read avidly by both the local populace and those further afield eager for news of the town's terrible ordeal. A number are from military archives, and others have been written up from interviews conducted during the 1970s by the author and journalist David Mould, and from my own research and interviews with the survivors. Now, for the first time in 85 years they describe, in their own words, the day Scarborough underwent its twenty-five minutes of hell, its never to be forgotten ***'Bombardment'***.

The author of the letter or verse always follows the piece. Notes relating to contemporary material are suffixed by the date (1914 or 1915), and notes about recent material are prefixed with 'This account was related by . . .' Maiden names have been used (where known) on recent material to provide a reference to 1914. All material is from, or related to, the 1914 attack on Scarborough.

In December 1914 I had just had my seventh birthday and was the youngest son of Warrant Officer Lawrence Reeve, who was in charge of the War Signal Station on the castle with a staff of nine coastguards, one policeman and one boy runner on permanent duty.

The morning of the raid was one of the kind of weather we often get on this coast, dry and mild with poor visibility because of the mist over the sea. The visibility on land was fairly good, but with the poor morning light that one expects in December. At this point I can tell you precisely what happened as far as the coastguards were concerned. We were having breakfast, my father having just returned from duty on the castle when the Royal Naval Volunteer Reserve rating, by name Durant, knocked on the door having come down from the War Signal Station and said (this I can quote verbatim without any hesitation), "There are some strange ships in sight and we cannot make out who they are."

THE CASTLE

1: The Yorkshire Hussars on guard duty at the 'old' barracks. Trooper Stanley Cunningham is third from the left in the rear row.
2: The damaged keep.
3: Chief Officer Arthur Dean outside the wreck of the 'old' barracks.
4: The damaged castle walls.

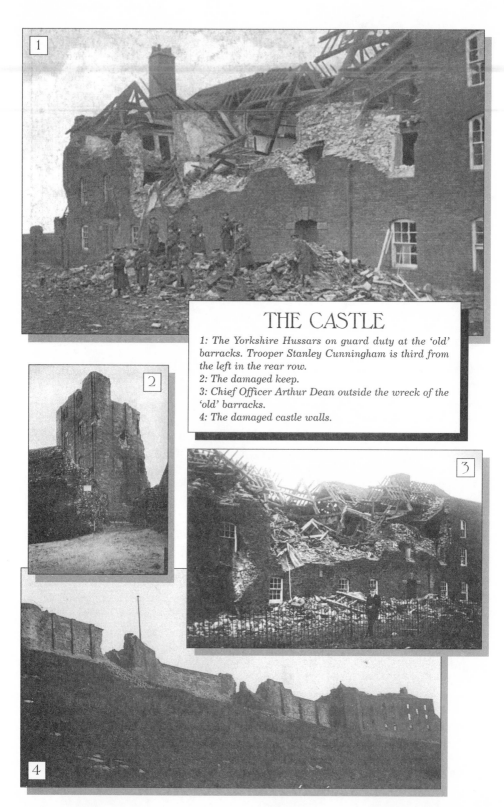

My father set off with him, quickly, running past Mulgrave Hall (where I think there was a military unit of some description billeted). By the time they got into the castle walls the firing had commenced. They crossed the main field (the yard) of the castle under fire which had now become heavy and arrived at the Signal Station only to see it disappear in rubble. The two men on duty at the station had already taken shelter in the arched vault of the Lady's Well, together with the policeman PC Hunter, whose shrapnel-riddled cape, which had been left on the railings outside, was the subject of a popular picture postcard of the time which showed it riddled with holes made by shrapnel.

The lead-bound code and other books were dumped into this well and for all I know are still deposited there. I believe the well has now been filled in.

The officer in charge had no telephone in his house - a matter that was corrected by their Lordships' order on the following day - and had there not been such an omission the lives of my father and his companion would not have been in such jeopardy during their crossing of the castle top, nineteen acres in extent and completely without shelter. I take a son's pride in recognising this as the act of a brave man.

During the bombardment my mother hid us children in the pantry under the stairs, believing we would be safer there. However, I remember seeing Mr Pickup's four girls (he was the custodian at the castle) come running down from the castle during the lull in the shelling, in just their night-clothes, and past our house.

There are one or two points about the conduct of the bombardment by the German ships that may shed a little more light upon what happened. Early targets were the red-brick barracks on the castle wall (ballium) probably on the assumption that troops were billeted there. All the damage to the barracks was at the back and it might be reasonable to assume that the shells that caused this damage were of comparatively small calibre, and taking the raid as a whole it would seem possible that no heavy calibre guns were in fact used.

I have pictures of British warships of the time and they have guns of all sizes stuck on all over the place and in view of the Kaiser's jealous obsession with the standards of the British Navy, there is perhaps little doubt that the German ships followed pretty much the same pattern. Weight is lent to my theory because along the waist of many British warships was a line of turreted medium guns and, since there was a short lull in the middle of the action, I am assuming that these were the guns that alone were used - the lull being the short time taken for the ships to turn around in order that the other side guns could be brought to bear.

In view of the length of the bombardment the damage and casualties were remarkably light and one cannot help but mention that many shells passed right over the town and landed in the fields on the outskirts. The ships had been at sea for some little time and it would be a prudent commander of such a force who would decide to retain his stock of heavy missiles in case of involvement in a naval action, at sea, before his ships could return to their home port.

Many of the shells used were of the shrapnel variety and burst in mid-air. Everybody picked up pieces of shell in the streets and in buildings for souvenirs - where are they all now? We kept for some years a piece of shell-case about three-quarters of an inch thick which was stuck in the door of an outhouse. I think it eventually went back to the Germans - twenty-five years later - when ironwork was being collected for munitions!

LAWRENCE REEVE

1: Warrant Officer Lawrence Reeve, (here pictured in 1913 aged 48) was Second-in-Command at the Coastguard's War Signal Station at Scarborough Castle when it was shelled and damaged in 1914. He also witnessed the submarine attack in 1917 and gave evidence at the inquests.
2: Reeve with the men who served with him at the Coastguard Station on Lundy Island in 1918.

I don't believe that the bombardment had any other than nuisance value for the Germans and in view of the fact that in those days the German people as a whole were humane, I feel that the Imperial Sea Command had no intention than to draw ships from other defence points in order to attack them. The putting out of action of the War Signal Station and knocking down the barracks were probably the only strategic benefit they had to gain; perhaps they made a mistake and intended to shell the Burniston Road Barracks.

I remember rushing upstairs once the shelling had ceased and saw what I believe to be the Kolberg steaming northward to catch up with the other two German ships.

There was no school that day - I attended St Thomas's School on Longwestgate at the time. I believe the school suffered some shrapnel damage. But I can still recall it was several days before I stopped shaking; the whole experience had been so unexpected and frightening.

This account was related by Aubrey Reeve, the youngest son of Warrant Officer Reeve. Aubrey was born on 11th November 1907 (what is now Armistice Day). He was the youngest of Martha and Lawrence Reeve's four children; Annie, Frank and Leslie preceded him. An accomplished artist and pianist, Aubrey served with the Royal Air Force during the Second World War.

Lawrence Edward William Reeve was born on 6th June 1865 in East Sussex. In his mid-thirties, Lawrence served aboard *HMS Mercury* during the 'Boxer Rebellion' of 1900-1901. He was posted to Scarborough in 1908 as second-in-command to Chief Officer Dean. He was 49 at the time of the 1914 bombardment. Lawrence gave extensive evidence at the inquests, and in 1917 he again gave evidence at the inquests of the victims of the U-boat raid, details of which can be found later in this book. In 1918 he was appointed to Lundy Island because of the growing German submarine menace. He died of cancer in October 1919 at the age of 54.

Whilst stationed in Scarborough the Reeve family lived in a house at the coastguard station, a row of Admiralty-built houses opposite St Mary's Church (at the castle end of Castle Road). It was from this house that Warrant Officer Reeve raced up the hill to the castle on that fateful Wednesday morning, 16th December 1914.

I had breakfast with my people about 7.30am, and, having collected one or two parcels and wished them 'goodbye' left the house shortly before eight o'clock. The morning was dull and rather hazy, but not so dark as you would suppose for this time of the year.

I'd not left Rothbury Street more than a few minutes when I heard an explosion. At first I could scarcely believe that it was anything other than firing at sea, but when there was another crash I realised that something out of the ordinary was happening. I rushed back to the house and as I expected found my mother and father in a serious state of nerves. They weren't quite sure whether the noise, which was still going on, was thunder, and were in that frame of mind when they liked to think it was nothing worse. I knew it was no thunder, but did not wish to alarm them. I told them that there was some firing at sea - a sort of practice - but added it would be just as well that they sat tight.

Then I left and made my way to the railway station, for my leave was up and I was due back at Sheerness in the afternoon. I hadn't gone far when the fragments

GENERAL DAMAGE

1: Damage to the interior of W. T. Petch's joiner's shop on Victoria Road. 2&3: Alfred Brown's home at 24 Rothbury Street (the clock on the wall stopped at 8.17am).

of a shell brought a chimney-pot toppling over in Barwick Street. Crash, it came as I was hurrying along! The experience, though it led to my wondering what was really going to happen, did not scare me, for a reason I cannot explain. It was a fascinating experience and I determined to take full stock of things.

Bang! Bang! Bang! I heard the guns go, and I counted seventeen distinct and separate explosions. I saw two houses in West Square struck and demolished, but, so far as I could make out, the firing was out of range; that is to say if the purpose was to damage the town - for the rest must have fallen in the suburbs.

The excitement as you may suppose was tremendous, and as it seems, people came rushing from everywhere, making for what they hoped would be a place of safety. The majority of these were women of the working classes, and most of them rushed along the street with their hair disordered. Many of them had their children with them and most of the little ones were crying. Not a few of them were without shoes and stockings. They made for the railway station, and their condition forced home the realities of war as nothing else has done or could do. These people came from Seamer and all the little places round about.

As I have said, it was shortly before eight o'clock that the first shot was fired. The last fell half an hour later. The flash of the explosives was quite distinct. Precisely what damage was done I cannot say, of course, for I was due to leave the town at 8.30am.

Colour-Sergeant Johnston of the King's Royal Rifles gave this account to a reporter from the *Daily Telegraph* on the afternoon of the bombardment when he alighted at King's Cross station in London on his way back to rejoin his unit at Sheerness. He had been in the town to visit his parents, his father being retired policeman, Robert Clarkson Johnston, living at 28 Rothbury Street. 1914.

Their first attempt was made upon the wireless station, but not a shot found its mark on the station. They next attempted to hit the electric light works, and also directed their firing upon the gasworks, but these shots also went wide. Nevertheless these shots did considerable damage to the property in the near vicinity.

Both my son and myself were injured by the same shell. Shortly after the bombardment commenced a reply was made by the guns at the castle. The east end of the town came in for more attention at the hands of the enemy vessels than any other part of the town. When the firing had ceased there were, I should think, quite a hundred homes in this part of the town in flames. Nearly all of the largest buildings in the town were affected in some way or other. Both the Balmoral Hotel and the Royal Hotel were struck. Nearly all the houses along the sea front sustained more or less damage.

So claimed Arthur Wood, the head book-keeper of the Scarborough Electric Supply Company (situated off Seamer Road and known to locals as the Electric Light Works), who resided at 7 Hanover Road.

Arthur was speaking to a reporter from the *Daily News* on the platform at King's Cross in London, after fleeing the town with his wife and son, Clifford. Both Arthur and twelve-year-old Clifford had sustained injuries from flying shell fragments from the shell which wrecked the Matson Temperance Hotel and Boarding House and sent a commercial traveller running for his life without paying his bill. Both their heads were

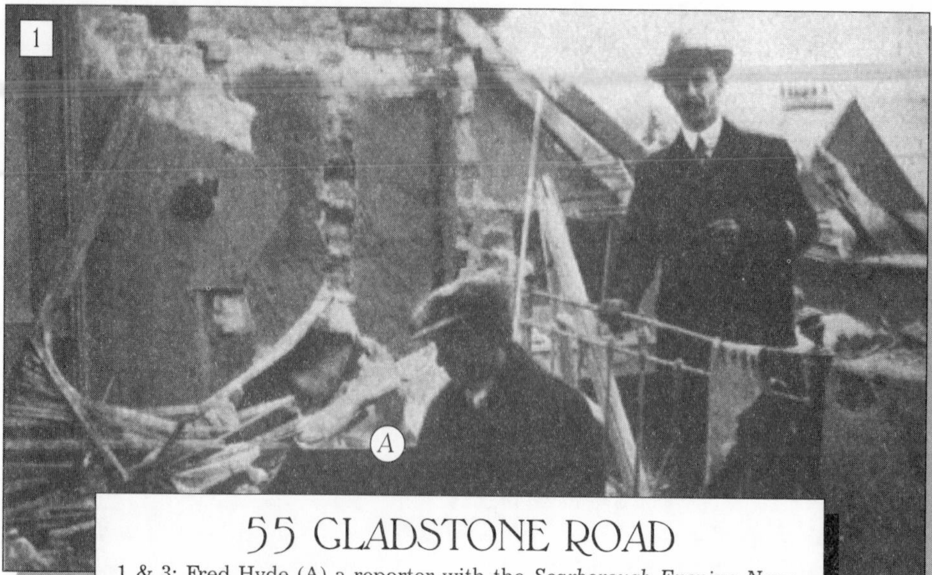

55 GLADSTONE ROAD

1 & 3: Fred Hyde (A) a reporter with the *Scarborough Evening News*, surveys the damage to his home. 2: Bedroom damage. 4: Roof damage.

swathed in bloodstained bandages when they alighted from the 5.10pm train to be accosted by eager reporters clamouring for the gory details of the enemy raid. 1914.

A SAILOR'S SONG!

The shores are blind, the seas are mined,
The wild sou'westers blow;
And at our posts on stormy coasts
We cruise and seek the foe.
Behind their forts in sheltered ports
Secure their ships may be;
But the sea was made for sailor men,
And sailors for the sea!

~

Through fields they sowed we clear a road
In weather they don't feel;
Long watch we keep while they can sleep
Behind the booms of Kiel.
They lock us out, and wait in doubt
For orders from Berlin;
But on the seas we hold the keys,
The keys that lock them in.

~

For blows they dealt below the belt
For mines their hirelings laid,
For things like these that spoil our seas
We're out until we're paid.
In safety they like captives stay,
In danger we go free;
For the sea was made for sailor men,
And sailors keep the sea!

A poem by S. R. Lysaght. 1914.

They steamed quite close to me, but I had no fear of them because I thought they were British vessels. One of them slowly turned and opened fire. I could see the shells flying into the town and clouds of dust and stone being thrown up as they hit the buildings. I thought we should not stand a dog's chance of reaching land safely, but after half an hour's firing the ships turned and steamed out to sea.

This was part of the account given by one of the local fishing vessel skippers on returning to port, after part of the Scarborough fleet, waiting to enter the harbour, had been passed by the German ships. 1914.

While at breakfast they heard a rumble which at first attracted little notice. This was soon followed by a noise which was put down by the pupils as thunder. However, one little Belgian girl who had gone through the horrors before, cried out:
"No! It is cannon!"

1

2

3

THE LIGHTHOUSE

Vincent's Pier, South Bay.

4

And this was soon patent to all, for a shell hit the upper part of the house, breaking all the windows, splitting walls and shattering desks, blackboards and other furniture. The school house was provided with concrete covered cellars, into which the pupils were taken in an orderly manner, where they prepared for an exodus when it was safe to go.

As soon as the firing became less intense, the roll was called, both in and out of the house and a march to Seamer - the first station outside the town - was undertaken. There they entrained for York, whence they were soon on the road to London, which was reached without further incident.

This report was made in the *Beckenham Journal* on the Saturday after the bombardment and was sent to the local paper by John Place, whose children were at the Westlands School, Westbourne Grove, at the time. Mr Place claimed that it was only due to the pre-arranged plans of Miss Wood, the Headmistress, that none of the children were hurt during the bombardment and that they were all able to get away safely. 1914.

SCARBOROUGH, DECEMBER 16th 1914

We mourn not for men who have fallen in battle!
We pine not for wealth we have lost in the strife!
We moan not in fear of the cruel guns' rattle.
We cry for the children, the maid, and the wife.
Their tears, like a river of fire, do torment us,
We suffer for them in our helpless dismay.
When humanity fails in her efforts to aid them,
We turn to Thee, Father - the Truth and the Way.

~

Those dear bleeding forms in their innocent terror,
Cry to us for succour, to aid their despair;
O help us to save them from death and destruction,
Be Thou at our side with Thy love and Thy care!
Our help in the ages long past and forgotten,
To Thee do we pray in our sorrow and woe,
Send Thy holy angels to bless and to cherish,
Look down on Thy dear tortured children below!

~

May we feel Thou art near us our trials to soften,
Let the dark mists of terror be swept from the world;
And over earth's battlements - fearful and beaten -
Let the black hordes of evil swiftly be hurled.
Then shall Thy peace come like balm to our spirits,
The world like a garden shall bloom once again;
Dread warfare shall cease for ever and ever.
No more shall be weeping and sorrow and pain.

This poem was signed simply 'R. S. of Manchester'. 1914.

THE GRAND HOTEL

Foreshore Road and St Nicholas Cliff.
1: The Restaurant. 2: The Yorkshire Hussars standing guard. 3: The roof damage. 4: The Restaurant.

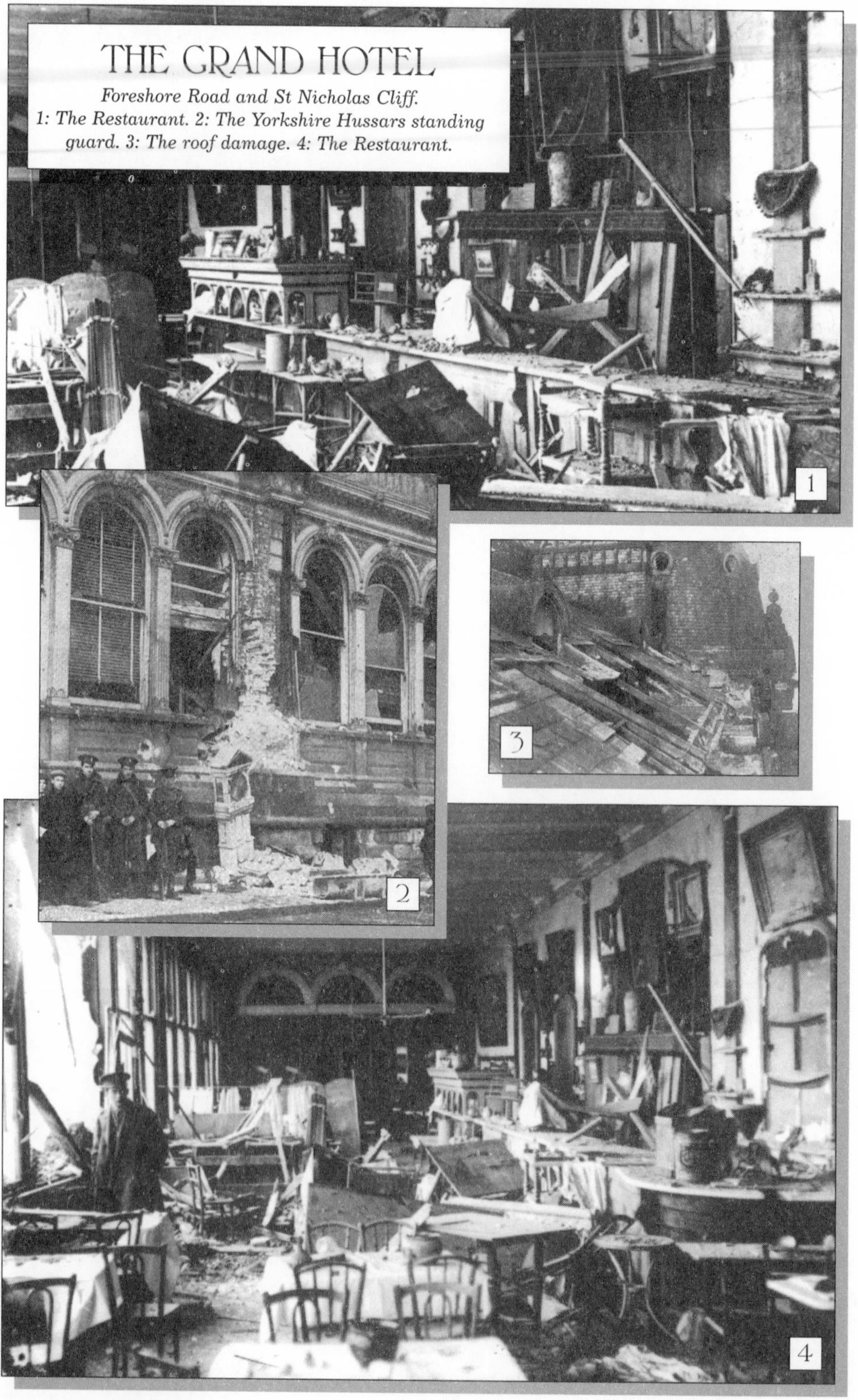

I was still in bed when the Germans paid us a surprise visit on December 16th.

At first I thought that a bad thunderstorm was coming - but that was soon settled. I got up then - about 8.10am - and, while I was dressing, thought it was a naval fight in the bay. I did not imagine that even the Germans would bombard an unfortified and undefended town. I got to the sea front at about 9.00am, but they had sailed off towards Whitby by then. I had been told that our Fleet was after them, but that must have been imagination, for they certainly never caught them. I then saw the wreckage.

There is a big hole in the Prince of Wales Hotel, and the large windows in the coffee room are shattered. The proprietor showed me later a piece of his railing found on the roof of a boarding house, also wrecked, as were other big boarding houses. 'The Grand' is badly knocked about and there is a big hole in 'The Royal'. As far as I can see 'The Crown' is the only big hotel not touched. A chemist's shop and a fine jeweller's shop in the same street, at the back of the Esplanade, were wrecked and two men killed in that street.

The inquest is not finished yet. I expect there will be nearly 20 killed - I have heard of 17 so far. They hit at least three churches, the Parish Church, St Martin's and All Saints'. Also they had a go at the castle - which had been left in peace since it was stormed by Roundheads in 1654 - and at Whitby Abbey too.

I am glad to say the stables, where I had a horse, got off very well; they hit only a large saucepan (in which linseed gruel is made), broke a window and splintered a little woodwork. The horses, of course, were very frightened; mine reared up, tried to get up the wall of her box and fell. I have ridden her since and she is none the worse for it. No horses there were hit. The owner of the stables wants to insure his horses, but war risks are £2 per horse, when it was only 5 shillings to insure before the war.

From the Crown Hotel to the top of the Esplanade there are few houses that have not been hit more or less. A shell landed in one house, went across the garden, through the back wall, across a road at the back, then through two semi-detached houses in West Street. The road crossed by the shell is a back road dividing the Esplanade from West Street. A maid servant was killed in one of the three houses.

Walking about afterwards I saw an unexploded shell in that garden with a sentry in charge of it. I am glad to say that the Royal Avenue got off very well, one house at the top being hit. I am a good half-way down. My servant picked up a small fragment of shell in the garden. I thought the Germans would excuse themselves on the grounds that they wanted to destroy the wireless station; yet it is one of the few things they missed! Though they destroyed a farm nearby. I have not been out there to see - it is between one and two miles away from where they did the most damage.

I have walked round most of the town: no doubt the most damage is done on the South Cliff. I suppose they singled this out as being the residential part of the town, but I am not certain there is not more loss of life in the other part, as they were bombarding us for nearly three-quarters of an hour. I wonder that some of our ships did not turn up. Some people said that the enemy's ships (two cruisers) were two or three miles away - but some people have not the least idea of distance.

I went to the Prince of Wales that evening for dinner; they do not use the big

5TH GREEN HOWARDS

The men guarding the Electric Supply Works premises, off Seamer Road at Beaconsfield Street in December 1914, where Private Bowman was seriously wounded. Captain Huddart (A) and Lieutenant Milburn (B), in front of whom is the nose-cone from one of the German shells. The civilian in the picture is the company's Resident Engineer, F. G. Holden (C).

coffee room (the wrecked room) in the winter. Some of the people belonging to the hotel told me the ships were quite close in and on reading the Coastguard's evidence at the inquest I see they were firing from 500 to 600 yards. I believe there were two or three other enemy ships lying off the bay, but they took no part.

We have had trenches dug and wire entanglements ready for a long time and the men were all in their places. I wish they had given them some volleys; they would probably have killed some of those on board. I do not think the ships could have stayed longer to do more damage. If they had, our fleet might have caught them in the bay and sunk the lot. Scarborough has been full of sightseers the last few days: the ubiquitous photographer began on Wednesday.

PS - One cruiser came from the North Bay, fired a starboard broadside and joined the other in the South Bay; then turned round, and both cruisers fired port broadsides with all their guns.

The unnamed 'correspondent' was writing on the 20th December for the *Green Howards Gazette*. The writer was almost certainly an officer of the Regiment stationed in the town, probably from the 4th or 5th Battalion, as both were part of the 50th (Northumbrian) Division, based at Newcastle, which was providing troops for garrison and guard work throughout the north and north-east, including Scarborough. As stated, he was billeted in a house in Royal Avenue. 1914.

I was born at Gristhorpe village, about six miles from Scarborough on the road to Filey. My father, John Francis Croft, then lived at Town Farm, Gristhorpe. Every morning he went to Scarborough with a one-horse milk float to take the morning milk in large cans to Paxby's Dairy. On the morning of the bombardment he had delivered the milk as usual and was in the middle of the Valley Bridge when the shelling started. A cabby who had just picked up a fare on South Cliff stopped and asked my father what all the noise was, whereupon my father jokingly declared that the Germans had landed. The cabby didn't stop to hear any more, but whipped his horse and galloped off into the town. A couple of days later the pair met up again and my father asked the cabby why he had driven off in such a hurry. The cabby explained that they had been in the middle of the bridge and if a shell had struck it both of them would have been done for. My father confessed he hadn't given it any thought - until then!

By this time his horse had become very frightened with the constant crash and bang of the shells and they galloped up South Cliff and had to pass over all the bricks and rubble outside 'Dunollie' on Filey Road. The shells continued screaming overhead as he galloped over Cayton Bay top. He was very relieved to arrive home safely with such a frightened animal and a light, four-wheel float.

This account was related by F. R. Croft of Norton, near Malton.

THE HUN'S VISIT TO THE EAST COAST

On that cold December morning,
Through the misty dawn they came.
Perchance they thought the coming,
Would add laurels to their name.

~

They shelled our dear defenceless homes,
Men, women, and children too.
To burn, to kill, and to destroy,
Is what they meant to do.

~

Bravely they fought with might and main,
Daring to do or die.
Bravely they fought, for well they knew,
There was nothing to reply.

~

No doubt they'll get the Kaiser's thanks,
For a raid so bravely done.
No doubt they'll get the Iron Cross,
For a victory nobly won.

~

The Guardian Angel saw their work,
And looked on it with shame.
To shell defenceless homes and babes,
Forever stains their name.

~

Fair play is a jewel,
But their Kultur knows no right.
They throw their deadly mines and run,
And shun an honest fight.

~

Base cowards, we shall meet them.
We've an insult to repay.
And when our tars do greet them,
They'll ne'er forget the day.

~

Fight on brave true Britishers.
Fight with all your might.
God will give you victory,
For God defends the right.

By G. A. Deacon of 63 Tindall Street. 1914.

My batman was giving me my bandoleer when there was a terrific noise. Outside the mist was lifting and I saw the ships firing at the coastguard station. We all fell in and were issued with rifles and twenty rounds of ammunition. For many of the recruits it was the first time they had handled a rifle. We were ordered to the gun emplacements behind the officers' mess. As we lay there, shells whistled over our heads; some fell in Peasholm Lake, but we were ordered not to return fire in case we gave our position away.

This account was related by Orderly Sergeant George M. Harrison, who was born in 1884 and was 30 at the time of the bombardment. George was already up and dressed when the alarm was raised at Burniston Barracks. Quite what the 14th King's Hussars stationed there could have done with their rifles against the might of the battleships is unclear. But it was widely felt by many at the time that the attack could well presage an enemy invasion of the town, and this could have been the main reason for the order not to return fire.

At the time the Germans fired on Scarborough in December 1914, I was a 'lad porter' for North East Railways, along with two mates, at Haxby Station near York. We lodged at 3 Railway Cottages and on the morning of the raid (as near as I can remember it would be about 8.00am) when we were taking breakfast there was a violent crackling of the roof tiles. We went out to see what it was, but could see no damage to the roof. We had just gone back inside to finish our breakfasts when it came again, three times, and it seemed as if the roof was moving!

Of course, we did not know then what was causing it as news did not travel as fast then as it does now.

At 11.15am our signalman received a message from the Station-master at Scarborough, saying that there had been a German ship firing shells into the town and he had arranged two excursion trains, containing people who wanted to flee. The trains would stop at Haxby (our station) to collect rail fares as they could not book them on at Scarborough.

We collected £35 in fares from the two trains. An army train went from York to Scarborough to see what had happened and it was three days before the Government told the people through the House of Commons.

Anyway, we put the crackling of the slate roof down to gunfire at Scarborough 35 miles away. People were a bit scared for a time, but it soon died down and life went back to normal.

This account was related by Sydney Allison of York. Born in 1897, he was 17 at the time of the bombardment. Sydney worked all his life on the railways, and rose to become a 'top signalman' at York Station, a post he occupied for 49 years and 9 months.

ARE WE DOWNHEARTED? NO!

German visitors to Scarborough,
Came unannounced one day,
Their stay was short and angry,
They shelled us from the bay.

~

They wrecked our homes and families,
And laid some mines as well,
To try and trap our Navy,
Should it turn up pell-mell.

~

Their plans were laid quite artful,
But they failed to draw us down.
Our tars will settle later,
For this raid on Scarborough town.

~

Our citizens were angered,
By their visitors, the foe,
And though the war has touched us,
Are we downhearted? No!

A poem written by H. H. Hollins of Scarborough. 1914.

My husband was in the Doncaster Yorkshire Dragoons and made me a small horseshoe out of some of the shrapnel he found after the bombardment - he was the shoeing smith.

This account was related by Mrs Sidney of Doncaster whose husband had been stationed in Scarborough during the bombardment (probably with the Yorkshire Hussars, or the 14th Kings Hussars).

We're sorry to hear that so many people have left Scarborough. The bombardment has been a very sad affair for a lot of poor people, judging by all accounts. I've passed the Pictorials on to some comrades in the West Yorkshires' trenches, as there are some local lads with them. William [elder brother] is still with the 7th Division. They are not far from here; in fact we've seen a lot of that Division lately. William goes back into the gun-pits tonight for 14 days, so I shall not see him till he comes out again. Their pits are only a mile from where I am at present, but we're not allowed to visit them. My word! The guns have done some firing this last week. But the weather is awful! On Monday it was snowing all day and William and I were walking round their lines with mud up over our boot tops; so you can tell what it's like out here. You say you wish the weather would take up and let us advance - so do we all out here.

Driver John Jennings, a Scarborough man serving with the Royal Field Artillery in France, was writing home to his father. 1914.

On the day of the bombardment my mother's house on Victoria Road was blown to the ground, behind the Co-op stores. I had visited her the day before and couldn't get there fast enough when I heard news of the raid.

This account was related by Mrs Shearing of Acomb, York. She was born in Scarborough.

As December approached, I was looking forward to the prep school end-of-term play, and to going home. On the morning of 16th December, between 7.00am and 8.00am, as we were getting dressed, the calm was shattered by loud booms. One small boy, thinking the sound was thunder, began to cry. The Headmaster, Lawrence Armstrong, quickly made the round of the dormitories to inform us that the town was being shelled by enemy warships in the bay, and to tell us to proceed with our dressing and then come down for breakfast. With that news the boy who had mistaken the disturbance for thunder stopped crying, whereupon another small boy, who disliked the idea of being under shellfire, took over the role vacated by his friend.

The dormitory in which I slept had a window looking seawards, onto land which contained a large commercial greenhouse. As we watched, the greenhouse received a direct hit and went down like a pack of cards. Not to be outdone by his dormitory mates who had witnessed the untimely end of the greenhouse, another boy gave utterance to the statement that he had just seen a shell pass between our house and the one next door - a remark greeted with a certain amount of scepticism until, on later crossing Filey Road to go to the college, we noticed a number of gashes in the bank between the school and the road where shells had exploded.

Having dressed, we went downstairs and started breakfast. A message arrived from the Headmaster (of Scarborough College) Percy Armstrong, to say that he was taking his boarders across the golf links into the shelter of Oliver's Mount. Lawrence Armstrong (the prep school's headmaster) asked the messenger to take back word that we would follow when we had finished our breakfast.

Breakfast having been finished and the shelling having ceased, we crossed to the college to find our big brothers only just returning from the shelter of Oliver's Mount. We were left to kick our heels while they had their breakfast and we could all go into school prayers together and thence into class.

The remainder of the day passed quietly, and it was announced that we would be sent home the following day, rather than await the previously arranged end of term some days later. That evening the prep school held its end-of-term party as planned, complete with Christmas tree. I still have the address book which was my present from the tree. The next morning we went home.

As to Mr Turner's promise to our father not to leave Scarborough unless accompanied by my brother and I, he had every reason for it slipping completely from his mind on the morning of the bombardment, given what transpired at his home on Filey Road, 'Dunollie'.

Early in the New Year our parents received a letter from the Headmaster informing them that the Governors had taken tenancy of the Park Hotel in Keswick, to which the entire college would transfer on the opening day of the Easter term.

This account was related by Sydney David McCloy who was 11 at the time of the bombardment. Born on 26th August 1903 at Kirk Smeaton, South Yorkshire, he was the youngest of farmer David and Lizzie McCloy's three children. The eldest child was Kathleen, born in 1900, and the middle child was Joseph, born in 1902.

The two McCloy boys were in their first term at Scarborough College (Sydney in the prep school) - having moved from Wakefield Grammar - when the bombardment occurred. Sydney was captain of the prep school's cricket team and can still recall having no difficulty in picking his eleven players as there were only twelve boys who could play anyway! The college was run by the Armstrong brothers; Lawrence, the younger of the pair, being in charge of the prep school.

Sydney refers in his account to John Henry Turner of *Dunollie* (31 Filey Road - where Margaret Briggs and Alfred Beal were killed) who was an established family friend. His wife had been Lizzie McCloy's governess, when Lizzie (then Hinchcliff) was a girl in South Elmsall.

Scarborough College returned from its self-imposed exile in the Lake District in 1916 and was the first of the town's boarding schools to do so. Throughout the war years Sydney recalls that life was a little more restricted, school meals a little plainer - with

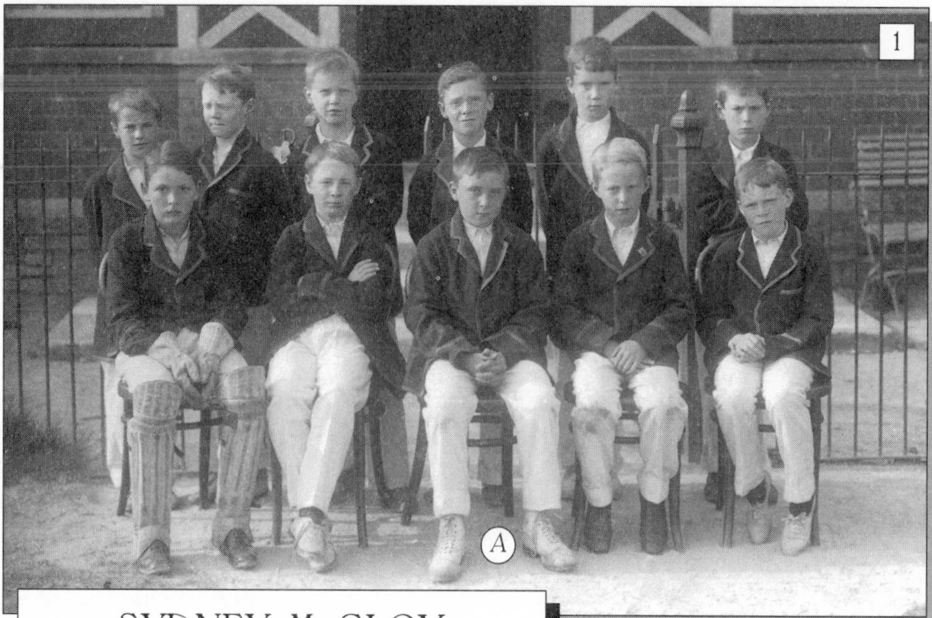

SYDNEY McCLOY

Following the bombardment, Scarborough College moved to the Park Hotel, Keswick. The school eventually returned to Scarborough in 1916.

1: The 1914 prep school cricket eleven, Sydney (A), aged 11, is seated centre and was the team Captain.

2: The prep school Headmaster, Lawrence Armstrong (B), with some of the boys including Sydney (C), during a walk around Derwent Water in 1915.

3: The older boys and Lawrence Armstrong (D) enjoy letting off steam in the ice-cold waters of Derwent Water.

the strict observance of 'meatless' days - and that only on Sundays was there jam or cake for tea, and any parent who ventured to complain was given short shrift by the headmaster. The other major intrusion of the war into the life of the school was the announcement, from time to time, of the death of a former pupil. One such sticks in Sydney's mind to this day; the death of Stanley Johnson of Bridlington.

Johnson had, on Sydney's first day at the college in September 1914, won his Royal Life Saving Silver Medallion at the Aquarium Baths (under the Spa Bridge). The entire school had gone to watch the long and exhausting test and Sydney recalls the hero worship Johnson's feat engendered in the young juniors. Johnson moved with the college to Keswick but left in 1915 to take a commission in the Royal Flying Corps. In 1917 his plane was shot down in flames and he perished.

Second-Lieutenant Stanley Morrell Johnson (pilot), 20th Reserve Squadron, Royal Flying Corps, died of his injuries on 25th May, 1917, aged 18. He is buried at Bridlington, East Yorkshire.

Sydney left school in 1921 and was articled as a solicitor to John Turner's well-established practice in York. Since qualifying he has practised in Derby, Helmsley and Scarborough. In 1935 he married Doris Whitworth (a junior-school teacher at The Mount School - the Quakers' Public Girls' School in York) and had two children; Patricia and James. In 1984 he retired after some 50 years' practising law in Scarborough.

I can still remember today the bombs going off. I was five at the time and lived on Overton Terrace (up the side of the Castle Hill). My dad was a fisherman and manned the lifeboat too. When the guns started he was sheltering under the pier and couldn't get home, I remember my mother got me in the corner of the bedroom and lifted her night-gown round me and kept saying, "God save my bairn."

This account was related by Mrs Shaw of Retford, Nottinghamshire. She was born in 1909 and was 5 at the time of the bombardment.

We were all surprised at the bombardment of dear old Scarborough and can't reckon the job up at all. I've been asked by several of the Scarborough lads here to express our deepest sympathy with the relatives and friends in their sad bereavement. It's very hard lines to be taken away so suddenly.

I can tell you candidly our boys are giving the German swine a hot time of it just now.

I get the newspapers every week and have just received the Bombardment number - when I've read them they find their way to the firing line to other Scarborough boys.

Our camp is knee-deep in mud and we've had rain every day for a fortnight. But I'm one of the fortunate ones. I had a pair of high-top rubber knee boots sent to me by a friend. I go dashing about in the mud with the horses while the other poor chaps in my tent have to pick their way through it; they've christened me 'Sinbad the sailor'.

Our horses are well looked after. We have them in big sheds and they seem very comfortable. I have to wade fifty yards from the sheds to bring the forage for our troops as their boots are no good to get through the mud. So you see, I save my chums from getting wet as much as I can. If we get much more rain we shall want a lifebelt, or else a Noah's Ark.

I hope the boys of Scarborough will see now what their duty is, after what the Germans have done at home. So tell them to enlist and get at the German swine, and avenge good old Scarborough.

Private H. Shaw of Scarborough, serving overseas at No.2 Base Remount Depot, Le Havre, was writing home. 1914.

My father, Alfred E. Anderson, used to tell me that during the bombardment he went up into the attic of our house in Granby Place, Queen Street and watched the shelling through binoculars. He said there was only one ship and after firing the salvos from one side, it sailed towards the South Bay bathing pool area and turned around and then fired the guns on the other side. He said he was surprised it did not get on the rocks it was so close in.

This account was related by Ron Anderson. His father, Alfred Ernest Anderson lived at 13 Granby Place, Queen Street, was married to Mary Elizabeth and was an undertaker.

I was there at the time of the bombardment of Scarborough. I had just joined the Green Howards (Yorkshire Regiment) at Malton. When the shelling took place I was a rookie being drilled on the excursion platform at Scarborough.

It was half an hour of hell and my first taste of war. Soon after it was over some of us were issued with white armbands painted with a Red Cross on them and were detailed to help in the rescue and relief of the wounded.

Rumour was rife and we were told of trainloads of evacuees fleeing to York as it was feared that there was to be a landing of German troops following the raid. Many of the evacuees were in their night attire. But by about 10.00am they had all returned to Scarborough, some only to find their homes had vanished during the bombardment.

This account was related by Herbert Potter from St Thomas, Devon. Private Potter joined the 5th Green Howards at Malton in November 1914. Born in 1897, he was 17 at the time of the raid and made a note of it in his diary.

I was born in Robin Hood's Bay and was 16 at the time of the bombardment of Scarborough and Whitby. Even now I can still remember seeing the ships pass by Robin Hood's Bay on their way to Scarborough and the loud reports soon after. We thought we were going to be blown to pieces.

This account was related by Olive M. Binns from Huddersfield, born in 1898.

WE SHALL REMEMBER

Because we could smite in an open fight,
And we sent your ships below,
You did not dare to stand up fair,
And give back blow for blow.
But by night you stole to your destined goal,

To win yourselves high renown.
What better fun to the murdering Hun,
Than shelling an open town?

~

You must have sighed for the summer tide,
When the little ones on the beach,
And the bathers too, a romping crew,
Would have been within your reach.
To have had a slam at nurse and pram,
On the crowded Esplanade,
Would have crowned your name with splendid fame,
That centuries could not fade.

~

You are shy to meet with a hostile fleet,
And we do not doubt you feel,
A bit of a qualm when you leave the calm,
Of your snug canal at Kiel.
You may turn and flee from our ships at sea,
But your records still shall tell,
How you had a go at an unarmed foe,
And gave civilians hell!

~

Such deeds as these your lord will please,
He will con the list of slain,
Though his heart, indeed, will doubtless bleed,
As it bled for fair Louvain.
You may truly boast of a raided coast,
But the last word is not said,
Till we humble your pride beneath the tide,
We shall remember our dead!

A piece which appeared in the *London Evening News* with the appended initials C. E. B. 1914.

My father-in-law's father was a policeman, PC Welburn, at the time of the bombardment and could always remember going with an inspector up to the top of Jacob's Mount to arrest the people who were signalling from there to the warships in the bay so they could knock out the naval wireless station at the bottom of Sandybed Lane.

This account was related by W. Milburn of Crossgates, Scarborough.

However, despite the claims of PC Welburn, I have been unable to verify the story that there were people signalling to the warships at the time of the bombardment. There appear to be no contemporary accounts and, if true, I would have suspected much to have been made of it in the local press, as tales and rumours of spies were rife at the time and a scapegoat - no matter how innocent of the charge - would probably have been most handy!

2ND/5TH GREEN HOWARDS

These were the men guarding the Electric Supply Works premises, off Seamer Road at Beaconsfield Street, in April 1915, the same month the 1st/5th Green Howards underwent their baptism of fire at St Julien, during the Second Battle of Ypres, and where they fought hard to avenge the shelling of their homes and so earned the nickname 'The Yorkshire Gurkhas'. Many of those pictured, including Lieutenant E. Hilary Weighill (A) were sent to replace the men lost in the Battalion's first action of the Great War.

We had not been up very long this morning, and I was feeding a dog in the greenhouse when I heard a loud noise and a shell went through the drawing-room. Soon after another one came into the kitchen. We made our way into the coal cellar, and had not been there very long before we had to leave our place of refuge. A fourth shell went into the maid's room. I believe altogether about six shells struck the house.

My husband goes away by the 8.30am train, and he saw some ships close in shore. He believes he saw the first shell fired. Making his way to the railway station he was on the front when the ships fired. We felt very anxious indeed about him, but he returned and called out to us. Our car is kept at a garage in Ramshill Road, and he brought it up and called out to us to come quickly. We drove away out of the town and large numbers of people were passed on the way to Seamer - refugees I suppose we can call them. My husband has gone back to Scarborough to look after our belongings. He says that whilst he was in the garage [Crown Garage] getting the car ready a shell came into the building and went through an old warming pan which was hanging on the wall.

Mrs Sanderson of *Mount Lea*, 44 Filey Road, related her experience after arriving safely at nearby Pickering with her husband, children and maid. The Sanderson house was situated on the side of Oliver's Mount where a large cluster of shells fell. 1914.

A nose-cap from one of the shells came through the roof of the house where I was born - 61 St Thomas Street - and landed in my cradle. My mother had just taken me out of it and come downstairs for refuge. Had she not done so, then I should have been killed.

The nose-cone weighed over 1lb. It was kept for a number of years as a souvenir, used as a doorstop and eventually it was thrown away (which I now regret).

This account was related by Clifford Crosby who was a mere 16-month-old infant at the time of the bombardment. He lived with his elder sister, Doris (age 7), brother Bernard (age 3) and parents Margaret and John above the fish and chip shop at 61 St Thomas Street. Had his mother, Margaret, not removed him from his crib he would indeed have been killed. By coincidence the 16th December was also his father John's 51st birthday. Due to the shortage of potatoes at the time John was employed as a tram driver.

Although I was rather young at the time I can still remember the visitation of part of the German fleet that December morning in 1914.

It was about 8.00am when my brother and I were awakened by the first salvo. We slept together in the top room of the house and sat up abruptly, asking each other, "What's that?!" Within seconds we could hear the rushing up the stairs of our parents and elder sister.

As the dormer window in our bedroom commanded an excellent sea view we were soon out of bed to join my parents and sister in the view of the German battleship that had fired the first salvo of shells into the town. We did not know at that time that two more battleships were out of view round the castle hill, also adding their quota to the bombardment, but we soon felt the results of their

79 COMMERCIAL STREET

Charles Herbert's house took a direct hit.

1

2

3

4

5

efforts by the house shaking in the successful shelling of the barracks on the castle hill. The effort to find the range destroyed part of the curtain wall of the old castle yard - it was these shells that were shaking our house. However, we could see the exploding shells hitting the three-hundred-room 'Grand Hotel' - the largest building in the town.

Then we saw the lighthouse clipped by a shell that ended up in the Grand Restaurant, and before that an explosion on the South Cliff. Later we learned this had been at 'Dunollie', a large private house where a postman and a maid, who had just taken delivery of the letters, lost their lives.

Another salvo from the out-of-sight gunboats shook our house to such an extent that my father thought it safer to go downstairs, but this proved to be the enemy's farewell gesture, for within minutes they steamed eastward into the mist covered North Sea.

My father, who was a local fisherman, went off to see if his boat was alright, and my mother stated it was time we got ready for school. So, at about 8.50am off we went to Friarage School - two streets away. But when within sight of the school we were stopped by a woman standing in her doorway who asked, "Where are you going?" When told we were on our way to school she said, "There is no school today. Go back home and tell your mother the school is all closed up."

Getting back home again we joyfully passed on this information to our mother, who told us to go and put our 'Sunday clothes' on and she would take us out to see the damage. Losing no time we were soon on our tour of the town, surveying the enemy's damage.

Out first call was to see the damage done in the Foreshore area, the Grand Hotel (hit scores of times), and the licensed place at the south end of the Grand Hotel known as the Glass House. Here I waded ankle-deep in broken glass from the plate glass windows and the mirrors from behind the bar counters, broken bottles and drinking glasses. Later a man was sent to prison for retaining a full bottle of whisky he found among the debris. Then on to see the Grand Restaurant on the Foreshore Road, and the ruined property at the back of Falconers Road.

Then, after receiving further information from a man in the crowd, we made our way to Wykeham Street to see the ruins of the gable-end house where four people had been killed, then on to see where the castle walls were broken down and the barracks in the centre of the curtain wall too, fortunately unoccupied at the time.

We collected fragments of shells as souvenirs to be swapped later at school for bigger pieces and given place of honour on the mantelshelf or china cupboard.

We were appalled at the number of deaths and of people injured in the raid. However, it was not until later that we learned of the large amounts of people who had left the town during the bombardment.

This account was related by John Cave, who lived at 8 Church Street in 1914.

My mother was one of the lucky ones to escape. She was living with and working for my Great Aunt who owned a tripe shop by the name of 'Lords' (on Victoria Road I think). They lived in a row of houses and mother had just returned to bed when the shelling started. She rushed downstairs just as a shell took the roofs off the houses.

ROBERT HUGHES

1: Robert 'Roy' Hughes, aged 4, in 1913.
2: Llewelyn Hughes with his son, Robert (then aged 2), in the yard of their home at 36 Ramsey Street. It was from this yard that the horrified father and son watched a shell crash through three houses in Ramsey Street.

Then began a nightmare journey to get back to her parents' home in Wombwell. The roads and railway station were crowded with people and she ended up travelling all the way to Wombwell in her night-gown as she had lost all her other belongings.

She told me that a skipper had been bribed to guide the German ships into the bay and that he was fired afterwards.

This account was related by Mrs Iris Burns from Wakefield, West Yorkshire. Her mother, Marion Outram, was born in 1893 and was 21 at the time. Whether she ever came back to Scarborough Iris did not say, and as to the story (and there were many such following the attack) that a skipper guided the battleships into the bay and was later sacked - I think, given the sentiment at the time, he would most likely have been lynched, and that would have made front-page news!

NOW

Shall Huns and Goths and Vandals rage
On hearths and homes fierce battle wage?
Shall riches treasured from the past,
Into fires of hate be cast?
Nursed in freedom shall we be slaves?
Or backward roll the flaming waves?
Now let the clock quick strike the hour,
Full armed hurl down this tyrant power.
With lightning's swiftness and its flash,
With right, with might, with thunder's crash,
Now smite their minions, sweep the sea,
And keep the Empire safe and free.

This poem was written by Bentley Benson. 1914.

During the scramble to leave the town my father took refuge in the fields just beyond Falsgrave Park. Lying prone he saw many shells explode in the vicinity. There was a naval wireless station at Sandybed Lane and it was this the ships were trying to hit.

Just before the war a team of German scientists had been entertained at the Town Hall and at the same time had done a recce of the town.

In Beaconsfield Street, where I was born, a shell burst, killing a soldier and I still have a fragment of the shell which was passed on to me.

This account was related by F. R. Craven. His father was Frederick Craven of 8 Beaconsfield Street. The soldier referred to was Private Bowman of the 5th Green Howards who was severely wounded (not killed) and taken to the hospital in Westborough Wesleyan Chapel.

It started off like any other day really; as the eldest I was getting ready for school - Gladstone Road Infants - and father was getting ready for work. I remember we suddenly heard this tremendous racket going on outside and we both rushed

ROBERT HUGHES

1: Robert 'Roy' Hughes (B), aged 1, with his father Llewelyn (A) and mother, Margaret (C), and grandfather Llewelyn Hughes Senior (D).
2: Llewelyn Hughes and son, Robert (aged 2), in the yard of their home at 36 Ramsey Street.

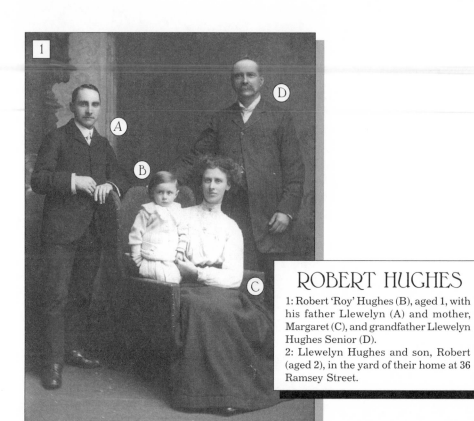

outside into the back lane. The noise was even louder, and suddenly Bernard Morley, one of the 'Jolly Rogers' came running hell for leather up the lane from his morning dip in the South Bay bellowing, "Battleships are shelling the town!"

To be honest though, by this time we had gathered as much. Mother, who was upstairs seeing to the little ones, pushed up the window and called down to us, "What's happening?"

Just then we heard the scream of a shell - in actual fact it sounded more like the steady swishing noise a traction engine makes - and father and I stood transfixed as we watched a shell coming straight at us, skimming the roofs of the whole row of outhouses in the street. It appeared to be tumbling over and over, rather than flying straight like an arrow and could have hit any of the houses in Ramsey Street, including ours, but it went on and crashed down a few doors further on at Mrs Brown's house at number 54. It crashed through her kitchen wall, and had she not been laying the dining-table in the next room at that instant she surely would have been killed outright.

Things quickly calmed down again and we went back indoors, I to finish getting ready for school and father for work - he was a real stickler for being on time and dependable. I think there were a lot of people that morning who were either late for work or who didn't go at all.

I can't remember if Gladstone Road School was closed for the day. I was in the infants and that was apart from the juniors, which was badly damaged.

Later that day I went to take a look at Mrs Brown's house and was very surprised at how small the hole in her kitchen wall was, just two feet across, but the room inside was absolutely devastated, nothing survived in there at all - she was very very lucky to escape.

I recall that for a time after the bombardment we would practice our drill for evacuating the school. When the whistle sounded we were lined up in pairs and marched off across the road to the basement of the dairy on the corner of Norwood Street. It was great fun larking about in those cellars.

After the bombardment there were soldiers everywhere and I can remember hearing the tramp, tramp, tramp of feet from quite a distance before the soldiers, four abreast, marched down the road towards the town and the Foreshore.

Later in the war, just as I was getting into my reading, I asked my father what they put in the newspapers when there wasn't a war on - because the pages were just full of lists of the dead, wounded and missing (I think it was around the time of the Somme in 1916). I was deadly serious, I wanted to know. He told me there were plenty of other things to go in the paper.

This account was related by Robert Llewelyn Hughes (known to his family as Roy) who was five at the time of the bombardment and lived with his family at 36 Ramsey Street. Robert was born on 31st March 1909 and was the eldest of the five Hughes children (Robert, Irene, Arthur, Amy and Betty). Robert's father, Llewelyn John Hughes, was originally from North Wales, though his wife, Elizabeth was a Scarborough lass born and bred.

Llewelyn Hughes was the Chief Clerk for Birdsall, Cross and Black of Huntriss Row at the time (the company later became Birdsall & Snowball). Robert recalls the pleasure of having the whole family; grandparents, aunts and uncles, together within a few streets of each other.

Shrapnel damaged a tree and headstones close to the Garfield Road entrance to the cemetery

Mary Brown's pantry and coalhouse were totally destroyed at 54 Ramsey Street

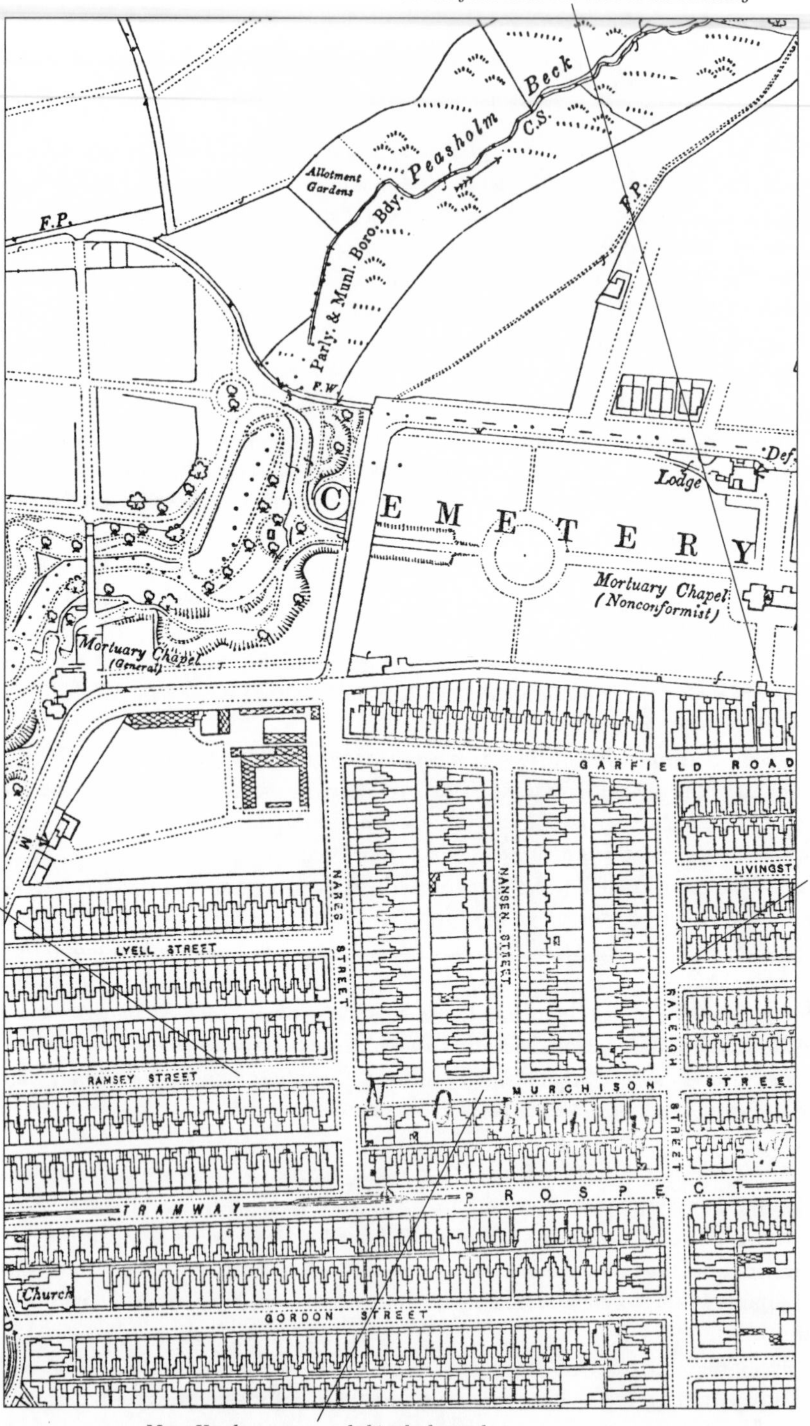

The front room of the sisters Devall at 16 Raleigh Street was completely wrecked

Mary Horsley was wounded in the leg and arm at 10 Murchison Street

During the Second World War Robert served with the Royal Signals and later worked for the GPO on the telephones.

The 'Jolly Rogers' mentioned in the above account was the affectionate name given by the townsfolk to the men who regularly took their morning constitutional in the ice-cold waters of the South Bay, though how many returned to this pastime after the bombardment is not a matter of record!

The ground seemed to lift to meet me. I looked out to sea through the gap in the cliffs and saw the ships coming out of the mist. They were firing - broadside after broadside, gunflash after gunflash.

Farmer's son Mark Newham, had been out feeding the chickens on the Newham Brothers' farm at Scalby Hall, Scalby, when a shell exploded somewhere nearby. 1914.

I was staying with my grandmother and aunts in the village of Scalby at the time of the bombardment in a house next to the church (the orchard and fields that were there then are now part of the burial ground). I remember it as though it was yesterday. A shell passed over the church tower which did not explode but buried itself halfway up Hay Brow Hill - as far as I know it is still there.

Crowds of families came through Scalby marching for the moors carrying their belongings.

The day after the bombing my aunts took me to Scarborough to see the damage - it was very bad, especially on the sea front.

My parents, concerned about my grandmother, family and myself came to Scalby by train and took me home.

I have a friend in Bradford who was stationed as a soldier in Scarborough at the time and he told me the bombing killed some of the horses.

This account was related by George Basil Cooper Halliday from Asenby, near Thirsk. George was born on 20th October 1909 and was 5 years old at the time. He later joined the family business (started by his grandfather in 1872) of agricultural engineers, blacksmiths, wheelwrights, joiners and undertakers. His parents were Basil James Halliday (1869-1953) and Anne Elizabeth Halliday (née Cooper) (1872-1943). George was the youngest of the Halliday children; Charles (born 14th January 1897), Sarah (born 12th October 1898), Lois (born 19th December 1900) and James (born 14th February 1906). He died on 31st December 1992 and is buried in Topcliffe Cemetery, Thirsk.

The grandmother George visited in Scalby was Annie Elizabeth Cooper, and his aunts (her daughters) were Barbara and Emily Cooper.

The last three days I have wished we could have been back in our own home - not for the sake of experiencing a bombardment over one's head, but for that of sharing more closely with the fellow townsfolk of one's lifetime in their distress of mind and soul, as well as to not a few in body.

It seems all to have been such an aimless bravado and outrage, with indiscriminate death and damage all over; government property escaping and churches, schools, hospitals and dwelling-houses, both of the well-to-do and the poor, being hit. When the chimney rattled down on the home of one of our scholars, the two parents and four children just drew their chairs nearer

1

2

3

THE GRAND HOTEL

Foreshore Road and St Nicholas Cliff.
1: Exterior damage. 2: Roof repairs.
3: Sea-facing bedroom. 4: The Restaurant.

4

together in the awful din, whilst the youngest boy, of seven, quietly said, "Mother, God will take care of us."

The ex-Alderman Hall who was mangled in his home and died as they were taking him into the hospital was our office-boy to begin with, afterwards Liberal Agent, always a man of goodwill to everybody. At times the temptation comes - have we failed wholly in life that this enlargement of hell made visible should come at the close?

But when one hears of the fine faith of so many of the young people, sees the brave but thoughtful witness for something better, fearlessly made in Manchester, Birmingham, Leeds etc., and all in a non-controversial spirit, one remembers the words 'in your patience possess He your souls: the coming nearer of the Lord draweth nigh'.

Thus wrote the elderly Joshua Rowntree of 3 Rawden Villas, 12 Ramshill Road, to a personal friend shortly after the bombardment. Joshua was a solicitor and Justice of the Peace. 1914.

Thank you for the Pictorial. We've had a rough time of it this week. No doubt you'll know by now that we've been in action and a very hot time we've had of it. We came under fire last Saturday and were hard at it until late last night. No one who has not been in it can possibly imagine what it's like. Our Battalion has done very well, though we've suffered a few losses. By degrees we got right up to the firing line, and I think we accounted for a few Germans.

I thought of Scarborough and of home while I was there, and did my level best to pay back a few scores. When shrapnel and 'Jack Johnsons' [a type of shell] are flying round you, you don't half think things. You cannot say you are frightened because it does no good being so. You are there to do your duty and that makes all the difference. We know what the Huns did at home after their half-hour's bombardment, but to see poor Belgium after over eight months makes our blood boil. To see the dead and dying men and horses is terrible, but it only makes one more eager to get at the enemy.

We've only had one wet night while we've been out, but we slept out in an open field without a bit of trouble. It's very peculiar, but when in the trenches, and the firing is going on, it does not matter how fierce it may be, you can get a real good sleep without a bit of trouble.

Private Harold Merryweather was writing home to his parents at the Chapman Hotel, Blenheim Street. The Merryweathers' daughter-in-law, Emily, was killed during the bombardment. Harold was an organist at St John's Road Primitive Methodist Chapel before the war. He survived and in 1923 played a major role in the unveiling ceremony of the Scarborough War Memorial. 1915.

Wednesday, 16th December 1914
I thought you might like a short account of today's proceedings. Harold was on duty at the hospital all night, and Lilian and Kath Gunner, the maid, Ethel, and myself were sleeping here.

Kath left here at 8.00am for Marshall and Snelgrove's. Lilian and I were sitting having breakfast, when, at 8.10am there was a huge bang. We surmised

Alice Duffield was killed on the steps of the Granville Private Hotel on the Esplanade

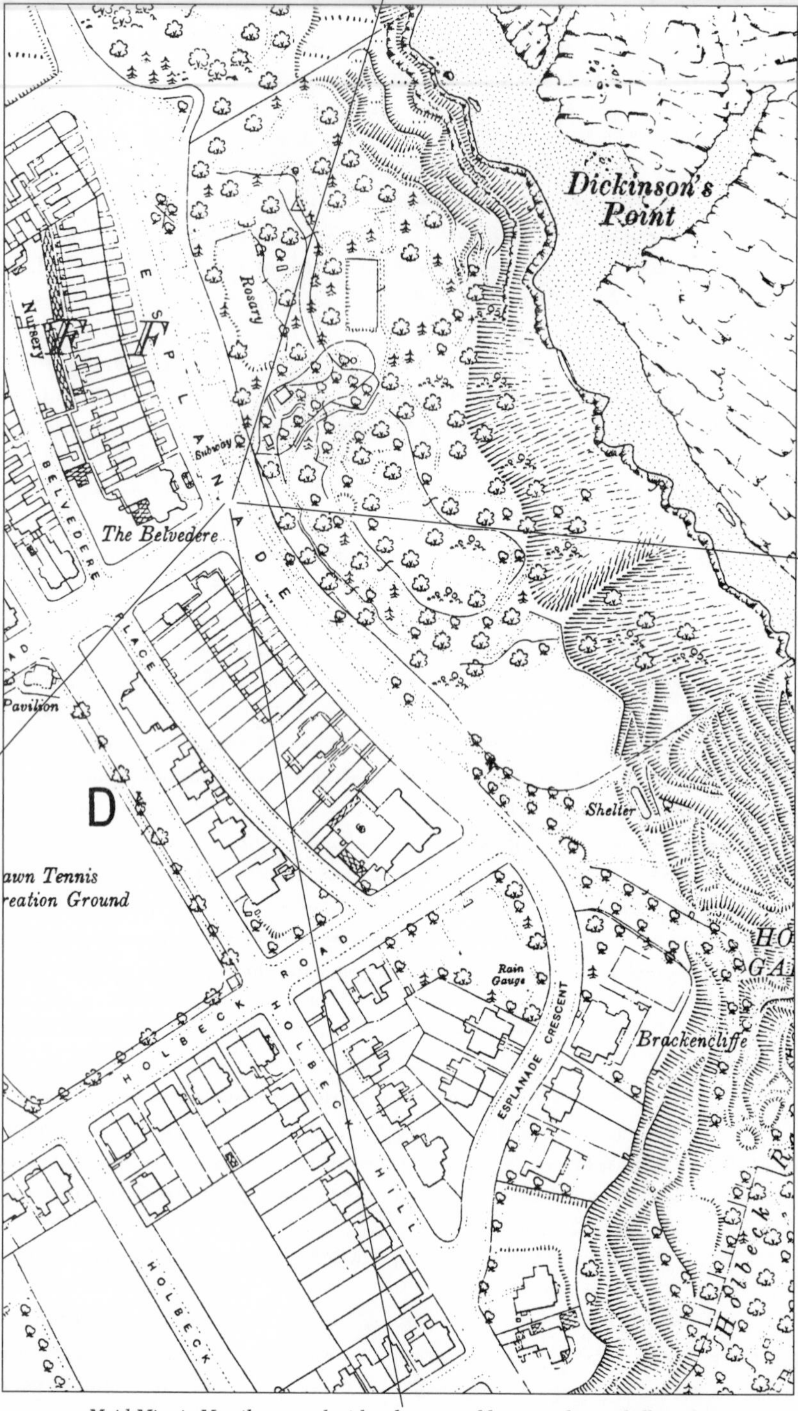

The Bingham property at 20 Esplanade was severely damaged

Two visitors, Mrs Bell-Irving and Miss Bertha Lee, were so badly injured at the Parade Private Hotel (41 Esplanade) that both needed a leg amputating

Maid Minnie Merrils escaped with only cuts and bruises when a shell crashed through the roof and two upper floors of 66 Esplanade, the home of Mr Beeforth thunder at first, but when several more followed each other in quick succession I knew what it was. Still, we both kept up the thunder idea and went on with our breakfast. Forks and flashes of fire were visible over the houses to seaward.

Shortly, Kath came back saying that houses were being hit right and left and that shrapnel was flying about. So we called Ethel in and told her to get her boots on, and Lilian did ditto. Then there was an awful bang close to - and then another tremendous one. I started putting on my boots.

Harold came running up and said, "Come out at once, they're falling all round here!"

So I sprinted with boots unfastened and overcoat on into Manor Road which was full of people. The Brightums were in an awful state. Harold took Lilian, Kath and Ethel over the fields towards Throxenby and I followed with the Brightums.

Shortly the shelling stopped, but we continued out. Heaps of people were only wearing night garb and overcoats. When we got to Scalby Road there were crowds of people with bundles of their whole belongings, handcarts etc., and one cart with a bed on it in which was an elderly lady! It was a regular troop of fleeing people.

Harold took the whole lot on to Throxenby Hall and I returned here and locked up the house which we had left open. I found Ethel's father and dying mother here and gave them some breakfast.

I found the house behind ours was smashed to pieces and there was a huge hole in the field adjoining. I went into this hole and got about a dozen pieces of shrapnel. The hole took me up to my chest!

I then started for the shop. The first damage I came to was a house in Wykeham Street which was knocked to pieces. They were just laying three people out, and I saw a fourth, his face cut to pieces and blackened, being bandaged. Further along, Gladstone Road School's roof was off and houses in almost every street were hit.

I got to the shop. There was no damage there, but there were very few men; many of them were out looking for their own people. A note was waiting for me asking for our van immediately in Lyell Street. The smaller van already had people in it to be taken to Seamer. We stopped this, and one horse rulley which we commandeered for ambulance work.

We heard that John Hall JP had had a leg and an arm blown off and that he had since died.

Ambulances and stretcherers were about in the street all morning. At about 11.00am a message came to the shop saying the father of one of the apprentices was killed. The boy came and told me quite calmly his father was killed and might he go. Then he broke down. One of Percy Cooper's men has died from wounds in the house in Wykeham Street. We closed at 1.00pm.

On the way up I saw more houses practically demolished in the 'common' district and I photographed a lot.

Lilian and Kath were back for dinner. Afterwards we went on an exploration. A summer house in the garden behind here was demolished, so we were fairly near! Three houses in The Crescent are knocked to bits and the Grand Hotel has about five holes. The Foreshore is cut up in two or three places and the Picture House and Foreshore restaurant are properly wrecked. But the Esplanade!

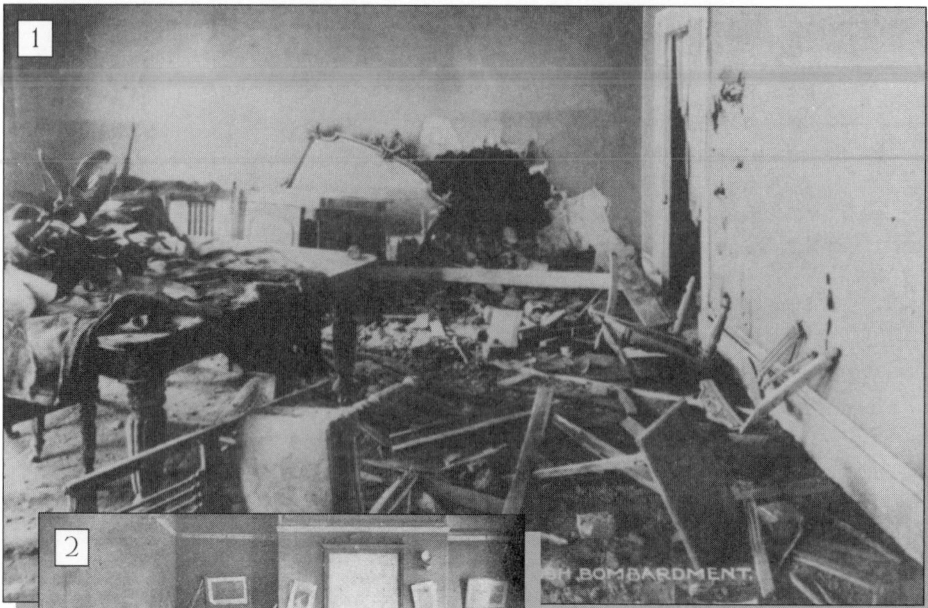

22 ESPLANADE

The damaged home of John Jaram.

MONTPELLIER HOTEL

The hotel on Alfred Street was empty, save for the caretakers, when it was struck.

At Montpellier Terrace and South Street corner there must have been a dozen shells - the place is fairly devastated. The Prince of Wales Hotel, Red Lea and Cecil are all hit, and Aunt Em's bedroom and sitting-room windows are smashed in. Queen Margaret's School Lodge and Hall are both hit and all the girls were marched to Seamer. Turner's house, 'Dunollie', was hit on the porch and the postman and a maid taking a letter were both killed. Dr Thompson's house is also hit, but only slightly. St Martin's and All Saints' are both hit and there are also two large holes in the castle walls. Uncle George saw most of the firing from Riseborough. On our way to Throxenby we heard the firing at Whitby.

On visiting my digs I found the house behind ours was hit and all my sitting-room window was gone and the glass in the room. If I had been in the digs and sitting at breakfast I should have had a sudden surprise!

Deaths are, I believe, 19 to 20, and wounded goodness only knows. Mrs Bethel Sharp is wounded and also her daughter Millie; the former is reported to be dying.

We have three gunboats in the bay tonight.

The damage here was one picture, which fell in my bedroom, and no windows broken marvellously.

The town is worth a visit, the damage is really awful. Heaps of people have had narrow escapes. The Post Office was besieged and the use of the telephone prohibited.

~

Sunday, 20th December 1914

Since the raid the 'lighting of shops at night order' is still more stringent; there are whole streets in which there is hardly a whole window pane, and hardly a street in which there is not some damage by shell or shrapnel splinters, although by now a lot is boarded up.

I should think quite half the people of the South Cliff have left town, and Christmas trade is at a standstill.

On Thursday [17th December] there was a great influx of sightseers into the town, and we also had some 2000 men of the Leeds Rifles brought here, with two machine guns and an armoured car. I am also told that some heavy guns - howitzer types - were also brought here.

On Saturday [19th December] all the shops closed from 11.45am to 1.15am; and from 12.00noon to 1.00pm the Archbishop of York conducted a memorial service at St Mary's. As luck would have it a customer or two, who thought it silly and absurd of us to close because they wanted goods, kept me away from the service. I saw one of the funerals however. The members of the Wykeham Street family [Bennetts]; the father (one of Cooper's RFA men), wife, child and another infant were all in one procession. Two hearses rode side by side for the seniors, the man's with a military bearing party, and then behind an open landau with the two little coffins, followed by a company of soldiers with their officers.

We are protected nightly now by several warships in the bay, and we hear the Germans left any number of mines in and near the bay. So there are a dozen or so minesweepers about. We heard later on Saturday that one of these had been blown up and the crew landed here. During Meeting this morning, at which Maurice Rowntree and George Rowntree were fine, we heard a 'special edition' being yelled out. On leaving Meeting we heard another minesweeper had gone and

THE FUNERALS

1: Albert Bennett with RFA guard. 2: John Hall. 3: Emily Merryweather. 4: George Barnes. 5: Bennett family cortège moves through the town on Castle Road. 6: George Taylor. 7: John Hall. 8: A huge crowd for Boy Scout George Taylor.

some of the survivors were being landed, so we tore down to the beach. The lifeboat was just in and the wounded and dead being taken up to various hospitals; we heard that there is some chance that they may get the boat towed in and save her.

We then wandered on to the harbour and there was the minesweeper that was blown up on Saturday with a hole under her bows big enough to drive a horse and cart through! She had been towed in stern first, but how they managed to save her I don't know.

There is a shell hole right through the lighthouse and it has to come down, as it's most unsafe. We next journeyed onto the Marine Drive. A shell has struck the steps in front of the café, gone underneath the floor, apparently hit against rock and come up into the ladies' lavatory. It isn't half in a mess! Luckily we are tenants, not owners, and our lease ran out this autumn!

No Rowntree house has been damaged, save a little glass at W. Rowntree & Sons furniture stores, and the rumour is already round that we are pro-German and had given particulars of the position of our houses etc. to them, and consequently have been saved!

More funerals of victims are passing here now.

Harold and I were just off for a walk when a doctor's car came round, stopped and took Harold off as he was wanted for ambulance work; where? I don't know.

I've got two rather extra good photos and I've sold the copyright of these to E. T. W. Dennis & Sons Ltd for picture postcards!

The above account was written by local grocer, Charles John 'Jack' Taylor, for his relatives. Jack lived on Manor Road at the time of the bombardment, in a house called *Moss Dene*. His shop was at 20 Westborough. He was obviously a keen photographer and took a large number of pictures immediately after the raid which he later compiled into an account of the event. The 'Uncle George' mentioned is local Justice of the Peace, George Rowntree.

Jack Taylor was a Quaker and thus not only held very strong pacifist beliefs, but also refused to take oaths. Such beliefs were greatly at odds with the general feelings prevailing in the town, and indeed the country at the time and it is highly likely that this is from where the accusations, made against him and his family, stemmed.

There had long been held the belief that spies operated freely and unhindered in the north-east. Many people were convinced there were German spies everywhere and many innocent folk were accused of conspiracy and treason. Local police, already over-stretched, were kept busy investigating and questioning locals and strangers alike. As if to prove the point of their spy theories, people stated categorically that it was no accident that the enemy had chosen the ports it had and at a time when the Navy was placed elsewhere and not within easy striking distance. 1914.

The Brightums referred to lived at 19 Manor Road.

Throxenby Hall, formerly part of Londesborough Estates, was a convalescent home run by Dr Pearce.

Had an awful time for five or six days and nights, as fighting seldom ceases, and one day got mixed up with another. The sights of this war must beat anything yet seen, and you have a faint idea of it in Scarborough, seeing the destruction there, but here you see not a single building left whole in town, village or countryside

KING STREET

1: Stretcher-bearers from the Yorkshire Hussars pictured in front of the wrecked premises of the Kingscliffe Holiday Camp's offices at 13 King Street.
2: Repair work gets started.
3: Troopers from the Yorkshire Hussars outside the badly damaged offices where twenty-nine-year-old Herbert Greenwood was seriously wounded, suffering two broken legs in the explosion which wrecked the building. He managed to drag himself into the cellar, where he stayed during the bombardment.

and added to that, other things, that must necessarily result from such destructive fire - the scene beats description.

Corporal Thomas Little was writing home to his wife at 1 Palace Hill. Thomas, an experienced NCO, saw 30 years' service, first with the Green Howards Volunteers, with whom he served in South Africa, and then with the Green Howards Territorials. 1915.

In 1914 we lived peacefully in the fishing quarter of Scarborough, separated by a narrow street from the Black Swan (known as the Mucky Duck). Nearby lived an undertaker, Mr Slingsby, who would jokingly complain to my father, a General Practitioner Surgeon, that he did not give him enough work, to which my father asked him if he expected his medical billheads to include the undertaker's name too!

But on 16th December 1914 this peace was rudely shattered.

It was soon after 8.00am, and my father was shaving before coming down punctually for morning prayers, which always preceded breakfast, when the first explosion occurred, followed by a rapid increase to a crescendo of deafening uproar.

Looking out of a shoreside window we could see flashes in the mist, and in the street crowds were hustling out of the fishing quarter in all stages of dress and undress, fearing there was an invasion. At that time many of the fishermen's wives wore black shawls instead of coats and men's cloth caps as headgear - but unshod children caused no comment in any season.

As we were being despatched to the cellar the doorbell rang and there stood a young parson holding a bloodstained handkerchief to his forehead. "I think I've been hit!" he said. Apparently he had gone to the sea front to investigate and a flying piece of shrapnel had produced a small flesh wound and a lot of blood.

Children can be thoughtless and one of us, probably quite unjustifiably, commented, "Serves him right for running away!"

Shortly afterwards he was transferred to an inland parish - just in time for a zeppelin raid!!

The shelling lasted for about fifteen minutes, followed by a short respite, only to be followed by a shorter second half, before the ships steamed away through the mist. At this stage we got down to essentials and had Finnan haddock for breakfast in the basement kitchen. That day we were permitted to miss school.

More damage was done to the already ruined castle walls and one shell passed right through the lighthouse at the harbour entrance, leaving a large hole which we saw amongst the other damage when we were taken round the town in the afternoon. On the south Foreshore I overheard one old fishwife declare, "Garn! Boys can do more harm than the Germans!"

In the evening our morale was boosted by a small troop of cavalry riding down the street; maybe they were a poor defence against the German fleet, but a great comfort to us nevertheless.

We children were later evacuated to Ripon for a year or so, where we lived in a cold house at the east end of a terrace with flickering gaslamps, deepening our discomfort.

Many years later, about 1929, when I was a student, I recall seeing the first 'talkie' with Al Jolson. Only part of the film was 'talkie', but we saw and heard a

FALSGRAVE AND STEPNEY

1: Shell hole in farmland near the Wireless Station. 2: Shell hole at Falsgrave Farm. 3: Damage to an outbuilding at Falsgrave Farm. 4: Damage to a house in Stepney Avenue.

news film which included the Battle Fleet exercising their heavy armaments, and, as the deep boom of the guns rumbled around the cinema I experienced a momentary sense of real and alarming terror . . . for the last time I had heard such a sound was during that 1914 bombardment.

This account was related by Hugh C. Maingay who was born in 1906 and was 8 at the time of the bombardment. He was one of the children of local GP Dr Henry B. Maingay of 33 Queen Street, and later followed in his father's footsteps, becoming a doctor too. Dr Henry Maingay and his wife, Kathleen, were on duty at the hospital throughout the 16th December 1914, when a number of local doctors were called on to minister to the town's wounded and injured.

By coincidence my great-grandfather's brother, George Stevenson, was Dr Maingay's chauffeur, and was the envy of everyone at Taylor's Yard, Friar's Entry, for having a telephone installed, so the doctor could summon him at a moment's notice.

The bombardment of Scarborough is my earliest recollection. I can remember our back yard at 43 Stepney Road suddenly being full of bricks as the house was hit. I was put in the front room (the holy of holies - only used on official occasions) and remember watching people running up the street. A lot of people panicked and thought the Germans were going to land. I particularly recall an old man in a 'furry coat' (it turned out to be a dressing-gown) and slippers, with a wall clock under one arm and a bread loaf under the other.

This account was related by Charles A. Pearson from Dewsbury. He was born in Scarborough in 1911 and was just 3 years old at the time of the bombardment. His father was Alfred H. Pearson of 43 Stepney Avenue, Scarborough. The house suffered some damage to the exterior brickwork and many of its windows were broken.

AN EXPERIENCE

'Twas eight of the clock in the morning,
When I heard a dread sound from the sea;
First thought: 'A signal for a lifeboat',
But the second: 'Bombardment - must be!'
So I looked from my bedroom window,
And there to my horrified gaze,
I saw the cause of the thunder,
I saw the German ship's blaze.
I hastily dressed and I washed me;
I gazed again at the ship;
It still blazed and still thundered its shell forth;
So downstairs I then made a dip.
I'd not long vacated my bedroom,
When the windows came shattering in;
And the crash of its breakage (and shell noise),
Made an indescribable din.
My first thought was, 'Down to the cellar!'
But requests that were never so strong,

GLADSTONE ROAD SCHOOL

1: Workmen repairing the roof take a break.
2: A general view of the damage to the roof.

Made me take to the streets, there to see -
A horrified, trembling throng.
So sudden! So startling! The happening;
Each acted his part best he could.
Thank heaven! 'twas eight and not later,
The time saved more shedding of blood.
The Germans may come - they may batter;
Their skill may out-wit for a time,
Our boats which are waiting to catch them;
They may come - they may scatter the mine.
But the end - ah, the end! Whene'er it shall be,
Must be Germany's power undone;
Must be Britain's entire command of the sea;
Must be - End of the new, savage Hun.

A. W. Roberts, a regular contributor to the local paper, writing from The Drawing-Room Lounge of one of the town's hotels. 1914.

I was ten at the time of the bombardment and remember it well. My wife's father was a local fisherman aboard one of the trawlers which arrived in the South Bay that morning. They were unable to enter the harbour because of the low tide and so were at anchor a short distance out. The German warships had evidently followed them in under cover of darkness and the mist to avoid minefields.

I lived with my mother and two sisters at 57 Gladstone Road (my aunt lived opposite us). I had just left my aunt's house to get ready for school (I attended Gladstone Road School - which was badly hit) when the shelling started. My aunt's house [Mrs Pickering, 36 Gladstone Road] was very badly damaged and had the roof torn off, and the bedroom floor blown down into the living-room below. My aunt had a very lucky escape. My uncle had already left for work by the time the shelling started, so he wasn't in the house when it was hit. Our house suffered a little damage, as did number 55 [Holborn Terrace, Gladstone Road]. We just left everything and fled along Seamer Road. We got as far as the Mere where some soldiers turned us back. Then we went to the railway station and in the afternoon caught a train to York, where we stayed with relatives.

This account was related by Ronald H. Ash from York. Ronald was born in 1904 and was 10 at the time of the bombardment. His mother was Rose Ash and the family lived at 57 Gladstone Road. They fled the town following the bombardment.

I had come downstairs for breakfast when I heard the bang of a shell and looked out of the window for signs of a thunderstorm. There were more bangs and then I knew we were being bombarded. I decided to go to the Town Hall. The thought crossed my mind that the Germans would land and as chief citizen, I felt it my duty to see what steps could be taken to resist an invasion, and what arrangements could be made for the speedy evacuation of the town.

As with many people in the town, Mayor Christopher Colborne Graham, *Oriel House*, Oriel Crescent, at first thought the bombardment was a severe thunderstorm. 1914.

14 LONSDALE ROAD

Mrs Kathleen Walker was out at the time a shell scored a direct hit on her house.

I was living with my parents within the precincts of the Scarborough Waterworks pumping station (my father being one of the engineering staff) situated some four miles south of the town [Cayton Bay] and built at the foot of the cliffs with the sea about twenty to thirty feet below. The house, adjacent to the sea wall, overlooked a wide expanse of the bay with a mainly sandy beach and, with a nor'easter blowing, the sea would splash the windows facing seaward.

It was a peaceful place until August 1914, the outbreak of war with Germany, and subsequently a guard was mounted by the Yorkshire Hussars. Three NCOs were billeted in our house, with the privates in other houses and farms close by. Their horses were stabled some ten to fifteen minutes' walk from the pumping station on the higher ground above it, where trenches were dug and machine-gun sites constructed.

The house served as their 'Headquarters' and small-bore ammunition, under the eye of an NCO was stored in the sitting-room. The room also acted as the off-duty quarters for the NCOs and I slipped in, when I could, to play board games with them. They were army reserves who had been called up on the outbreak of war and were family men as far as I can recall; Sergeant Rook was from York, Corporal Turner from Thirsk and Lance-Corporal Prosser . . . I can't recall where he was from. They eventually moved on to serve elsewhere, but the memory of them lingered on.

Of those who replaced them I remember only a sergeant who called himself 'Tiddlywinks' Webster because he was so fond of the game - and my word couldn't he play! To my profound sorrow he was called away suddenly, but managed to post me a tiddlywinks set from Scarborough before leaving altogether.

As I recall there was considerable fog at sea that particular morning, the 16th December, but it was beginning to clear by dawn. Visibility in the North Sea had been poor, enabling a section of the German fleet to slip through the British lines. A warning was issued to all coastal defence units.

My friends, the NCOs, were reporting for breakfast at 8.00am, and we were all together sitting near a window overlooking the sea when the flash of the first broadside salvo was fired - a terrific noise! I thought the house would be shaken down with the vibration. The order 'Action Stations' was immediately issued, but mother - despite all the din and coping with a frightened nine-year-old - exclaimed, "Have your breakfast whilst it's still hot!"

The continuous shelling cleared the fog to reveal a battleship supported by two other ships (I can't remember the class), plus an armed minelayer. Whilst the former continued the bombardment, the minelayer sailed on a southerly course. This caused the pumping station guard to anticipate a landing party being put ashore to blow up the works, in addition to the minelaying operation.

Alarmed for the safety of mother and me, the corporal remaining at HQ (the house) escorted us out of the works, suggesting we go to the village about a mile inland [Cayton]. So no breakfast for me! And no school!!

The bombardment lasted about 18 minutes, but no shells fell anywhere near the pumping station, neither was there an attempted landing. There was damage in Scarborough and fatalities and injuries, but the damage was small by comparison with the amount of shelling, perhaps because the ships had come too close inshore (due to the fog) and used too much elevation on their gun settings, causing the majority of the shells to fall on the open hillside behind the town.

MARINE DRIVE & SEA WALL

Minor damage was done to the sea walls and property on Marine Drive.

We were allowed home before nightfall to the accompaniment of more noise, for a flotilla of British minesweepers had arrived and explosions continued at intervals over three or four days as the mines were detonated. One of the minesweepers was lost in the operation. Obviously, the object of the mine-laying operation by the Germans was to sink any British ship which might be in pursuit.

One wonders why they targeted a largely residential town with such gun power. Despite a common rumour that a German Brass Band who visited the town previously were spies, error by the navigating officer on the flagship was more likely to have been responsible. With poor visibility the coast at this point might have been mistaken for Teesside, where the ships sailed after shelling Scarborough. Maybe the real target was the Wearside shipyards.

Some of the guards were more nervous than us and at times we felt safer at home without them, especially when they held a loaded rifle with a fixed bayonet attached - perhaps they were not used to the cry of the sea birds and mistook them for the enemy!

This account was related by Stanley Sewell who was nine years old at the time of the bombardment. He was born on 14th January 1905 and was the only child of George and Eleanor Sewell. At the time Stanley attended Cayton Village School and later worked on Cliff Farm for local farmer Edwin Jackson. Educated through correspondence courses, Stanley went on to work for Scarborough Corporation Waterworks and later went into the construction industry. After retirement he went to live on the Isle of Man.

WAR ON EARTH, ILL WILL TO MEN

Ere yet the orb of day the cliffs had kissed,
The German raiders came on through the mist;
Before the people knew the foe had come,
The shafts of death found many hearths and home.
On wings of death, the shells flew thick and fast;
The victims little thought that day their last.
Ah, no; they knew it not; oh! Mighty God:
Help us to bow before the chastening rod.
Strange paradox; in season of goodwill,
How deep the stain: the innocent to kill.
Their dreadful work began, and with the sound,
Of vibrating thunder shook the ground.
The peaceful residents shot down by shell,
Their homes destroyed in mangled ruin fell.
Devoted town, lulled by the night to rest,
Ere, yet, night's shadows cleared - were deep distress,
By mortal woe - by remorseless foe,
Who broke all ties, and laid all comforts low.
The mourners for their loved ones sigh and weep.
For the untimely end of those that sleep.
All those cut down in childhood's early bloom,
Bereaved ones fain have saved them from the tomb.

Relentless foe, thy sun will set in blood,
For vengeance will o'ertake thee like a flood.
Thy murdered victims speak as from the sod,
Whose cry will reach the ear of the just God:
Soon time, resistless time, a change will bring,
When he that caused the war be a breathless thing.
And my last prayer shall be for England's weal,
Helper of the weak - for their sorrows feel;
The day of peace will dawn - though hid from sight,
And liberty once more shall conquer might.
Summer winds shall sing o'er our fallen brave,
And gently sigh around our heroes' grave.

By Thomas Lonsdale of Scarborough. 1914.

The first thing I remember was my father calling upstairs to my brother [Ted] and myself that we had to get up as we had all overslept and that it had gone 7.30am. I got up straight away, went to the window to draw the blind up and let some daylight in, but it was no use - it was still a very dark morning. There was a dismal and sinister outlook, as well as a humid atmosphere.

When we got downstairs mother had prepared the breakfast and father was having a shave in the scullery. It was about five minutes to eight. Mother said she would go and open the shop doors; father always believed in having the shop open at eight o'clock.

At 8.00am I heard the first sound of what I thought was thunder, but turned out to be gunfire. Mother dashed back to the kitchen and asked in a very frightened voice, "Whatever is it?"

The sky to the east was lit with flashes of fire. What could it be?

It turned out to be gunfire and it was the start of people moving along Gladstone Road in large numbers, making for the country outside the town and away from the buildings.

In Brook Square there lived a small colony of Italians. They were the ice-cream sellers. They took the ice-cream churns out of the carts and put in some of their belongings and off they went. It was several months before we saw them again.

At about 8.15am the gunfire stopped, but only for a few minutes. In that stoppage I ran out of the shop and picked up a piece of shell which was in the middle of the road. It was hot when I picked it up, but I was able to get back with it and kept it as a memento of the occasion. One of my grandsons has it now.

Then the gunfire started again and more people were going past the shop. Father told us to open the cellar doors and people went down there for shelter, but it soon got full. At 8.30am the gunfire stopped altogether. The people in the cellar came out and went home. The St John Ambulance people started to carry past dead people on their handcarts on their way to the mortuary on Dean Road. The men looked pale and nervous. It was an unpleasant job for them to do.

The nearest bad damage to us was at the corner of Gladstone Road and Candler Street. Our house was 45 Gladstone Road and these two semi-detached houses were numbers 53 and 55. A shell had taken most of the roofs off. A lot of roof timbers and slates were scattered over the front gardens as far back as our corner. At Norwood Street, number 36 was hit at the rear and when the occupants opened their bedroom door they found the landing and staircase had been sliced clean off. In Rothbury Street number 24 was a complete mess. All of these were in our area and although bad, they were nothing like what had occurred in other parts of the town.

At 8.45am our provision hand and the apprentice arrived; a postman was delivering letters; milkmen were on the move with their churns; a horse-drawn lorry was on its way to the Roscoe Street coal depot.

One daily job that had to be done was to go and collect orders from our customers. They all had special days when they had their usual weekly order. Wednesday was not a very long list as it was half-day closing at one o'clock. The orders were packed into boxes and our horse-drawn dray delivered them. Before I set off on my round I went on my bike to Aberdeen Walk where my girlfriend [Violet Wroe] lived, to see how they had managed during the bombardment. The house was locked up back and front, so I put a note through the letterbox to say I would be back in the afternoon.

At one o'clock the shop was closed and we went in to have a good dinner which mother had prepared for us; and we were all ready for it. By 2.30pm I had changed and went again to Aberdeen Walk to find they had all returned. They had done what a lot of people had done and joined the scores of those making for the country.

My friend and I then went for a walk up on the South Cliff. All along the Esplanade houses and hotels had been hit and big holes had appeared in the buildings. At the Belvedere, a large shell had gone through the front of the house, right through the building, out through the back wall, across a rear lane, and then through the rear of a house in West Street, killing a maid who had been preparing breakfast, then it smashed its way out through the front of the house and ended up on the grass lawn unexploded.

We went through to Filey Road and saw what had happened there. The worst damage was at the building called Dunollie. A postman had been delivering letters to a maid at the door when a shell hit the building and blew the postman and the maid and the bag of letters to bits.

We made our way home after this. I had tea with my friend and then decided we would do without going to the theatre or the pictures. I wasn't sorry. It had been a trying day and I think many people were dreading the night and what might follow. That evening the Mayor had a message in the Evening News asking people to stay calm and not to take any notice of the baseless rumours that were being circulated.

This account was related by Harold Charles Atkinson who was 23 at the time of the bombardment. He was born on 21st August 1891 in Scarborough (at the family grocers shop at 1 Rothbury Street).

The shop mentioned above was that of his fifty-one-year-old father, Charles Atkinson (born 30th April 1863), and was a general grocers situated at 1 Rothbury Street. The Atkinson family lived in an adjoining house at 45 Gladstone Road. Harold's mother was called Annie (Tomlinson) and she was born on 4th May 1864 making her fifty at the time. His brother, 'Ted' (Edward), was born on 28th December 1896 and was eighteen at the time of the bombardment.

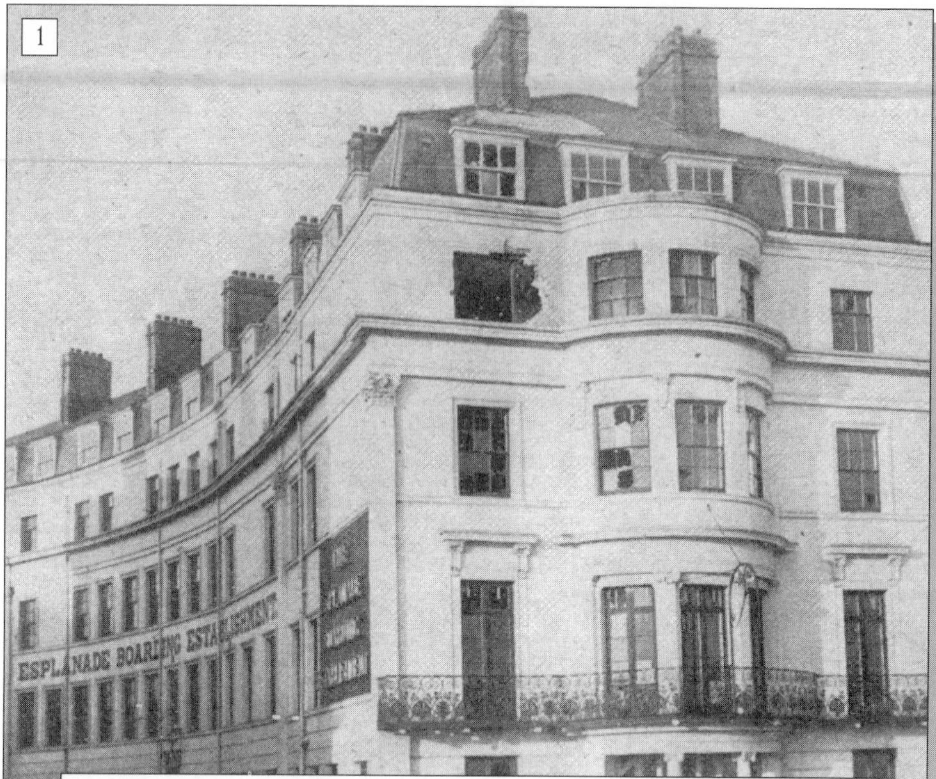

ESPLANADE BOARDING ESTABLISHMENT

Councillor Frank White's hotel suffered substantial internal damage.

Later in the war Harold Atkinson served with the King's Own Yorkshire Light Infantry in Tipperary, Ireland. He became a Corporal and a Lewis Gun instructor. After the war he rejoined his father in the family business and remained in it all his working life.

The girlfriend mentioned in the account was one Violet Wroe, whom Harold married on 22nd September 1920. Harold was a founder member of the Bulk Order Buying (BOB) organisation and remained as a director after retirement until the age of 70. He was President of Scarborough Grocers' Association, a member of the Conservative Club (since 1914), an honorary member of Scarborough Cricket Club and a member of the local Probus Society. He died in 1980 aged 89, but had wisely thought to write down his memories of that fateful day for his daughter Dorothy.

I remember a shell whistling over Scalby village and embedding itself in the earth bank above Prospect Farm, but it didn't go off.

This account was related by May Thompson who was just four at the time. She was born in 1910 and lived at 10 Mount Pleasant, Scalby, in what was the telephone exchange run by her mother and father, Oliver and May Thompson. May recounted this snippet to her son (John) many years later. Strangely, her brother Arthur, then aged six, never mentioned the bombardment. Oliver Thompson, a joiner by trade, served with the Royal Flying Corps in France. He 'dropped dead' in the *Nags Head*, Scalby, at the age of 72.

Dear Harry & Ethel,
You will know by this that we have been shelled and I suppose exaggerated accounts will have reached you. We are all safe and sound but most people we are interested in live next door but one to a house that has been struck.

Mabel thought they were delivering coals rather noisily next door and then we decided we were having an unseasonable thunderstorm; she went into the yard to see what was happening and saw a shell strike 54 Ramsey Street [Mrs Brown's] - it smashed in the scullery and made a sad mess of the whole back of the house. A bit of the iron fall pipe fell in our yard and bits of shell further away, so Mabel had a narrow squeak.

A house in Ireton Street, two doors from yours [number 22], was similarly smashed. A shell struck the house next door but one to Mrs Dobson's and smashed all the windows within 100 yards. Another fell in a yard close to George Dobson's, but didn't burst.

Merryweather's wife killed. Postman Beal was delivering a letter to a servant girl on the South Cliff when a shell fell and killed them both.

Ex-Councillor John Hall was killed.

Uncle Robert was delivering milk at a house in Falsgrave when a splinter struck his trousers pocket and scattered his money: he has a rather nasty flesh wound.

Aunt Mary's house is the first uninjured one in the row - all the windows smashed in 136, 134, 132 and so on. Gladstone Road school is 'broken up' in a literal sense, a shell through the hall roof - much damage in all rooms overlooking Wooler Street. Central Junior School also damaged, All Saints' Church also; Castle walls damaged - keep untouched. The Grand Hotel was struck in several places; also Royal Hotel and Town Hall.

MARSHALL & SNELGROVE

1,2&3: Damage to workrooms facing the sea.

1

2

3

MAC'S CAFE

4: An unbroken mirror.
5: Interior damage.
6: Exterior damage.

4

5

6

I counted four holes dug by shells in the gardens - one in Hopper's, one in Morley's, close to the greenhouse which is demolished, one in Collier's, just beyond mine. My corporation hut is damaged and some panes in the greenhouse broken.

The wireless station is intact, but Falsgrave Park and the fields all around are pitted like a smallpox patient. We can't get to know the number of killed, rumours vary from nine to seventy. There are very large numbers of injured. Amy King has a bullet in her back - nothing serious. A woman and two children killed at the end house in Wykeham Street - the first house on the right after crossing the bridge.

They must have fired hundreds of shells - it lasted half an hour. Began, I think, a few minutes before 8.00am. We sat down to breakfast just after 54 had gone, but we didn't eat much. Mabel couldn't manage more than a cup of tea. The boys and I did fairly well.

Frankie wouldn't believe it - "The British were practising." When he did believe it he shed a tear or two, but nobody set him the example of getting excited. Geoff was very pale. Walter asked questions and made jokes and looked worried by turns and I felt rather shaky and ready for breakfast all the same.

I went to school but the children didn't come in large numbers. Panic-stricken people tramped half-dressed to Seamer, Scalby and Ayton and went to York and Leeds by train. The tramps tramped back - many only half-dressed, for shells fell in all the villages. It's a day we shall never forget. The town is a sight! Scarcely a street without a damaged house.

I saw a corner knocked off a house on the South Cliff and bloodstains on the broken stones. A servant maid had been killed in the corner room. The north side seems to have suffered least. I only saw one damaged house on the front. A shell seems to have burst in the air in Murchison Street. No sign of anything struck, but the windows shattered in about twenty houses on both sides of the street.

Everybody has splinters of shell as souvenirs - a piece was picked up under Mr Northorp's chair in his private room, it had cut a clean hole through the window.

There is no news in the paper but the Press Bureau News, so we are wondering what has been done at Hartlepool. Rumour says 'hundreds killed'; but probably that is an exaggeration.

We feel very tired - I feel as though I had been awake about two days and nights - very heavy eyes and sleepy.

The boys have essays on the way about 'Boyes' Christmas Display'.

Frankie gravely expressed the opinion that if he had been writing during the bombardment he would have made a mess of it. I dare say he would!

Dare you come home for Xmas now?

I've heard nothing of any of Ethel's people, but no news is good news and I suppose they will be writing.

No more now,

From your affectionate brother, Frank.

This letter was sent by schoolteacher Frank Drake of 44 Ramsey Street to his family staying at 57 Cartington Terrace, Heaton, Newcastle. It was posted at 9.50pm on 16th December 1914, the evening of the bombardment. Mrs Dobson lived at 15 Ireton Street, and George Dobson (the son of John Dobson) at number 20. 1914.

PROSPECT ROAD AREA

1: Alfred Coates' roof at 69 Gordon Street. 2: Mary Horsley of 10 Murchison Street was wounded in the leg and arm. 3: Shell hole in a field on Manor Road. 4: View of damaged roof on Manor Road from *Moss Dene*, home of Jack Taylor. 5: Thomas Place was wounded outside 153 Prospect Road.

AFTER THE RAID

Durham and Yorkshire, honoured names ye bear,
Noble your record and your role of yore.
Struggle and triumph have been yours to share,
Oft with your sister counties. Now once more
Trial hath come upon you, and the roar
Of hostile cannon, dealing death and pain
In spiteful mockery of the code of war,
After long quiet hath been heard again,
Leaving a ghastly tale of babes and women slain.
Yours is the loss, the honour yours as well.
These, whom you mourn, as faithfully have died
For King and country, even as if they fell
In that grim battle by the Yser's side.
Spread ye the tale of slaughter far and wide
To rouse the anger that these deaths demand.
Be the effects of war exemplified
To young and old throughout our native land,
That seeing they may know, and hearing understand;
That they may learn, and act on what they know,
At last persuaded where their duty lies.
'Tis here we suffer; yonder let the foe
Feel our attack. What boxer wins the prize
Who upon nothing but his guard relies?
If by this blow the backward shall be stung
To see, not visions, but realities,
To hear the trumpet that so long hath rung,
Not vainly have we lost our innocent and young.

Written by R. H. Forster. The reference made to the Yser regards the fighting in Flanders about the Yser Canal. Within a matter of four short months the 4th and 5th Battalions of the Green Howards would be fighting almost hand to hand against the Germans on those same canal banks. 1914.

I hear the Germans have bombarded your town and I want to know who is killed. We are all right here.

Tell the lazy young men of Scarborough that they would be blown off the face of the earth if it was not for the Army and Navy. People will know now whether it was right or not to remove the Garrison Artillery from Scarborough.

The beer is not worth drinking out here, but we get plenty of cigarettes and tobacco.

It is a disgrace to hear of so many watching football when there are hundreds of poor people being turned out of their homes by these awful cowardly Germans!

Private R. Banks of the 3rd King's Own Hussars, part of the Corps of Hussars with the BEF, was writing home to his parents at 23 Trafalgar Street West. 1914.

SOUTH STREET

1: Charles Smith outside his boarded-up shop holding a piece of the shell which did the damage. A portrait of Lord Kitchener hangs from the boards and below it the insciption reads 'Are we downhearted? No.'
2&3: Clare & Hunt's Chemist shop.

I was getting ready for school, when at about 8.10am I was frightened by the shattering noise of a bursting shell. Half-dressed, I ran downstairs and heard our charlady telling mother it was only gun-practice from the castle. But the firing went on and the woman eventually ran home.

Mother thought it must be an invasion and started collecting her valuables, and gave me some new boots to carry in case we had to run away. I remember she put on two warm coats, but in her hurry put the shorter one on top!

After a time there was a lull in the firing as the ships turned round, but not for long.

We lived in Albion Road, opposite Sarony's (now a car park) and that large house was full of soldiers. There were trenches cut into the Spa grounds and some soldiers who had been in them that morning were now running away - which I thought very strange, especially if we were being invaded.

When the firing finally stopped I ran outside, hatless and coatless, and joined my school-friend at the end of South Street. Clare and Hunt's chemist shop had had a shell through it (which killed a Salvation Army man who was cleaning up outside). The shell had travelled across the road and through Charles Smith's antique shop, but it did not explode. The windows were shattered, but a photograph of Lord Kitchener hanging inside was untouched.

I picked up many pieces of shrapnel, but dropped most of it as it was hot. I thought there would be bullets on the ground, not sharp bits of metal. We dare not go to bed that night, thinking the Germans would come back again.

This account was related by Muriel Brown. Born in 1902, Muriel Brown (married name) was twelve at the time of the bombardment and lived on Albion Road. Sarony's was one of the town's most well-known local photographers. It would appear the house was being used as billets for one of the military units stationed in the town.

From the safety of Ravenscar there was nothing sinister-looking about the three battleships which ploughed their way southward that morning. In fact, those villagers who did see them quickly turned back to their labours without giving them much thought, and mothers with children attending the Municipal School in Scarborough urged them to hurry up or they would miss the school train.

I lived with local businessman Sidney Carter at the time, and had been sent to the chauffeur's house to tell him the car would be needed at 9.30am to go into Scarborough.

I had a very clear view of the ships as they passed opposite Station Square, but thought no more of them until we neared Scarborough on the coast road, when we saw far more people than usual walking away from the town.

Arriving at the station, where crowds were packed around the booking office, we learnt of the tragic events that had taken place earlier that morning. Mr Carter nevertheless decided to travel to his Leeds office as intended.

After seeing the train off we drove down Westborough to the Post Office to send telegrams to his office and relations in the West Riding. Whilst the chauffeur was in the Post Office, fighting his way through the crowds to carry out his task, we (my younger brother and I) sat outside in the car until an army officer approached.

After asking us what we were doing there he ordered us out, saying that he was commandeering the car and chauffeur to take him to West Hartlepool.

SPRING BANK

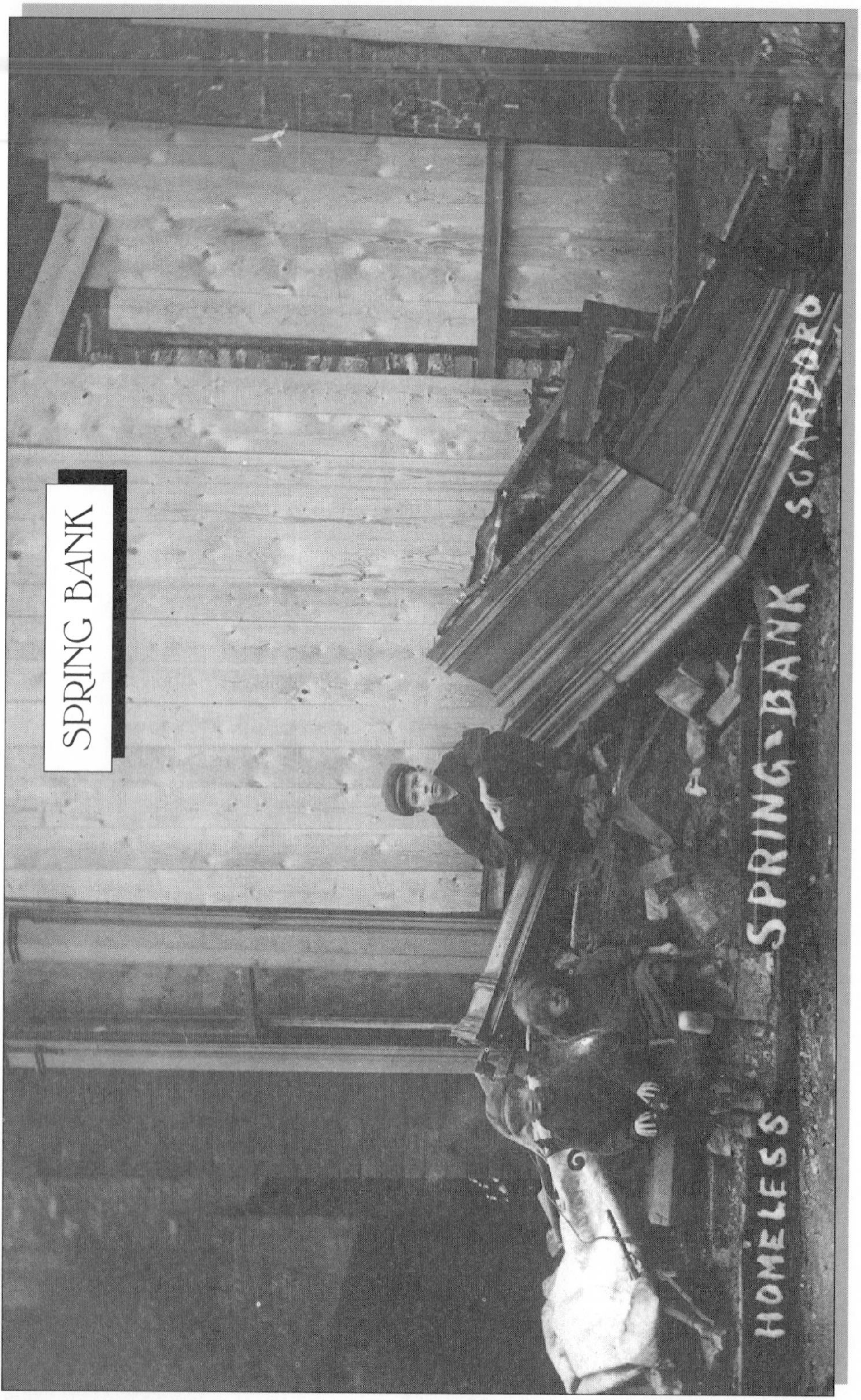
HOMELESS SPRING-BANK SCARBORO

I remember that my brother and I were delighted with this news as it gave us an opportunity to travel by train back to Ravenscar.

This account was related by Frank Green.

AN INNOCENT VICTIM

Doctor and nurse were busy,
'Twas through the German raid;
And many were the victims,
In the hospital laid.

~

On one white cot was lying,
With grim, determined face,
A badly wounded youngster,
A most pathetic case.

~

His feeble voice, when speaking,
With eagerness did ring;
'My daddy is a soldier brave,
Who's fighting for the King.
And when he hears they've hurted me,'
He said with eyes aglow,
'You bet your life my daddy will,
Give them what for, I know!'

~

Then to the eyes of those around,
The tears came fast and hot;
To see the youngster racked with pain,
So bravely bear his lot.

~

Poor child! He never lived to see,
The Germans made to pay;
The little hero's spirit fled,
To heaven the following day.

This moving piece was written by Edythe Barker of 129 Queen's Parade. 1914.

With the exception of our maid [Ida Coates] we were all in bed at the time of the first shot. I was just sitting up preparatory to getting up, and from the window at the foot of my bed I could see the flames in the sky as the shots raced across. The first one sounded like an extremely loud peal of thunder, but at the second I shouted out to Mabel, [sister] "It's the Germans!"

We all dressed more quickly than we ever did in our lives, into our best clothes. We thought that if we had to leave home and everything, we would at least be as well clad as possible.

The whole bombardment only lasted for about half an hour, from 8.00am until just after 8.30am, with a short interval in between, during which the ships turned

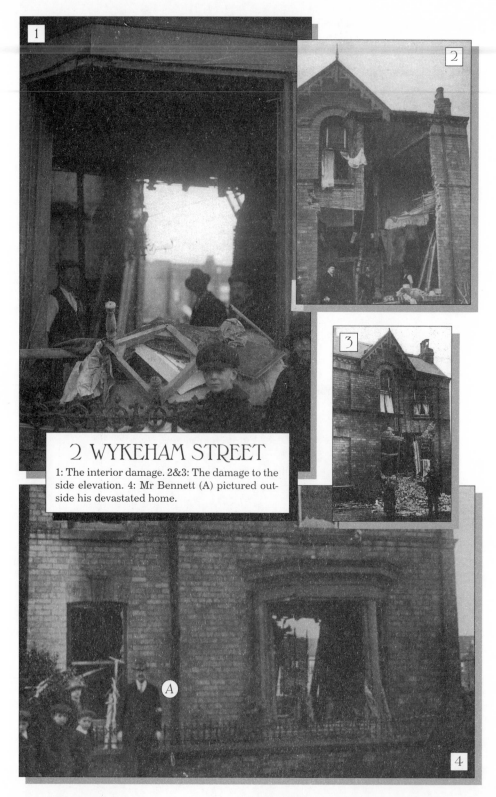

2 WYKEHAM STREET

1: The interior damage. 2&3: The damage to the side elevation. 4: Mr Bennett (A) pictured outside his devastated home.

round. It is estimated that 250 shots were fired from either broadside, and we did the best thing which was to be done under the circumstances, that is to keep in the lowest room at the side of the house which was furthest from the sea, our kitchen; but oh for a cellar cool! They are certainly the safest place during either a naval bombardment or an air-raid.

All of you will readily believe that that half an hour was in some respects an eternity of time. Awful and paralysing. Besides the crashing of the bursting shells, masonry falling, glass breaking, was to be heard the frightened screams of women and children, as men, women and children, lots of them only half-dressed, rushed past our windows making for the country. What was most paralysing was the knowledge that one could do nothing for anyone else, could not save a child or shield it, could not run away. It is far worse to be in the streets than in a house. The only thing to do was to wait as patiently and cheerfully as possible.

Later, when the bombardment had ceased, mother and Mabel went to see what had really happened and to see what harm had been done, and how our relatives here had come through it. We were thankful to escape with only the windows of the two sitting-rooms and one bedroom broken, but round about us on all sides there has been an immense amount of damage done to property and a number of people killed.

The South Cliff has also suffered a heavy toll, but considering the very great destruction of property, there has been a miraculously small number of lives lost. Indeed, in a number of ways Scarborough has been blessed. For one thing, if the raid had been an hour later whole classes of children, including Mabel's, would have been killed practically wholesale. Two of the schools have been rather badly hit. Mabel went down to hers later in the day and besides counting seven holes in the roof of her classroom, collected several bits of shell from the debris. Then too, after having had very wet weather, the day of the bombardment and the one following were beautifully fine.

To me it was simply wonderful how very quickly the news that the Germans had gone spread abroad, people returning home from the surrounding villages by 10.00am, having walked both out and home.

Whilst mother and Mabel had gone to seek out friends, I looked after Audrey and baby (in her pram) just around about the door, and saw scores, hundreds of people returning home, half-dressed, tear-stained, cold and frightened. Women who had none, helping to carry other women's children, some carrying pet dogs and cats.

I was drinking a cup of tea outside and offered some to an old woman who had taken someone's stray pussy with her; she was dressed, but had no outdoor things on and was so cold and frightened that she could hardly hold the cup.

One man on Seamer Road was driving with a load of manure; he instantly tipped up his cart and loaded up with children walking out to Seamer. It was truly a time of 'doing unto others as you would they should do unto you', regardless of age, sex, riches or their lack.

I saw one woman half leading a young fellow down Mill Street; he looked dirty, as though he had been working amongst wall plaster or lime and was almost crying. When she came back alone a few minutes later I asked her what had been the matter. He was the young man from Wykeham Street [Christopher Bennett] whose mother, brother, nephew, and another little boy had been killed, whilst his

DUNOLLIE

The imposing home of York solicitor John Turner at 31 Filey Road was the scene of two deaths. Contrary to popular misconception, maid Margaret Briggs was killed in the library, whilst local postman Alfred Beal was killed in the driveway leading up to the house by the blast from the first shrapnel shell which burst over the stone portico.

father had also been hurt; he himself fell from his bedroom into the kitchen when their house was struck.

Everyone spoke to everyone else whether they were acquainted or not and it was most exhilarating and reviving to see and hear of the preservation of friends and relatives, one after another. Indeed, the whole day abounded in superlatives.

We did not know if it was going to be an invasion. That is what I dreaded personally, the being killed by shell or falling masonry does not seem to me half so terrible as having the men themselves in our town.

Although £600 was taken at the railway on the memorable Wednesday, hundreds and hundreds of people travelled without tickets, some of them meeting and succeeding in stopping the trains further out of town. The inhabitants in the towns and villages were extremely good to the people who reached them, giving away lots of hot tea, soup, coffee etc.

One of the most wonderful things was the rapid and cool way in which practically a few minutes after the firing ceased the corporation men, plumbers, glaziers, joiners, shop men and women, and private people were sweeping, brushing and generally clearing away the debris, boarding up or glazing windows, mending roofs, building up chimney stacks and pulling down, by means of long lengths of rope, loose pieces of masonry from the tops of houses.

A gentleman on the South Cliff [John Henry Turner], under whose bedroom window his maid [Margaret Briggs] was killed whilst taking the letters from the postman [Alfred Beal], a shell bursting between them and killing both, who said that Scarborough was no place for women at present, has been keenly criticised both by ministers and others. You see a great majority of the women and children must stay, and nearly all the men are obliged to do so. Some women who have relatives inland have left their children with them and come back to share things with their husbands.

The basement of Westborough Wesleyan Chapel (our chapel) has been taken as the 2nd Military Naval Base Hospital. It is used for east coast camps. A number of people wounded in the bombardment were also taken there. The members of the local Red Cross and St John Ambulance nursing corps take alternate duty there. I am a member of the latter, but have not been to nurse there yet, having only just got my uniform. We started to work for our exams as soon as war broke out. The students in Darlington College are all working for the Red Cross exams. In fact almost every other woman here is taking up either one or the other.

When some mines were shot the other day by the minesweepers, Mabel and her friend were on the pier; they ran for dear life at the first shot; scores of other people ran also. The people on the Foreshore ran out of their houses with large parcels. They have had orders to be ready to leave at a moment's notice. Ever since the bombardment there have been a number of minesweepers constantly at work, several of which have been struck, with several lives lost.

This letter was dated 30th December 1914 and was hand-written by the then twenty-seven-year-old Gertrude Harrison to her cousin living in Toronto, Canada. Miss Harrison was born in 1887 and lived with her family at *Calthorpe House* on Victoria Road. Her father, Albert Prince Harrison was the owner of the mill on Mill Street (just off Victoria Road). 1914.

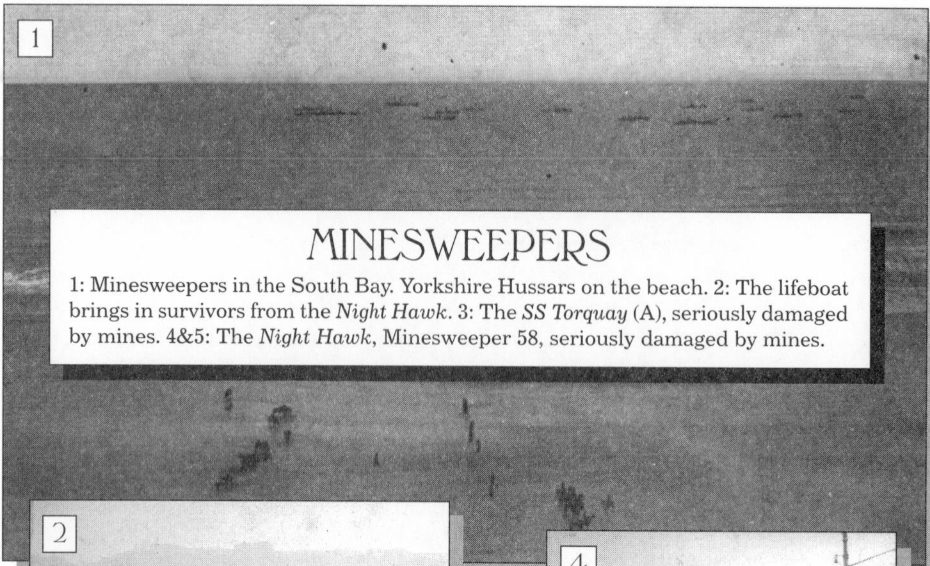

MINESWEEPERS

1: Minesweepers in the South Bay. Yorkshire Hussars on the beach. 2: The lifeboat brings in survivors from the *Night Hawk*. 3: The *SS Torquay* (A), seriously damaged by mines. 4&5: The *Night Hawk*, Minesweeper 58, seriously damaged by mines.

ENLIST

When you've talked about conscription,
and your country wanting men,
And you've finished slandering Kitchener
by word of mouth or pen;
When you've tried to teach your country
how the war it should be won
Will you kindly join the army
and help to get it done?

~

To you young men of England
I write these verses few,
Asking you to join the army
your duty there to do.
And when the war is over,
I feel sure you'll not regret
That you fought for the country that bore you,
England - don't forget.

~

You've perhaps forgotten Scarborough
and Hartlepool as well,
You've perhaps forgotten Belgium
and deeds I dare not tell.
Don't let the cries of outraged women
call to you in vain,
Enlist whilst you've the chance to avenge
the dastards of Louvain.

~

You who have wives and children,
and sweethearts ever dear,
Picture the fate they'd suffer
if that alien horde got here.
Don't let us call you shirkers,
don't turn your head away
When you see in the street a poster
'Enlist in the army today'.

~

You athletes of England,
of football, bat and blows,
Don the suit of khaki
and make footballs of our foes.
Show them that German Kultur
shall never come to pass;
Remember our sons she has murdered
by her asphyxiating gas.

~

Rise up young men of England
be soldiers one and all.
Tear off your ties and collars,
throw your straw hats to the wall.
Come and help us in the trenches
thereby victory bring.
For the sake of home and freedom
for your country, God and King!

~

If you cannot get a girl on the promenade
by winking your saucy eye,
If you cannot get a girl in your nice pink socks,
and new straw hat and tie,
If the rattle of your pocket won't bring them
- and they say that money talks -
Tear off your suits, and patent boots
and enlist in the 3rd West Yorks.

This stirring poem, a call to arms to those men reluctant to join the colours, was penned by T. Hobson of the West Yorkshire Regiment and appeared on Wednesday, 24th November 1915, almost a year after the bombardment, when its effects were already well overshadowed by mounting casualty lists from the Western Front. 1915.

I was getting ready for school at the time of the bombardment, although I didn't know what it was. We thought all the noise was just a really bad thunderstorm. I remember coming down from the attic room and passing grandma's bedroom. She was on her knees by the side of the bed saying her prayers.

I went out and off to school - Central School - like every other morning, with my friends. We were rushing along Dean Road and had just got to the bottom of Penny Back Lane when a policeman stopped us and told us to turn around and go straight back home as there would be no school that day. He didn't give us any explanation, so we turned around and trooped off back to our homes. It was only then I realised there had been a bombardment, because I confess I hadn't noticed any damage on the way to school!

I learned that uncle Thomas Dixon's house in Oxford Street had a shell go clean through the front room window and embed itself in the glass back of the chiffonier, but no one was hurt - I think he was out at the time. And anyway, in those days the front room was usually only used on special occasions - like Sunday best.

After the bombardment we were subjected to regular drills at school. A teacher would blow a whistle and we would form up, two-by-two, and march down into the school basement, where it was hoped we would be safe from another bombardment.

This account was related by Lilly Fell who was seven at the time of the bombardment. She was born on the 8th October 1907 in Scarborough, the eldest of four children - Lilly, Arthur, Edith and Francis - born to Herbert and Sarah Fell. The family lived at 20 Hope Street. Herbert worked for Jewison's on North Marine Road and drove a horse and cart. Lilly's grandparents lived on Seamer Road. Shortly after, they moved to Stockton where Herbert joined the Green Howards. However, he required compassionate leave when three-year-old Francis contracted pneumonia and died. In 1921 they had another son, Robert.

The uncle mentioned was John Thomas Dixon of 7 Oxford Street. He and his wife Elizabeth had a narrow escape when the fragment of shell crashed into their room and embedded itself in the chiffonier (an ornamental cabinet, often with drawers).

> *Father was just about to go off to work in York - he was a land agent - when the bombardment began. I wasn't quite out of bed yet, but he immediately called up for me to get up at once and to come downstairs. I flung my clothes on and rushed downstairs amid deafening bangs going on outside. Father took us all - including the maid and handyman - down into the cellar and there we waited until it was all over and everything had gone quiet.*
>
> *Our house had not been damaged, but others had and we stood together in the back yard to survey the nearest damage and wait for news of what to do.*
>
> *Peter was sent off to see how a friend of my mother's had fared on West Street and also another family friend at the Red Lea. He came back very shook up, with the news that two ladies staying at the Red Lea had been seriously injured in their legs. Father did not go to work that day, instead he stayed at home. He told us we were not going to leave, as some were doing, and that if anything happened we would be here when it did. We could look out over the main rail line to York from Westwood and could see the amount of people crammed into the trains.*
>
> *My brother and his friend, excited at the prospect of exploring the town and the damage, went off in search of souvenirs and came back with bits of shell-casing. On their travels they saw the German ships departing in the fog.*
>
> *We later learned that Mrs Kathleen Walker's house at 14 Lonsdale Road had been badly damaged. She was a friend of my mother's and luckily was away at the time. Her husband was the captain of a merchant ship and was also away at the time. They used to have a beautiful Chinese-style garden, but it was also wrecked in the bombardment. To the best of my knowledge Mrs Walker never returned to Scarborough after that.*

This account was related by Lucy Ursula Surtees Hornby who was nine years old, and just four days short of her tenth birthday at the time of the bombardment. She was born in York on 20th December 1904. Lucy lived at 11 Westwood with her parents, Robert and Constance Hornby and her brother, William (known in the family as Peter), two years her senior. Robert Hornby was a land agent and worked in York.

Following the bombardment Lucy's mother scrapped plans to send her to Filey Convent School and instead enrolled her at the Convent School in Scarborough, which was situated on Queen Street. Although the Hornby family home was undamaged, a number of houses close by had their windows smashed, and the home of family friend Mrs Kathleen Walker at 14 Lonsdale Road was almost demolished. The image of the house, transferred onto postcards, became one of the abiding images of the day.

Lucy's paternal grandfather, Valentine Fowler, was a former Mayor of the town and an Alderman. In her teens Lucy played hockey for Scarborough, whilst her brother played for Yorkshire. Peter later became a doctor.

LUCY HORNBY

1: Lucy aged 11, pictured with her parents and grandparents whilst on holiday at West Ayton.
2: The Hornby family, taken shortly before they experienced the horror of the 1914 bombardment of Scarborough, from their home at 11 Westwood. Robert and Constance, with children William (known as Peter) and Lucy.

Although I was only twelve at the time I still have very vivid memories of that day. I lived in Commercial Street. It was a terrifying experience as the goods depot and Scarborough to Whitby rail line were at the back of the house.

At the time my sister was ill in bed, but when she heard the noise she got up and looked out of the bedroom window in time to see a shell explode over the goods depot. All our back windows were blown in and the back door was riddled with bullets. Later we found a lump of shrapnel on the hearth.

We only lived yards away from the house on the corner of Wykeham Street where the Bennett family lived - and died. I well remember one of the sons standing in the devastated front room begging for help from passers-by - none would help him. It was terrible.

Mr Harper, who had a removals and taxi cab firm near us took us out to Scalby, along with another couple and an old lady in a bed. We certainly were refugees!

We were taken in by a very kind family called Halliday-Huggan (I think) for the rest of the day. They fed us and gave clothes to those who had not had the time to dress properly at home. My father came up for us in the afternoon and we didn't know what to expect when we got back home.

I went to Gladstone Road school at the time and we would assemble, boys and girls together, in the hall. Had it been 9.00am instead of 8.00am there would have been very many casualties because a shell went straight through the hall roof.

This account was related by Marjorie Davison from Leeds. Born in 1902, she was 12 at the time. Her father was Robert Davison, a 'rulleyman', of 99 Commercial Street.

The Mr Harper mentioned was furniture remover George Harper of 81 St John's Road, who put his transport at the disposal of Scarborough's fleeing populace. The Huggan family lived at *Crimbles Court*, Scalby, and took in a large number of refugees.

BOMBARDMENT OF THE EAST COAST

Out on the German hound
That came like a thief in the night
To the shores of our dear homeland
The home of right, not might.

~

Across God's ocean fair
He crept 'midst a shroud of fog
Like a beast from his filthy lair
Like a snake from his loathsome bog.

~

Did he dare in the light of day
To face our boys in blue;
Did he dare to test in the fray
And fortune's favour woo?

~

Would he stand to it ship 'gainst ship
And fight like a foeman stout
'Midst the shock of the battle's grip
For victory: or rout?

~

Did he think that the one on high
Whose name he so blasphemes,
Would view with lenient eye
Such ghastly, murderous schemes?

~

Do the cries of the wakened babes
From innocence's sweet slumber
Or the shrieks of the distraught maids
Make music to his thunder?

~

Do the ghastly gaping wounds
Of the spreading, shredded shell
Or the picric's stifling fumes
Their heaven; but our hell?

~

Will the sound of the orphan's wail
Bring comfort to their ears
What sympathy prevail
And dry the widow's tears?

~

Back to your dens, then hounds
Back from the gory meal.
Leave us our shattered towns
Stamped with your gory seal.

~

But cravens: mark! The day's at hand
When vengeance full and dire
Shall fall upon your boastful land
A nation's righteous ire.

~

Our heel upon your serpent neck
Shall crush your writhing form,
And not one atom from the wreck
Shall e'er again be born.

~

You've toasted to your boasted day
Whatever else betide
Old England's got a debt to pay
And God be on our side.

Written by J. C. Rokeby-Hailen of Brighton. 1914.

I still have in my possession a book that came from the library of 'Dunollie' (31 Filey Road) and was hit by a fragment of shell. Would you believe its title is 'The Death Whistle'!

This account was related by Mrs E. Bolton from Sheffield. Of all the souvenirs that have turned up from the bombardment over the years this must be one of the most curious - given its title.

It was a dull morning and my father had just set off for work, leaving mother and us six children (aged from seven months to twelve years) at home.

Mother had just served out porridge for breakfast when there were a number of very loud bangs. We were terrified.

Mother rushed to the door and saw half-dressed men, women and children running down the street in terror.

We were living at 71 Hampton Road, and a shell exploded on a house at the bottom of Wykeham Street, killing the whole family; but a cat, which had got into a copper, survived. A piece of shrapnel from this shell flew over into Hampton Road and hit my baby sister.

Mother panicked, but my father, who had rushed home, kept his nerve. He put the baby in the pram and we all set off running, along with the rest of the panic-stricken crowd, along Scalby Road, heading for the open countryside.

We reached a lane (now known as Coldyhill Lane) and a man directed us to a doctor called Tenison. He attended to my baby sister's wound and she recovered.

The people of Newby and Scalby were marvellous and served the shattered Scarborough people with hot tea and food.

We were then taken to a family called Huggan, who were very kind to us.

After a while Dr Tenison sent us home in his car (my first ever motor ride). We reached home at about dinner time, still very shaken.

I recall we did not go back to school until well into the New Year.

This account was related by A. N. Warley from Tunbridge Wells. His father was George Warley. The Huggans mentioned were the family at *Crimbles Court*, Scalby, who took in many refugees. Dr Adolf Tenison lived on Station Road, Scalby.

I was getting ready for school when the bombardment started.

As the shells fell (I don't think there were 500 as some suggest) I was more concerned for my little black and white rabbit in its hutch in the back yard than for myself.

My school, Gladstone Road, was hit and had to be closed for repairs, so there was no school for the rest of the day.

After the shelling, which lasted perhaps twenty minutes, I went off and found some souvenirs, fragments of shell and the like.

There were rumours that the Germans had landed on the south sands, but it wasn't true.

By teatime, those who had fled into the country began returning home.

The next day life went on as normal and they moved us all to Falsgrave School until Gladstone Road was repaired.

This account was related by Cyril William Saville, who was nine years old at the time of the bombardment. Born on 17th May 1905, he lived with his family at 34 Lyell Street, one of the fortunate houses not to be damaged, despite a large number of shells falling in the Manor Road area. His father was Thomas Saville and his occupation was listed as 'a traveller' in the local directory of the day.

1

2

ST NICHOLAS PARADE AND MARINE PARADE

1 & 2: The rear of Mr Ashley's Spa Boarding House, St Nicholas Parade. 3: 'Fine Art Saloon', Marine Parade.

3

YORKSHIRE'S REPLY TO THE RAID

For the death they dealt in the morning mist,
For the coward blow of the mailed fist,
For the Yorkshire blood set flowing then,
This is the vow sworn by Yorkshire men.

~

For the deaths they dealt in the morning mist,
In an undefended town,
For the sorrows of their sowing,
For the wounds of their bestowing,
For the griefs that pass all showing,
We will hunt the raiders down.

~

We'll pay in full the debts we owe
Though red with blood the rivers flow.
Yet once again our foes shall know
That blow for blow is Britain's way,
And what Britain owes she'll surely pay.

~

The guns may roar over Scarborough town,
Its churches reel and roofs crash down.
But gun for gun and town for town,
Measure for measure and pressed well down,
Two and six for each half-crown,
What Britain owes she'll pay cash down.

~

The foe shall surely rue the day,
Though long the road and rough the fray,
What Britain owes she'll shrewdly pay.
Such debts in full is Britain's way.

Written by the prolific J. T. Mullett this poem originally appeared in the *Leeds Mercury* before being reproduced in the local paper. 1915.

The day dawned dull and foggy and the sea was flat calm. My father and I had just been down to the harbour: it was high tide and almost all the fishing fleet was at sea. We arrived back home just before 8.00am, and not many minutes later, as mother was putting out our porridge, there was a heavy whining sound overhead, followed by explosions.

"That's gunfire!" father exclaimed incredulously and closed the wooden shutters of our living-room windows to prevent flying glass. He also put out the gas light and lit a couple of candles. "Eat your breakfast and stay in," he said. "If we go, we go together!"

Meanwhile the firing went on, and now there were also heavier shells with a slower buzzing sound and much louder explosions; these were the heavier shells used on the castle walls and keep.

There was a lull of a few minutes, then the firing resumed. After a quarter of

1

2

3

4

14 LONSDALE ROAD

The home of Mrs Kathleen Walker was devastated by a direct hit.

an hour the firing ceased and all the neighbours came out into the street, giving various opinions of what should be done, not only to the Kaiser, but to the Commander-in-Chief of the Home Fleet too. There were loud demands of, "Where's the Navy?"

Wild rumours were circulating about people in their night-clothes seizing a train and going to York; that hundreds had been killed up on the common; that many children had been killed in Gladstone Road School and the buildings themselves flattened; that there had been an attempted landing on the North Bay, repulsed by soldiers in the barracks; that the German ships had followed the local steam trawler St Cloud in through the morning's fog. There were demands to know how the Germans could shell the town from only a mile off shore, when the British Fleet always anchored three miles off when visiting the town.

Having heard the fate of Gladstone Road School I immediately ran around to see if Friarage School was still there. Much to my dismay it was. However, a boy running past bellowed at me that there was a great hole in the lighthouse, so I hurried over there instead. There was no one on Sandside or Vincent's Pier (where the lighthouse stood). I crossed the bridge and stood looking at the hole in the lighthouse, when the door opened and the harbour-master, Captain Cass Smith, came out and with many threats from his hands and boots, drove me away.

I crossed the bridge only to have him call me back. I went warily and ready for flight, but he did nothing more than give me an apple. I wandered back along the Foreshore and somehow got into the Crescent, where I found a piece of shell four and a half inches by one and a half inches. Then I went home.

The shelling had been unhurried. The first reports said there had been 500 shells, but later reports put it at 200 shells in about thirty minutes. The German ships had come in from the north and were the battle-cruisers Derfflinger and Von der Tann, while the Kolberg had lain a minefield. After that had been done at Scarborough they steamed away northward. The Germans claimed great prestige from the raid, claiming that Scarborough was a fortified town, which it was not. Yet years later in 1930, when I was a navigating officer in the Merchant Navy, I saw the Admiralty chart for 'Flamborough Head to Hartlepool' (which anyone could purchase) and it bore the legend 'CAUTION - Gunfire takes place periodically from the fort at Scarborough. Mariners are warned accordingly.' This referred to the South Steel Battery, disused since the turn of the century!

This account was related by Sydney Thomas Smith who was born in Scarborough on the 11th December 1907, and was seven at the time of the bombardment. He lived at 24 Cook's Row with his father, fisherman Thomas Smith, and his mother Violet. Sydney could still remember the thrill of running around the town after the shelling to see all the damage that had been done and in picking up a large lump of shell fragment which took pride of place among his boyhood possessions until, *"someone helped themselves to it!"* He also recalled the disappointment of having to attend school the following day because Friarage had escaped damage.

Sydney went to sea alongside his dad at the tender age of seven on the *Prairie Flower*. He later attended Graham Sea Training School, was a member of the Sea Scouts, and at the age of 16 went to sea as a fisherman with local coble fisherman, Fred Megginson, aboard the *Togo*. He then joined the Merchant Navy and served on the *Loyal Devonian*. In 1935 he married Gladys Metcalfe (whose family had lived at the top of Cook's Row,

1

KINGSCLIFFE HOLIDAY CAMP

The canvas huts of the camp were situated below King Street.

2

3

SYDNEY SMITH

Born in December 1907, Syd Smith was seven and lived on Cook's Row in the old town, close to the Foreshore and harbour. With no school that day Syd went out collecting fragments of shells.

2: aged 10, 1918. 3: aged 12, 1920.

when Sydney lived at the bottom). Before the outbreak of the Second World War Sydney joined the Royal Naval Reserve and won a King's Commendation for Bravery on 7th March 1944 whilst Master of the *SS Empire Trent*. As a Captain he returned to the Merchant Navy after the war and eventually became the Deputy Harbour-Master at Scarborough and President of Scarborough Trinity House Merchant Seamen's Homes. Of all the places he visited throughout the world his favourite was River Plate, *"Because it was lovely and warm!"* and of all the honours and accolades Sydney has earned throughout his life - including the MBE awarded in 1998 - his most prized was the Masters Certificate he gained on 6th February 1936.

The battery Sydney refers to above was made up of five guns, museum-piece cannons, four of which dated from the 18th century, while the fifth gun [beside the Grand Hotel] was a souvenir of the Crimean War (1853-1856). Even if they had still been in place and capable of being fired, they would have proven no match for the grey-steel might of the German Navy.

THE EAST COAST RAID

One cold December morning grey,
Scarce had the darkness fled away
Than through the haze
The masts of giant warships reared
And fiends in human form appeared
Whilst guns did blaze.

~

With loud reports the air was rent
As messengers of death were sent
Upon our shore.
Victims of cruel shot and shell,
Defenceless women and children fell
To rise no more.

~

Then gloating o'er the maimed and dead
The treacherous cowards turned and fled,
Leaving behind
A deed which ever will disgrace
The much refined and cultured race
Upon our mind.

~

Tyrants who do not hesitate
The laws of man to violate
At every turn.
Eye fails to view, but with disgust
The human heart then surely must
With hatred burn.

~

Base monster, thou who seeks to slay
The innocent in such a way
Take this to heart -

Just retribution comes always
To each and every one who plays
The cowards part.

~

Dost not thine heart within thee bleed
With recollections of the deed?
The beast would shun,
In recognition of our loss,
Thou may receive an Iron Cross
By treachery won.

~

Fools but imagine they may pierce
Our hearts of oak with onslaught fierce.
Make terror reign,
They knoweth not the English man
Nor realise their futile plan
And purpose vain.

~

Thou cruel murderer pray take heed -
Who dares to rouse the bulldog breed
Shall dearly pay.
The British Lion reigneth still
And take a swift revenge he will,
As sure as day.

This poem was penned by George N. Chappell, a prolific poet, from his home in Huddersfield, West Yorkshire. 1914.

My Darling Len,
Whew! We have had a day. I'm sure you'll want to know all about it as they censor things so terribly in the papers.

We, in Scarborough, have been bombarded, between 8.05am and about 9.00am.

Well, I'll start at the beginning. We were all at breakfast and mother said to me, "Doesn't that sound like thunder?"

I said, "Oh no, it's only the wind."

Then the gardener knocked at the window and said, "My word, the Germans have come!"

We rushed out and heard from the sea, but terribly near, heavy cannon firing. BOOM! BOOM! BANG! SKWISH! - as cannon after cannon and shells sounded. You can't imagine what it was like. It sounded like terrible thunder, but incessant, and a thousand times worse.

Everyone was in a panic. All the carts etc., which had been going towards Scarborough came flying back. I was all shaking and mother ditto. I heard and saw a shrapnel shell come right over this house, it must have exploded somewhere over Hay Brow.

Dad thought it was only a naval action near in, so he and I rushed off up the hill near the fever hospital. This was about twenty minutes after, and when we got there the cannon stopped.

We saw a man who said, "You're just too late, it's very foggy out to sea, but I saw two or three big cruisers very near in firing on the town." He said he too thought it was part of a big naval engagement and that the cruisers were being chased north by some of our fleet. He didn't seem to know much. We know now that it was not correct, as none of our ships were on the scene of action.

Dad said we had better go home. We went and saw streams of men, women and children coming from Scarborough, many with no shoes on and not half-dressed, carrying babies etc. A man brought two kids in our house. They'd no shoes or stockings on and were bitterly cold. He said he was bringing a few more. Of course we said all right, and kids and mothers (poor people) came streaming in until we'd 25 people in the house!!! We had them in the kitchen and gave them tea and bread and jam. Some of their houses, and houses near them, had been all blown up by shells. Some people had been killed and they had seen houses falling as they came along.

I, going for some bread, heard, as many others did, heavy though distant firing towards the north. We supposed that our ships were chasing them up towards Whitby. But we knew nothing for certain. People were off their heads. Some passing through here said, "Scarborough is in flames!" Others said the Germans had landed.

Of course, we knew the latter could not be true, but we were afraid of the former.

We had the 'refugees' in our house till 11.00am, then they said there was no more firing off Scarborough. They went.

I must hurry, it's almost post time so can't give the awful details. We all went to Scarborough. Scarcely a house not hit by a shell. Some in absolute ruins. It is not certain to the number, but about 30 to 60 are killed.

The Grand Picture House, lighthouse, many hotels and houses are wrecks. Troops are being sent to Scarborough. If only we had had cannon on the castle hill we should have sent the pigs of German cats to the bottom.

They say Whitby and Hartlepool are also bombarded. All is quiet now. We hope we will not have a fresh attack, though some people think there will be worse to come. They say there were four big German cruisers, and none of our fleet was near. However, they evidently are near, for I have seen three English torpedo destroyers passing near the bay.

Goodbye. Ever your own loving, Audrey.

Details later, no time now . . .

The above letter was sent from Newby at 7.00pm on the evening of Wednesday, 16th December 1914. Unfortunately, there are no further details as to the identities of either Len or Audrey. 1914.

I was eleven years old at the time and was in the first intake of boys into the Scarborough Sea Scouts School (known nowadays as the Graham Sea Training School). I was full of reading, thinking and dreaming about the Royal Navy, which I always thought I'd join - in fact I joined the Royal Air Force!

We wore the Sea Scouts' uniform for school and I never wore any other clothes for four years for I had no ordinary clothes to wear.

At the time of the bombardment we were living two doors from the Sea Bathing

THE GRAND HOTEL

Foreshore Road and St Nicholas Cliff.
1: Exterior damage. 2: Roof damage.
3: Exterior damage. 4: Bedroom damage.

Infirmary (on the Foreshore) in a row of houses behind the main houses on the sea front, separated from them by a six-foot passage.

Two doors to the left and across the passage was Neptune House (13 Foreshore Road), in which my grandmother (Mrs Rose Jarvis) lived with her daughter Violet. This house was right on the Foreshore and in front of ours, as were others, so we could not see the sea. Due to invasion precautions, all the steps leading from the sea front up the cliff (about 70 feet) to the main street of the town were barricaded with barbed-wire six feet high, only one narrow path being left free for our use. All the main streets, and the lesser ones, to the sea were likewise wired - real 'Western Front' type jobs they were too, no half-larks.

We therefore had no access to the town save this one narrow stairway. And, as if to put the thought of invasion even more into our minds, there were two machine-gun pits, one at each end of the Foreshore, one on the West Pier and the other on the Spa sea wall.

Furthermore, where we emerged from our 'stairway' - which was covered by houses at the top - our first sight was a tremendous sandbagged barricade across Eastborough, six feet high and six feet thick, with a staggered passage through it so that there was no gap where a bullet could find its way through.

The soldiers who put up the barricades were looked after by our families and others with cups of tea and biscuits etc. They left us all their wire cutters, which we kept for years afterwards, and they were real good heavy jobs.

On the great day, my sister and I were downstairs getting ready for school. The gas stove had the kettle on it when suddenly a very loud, deep rumble commenced and died away. We all looked up, but not for long, for bangs and crashes started regularly, many of them of a 'whip-like' intensity which made me pull my head into my shoulders. I learned later that this noise was caused by the actual discharge of the guns and not the explosions of the shells - my father also tried to have me believe that the noises were the sound of the 'Steel Battery' on the castle hill replying to the warships! Absolute nonsense of course, for no such guns existed.

After about three minutes of this, and wondering what sort of a naval battle was going on at sea, we suddenly found it was our battle, not the Navy's, for all the light at the window was completely blacked out by a thick cloud of what we later realised was brick dust and debris.

Strangely enough we didn't hear a sound from this little turmoil and it didn't occur to us that a shell had hit Neptune House where granny was.

What happened next is a little unclear. Granny and Violet suddenly appeared, having come down a back staircase, as their own normal one was blocked with bricks. I recall hearing the word 'invasion' used. Then we all trooped off towards our 'stairway' to the town. Violet had no shoes on, and neither did granny, as they had been in bed when it had all started.

Going through the six-foot passage behind Neptune House, which had a 'semi-basement' kitchen with a windowsill at floor level, I noticed all the windows were out and the room was half-filled with rubble.

Then, right in my way as I hurried past was a 5.9-inch shell - it was just lying there, unexploded. I jumped over it and noticed as I did that it was armour-piercing and that the copper driving band had become dislodged and was half-way down the body of the shell.

1

2

3

4

FORESHORE ROAD

1: The patients moved from the Royal Northern Sea Bathing Infirmary & Convalescent Home, including British and Belgian wounded soliders, to make way for the injured.
2: Damaged buildings on the Foreshore behind the lifeboat house. 3: The Olympia Picture Palace café. 4: The Olympia Picture Palace looking back from the veranda towards the castle.

We Sea Scouts knew all about such things from the cigarette cards then current!

It is here that the effects of the 'invasion' scare come in, for we would have been far safer to have stayed where we were than to have trudged a mile into town where more shells were falling. We ended up at my other granny's house (my dad's mother) and after all had quietened down we all trudged back again to Neptune House.

Just whose shoes granny and Violet borrowed I don't know, but it was a typical damp December day and their feet must have been soaking by the time it was all over.

When we got back we found that bricks shooting through the kitchen window had cleared everything off the windowsill, which was usually fairly cluttered. Only one thing was left there, the cup full of water in which my granny nightly deposited her false teeth! The cup was there, the water clear and unsullied, but some delightful Britisher had pinched the false teeth! She later included them in her compensation claim. We also found we had left the gas on and there was a hole in the bottom of the kettle!

Another thing missing was the shell I had jumped over, which was a relief! Apparently a local rock-maker a hundred yards further along the Foreshore had been snooping about and had picked up the shell and carried it to his house where he deposited it on his dining-table as a war trophy, while his wife and daughter ran screaming from the house to tell the nearest troops. He got a good dressing-down from the officer when he arrived on the scene. A 5.9-inch shell is no light weight and he must have been a strong chap to have carried it a hundred yards, for they don't have handles on them.

Then we talked about it all. I think we must have talked for a whole week.

It seems granny, on waking, had gone to the front window to see what all the noise was about - she was on the first floor, the room beneath her being a sweet shop (Vose's Toffee Shop). A tremendous flash occurred on the road in front of the house and suddenly there was dust everywhere and she found the stairs full of bricks and came to us the other way. The shell had hit the edge of the pavement on the Foreshore, bounced upward through the shop, gone through two walls, over the stairs and then through an eight-inch wooden beam over the back door, and still travelling upwards, had crossed the six-foot passage into the fanlight over the door of the house next to ours - which was empty. It struck the ceiling of the room and dislodged a whole heap of plaster and then fell vertically to the floor which it dented. It then bounced out of the house via the bottom panel of the door through which it had entered.

At first no one could understand what had caused the damage in this room, as no bricks or rubble were inside it, but I soon sorted it out for them - being a Sea Scout it was easy!

The Sea Bathing Infirmary took a shell which went right through the first floor and, like ours, did not explode, but did some damage, though I don't think anyone was badly hurt. For the inmates of the ward it must have been a case of 'out of the frying pan and into the fire' for they were wounded Belgian soldiers recovering from their ordeal with the Germans.

A firm called Maynards took over the shop at Neptune House and the square, two-foot-six hole at the back was boarded up and left as it was, framed in a

1

GENERAL DAMAGE

1&4: Mrs Bethel Sharp and daughter Millie, both wounded at 31 Norwood Street. 2: Damage to a house on Norwood Street. 3: The George Hotel, Newborough. 5: Damage to the interior of Petch's joinery shop, Victoria Road.

2

3

4

5

wallpaper surround as a curio to attract visitors. It was very successful actually and I suspect granny got a bob or two out of it.

This account was related by Norman Hodgson from Hayes, Middlesex. Born in 1903 he was 11 at the time of the bombardment. He also witnessed the 1917 attack and his account is included later in the book. Norman's sister was Marjorie, born in 1904 and aged 10 at the time of the bombardment.

Miss Fowler had been warned (whether by Scarborough authorities or the War Office, I do not know) of the possibility of east coast raids. She had sent a letter to every parent warning them of this, and also telling of the precautions the school was taking. They were asked to decide whether they would like their children home or prefer them to stay at school. From the beginning of term she had made preparations, and in those last few days little bags of money and rations were stored ready for any emergency. Out of 170 girls, I think quite 130 of us left in 36 hours - amid anger and scorn and contempt for the cowardice of our parents! I felt I could never forgive them, but 14 days later they were more than justified.

This account by Winifred Holtby was sent to a school-friend at the time of the bombardment and was given - in November 1938 - to her friend, the writer Vera Brittain. It was included in her work 'Testament of Friendship'. As well as this brief account of the readiness of Queen Margaret's School (at which she was head girl) the school-friend also forwarded to Vera Brittain an original letter (which follows) by Winifred Holtby, sent to her the day after the bombardment - Thursday, 17th December 1914.

When I got up on Wednesday morning, if somebody had told me it was going to be the most exciting day I ever had, I should have laughed and said, "Rats!"

I went down to breakfast in high spirits. There was an end-of-termy feeling in the air, and breakfast was at 8.00am. I was sitting next to Miss Chrichton, and I distinctly remember she had just passed me the milk and I was raising my first spoonful of porridge to my mouth. I never tasted that porridge! Crash! Thu-u-d!

I sat up, my spoon in the air, all the nerves in my system suddenly strung taut, for the noise was like nothing I had heard before - deafening, clear-cut, not rumbly - as though a heavy piece of furniture had crashed in the room overhead. I looked at Miss Crichton, saying with a laugh, "Hello! Who's fallen?" when the look on her face arrested me. She was deathly white, and with fixed eyes was looking towards Miss Bubb. Suddenly I felt a tightness across my chest and an icy hand laid on my spine. I could see the hand that held my spoon was trembling, and yet I had not realised what was happening, only something caught at my heart and for an instant it stopped beating.

I was about to speak, when CR-R-ASH - a sound more terrific than the first - and then all the windows danced in their frames; each report was doubled, first a roar and then an ear-splitting crash as the shell exploded. Then someone whispered, "guns". The word, like magic, passed from mouth to mouth as we sat white-faced but undismayed, with the uneaten food before us. Another crash, and two mistresses rose and spoke together a moment and went out. Still not a girl moved or spoke; all sat as under a spell. Another crash, and another; then one by one the girls rose to their feet; that was the moment - the only moment -

WINIFRED HOLTBY

Winifred (aged 11) seated left,
with her elder sister Grace (aged 14)

Winifred Holtby was born on 23rd June 1898 at Rudston, near Bridlington, East Yorkshire. She was educated at home with her sister, and was then sent to Queen Margaret's (Anglican) School for Girls in Scarborough. She witnessed the bombardment of the town on Wednesday, 16th December 1914 and wrote an account of it which was later published in the *Bridlington Chronicle*.

After a short spell as a temporary nursing assistant in a London nursing home she attended Somerville College, Oxford in 1917. The following year she became a hostel forewomen in the Women's Army Auxiliary Corps (WAACs) serving in France. In 1919 she returned to her studies.

Once dubbed 'the most brilliant journalist in Britain' she is perhaps best remembered for her friendship with the author Vera Brittain, her fight for female equality and for the novel 'South Riding'. Winifred died in September 1935, aged just 37, and was buried at Rudston. In her Will, she bequeathed her entire library to Queen Margaret's School, in recognition of the happy time she had spent there.

when panic could have occurred. We did not know, we could only guess what was happening, but a steady voice brought us to our senses.

"Lead out to the cloakroom and wait there."

We led out; yes, but not as sedately as usual; quite slowly and quietly, and then we stood awaiting orders. If anybody felt fear, and I know that some did, no one showed it save by a white face or an excited laugh. We talked quietly, in awed tones. Each time a shot was fired some started and flinched, others stood calm and motionless. Then Miss Bubb appeared on the stairs, with her dear, familiar smile and her steadying voice, and we seemed to have caught, in a bad dream, on to something that was safe, and real, and solid.

She was our saviour. And yet the words she said were so absurdly familiar and commonplace; "Put on your long coats, tammies [hats] and thick boots; we are going for a walk into the country till it is over."

We dressed and we started, Nellie calm and placid as ever, waiting till we were all in line. Just as we got through the gate another shell burst quite near and, "RUN!" came the order - and we ran. Ran, under the early morning sky, on the muddy uneven road, with that deafening noise in our ears, the echo ringing even when the actual firing stopped for a moment - it never stopped for more; ran, though our hastily clad feet slipped on the muddy road.

Over the town hung a mantle of heavy smoke, yellow, unreal, which made the place look like a dream city, far, far away. Only the road was real, and the tight pain that caught us across our breast - it was not fear, but something inexplicable that hurt, and yet in some strange way was not wholly unpleasant. Round the corner leading down to the Mere we ran, now all puffing. Someone was down; with a bang they fell full-length on the road and lay winded; then somebody picked her up and they ran together.

In an instant's pause I looked round. I heard the roar of a gun and the next instant there was a crash and a thick cloud of black smoke enveloped one of the houses in Seamer Road; a tiny spurt of red flame shot out. Then I was swept on down the hill to where the Mere lay grey and placid in the cold morning light. Where the road joins at the foot of the hill we hesitated a second; we were moving to the level-crossing, when a shell struck the ground some 50 yards away, throwing up earth and mud in all directions.

"Back! Back!" came the cry, and we turned and ran with dragging feet along the Mere path. It was all so like a bad dream, I wondered if I should wake and find myself in my dorm! Well, we just had to jog on and we tried to keep our spirits up by singing 'Tipperary', but it took too much breath.

We left the Mere path where it turns and went along 'no-man's-land', strewn with old tins and broken crockery; we tripped on the pottery and slipped on decaying refuse and staggered along through the mud.

Miss Trethowan still ran behind, helping the stragglers, encouraging, laughing and being just the brick she is. It was an awful responsibility but she bore it capitally.

We crossed the [railway] line into the Seamer Valley. Along the road was a stream of refugees; there was every kind of vehicle, filled to overflowing with women and children; yes, and men too. I saw one great brute, young and strong, mounted on a cart-horse, striking it with a heavy whip, tearing at full gallop down the road, caring nothing for the women and children who scrambled

1

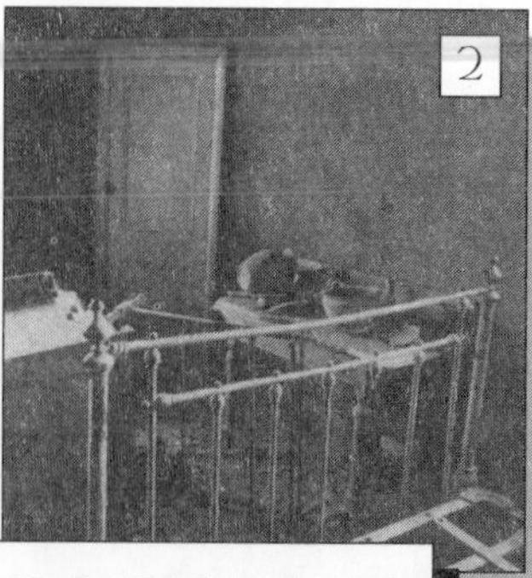

2

ESPLANADE BOARDING ESTABLISHMENT

Councillor Frank White's hotel suffered substantial internal damage.

3

4

RED LEA BOARDING HOUSE

5

CHARLES MACKARNESS

Archdeacon Charles Mackarness carried on with his service at St Martin's Church despite its being struck by a shell.

6

piteously out of his path, with the fear of death on his craven face. I could have killed him with pleasure.

Oh! Those poor things on the road. There was a young mother with a tiny baby clutched in her arms; an old woman, only partly dressed, with her pitiful bundle of worldly goods on a rickety perambulator; there were mothers with tiny children clinging to their skirts crying for fear of this unknown horror. There was one particularly touching old couple, tottering along side by side, perhaps the last time they would ever walk together. I think I shall never forget them - those people of 'the dream that was real'. With white faces they passed on. Whither? Where to go? Only an instinct urged on their weary feet, and fear lent wings to the old and tired.

We paused at the foot of the hill that leads to Seamer [Stoney Haggs Rise] to rest for a moment, for shells had been bursting not far from the top, and we knew that when we were half-way up we must run for our lives; all our strength was needed for that, so we stood for a moment and watched the living stream sweep past. I saw a rulley [cart] laden with children pulled at an unsteady amble by an old, old horse, driven by a young girl; then a motor built for two with at least five in it; then a country cart with old women and children driven at full gallop; then with a warning 'Honk! Honk!' a splendid car swept by at a terrific speed with one occupant - a woman wrapped in costly furs, alone in that great car, yet she would not stop to take up one of the poor old women who staggered on, weary to death, yet fleeing for their lives.

Here also, some of the girls found four tiny mites, half-dressed and almost mad with fear, yet not understanding in the least why. They had lost their mother, so we took them with us; some put coats round them and carried them. At the top of the hill we found their mother. The poor thing was almost wild with joy when she saw her 'bairns' safe and sound.

Just outside Seamer we sat down, tired out. As we sat, newcomers came with dreadful tales;

'The school was shattered', (two mistresses had stayed in).

'The Grand Hotel was in flames.'

'The South Cliff lay in ruins.'

'The Germans had landed.'

All this we took with salt, and waited for the mistresses to come - they had carried on their hands a mistress who was ill. Some of the servants came up and told us Miss Fowler was on the road with our breakfast. Our breakfast! At this awful moment they had stopped to get chocolate, dates and biscuits, parcels of which they had ready in case of emergency. How good those biscuits were, eaten as we sat by the side of the road and shared them with other refugees.

While we sat there a nice looking officer, who seemed to be directing the traffic, came up and said he was the Vicar's son, and we were to go to the vicarage. Miss Fowler demurred; how could she land fifty dirty, tired schoolgirls and maids on the Vicar's wife? But he waved away her hesitation with a kindly gesture, saying, "Tell them I sent you." Bless him!

We went and the kindness of the Vicar of Seamer and Mrs Stapleton will never be forgotten by any of us. They set us to make tea and cut bread and butter, knowing that occupation was the best thing for our overstrained nerves.

Then Miss Fowler appeared, armed with a time-table and read out the names

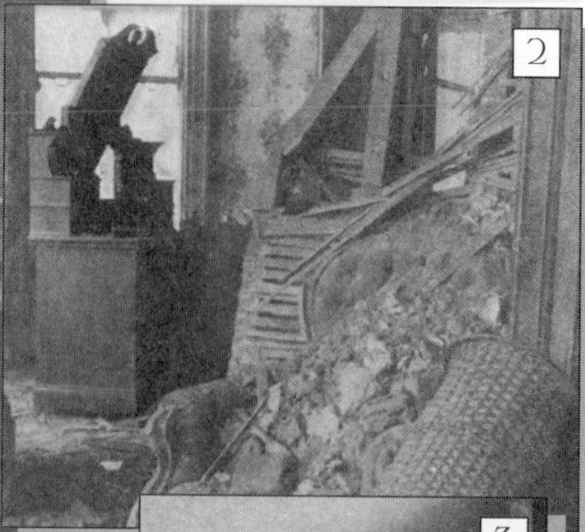

ROYAL HOTEL

St Nicholas Street.
1&4: Exterior damage.
2&3: Damage to a bedroom.

of the London girls who had to be put on the train just due. The Leeds girls had to wait some time, so the Vicar had a fire put in the parish room and turned us in there to give vent to our high spirits in songs and games; and some of us he took to see the quaint old church.

How strange it all seemed! Only an hour or two ago we were sitting calmly at breakfast. Another few minutes - seven to be correct - we were running for our lives in the chill morning twilight, and here we were in the peaceful village street which seemed miles and miles away from guns.

Finally we returned to school by train to find a meal ready for us. I just can't describe the cool way everything was arranged. Poor Miss Miller had been brought back by car and put to bed again. We set to work to pack, and then walked round the town to see the havoc.

The South Cliff looks pretty bad. The poor old Prince of Wales Hotel has a good many shells through it, and the darling Hall has had its hat knocked off by a German shell . . . Don't you wish you'd stayed at school?

I can only finish with an earnest hope that never again will England suffer as she did on that awful December 16th, 1914 - but if she does, may I be there to see.

At the age of 16, Winifred Holtby was a pupil at the then Queen Margaret's School, an Anglican school situated below Oliver's Mount, on Queen Margaret's Road, and overlooking the town. The building had, when first built in 1859, been the Princess Royal Hotel and had subsequently been the Oliver's Mount School for Boys, before becoming the all-girl Queen Margaret's. The school was intended for middle-class girls of moderate means who had a living to earn. Some slight damage was done to some of the buildings which comprised the school from the large cluster of shells which fell around Oliver's Mount. Princess Mary later planted a beech tree in a shell hole, made during the bombardment, in the garden of the school.

Winifred Holtby's mother, Alice, ensured the letter was submitted to the *'Bridlington Chronicle'*. The newspaper not only printed the letter on Friday, 1st January 1915, but arranged for its syndication in Australia too. Prints of the letter were made and sold by Winifred and Mrs Holtby at the princely sum of threepence each, with the proceeds being donated to the Red Cross.

Winifred followed up her account with a long letter to the press, in which she earnestly protested against Britain adopting a policy of reprisals against Germany after the war.

Following the bombardment the school was moved to the Atholl Palace Hotel, Pitlochry, Perthshire, where it was well out of reach of the guns of any German warships.

The harvest fields of fair Lorraine
Were crowned with yellow corn,
And 'midst the gold were crimson heads
By poppy stems upborne.
In dewy morn the peasants reap,
In quivering heat of noon,
Till o'er the purple hill-top glides
The primrose harvest moon.
The harvest fields of fair Lorraine
Are not so gold as then,

WINIFRED HOLTBY

Queen Margaret's School,
Scarborough, 1914.
1&2: Winifred (A), aged 16.

And midst the gold are crimson stains,
The blood of slaughtered men.
And by the light of one lone star
And the chill wind's sobbing breath,
A reaper gathers his harvest there -
And the reaper's name is Death.

In 1915 Winifred wrote a play she titled 'Espinage' (a dreadful speller, it should have been 'Espionage') which contained the above, which was described as 'a mournful ditty, set to music and sung as a prologue'. The war had a profound effect on her and this was evident in her later writings. Below is the poem she wrote for the school magazine in 1915 (then at Pitlochry), titled simply 'Queen Margaret's School, Scarborough'.

There's a lone grey school on a wind-swept hillside,
Where over the garden the wild sea-birds cry;
There's a red-roofed town that the waves wash over,
And a castle stands guarding it regally high.
And far away from the eastward coastline,
Where the wind from the moorland heights blows chill,
We suddenly pause in our work to remember
That red-roofed town at the foot of the hill.

~

When the valley lies still in the soft morning sunlight,
And the looped river gleams like a silver snake,
And the misty clouds that enwrap the shoulders
Of the mountain giants grow tattered and break,
Then we think of the waves in the golden morning,
When the great sun rises beyond the sea,
Throwing living flame on the grey, cold water,
And the fresh salt sting of the wind blowing free.

Winifred Holtby was born on 23rd June, 1898, at Rudston (near Bridlington), East Yorkshire. Her father, David Holtby, was a prosperous farmer. Whilst still young Winifred was educated at home with her elder sister, Grace, before she moved on to Queen Margaret's School in Scarborough. There at the time of the bombardment, she wrote the long account of her 'adventure' which later appeared in the local press. Following a short period as a temporary nursing assistant in a London nursing home she attended Somerville College, Oxford, in 1917. The following year she interrupted her studies to become a hostel forewoman in the Women's Army Auxiliary Corps (WAACs), serving in France.

In 1919 she returned to Oxford to take a degree in Modern History. It was whilst there she met Vera Brittain and the two became lifelong friends. In 1921 Winifred moved to London to share a flat with Vera and to pursue her literary career.

Once dubbed 'the most brilliant journalist in London', Winifred was a regular contributor to many of the leading newspapers and periodicals of the time, as well as writing a number of books. She was also active in the fight for equality for women, and in the cause for world peace. In 1931 she collapsed after working for the Labour Party. The following year she was told she had an incurable kidney disease. She was given just

THE GRAND HOTEL

Foreshore Road and St Nicholas Cliff.
1: The Grand Restaurant. 2: The kitchens.
3: Exterior damage. 4: The Yorkshire Hussars.

two years to live. As it transpired, she survived for three and half years and in that time completed perhaps her two most important works, 'Mandoa, Mandoa!' and 'South Riding'. On the evening of 29th September 1935, the BBC announced Winifred Holtby's death to a stunned nation. Following a memorial service at St Martin-in-the-Fields she was buried at Rudston on 2nd October. In her Will, Winifred left her library to Queen Margaret's School. Alas, space does not permit me to do her justice, and I can do no better than to point interested readers towards Marion Shaw's biography of Winifred Holtby (see acknowledgements).

I was in the 8th Battalion of the West Yorkshire Regiment - The Leeds Rifles - at the time of the bombardment of Scarborough. We were stationed at York. On that day we were marching to our training ground when a motor cyclist came to our Colonel. We were at once halted and ordered to 'About Turn' and were marched sharply back to York. We had no idea of the reason.

We were given a ration of bread and cheese and an extra ration. We had no idea why. The next order was to 'Fall In' on the parade ground in full fighting order, with rifles and ammunition. Still we didn't know why.

We were marched to York Station, where we saw plenty of women and children who were arriving from Scarborough.

We arrived in Scarborough in the mid-afternoon and saw that the station had suffered a lot. We went down to the sea front and dug trenches in front of the Grand Hotel. We later went back to the station for more cheese and bread and to clear up the debris. At night we marched around the town to give the people some reassurance, before sleeping in the railway carriages that had brought us.

Before dawn the next day we marched to the sea front and occupied the trenches in front of the Grand Hotel. At dawn we saw a boat coming towards us and were ordered to load with five rounds of ammunition and told to close our ammunition magazine. As the boat came towards the shore some women and children came down to the shore. It turned out to be a fishing vessel.

We returned to the railway station and during the morning marched around the town again. We saw several dead shells in the castle. Then we marched back to the station and cleaned it up. Then there was more bread and cheese before we returned to York.

That was the beginning and the end of the Battle of Scarborough. Many buildings were badly damaged, but our next battle was in France . . .

This account was related by W. K. Reynard from Horsforth, Leeds. 22221 Private W. K. Reynard of the Leeds Rifles (8th West Yorkshires) survived the war.

The 1914 bombardment had repercussions in Leeds, for we went to Scarborough every year for our holiday. As I was on my way to school I read a placard saying 'Scarborough bombarded by the Germans!'

I arrived at school absolutely heartbroken and the headmistress took me into her room to find out what the trouble was.

"Oh dear," I blurted out, "The Germans have blown up Scarborough and I can't go for my holidays any more!"

This account was related by Marie E. Flounders from Temple Newsam, Leeds.

REG WEBSTER

Seaman Reginald Webster (18), served aboard *HMS Ramillies* and found three German post-cards of the raid on Scarborough on the deck of the *Von der Tann* whilst escorting the ship's crew, as prisoners, off the ship at Scapa Flow where the enemy fleet was interned in 1919.

HMS RAMILLIES

At the time of the raids on the east coast I was a signal boy on Admiral Sir David Beatty's flagship, 'HMS Lion', in company with the 'Princess Royal', 'Queen Mary', 'Tiger' and 'Indomitable'.

Information had been received that a squadron of German battle-cruisers were steaming north from their base in the Kiel Canal. We sailed from Rosyth on 15th December and steamed at full speed.

We were unable to intercept the enemy before they had carried out the bombardment, but steaming at about 28 knots we sighted them steaming southward at full speed. We increased to maximum speed (about 30 knots) and eventually sighted them. We were almost within gun range when a heavy mist came down - very common in the North Sea at that time of year - and visual contact was lost and not regained.

However, on 27th January 1915, the German battle-cruisers, 'Seydlitz', 'Moltke', 'Von der Tann' and 'Blücher', again sailed from their base on a similar expedition of bombardment; on this occasion they were not so lucky.

We sighted them early on the morning of 28th January and gave chase. We were about 4 knots faster than they were and opened fire in the vicinity of Dogger Bank. We opened fire and very soon hits were registered. The Blücher was sunk and all the other German ships received very severe damage, but managed to struggle back home.

The British ships naturally received some damage. 'Lion' sustained an 11-inch shell in the engine-room which necessitated having to draw the fires in the boiler room and so could not steam more than about 5 knots.

Admiral Beatty called the destroyer 'Oak' alongside and transferred his flag to 'Princess Royal' and continued to chase the enemy all the way back to Heligoland, inflicting further heavy damage on them. So much so that they never came out again until the Battle of Jutland on 30th May and 1st June.

I was still serving on Admiral Beatty's signal staff and was fortunate enough to be awarded the Distinguished Service Medal (DSM), being the youngest boy ever to receive this honour.

'Lion' was taken in tow by 'Indomitable' and towed more than 300 miles to Rosyth. A famous painting of the two passing under the Forth Bridge was titled 'Towing home the wounded Lion'.

This account was related by Lieutenant-Commander Alec S. Tempest who served throughout the war and survived. Later he was Commanding Officer of Leeds Sea Cadets and added the MBE to his DSM.

In 1919 I was serving as 'Boy 1st Class' on HMS Ramillies in the First Battle Squadron of the British Grand Fleet, which at the time was guarding the German Fleet interned at Scapa Flow. One day we left Scapa Flow for 'torpedo running', the Grand Fleet having been dispersed some months ago.

Whilst at sea we received a message that the Germans were 'scuttling' their ships in Scapa. We put on all speed to return and as we entered Scapa we were given orders to save, if possible, any of the ships still afloat and to round up all the crews. We rounded up hundreds of German sailors and herded them into the Forecastle Mess Deck. Whilst doing this, one of the German sailors hoisted his kit-bag onto his shoulder and out came three postcards which I picked up off the

HMS RAMILLIES

View from the deck of the ship's guns as she passes under the Forth Bridge.

HMS RAMILLIES

Firing a broadside salvo, North Sea 1918.

HMS ROYAL OAK

View from the deck of the Ramillies, as the Royal Oak passes under the Forth Bridge.

deck. Owing to the hustle and bustle at the time I just put them in my pocket and forgot about them. Later I discovered they were German postcards of the raid on Scarborough. Most of the men we had picked up came from the Von der Tann.

This account was related by Reginald Webster from York. Reg was born on 19th December 1900 in Dalton, Huddersfield. His parents were Richard (a tailor) and Emily. In 1917 Reg attempted to join the Army but was too young. He joined the Navy on 19th December 1918 on his 18th birthday. He served on the *Powerful* and was then sent to the *Ramillies* in March 1919. It was whilst serving on the *Ramillies* that the events related in the above account occurred. Reg continued with his 12 years and saw service aboard the ships *Vivid, Highflyer* and *Victory* amongst others. He left the Navy in 1923, married Jane Wear of Bradford two years later, and worked as a glass founder. He died on 7th November 1980 and is buried in York.

WHITBY

AN ACCOUNT OF THE GERMAN NAVAL RAID ON WHITBY ON WEDNESDAY, 16TH DECEMBER 1914

As the German warships steamed northward William Lee, a tailor and the Chairman of Burniston Parish Council watched them go, the sky black with the clouds of smoke belching from their funnels. The guns continued to fire and William could clearly see the flashes of flame from the barrels of the guns as the bombardment, sounding like heavy thunder in Burniston, came to an end. As the ships steamed away, the *Kolberg*, now steaming to rejoin the group, scattered mines in its wake to put off any Royal Naval pursuit which might materialise. At 9.00am William again heard the terrible din of gunfire as the two great battleships shelled the small fishing port of Whitby further up the coast. This time, thanks to the direction of the wind, the noise of the guns was distinct, and he recognised it for what it was.

June 1636
Not since June 1636 had Whitby been subjected to enemy naval action. On that occasion two Dutch warships had chased a Spanish ship into the harbour and boarded her. Incensed by this blatant defiance of Britain's neutrality, the Governor of Whitby, Sir Hugh Cholmley, had taken local ships, retaken the Spanish vessel and arrested the Dutch captains.

The Story of the Rohilla
The war had, however, come painfully close to Whitby some weeks earlier, in late October, when the hospital ship *SS Rohilla* had been wrecked off Saltwick with the loss of some ninety lives. Now it was to visit them in their homes and on their streets.

The *Rohilla*, having left the Firth of Forth on the afternoon of Thursday, 29th October, was bound for Dunkirk to pick up British wounded. The course had been set, but with no lights along the coast (because of war restrictions), navigation could be difficult. Towards evening a storm sprang up. By the time the ship passed Whitby the following morning (30th October) it was found to be closer to the coast than it should

ST HILDA'S ABBEY

1: The wreck of the *Rohilla* off Whitby.
2: The damaged western end of the Abbey.
3: The damage to the Abbey Lodge.

have been. Indeed it was only some two miles off the coast, when it should have been eight. It was about this time that the Second-Officer on the *Rohilla* reported seeing Morse lights flashing. However, the signalling was too fast and the message could not be read. At Whitby, coastguard Albert Jeffers continued trying to warn the ship she was too close in, unaware his message had not been deciphered.

Before soundings could be made to determine the ship's position it struck Whitby Rock violently and was lifted vertically and sideways, throwing the crew off their feet. Had it not been for the war, a light-buoy and bell would have marked this dangerous coastal feature. Captain Neilson, however, felt sure they had struck a mine and gave orders to steer to shore in the hope of finding shallower water and thus avoid sinking altogether. Some minutes later the ship ran aground on a submerged shelf of rock jutting out from Saltwick Nab (about a mile south of Whitby). There was nothing to be done but cut the engines and wait for daylight to see what action to take.

Ashore, the lifeboat had been called out, but it too waited for daylight. As soon as daylight dawned, however, it was clear the appalling weather conditions made a launch from the harbour impossible. It was then decided to haul the smaller of Whitby's two lifeboats along the shore to Saltwick. This feat was only accomplished by many pairs of willing hands from the good folk of Whitby, who by this time had turned out in droves, and the company of Territorials stationed in the town, the 7th (Cyclist) Battalion Devonshire Regiment.

Along the cliff top the 'rocket brigade' gathered and shot lines to the stricken ship, hoping to attach a bosun's chair and bring the crew to safety, but all the rockets fell short of the mark. The brigade then moved onto the beach and managed to get several lines onto the ship, but in such a position they could not be reached by those on board.

By the time the lifeboat reached Saltwick the *Rohilla* had broken in two on the rocks and was being pounded mercilessly by huge waves.

A little after 7.00am the Second-Officer and a volunteer crew of seven pulled away from the ship in the last remaining lifeboat (the others had all been smashed to matchwood by the sea) trailing a line they hoped to get to shore. However, with the constant threat of capsize the line was severed and the boat finally reached shore safely.

At 9.30am the lifeboat *John Fieldon* was launched. The *Rohilla* was just four hundred yards offshore, yet it might as well have been miles given the state of the sea and the prevailing conditions. In all, seventeen of the crew (five of whom were women) were taken off, including a stewardess named Mrs Roberts who had been a passenger on the *Titanic!* On the second attempt by the lifeboat eighteen further crew were taken off the *Rohilla* and landed safely. The people of Whitby rallied round and took them to shelter. By this time it was deemed too dangerous to launch again, and a plan was hatched to bring a heavier lifeboat from Upgang. However, when they finally got it to Whitby, it was impossible to launch it.

At noon the stern of the *Rohilla* broke away and sank, taking with it some thirty men. By now the cry for help had gone out up and down the coast. To the north the South Gare lifeboat put to sea, but took such a pummelling it had to be towed into Redcar. From Scarborough the steam trawler *Morning Star* towed the town's lifeboat north towards Whitby. But by the time it arrived it was considered too dangerous to attempt to launch the rowboat and it was stood by in readiness. Darkness drew in and finally closed over the dreadful scene. There was nothing to be done but wait for morning.

Come daylight another lifeboat attempt was made but was beaten back. Neither was the Scarborough boat able to get to the *Rohilla* and eventually it returned home.

7th (CYCLIST) BATTALION DEVONSHIRE REGIMENT

'B' Company at Headquarters, Guisborough Town Hall, December 1915.

1

2

Fearing the ship would soon break up, Captain Neilson advised all who could swim to take their chances and head for the shore. Horrified onlookers watched as men dropped over the side into the mountainous seas, battling for survival. Human chains were formed from the beach and swimmers went out as far as they could to bring in survivors. One such was George Peart (later awarded a Silver Medal by the Royal National Lifeboat Institute), who, time and again put his own life at risk to dive among the rocks to bring in members of the *Rohilla's* crew; another was Edward Griffin who saved four men and brought them to shore, a third was Colour Sergeant Hearn of the 7th Devonshires.

The drama continued through Saturday afternoon. Eventually, fifty men remained on the ship and there they spent another cold and hopeless night. At 1.00am (Sunday) the Tynemouth motor-lifeboat arrived on the scene, poured oil on the heaving waters in an attempt to calm them somewhat and, at first light, made for the *Rohillla*. The fifty remaining crew were taken off without mishap, Captain Neilson being the last to depart. Suddenly a huge cry went up from the stunned onlookers as a huge wave almost overturned the lifeboat. Fortunately it righted itself and sailed into Whitby harbour without further mishap.

Of the 220 aboard the *Rohilla*, 90 died and 130 survived. Today a monument stands in Whitby Cemetery to the lost, erected by the owners of the ship.

So it was that the good folk of Whitby were no strangers to disaster. However, not even the events of those few days could have prepared them for what was to come.

The Devonshires Report In

Part of the defence of the east coast, in an area stretching from Scarborough to Seaton Delaval in Northumbria, was entrusted to the men of the 7th (Cyclist) Battalion Devonshire Regiment, a Territorial unit. The battalion had been embodied for war in August 1914 - Regular units were 'mobilised' for war, Territorial units were 'embodied' - and were moved to form part of the Northern Command's Coastal Defence. The battalion would never see active service abroad in its own right, but throughout the war was to be used to provide reinforcements to other battalions of the Devonshire Regiment. The companies of the battalion were spread thinly along the east coast with detachments at points including Ravenscar, Robin Hood's Bay, the East Cliff Coastguard Station (War Signal Station) Whitby, Sandsend, Runswick Bay and Staithes. The Whitby detachment's Headquarters were at the Drill Hall, whilst Battalion Headquarters was based at Guisborough Town Hall. Hornsea was the Headquarters for the Yorkshire Mounted Brigade, which had command over this area of the coast and its defences.

On the evening of 15th December, Corporal Booth of the 7th Devonshires received a telephone call warning him and his men to keep a sharp lookout the following day. He was also told to ensure he and his men were in their trenches (at the coastguard look-out point at Staithes, north of Whitby) by 5.45am.

Sensing something was afoot, Booth was little surprised to be roused in the early hours of the next morning to receive a telegram telling him exactly the same thing. As instructed, Corporal Booth kept his eyes peeled and at 7.45am reported to the Coastguard Station at Whitby the sighting of three unidentified cruisers perhaps two miles off, steaming northward at full speed (the *Moltke*, *Seydlitz* and *Blücher*).

At 8.10am the Corporal again contacted the Coastguard Station at Whitby to report the sound of heavy gunfire to the north. It was assumed by all that a naval engagement was being fought and because of these reports the last thing anyone expected was two

THE EAST CLIFF

1&2: Before and after views of the Signal Station on the East Cliff.
3: The damage to St Hilda's Abbey. 4: The damage to the Abbey Lodge.

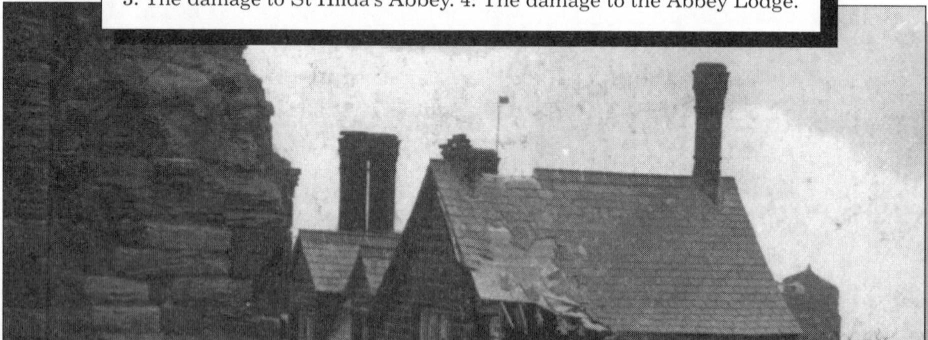

unidentified ships steaming in from the south towards them. At 8.50am, on the lookout post at Ness Point (just above Robin Hood's Bay, situated between Scarborough and Whitby), Private Light of the 7th Devonshires, on his way with a message for his Corporal, saw what he thought were the sterns of two ships disappearing northward. Private Manning, on telephone duty at the post, also saw the ships disappear into the mist, but thought nothing of it. Neither man saw fit to report the sightings to a senior officer (until after the events which were to follow).

First Salvo ~ First Fatality ~ East Cliff

It was at precisely 9.00am when a coastguard on watch on the East Cliff above the small, picturesque fishing port, spied a ship he did not at once recognise. The message, "What ship is that?" was run up the flagpole and in response the leading German vessel let loose a salvo of shells.

As with the inhabitants of Scarborough, the good folk of Whitby were caught completely off guard. Again, many thought the ships were part of the British Navy on manoeuvres. Others believed the thunderous noise they were hearing came from local shipbuilders blasting large pieces of iron. But they were quickly enlightened as the shells rained down from on high for a full eleven minutes.

The first two shells struck the cliffside in front of the East Cliff coastguard's station, while the third shell claimed the life of Coastguard Boatman Frederick Randall. Having just sat down to breakfast after coming off duty, Randall had risen from the table on being hailed by his wife upstairs that there were ships in the bay, and had gone to stand outside on the front step of his coastguard's cottage, situated next to the station, to get a better look. There he could clearly see the great grey warships in the bay, the barrels of their guns spitting orange flame. No sooner had he stepped outside to shout the warning to others than a large fragment of shell tore off the top of his head, taking a goodly portion of his face with it. He died instantly amid the debris of the explosion.

Those at the coastguard station, including Robert Parkinson, the telegraphist, who was wounded in the hand and leg by flying shrapnel, and several Royal Naval Reservists, beat a hasty retreat. It proved to be not a moment too soon as the station was hit and partly demolished.

A Territorial solider, 918 Private Favis, from the 7th Devonshires (a full company of which was stationed in the town) was injured slightly by flying shrapnel which tore the back off his greatcoat leaving it in shreds and him in shock. However, a Boy Scout, Roy Miller, also on duty at the coastguard station and acting as a runner (to carry messages) was less fortunate and was hit in the legs by shell splinters, his right being particularly badly hit. Despite this he remained at the station in the company of the Devonshires' Sergeant Foxworthy, who dressed his wounds. Once the shelling was over the Sergeant sent the lad to the hospital under the care of a St John Ambulance Brigade stretcher party. At first the wound did not appear that severe, but infection soon set in and in the end the doctors could not save the leg and it was amputated. It was said that Roy - a former pupil of the Municipal School in Scarborough - had the dubious honour of being the first Boy Scout to be wounded during the war (Scarborough Boy Scout George Harland Taylor being the first and only one to die).

St Hilda's Abbey and the Parish Church

Just as the Castle at Scarborough had proved an easy and identifiable target to the German gunners, so St Hilda's Abbey proved also. A shell took out the arch above the

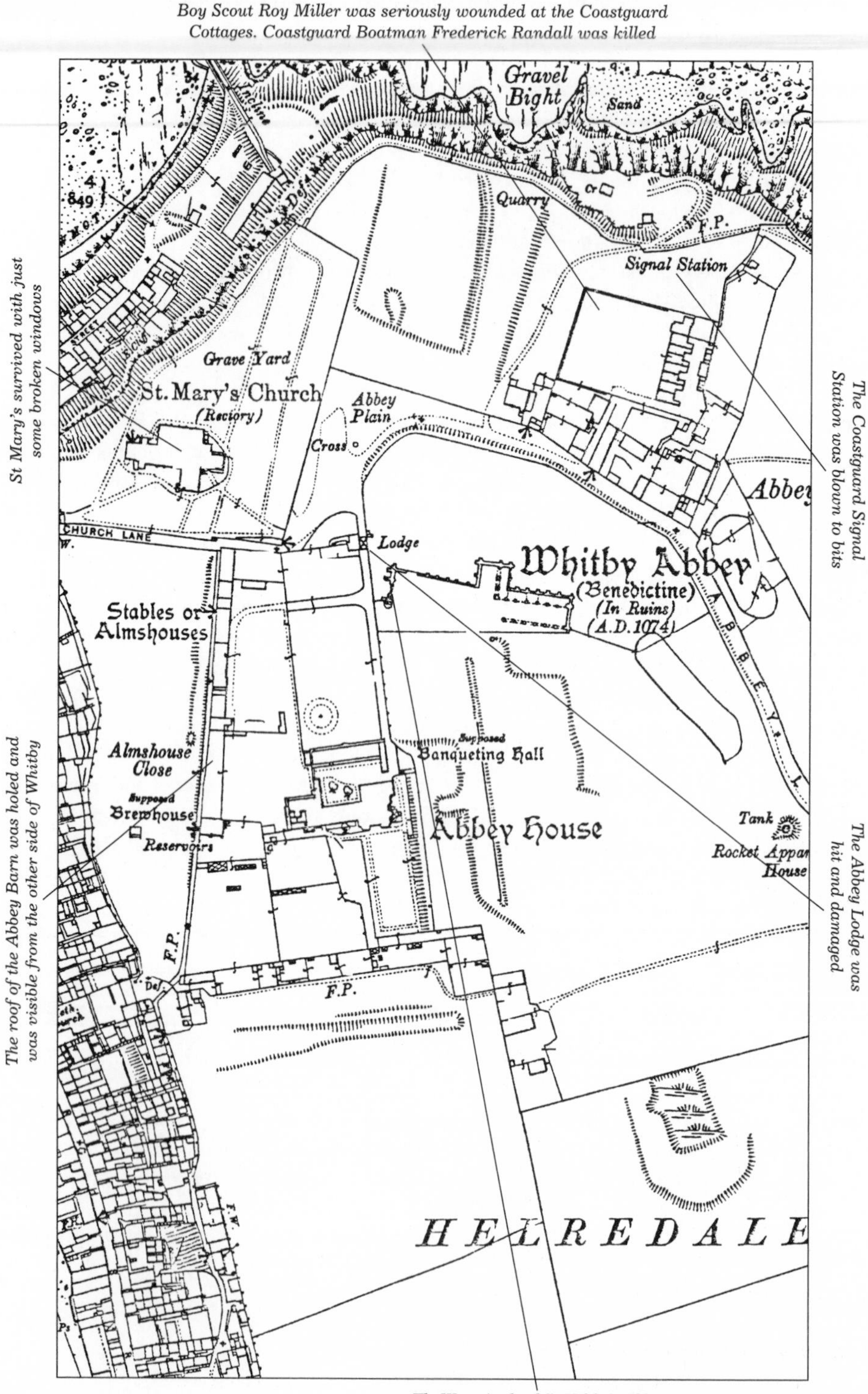
Boy Scout Roy Miller was seriously wounded at the Coastguard Cottages. Coastguard Boatman Frederick Randall was killed
St Mary's survived with just some broken windows
The Coastguard Signal Station was blown to bits
The roof of the Abbey Barn was holed and was visible from the other side of Whitby
The Abbey Lodge was hit and damaged
TheWest Arch of St Hilda's Abbey was knocked out by a direct hit
Gravel Bight
Sand
Quarry
F.P.
Signal Station
Grave Yard
St. Mary's Church
(Rectory)
Abbey Plain
Cross
CHURCH LANE
Lodge
Whitby Abbey
(Benedictine)
(In Ruins)
(A.D.1074)
Stables or Almshouses
Almshouse Close
Supposed Brewhouse
Reservoirs
Supposed Banqueting Hall
Abbey House
Tank
Rocket Appar House
F.P.
HELREDALE

west doorway and the Abbey Lodge was damaged too. However, the old Manor House and the Abbey House, both close by, escaped serious damage. An old tithe barn, stables and almshouse nearby had a large hole blown through its roof which could be seen clearly from the other side of Whitby.

The parish church of St Mary's, high on the East Cliff overlooking the harbour, escaped with a few broken windows.

Lady Emerges Unscathed from Devastated Cottage ~ Postmaster Injured

Close to Albion Place, the cottage of Mrs Filburn was all but demolished by a direct hit and she was injured, though not severely, by flying masonry and glass.

On his way to work William Watts, the Postmaster, of 28 Esk Terrace, was struck on the leg by a stray piece of shell from the blast at Mrs Filburn's on Albion Place. He escaped with just severe bruising.

Invalid Winefride Miller Mortally Wounded

In the town itself, Gray Street, George Street and Falcon Terrace were all badly mauled.

Frederick Robinson's house at 2 Gray Street was hit and severely damaged. Across the road at number 3, the house was also severely damaged and the owner's wife, Mrs John Marshall was badly wounded in the leg by a lump of shell. Further along at number 22, John Laws' roof was hit and almost blown off completely.

On Falcon Terrace behind George Street, the home of the local sanitary inspector, Oscar Graham, was severely damaged when a shell struck it and started a fire. The fire was extinguished before it could take hold, but the house was left devastated.

More damage was done on Spring Hill Terrace, which runs at right angles to Gray Street, George Street and Falcon Terrace. A shell hit *Springfield House* at 3 Spring Hill Terrace doing severe damage to the lower front elevation, completely destroying the bay window and fatally wounding the invalid owner, Winefride Miller, who was in bed in the room above the blast, having been confined there for almost three years. Two single ladies in the same house emerged shaken but otherwise unhurt. Suffering from serious injuries, Mrs Miller was taken to the nearby Convent Convalescent Home on Chubb Hill Road run by the Convent of the Sisters of Mercy. However, her condition suddenly deteriorated on Christmas Eve and by 3.00pm on Christmas Day (25th December) she had succumbed to tetanus as a result of the injuries sustained during the attack.

At Thomas Parratt's house, *Falcon House*, the roof was damaged and the windows were broken.

On Spring Hill Road at *West Hill House* a shell ripped off the side of the property and passed through into the garden beyond where a tree was struck and the high stone garden wall was left pitted with shrapnel. The owners, Mr and Mrs Bulmer, had only a few moments earlier taken refuge in the cellar and were thus saved from injury, or worse.

Amidst all this damage, the flying shells, debris and shrapnel, thronged hundreds of schoolchildren, sent home by their teachers, and their frantic parents, running anxiously through the streets looking for their offspring. It is a wonder more people were not killed.

Trapped on a Windowsill

On the corner of North Road and Falcon Terrace, Henrietta Fisher was busy cleaning

GENERAL DAMAGE

1: Mr Blewett's home at 1 Grove Street. 2: General damage on Gray Street. William Tunmore, mortally wounded at Boghall, lived at number 14. 3: Captain William Barton's home at 15 Esk Terrace. 4: *West Hill House*, the home of the Bulmers who took refuge in the cellar.

the windows of her family's greengrocers shop when the bombardment began. Sitting on the sill, she was trapped at the waist when the force of a nearby explosion brought the raised sash window down across her thighs. Unable to open the window the terrified girl spent some fifteen minutes struggling to get free, her cries for help unheard above the cacophony of exploding shells and the great thundering roar of the huge naval guns.

St John's Church of England School

The Fishburn Park area bore the brunt of the attack and thus most of the damage. However, St John's Church of England School, situated on Windsor Terrace (which suffered hugely) escaped unscathed.

At the start of the shelling the school's headmaster, William Hamilton, had assembled the children in 'drill order' and promptly marched them out of the place in an orderly manner. Once free of the school precincts most of the boys scampered off towards the countryside in the general direction of Ruswarp, blithely singing, *'It's a Long Way to Tipperary'* at the top of their lungs. With shells raining down all around the area it was a wonder none of them were hit!

Second Fatality

A trolleyman, William Tunmore, with the North Eastern Railway was hit in the chest by a piece of shrapnel as he struggled to bring his terrified horse under control having just passed Ford Crossing and reached Boghall; mortally wounded, he died on his way to the Cottage Hospital on Grape Lane. He was later awarded a silver medal for bravery by the Royal National Society for the Prevention of Cruelty to Animals in recognition of his efforts to save the horse. It was collected by his son.

Meadowfield Hall School

Considerable damage was done to Meadowfield Hall School. The main house was struck by a number of shells and the roof and four upper bedrooms were severely damaged. The coachhouse and various outbuildings were also hit and damaged, although the actual schoolroom escaped unscathed. The grounds of the school also suffered, with a wall and greenhouse being demolished. The glass in the vinery was shattered, a large tree blown out of the ground - roots and all, whilst another was cut in two. Luckily none of the pupils, all boys and at morning assembly at the time, were injured.

Mrs Gibson's Sweet Shop

A number of shells fell short of the town and crashed into the upper harbour sending up great gouts of mud and brine. One of the few places to suffer close to the harbour and pier was the Fancy Repository, next to the Marine Hotel, at 12 Marine Parade belonging to Laura Gibson. Here a splinter of shell smashed through the window and the thin wooden display partition into the shop, where it apparently tore through a leather purse, passed through a box of chocolates and a glass-covered picture and came to rest in a box of ladies' purses on a shelf behind the counter. Rather fortunately there had been no one in the shop at the time.

Final Salvos

As the ships made haste away from the devastated town the last few shells fell at Ruswarp and Sleights, where two unexploded shells were found and were 'examined' by wounded

MEADOWFIELD HALL BOYS' SCHOOL

British soldiers being nursed at the Red Cross Hospital housed in Sleights Institute. One of the shells was buried as a precautionary measure by Major-General Trotter, and one Sergeant Curtis, an inmate of the hospital.

A shrapnel shell, which had failed to explode, was later dug out of Dobson's Field at Ruswarp. The shell had buried itself to a depth of five feet.

Many people at Sleights had initially thought the shells were strays fired from a British warship in pursuit of a submarine! It was not until the many schoolchildren began arriving on their doorsteps from Whitby that they learned the truth.

Whitby Begins to Count the Cost

In just eleven minutes the German warships had sent some one hundred and fifty shells screaming into the little port - defended by just twenty-six soldiers - and had claimed two more lives outright, while a third, that of Winefride Miller, hung precariously in the balance. Nine days later the official death toll had risen to three.

In the aftermath of the bombardment the Whitby Division of the Red Cross were kept extremely busy and the following account of their day was entered into the Divisional logbook and signed by Honorary Sergeant and Secretary Hood and the Officer in Charge, Sergeant Knaggs:

> *Whitby was bombarded at 9.05am by two German war vessels, probably battle-cruisers. The bombardment lasted about seven minutes, and one hundred shells, at least, were fired into the town, chiefly in the direction of the coastguard station.*
>
> *No formal call was sent out, but members of the Brigade were at work before the bombardment had ceased.*
>
> *By 9.15am the Brigade was in communication with the Abbey House, a part of which was stated to be seriously damaged, and news was received that a boy scout [Roy Miller], and also a Territorial, were seriously injured. Sergeant W. R. Knaggs and Honorary Sergeant and Secretary C. H. Hood took charge and three bearer parties, each in charge of a senior, were despatched to the scene of the wrecked building.*
>
> *Squad No.1 met and took charge of the boy scout, Miller, who had received severe shell wounds in the back and legs. After being attended by a local doctor, Miller was conveyed to the Cottage Hospital, having subsequently one leg amputated.*
>
> *Squad No.2 attended the wounded Territorial, who was able to walk down to the hospital and within a few days recovered.*
>
> *Squad No.3, in searching the ruins of the coastguard station, discovered the body of coastguard Randall, whose head was almost blown away, having been hit by a shell. The body was removed by members of the Brigade to the mortuary, where the squad also assisted in the removal of another victim of the bombardment.*
>
> *Squad No.4 was then sent to Spring Hill Terrace, and removed a lady, Mrs Miller, who had been injured by shell and falling brickwork. This patient was removed to the Convent Convalescent Home, where she subsequently died.*
>
> *The following minor cases were also reported: five cases of shock and fainting, requiring skilled attention, two cases of shell wounds, one in leg and one in body, treated by nurses Birch and Philips, who are attached to the Brigade as nursing*

Invalid Winefride Miller was mortally wounded at Springfield House, 3 Spring Hill Terrace

Henrietta Fisher of North Road was trapped on a windowsill during the entire bombardment

Railway worker William Tunmore was mortally wounded at the cabin, Boghall

Mrs Marshall was wounded at her home, 3 Gray Street

Postmaster William Watts, of 28 Esk Terrace, was hurt on the leg on his way to work

The local sanitary inspector, Oscar Graham, had to face a fire at his house on George Street sisters, and several minor cases were attended by various members. Whilst assisting in the treatment of a lady, Nurse Birch was injured in the leg by a large piece of shell and was confined to the house for several days.

At noon the officer in charge and the senior member were conveyed to the Whitby High Lighthouse, it having been reported that it had been shelled. At the same time the secretary was taken to Scarborough - all in motor side-cars.

All telegraph and telephone wires being down, we were unable to communicate with other towns, and it was decided to offer assistance to Scarborough, if required. The Scarborough Division were interviewed, also Dr J. G. Murray, but assistance was not required.

As there were no further calls the Brigade dispersed at 4.00pm, but one stretcher squad remained on duty until 10.00pm.

The death toll at Whitby, as a result of the bombardment, was six, In the event of a return of the enemy, the Brigade will be on duty at once.

The number of dead given in this account is double the 'official' tally of three. However, it is interesting to note that there were three other deaths registered on the 16th December and it could be that this has confused the issue.

We already know of Randall and Tunmore who both died on the 16th, their deaths attributed to the bombardment, and also of the death of Winefride Miller, who died on Christmas Day from injuries sustained during the attack. The other listed deaths are those of Myra Jackson, Mary Elizabeth Warters and Annie Margaret Stephenson, though it has to be said there are no concrete details of their deaths being caused by, or having occurred during the bombardment.

There is also the story of seventy-three-year-old William Graham, who was found dead in his home on Church Street on the 17th December. It was later claimed he had died from the shock of the bombardment. His death would take the unofficial tally to seven. I believe, given the material available, that there were four deaths at Whitby caused directly or indirectly by the bombardment, those of Randall, Tunmore, Graham and Miller.

Brave Lad Rides Terror-Stricken Horse Bare-Back

Immediately the shelling was over stories of 'strange' and 'miraculous' incidents, 'near misses' and 'heroes' began to emerge.

There was the story of local lad, sixteen-year-old James Mitchell of Scoresby Terrace, who had been delivering flour in Baxtergate when the shelling began. His horse had quickly become skittish and had bolted, taking its dray with it. Luckily young James had hauled himself onto the back of the horse and managed to divert the terror-stricken beast along Wellington Road towards the railway station. He guided it on past Windsor Terrace, where shells were falling heavily, and onto Esk Terrace. Here he apparently executed a nifty about-turn, without overturning the dray, but knocking down a lamppost in the process. It was at this instant that a shell crashed into the road ahead of the horse, forcing it to pull aside. The front wheel of the dray caught fast in the hole in the road and tore itself free of the animal, which galloped off with James still aboard. Later the boy and the horse were found, worn out but otherwise unscathed after their ordeal.

Young James was later awarded a silver medal for bravery by the Royal Society for the Prevention of Cruelty to Animals, on which was inscribed 'For animal life-saving.

William Kipling and other boys from Mount School hid in a tunnel on the Khyber Pass

James Mitchell's horse bolted whilst delivering flour, but the lad guided the terror-stricken beast through the streets from Baxtergate to Esk Terrace

William Graham was found dead at his home on Church Street on 17th December and is believed to have died from shock during the bombardment

Four plucky lady postal workers refused to leave their posts at the GPO on Baxtergate whilst their colleagues fled

For humanity.' The medal was presented on behalf of the Society by its local representative Major Bentley Buckle (who also presented William Tunmore's posthumous medal to his son). Both silver medals were, for a time, proudly on display in the window of the *Whitby Gazette* offices at 17/18 Bridge Street, the premises of Horne & Son Printers and Stationers.

Lady Postal Workers Refuse to Hide ~ Breakfast Interrupted

Then there was the account of four lady workers at the Post Office who stoutly stayed at their posts at the main GPO on Baxtergate throughout the bombardment, even though others sought shelter.

At the Bruce home, *Hill Crest* on Prospect Hill, a lump of shrapnel crashed through the house and straight through the middle of the dining-table, at which the very startled Mr and Mrs Bruce were breakfasting!

Local Livestock Killed

There was also the story of the pig which had been out in its field and had its back sliced off by a lump of shell. Needless to say the poor animal had to be destroyed. However, it could be that this story was a corruption of the tale of Isaac Fisher's pig, which had its head neatly severed by a piece of shell.

There were also two sheep struck and killed near the Abbey.

Gas Works and Police Station Unscathed

The gas works was reported to be unscathed, though on later inspection lumps of shell and shrapnel were found littering the tops of the gas holders. Likewise the Electric Power Station at the top end of Church Street emerged unscathed, though houses close by were damaged.

It was also reported that some twenty shells had fallen all about the Police Station on Spring Hill, and although some of the policemen's houses were damaged, the station escaped entirely.

Tussaud Collects Relics

In a contemporary account a young man named Tussaud, whom it was claimed was descended from the famous Madame Tussaud of the London waxworks, visited Whitby after the bombardment for the sole purpose of collecting interesting relics and curios of the event.

Near Misses

Near misses and close calls were reported by a soldier from the 7th Devonshires, a Despatch Rider, Private Moysey, who claimed a shell had passed close to him only to crash into the road at the seaward corner of Royal Crescent as he was making for the lookout post situated at the Spa and his Commanding Officer Captain Goodridge; and another by Mrs Rhodes, who was passing down Ruswarp Bank when a shell struck the retaining wall ahead of her, doing damage to the wall and the overhead telephone wires, but missing her completely.

Birth of George Shrapnel Griffin

One of the most remarkable stories to emerge in Whitby, and by far and away the most endearing tale that day, was that of the birth of Edward Griffin's seventh child.

Despatch Rider Moysey of the 7th Devonshires had a narrow escape on Royal Crescent

Dr Lionel Pern of 27 Skinner Street delivered the bombardment baby, George Shrapnel Griffin

The Kipling family lived at 6 Hunter Street and John Kipling joined up shortly after the bombardment

Harold Parkin hid behind a wall in Duck's Field after St Hilda's School sent the children home

The child, a boy, was born on the morning of the bombardment, during the raid. The noise and fear of the bombardment had induced labour in a way few modern drugs or techniques could possibly do and Dr Lionel Pern was called from his home at 27 Skinner Street. The poor, petrified Mrs Griffin lay in her bed at 52 The Cragg, bearing down, whilst all about her was mayhem and madness. At first she thought the noise to be thunder and said as much to the doctor, but he did not reply for fear of upsetting her and adding to her obvious distress. However the young woman with Mrs Griffin, in an attempt to turn her mind from the noise, lied and said she thought it was a 'rocket' - the signal to call out the lifeboat when a ship is in danger of coming ashore. As she listened to the shrieks and explosions of the first few shells falling on the town and the cries outside in the street the trembling Mrs Griffin was left in no doubt that the Germans had come, and became terrified that at any moment a shell might crash through the thin walls of the house and carry them all off into oblivion. It was at this point the child, a boy, emerged screaming into the world, all ten and a half pounds of him.

On satisfying himself that the child was healthy and the mother was in no danger, save that which they were all in, the doctor advised the family to put their trust in God and seek comfort in prayer and left to see to his own residence - only to be called away to the home of another patient, the invalid Mrs Miller.

The Cragg escaped damage and all was well. Louis Tracey, the Commandant of the Whitby District Volunteer Training Corps, one of the boy's soon-to-be godparents, was asked to choose the child's names and settled on George 'in whose glorious reign England is rendering her greatest of many services to humanity by crushing Prussian militarism' and Shrapnel 'as commemorating the German attack on our undefended town, so dear to all Yorkshire folk and so famous in its history'. And thus the child who came into the world amidst the murderous bombardment of Whitby was named. So taken with the child and his naming was Louis Tracey that he actually wrote to the King to inform him of the event, and of the child's father's long history of meritorious service in the saving of lives. Teddy Griffin, a 'holder-up' in a shipyard, had saved some thirty-six people from drowning, had been awarded the Royal Humane Society's bronze medal on 12th December 1911, and had, earlier in 1914 saved four men from the crew of the stricken hospital ship the *Rohilla*.

On the first day of 1915 Mr Tracey received a reply from the King's Private Secretary, Stamfordham:

> *I have received and laid before the King your letter of the 30th December, reporting the remarkable circumstances attending the birth on the 16th December of Mr and Mrs Griffin's seventh child, who has been christened in memory of the occasion 'George Shrapnel Griffin'.*
>
> *The King is glad to learn that the mother and child both escaped injury and are now making good progress. I am commanded to express to Mr Edward Griffin His Majesty's congratulations upon his magnificent record for saving life from drowning.*

Following the exchange of letters the *Whitby Gazette* interviewed the mother of 'the famous baby' and the reporter commented on how well they both appeared given their ordeal. "Poor little fellow," Mrs Griffin was reported to have said, holding the baby up for the reporter to get a better view before hugging him to her bosom, "Shot and Shell they already call him about here, but he knows nothing about it."

GENERAL DAMAGE

1: Windsor Terrace. 2: Cleveland Terrace.
3: *West Hill House*. 4: Esk Terrace.

Whitby Spy

There was much speculation both in the town and reported in the local paper, that somewhere in Whitby there was a spy with a hidden wireless set, which had been used to communicate with the enemy prior to the bombardment. It was said that the Germans knew of happenings in the town almost as quickly as did the locals themselves! A spy was never found however, nor were any spies uncovered at the time, although the *Daily Express* endeavoured to pin the blame on a German intern:

> *There can be little doubt that the Germans, in their raid on the east coast, acted on information supplied to them by spies. For years past, the German secret service, under the lead of Steiuhauer, the Kaiser's master spy, has been specially engaged in obtaining the latest plans of east coast towns and their approaches from the sea.*
>
> *Admiralty charts, showing navigable channels, depths of water, lights and precautions to be observed on entering harbours have been sent to the German naval authorities by their secret agents here, and they have also been reliably informed of the strength of defence works, stores, and public buildings.*
>
> *There is now, in one of the concentration camps, a notorious German spy who lived for some years in Whitby, one of the places bombarded on Wednesday morning. The authorities knew him well, but he was not arrested until war broke out, and it may be safely assumed that long before being deprived of his liberty he sent over to his imperial master information which was useful when the German ships made their sudden raid on the town.*

That the information mentioned was readily available to anyone who cared to have it was conveniently overlooked by the journalist. There may very well have been Germans operating out of both Scarborough and Whitby, but as neither were of any military or naval significance (apart from the war signal stations) there can have been very little useful information passed back to Germany. Hartlepool was perhaps a different matter.

As if to lend credence to the story of the Whitby-based spy, the story of the arrest of a Manchester man in possession of a wireless appeared alongside it. The man, unnamed, was said to have been in possession of an 'apparatus complete in every detail - consisting of dozens of feet of wire, two or three batteries and other mechanical devices'. There were no details about what the man had been doing with the 'apparatus' nor was there any further information as to what became of him.

After the raid on the town, reports of bright lights being 'flashed' out to sea by spies became almost commonplace.

Local Newspaper Condemns German Atrocity

As at Scarborough, the local paper, the *Whitby Gazette*, was full of details of the raid on the town over the next few days and weeks. By Friday, 18th December, two days later, the paper carried the following editorial, intended to show how unbowed the town was by the incident and how its citizens still had both faith and pride in the country's Navy (despite its having been unable to prevent the raid in the first place):

> *Like a bolt from the blue to the people of Whitby came the naval bombardment on Wednesday morning. It came when business and working people generally had*

just got nicely settled down to the duties of the day. Bang! Crash! came their first shell, and, with the second boom and nerve-racking crash, every intelligent person was immediately impressed with the idea that the Germans had opened fire on the town.

It was unlike anything they had ever heard overhead, either in the way of thunder or shipwreck signal; and then for every two or three seconds of seven momentous minutes, four-inch shells were rained over the old town.

With long-fixed calculation, the two fine cruisers had chosen their stand with such a nicety that every place and structure of importance - signal station, electric power station, gasworks and viaduct - came within their line of fire.

The place selected for opening fire happened to be but a very short distance to the northward of the scene of the wreck of the hospital ship 'Rohilla'.

The warships first appeared round the bend of the cliffs three miles to the south of the harbour; they came through the foam and spume of an angry, though windless sea, and dimmed by a haze which formed a fit backing for their evil work. How the men of Whitby - especially those who had handled the forty-pounder breech-loader gun, which at one time was mounted on the cliffs, wished for something of the kind to reply with!

There was a calm but indignant spirit shown by the men of Whitby; but the women, they were naturally distressed, because they did not fully comprehend the nature of the danger and the best way to avoid it.

Most people kept in their houses; though many showed a restless move towards the country. As a whole the town stood the punishment with marvellous composure. The spirit of the men was typified by the young man who, immediately the ships steamed away, went off to the Recruiting Station to enlist.

Doctors, Devonshires, police and ambulancemen, were cool and collected and ready for any call upon their energies.

This incident of war - so disastrous to us as a town - was considered but as an incident in the great war which is testing the spirit of the nation.

Admiral von Tirpitz makes a mistake if he thinks to hearten his Berlin friends by a demonstration of cowardice on the part of the people of Whitby. They snap their fingers at him and ask him to send still more of his ships into the North Sea, that our 'Jacks' may have a chance to send them to 'Davy Jones's locker'.

Very naturally our readers are anxious to know what has become of these particular warships, but all we seaboard people know how wide and free is the ocean and how difficult it must be to round up or make fight vessels possessing great powers of speed.

Of course, it is presumed they have come out of the Kiel Canal, and that their main objective was a demonstration along the coast, so they could wireless to the Kaiser, "Hoch, hoch, we have invaded England, destroyed their big ports and shipping, now await attack by British Grand Fleet. Hoch, Hoch!"

We have unbounded confidence in our fine old Admiral, whom we lovingly call 'Jacky Fisher' to deal, in a seamanlike fashion, with the enemy.

The paper also carried calls for more men to enlist in order that any invasion attempted by the enemy could be repelled in a controlled fashion, rather than by individuals 'taking the law into their own hands'. The Duke of Norfolk and the writer H. G. Wells were vocal advocates of the call to arms.

1

COASTGUARD COTTAGES

The coastguard cottages, where Boatman Frederick Randall was killed, Boy Scout Roy Miller was seriously injured and Private Favis was slightly wounded, were situated next to the Signal Station. Both pictures show the damage done to the properties, and coastguards and troops from the 7th (Cyclist) Battalion Devonshire Regiment who were posted in the town and along the coast, clearing the debris.

2

The Inquests of Randall and Tunmore

The inquests into the untimely deaths of Coastguard Randall and railway worker Tunmore were conducted on the afternoon of Thursday, 17th December, by the Whitby Coroner, George Buchannan, and were held in the Board of Guardians' Room on Church Street. The jury was sworn in under the foremanship of Mr Crawther.

"Before beginning the enquiry on this occasion, I think it wise to make one or two remarks," began the Coroner. "We live in very strange times, and this enquiry is quite unprecedented in either your experience or mine, but that is no reason why it should not be a plain common-sense enquiry, and that is what I propose to make it.

"These are days of excitement that call for quiet, steadfast courage, and those of us who cannot serve our King in arms, will do our best by going about our ordinary work in our ordinary way, with as little excitement and heroics as possible.

"With that preface, I will now call upon the first witness."

The Chief Officer of the Coastguard at Whitby, Charles Davie, took the stand. He began by stating it was 8.55am when they, those on duty at the coastguard station on the East Cliff, had first spotted two German cruisers through the haze. At that time he was inside the War Signal Station and could not see if the vessels were flying flags of any description. Davie estimated the ships to be some three miles off the coast.

The staff at the War Signal Station then carried out their orders as required by the Admiralty, claimed Davie.

"And they were?" asked the Coroner.

"I'd rather not say, sir," answered Davie.

"Very well," nodded the Coroner, making a note, "What happened then?"

"In about five or ten minutes the vessels bore about east, and then they commenced to fire. The foremost vessel eased down a bit and closed in on her, opening fire . . ."

He went on to say he could not swear as to what size guns had been used, but that the fire was directed at the War Signal Station. The first salvo hit the face of the cliff, underneath the station and this gave them time to clear it. The second salvo, in which Davie claimed three or four shots were fired together, took the top off the station, practically demolishing it, and carried on towards the coastguard cottages behind.

Boatman Randall, Davie informed the inquest, was not on duty in the Signal Station at the time, for he had gone off duty at daylight and gone home for his breakfast. He could not tell how many shells were fired, but estimated between 100 and 150, and they being common shells, not of the shrapnel variety. It was Davie's impression that all the shots were fired at the Signal Station, but that some went wide of the target. Not that that was intentional, in his opinion, but was made so by the rolling of the ships as they fired. The East Cliff was some 250 feet above sea level and, in his opinion, this had necessitated the enemy guns firing high, which is why shells had fallen in the town. He judged the bombardment to have lasted for between fifteen and twenty minutes, but could not be exact on this point.

It was only after the shelling had stopped that he heard that Randall had been hit and taken to hospital. Davie had then gone to the hospital to see him and had found Randall with a large part of his head blown away, evidently by a shell or piece of one. Davie stated death must have been instantaneous. He had also seen the place where Randall had been hit, and it was evident that Randall had come out of his cottage onto the porch when he had been struck. Davie understood Randall was on his way to tell the Territorials on duty at the station to go for their breakfasts. The pavement outside the cottage was covered with blood, but as far as he was aware, no one saw Randall hit.

GENERAL DAMAGE

1&2: Cleveland Terrace. 3: Windsor Terrace. 4: *West Lea*, Falcon Terrace, the home of solicitor's clerk, John Gaskin.

Davie then confirmed that Randall was thirty years old and that his position with the coastguard was that of a Boatman. The deceased was a married man with four children, the youngest being six months old. He also confirmed that a boy scout had been injured, though he did not see how it had occurred, and that no others had been killed or wounded.

After declaring that a good many shots hit the station, the foreman of the jury asked Davie, "Then you consider the marksmanship was good?"

"I cannot say that sir," answered Davie.

"What do you consider to be bad?"

"I am not going to say sir." Davie had no further evidence to give and was allowed to stand down for the moment.

No verdict was given on the death of Randall at this point, as the Coroner was intent on hearing all the evidence in both cases before asking the jury to give a verdict. There was a short pause and then Ernest Lorains, a goods porter with the North Eastern Railway Company was called to the stand to give evidence in the case of William Tunmore.

Lorains confirmed that Tunmore had been a 'rulleyman' with the company and that he was sixty-one years old. He was then asked to give his account of the events of that morning.

Lorains had been with Tunmore near Boghall Cabin at about 9.15am. He was leading his horse along the railway line and Tunmore was walking with him. Several shells had burst on the houses close by and the pair had wanted to get out of the line of fire. Just as they had passed through the gate at Boghall Cabin, a shell exploded in the cattle dock and a piece of it hit Tunmore in the chest. Though not killed outright, Tunmore expired as Lorains and others carried him to the hospital.

This was the sum of Lorains' evidence and he stepped down.

The jury quickly returned a verdict that 'the men were killed by shells fired by German vessels on 16th December.' The jury then directed the Coroner that their fees should be handed to Coastguard Randall's widow with an expression of their sympathy.

The Archbishop of York

On the evening of the day of the Whitby inquests (17th December) the Archbishop of York, Dr Cosmo Gordon Lang, whilst instituting a new vicar at Wistow, near Selby, made the following reference to the bombardment of the north-east coast:

> *It is very natural that at this present time a cry of anxiety and concern should be rising from our hearts, for at last we have had a vision of what the reality of war means. The hideous spectacle of death and destruction has knocked at our own door. War, with its ruthlessness, its ferocity, its wanton destruction of life, has, though only for a short hour, invaded the coasts of this diocese.*
>
> *Peaceful citizens have been killed and wounded, peaceful homes of our own people have been scattered and four of our parish churches have been damaged. We cannot be sufficiently thankful that though for a moment, there seemed a danger that one of the most venerable of our Yorkshire churches, the Abbey of Whitby, might be desecrated, the danger has passed.*
>
> *It is quite near enough to make us here in this diocese of York feel a new sense of kinship and sympathy for the members of Christ's church at Malines, Louvain and Rheims. While there arises from us very naturally the cry of distress, there*

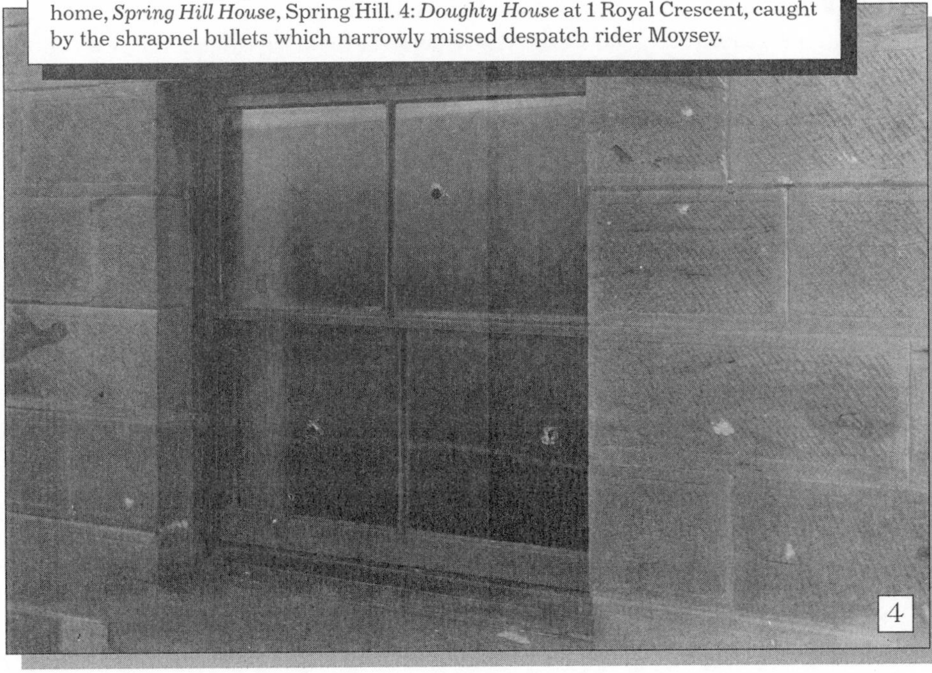

GENERAL DAMAGE

1: The Old Ropery, Spital Bridge. 2: *West Lea*, Falcon Terrace. 3: Dr Herbert Raw's home, *Spring Hill House*, Spring Hill. 4: *Doughty House* at 1 Royal Crescent, caught by the shrapnel bullets which narrowly missed despatch rider Moysey.

arises also a stronger and deeper note - the cry of a righteous indignation. Our hearts burn when we think of this cruel and ruthless violation of the sanctities of international law. We have witnessed an attack not only upon our coasts, but also upon all the principles which we had hitherto hoped were to govern the warfare of civilised nations.

The object of the enemy was at least twofold - to create alarm in the hearts of our people and to make it difficult for our troops to be sent across the channel to take part in carrying on our righteous cause. Let us show that we are not going to be rushed into panic. When the first excitement was over, the people of these towns sensibly returned to their homes and resumed their ordinary lives. Let the spirit of the whole county and country follow that example.

This attack upon the sanctities of our own Yorkshire coast will bring many more recruits to the front and will, therefore, result in more men being able to cross the seas while there will be more available for home defence.

The Archbishop had a remarkably succinct grasp of the situation and the realities of the raid and its repercussions. Recruitment did indeed benefit, as has been previously stated, and not just in Britain. One contemporary report claimed that two recent immigrants to Australia, both men hailing from Whitby, on hearing of the raid on their home town, had packed up at once and returned to England forthwith to enlist.

The reference in the above passage (and elsewhere in this book) to Louvain concerns a Belgian city occupied by the Germans on the 19th August 1914. The city was to become synonymous with the 'atrocities' perpetrated by the advancing Germans and the name Louvain a byword for Hun barbarism. During the first few days of occupation a number of hostages were taken from the civil populace and shot - standard German practice during the time of the invasion. However, around the 25th August German rearguard units were attacked by units of the Belgian army (such as it was) from Antwerp. The German rearguard fell back on Louvain in chaos, during which shots were fired and violence erupted in the city. Believing themselves the victims of determined Belgian resistance the Germans retaliated by systematically sacking, looting and burning the city over a period of five days and nights, and in rounding up civilians, among them clergymen, women and children and shooting them en masse.

Diplomatic outrage followed, with many neutral countries shocked and horrified by this new type of warfare - a reign of terror practised against a civilian population the Germans felt was a legitimate extension of war, and one which would quickly subdue and pacify a hostile populace. That the Belgians claimed German troops had shot at, and killed each other in the chaos and confusion of their retreat brought fresh condemnation from across the globe.

Messages to the Wounded Boy Scout

Languishing in the Cottage Hospital on Grape Lane, minus a leg, wounded Boy Scout, Roy Miller received many messages both directly and indirectly from far and wide to cheer him. His most treasured message however, was from the head of the Scout movement General Baden Powell:

To Scoutmaster Vivian,
Seaton Gray, Whitby.
Extremely sorry to hear of severe wounds received by King's Scout Robert Miller,

who holds the honour of being the first Scout wounded in defence of his country.
Only hope you will be able to send better news of him tomorrow.
Baden Powell.

To King's Scout Miller,
Hospital, Whitby.
Scouts are all proud of you and admire the plucky way you bear your wounds.
Keep smiling.
Baden Powell.

To Scout Miller,
Coastguard Station, Whitby.
Glad to learn you are still smiling. Can you whistle old chap?
Second-Lieutenant Nicholls,
Royal Engineers, Aldershot.

To Captain Miller,
Victoria Square, Whitby.
Please say how Roy is today. My best wishes for our brave Scout.
Lady Ley,
Epperstone Manor.

To Captain Miller,
Victoria Square, Whitby.
The Cambridge Boy Scouts wish to enquire as to the condition of Scout Roy Miller.
Councillor Church,
Guildhall, Cambridge.

Funeral of Frederick Randall

The next day, Friday, 18th December, the funeral took place of Coastguard Boatman Randall under the direction of the undertakers Pinder Brothers.

The cortège moved off from the Cottage Hospital on Grape Lane at 2.00pm and present were representatives from the military, navy, police and St John Ambulance Brigade - all in uniform. The coffin was of polished oak, with heavy brass mountings. Members of the coastguard acted as pall-bearers and the coffin was draped with the union flag, upon which were placed Randall's cap and side-arms, together with wreaths and floral tributes. Among the many tributes were those from the Naval Centre at Newcastle, the wives of the coastguards, Randall's colleagues, and from 'F' Company of the 7th Devonshires. The cortège was preceded by a firing party drawn from the Devonshires, led by a Boy Scout bugler named Gale. Many local people turned out to pay their last respects.

Randall was buried in Whitby Cemetery and a single volley was fired over the grave. The service was conducted by Reverend Snushall and Reverend Walter Bancroft. The last post was then sounded by the boy bugler.

Special Meeting of Whitby Urban District Council

On the evening of Friday, 18th December a special meeting of the Whitby Urban District Council was convened at the Council Chambers on Flowergate for the purpose of *'Considering as to the advisability of applying to His Majesty's Government for compensation to those who have suffered loss in Whitby through the German bombardment, or any other suggested method of compensation.'*

Many of the councillors attended the meeting direct from the funeral of Coastguard Randall, held that afternoon.

Before the matter of compensation could be addressed the Chairman, Councillor James Egan Harmston, proposed the council spend a moment or two in contemplation of those who had lost their lives in the town.

"Property damage," he said, "could be repaired, but life forfeited could never be brought back."

There were nods of assent and mutterings of "Hear! Hear!"

A resolution, expressing the sympathy of the council to the families of the deceased was proposed and passed. The Chairman then went on to say how fortunate the town had been compared to its neighbours, Scarborough and Hartlepool, at which much greater loss of life had been sustained. He then progressed to the damage done to the town itself and the first rough estimates which were to hand of between £5,000 and £10,000 in repairs - much of which, he stated, had fallen to those least able to pay it. He went on to say how proud he was with the behaviour of the townsfolk during and after the bombardment, and gradually moved on to the various messages he had received:

> *I am very much concerned to hear of the ordeal Whitby has been called upon to endure. Kindly express my deepest sympathy with those who have suffered. I am quite sure that, however great the damage done to Whitby, the courage of her people will be greater than ever.*
> Gervase Beckett, MP for Whitby.
>
> *We wish to extend our heartfelt sympathy at the loss of life and damage occasioned by the visit of our inveterate foes.*
> Chairman and members, Orsett Urban District Council, Kent.
>
> *We deeply regret Whitby's experience and extend sympathy with all who have suffered.*
> Mayor and Corporation of Bridlington.
>
> *A vote of condolence and sympathy was passed with the inhabitants of Whitby in their terrible suffering caused by the bombardment of the town by German warships.*
> Cardiff Chamber of Commerce.
>
> *We offer our deepest sympathy in the terrible events you have just experienced at the hands of the enemy, whose ideas of warfare are in such marked contrast to our own. Please convey our condolences to the relatives of the dead and we hope for a speedy recovery of the wounded.*
> Mayor and Corporation of St Albans.
>
> *We tender our deepest sympathy with the inhabitants of Whitby in the sorrowful loss of life and destruction of property caused by the bombardment.*
> Musical & Social Bodies to Assist the War Charities, Stockton.

The Daily Telegraph here [Hartlepool] is in touch with the Mayors of Hartlepool and West Hartlepool with regard to joining a national appeal by the Daily Telegraph to compensate the unfortunate losers.
Mayor of Hartlepool.

We express deep sympathy with the sufferers, and, if any children are rendered destitute of homes, homes will be prepared for them and prompt help given.
Council of Dr Barnado's Homes.

I wish to express my deep sympathy with all three towns. I trust people will not be driven from their homes. In case such a need arises I will gladly offer a home to two or three, and promise that every care and consideration will be afforded them. We are only a small family, but will do our best.
Mrs C. M. Russell, Stoke Newington.

It is probable that some poor people may be suffering from the Hun's gunfire on the defenceless town. Please find enclosed the sum of £1. 1s. [one pound one shilling] for the relief of any such cases.
Messers B. & L. Philips, London.

This brought the messages to a close and the Chairman began in earnest on the main reason for the hastily convened meeting:

And now it rests with us to see what can be done. The loss, we know, is great, and if some steps can be taken whereby we can get help for those people, it will be a very good thing. We have had a visit today from Mr Bushel, an Inspector of the Local Government Board, and the vice-chairman and the clerk have been round the town with him to inspect the damage. There was one suggestion he made and that was that all damage which had occurred should be tabulated and the approximate damage scheduled out.

The Chairman went on to enlighten the council members as to what they could expect in terms of financial help. Apparently the Prince of Wales' National Relief Fund was not applicable to Whitby's case (for reasons not given), and the town's own War Aid Fund represented only 'a drop in the bucket,' according to the Chairman. And as to the setting up of a local fund, he claimed that was impossible owing to the drain on the public purse. Nor was it thought relief would be adequately met from private assistance or from newspaper appeals. All in all, it was decided there was no one else to turn to for help but the Government.

Councillor Thomas Woodwark, acting as Vice-Chairman, then told the council how he had been approached and asked how local people stood with regard the damage to their property. One suggestion which had been made to him was that if the country was victorious in the war, the Germans could be made to pay for the damage. But there was a feeling that there may very well be a long wait if this were the case. Woodwark recommended that collective action to secure compensation be taken as opposed to individuals all fighting their own claims. Indeed, he proclaimed, if the Admiralty had seen fit to keep the fleet at home while the town was left open to attack, then surely some burden of responsibility and, to an extent, culpability, rested with them, and compensation should perhaps come from the Government's coffers. He also felt that the town should put its case as a matter of right, rather than as a matter of charity.

The Vice-Chairmen informed the meeting that a Mr Welburn had been engaged to survey the town and prepare an official report for the council on the extent of the damage done. He further proposed the Government be approached with a view to setting up an insurance scheme for properties in coastal towns, similar to one which had been set up for the mercantile marine.

There was much heated discussion over the matter of insurance and who should foot the bill for it before the meeting was brought to a close with a motion for the council to send a letter of *'appreciation for their bravery for standing at their posts at such a time'* to the wounded Boy Scout, Roy Miller, and the injured Territorial from the 7th Devonshires. This motion met with hearty cries of "Hear! Hear!" and a round of applause.

As at Scarborough, the matter of compensation would rumble on and on and eventually fizzle out altogether by the end of 1915.

Funeral of William Tunmore

On Saturday, 19th December, the funeral of railway worker William Tunmore was held. The service was conducted by the Reverend Austen, the Vicar of Thirsk, and held at St John's Church.

As with Randall's funeral the day before, the service and internment at the Whitby Cemetery was well attended by local people, and many wreaths and floral tributes were laid from work colleagues and friends from St John's Church, where Tunmore had been a warden.

The following evening at St John's Church the Reverend Snushall gave the following eulogy for a man he and many others obviously respected greatly:

> *Some few weeks ago a sermon was preached in the old church on the East Cliff by the Rector from the text 'Sorrow on the Sea'. It was a memorable sermon, for it was preached on the occasion when eleven of the local survivors of the crew of the three British cruisers, 'Aboukir', 'Hogue' and 'Cressy' were present in the church to give thanks to Almighty God for their safe deliverance from a watery grave.*
>
> *Not far from the same old church and hard by the old Abbey of St Hilda, there has been, during this week, sorrow on the land, for from out at sea the naval guns of the German enemy have struck two of our brothers who were defending this coast and their country, killing one and injuring the other, only a young brave boy, for life. Our hearts are full of sorrow for the families of these two tonight, and we pray that God the Holy Ghost, will comfort them in their great trouble, and, if it be His will, will restore to health that young lad who is now lying in the Cottage Hospital in a critical condition.*
>
> *But, dear people, that is not all, for bad enough as that is, sorrow indeed has filled hearts who are gathered together in this church of St John's tonight. Instead of the presence of one to give thanks for his perseverance from the perils of last week, there is absent from this house of God, which he loved so much, our dear brother who, in this cruel bombardment, has been murdered by the German people in another part of the town.*
>
> *Nobody, I think, even if they could not always see their way to agree with, could help admiring him who tonight is in the paradise of God, and who, to the*

time of his death, was one of the wardens of this church. May I speak of him to you tonight for a few minutes?

I think of him, first, possibly in connection with his associations with this church. Was there ever a more loyal member of this congregation than Mr Tunmore, who has met with so sudden and tragic a death?

His interest in the welfare of St John's was most marked. I could not possibly go fully into all the many details of his work in connection with this church tonight, but every time you and I kneel at the communion rails we shall be reminded of his life here, for he it was who, a few years ago, suggested them to the Rector, and undertook to collect the money to defray their cost.

Again I look at this church tonight and I believe I should not be far wrong if I were to say that, but for a certain remark made by him, whose loss we mourn over, this church would certainly not have been at this present moment in this beautiful condition.

At a meeting with reference to the decorations of the church, it was he who said that he would be pleased if the church could be beautiful during the lifetime of some of the elder members of the congregation. This I told the Rector and, to a certain extent, the work was commenced and only this week has it been completed. He saw the church the last time with me Tuesday evening, when we were talking over further improvements, and he saw it then practically as it is now.

After the church I picture him in his home. He was a man rightly proud of his home and a devoted husband to her with whom he shared that home and where tonight there remains his vacant chair.

I think of him also as a father and I do not think I shall ever forget his talks with me about his children. If ever a child had a good father, I have no hesitation in saying that the Tunmore family most certainly had. And oh! What a good father means in the home. To you who are fathers in this church tonight, strive as he strove to be good fathers to your children.

From his home and his family I go to his employment. As a railway man I wonder if the North Eastern Railway Company ever had a more trustworthy and dutiful servant in the whole of their employ. A man who was always patient with those with whom he had to do, and who always gave to any fresh comer to the town that hearty welcome which was by many so much appreciated. But amid all this sorrow that has filled our hearts, should I not be doing wrong were I not to sound a note of thankfulness to Almighty God for His most watchful and merciful deliverance of us who have been spared from the dangers and perils of the past week, as also for the spirit of comradeship which has been brought about between all classes of people and which I would like to see still more of.

When I think of the number of lives that have been so miraculously spared, should we not be doing wrong were we not to pause in this church tonight and thank God for His mighty arm, which has shielded us from the hands of the enemy?

I shall therefore ask you, at the conclusion of this service, to kneel silently in your places and to thank and praise God for what He has done for us.

Devonshires' Official Report

On Saturday, 19th December, Captain Alan Goodridge, commanding 'F' Company of

7th (CYCLIST) BATTALION

1: Colour Sergeant Stanley Hearn, 'F' Company, based at Whitby. Helped bring survivors ashore from the *Rohilla*. 2: Shoulder title. 3: Signallers in 1916. 4: Transport in 1916.

the 7th (Cyclist) Battalion Devonshire Regiment in Whitby, was finally able to send the following report to his superiors via the battalion Adjutant after a hectic three days of clean-up operations and preparations in case another attack was launched, as many feared:

On Tuesday night, at about 11.15pm, I received telephone messages from Hornsea and Headquarters, Guisborough, to keep an especial lookout and to man all trenches and defences from before dawn until after daybreak. On receipt of these messages I telegraphed instructions to detachments at Robin Hood's Bay, East Cliff Coastguard Station (War Signal Station), Sandsend, Runswick Bay and Staithes.

On Wednesday, 16th December, at 6.45am, I manned all my trenches and defence posts until 8.00am, when the men were marched back to quarters and sent to breakfast by detachments. The sea was rough and the weather hazy. Second-Lieutenant R. A. Ball went to his breakfast at 8.30am and on his return, just before 9.00am, a telephone message was received from the War Signal Station to say that heavy firing was heard off the Tees and off Scarborough. I immediately sent a message, through the War Signal Station, to all my coast detachments, to man all defences until further orders, and the men who had returned from breakfast to stand by.

I was just arranging to go to my own breakfast when the first shot was heard. Second-Lieutenant Ball and I got into our equipment and I sent Second-Lieutenant Ball and Colour Sergeant Hearn with all available men to the Harbour sandbags and to the Spa trench. I also arranged for the collecting of the other men who were at breakfast, and their subsequent distribution to the several stations, and a supply of reserve ammunition. I then proceeded to take up my station at the Spa gates (where there is a telephone) which I use as my lookout station, and on my way there was met by Motor Cyclist Moysey, who informed me as to the bombardment which was now very violent. In order to save time I told him to go to the Drill Hall ('F' Company Headquarters) and ring up Guisborough 15 and report to the Colonel.

While running to the Spa a shell pitched on the sea-front end of the road and ricocheted away somewhere, and I got to the Spa box in time to see the last shots fired. I immediately rang up Hornsea 47, Headquarters Yorkshire Mounted Brigade and Guisborough, and, while waiting for the call to go through, I lost sight of one ship in the haze. I saw the other ship turn and at great speed make off in a north-east direction.

There were two ships firing, one looked to me like a battle-cruiser of the Goeben type and the other a heavily armoured cruiser of the Seydlitz type. I cannot say definitely if they were flying ensigns.

There were two tramp steamers in the vicinity going south - these did not seem to be molested. As the raiding cruisers were disappearing in the haze, I saw two small steam craft approaching from the north-west. I saw no British warships to account for the sudden and speedy retirement of the enemy. I reported to York by wire after the bombardment ceased and by telephone to Hornsea and Guisborough. The firing lasted about 10 minutes, during which the enemy fired between 40 and 50 rounds from guns of various calibre.

I saw that the War Signal Station had been knocked out but the ensign was still flying. As a precautionary measure I arranged with the local Guides for the removal into the county of a large quantity of petrol. The local corps of Guides were soon on the spot with their motor cars and cycles and I put them under cover in the vicinity in case their services should be required. I would mention here that on hearing the firing, several of the Guides came along roads immediately in line of fire and had many narrow escapes. My detachment at the War Signal Station, under Sergeant Foxworthy, received the brunt of the enemy's attention, and although under fire for the first time, they behaved with great coolness and did excellent rescue work.

One man, No. 918 Private Favis, was slightly wounded by fragments of a shell, which burst close by him. His rifle, greatcoat and cap were badly damaged. This man was attended to by his comrades and taken to the Whitby Cottage Hospital. When I considered there was no likelihood of the enemy returning, I ordered the men back to quarters, but told them to stand by for any eventualities.

I append reports by Second-Lieutenant R. A. Ball and Sergeant Foxworthy. Also a map showing the dispositions of the ships and their lines of fire.

After I could get away from the telephone I made a tour of inspection of the damage caused by shellfire. The small list of casualties and the absence of fires were most remarkable. I would like to say that all ranks under my command behaved with great promptitude and were exceedingly cool and steady under the new and unexpected conditions of things. 'F' Company's casualties were Private Favis - slight wounds in right thigh and leg.

The other casualties were: killed - Coastguard F. Randall - Civilian W. Tunmore. Wounded - Boy Scout R. Miller (seriously) - Mrs Miller. There were several cases of cuts and abrasions among civilians not reported to me.

I append hereto reports from Second-Lieutenant Whitehead [Ness Point, Robin Hood's Bay], Sergeant Foxworthy [War Signal Station, Whitby], Sergeant Lawrence [Runswick Bay] and Corporal Booth [Staithes].

The only detachment not mentioned in the above report was that under the command of Sergeant Buynon at Ravenscar; but it reported seeing nothing.

The SS Hydro

Many years later the story of the *SS Hydro*, part of the Ellerman-Wilson Line, came to light. She had been sailing down the east coast on the morning of the 16th December. At 5.30am she passed four destroyers of the Hartlepool Flotilla on patrol. At 6.50am she passed the three German warships, *Blücher*, *Seydlitz* and *Moltke* off Hunt Cliff (between Hartlepool and Loftus, above Brotton), and at 9.05am passed some 400 yards under the belching guns of the *Von der Tann* and *Derfflinger* then engaged in the bombardment of Whitby. The *Hydro's* master, Captain George Sharp, of 134 Cromwell Road, Grimsby, drew a hurried sketch map of the encounters and, on safely making port, handed the map to his brother for safe-keeping. Unfortunately the *Hydro*, and George Sharp, were lost in early 1915 when sailing from Liverpool.

The map and the *Hydro's* story then remained hidden until coming to light in 1982 when the family of George's brother discovered the map and passed it on to the Whitby Museum. Although no written or verbal account survives, the map speaks for itself and is perhaps a unique document of the events of 16th December 1914. The account is confirmed by a reference in the above report by Captain Goodridge and a short mention in the war's 'Official History' which reads '. . . *they made off in an obvious hurry, for they left unmolested two tramp steamers that were passing southward at the time.'*

A Rumpus over the Message to the Town from the King

A week after the attack the King sent a personal message to the people of Whitby via the Lord Lieutenant, Sir Hugh Bell. The message was short and succinct:

> *The people of Scarborough and Whitby have been much in my thoughts during the past week, and I deeply sympathise with the bereaved families in their distress. Please let me know as to the condition of the wounded. I trust they may have a speedy recovery.*

However, a small storm of etiquette erupted in Whitby when it was discovered that the message had simply been telephoned through to the police station and that the Mayor, for whom it was intended, had not seen it prior to its being printed in the *Yorkshire Post*. The row over the alleged 'slight' rumbled on for several days and the correspondence between the Mayor and Sir Hugh Bell was made public shortly afterwards in the local paper following a statement of the affair being made to the council by the Mayor.

As it transpired, the first the Mayor had known of the message from the King was on reading it in the press, where it was stated that the message had been sent to the Chairman of the Whitby Urban District Council - Mayor Harmston. Knowing it had not been sent to him, he had sent a messenger home to see if anything had arrived there in the meantime. The messenger came back empty-handed. Harmston then visited the Clerk of the Council to see if he had received the original message. He had not. Determined to get to the bottom of the matter Harmston next consulted with the Vice-Chairman. The pair agreed they needed to find out where the message was, and to whom it had been sent. They also endeavoured to contact Sir Hugh Bell by telegram, but he was away and could not respond.

That evening (Tuesday, 22nd December) Harmston visited the local police station and, whilst talking with some of the constables, discovered that the King's message had been telephoned through to the station. The following day, after receiving a wire from Sir Hugh Bell confirming this, Harmston visited the Superintendent and discovered that on reaching home at about 9.00pm on Tuesday evening the Superintendent had discovered the King's message, as telephoned, on his desk. The message, he said, had simply asked for information on the wounded and the numbers killed. The Superintendent had replied forthwith, but had not passed the message on to anyone for there were no instructions to do so and he had thought nothing more of it.

The Mayor went on to express the hope to the council that they would see that it was due to no fault of his or the council's generally that the King's message had not been published to the townsfolk of Whitby and a reply sent by return, as had been the case in the other towns affected. It was made abundantly clear that Mayor Harmston set the blame fairly and squarely at Sir Hugh Bell's door and he produced the following correspondence to prove it:

> *To: J. Egan Harmston, Mayor.*
> *Wednesday, 23rd December 1914*
> *The King's message of sympathy, as printed in the Yorkshire Post, was telephoned*

to the Police Superintendent last night (22nd) when I made enquiries to enable me to reply. I expected the police would communicate with the persons concerned.

I have heard this afternoon that the Government will compensate for loss sustained by the bombardment. This is not official, but may, I believe, be accepted as fact.

Sir Hugh Bell.

To: Sir Hugh Bell.

Wednesday, 23rd December 1914

I have just received your wire. I have received no communication whatever concerning the King's gracious message to Whitby. If there is such a message from His Majesty, I shall feel obliged if you will please forward it to me direct, and not through an intermediary, so that I may have it published to the inhabitants.

J. Egan Harmston, Mayor.

To: J. Egan Harmston, Mayor.

Thursday, 24th December 1914

On my return from York last night, I found your telegram and at once replied to you explaining the circumstances under which I had dealt with the King's telegram of the previous day. Owing to the disorganisation of the postal arrangements I was not able to write to you last night. I now supplement my telegram by informing you that on receipt of the King's telegram I considered with whom I should communicate. Neither you, nor the Urban District Council appear in the telephone directory. It then occurred to me to telephone Mr Pyman, as Chairman of the Local Emergency Committee, but his name also does not appear. I then communicated with the police and in the absence of the Superintendent received the information I required to enable me to reply to the King's question from the officer in charge. I am under the impression that I asked him, as I asked the officer at Scarborough, to communicate my message to the persons interested. I am exceedingly sorry that this was not done, and that you were left to learn from the newspapers the fact that His Majesty was enquiring. From what I have said you will see that I did my best to communicate with the people of Whitby and I am exceedingly sorry that I did not succeed better. You will, I feel sure, understand that I am especially anxious to avoid the appearance of slighting the important position you hold as Chairman of the Local Government Authority in Whitby.

I hope the wounded at Whitby are doing well. I was sorry to hear there are two somewhat serious cases. The letter from Mr Asquith to Mr Walter Rea MP, will no doubt be the source of much satisfaction to the inhabitants of Whitby who suffered by the outrageous act of the Germans.

Sir Hugh Bell.

To: J. Egan Harmston, Mayor.

Friday, 25th December 1914

Your somewhat ungracious note of the 23rd did not reach me until this morning. You will in the meantime have received my letter, which will show you that I took a great deal of trouble to make known the King's message to Whitby. I cannot accept any responsibility for failure, though I may feel some surprise at the terms

in which you draw my attention to the fact. I wrote to you yesterday explaining very fully what I had done and I have nothing to add in further explanation.
Sir Hugh Bell.

To: Sir Hugh Bell.
Saturday, 26th December 1914
Your letter of 24th December I received on 25th December and had prepared a reply to the same on my return home from wiring you with my reply to His Majesty's message. Your letter of 25th December was awaiting me and after reading the same I have nothing else to explain and shall place the whole correspondence before my council at their first meeting.
J. Egan Harmston, Mayor.

To: Sir Hugh Bell.
Saturday, 26th December 1914
The following is a copy of the telegram I forwarded to you this morning in reply to the King's gracious message of sympathy to Whitby sent to us through you:

*

May it please your Majesty
The Lord Lieutenant, Sir Hugh Bell, yesterday communicated to me your Majesty's gracious message of sympathy with the people of Whitby, in the trying ordeal through which they passed during the bombardment of their town by the enemy's fleet. Your Majesty's gracious consideration for the bereaved and the injured is gratefully appreciated by my fellow townsmen.
I have the honour to remain,
Your Majesty's most humble and obedient servant
J. Egan Harmston
Chairman of the Whitby Urban District Council

*

In anticipation, thanking you for forwarding the same to His Majesty.
J. Egan Harmston, Mayor.

To: J. Egan Harmston, Mayor.
Saturday, 26th December 1914
I am in receipt of your telegram of today, to which I have replied as follows: 'Telegram received. In my judgement it is not necessary to make further communication. I replied fully on the day the message reached me. If you hold a different opinion I would prefer you telegraphed direct from Whitby.'
In confirming this message I should like to add that a telegram from here would bear the name of this as the office of origin, and as I do not agree in the necessity, or indeed in the desirability, of sending a further reply to the King's message, I should much prefer that this should not be the case. At the same time, I wish to leave it entirely in your hands to decide whether you will telegraph. It is for that reason that I have at once replied to your message in the terms set out above.
Sir Hugh Bell.

On hearing the communications which had flown between the Mayor and the Lord Lieutenant, the council approved of the stand Harmston had taken over the matter and decided that Sir Hugh Bell could not be exonerated of all blame as he appeared to wish. The council was much aggrieved by recent events, for this was not the first such incident where messages had gone astray. Apparently the Chairman of the North Riding County Council had wished to convey his sympathy to the people of Whitby and instead of being sent to the Chairman of the Council or the Clerk, it had been passed on to one of Whitby's County Councillors. As the meeting and the affair came to a close Councillor Brown commented upon the fact that Whitby appeared to be "*. . . very much outside things, and the only uses it seems to have are to be bombarded by the Germans, and ignored by the County Council!*"

Fears of Another Raid

Many people in Scarborough and Whitby, and other towns along the east coast, were justifiably worried that another attack may be levelled on them before too long. If the Germans could strike so freely once, what was to stop them doing so again, perhaps with even more ships and with greater loss of life? Whitby's local paper had advice of its own to give on the subject, and on the ever-constant threat of local spies:

> *There is much speculation as to whether the German warships will again bombard Whitby. Our answer to the query is that no one can be certain. If we may say so without egotism, we did expect a bombardment sometime, and it was a lucky thing for the town that there was a very heavy surf rolling in at the time when it did occur; but if the enemy tried the same feat again, they would, for several reasons, find it much more difficult of accomplishment and would run infinitely greater chances of being sunk. We have had assuring evidence, which it would be unwise of us to mention, that in the case of another attack we shall be much better looked after.*
>
> *The sneaky work of last week was done under cover of a mist which greatly facilitated their movements, and their Admiral must now understand what a really hazardous enterprise he had sent them upon, for had he lost those ships, the very flower of his grand fleet, he could not have put up a fight against our fleet without still more reducing the odds. This fact, and the realisation that the whole of the neutral countries of the world have condemned their action, make it very unlikely that they will be anxious to repeat the exploit. It had absolutely no military significance; indeed, from every point of view, it has done them more harm than good. It has also proved to our mind that there will be no raid or invasion of the English coast, and that the worst that is possible to happen is that some lame duck, from an engagement or battle, may vent its spleen on the handiest place it comes across. Such an event might signal the crushing of the enemy's sea power for ever and spell the close of the war. Every day that lengthens now decreases the chances of success of the German vessels in any possible dash they might make across the ocean again.*
>
> *Just supposing the Germans did return, would it not be advisable, in addition to the Emergency Committee already appointed, to have a Committee consisting of gentlemen of the town, with particular streets allotted them to control? How useful would such have been last week! We would urge Mr Harmston, the Chairman of our Council, to seek the co-operation of some active citizens pledged to immediately assist and give advice to their neighbours, should there be another bombardment.*

Another requirement is some specially trained detectives from Scotland Yard, for a few nights to ferret out the spies who every night in and out of our town flash signals to the enemy. We spoke of this many weeks ago, and it was ridiculed; but now hundreds of people have seen the same thing, or some other kind of signals and the authorities dare not pooh-pooh it any longer. The fact is that the spies are exceedingly clever, and the energies of the cutest minds must be exercised in trapping them. How far they had any connection with the attack last week, or may have in connection with any possible future attack, we cannot precisely say. It was only last Friday night that powerful streaks of light were sent up from a particular building on the West Cliff, a fact which was notified to the police by a professional gentleman; and again this week the peculiar kite variety of signal light has been seen on the East Cliff and in several places in the district.

Were we likely to have our request granted, we would ask the War Office to send us a battery of guns of sufficient calibre to keep the enemy ships at a proper distance, but that would be at a cost of several thousands of pounds, and they need all the guns they are getting ready elsewhere, so we cannot be like the German coast, fully protected from its enemies on the sea.

If the War Office could see their way to billet at Whitby one or other of the regiments now in training inland, it would have a reassuring influence on the people of Whitby and greatly make for easiness of mind. Indeed, we almost think we have a right to such consideration after the terrible shock we have had. In the matter of the spies, we would ask the Home Office to do its duty; and, in order to encourage a more comfortable feeling, again urge Councillor Harmston to get round him a band of civilian workers.

Had a regiment been billeted in the town as suggested there is little it could have done should another bombardment occur, save perhaps add yet more numbers to the list of the dead and wounded.

Bonar Law

Speaking at a recruitment meeting in Bootle, Merseyside, in the week leading up to Christmas 1914, the MP Bonar Law presaged his call for national conscription with references to the east coast raids:

After all, what have they gained by it?

They have not frightened us, they have only steeled our hearts to see this thing through, and have only still further alienated the sympathy of the world.

We were quite right to take it calmly and I am glad our people are not uttering hysterical cries for sympathy. This sort of thing would be crushed not by words, but by deeds, and the time for deeds was coming.

The raid has had no effect upon us, except to make us realise even more clearly the nature of the foe with whom we have to deal.

It has made us realise that we are fighting not against a superman, as the Germans would have us believe, but against a wild beast, which is only the more brutal because it has at its disposal all the resources of science and invention.

It is rather depressing to find that at this time in the world's history, war is carried on by methods such as are used by our enemy. We have seen in the attack on defenceless men, helpless women and children, a symbol only of what is in store for us here if the shield of our Navy should ever fail us. It was a symbol here, but it has not been a symbol in Belgium, for there it has been on a scale which ought to have been impossible; and what makes these cruelties so terrible was that they were not done in hot blood, or by the ordinary soldier in the heat of action, but were deliberately planned.

This murder of women and children is part of a scheme to make German arms terrible and thus win their victory. The Germans have to win by any means. But they are not going to win. Indeed, the German Emperor, after all that has happened, still speaks as if he were the leader of the chosen people, and as if the god of battles was on his side - he will find he is mistaken.

Each has to do his part to make the German defeat certain, because upon it everything we value depends.

For months to come the east coast raids would provide enough fodder for the recruitment boards to ensure that Kitchener's New Army would be raised in record time and would be ready to be thrown into the fray on the Somme front come July 1916 - a fray from which most of them would never return.

Whitby's Christmas Message

The day before Christmas, Thursday, 24th December 1914, the *Whitby Gazette* featured the following verbose editorial seasonal message:

This is the first time in the history of this newspaper that instead of using the ancient rendering, 'Peace on earth, goodwill to men', we have to adopt the more correct form of the text, 'On earth peace to men of goodwill.'

Peace. Peace of mind and joy of soul be to those of goodwill and to those who do battle for the right; but war swift and vengeful to the fiends of hell who slay priests of God, doctors of healing, innocent women and young children. Consolation be to the bereaved and stricken in our midst, and to those whose sons have fallen, like the good Saint Michael, in fighting against the powers of hell, as incarnated by the war staff of Hanover.

The devil is revelling in what must surely be the greatest licence he has ever had upon the earth; therefore why cry, 'peace, peace' like the Israelites of old, when there is no peace?

Is it within the bounds of belief that there remain in Whitby today any fit men who stand idly by and watch the movements of the Beast in the world, without joining in the attack upon his throat, like the valiant Saint George of Merrie England (what a mockery in the term) who slew the dragon aforetime?

All khaki men of goodwill who have fallen in the fight should be canonised like our patron saint. But that is not the habit. The men of peace say, 'Let the Beast alone, we will tell it to go home again.'

Was this what St Michael did?

In plain English this is a fight between Good and Bad, between Heaven and Hell, and all the fearful wickedness typified in the world; against the powers of darkness enthroned in high places. How can we say 'peace' to our readers who are leaving and have left their homes in distant parts of the earth to do battle for the right?

Peace of course, they have, the peace of an easy conscience, and good honest British pluck mixed with Christianity without cant.

Good men in the world are fighting for peace, but it is not yet; and the men in khaki who pay their devotions to the Prince of Peace tomorrow morning are among the saviours of the world. Our motto is this Christmas; 'to war - avenge the innocent, the good men we buried last week, the boy-hero who has so narrowly missed death and whose blood stains the sod of our East Cliff'.

Merry we grown-ups cannot possibly be this Christmas time, but we must do our best to make the children merry. They need and deserve the best we can do for them. Though we cannot urge merriment, there is no reason why we should not do our best to copy the happy warrior and make as light as we can of our trials. It would be rank injustice to doubt the valour and prowess of our soldiers and sailors to bring us an eventual victory, so let us, with real British grit, rise as well as we may to the spirit of King Christmas and, with our warmest thoughts thrown to the long khaki line in Flanders, try to enjoy at home, and wish for all, a happy Christmas.

An admirable sentiment, but one which was not to be extended by the larger populaces of Scarborough and Whitby towards the enemy. And when word later came back from the front of the strange Christmas truce on the Western Front, many were angered anew - their wounds ripped open to gape wide afresh. How could good old British Tommy Atkins consort and share with the dastardly Hun?

Indeed it was a strange Christmas, and one that was not to be repeated on any front, home or military, again.

Death and Inquest of Winefride Miller

In the early evening of the 24th December the condition of Winefride Miller, seriously wounded at her home, *Springfield House*, during the bombardment, took a turn for the worse and the doctor was called to the Convent Convalescent Home to attend her. Tetanus had set in and her mouth could not be opened. Despite administering a serum she died at 3.00pm on Christmas Day.

On Boxing Day, Saturday, 26th December, Whitby witnessed its third and final inquest into the death of one of the bombardment's innocent victims. The inquest, conducted by the Whitby Coroner, Mr Buchannan, was held at the Convalescent Home. Captain McGregor was chosen foreman and the first person to give evidence was Mrs Miller's family doctor, Dr Lionel Pern, who had been treating her for the last three years.

On the morning of 16th December he had been sent for to come at once to the home of Mrs Miller for she had been wounded. On arriving there he found that she had been moved to the Convent Convalescent Home, where Dr Edward Baines had already arrived and was treating her. Mrs Miller was conscious and the pair examined her thoroughly and found her seriously injured, so much so, that in her invalid state, they feared for her life. They put the wounds she had received down to the shell which had exploded in the room below her own and which had devastated half of the house. Mrs Miller's wounds were extensive, but did not impact on any of the major organs. However, because of her frail health and the extent of the numerous injuries, they considered her in grave danger. All that could be done was done and as several days passed it appeared that she was doing well, better indeed than had been expected.

Invalid Winefride Miller was taken to the Convent of Mercy but died on Christmas Day

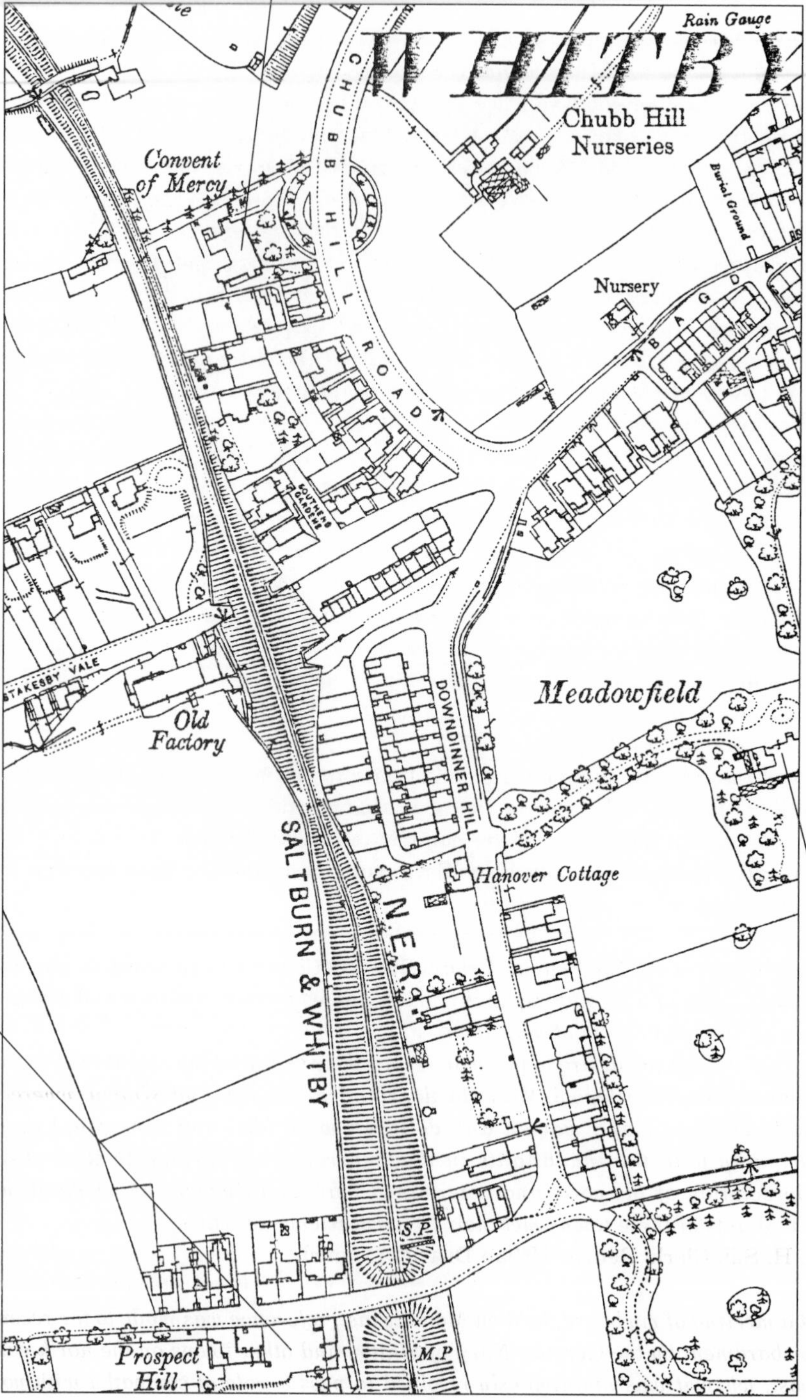

At Hill Crest, on Prospect Hill, Mr and Mrs Bruce were rudely interrupted at breakfast as shrapnel burst through the window and smashed clean through the table

Meadowfield Hall Boys' School off Downdinner Hill suffered considerably, but no one was hurt

However, at 6.00pm on Christmas Eve, Dr Pern had been urgently sent for and on arrival found that tetanus had set in and Mrs Miller could not open her mouth. He treated her with a hypodermic of serum but to no effect and she eventually died at 3.00pm on Christmas Day.

The doctor was of the opinion that the injuries sustained from the blast of the shell were the cause of her death, and was adamant that nothing in her previous condition, medical history or subsequent treatment was a contributory factor.

The Chief Officer of the Coastguard, Charles Davie was then called to give his evidence of the 16th December (as he had at the inquests of Randall and Tunmore several days earlier).

Following this Raymund Collier, the brother of Mrs Miller, took the stand and confirmed that the deceased was fifty years of age and the widow of the late John Miller, Master Mariner. He also confirmed that she had been an invalid, confined to her bed for the last three years and that on the morning of the bombardment he had assisted in removing her from her destroyed home to the convalescent home.

The jury returned the verdict that Mrs Miller had died as a result of tetanus, resulting from wounds sustained from the explosion of a shell fired by a German vessel of war on 16th December.

Thus ended the story of the last of Whitby's innocent victims.

A Subdued New Year ~ Messages Flood In

The New Year was ushered in in much quieter style than usual at Whitby and there was almost an entire absence of any happiness at all. Even the bells of St Mary's Parish Church high on the East Cliff were silent for the first time in living memory. Services and events were not well attended and there were no football matches as there had been in previous years.

Truly the bombardment had brought home to the close-knit little port the true meaning and horror of the war her sons, husbands and fathers were engaged in. And they had yet to feel the weight of the Somme and Passchendaele.

Meanwhile messages of goodwill and sympathy continued to flood into the town in their hundreds:

> *I am directed by the Redcar Urban District Council to forward to you the enclosed copy of a resolution, unanimously passed by them, relative to the recent raid on the inhabitants of your town.*
>
> *'That the council desire to place on record their horror at the recent raid on the inhabitants of Hartlepool, West Hartlepool, Scarborough and Whitby, whereby the lives of so many women and children were lost, and to express their sympathy with the inhabitants in their sorrow; and further, to state their appreciation of the calm and determined manner in which the whole of the inhabitants of these towns met their first experience of war.*
>
> A. H. Sill, Clerk. Redcar Urban District Council.

> *At a meeting of my board, held on Monday last, reference was made to the recent bombardment by the German Navy of Whitby and other towns on the north-east coast, when it was unanimously resolved to pass a vote of sympathy with you and your townspeople who have been made the victims of so barbarous an outrage, entailing considerable loss of life, suffering, and damage to property;*

this attack by a ruthless enemy on peaceful and unarmed citizens being a complete violation of the laws and customs of modern warfare. I was accordingly directed to convey this vote of sympathy to you from my board.
H. R. Peters, Clerk to the Berwick Guardians.

At a meeting of my council last evening it was unanimously resolved that I should write to you expressing the sincere sympathy of my council with the inhabitants of your borough, who have suffered bereavement or damage to person and property through the dastardly bombardment of your town on the 16th instant.
Norman Dixon, Clerk. Withernsea Urban District Council.

At our evening service on Sunday last at which three hundred friends were present, our speaker, Mr G. H. Bibbings of Beauchief, Sheffield, asked the friends to support him by rising while he moved that a message of sympathy be sent to our brothers and sisters in your town who have suffered so heavily from the shells thrown by an unscrupulous foe. May I humbly ask of you to kindly convey to those despairing ones our profound sympathy and we sincerely hope that ere long the right will triumph over might.
John H. Hawkins. Belper Spiritualist Society.

At a Ward-Mote for the ward of Aldersgate in this city, held on St Thomas's Day, the Right Hon. The Lord Mayor in the chair, it was moved, seconded and carried unanimously 'that this Ward-Mote desires to express its great sympathy with the towns of Scarborough, Whitby and Hartlepool in the great damage and loss of life they have sustained by the German bombardment on Wednesday last, and their sincere condolence with the relatives of those killed and earnest hope that the wounded may recover and that a copy of this resolution be sent to the mayors of those towns.'
Leonard Tubbs, Ward Clerk. Aldersgate, London.

I am directed by the Guardians of the parish of Newcastle-upon-Tyne to inform you that at their meeting held on Tuesday last they passed a resolution expressing their horror at the recent unjustifiable bombardment of your peaceful borough, and I am to ask you to receive their deepest sympathy and condolence with the citizens in the frightful losses they have sustained in both life and property.
G. Walker, Clerk to the Guardians. Newcastle-upon-Tyne.

On behalf of the fraternity I am instructed to convey to you, and the people of Whitby who have been rendered homeless and bereaved by the bombardment of your town, our sympathies. Also we wish to congratulate you on the splendid fortitude shown by your people during this dreadful calamity and pray that God's richest blessing may rest on them and protect you all during this very trying crisis. Will you kindly convey the same to your people.
Rev. David Pughe, President. Merthyr Central Brotherhood.

We were all very grieved to read of the appalling disaster which occurred last week, in which so many young people lost their lives. We are trying at our

Sunday School to prepare young lives for life or death, so that we shall be ready if the call of God should come to us suddenly as it has done to so many during the last three or four months. We pray that our God may give special grace and comfort to the bereaved ones and that we may shortly be able to rejoice in an everlasting peace. On behalf of the class I ask you to please accept our most heartfelt sympathy.
Mary Pointon, Class Secretary. Wesley Place Sunday School, Tunstall.

The officers, teachers and scholars of the school on hearing of the terrible calamity that has come upon your town through the outrage of an enemy of us all, passed by a standing vote their sincere sympathy and condolence with your distressed people, realising that it was as likely to have been our town as well as yours. We also pray that God in His divine power will protect you as well as ourselves against a repetition of slaying innocent women and children as well as men civilians.
Frank Wood, Superintendent. Wesleyan Sunday School, Skegness.

I beg to send you herewith a copy of a resolution passed by the Town Council of Stafford on the 21st instant, with reference to the recent bombardment of the three east coast towns by the Germans; 'That this council desire to offer their deep-felt sympathy with the towns of the Hartlepools, Scarborough and Whitby in the loss of innocent lives sustained through the recent ruthless bombardment by German vessels of war and record their utter abhorrence of so dastardly an act upon open unfortified towns. They also fervently trust that the Allied Armies will so vigorously prosecute the campaign as to bring about an early victory and cause wars to be impossible in the future.'
Richard Battle, Town Clerk. Borough of Stafford.

Along with the myriad messages came donations, both large and small, and some just downright peculiar, from across the nation:

Please use these few shillings (10s) at your discretion in the relief of distress which has been caused in Whitby through the recent raid. I only wish the sum could have been a larger one.
Miss Alice M. May, North Kensington, London.

Please accept the enclosed £1 on behalf of the dependants who lost their lives by the Butcher of Berlin.
D. Nimmo, Hamilton, Scotland.

I felt I must take the liberty of writing a few words to express to you my deep sympathy with the people of Whitby in the sad calamity which has befallen their town and noble Abbey, so dear to the readers of Scott's 'Marmion'. Should our turn here come we hope we shall bear it as bravely as they have done. Will you please accept also the enclosed little book, which I think is very good for recruiting. I am a widow of very limited means and am unable to help in any other way.
Mrs H. Watson, Ramsgate.

SHELLS ON THE BEACH

Will you please accept my humble donation for your Relief Fund, namely ten pairs of valuable long-distance racing pigeons to be sold in suitable pairs at £1 per pair for the fund. These are the best it is possible to procure for money, many of them being bred like Higham Brothers' national winners, also Barlow and Barton's soffles advertised at £7/7s. each squeaker. Postal orders or cheques to be sent to you; letters or address of purchasers to be sent on to me and I will forward the birds on with full particulars of performances and pedigree. Trusting that my proposal will meet with your approval and thanking you in anticipation.
M. Bolton, Cambridge.

As to this last, the offer of pigeons, the Council was undecided as to whether to accept, for there was a prohibition on the sale of such birds. It was left for the Mayor to look into the matter further before a final decision was made.

We have heard with feelings of great indignation of the crime which has been committed against your beautiful town. As you will see by the enclosed prospectus we are projecting a series of Rolls of Honour for those who have offered their services to their country and we think that such a roll of honour should be made for those who have been killed and wounded in this the latest crime against humanity. We should be very pleased to present the town of Whitby with a fitting memorial containing the names of those who have been killed and wounded if you will furnish them to us together with the arms of your town, when we shall be happy to execute this for you in due course.
The Fine Art Society Limited, London.

This offer was put aside to be discussed in Committee. The fact that Whitby's civilian dead were not included on the town's war memorial which is carved of wood and hangs in the Parish Church begs the question; how was Whitby going to remember the dead of the bombardment?

Kitchener's Army to Defend Whitby

As was stated at the beginning, one of the reasons for the raids on the east coast may well have been due to Kitchener's 'first hundred thousand' having been raised. The Germans may well have hoped to create a public outcry for Kitchener's New Army to be kept in England and used for home defence and in its first issue of 1915 the *Whitby Gazette* duly obliged:

We would revert to our suggestion of last week, that it is desirable and a wise thing to locate a regiment of Lord Kitchener's New Army for training at Whitby. Further alarm has been caused by the methods adopted to endeavour to advise people in case of another possible shelling of the town, and many have left their homes in consequence, and either taken houses in the country or gone away to friends and relatives at a distance. The mere fact of the issue of certain literature suggests to timid folk that another bombardment is not improbable. In these circumstances, though the inhabitants of Whitby of the old stock may not fear the enemy so much as some of those, especially ladies, who have but a residential or business connection with the place, there is no reason why we alone, a town and port of a certain national value, should remain on the most vulnerable (to the

SOUVENIRS

1: An intact Red Ensign from the Signal Station. 2: Repair work. 3: The Griffins with son George Shrapnel Griffin. 4&5: Shell fragments from around the town.

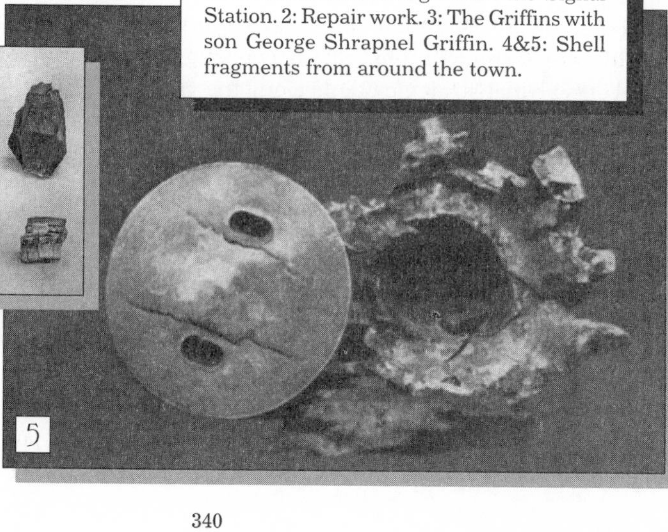

enemy) portion of the English coast in a state of unprotection, isolated from military aid by unsuitable lines and geographical situation, and distant by sea many miles from any port of any naval importance. We need some ocular and substantial accretion of military strength to reassure the women and children of Whitby and steady their nerves.

If men of over military age hastened to join the recently formed Volunteer Training Corps as they should do, and were armed with rifles which they knew how to use, there might be no need to ask for men of the New Army to be stationed here; but we would ask what effective control has the town over the spies and enemies in our district when, in case of emergency, the only men allowed to use or carry firearms of any description are the handful of Devon Cyclists, who would be fully employed with other duties and the national reserve, who, however, have not yet been served with either uniforms or rifles. Police and special constables would be impotent in the face of an armed enemy intent upon destroying bridges, severing telegraph lines or doing other serious damage.

Failing a granting of a request for a regiment of regulars at Whitby, the reassuring effect of three or four hundred armed volunteers, who would assemble at a moment's call, would be great. The number mentioned is well within the power of the town to supply if the men do their duty. Means ought to be found to supply rifle and uniform without cost to the individual volunteers; and the town should be equipped with an electric alarm to summon all bodies of men to their posts. The Lord Lieutenant, Sir T. Hugh Bell, says that no man must take part as a combatant unless he is a soldier or a member of a Volunteer Corps; and everyone otherwise who possesses any kind of firearm must surrender it when called upon to do so. Thus, the man who is un-uniformed will be of no service in repelling any possible or prospective foe.

Surely no further words are necessary to denote to every man his bounden duty. The men of Whitby need to drill and school themselves for whatever the future may have in store.

Whitby never got its Kitchener regiment, nor its hundreds of armed volunteers. Indeed, the *Whitby Gazette* also joined Robert Blatchford of the *Weekly Despatch*, in calling for the placement of heavy naval guns along the threatened east coast. The stationing of specially built ships was aired but ruled out due to the length of time it would take to build them. But it was suggested that groups of four naval guns, well-concealed at strategic points along the vulnerable north-eastern coast might be all that was required to deter the Germans from again attempting to bombard coastal towns, or at the least, repel any such attack. A counter-argument was launched by the correspondent for *The Times*, who, in effect, suggested that nothing could be done to protect the vulnerable ports and towns. He also went on to say that were naval guns of the calibre required actually available they would be better served mounted on the ships they were intended for so as to become a mobile squadron and thus provide better overall strategic defence. Robert Blatchford reiterated his argument and concluded cynically:

No squadron, however mobile, could possibly defend the entire east coast. But a few heavy guns of the latest type at each vulnerable point would prevent the repetition of such dastardly raids as those upon Whitby, the Hartlepools and

Scarborough, simply because they would make such raids too risky to be worthwhile attempting. If a neighbourhood is in danger of visits from armed and desperate burglars which is best, to depend upon a couple of local policemen for the protection of a district four miles square, or to fit up each household with good locks and revolvers?

If any gentleman of the 'Blue Water School' will explain to me how the Navy can possibly defend the east coast of Britain against such raids as the recent one I shall be grateful. The Admiralty says it cannot be done. If the Navy cannot do it, are we to understand that towns on the east coast must wait and suffer in patient and defenceless silence?

Or are we to suppose that proper batteries of the heaviest guns would be useless for defence unless they were on board mobile ships, whose mobility carried them too far away to get back in time!

Though the arguments raged nothing was ever settled, and as the war progressed England's preoccupation with naval bombardment gave way to the aerial menace of zeppelins and warplanes.

WHITBY

IN THEIR OWN WRITE
PERSONAL ACCOUNTS OF THE GERMAN NAVAL RAID ON WHITBY ON WEDNESDAY, 16TH DECEMBER 1914

The following extracts from letters and verse were written largely by the men and women of Whitby. Some have appeared in local papers, others are from military archives, a number have been written up from interviews conducted during the 1970s by the author and journalist David Mould, and others are from my own research among the survivors. Now, for the first time in 85 years they describe, in their own words, the day Whitby underwent its eleven minutes of hell, its never to be forgotten ***'Bombardment'***.

The author of the letter or verse always follows the piece. Notes relating to contemporary material are suffixed by the date (1914 or 1915), and notes about recent material are prefixed with 'This account was related by . . .' Maiden names have been used (where known) on recent material to provide a reference to 1914. All material is from or related to the 1914 attack on Whitby.

I had a telephone message on the 15th December at 11.55pm warning me to keep a sharp lookout and to be in the trenches by 5.45am. I also received a telegram of the same message at 1.00am on Wednesday, 16th December.

I reported to Whitby Coastguard Station at 7.05am on 16th December three cruisers steaming full speed going north. We could not see to distinguish the boats; they were about 2 miles out. At 8.10am I reported to the Coastguard Station heavy gunfire was heard north.

So wrote Corporal Booth of the 7th (Cyclist) Battalion Devonshire Regiment in a report to the officer commanding 'F' Company at Whitby from his detachment's post at Staithes further up the coast.

On receipt of messages during the night of Tuesday, 15th December, special measures were taken so that at least half the men should be ready to turn out

ABBEY BARN

The hole punched through the roof of the Abbey Barn on the East Cliff could be seen from the other side of Whitby.

fully equipped at a moment's notice. At 8.30am on Wednesday morning, the bay being quite clear of ships, though misty, the men returned to their billets for a wash and shave preparatory to breakfast. At 8.45am Private Purnell went out to get some cigarettes; he reports that he had a look out to sea but saw nothing.

At 8.50am as Private Light was taking this message down to report it to Corporal Bryant, he says he saw the sterns of two very dark boats disappearing round Ness Point. They were going very fast. Private Manning, up at the telephone, also saw the ships, but did not know what they were and thought no more of the matter.

At about 9.00am Corporal Hutchings came up to report the message to me and to get orders; as he was doing so we heard the guns being fired off Whitby.

Sergeant Buynon says he saw nothing from Ravenscar, but even if he had he would not have been able to communicate in time. It was very misty, especially out at sea that morning.

So wrote Second-Lieutenant B. Whitehead of the 7th (Cyclist) Battalion Devonshire Regiment in a report to Captain Goodridge on the morning of Saturday, 19th December. Whitehead's detachment was situated at the coastguard lookout point above Robin Hood's Bay at Ness Point. 1914.

On the morning of Wednesday, 16th December, at 9.00am, I was on duty at the War Signal Station on the East Cliff at Whitby, and had just gone to my lodgings to get a cup of tea when I heard a terrific explosion. I ran outside and found that two German battle-cruisers had opened fire on our houses and the War Signal Station. I reached the yard just in rear of the station when a shell burst over my head and stunned me. The exact time I was on the ground I do not know. I remember recovering somewhat and sending my men to help to get the women and children away from the station.

We were quite helpless with rifles against the ships which were about a mile and a half from the cliffs. During the bombardment I discovered a Boy Scout [Roy Miller] coming through the yard with two very bad wounds in the legs. I rendered first aid and stayed with him until the firing ceased. I then sent him to the local hospital. We then discovered Coastguard Randall amongst the debris of the shattered houses. He had the top part of his head blown off. Private Favis, the sentry on the War Signal Station door, was struck by a piece of shell which tore the back of his greatcoat off, but only wounded him slightly. Favis was badly shaken so I sent him to the hospital for treatment as well.

The above is from a report addressed to the Officer Commanding 'F' Company of the 7th (Cyclist) Battalion Devonshire Regiment and was sent by Sergeant Foxworthy who was in charge of the War Signal Station detachment. Louis Henry Foxworthy was born in Dartmouth and enlisted there. Although a Sergeant whilst serving with the 7th Devonshires at Whitby, he was killed in action on the Western Front on 8th October 1918 as 290034 Corporal Foxworthy, serving with the 9th (Service) Battalion Devonshire Regiment. 1914.

With reference to your telephone message with regard to the bombardment of Whitby, I have to submit the following report:

The bombardment of Whitby took place on the morning of 16th December 1914, starting at 9.05am. Two battleships suddenly appeared out of the mist, coming from the south, and immediately on being challenged by the War Signal Station opened fire at a range of about a mile. The vessels resembled the Moltke and Von der Tann. About 100 shells were dropped into the town. The battleships opened fire with a salvo from their 6-inch guns on the broadside. Three people were killed and two injured as a result of the bombardment. The former were a coastguard, a civilian and a woman, and the latter a private of the 7th (Cyclist) Battalion Devonshire Regiment [Private Favis] and a Boy Scout [Roy Miller].

The War Signal Station was wrecked by a shell which passed through the front window and knocked out the back wall, cutting off all telephonic communication with other stations. The coastguard cottages in the rear of the station were badly damaged, being struck by a number of shells.

A number of shells also struck private houses, doing considerable damage. The coastguard [Frederick Randall] was killed in the yard of the coastguard cottages, a shell taking off the top of his head and face. The civilian [William Tunmore] was killed while leading his horse to its stable; and the woman [Winefride Miller], who was an invalid, was struck by a piece of shell, dying a few days afterwards.

The above report was written by Captain T. O. Endle, Commanding 'F' Company, 7th (Cyclist) Battalion Devonshire Regiment. It was dated 8th January 1915, was accompanied by a sketch map showing the line of fire from the ships and was sent to Headquarters of the Mounted Brigade at Hornsea in response to their telephone enquiry for information. 1915.

At the time of the bombardment of Whitby I was only seven years old, but still have vivid memories. I was at St John's Church of England School, near the War Memorial Hospital.

At 9.05am that morning the first bang knocked the clock off the school wall and then the barrage started. We were assembled outside and dismissed as shells were pumped into the town and surrounding areas. We had to run the gauntlet of flying shrapnel, brick, glass and the like. Everything was seen as if through a red fog because of all the red brick dust.

My uncle [Robert Burnett] lived at 1 Gray Street, while Mrs Robinson and her family lived at number 2 - I saw them both get direct hits. The shells tore a hole through the back room walls and went out through the front walls.

I saw Falcon House hit. My teacher, Mrs Polly Parratt lived there. And I saw many other properties hit.

We lived at Airy Hill Farm and I eventually arrived there to find the pig sty and coalhouse adjoining the house had been demolished and our dear old sow was no more. I found my mother and my younger brothers and sister hiding under the settee.

Altogether we had 18 shell holes in the farm, and we spent many hours digging the brass nozzles out as souvenirs.

There is never a crisis but there is an amusing incident . . . Looking back I remember my aunt, Mrs J. Phillpot, of 12 Gray Street, arriving at the farm with her Christmas cake stuffed under her arm which she said she was not leaving for the Germans!

I also remember the arches of the viaduct which carried the Scarborough rail traffic being hit. I saw things that day that I shall never forget.

This account was related by Ernest Burnett from his home in Keighley, West Yorkshire. He was born in 1907 and was seven at the time of the Whitby raid. His father was John Hassell Burnett of Airy Hill Farm. The War Memorial Hospital referred to was pulled down and replaced with a modern hospital, and where once the C of E School stood there are now houses.

At the time of the Whitby bombardment I was a little girl of seven, living at 41 Cliff Street with my mother and older brother. My father was a ship's carpenter and was away at sea at the time.

I attended Cliff Street School (since demolished). On the morning of the raid I went to school as usual. We were just starting our first lesson when we heard several loud bangs, which I thought was thunder. Then I heard someone say, "The Germans are coming!"

The teacher, Miss Boyes, asked us to go out quietly and to go home. There were steps down to the road outside and I remember one of my friends fell and hurt her leg. Outside men and women were running about, some of them still in their night attire.

Of course I hurried home to look for my mother and was very upset when I couldn't find her. Someone eventually told me she was with a neighbour who was ill. She was an old lady called Mrs Boyes who lived alone. From the window of her room you looked out across to the East Cliff and could see the Abbey and St Mary's Church, the Spa and the East Pier, and, just out to sea, were two ships, from which you could see shells being fired. They made a swishing sound as they came. The old lady was in bed and my mother lifted her up so she could see what was happening. As we watched through the window a shell hit the top of the Abbey and the wall collapsed like a deck of cards. I was very frightened and clung to my mother. After a short while she said, "Look, the ships are leaving!"

We watched them sail away.

I remember afterwards we had to take money to school for a fund which had been started for a Sea Scout called Miller who had had his leg blown off.

This account was related by Edith M. Palmer (later Rochester). She was born in 1907 and was just seven years old at the time of the raid. Her mother was Margaret Palmer and they lived at 41 Cliff Street.

The Cliff Street Girls' and Infants' School was opened in 1894.

I was ten years old at the time of the bombardment and still recall it vividly. I attended St Hilda's Roman Catholic School at the time. We were just beginning prayers, at about 9.00am, when we heard the noise of what we thought was thunder. No one had ever heard gunfire before, but a boy shouted, "It's Germans!"

The teachers ran to the door to stop us going outside, but they were knocked down and trampled on as we ran out into Windsor Terrace. At that moment a shell went through a gate and smashed through all the cocklofts in the street before emerging at the other end. All the slates were flying from the roofs and into the street. It was a miracle no one was hit. Nearby was a green meadow with

GENERAL DAMAGE

1: *West Lea*, Falcon Terrace. 2: Cleveland Terrace.
3: *Springfield House*, Spring Hill Terrace.
4: Esk Terrace and James Mitchell's delivery cart.

cows grazing and around the field (Duck's Field) ran a stone boundary wall. We all crouched behind it and were lucky again as another salvo burst in the field on the other side. Again no one was hurt, but a piece of shell hit the school clock. After about ten minutes the shelling stopped.

Then all the children started to run inland. I carried my sister on my back and led my younger brother by the hand. We finished up at Sleights Institute, about four miles away. It was being used as a hospital for wounded Belgian soldiers and I remember them well. There was no khaki then, they had blue uniforms on. They gave us tea and eventually sent us home!

One Whitby lad finished up in Pickering, 21 miles away. He came home that night in the guard's van of the train.

When we arrived home our parents were frantic with joy as they didn't know what had happened to us.

It was a grey morning when they came up to the Rock Buoy and opened fire over open sights with their secondary armament. The next day I had a walk around and saw the damage. The cliff was hit by shells and there were landslides all over. When the tide went down there were unexploded shells laid on the beach, some in pairs. I can still recall the shell holes at Boghall, and the end house of George Street that was hit. They were white brick houses, but they had no white bricks and so patched them up in red. It was only a few yards from where we all crouched behind the wall in Duck's Field. It is the site of the War Memorial Hospital.

Looking back I think we were all very lucky indeed!

This account was related by Harold Parkin. He was born in 1904 and was 10 years old at the time of the Whitby raid. The St Hilda's Roman Catholic School was a mixed school on Spring Hill and was opened in 1874 under the administration of the Sisters of Mercy (whose convent was on Chubb Hill Road). They also administered St Patrick's Roman Catholic School on Church Street.

I am sure you will be wondering how we fared during our visit from the Hun. I am thankful to tell you we are all alive and well after our terrifying experience.

I had just sat down to my breakfast with my little ones when the first bang came, the like of which I had never heard before. I started to my feet to see what it was, when another came, more awful than the first, and still more, and I soon realised that we were indeed in the hands of the enemy.

I was dumbfounded. I took my children into my next-door neighbour, who is an old lady of 75 years, and nearly blind and who lives alone. There we stayed until the bombardment was over. I was afraid for my children; Laura trembled like a leaf and my dear little boy, I thought he would have died in my arms; he lay with his eyes closed and never moved until the firing ceased.

Jack [husband] had a narrow escape. He was working on the East Pier with four or five more men and was watching these two ships, thinking they were English battleships, when they opened fire and shells flew all around them. They scrambled over the pier side and fortunately the tide was low and they were able to get onto the concrete ledge which runs along the piers on the harbour side, and there they had to stay until the bombardment was over. He

ST HILDA'S ABBEY

1&3: Before and after views through the west window.
2: Another view of the damage.

saw every shell that was fired come over the town and explode, and it was agony for him, for he did not know what might be happening to us, yet they dared not move for fear of their lives. You can imagine the joy when he came home and found us all safe; he went back and picked up several pieces of shell.

It is impossible for me to try to explain to you what it was like; the noise of the shells as they whistled and exploded over our heads was terrifying and much worse than the heaviest peal of thunder I have ever heard.

We live in fear of their return. Three or four hundred people have left the town, and I feel I would like to take my little ones to a place of safety, but one hardly knows what to do for the best.

But we thank God we are alive and we pray we may never hear the sound again.

This extract from a contemporary letter appeared in the Times History of the War and is unattributed. 1914.

I left Malton at 6.50am and reached Whitby at about 8.25am on Wednesday morning (16th December). About a quarter-past nine o'clock I was in the guard's room at the station when I heard a crash - a bigger noise than I have ever heard before. I rushed out to the square and then heard ten or twelve shots. I think I saw one hit the Abbey - a big piece of shell, as big as a man's hand, and hundreds of splinters then flew around me and I had to stoop down to escape. I saw one man knocked down and afterwards dozens of persons were picking up shells. I was frightened for the first time in my life and I can tell you I was very glad to get away from Whitby.

Thus spoke Tom Hall of Norton, near Malton, North Yorkshire. He was a guard with the North Eastern Railway and gave this account to a reporter shortly after the event. 1914.

I was in bed at the time of the bombardment, but my daughters had already risen. At about 9.05am we were all surprised by a loud report. At first it did not alarm us, for we imagined it to be a rocket or some such. The report was followed by another explosion which made such a tremendous noise that it was apparent the town was being fired upon. Shot followed shot, and they were so rapid that it was difficult to estimate how many there were. The noise they made was appalling - much louder than any thunder claps. It sounded almost as if bricks were falling in cart loads on the roof.

We did not leave the house, but the girls glanced through the window and saw stones and mortar falling so densely they could see no distance at all.

At the second shot the back windows were shattered. The cannonade lasted for some considerable time, and when it had died down we made fast the house and made off inland. On the way we noticed that the houses of our neighbours had been very much damaged on either side of us.

A stretcher passed by with a man on it, who I believe was the railway rulleyman. His horse had become unharnessed and was walking aimlessly along, up the street. The cart had been blown several yards away.

There was a neighbour's venetian blind in the garden and the houses on either side had had their roofs blown off. A house in Windsor Terrace seemed to have its insides blown out and only the outside shell was still standing.

We returned home later in the day and packed some luggage. We then left Ruswarp for Northallerton. I had had no information how to act or what to do in this situation, and those about did not know how to act for the best.

Mrs Jane Heselton of 13 Normanby Terrace and her four daughters fled Whitby after the bombardment and stayed in Romanby near Northallerton for a time. 1914.

Just a few lines in answer to your kind letter. I was glad to hear you were all well, as it leaves me very uncomfortable until I get the full details of the bombardment. I see you have lost half of the Abbey. I told you you did not know what dirty cowards the Germans are. To think they should fire on an undefended town like Whitby!

But never mind, they will have to come in. You will know now what shells are like, and the men left in Whitby will know they are wanted.

I do not think they have done so much damage in Whitby as they have at Scarborough and Hartlepool. We are waiting to hear whether they have caught them; but we shall catch them in the long run.

Why don't they come out and fight, and then we shall see who is the best, the dirty dogs.

Stop in your homes. I don't suppose they will come again. And see if you can't rouse a few men to come out. I know there are not many left, but it is time those who do remain thought about it. It will give you just an idea of what Belgium is like.

As I am writing the big guns are booming and I can't tell you what it is like. The weather is very bad out here and it is very cold at night. I have got my skin coat and I can tell you it is warm.

Wishing you and yours a Happy Christmas and a bright New Year.

From your chum, W. Purvis.

This letter was received by Mr T. E. Todd of *Westoo House* on Church Street, Whitby. Private Purvis was with the Royal Army Medical Corps, part of the BEF serving on the Western Front. 1914.

Our house faces the west coast and singular to say, there are some houses near the sea called Falcon View. Our name is Gaskin (John). We (my wife and I) thought we would like to congratulate you and yours in escaping injury, and sympathise with you in your upset and damage. I have had two or three messages of enquiry thinking it was our family. I do not know if we are in any way related. We also reside in Manchester, where I first had my attention drawn to it.

Hoping you will escape any further trouble.

Mr and Mrs John Gaskin of *West Lea*, Falcon Terrace, received this letter three days after the bombardment (19th December) from Mr and Mrs John Gaskin of *Bank Cottage*, Waberthwaite, Cumberland. The Whitby Gaskins' recently built semi-detached villa, *West Lea*, was struck by a shell and severely damaged, though the occupants were unhurt. John Gaskin was a solicitor's clerk. 1914.

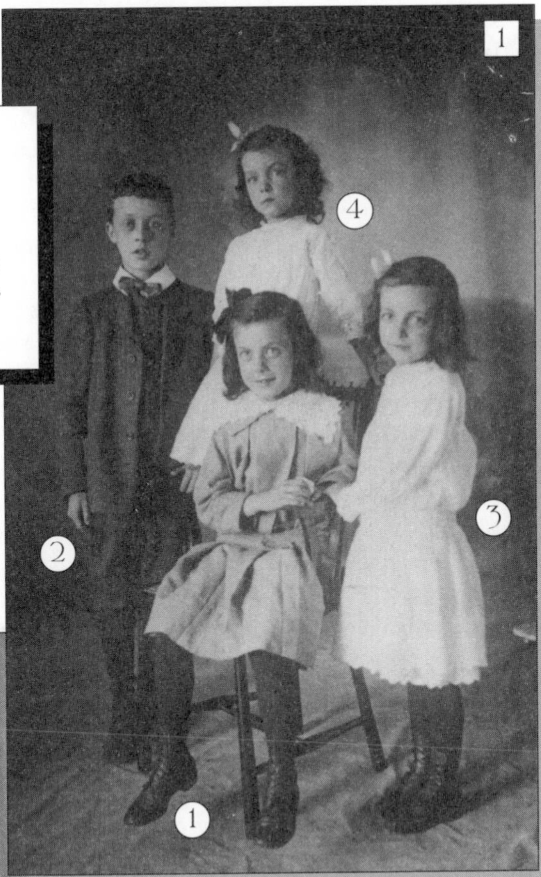

EVA WOOD

Eva (1) aged 8, with her siblings Harold (2) aged 10, May (3) aged 6 and Edith (4) aged 4. Eva was at St Michael's Girls' School when the bombardment began and ran through Whitby to her home at 7 Horner's Terrace.

JOHN KIPLING

In 1914, at the age of 23, John was an assistant with Jackson & Company Outfitters on Bridge Street, Whitby. As a result of the bombardment he joined the Royal Army Medical Corps. He died from kidney failure, as a result of exposure to gas, in June 1917, just fifteen days before his only daughter, Jessie, was born.

I was eight at the time of the bombardment of Whitby and went to St Michael's Girls' School [Church Street]. The school was just above the bridge and we were on the second floor. The headmistress was Mrs Bancroft and she was very handy with a cane and I have good cause to remember this fact!

On that morning we were stood for assembly and had a good view of the harbour. Suddenly there was a loud explosion and I remember looking out of the window and seeing a shell go whizzing by . . . then it was pandemonium. One of the teachers fainted and mothers ran up the stairs shouting, "Where's me bairns?"

The next thing I remember is running down Church Street to my home. I lived on Horner's Terrace and the sitting-room was downstairs. My mother had got the youngest baby [brother Tom] in the pram (I was one of seven).

"Have you got the Xmas cake in there mam?" I asked.

My father, a sensible man, would not let us leave the house for fear of injury. But he ventured out and up towards the bridge to see how things were going.

I remember looking out of the window at the houses on the other side of the river and seeing the roofs crashing in as they were hit. One shell just missed the Electric Light Station chimney and went straight through the roof of poor Polly Hustler's house; she had two spinster daughters. They were all in the cellar and survived.

People were streaming past our house making for the country, carrying babies and old people. They thought we were being invaded. It was a day or two before some of them came back.

We thought it was all very exciting and I don't recall being afraid at all.

Dad came home finally and put our minds at rest.

Later in life I endured two blitzes on Sheffield, but by then I already knew what war was all about.

This account was related by Eva Wood (now Emmett) from her home in Towcester, Northants. Born in Whitby on 13th June 1906, she was 8 at the time of the bombardment.

Eva's parents were Alexander and Jane Elizabeth Wood. At the time of the bombardment the family lived at 7 Horner's Terrace. As stated above Eva was one of seven children and she was the second eldest. The Wood children were; Harold (born 13th May 1904), Eva, May (born 22nd February 1908), Edith (born 12th April 1910), Thomas (born 14th September 1914), Alexander (born 21st January 1917), and Arthur (born 8th March 1918).

On leaving school Eva worked, for three years, for the *Whitby Gazette* (as did her Father and her brother Tom's son, who is now sub-editor), which was owned and produced by Horne and Son at 17/18 Bridge Street. Yorkshire Regional Newspapers now own the title.

My father was a coastguard on duty in the lookout tower at the time of the bombardment of Whitby, and mother was in the coastguard houses on the station.

That morning father had his attention drawn to the ships by another coastguard who had not identified them for what they were. On seeing their profile father drew the attention of the senior man to the fact that British cruisers had four funnels, but these had only three.

Shortly after this the enemy opened fire on the lookout - father thought it was to silence the telegraph line connecting coastal stations. The Abbey was immediately behind the station and received some of the shots aimed at the tower.

A shell struck the top of the tower removing the roof and the tower was then abandoned by the men on duty.

Meanwhile, my mother was in one of the upstairs bedrooms making the bed and upon hearing the commotion looked out into the yard below. A coast watcher shouted at her to evacuate the building and take cover down the road. The poor chap who cried the alarm was killed immediately afterwards when a shell struck one of the outhouses and removed half his head. Splinters of shell flew everywhere, peppering the buildings and breaking the window at which my mother was stood. She received a minor wound on the chest but ran outside and took shelter with the other families behind a wall on the Hawsker road near the Abbey.

I have a book from the library at the Signal Station which has a fragment of shrapnel embedded in the binding.

This account was related by John Jeffers from his home near Bideford in Devon. John was the son of Coastguard Albert James Jeffers, who was on duty that day, and of local girl Nellie Jeffers (née Corner). Albert was one of the pall-bearers at Randall's funeral.

In July 1914 I was on holiday at the 'Abbey House', Whitby, which was the guest house belonging to the 'CHA Holiday Association'. At the time there were some 80 guests there, of whom 16 were Germans.

It was rather suspicious that at dusk there was always one of them on the cliffs around the church and they always managed to lead you away if you went near them.

Also, on the 'free day' every one of them went to Scarborough taking photographs. Afterwards they travelled to different parts of the country to other CHA guest houses.

Perhaps there wasn't anything in it, but on looking back it was rather strange.

This account was related by Mrs C. Howe from her home in Bingley.

My great-great-grandfather, Isaac Fisher, was working in his market garden when the guns opened on Whitby. Much to his disgust his prize pig, which was rooting around the garden, had its head neatly severed from its body by a piece of shrapnel. He said the threat to his own safety didn't enter his mind as he watched the pig, minus its head, career around the garden for several minutes before dropping down dead. His garden was situated where the Memorial Hospital was.

At the same time his daughter, Etty Fisher, then in her early twenties, was sat on the windowsill of their grocer's shop in North Road washing the windows. The shock of the explosion caused the raised window to slam down trapping her. Her calls for assistance were ignored and she spent the whole of the bombardment trapped in the window!

This account was related by Christopher Hogg from his home at Haxby, York. The Fishers' shop was situated on the corner of North Street and Falcon Terrace.

1

2

JOHN KIPLING

1: John Kipling and his sweetheart Florence Fowler, whom he married on the day he enlisted, 8th March 1915.
2: Private John Kipling, Royal Army Medical Corps. John was sent home in July 1916 after 16 months on the Western Front. He spent a further 4 months in Nottingham Hospital before being sent home to Whitby, where he died of liver failure, due to gassing, on 8th June 1917.

I am sending you a postcard of the Abbey where the Germans have left their mark. You will be able to see what they have knocked down.

We are all in darkness at Whitby at night, no lights in the shop windows and no lights in the streets. We are going to start to close at 6.00pm next week, trade is only very poor. A lot of people have gone out of here into the country to live, but we had no panic on the day. In fact people were watching them firing. Harry was watching them out of the window.

This is part of a postcard (dated January 1915) sent by John Kipling of Whitby to his sister, Mary Ann, a novice nun, shortly after the attack.

John Stephen Kipling was born on 25th October 1891 and was 23 at the time of the bombardment. He lived at 5 Hilton's Yard, Baxtergate with his family. On leaving school he served his Draper's apprenticeship with H. Duck of Whitby, and at the time of the bombardment was an assistant with R. Jackson and Company Limited, Outfitters, Bridge Street. It was from here he joined the Royal Army Medical Corps on the 8th March 1915; the same day he married his sweetheart Florence Mary Fowler. One of the main reasons for his joining up was the bombardment of Whitby.

In July 1916 (after 16 months) John was sent home from the Western Front after being gassed and contracting a kidney complaint. He endured four months in Nottingham Hospital, before being released home to his house in Poplar Row, Whitby, where he died on 8th June 1917 from kidney failure as a result of the gas (just fifteen days after the birth of his daughter Jessie). Following the funeral service at St Michael's Church (at which he had been a sidesman) John was buried in Whitby Cemetery and the local Cadet Batteries provided a firing party.

The Kipling family, living at Hilton's Yard at the time of the bombardment, was large and consisted of; George (father), a shopkeeper with premises at 6 Hunter Street, Mary (mother), Sarah, Mary, John, Euphemia, George, Emily, Harold and William.

John's sister, Mary Ann, was 25 at the time and a novice nun with the Community of the Epiphany. The 'Harry' mentioned in the card is believed to be his young brother Harold, who would have been 11 at the time. William, who was 8 at the time, hid in the tunnel from the Khyber Pass to the brig with other boys from the Mount School during the shelling. 1914.

I was manager of the Scarborough and Whitby Breweries offices on St Ann's Staith in 1914 - a company previously owned by Corner and Readman whose brewery was at Eastrow, Sandsand.

I was there, at the offices, when the Germans began the bombardment. I went outside and could hardly believe it. One shell hit the Abbey and another the Abbey stables, one dropped in the harbour opposite our office and I thought it was high time I shifted.

I went to my mother-in-law's home in Falcon Terrace and we sheltered in the cellar. Part of the house was blown away but the worst thing was the soot and muck that came down the chimneys!

Anyway, I went on up to the Gas Works (where I lived with my parents) and found mother boiling plum puddings for Christmas. She was more worried about them puddings than she was about the shells. I turned the gas off and said, "Let's get out of here!" because shrapnel was peppering the gas holders which were full of gas.

ADA KELLY

Second eldest daughter of fisherman Thomas McGarry Kelly and Sarah Elizabeth Kelly of the Monkshaven Public House on Church Street, Whitby, pictured in 1914.

THE KIPLING FAMILY

In 1914 the family lived at 5 Hilton's Yard, Baxtergate, Whitby. Sarah, aged 26 (A), George, father, aged 51 (B), William, aged 8 (C), John, aged 23 (D), Euphemia, aged 21 (E), Harold, aged 11 (F), Mary, aged 25 (G), Mary, mother, aged 51 (H), George, aged 16 (I) and Emily, aged 14 (J).

The men from the works had already fled further up, towards Ruswarp fields and had left father to cope there on his own.

This account was related by Arthur Melton. Arthur was born in 1889 and was 25 at the time of the bombardment. As stated he was the manager of the Scarborough and Whitby Brewery offices, and his father was the foreman at the Gas Works. Arthur married Edith Coates - whose family had an antique and cabinet maker's business on Baxtergate - in 1916.

The bombardment of Whitby occurred on Wednesday, 16th December 1914 and I'll always remember it because it was the day before my 8th birthday; unfortunately forgotten in all the hullabaloo after the bombardment. However that's a minor point compared with the strange things that happened.

I went to St Michael's School. There was a girls' school, boys' school and an infants' school - three sections. There were about 150 of us in the boys' school, and I remember we were all congregated in one room just after assembly. The schoolmaster gave the order for us to get into our desks.

I must tell you something about the schoolmaster. He was a very very harsh man, he believed that if you spared the rod you spoiled the child. Well, he was going to see to it that none of us were spoiled. But he was unreasonable with it. He was a bachelor and really liked punishing small boys. Unless you started crying straight away he would beat you until you did cry, he was that type. I didn't know the meaning of the word sadist at the time, but now I do that is the word I would have applied to him. It was unfortunate, because he was a good teacher in many ways, but he couldn't teach without a stick.

Anyway, he gave the order to get into our desks. He did this by numbers you see, nothing had to be done until he said so and everything was done at the double, in real regimental style. One, two, three. He gave the order to get into the desks and we jumped in on the count of three. Then the first report was heard. It sounded like a maroon summoning the lifeboat, so we waited for the seconds to elapse before the second one went up. But when that went off we knew it wasn't a maroon, it was a salvo of shells. Immediately everyone realised it was a bombardment. And we thought, as everyone else did, that it would be preparatory to a landing.

Now the schoolmaster, who was standing at his desk on the dais, turned around to the class and his face, I shall never forget it, was drained of blood, it was a real putty colour and, with terror in his eyes, he said, "Boys, the Germans are coming, get away home as fast as you can!" and with that he disappeared, fled, and I never saw him any more. It was rather funny to think of him breathing fire and brimstone at little boys when things were normal, but when it came to the real test he shook like an aspen leaf. I and many other boys never forgot the day that 'Buttery' was frightened.

It struck many people in different ways of course. It was the practice for some of the shopkeepers to leave their staff in charge first thing on a Wednesday morning and take a stroll down to the pier, a constitutional. I know some of them were down at the pier end around about 9.00am and they were peering through the fog and mist watching the hazy outline of these two battleships coming into view, and they passed comments to one another about how nice it was to have the

At St Michael's School Jack Kelly's schoolmaster fled, leaving the boys to find their own way home through the shelling

"Have you got the Xmas cake in there mam?" asked Eva Wood, dashing in from St Michael's School, and finding her mother ready to make off with the baby in its pram

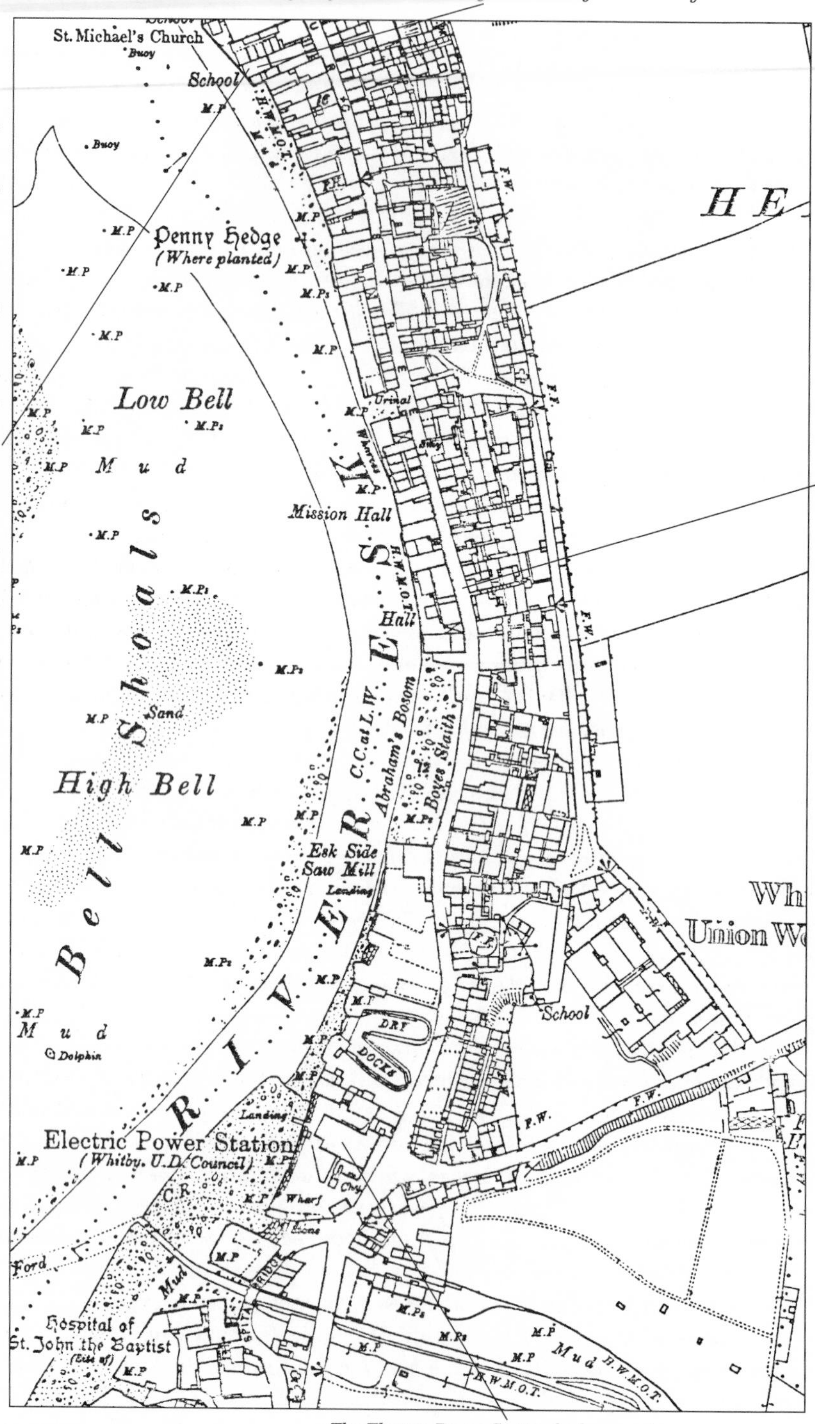

George Buchannan, the Coroner, held the inquests at the Board of Guardians' Rooms on Church Street

The Electric Power Station had near misses and emerged unscathed

Navy on our doorstep protecting us in these days of war . . . until they saw the guns belch. Needles to say they made a hasty retreat and I don't think they ever came back from their walks as quickly as they did that day.

Well, we scrambled out into the street from the school and I wish you could have seen Church Street. There were literally hundreds and hundreds of people living in Church Street in the many yards (there's nothing there now compared to what there was) - I think the majority of Whitby's population lived in and around Church Street, packed into those yards. When they turned out (I should think there have never been so many who vacated their houses so quickly at one time) the street was dense, packed with them. I saw my mother and sisters outside in the street, coming to collect me from the school and we went off down the street and joined the procession, all of us hurrying as quickly as we could. As each salvo of shells whined overhead (the whine was rather frightening the first time you heard it) everyone set off with little bursts of speed, but once they had passed over everyone slackened to their normal pace heading towards the country where they thought to escape the shelling. I couldn't understand why we all ran when the shells came over the top and then when they stopped we all walked slowly. Perhaps we thought they couldn't hit us that way!

We couldn't see anything until we got to the Staithe (which was near where Smailes had a sawmill - it's open now) and I looked across and could see Esk Terrace. There was some smoke hanging about the houses where an explosion had occurred and a shell had fallen in among them. Mother grabbed me away, and we carried on until we got to the bottom of Spital Bridge, near the electric light station with its big tall chimney (it's not there now). We all gathered there, at the bottom of Green Lane, Spital Bridge and part of Church Street. Dense we were, hundreds of us, and if a shell had fallen down there there would have been hundreds killed, but fortunately they went over the top.

There was a house there which had a shell hole right through the roof, as clean as a whistle. An old lady lived there, but fortunately she was busy feeding her hens at the bottom of the garden at the time. But the sight of it was sufficient to make people realise that instead of running away from the trouble they were possibly running into it. So we all stopped there.

We stayed there until the firing ceased. No one wanted to go home and it wasn't until a policeman arrived and told us we could all go back to our homes that we began to go back.

They questioned the policeman very closely; had the Germans landed? Had they been driven back? But he didn't know any more than that it had been a bombardment and he persuaded people to return to their homes. Off we went home.

The German ships had tried to knock out the coastguard station. A shell went through the west arch of the Abbey and a few days later it fell in. The shells that missed the coastguard station went over the harbour and landed on the railway; Esk Terrace, Windsor Terrace, Spring Hill and that locality and quite a few houses were knocked about.

Two people were killed as I recall, one was a coastguard on duty at the station, and the other was a railway rulleyman, whose horse had taken fright. He had tried to calm it and a splinter from an explosion had killed him.

But there was a young Sea Scout, called Roy Miller, who subsequently worked

THOMAS & SARAH KELLY

Herring fisherman Thomas McGarry Kelly (2) and, inset, his wife Sarah Elizabeth Kelly (née Redman) (1), both pictures circa 1914. Thomas, Sarah and their seven children lived through the bombardment of Whitby at their home in the Monkshaven Public House, Church Street. Eight-year-old Jack, the Kelly's only son, and their youngest child, was at St Michael's Church of England School on Church Street when the bombardment began.

1

2

at Barclays Bank, who had a leg severely injured which later had to be amputated.

The gossip at the time was that the bombardment was the result of a German band which used to visit Whitby before the war. There were about eight of them. And these poor fellows, only trying to earn a living, very humble and very decent fellows, when war was declared were rounded up and carted off to the castle at York, where they were imprisoned until after the war.

Shortly after the raid, when things began to cool down, I met up with some of my pals and we went up onto the coastguard station searching for shrapnel and shell splinters. They were very much desired at the time. We started digging in one place where a shell had exploded and were digging pieces out (I don't know what we would've done had it still been live) until the coastguard came along and shifted us off. He made us turn out our pockets and took most of the shrapnel off us but we managed to secrete a few bits away. The place was called the Old Quarry, but it's long since fallen into the sea. Even then it was right on the edge and I shudder to think of it now.

I must have been a lot braver as a boy, because I wouldn't have gone down there now. We used to sell the shell splinters and shrapnel; they were offering good prices for them.

Incidentally, the fearlessness of little boys is remarkable really. My pal, Frank Stonehouse, was a little younger than me (he was in the infants at St Michael's School), and he was turned out of school like the rest of us, but he and his pal, instead of going home, had sneaked off and gone to play marbles. His older brother was sent to find him later and found him still playing marbles - he'd played right through the bombardment!

This account was related by John 'Jack' Kelly from his home in Whitby. Jack was born on 17th December 1907, and was just one day short of his 8th birthday at the time of the bombardment. He lived on Church Street at the Monkshaven Public House (for which his father held the license). His parents were Thomas McGarry Kelly (1863-1950), the Coxwain of the Whitby lifeboat, and Sarah Elizabeth Redmond (1866-1931).

Jack had six elder sisters; Catherine, Ada, Minnie, Hilda, Betty and Ethel. He attended St Michael's Church of England School and began his working life as an apprentice painter and decorator, before an uncle helped him pass the exams to become a clerk with North Eastern Railways. Jack worked all his life for the railways and lived largely in York. However, during World War Two he was in charge of troop movements in Hull and for a short time at Newcastle. He retired in York and died at the age of 87 in 1994.

On the day of the bombardment I was outside, playing with my brother, Ben, on some steps called 'The Walk' at the rear of our house on Pier Road.

The shells started to fall and a local fisherman, Mr Winspear seemed to realise what was happening, and he picked us up and rushed us off home.

Later, my grandfather, Thomas Welbury, carried us to the railway viaduct near Factory Field - Edward's the confectioners had a sweet factory nearby. I recall all the folks shouting. A lot of the shells fell in the Fishburn Park area of the town. I remember Mr Randall, who lived at the coastguard cottages on the East Cliff was a casualty.

GENERAL DAMAGE

1: *Springfield House*, 3 Spring Hill Terrace, where the invalid Winefride Miller was mortally wounded. 2: The rear of Gray Street. 3: Windsor Terrace.

I can still remember what I was wearing that day - a velveteen jacket with braid round it and a pair of high boots with buttons down.

Bombs seemed to follow me about, for during the Second World War we were bombed out at Loftus!

This account was related by Elizabeth Welbury Jackson (née Marsay - no relation). Elizabeth was born on 15th March 1909 and was one of twins. Both she and her twin brother, Benjamin Garminsway Marsay, who died in 1991, were five at the time.

The family lived at 23 Pier Road. Thomas Welbury, her grandfather, was a Master Mariner and lived at *Fair Isle Cottage*, Tin Ghaut (just off Grape lane).

It was a cold hazy morning. We were singing our morning hymn in Cholmley School on Church Street when there was a shattering noise like the loudest thunder. It seemed to rock the school.

Mrs Ward left the piano and climbed into the bay window which overlooked the harbour.

"I can't see anything Miss Parratt," she said to our Headmistress.

The terrible explosions continued. We were filed out of the school. I wanted to go into the infants' room for my little cousin, Nora, who I had taken in that morning, but when I looked in the room was empty, the little ones had been let out first. I learned afterwards that Uncle Jack had taken Nora home under his coat!

"Your mother is outside," said Mrs Ward as she passed me.

It was surprising how many parents were already at the school door. People were surging down the street, some were carrying invalids. The noise was terrifying. I wanted to go with the rest of the people down the street - away from the sea, but mother wanted to go back home to lock the door after getting some money, which she said we would need if we had to leave town (people were saying the Germans had landed).

We saw an old friend of mother's being led by her daughter on the opposite pavement and mother said to me, "Go and take Mrs Holmes' other arm."

I did. And mother went back to our house at the foot of Church Street. She picked up some pieces of melting lead which must have fallen onto our doorstep from the shells as they went over. She was soon back with us and by now the firing had stopped. Mrs Holmes was taken to her relatives down the street.

Mother was anxious to know if my sister Nellie and her little girl (also called Nellie), who lived at New Gardens, were alright. We went up Green Lane and a Welsh Officer who was stationed at Whitby stopped his motor-bike and told mother she could go home now, the Germans had gone. She thanked him and we carried on to my sister's. They were alright, but a bit shocked. I remember having a cup of milk and some biscuits.

On our way home mother opened aunt Hannah's door. There was another woman and some children sitting around the table having a meal.

"Wasn't it awful?" mother said. "They say a young coastguard has been killed."

The other woman looked up and said, "Yes. My husband."

Mother was shocked, and could only say, "Oh dear, God help you."

My aunt Hannah had the coastguard's family staying with her for about three weeks, then they went to relatives in London. All the coastguard houses were shattered and the coastguards and their families moved to the Custom House

Hotel (now the Dolphin). But apparently the wife of the coastguard who had been killed, had begged my aunt to let them stay with her.

This account was related by Mrs D. L. Jackson. Her home had been at 16 Kiln Yard, Church Street, at the time.

The Cholmley School on Church Street was opened in 1869 and endowed by Mrs Hannah Cholmley as a memorial to her late husband Colonel George Cholmley. The school had room for 150 children and the headmistress in 1914 was Miss Emily Parratt.

The coastguard's family mentioned in the account was that of Frederick Randall.

A Whitby Man at Hartlepool

An extract from a letter from a 'native' of Whitby who was serving with the Royal Army Medical Corps in Hartlepool at the time of the bombardments later appeared in the *Whitby Gazette* and was most graphic in its description of what the writer, sadly never identified, had seen:

Just fancy the Germans calling upon poor old Whitby. But it is quite in keeping with all the rest of their doings. I think you escaped very luckily, compared with the Hartlepools.

I had a very busy day. I did about two hours' work on my own, and then reported to the hospital where I was engaged all day. The first case I saw was a woman shot through the chest, a big splinter having passed right through the lung and out at the back. It was fatal.

I saw a little chap, aged seven, with a shattered thigh. He didn't lose consciousness, but, as we set him up he kept saying, "Oh! Don't do that . . . you are hurting me."

I saw a woman carrying a dead baby. I saw an old man of sixty, all torn and bleeding and dozens of other horrors.

In this way Germany has added to its laurels. As one paper puts it, 'All these poor souls have suffered and died in vain unless every eligible man falls in'.

However this may be, I'll bet the North Country boys won't forget those murdered babies. There's some stick waiting for the bloody butchers and I give you my word that until they are paid in full there will be not an ounce of my mercy for any one of them who comes my way.

It knocked the bottom out of my holiday and that's another debt to wipe off!

HARTLEPOOL

A Brief Account of the German Naval Raid on the Hartlepools on Wednesday, 16th December 1914

The old town of Hartlepool, on the north side of the entrance to the Tees, denied expansion due to its position on a promontory, had been outgrown by the younger West Hartlepool. Together the towns were known as the Hartlepools, and although closely adjoining one another each was separate, with its boundaries clearly defined. Separated by Hartlepool Bay and the docks, the towns were officially one port which included six docks, four large timber ponds, one basin, and two tidal harbours, one of which was known as the Victoria Dock.

The last time the old town had been significantly attacked from the sea had been by Danish Vikings in 800AD, when they landed and destroyed a monastery.

The Hartlepools' Defences

Throughout the Great War, the defence of the Hartlepools was, except for a smattering of regulars and reservists, given over to the Durham Royal Garrison Artillery (Territorial Force). At the outbreak of the war the unit's strength was 320, but by the end of hostilities some 85 officers and over 2,000 other ranks, including the personnel of eleven siege batteries, had been raised, clothed, equipped and given preliminary training prior to despatch to the various fronts.

The Durham Royal Garrison Artillery (11 officers and 155 other ranks) manned Hartlepool's two coastal defence batteries, 'Lighthouse Battery' and 'Heugh (pronounced 'Yuff') Battery', both of which were situated on the point of the promontory in the old town and within 150 yards of each other. The batteries were separated by a broad path leading to the promenade which formed the boundary of the batteries on the seaward side and continued for a mile or so northwards.

The Lighthouse Battery, built in 1855, seven years after the lighthouse from which it took its name and which stood in the battery's precincts, lay on the south side of the path. Its only armament was a 6-inch gun, sited twenty-five yards to the south of the lighthouse. Some fifteen yards to the rear of the gun emplacement and running roughly

Annie and Florence Kay, of Cliff Terrace, were killed by one of the first shells fired

Three children of the Dixon family, from William Street, were killed outside Church Close School. Mrs Dixon and two of her other children were seriously wounded

Etta Harris was killed when a shell demolished her lodgings at Ivyholm, South Crescent

The Baptist Chapel received a direct hit

St Hilda's Church was damaged when a shell crashed through its roof parallel to it, was a road which formed the boundary of the battery on the landward side.

The Heugh Battery, built in 1859, lay on the north side of the pathway and had as its landward boundary the ground of Hartlepool Rovers Rugby Football Club. The ground adjoined the southern boundary of Hartlepool's small triangular Town Moor. Heugh Battery was armed with two 6-inch guns, with a maximum range of 11,200 yards. Both batteries were 'low-sited'; being level with each other and just fifty feet above sea level.

These three Mark 7 coastal defence guns, a model introduced in 1898, were the sole land defences of the port.

The Fire Commander's post at Fairy Cove, about 500 yards north of Heugh Battery, was built into the high wall flanking the inner side of Hartlepool's promenade. Like the batteries, it was low-sited. The view to the south, and of the harbour entrance was interrupted by the small bluff on which Heugh Battery stood and by the lighthouse. As a result of the representations of the Fire Commander, Lieutenant-Colonel Lancelot Robson, who was also the Commanding Officer of the Durham Royal Garrison Artillery, the Fire Command Post had been moved to the Battery Command Post of Heugh Battery a fortnight earlier. Although this new position gave better observation, the view to the south-east was still restricted by the lighthouse some one hundred yards away.

At the outbreak of war the Port War Signal Station (under the command of a naval Petty Officer) had been a little north of Heugh Battery, but again, owing to restricted views it had been moved into the lighthouse itself.

The Fire Command was in communication by telephone with the South Gare Battery five miles to the south, Fortress Headquarters at West Hartlepool and with the Lighthouse and Heugh Batteries.

The Port War Signal Station was in direct communication with the commander of *HMS Patrol* (berthed in the Victoria Dock) Captain Alan Bruce, Hartlepool's senior Naval Commander.

The batteries' infantry defence was provided by two companies of the recently raised 18th Battalion Durham Light Infantry (The Durham Pals). The electric lights and communications in the area of both batteries were manned by a detachment of Royal Engineers (Durham Fortress Territorial Force).

Based at Hartlepool were four 'River' class destroyers; the *Doon*, *Waveney*, *Moy*, and *Test*, along with a submarine; *C9* and two light cruisers; the *Patrol* and *Forward*.

Wednesday, 16th December 1914

This then was the general scene at Hartlepool when, a little before midnight on 15th December, the Fortress Commander received a message from Fortress Headquarters:

> *A special sharp lookout to be kept all along east coast at dawn tomorrow, 16th December. Keep fact of special warning as secret as possible; only responsible officers making arrangements to know.*
> Troopers, London.

Beneath this was written:

> *In connection with above, the Fortress Commander wishes you to take post from 7.00am to 8.30am. If all quiet at latter hour, troops may return to billets.*

Edwin Ashcroft of 19 Penrith Street was killed outside the gates of Richardsons Westgarth & Company

Charles, Polly and Jane Cornforth, of 3 Lilly Street, were killed when a shell demolished the rear of their house

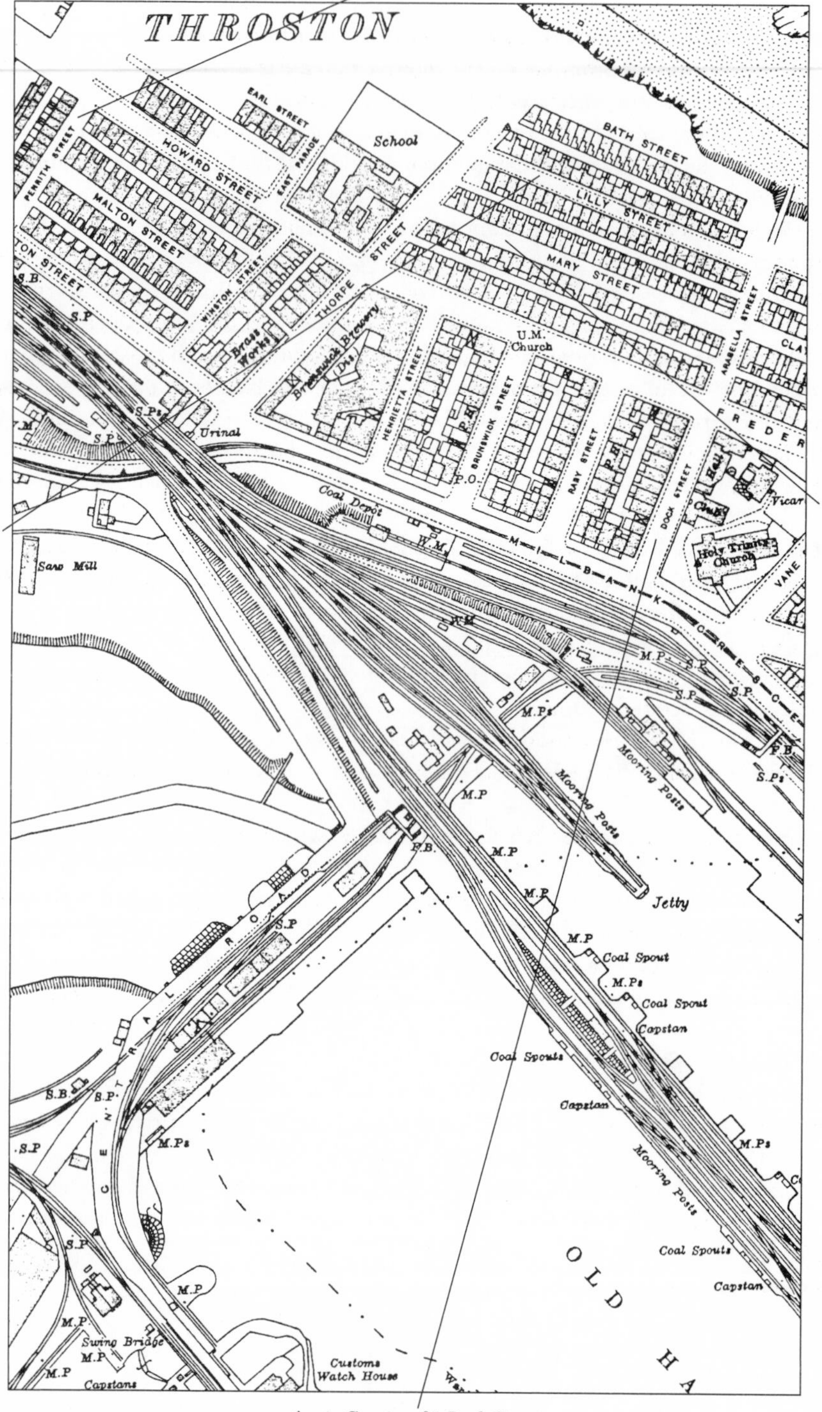

Two inhabitants of Mary Street, Catherine Marshall of number 41, and Charles Hudson of number 43, both died in the bombardment

Annie Corner, of 1 Dock Street, was killed

The special warning had been received by Fortress Headquarters direct from the War Office and this was unusual, as all previous warnings of the movement of enemy vessels had been passed through the normal source, which was the Port War Signal Station.

The following morning, Wednesday, 16th December, in accordance with normal daily routine, the detachments took up their stations an hour before dawn and the guns were prepared for action. Both batteries reported ready by 6.30am.

The four destroyers had left the harbour at 5.00am to follow their normal daily routine of patrolling parallel to the coast some five miles off. The light cruisers *Patrol* and *Forward*, and the submarine *C9* remained at their berths in the Victoria Dock.

The morning dawned with a heavy mist, and a bank of fog lay off the Hartlepool batteries bringing visibility to the east down to 4,000 yards. Visibility southwards was a little better, being clear up to about 6,000 yards. The sky was heavily overcast, leaden. There was a slight breeze from the north-east and, except for a slight rolling swell, the sea was calm. This then was the scene the *Seydlitz*, *Moltke* and *Blücher* were steaming towards as the other ships from their group steamed towards Scarborough.

Hartlepool Flotilla Engages the Enemy

Engaged on routine patrol, it was 7.50am when the *Doon* spotted the tell-tale smoke from the funnels of the approaching German warships closing from the south-east at a range of some 9,000 yards. She altered course and increased speed to 18 knots. At 8.05am the *Doon* confirmed the sighting of three enemy battle-cruisers. At 8.07am the *Waveney* too confirmed sight of them and sounded 'action stations'.

As it turned out the German ships had also spotted the British vessels and, although already engaged against Hartlepool, opened fire on them at 8.08am. The *Waveney* returned fire from one forward gun. The *Test* was hit and, along with the *Waveney* and *Moy*, withdrew. The *Doon* then attempted to launch a torpedo but was forced to turn away under heavy fire and she sustained severe damage. She also lost a member of her crew; Stoker 1st Class James Fraser was hit by a shell and carried overboard.

Meanwhile, as the bombardment of Hartlepool continued, the *Patrol* and *Forward* attempted to put to sea. At 8.20am as the *Patrol* made to pass the entrance to the harbour she was hit twice and Captain Bruce had no choice but to ground her to effect emergency repairs. The *Forward* was unable to raise enough steam to be of any use and the submarine, *C9*, perhaps the biggest threat to the enemy battleships, had dived to avoid shellfire and then grounded herself when attempting to negotiate the 'bar' at the harbour mouth.

The four destroyers and the two light cruisers (the *Forward* escorting the *Patrol*), outgunned and outclassed by the enemy ships, all made eventually for the sanctuary of the Tyne, there to lick their wounds. During this brief naval engagement the Germans had continuously bombarded Hartlepool, their only opposition the three 6-inch guns of the two batteries.

The Bombardment of Hartlepool

At precisely 8.00am the Fire Commander had received a telephone message from South Gare Battery further down the coast.

"Dreadnoughts steaming north."

This was followed almost immediately by a message from the Port War Signal Station. "Three warships coming in at great speed!"

HIMS SEYDLITZ
Kapitän zur See von Egidy

FLAGSHIP
Admiral Franz von Hipper

Ship's War Complement: *1,400*
Armament:
10 x 11-inch (28cm) guns
(average 88 rounds per gun - 880 rounds)
12 x 5.9-inch (15cm) guns
(160 rounds per gun - 1920 rounds)
2 x 22-pounder (8.8cm) anti-aircraft guns
4 x machine guns
4 x 19.7-inch (50cm) torpedo tubes
8 x 43.3-inch (110cm) searchlights
Speed: *26.5 Knots (63,000 horsepower)*
3,543 tons coal - 197 tons oil
Length: *656 feet 2 inches*
Breadth: *93 feet 6 inches*
Displacement: *24,610 tons*
Built: *Blohm & Voss, Hamburg*
Launched: *30th May 1913*
Cost: *£2,186,154*

As the approach of the ships was obscured from the Fire Commander by the lighthouse, he asked "What nationality?"

"They're our ships. They're flying the White Ensign and have answered our signals," came the reply from the Port War Signal Station.

"What class?" asked the Fire Commander.

"They appear to be of the 'Indomitable' class, sir," stated the Port War Signal Station. As this exchange went on the guns of both batteries were manned. It was precautionary, nothing more.

Following the Fire Commander's conversation with the Port War Signal Station the ships were heard to be firing seawards.

"What are they firing at?" demanded the Fire Commander.

"I presume it's the enemy, sir," was the reply.

"Are you sure they're not firing at our destroyers?" snapped the Fire Commander, astutely gauging what was happening at sea.

"I can't see what they're firing at, sir."

At that instant the leading ship loomed out of the mist from behind the lighthouse and by its colour and silhouette the Fire Commander was able to identify it as a German vessel. All doubts were dispelled when the other ships came into view and the lead ship (contemporary accounts cannot agree on which ship this was) opened fire on Heugh Battery.

The time was ten past eight.

The Battle of Hartlepool

The first enemy round fell beside the low wall which formed the boundary between Heugh Battery and the pathway leading to the promenade just twenty-five yards to the left of the guns. The blast killed the sentry, Private Jones, and three other members of the 18th Durham Light Infantry, Privates Liddle, Clark and Turner, and wounded many others.

Private Theophilis Jones was later declared to be the first soldier killed on British soil by enemy action during the Great War and a plaque now marks the spot where he fell (the original was stolen in 1966 and was later replaced). However, given that the first shell killed four men, and that the plaque does not specifically name Private Jones, it is impossible to be absolutely certain this was the case and the fact was probably used more for propaganda purposes than anything else.

Wounded men lay crying in agony among the dead as two medical orderlies from the Durham Royal Garrison Artillery, Gunners Houston and Spence, dashed out from the protection of Heugh Battery to tend to the injured. The second shell from the lead ship landed almost where the first had, killing both men outright, and wounding many more, among them Privates Rogers and Minks of the 18th Durham Light Infantry who were fatally wounded and subsequently died from their injuries. The shell also brought down the telephone poles, severing all links with the battery.

Another shell struck the end house of one of the terraces immediately to the rear of the Lighthouse Battery, instantly killing two of the occupants, the Kay sisters.

The *Seydlitz*, steaming north, was engaged by both guns of the Heugh Battery at a range of some 4,000 yards and fire was opened with high explosive. The Lighthouse Battery, in accordance with the pre-designated 'fire scheme', immediately engaged the rear ship of the three, the heavy cruiser *Blücher*.

The action had now become general, all three ships pouring broadsides of 11-inch,

HIMS MOLTKE
Kapitän zur See von Levetzow

Ship's War Complement: *1,400*
Armament: *10 x 11-inch (28cm) guns*
(average 88 rounds per gun - 880 rounds)
12 x 5.9-inch (15cm) guns
(160 rounds per gun - 1920 rounds)
4 x 22-pounder (8.8cm) anti-aircraft guns
(287 rounds per gun - 1148 rounds)
2 x machine guns
4 x 19.7-inch (50cm) torpedo tubes
mines (additional)
8 x 43.3-inch (110cm) searchlights
Speed: *25 Knots (52,000 horsepower)*
3,050 tons coal - 197 tons oil
Length: *610 feet 3 inches*
Breadth: *96 feet 10 inches*
Displacement: *22,640 tons*
Built: *Blohm & Voss, Hamburg*
Launched: *7th April 1910*
Cost: *£2,156,555*

8.2-inch, 6-inch and 5.9-inch shells onto the two Hartlepool batteries. The *Seydlitz* and the battle-cruiser *Moltke* engaged the Heugh Battery, while the *Blücher* engaged the Lighthouse Battery. Due to the action taking place at such short range, many of the German shells, fitted with delay fuses, were being fired almost point-blank and thus did not explode, for which the batteries' gun detachments would be forever grateful. Had this not been the case the loss of life would have been doubled at the very least.

Two 6-inch shells landed on the concrete aprons of the Heugh Battery guns and ricocheted off to burst in the field behind the battery, killing a cow. The narrow strip of land in front of the battery and the ground around it was continually ploughed up by enemy shells, yet the detachments stuck to their guns. With their puny 6-inch shells being no match for the heavily armoured ships it was decided to elevate the guns and aim instead for the 'above decks' structures.

The two leading ships, some 1,000 yards apart, steamed northwards, the *Seydlitz* followed by the guns of the Heugh Battery. As the range was long and observation was difficult, both guns were ordered to change target and take on the *Moltke*. The Battery Commander of the Heugh Battery, who had given no thought to the third ship, the *Blücher*, now realised she was practically stationary and was not being engaged by the Lighthouse Battery. Immediately both the Heugh Battery's guns were brought to bear on her. At this point the *Blücher* was firing black powder-filled shells on to the rocks in front of the battery in an attempt to produce a smoke screen (one of the earliest recorded incidents of its use). The dense black smoke proved fairly effective and interfered with the sighting of the guns and the observation of fire. The *Blücher*, perhaps taken by surprise as much as anything else, turned and steamed eastward at high speed, engaging the battery with her aft guns.

The *Seydlitz* and the *Moltke* meanwhile elevated their guns and purposefully bombarded the Hartlepools, their objectives the steel works, docks, ship-yards, gasworks, and railway goods and passenger stations. After some fifteen minutes of heavy shelling the ships turned about and steamed south-easterly at an oblique angle across the front of the two shore batteries, opening fire on them again with their guns. As the *Moltke* re-entered the area of fire from the Lighthouse Battery she was again engaged by both guns of the Heugh Battery until she disappeared into the rolling mist to join the racing *Blücher*.

With two of the three German ships now out of range and view the batteries turned their attentions to the *Seydlitz* as she raced to follow in the wake of the *Moltke* and *Blücher*. The batteries poured fire after her until she disappeared into the mist, the last round from the batteries being fired at precisely 8.52am. The British gunners had managed to get off 123 rounds (70 at the *Seydlitz*, 20 at the *Moltke* and 33 at the *Blücher*) and had inflicted some serious damage and killed and wounded a number of men from the enemy's crews.

Few Military Casualties

That there were no casualties inside the batteries was put down to the foresight of Lieutenant-Colonel Robson, who had been responsible for the creation of a camouflage extension along the top of the wall at the rear of the batteries a few days earlier. It was thought this extension, as well as making it difficult to 'locate' guns from seaward, also gave a false impression of the height of the batteries. This would account for the large number of shells which passed over the batteries into the towns.

HIMS BLÜCHER
Fregattenkapitän Erdmann

Ship's War Complement: *847*
Armament:
12 x 8.2-inch guns
8 x 6-inch guns
16 x 24-pounder guns
3 x torpedo tubes
Speed: *25.86 Knots (43,886 horsepower)*
900 tons coal - 200 tons oil
Length: *493 feet*
Breadth: *80 feet*
Displacement: *15,500 tons*
Built: Kiel Yard
Completed: *September 1909*
Cost: *£1,349,00*

Nearly all the military casualties were caused when the troops left their billets to fall in on parade, or went to the aid of those already wounded. Private Jones of the 18th Durham Light Infantry is the exception as he was on sentry duty when he was killed.

The casualties were; Durham Royal Garrison Artillery - 2 killed; 18th Battalion Durham Light Infantry - 6 killed, 10 wounded; Royal Engineers - 6 wounded; *HMS Patrol* - 4 killed or died of wounds, 7 wounded; *HMS Waveney* - 6 wounded; *HMS Doon* - 3 killed or died of wounds, 9 wounded.

The Aftermath

Of the three German attacks that day, the one on the Hartlepools was by far the most destructive, not just in loss of life and injury, but to property and the general infrastructure of the towns. Casualties among the civilian population were reported as 112 killed (comprising 43 men, 32 women and 37 children) and about 200 wounded. Of those killed, only 23 died in their homes, the rest were struck down in the streets where panic and mayhem had ensued. However, six more names have been added to the list of the Hartlepools' dead as others died later of their wounds; the last of these, making the total 118, was reported as having died in 1916.

Property damage was extensive. The three gasometers at the Hartlepool Gas and Water Company were struck and engulfed in flames and the explosions from them were said to be visible for many miles. The damage left the Hartlepools without a gas supply for a number of days whilst emergency repairs were undertaken. That night many of the residents had to sit in partly damaged houses with little more than a candle for comfort, light and warmth. In those houses whose roofs had been seriously damaged the rain fell on blistered and battered furniture and the shoulders of the forlorn.

Many of the ships in the harbour received direct hits and were seriously damaged, while the shipyards and docks were badly hit. Two fishing boats, the *Constance* and the *Wayside Flower* were reported sunk by the German battleships, though with no loss of life.

The railway station and goods yard suffered too. Indeed, one shell narrowly missed the packed 8.27am train to Leeds as it steamed out of West Hartlepool station, crashing through the wall and onto the station platform.

Many shells fell in the grounds of the Workhouse, causing damage to the buildings, but no loss of life among the inmates. In both towns many houses were completely wrecked. The damage was not confined to any particular area, but extended practically the length and breadth of the Hartlepools, and in a few cases to the countryside beyond. It was reported that seven churches, ten public buildings, five hotels and over three hundred houses had been destroyed or damaged in some form or another. The damage to property was estimated to be between £100,000 and £200,000.

Message from Bishop

That evening the Bishop of Durham wrote to the Hartlepools from his sickbed:

> *I hear with great distress this evening of the naval bombardment. It is terrible to read of the destruction of so many dwellings and the loss of lives as well as other outrages. You need not be told how sad I feel at having to be passive here, though under kindest care and steadily, but slowly regaining strength, while dear County Durham is thus assailed. My prayers are always there.*

Two-year-old Charles Peart of 30 Turnbull Street died from abdominal wounds. His five-year-old brother, William, was also killed

Richard Theaker of 63 Turnbull Street died at the back of the Central Marine Engine Works. Some 9 residents of Turnbull Street perished, 6 of them children

Barney Hodgson of 9 Water Street died outside the Scandinavian Church trying to turn people away from the shelling

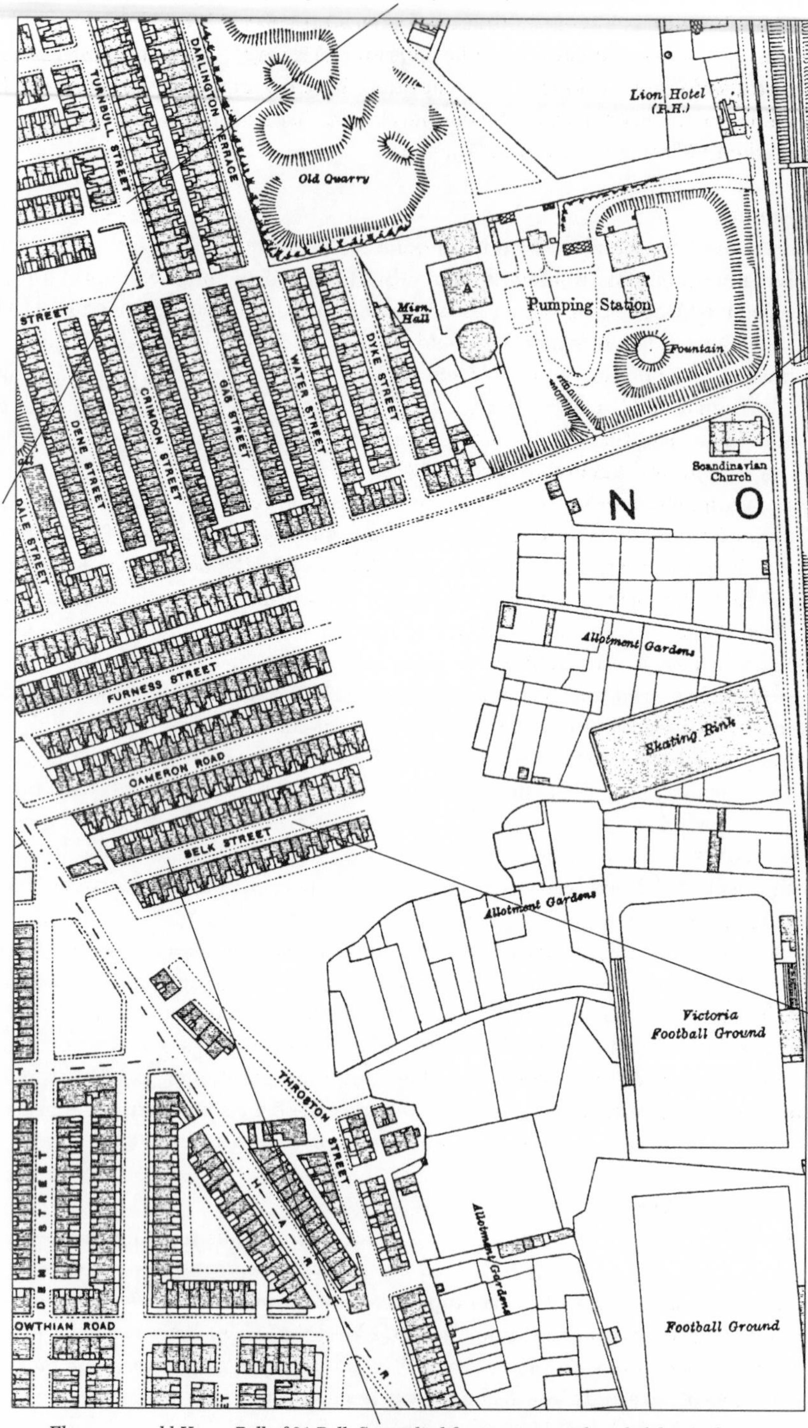

Seven-month-old Benjamin Lofthouse, of 25 Belk Street, died from severe head injuries

Eleven-year-old Henry Bell of 31 Belk Street died from serious neck and abdominal wounds. Some 5 people from Belk Street were killed, 4 of them children

The Inquests

The following day, Thursday, 17th December, the inquests began in West Hartlepool, where 37 were listed killed, with a lengthy statement by the Deputy Coroner. At the same time Coroner Bell conducted the inquests at Hartlepool where 40 more were listed killed. About half of the inquests and details of the deaths appeared in the local papers. By far the saddest stories were those of the deaths of the children, many of whom had been in the streets either playing or walking to school.

The first death dealt with was that of forty-one-year-old Jane Stoker. Her employer, local shipowner William Ropner of *Ambleside* described the circumstances of his cook's death. At the outbreak of shelling, fearing for their lives, Ropner and his family had hurried to the relative safety of the cellar. When the bombardment ended he had emerged into the devastated house to discover the lifeless body of Jane crumpled at the top of the steps leading down to the cellar - a sanctuary she had only just failed to reach when she was killed by the shell which devastated the house.

The Kay sisters, Annie aged thirty-four and Florence aged thirty-two, were killed outright when a shell, an overshoot intended for the Lighthouse Battery, smashed into their home, *Rockside*, situated on Cliff Terrace just behind the battery. The sisters were the first of Hartlepool's civilians to die.

From 31 Belk Street, eleven-year-old Henry Bell had died from wounds to his neck and abdomen.

Another eleven-year-old, Thomas Highan of 9 Henry Street, died from his abdominal wounds.

In the case of twenty-five-year-old Dorothy Caws, of 57 Grosvenor Street, her father William told how she had been about to have her breakfast in the back sitting-room, along with the rest of the family (father, mother and brother) when a shell had smashed through the roof, crashed through the ceiling and killed her instantly as she sat by the fire.

A four-year-old, Catherine Frankland of 3 Leeds Street, died from severe wounds sustained to her chest, head and arms.

Sixty-eight-year-old Julia Moon, of 11 Dover Street, was identified by her daughter, Julia Grainger. On the morning of the 16th December Julia and her husband had rushed through the shelling to Dover Street in order to take Mrs Moon to safety. However, on their arrival they found the house partially demolished by a direct hit and on searching the rubble discovered the limp and lifeless body of Mrs Moon in the back passageway to the house.

A babe in arms, seven-month-old Benjamin Lofthouse of 25 Belk Street, died from severe injuries to his head.

Chas Owen of 1a Pilot Street identified the body of his forty-three-year-old wife, Rose, for the inquest. Rose had been found lying face-down with her arms outstretched in a passage on Dock Street, in Old Town, by Richard Stamp. On further investigation he discovered she had been killed by a lump of shell fragment which had passed clean through her body. Mr Owen also lost his daughter, seventeen-year-old Mary Ellen, during the bombardment. Rose had been carrying a neighbour's youngest child, six-month-old infant Eleanor Necy of 2 Pilot Street, when she was killed. The baby was also hit and died from a severe abdominal wound.

The Jobling sisters, Sarah, aged 6, and Hannah, aged 4, of 22 South Street were identified by their aunt, Lily Jobling. The pair's father, a stoker with the Royal Navy, was away on duty at the time of the bombardment and it fell to grandfather George Jobling

Edith Jackson, of 49 Perth Street, was killed

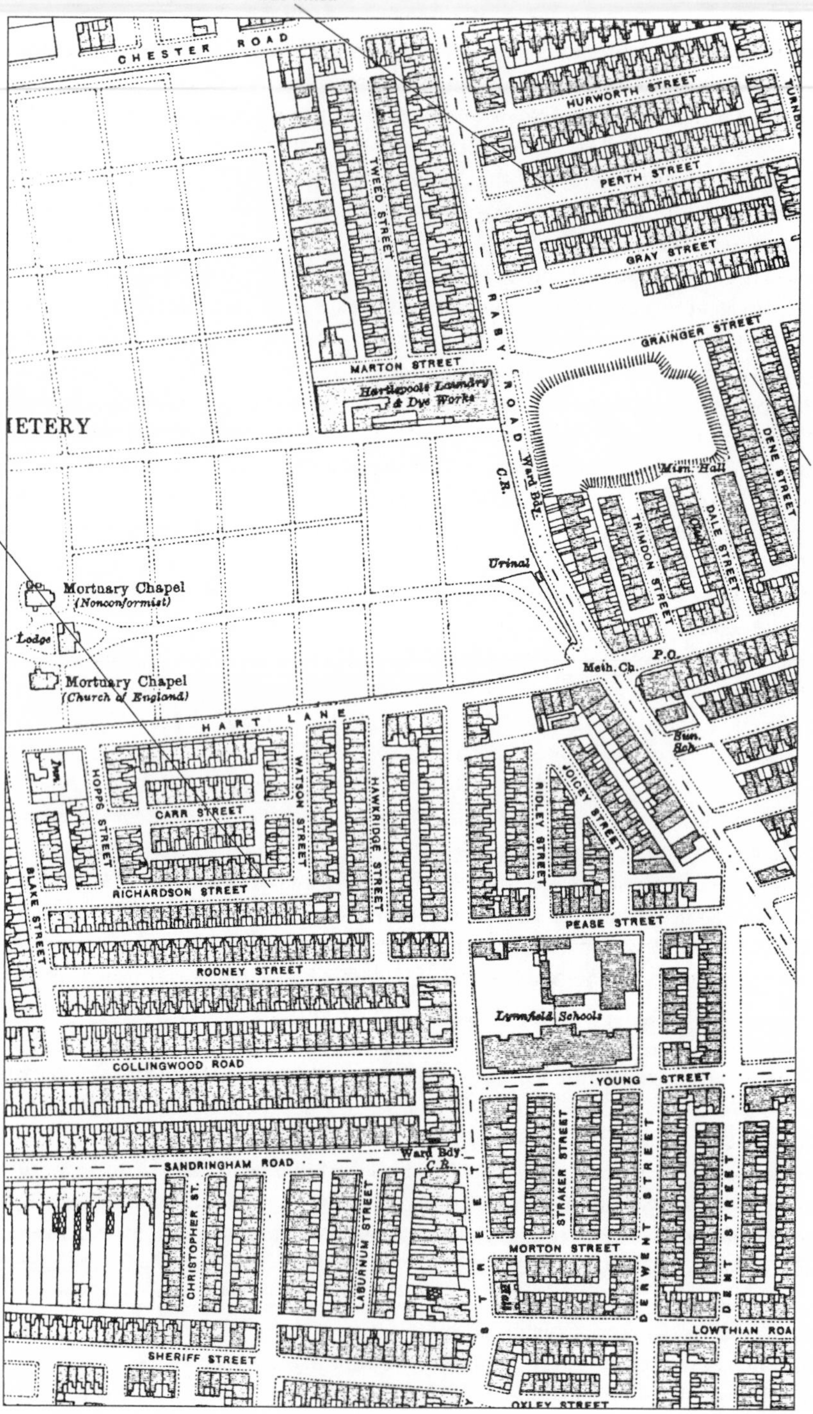

Thomasina Scarr, of 1 Richardson Street, was killed

Laura Wilkinson, of 20 Dene Street, and Mary Ann Harrison, of number 24, were killed to give an account of the girls' deaths. On hearing the rattling of the guns George had gone to the street door, from where he saw lots of folk running down the 'Old Town Tunnel'.

"I never thought it was the Germans," he said, "I thought they were just practising. I went to the door and saw people running round. I turned back into the house again and was just going to get a drop of tea when all at once *smash!* went the corner of the house. I was knocked to the other side of the room and it took me a few minutes to recover. When I did so I went round to the front door and found three children among a lot of bricks, two of them being my son's children. They had been killed by the shell which struck the house."

The third girl was eight-year-old Margaret Henighan of 18 Dock Street, Old Town. The girls had been playmates all their lives. Now all three were dead.

In the case of seventeen-year-old tailoress Hilda Horsley of 9 Wood Street her father, William, identified her for the inquest and confirmed her occupation before stating she had left home that morning at 8.00am to walk to work. Local dressmaker Sarah Philips then took up the account, for she had met and walked with Hilda through Middleton. Then the bombardment had started and they had raced to take shelter behind the Customs House office. No sooner had they arrived than a shell burst practically at their feet and Hilda, taking fright, had bolted. Sarah never saw her again, but learned later that she had been killed whilst running away.

In the case of forty-one-year-old John Staunch of 44 Alliance Street, Samuel Wilson claimed he saw a shell burst among a group of some fourteen men standing on the railway line near Old Town. Staunch had been felled by what Wilson claimed was a piece of shrapnel, but was more likely to have been a shard of the shell-casing (as most of the others in the group would have been killed too, had it been a shrapnel shell).

Once the body of thirteen-year-old Joseph Jacobs, of 32 Belk Street, had been identified, John McDonald told how he had seen the youngster run out of his house and into the road where he had been blown over by the blast of a shell which fell in the street at that instant. McDonald believed the boy to have been killed outright, but Dr Strain, the acting house surgeon giving evidence for the mortuary, stated that Joseph had been brought in with severe injuries to his head and that his right leg was smashed to a pulp. He died from his injuries.

Dr Strain also gave evidence in the case of sixteen-year-old Samuel Hunter, of 1 Alexander Terrace, Hart Lane. Samuel too had sustained serious wounds to his head and legs and, after a long struggle to save him, had subsequently died at 9.15pm.

The evidence from the mortuary continued with the case of another sixteen-year-old, Edward Cooper of 2 Exeter Street. He died from the shock after his thigh had been hit and mangled to a pulp.

Two-year-old Charles Peart of 30 Turnbull Street died from an abdominal wound. His elder brother, William, aged five, was also killed.

Thirty-year-old teacher of English and Latin, Etta Harris, based at the Henry Smith School for the past eighteen months, was killed outright when her lodgings at *Ivyholme*, South Crescent (the home of Mrs Jackson) received a direct hit and the back of the house was demolished.

The body of forty-seven-year-old George Dring of 30 Elliott Street was identified for the inquest by his son. George had been killed when a shell splinter hit him whilst he was at work at the Dock End.

The body of forty-nine-year-old Elizabeth Harper was identified by her husband.

A shell smashed through the roof of 57 Grosvenor Street, killing Dorothy Caws

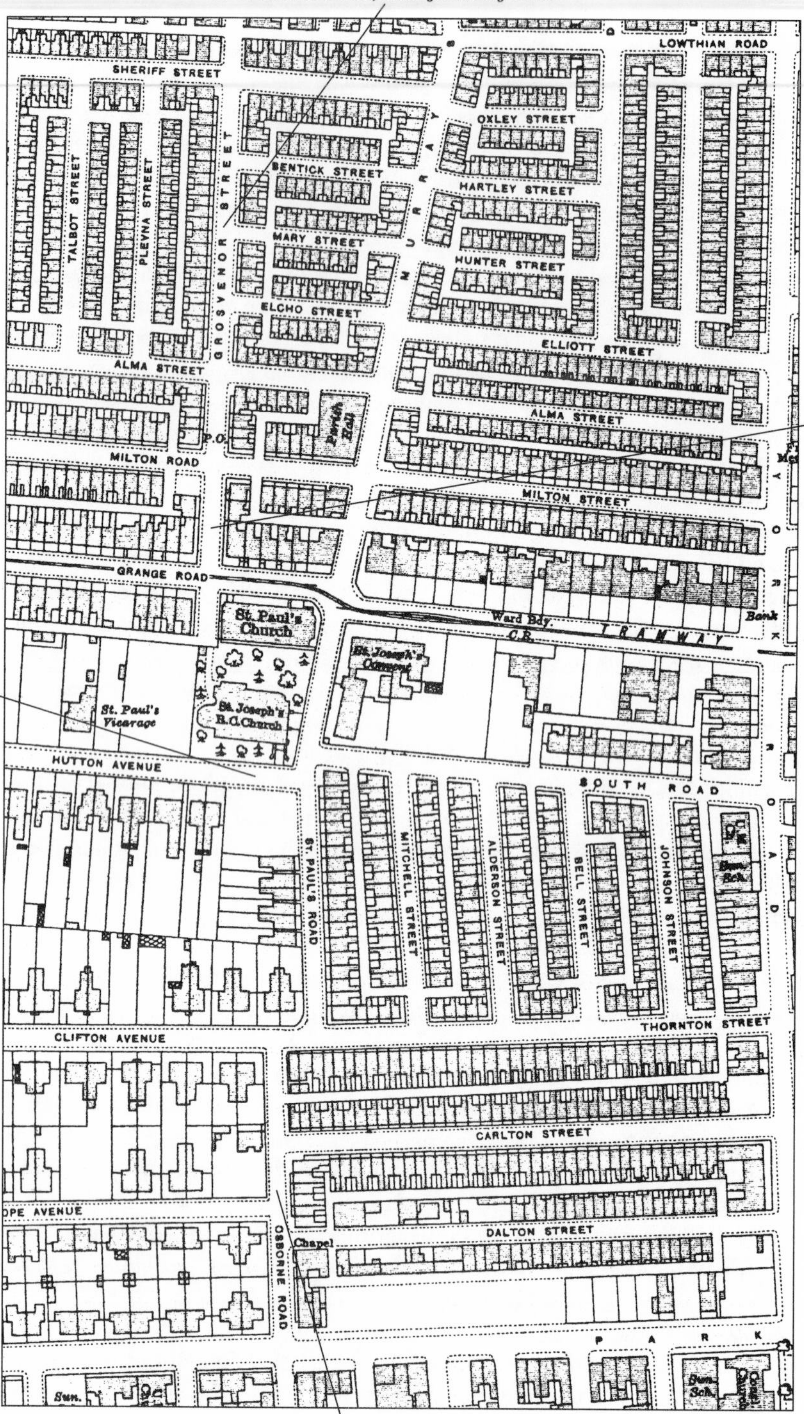

A shell went through the roof of 34 Hutton Avenue doing considerable damage

Mustard's tailor's shop on Grosvenor Street was practically demolished

Charles Ramsey, of Osborne Road, was killed on his way home from Richardsons Westgarth & Company

Elizabeth had been fatally wounded when her house, at 4 Moor Terrace, received a direct hit from a shell. Despite being rushed to Hartlepool Hospital her injuries were too severe and she died at 11.30am.

In the case of thirty-one-year-old Ivy Williams, a neighbour identified the body for the inquest and gave an account of her death. The neighbour had been called to the shattered remnants of the Williams' home at 8 Beaconsfield Square by Ivy's husband and had found her lying, already dead, amidst the debris of what had been the house.

Twenty-nine-year-old Albert Cressy's mother identified his body. On the morning of the bombardment she had had no news of her son, a beltman at Richardsons Westgarth & Company. But when he failed to return home for his dinner she had gone out to look for him and discovered that he had been killed at work. At the same works twenty-nine-year-old Edwin Ashcroft of 19 Penrith Street and thirty-seven-year-old James Cook of 28 Rokeby Street were both hit by shrapnel outside the gates. Edwin fell to the ground and died where he fell. James was dragged into the gatehouse, but despite the best efforts of those who had helped him he died shortly afterwards.

Among those who died when the iron-dressing shop at Richardsons Westgarth & Company, and the office block on the corner of Sea Terrace were hit was fifty-six-year-old James Leighton of 16 Clifton Street. Thirty-three-year-old Robert Ambrose of 65 Everard Street was also hit and fatally wounded. He later died from his injuries.

Pattern maker George Langdale of Belk Street then gave evidence in the case of his friend and colleague, thirty-seven-year-old Charles Ramsey of 24 Osborne Road. Both men were employed by Richardsons Westgarth & Company and on the morning of the 16th December, a little after 8.00am, had been startled by the sound of gunfire. Shortly after this the roof of the workshop in which they were working was hit by debris and shell fragments and the forty or so men at work there had made a hasty exit into the yard. However, they soon realised that their now exposed position was far more dangerous and so hurried back inside the workshop. It was then decided that the men should go home and see to their families. On exiting the works George went one way, Charles the other, and that was the last time they saw each other, for shortly after this Charles was killed.

It was the custom of twelve-year-old Alfred Claude of 11 Gordon Street to walk to the dairy on Mulgrave Road every morning to fetch his mother's daily order of bread and milk. It was to cost him dear, for the lad had been struck by a piece of shell which had exploded in Bright Street. Afterwards, those passing out of the town along the road passed either side of a hole in the road in which lay the lad's bloodstained cap which no one had the heart to remove.

At 3 Lilly Street a family tragedy occurred when a shell struck the house killing sixty-three-year-old Charles Cornforth as he stood on the back kitchen step looking into the yard. The shell demolished the rear of the house and killed his two daughters Jane aged seventeen, and Polly aged twenty-three.

Forty-year-old Mary Watson had been dressing at 164 Hart Road when a shell burst through the roof and ceiling and exploded in the bedroom, killing her instantly.

A twenty-three-year-old employee of the North Eastern Railways Company, platelayer Richard Theaker of 63 Turnbull Street, was killed by the blast from a shell whilst on the railway line behind the Central Marine Engine Works.

Apprentice engineer twenty-one-year-old Charles Hudson of 43 Mary Street was fatally wounded by shrapnel whilst working in the engineering shop at Richardsons Westgarth & Company. He died later that day.

J. Ballantine, on his morning newspaper round, thought the loud bangs were gunnery practice

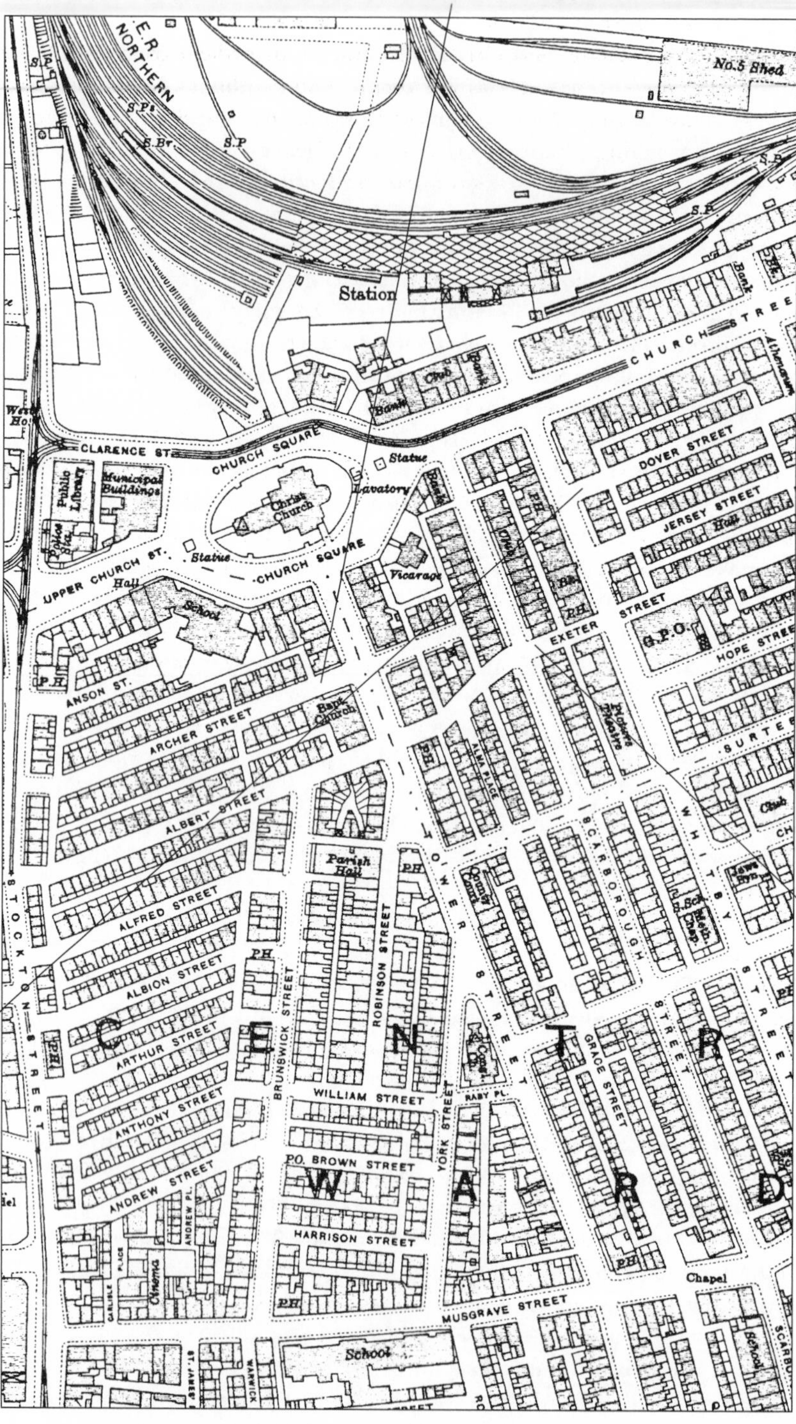

Julia Moon, of Dover Street, was found dead amongst the ruins of her house

Edward Cooper, of 2 Exeter Street, was killed

Daniel Sullivan was on his way to work from his home at 3 Harrison Street to Irvine's Harbour Dockyard when the bombardment began. The forty-seven-year-old plater's helper was killed outright on the street.

Sixty-three-year-old John Healey of 18 Hart Street was killed instantly by a shrapnel bullet which entered his back whilst he was at work in one of the shipyards, whilst fourteen-year-old Frank Unthank of 24 Wood Street was also reported killed at the same yard.

At the inquest into the death of five-year-old Stanley Simmons of 22 Campion Street (whose father was a gunner with the Royal Field Artillery), his mother told how a shell had struck the house and she had found herself in darkness amid the debris and almost suffocated. She struggled free and discovered Stanley badly wounded in the leg. Despite being rushed to hospital he died from his injuries.

In the death of twenty-five-year-old Nicholas Capeling of 4 Darlington Street, the inquest was told he had just left the shipyard after a night shift and was walking home when he was struck in the face by shrapnel. At first he did not appear to be too seriously wounded for he managed to walk to an ambulance, exclaiming that he wished he were dead. He was transported to hospital and there died.

The home of the local Salvation Army Adjutant, forty-nine-year-old William Avery at 7 Victoria Place received a direct hit and the roof and upper storey were completely destroyed in the blast which also killed William.

An act of kindness on the part of forty-seven-year-old Margaret Redshaw caused her death. Throughout the night the local shopkeeper had sat at the bedside of her close friend and neighbour Cissie Carr who lay seriously ill. Exhausted by her night's vigil, Margaret left Cissie for just a few moments to walk the few yards to her own home at 50 Watson Street in order to get her children up for school. At the sound of the guns Margaret ran out of her shop's kitchen and into the street to see what was happening only to be struck and killed by a fragment of shell.

Local widow Martha Measor walked to work across Sandwell Chare unaware she was about to lose a child. At her home at 11 Well's Yard her children, among them ten-year-old Christopher, were dressing for school. As the bombardment began the terrified children rushed into the street and Christopher was killed by a splinter of shell-casing.

As with many other families, the Dixons fled their home at 30 William Street the moment the bombardment began, hoping to run out of the town and into the countryside and to safety. They were hurrying past Church Close School when a shell hit the street in front of them. Fourteen-year-old George, eight-year-old Margaret and seven-year-old Albert all died instantly. Their mother was blown from her feet to the ground, and though seriously injured (one of her legs had been torn off) she still clutched to her bosom the blood-covered baby of the family, John. Hardly conscious she urged the wounded twelve-year-old Joseph, one of her remaining three sons, to take three-year-old Billy (also wounded) and run for all he was worth. Needing no second bidding Joseph picked up his brother and, with blood pouring from the wounds in his legs, ran off. The pair reached the gas works but were turned back. Joseph finally collapsed outside the Trinity Church. The pair were discovered by soldiers who took them to hospital and there they stayed for several weeks. Joseph had seventeen pieces of shrapnel taken from his wounded legs. It was a miracle he had been able to walk at all, let alone run, carrying his brother. Their father returned home following a compassionate discharge from the army.

T. S. Cassidy, an apprentice at Richardson's Foundry, saw bodies lying around in Commercial Street after an office block was hit

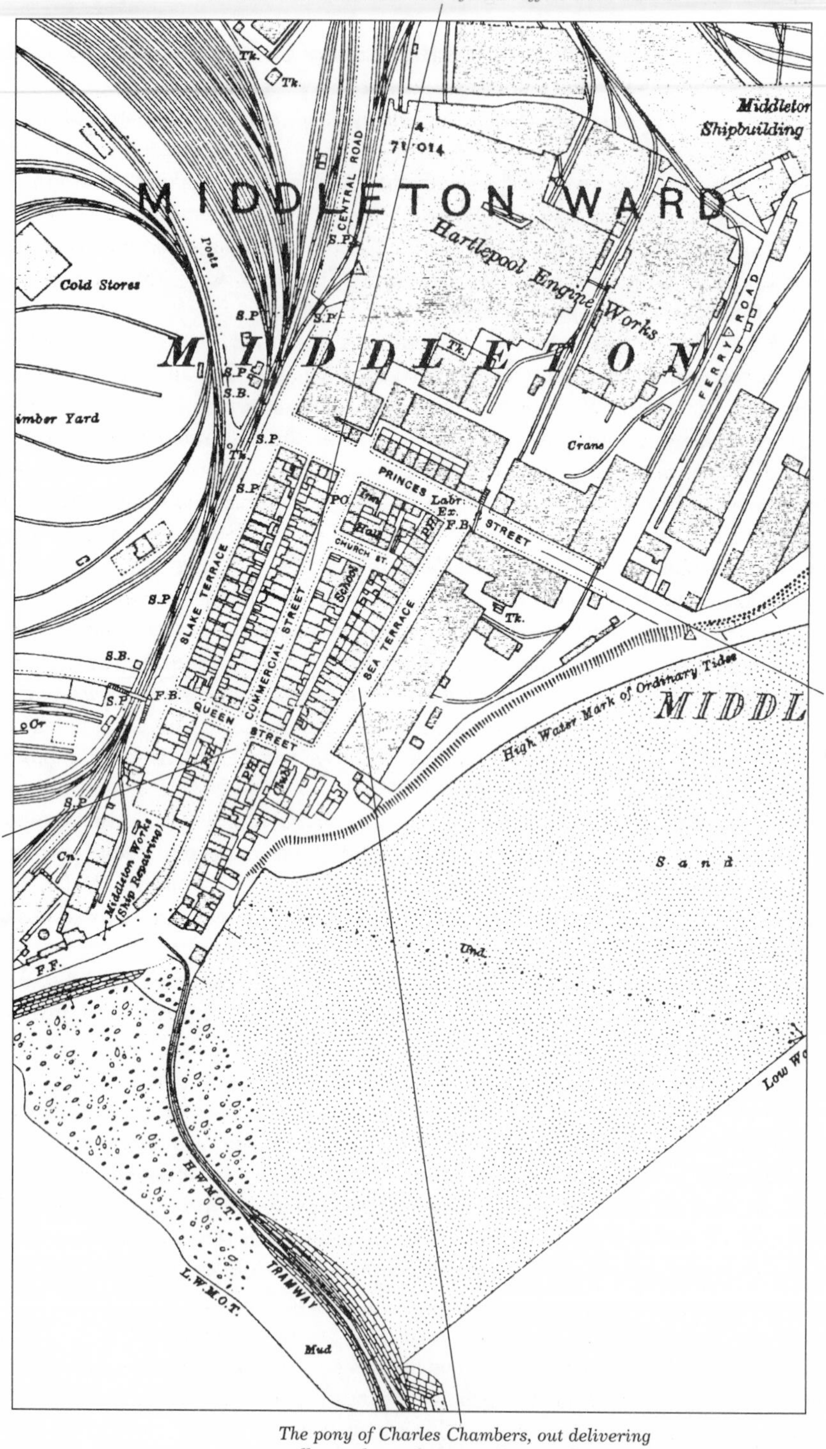

Also killed was James Bunter of 13 Commercial Street

Bertie Young of 7 Princes Street was killed with his face pressed to the window of his bedroom watching the bombardment

The pony of Charles Chambers, out delivering milk, was hit in the jaw and seriously injured

At 7 Princes Street, Middleton, thirteen-year-old Bertie Young was killed when, with his face pressed to the glass watching the bombardment, a stray shrapnel bullet hit and killed him.

Two local women, Margaret Bedlington and forty-seven-year-old Margaret Hunter had been on the beach collecting coal when the shelling began. Although the pair left the beach in something of a hurry Margaret Hunter, of 11 Bridge Street, believing there to be no immediate danger decided to turn back and continue with her coal-scavenging. She was about to cross the railway line and descend onto the beach again when a shell exploded nearby killing her.

Fifteen-year-old John McGuire of 58 Cameron Road was found by a young chap named Bell sprawled face-down across the tram lines at the junction of Middleton Road and Hartlepool Road. On reaching the boy he had turned him over only to discover half of the lad's chest blown away.

It was as if the Bedlingtons were blessed that morning, for Margaret's husband, Thomas and his best mate thirty-seven-year-old Robert Burgon of 7 Mill Street, left work at Irvine's Shipyard to race home to see to their families. On reaching the sea wall at Old Town, Thomas scaled it and dropped to safety on the other side. However, as Robert, following closely on his heels reached the top of the wall and made to drop down he was hit and fell dead at the feet of his friend.

Aboard the *SS Phoebe*, at rest in the harbour, twenty-five-year-old second officer James Pearson, of Robin Hood's Bay, was hit and fatally wounded. James had previously served aboard the *Birdoswald*, *Resolution* and *Roma* and had just returned from a trip to Archangel. Along with the *Phoebe*, James had been at Hartlepool for little more than a week and was greatly looking forward to some home leave on the weekend of 19th and 20th December. Although rushed to hospital and treated James died from his wounds at 3.15pm before any of his family could reach his bedside His father, the late Captain Richardson Pearson, had previously lost his life in a tragic accident when he had fallen from the bridge of his ship, and this, coupled to James's own untimely end, brought forth an outpouring of emotion and genuine sympathy from the good folk of Robin Hood's Bay towards his next of kin; his mother and two sisters. At the funeral on Saturday, 19th December, the little parish church was crowded to overflowing with mourners. No one would forget the loss of one of the Bay's own.

Aboard the *SS Munificent* in Gray's Shipyard twenty-three-year-old engineer's steward William Gray of 3 Ballast Hill, Blythe, was severely wounded. Among his numerous injuries one of his legs was completely shattered. He later died from his injuries.

The inquest heard how forty-three-year-old William 'Barney' Hodgson of 9 Water Street, on his way to work, saw the gas holder on the corner of Middleton Road and Clarence Road receive a direct hit and collapse in a burst of flame. A group of schoolboys were blown off their feet by the blast. One was reported killed, the other two were seriously injured. Realising the danger in the area, William took it upon himself to stand at the junction and warn people away, especially the children who were making their way past him. He was hit twice by shrapnel as the Scandinavian Church he was standing outside was hit. He died in the road with an arm blown off.

Fifteen-year-old John Crake of 19 Wood Street died outside 5 Prissick Street when a shell exploded almost on the doorstep. The Jacques family who lived in the house had to clamber over the boy's lifeless body amid the debris to get out and off to safety. However, they had gone barely a few yards before they came across the crumpled body

Eleanor Necy from
2 Pilot Street was killed

Sisters Hannah and Sarah Jobling of 22 South Street, and their friend, Margaret Henighan of Dock Street, were all killed together

Margaret Hunter of 11 Bridge Street was killed coal-scavenging on the beach. Her friend Margaret Bedlington survived

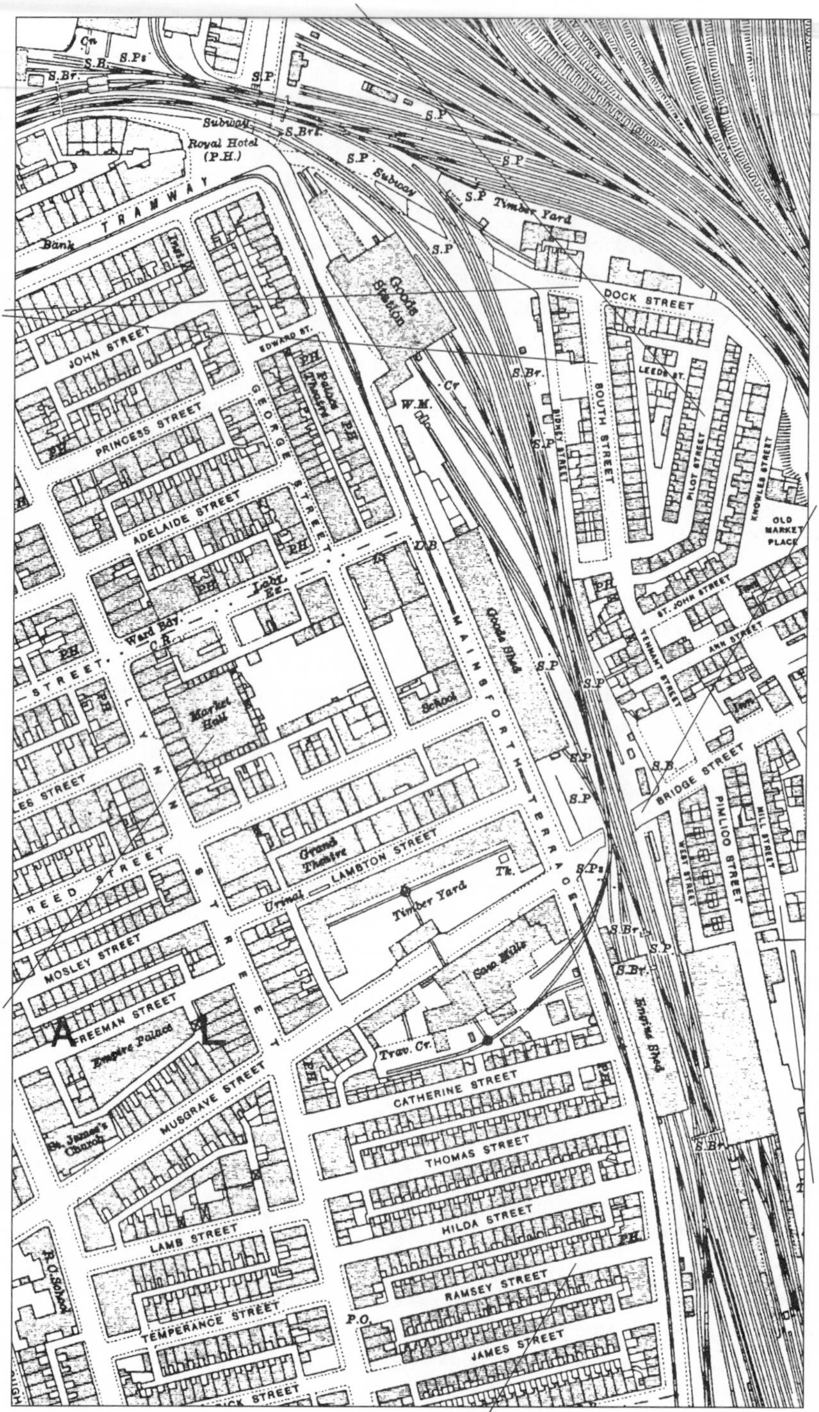

Glass roof panels at the Market Hall were shattered. The 'Dead House', or Mortuary, was situated here

Thomas Bedlington's pal, Robert Burgon, of Mill Street, was killed climbing the sea wall at Old Town

Samuel Binns of
21 Ramsey Street was killed

of nineteen-year-old Freda Wainwright of 10 Henry Street who had been killed by the same blast as had done for John Crake.

It was confirmed for the inquest that forty-four-year-old James Lynett of 11 Staindrop Street had died as a result of the wounds he received whilst on Scarborough Street.

Charles Tate was reported as having died of abdominal wounds at the inquest, yet his name does not appear among the list of Hartlepool's dead.

Praise for the Garrison

The day after the bombardment General Plumer, the officer commanding Northern Command, visited West Hartlepool and addressed officers and men of the town's defences, praising them for their coolness and courage. He also read a message to them from Lord Kitchener who commended them and the civilians of the Hartlepools for their calmness and absence of panic.

Local Newspaper Comments

Thursday, 17th December also saw the following editorial comment appear in the *Northern Daily Mail* in response to the release and publication of the Admiralty's statement of the previous day (see Scarborough p105/107), which made reference to a certain amount of risk having to be expected and borne by those living on British coasts:

> *It was of course disappointing to people here to learn that the raiders had escaped. The first statement issued by the Admiralty led us to hope that some comprehensive operations, with a view to forcing a decisive fight, were afoot. The despatch spoke of 'German movements of some importance' and added that 'the situation is developing'.*
>
> *From this we assumed that the raiders were being forced to fight, but in a later message it was reported that they had escaped in the mist. True, the enemy were engaged by patrol squadrons, but these were possibly not in greatly superior strength if they were strong at all.*
>
> *In the statement issued last night, the Admiralty pointed out, quite rightly, that 'demonstrations' of this character are devoid of military significance and that such demonstrations must not in any circumstances be allowed to modify the general naval policy which is being pursued. But we hope that the authorities will not forget that although the shelling of a town may be insignificant from a military point of view, it is significant enough to the people who live in the town. No doubt the larger questions of naval strategy must take precedence over the defence of particular localities, but at the same time we may be permitted to hope we are not to be made a target for the German ships even in the interest of a higher strategy.*
>
> *The Admiralty have a duty to perform to the inhabitants of the coast towns, who naturally look to the Navy to protect them from such events as occurred yesterday. We do not wish to write a harsh word of criticism, for the responsibilities of the Admiralty are great, but it is certainly disappointing that so many German ships should be able to pay a surprise visit to our coast, do so much damage, and escape with immunity.*

The question, though phrased a little differently, was being put yet again. And, yet again, the answers were not forthcoming. In the face of growing hostility the Admiralty

Major Hill's Company, 3rd Green Howards, were billeted at the Town Hall and had a close shave when a shell exploded nearby

The Grand Hotel was the home of the Regimental Headquarters of the 3rd Green Howards

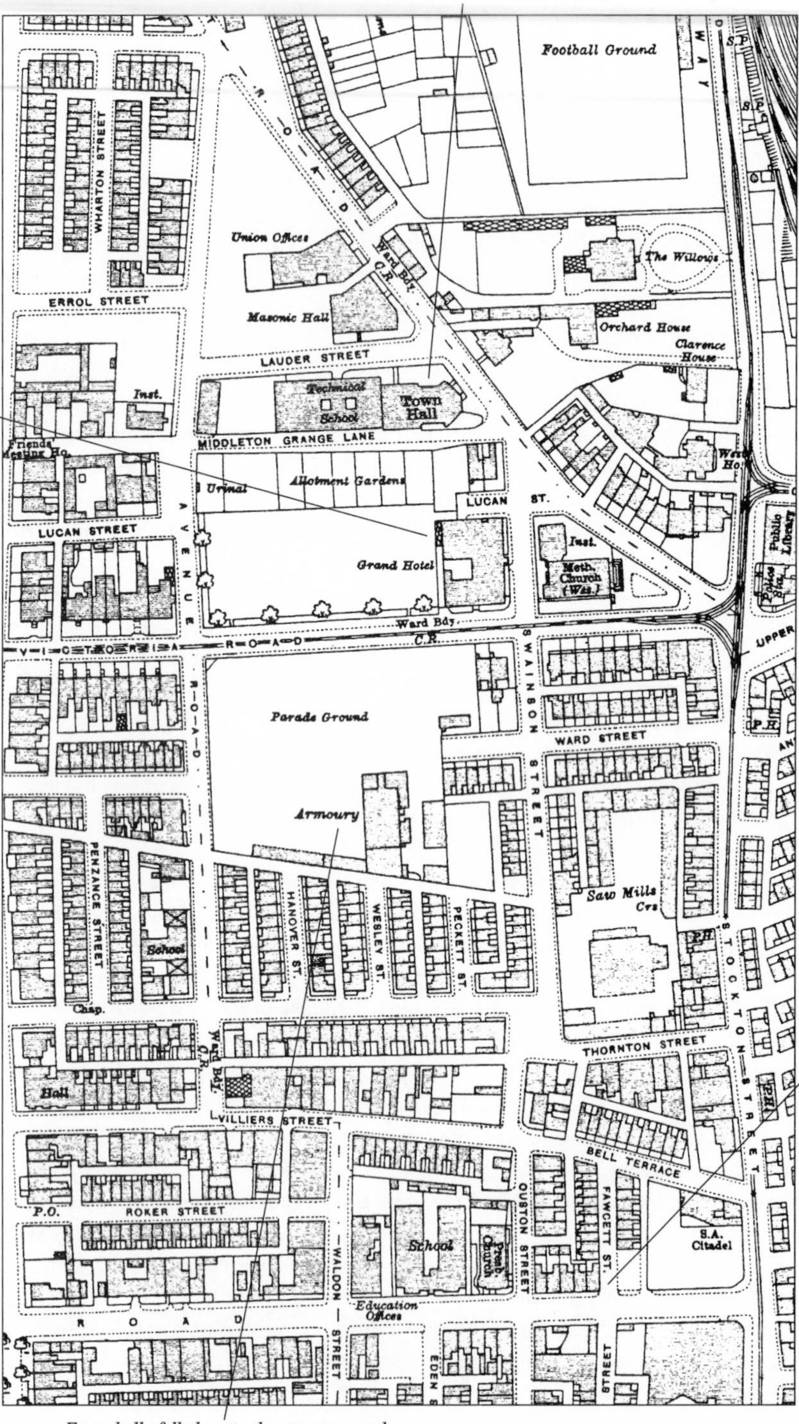

Charles Brookbanks of 4 Fawcett Street was killed

Four shells fell close to the armoury and it was slightly damaged could only keep its own counsel and trust that information about the breaking of the German naval codes did not surface. This, if nothing else, was the only positive thing to emerge from the bombardments of the 16th December.

Citizens Flee in Panic

On the morning of Friday, 18th December, hordes of people left their homes fearing another German attack as rumours spread like wildfire throughout the Hartlepools. However, the rumours were quickly disproved and people slowly drifted back to their homes, sheepish, but much relieved.

Later in the day a telegram was received by West Hartlepool's Town Clerk in reply to the Mayor's request of the Admiralty for an inquiry into the bombardment of the Hartlepools:

> *The Admiralty appreciate the composure with which the Hartlepools have borne themselves in their first experience of German fire. All the facts of the situation are known to the Admiralty and no further statement upon them can be made at present.*

Although all the facts were indeed known to the Admiralty, they were not made public until much much later.

On Sunday, 20th December, church services were held as usual, though they were far sadder affairs than was usually the case. Many of the churches themselves had been victims of the shelling, and even those which had survived intact had losses to bear in their congregations.

Letters of sympathy and messages of support flooded in from around the country as they had at Scarborough and Whitby, and from the King came a gift of pheasants for the sick and injured at Hartlepool Hospital. It was reported that when the patients discovered who had sent the gift each asked for a feather as a memento.

Seamen's Funerals

On the afternoon of Monday, 20th December, Able Seaman Woolgar and Leading Seaman Rigsby, of the *Hardy* were buried at Immingham Old Village, both having died as a result of the ship's involvement in the preliminary defence of Hartlepool. Several staff officers and a company of one hundred soldiers attended and the Last Post was blown as they were lowered into the earth.

The *Hardy*, along with the *Lynx*, *Ambuscade* and *Unity*, had formed part of the Third Cruiser Squadron which had come into contact with the cruisers forming one part of Admiral von Hipper's screening flotillas at 5.15am on the morning of 16th December.

The lead German cruiser had given the wrong signal when challenged and had been engaged by the British flotilla. During the engagement the *Lynx* was holed and was forced to withdraw. The German vessels then made off and *Lynx* rejoined her group.

At 5.58am the ships sighted another cruiser and opened on her at a distance of some 700 yards. The cruiser was the *Hamburg* and she returned fire. The *Hardy* was particularly badly hit and withdrew from the engagement at 6.00am.

It was in this engagement that Woolgar and Rigsby had been killed. The *Hamburg* then doused her lights, disappeared southward and contact with her was lost.

Message from the King

On Tuesday, 22nd December the Hartlepools received a message from the King via Lord Durham, the Lord Lieutenant of the County:

> *I have felt keenly for the people of Hartlepool during the past week and heartily sympathise with the bereaved families. Please inquire as to the progress of the wounded. I wish them all a speedy recovery.*

Mayor Watson replied;

> *Please inform the King the people of Hartlepool fully appreciate his gracious message of sympathy. The condition of the wounded is still serious but there is some improvement. We thank his Majesty for the kind wish for their speedy recovery.*

Admiral Von Scheer's Account of the Raid

The following is a portion of Admiral von Scheer's account of the raid written after the war:

> *In the first months of the war many efforts had been made to conduct our operations in such a way that would cause the enemy such losses as would enable us to speak of a real equalisation of forces. But in vain. The results of our mine-laying were unknown, while the successes of our submarines did not weigh much in scale, as the ships they torpedoed had no fighting value. On the other hand, raids by our cruisers were much more likely to bring considerable portions of the English Fleet out of their harbours and thus give our fleet a favourable chance of intervening if kept in close touch with the cruisers.*
>
> *On 15th December, the big cruisers under the command of Vice Admiral Hipper sailed under orders to bombard the fortified coastal towns of Hartlepool, Whitby and Scarborough and to lay mines along the coast, for there was constant traffic between the east coast ports.*
>
> ~
>
> *Shortly before they were off Hartlepool the cruisers were attacked by four torpedo-boat destroyers of the 'River' class, that ran out to sea and were brought under fire at a range of about 50km. The sinking of one destroyer and heavy damage to another were observed. After firing some torpedoes without result, they turned away. We gave up pursuing them so as not to lose time for the bombardment. The Seydlitz opened fire on the Cemetery Battery and scored several hits, so that at last the fire was only returned by one 15cm gun and one light gun from the battery. The Moltke was hit above the waterline, causing much damage between decks, but no loss of life. From the first, the Blücher came under a lively fire from the land batteries; she had nine killed and three wounded by the one hit alone. 15cm howitzers and light artillery were used on land and the Blücher was hit six times altogether.*

The first part of the account gives some rationale for the raids, but the account of the Hartlepool raid is inaccurate in some respects, as although all the British destroyers, except the *Waveney*, received damage, none of them were sunk, and all made it back to port in the Tyne. The Cemetery Battery referred to, some two and a half miles north of the Heugh Battery, had been derelict for many years before the war and no shells fell near it during the raid. There had been no howitzers or light artillery used on land, only the three 6-inch guns of the Lighthouse and Heugh Batteries.

German Medal Struck

According to a report made by the German press, their own casualties among the three ships amounted to 80 killed and some 200 wounded. All three ships were reported damaged, the *Blücher* more seriously than the others. However, the news of the bombardment was received in Germany with great acclamation; the action considered of sufficient import to warrant the award of the silver medal, specially struck, to each one who took part.

According to the German official historian, the three ships fired some 1,150 shells during the forty-two-minute bombardment of the Hartlepools.

Defences Strengthened

Soon after the raid on the Hartlepools their defences were strengthened with the addition of a 'monitor' carrying two 12-inch guns. The monitor was allotted a position for mooring, and when moored formed part of the shore defences under the orders of the Fire Commander. However, the commander of the monitor was also given a 'roving commission' and was able to put to sea at will; thus the monitor was often away from her moorings. This unusual situation prevented any complications arising from a naval vessel being under the orders of an artillery fire commander.

Awards and Decorations

The 'good and efficient service' of the Durham Royal Garrison Artillery (Territorial Force) during the action was officially recognised by the award of the Distinguished Service Order (DSO) to the commanding officer Lieutenant-Colonel Robson. When the King and Queen visited the Hartlepools in June, 1917, Robson was invested with the insignia of the Most Distinguished Order of St Michael and St George, in recognition of his valuable services.

The Distinguished Conduct Medal (DCM) was awarded to Sergeant Douthwaite of the Durham Royal Garrison Artillery stationed at the Lighthouse Battery - the first to be won on British soil in the Great War - who, according to the official citation *'Extracted a live cartridge from the breech of a gun which had misfired.'*

The Military Medal (MM) - instituted in the early days of the war - was awarded to Acting Bombardier Hope and Acting Bombardier Mallin of the Heugh Battery. The medal awarded to Hope was the first Military Medal to be struck at the Royal Mint and the first to actually be presented.

It was not until some years after the war that it was decided to award the British War Medal to all ranks of the Durham Royal Garrison Artillery (Territorial Force) who took part in the Hartlepool action, but there were very few who were not then already entitled to the medal by virtue of their service overseas subsequent to the bombardment.

Hartlepool Commemorative Medal

In 1915, in an effort to raise much-needed funds for the hospitals at Hartlepool, all of which had been hard pressed to cope with the influx of injured and wounded during the bombardment, it was decided to hold an annual 'Bombardment Thank-Offering Day' on the 16th December each year and a brass medal was struck and issued. It was oval and measured some two and a half inches. Emblazoned around the edge was the legend 'Thanks offering to Hartlepool Hospitals'. The medal was given to anyone who contributed to a collection held in the Hartlepools in 1915.

The first 'Thank-Offering Day', held on 18th December 1915, saw the Durham Royal Garrison Artillery take on the Green Howards at rugby on Friarage Field and the Royal Naval Air Service take on the Royal Flying Corps in a football match on the Victoria Ground. There were also many sideshows, and theatrical events were held in the evening. At the end of the weekend of festivities £2,330 had been raised for the hospitals. In 1916 the sum raised was £2,960 and in 1917 it jumped to £3,150. In 1918 'Thank-Offering Day' was held on 21st December and a German submarine, *U94*, was put on display at the Union Dock.

However, in 1920 it was decided to abandon 'Thank-Offering Day' in favour of other means of fund-raising. Occasionally, in the years between the wars and at irregular intervals after the Second World War, the Durham Royal Garrison Artillery held 'bombardment' dances in December; though by then two world wars had been fought and the wound at Hartlepool, by no means healed, was no longer as open and sore as it had been.

Hartlepool

In Their Own Write
Personal Accounts of the German Naval Raid on the Hartlepools on Wednesday, 16th December 1914

The following extracts from letters and verse were written largely by the men and women of Hartlepool. Many have appeared in local papers, or are from military archives, and a number have been written up from interviews conducted during the 1970s by the author and journalist David Mould, and the Hartlepool author John Ward. Now, for the first time in 85 years they once more describe, in their own words, the day the Hartlepools underwent their forty-two minutes of hell, their never to be forgotten ***'Bombardment'***.

The author of the letter or verse always follows the piece. Notes relating to contemporary material are suffixed by the date (1914 or 1915), and notes about recent material are prefixed with 'This account was related by . . .' Maiden names have been used (where known) on recent material to provide a reference to 1914. All material is from or related to the 1914 attack on the Hartlepools.

Hartlepool, or rather the Hartlepools, for the new town of West Hartlepool immediately adjoins its ancient sister, possesses fine mercantile marine shipbuilding yards, and is the home port for a large fishing fleet. There are also immense marine engineering works. These were cogent reasons for arming the place and it had been a defended port many years previous to the war. But a pretty weak armament it was; two forts, one containing two six-inch guns, the other, a hundred yards to the south having just one six-inch gun.

Three and a half miles farther south, across Tees Bay, lay the mouth of that river, defended by a fort with two 4.7-inch guns. The steelworks, dotted up its banks as far as Middlesbrough, were too far inland to attack, the river's mouth was an important anchorage for in and outgoing vessels.

In other words, the authorities, when arming the place, had never contemplated this sort of attack. But nothing in war ever happens as per the book!

GENERAL DAMAGE

1: *Rockside*, Cliff Terrace, where sisters Anne and Florence Kay were killed. 2: William Avery's house at 7 Victoria Place. 3: Dock Street. 4: A damaged gasholder.

During the night of December 15th/16th, three battle-cruisers, the Seydlitz, Moltke and Blücher gathered off the coast and must have edged in a bit closer to the shore, as they were inside our extended patrol area by dawn.

Shortly before 8.00am on the 16th, the ships steamed across Tees Bay from the south-east. The morning was cold, but there was not a breath of wind, for the smoke went straight up the funnels of the hostile ships as they eased down on their speed.

The sea was like oil, and the tide dead low - a combination which considerably helped the defence as I will explain later. Pocketed in the bay was a dense mist which slowly, but never quite, dispersed. These conditions considerably hampered the style of South Gare (the 4.7-inch battery). Our tiny intercept patrol pluckily closed with the three monsters, who naturally bashed them unmercifully, quickly causing damage to both personnel and material. It was a hopeless fight from the first and our boats had to draw off. It was difficult to distinguish the ensigns of the various ships, for the flags, at such a distance and when fouled by funnel fumes, appeared the same. As a result, the South Gare Battery, on hearing the firing and seeing what they thought to be three English cruisers being attacked by German destroyers (for the Germans were only using their seaward or starboard armaments at this point) swarmed on to the parapet and took up what they thought were front row stalls for a most interesting fight. Only when they later saw those same ships firing on the Hartlepool forts did they realise the mistake, by which time the ships were out of their range.

Out of the mist, and almost head-on at a range of about 4,000 yards, came the leading ship. Identification was difficult under such conditions, but within seconds the position was clarified. A large red light suddenly showed from the foremast of the Seydlitz, and the Germans opened immediately with some ranging rounds. Between them the ships had twenty 11.2-inch guns, eight 8.2-inch guns, eighteen 5.9-inch guns, besides a host of lesser armaments for 'port side' fire. To reply we had three 6-inch guns, two of them at Heugh and one at the Lighthouse. The three German ships ranged quickly, the forts even more speedily. The guns in Heugh engaged the leading ship, while the Lighthouse gun took on the Blücher, the last ship in the line, and the only one in the arc of fire from the battery. The third round from the Lighthouse was a 'juicer'. An immense sheet of flame shot up from the Blücher's after-deck; the deck supply for one of its 5.9-inch guns had been detonated by our lyddite shell, and the effect was passed on to the next gun whose ammunition did ditto. Half the after-bridge was brought down and eleven seamen killed.

I previously mentioned the fact of it being low water. Both Heugh and the Lighthouse are very low-sited batteries. The range was short, the mean range during the fighting being only 5,300 yards; consequently the trajectories of the hostile guns, designed for fighting at 20,000 yards, were, at this distance, absolutely rigid, i.e. straight lines - the smallest error in laying was a miss. Each 6-inch gun had to be hit to damage it, and each presents a relatively small target even at short range. Clods of earth and chunks of masonry there were in plenty, but the guns remained intact, though the three of them had several hairs-breadth escapes.

To render things more difficult for the Germans, Colonel Robson, the Fire Commander, had a few days earlier run a camouflage extension along the rear fort wall of Heugh. It gave a jagged skyline from the sea and an appearance of false height. This and low water gave a most exaggerated height to the battery, and the enemy projectiles hummed over - only just - to burst in the houses behind. Naturally the enemy then shortened the range and his shells burst just in front of the guns. Here the defences scored heavily, for he used delay armour-piercing projectiles, which struck and bounced off, bursting far over in the air. The pieces however killed and wounded many inhabitants, who were now in the streets and getting a move on for the nearest countryside.

A pilot cutter, becalmed halfway between the combatants, was in a somewhat unique position. The Germans left her alone. Her captain could actually see some of our six-inch projectiles whirring away after they had failed to penetrate the tough armour of the battle-cruisers. When the range was adjusted to hit the upper works, considerable damage was seen on the funnels etc. From the battery came the shout, "Go on! Shove 'em through! Shove 'em through! Give the buggers hell!" and the reply, "Do stop dancing about there and save your breath for your gun corrections!" The worst thing of all was seeing each ship lit up by a nasty yellow glare, that seemed to trickle along their sides, while we waited for the result. It was only a matter of seconds at that range. As each salvo arrived it was preceded by an appalling 'onde-de-choc', that curious double report which occurs when you are stationed in line with a high velocity gun at short or medium range. The shells were so low that the wind of each salvo knocked down any men who happened to be on the manning parade, and caps were snatched off heads and whirled away like leaves.

Behind the Lighthouse Battery, marching on his post in the approved Buckingham Palace style, was a sentry of the 18th Durham Light Infantry, backwards and forwards, one-two-three-four-about. His officer asked him afterwards why the hell he had not gone under cover. His reply was classic, that of a Durham pitman, "Eeee, bugger! I was that feared, had I done nowt I'd have run away!" The little fellow's beat, I have to say, was fully exposed and the opening salvo had bashed up the row of houses in front of which he had to continually pass.

Our total casualties among the two forts were extraordinarily light, thanks to the enemy's use of delayed action projectiles - direct action fuses would have wiped everything and everybody out, as by now the range had been found and the Germans were at 'fire for effect'. Four gunners, one sapper and eight infantrymen were killed, and between twenty and thirty of the garrison were wounded - these mostly in reserve at their billets. Four infantrymen, comprising a beach-situated machine-gun nest just outside the entrance to Heugh, were 'done in' with the very first salvo. Two gunners - relief detachment men - who rushed out to render assistance were killed by the next. Seydlitz and Moltke now moved north to swing round and rake the Hartlepools. This ended the second phase of the fire from the Germans which had commenced at 8.05am. The concentration ceased at 8.20am.

In spite of their close range no material damage had been done to the defence, except that the scarps and parapets of each fort were a mass of ruined masonry.

The two battle-cruisers now left the Blücher to engage the two forts with harassing fire. The Blücher, by luck or design, had taken station directly in line with the Lighthouse, thereby causing the single gun of the battery to go out of action for something like twenty minutes. With one gun short, Colonel Robson could only follow the leading ship, Seydlitz, with the remaining guns in Heugh, until she passed out of the fort's arc of fire, when he switched his attention to the Moltke. When she too had disappeared, he swung on the Blücher. Directly the guns in Heugh engaged the Blücher she began to move out to sea. She cleared the lighthouse and that battery came into action again, engaging the ship. A dense white cloud issued from one of her funnels, and it was thought that a steam pipe had been cut, or that the 'black squad' (the stokers) were raising a head of steam for the home run and that it was only the safety valves lifting.

Before being engaged by Heugh, the Blücher, in order to blind the fort from firing on the other ships, had been firing salvos of old pattern powder-filled 8-inch projectiles at the rocky Foreshore just below the battery. Owing to the absence of any wind, a quite efficient smoke screen was put up. It cut down the rate of fire tremendously, but our gunners, availing themselves of every opening in the screen, continued to fire on the Seydlitz and the Moltke, until these drew out of the arc of fire. The work of destruction now began on the two boroughs. A group of enormous gas holders were the first to go, 'picked off as clean as a whistle'. Each became a roaring column of flame. No area seemed to have been untouched. It was as if a gigantic rake had been drawn across each spot. Shipyards, marine engineering works, railway stations, churches, schools, streets and even the private houses of the heads of businesses on the low ridge above West Hartlepool, received shells of various calibre. A total of 119 were killed and 300 wounded (of both sexes) while some 600 houses were destroyed or damaged. The Germans claimed the silencing of an old battery known as 'Cemetery'; as this work had been dismantled in 1906, they merely wasted their salvos.

As soon as the Blücher was well under way, the two other vessels ceased firing on the Hartlepools and steamed off, converging on her. As they once again crossed the arcs of the batteries they gave Heugh and the Lighthouse a few parting salvos. These were replied to, and as the last ship disappeared into the mist our final round was fired at a range of about 9,300 yards.

The whole action lasted some forty-three minutes, from 8.05am to 8.48am. In the whole German squadron there were 80 killed and 200 wounded.

The above account was related by the officer in charge of the Hartlepool defences to a contemporary magazine shortly after the event. However, some of the details are incorrect, especially with regard to those killed - only 2 gunners died, 6 infantrymen and no sappers. The figure of 119 civilians is thought to be out by 5 - as I have only been able to trace 114 named civilians (recorded in the indexes) as having died. 1914.

My recollection of that tragic memory remains as vivid as ever. When I look back I can still feel the atmosphere of excitement in the Battery; flurried excitement to begin with, but changing to a cold deliberation as we took command of our nerves. I still have flashlight impressions of the men at work and I'll never forget Captain Dickie Trechmann pacing about as calm and collected as an undertaker, with his monocle in position and his eyes staring with hardly a trace of perturbation. In another flash I see Captain Jack Farmer smiling all over his face as the shells streamed steadily out of the guns without a hitch and then bursting violently into explosive words when the guns went out of action through being masked by the lighthouse.

The most spectacular thing about the whole bombardment is that I never felt a single qualm of fear, even while the enemy shells were banging up against the concrete, not quite as thick as hailstones, but often enough to be dangerous.

That was my first experience of being bombarded. I went through many others during the war, but in none of them did I feel so completely at ease and free from anxiety. I found that the more bombardments I went through the more my confidence seemed to disappear and towards the end of the war they were terribly frightening experiences. Many of my colleagues say the same thing. I suppose we were too surprised at the German ships actually turning up and too intent on getting our blows in to think about what might happen to us.

I was No.1 range-finder in the Lighthouse Battery when the German ships came into sight. At first we thought they were British cruisers. Ready as we were, and waiting for the German ships, none of us seemed to believe that these splendid, powerful-looking vessels could be any other than British. I remember the tension rising a fraction when there seemed to be no satisfactory answer to the coastguard's challenge, but almost before we could suspect them they settled the matter by letting off one of the big guns at us. The shell landed behind the battery.

We engaged the Blücher, and thus, almost without warning, we were thrown into our first battle. Theoretically, firing at real enemy ships ought to be no different from placing guns on towed targets, but we soon found how different the two things can be. At practice you take your range and give your orders quickly and confidently because you know that if you make a mistake the effects will not be very serious. But in war you are obsessed by the peril of making an error. Your confidence deserts you, you try to take infinite pains over everything and consequently get yourself into such a nervous state that you find it difficult to do the simplest of things correctly.

We soon warmed up to the job and it was not very long before the chain of actions, from the lifting of the shell from the magazine to the actuation of the trigger, was proceeding as smoothly as possible. When we changed from armour-piercing shells to lyddite the gunners got so excited they brought up scores of projectiles from the magazine and had them strewn all over the floor. I shall always remember the sad look of disappointment on their faces when they were ordered to take them back. It was a look of tragic frustration.

We got the range of the Blücher at 6,000 yards. Then we changed to lyddite. We got two or three direct hits almost at once and there was a great flare of fire and smoke. I was certain the ship had been blown up, but the German ships were not so easily disposed of. We had only carried away the forebridge and dismounted a gun. It is possible the flare was caused by some loose ammunition which our shells ignited. At that range it was almost impossible to miss such a big target as a battle-cruiser and I do not think there would have been much left of her had she stayed so close in and had the lighthouse not masked our gun.

Heugh Battery engaged the Moltke and Seydlitz in a sustained action lasting thirty-three minutes. The ships were eventually driven off and proceeded north. The battery then turned on the Blücher and she was driven off by the combined fire of both batteries. I can never understand why they came in so close. They could have done their work just as easily and without danger to themselves by standing well out of range and pumping long distance 11-inch shells into the town. Closing the range as they did gave them no advantage except to enable them to use their smaller guns. Perhaps they hoped to put the batteries out of action and they would have done so, had they not used the wrong fuses. The shells they fired had delayed action fuses, so they hit the concrete, ricocheted over the top and exploded in the town. If the fuses had been instantaneous they would have burst as they struck the concrete and probably have destroyed us all. There were two direct hits on the guns at the Heugh Battery and one shell just cleared the front of the gun in Lighthouse Battery. They would have made a much better job of the attack if their shells had not contained such a high proportion of duds. Unexploded shells were found all over the town and when I got back to my own house I found one in my kitchen, having come through the wall. It would have made a considerable mess had it not been a dud, but exploded inside.

Their coming in close may be explained by the fact that about a week before the bombardment some buoys, fixed a good distance from the harbour, had been brought much nearer the shore. The Germans may have known of these buoys and perhaps were ignorant of their change of position.

We had a submarine lying in the harbour that morning. I don't suppose that in the whole history of the war so tempting a prize was damaged so near it. If it had been patrolling the coast . . . Still regrets of this sort are in vain.

The above account was related by Tom Pailor. A Sergeant-Major, he was the No.1 range-finder for the Lighthouse Battery during the bombardment. He later went on to become a Councillor.

I was an apprentice in Richardson's Foundry, and started work at 6.00am on that fateful morning. At 7.40am we heard gunfire quite a distance away. By 8.10am shells were screaming overhead and clouds of dust filled the foundry. The ground trembled as we made for the gatehouse.

In Commercial Street, Middleton, many bodies were lying around, the office block having been damaged, and soon I was running for West Hartlepool via the dock gates.

I reached the big chimney just as it was hit by a shell and I turned back and ran onto the pier where I noticed two destroyers leaving Hartlepool under fire. It was too hot there, so I ran back and tried getting up Middleton Road. I got as far as the swing bridge, but it was chaos there, flames reaching to the sky from the gasometer. The telegraph wires were all down and pit props were flying around with crowds of people milling about not knowing which way to go.

One old lady, with a birdcage, appealed for anyone to help her. She was only dressed in her nightclothes.

I eventually got back into Middleton again, passing down a back street where two coal carts with horses were abandoned by their drivers. The animals were causing quite a commotion. I dived into the cellar of a house where a cosy fire burned in the grate and there I stayed until quietness returned.

The above account was related by T. S. Cassidy.

On the day of the bombardment I was 16 years old and worked at Gray Peverells. My mother came in and told my sister and me that there was a naval battle in the

GENERAL DAMAGE

1&2: Rugby Terrace.
3: Shell nose-cones. 4: Hunter Street.
5: Knowles Street.

North Sea, but I still set off to work as usual, walking from Cleveland Road on the Central Estate to West Hartlepool. When passing the prop yard on Union Road I saw pit props dancing out of the wagons and I thought it was the vibration from the naval guns.

By now the noise was terrific and when I reached Greenland Bridge there were great bursts of shrapnel in the sky, so I decided to turn back, but soon changed my mind when I saw that the Tram Offices I had just passed were now strewn across the road. I ran on.

The gasometer in Montague Road was blazing and in front of me a tramcar was throwing off coloured lights - it was really frightening.

I saw the Middleton Road gasometer blazing and all the workmen were running up Middleton Road from the shipyards. Outside the wrecked Scandinavian Church a poor workman lay with his arm blown off [William Hodgson].

I eventually got to Ward Jackson Park and was there until a man on horseback came and told the hundreds who were there that it was safe to go home again. When I got back to Cleveland Road it was to find that two huge pieces of shell had come through our roof and the debris was all over the bed where my sister and I had been sleeping earlier that morning.

We made do with an improvised bed in the kitchen for weeks after, with no windows anywhere and no gas.

The above account was related by T. M. Temple. Born in 1898 he was 16 at the time of the bombardment.

I lived in Middleton at the time of the bombardment. I remember winding up the window blind and seeing an old lady with a bag of cinders on her back running through the passage dropping cinders as she ran crying, "The Germans are here!"

An old friend ran in to tell us to stay indoors near a double wall. Mother, younger brother and I went out to look for a friend who was blind. The first thing we saw was a coal cart and a man sat wrapping up his bleeding leg. We could not get to our friend's house for the fallen walls. We then went to look for our grandfather, but uncle said he was alright and was on the banks watching a 'fine display' with an old friend.

The above account was related by Mrs S. Clayton.

On the 16th December the 3rd Battalion [The Green Howards] received its baptism of fire in the shape of a rain of shells fired from German warships. The bombardment of the Hartlepools was in keeping with other German exploits. They followed their reputation for striking hard, quickly and unexpectedly.

Though the incident is of 'no military importance', it has had the effect of stirring the imagination of our recruits under arms, quickening the military spirit of all ranks, and giving to those who have returned from the front a further taste of war. The details of the raid have been well described in the newspapers; but, of course, almost entirely from the civilian point of view, and naturally so considering the havoc to property and the great loss of life; the death-roll amounting to 110, and the wounded to over 400, many of them women and children.

Our Companies [of the 3rd Green Howards] are stationed over a wide area from South Gare to the Naval Barracks at Hartlepool, some five or six miles of coastline, and then again we have Companies in West Hartlepool in various billets, and a couple at Seaton Carew on Coast Defence. All the Companies billeted in the Hartlepools came under the zone of fire. The Germans contrived to annihilate any jealousy in that respect, as their fire was well distributed over the whole of Hartlepool and West Hartlepool.

The bombardment commenced at 8.05am and continued until nearly 9.00am. During that time it is estimated that some 800 to 1,000 shells of all sizes, up to 11-inch, were hurled at the towns, over the towns and far beyond into the country. The fire was replied to by the batteries at Hartlepool manned by Durham Royal Garrison Artillery Territorials, who served their guns with conspicuous coolness and gallantry. The guns being of 6-inch calibre, their shells were not able to penetrate the heavy armour of the battle-cruisers, but the gunners claim to have damaged the decks and to have carried away the bridge of one of the vessels.

The German warships, three in number, steamed past the Hartlepools, coming from the south, at a distance from the shore of some 3,000 yards. As they were said to be flying the White Ensign their identity was not at first established. Before shelling the town they fired out to sea, probably to allay suspicion.

The German fire was directed in a systematic fashion, evidently on a pre-arranged plan. They tried to knock out our guns. However, they did not succeed in actually hitting any of them, although great holes were rent in the sea wall; and the stone parapet, behind which are the gun emplacements, was severely battered. Immense havoc was wrought amongst the houses which lie clustered together in the vicinity of the batteries. The historic church of St Hilda received a shell through its roof. The gasworks were badly damaged. Fire was directed on the waterworks, but the injury done was trifling. Five shells were found in a field about one and a half miles west of . . . . [name censored], the billet of No.5 Company. These shells seem to have been intended for either Tunstall Court or the waterworks, probably the latter. Tunstall Court lies about half a mile west of the waterworks in a direct line, the waterworks being about half a mile from the sea. Many shells fell near Seaton Carew and several passed over . . . . [name censored], the billet of Captain Fish's Company. The shells which fell in the fields onto the soft ground failed to explode, but tore great holes in the earth. The scene from the swimming baths at . . . . . . [name censored], the billet of Captain Rollo's Company, was majestic and superb. Until the mist lifted the hostile ships were hidden from view, but the flashes of their guns were clearly seen. Shells falling short were observed splashing into the sea, raising great columns of spray.

Several shells burst on the seashore just short of our trenches, throwing up clouds of sand and dust. Captain Fish was blown off his feet by a shell which burst near Staincliffe, the shell exploding some 70 yards away from him; he was unhurt. The Regimental Staff at the Grand Hotel had several shells unpleasantly near to them, no less than four falling into the Armoury Field where we have a miniature range, about 50 yards distant from the Grand Hotel. Three of these shells exploded, doing little damage. A shell fell into the grounds of . . . . [name censored], where are situated the offices of the Fortress Staff. This shell burst and some of the pieces fell among the men of Major Hill's Company, whose billet is at the Town Hall. The Grand Hotel, Town Hall and Orchard House are within a stone's throw of one another.

Those of the Service Companies whose war stations lie in close proximity to the shore manned the trenches which overlook the beach and sea. The ships were too far off for our rifle fire to be effective.

The experience will not be forgotten by those who saw the flashes and heard the boom of the guns, as the great cruisers steamed northward sending forth a fateful message of death and destruction.

Captain Richardson had a near escape when a shell came through the roof and burst in his bedroom. Captain Richardson being an early riser was, fortunately for himself, not in the bedroom; but he had only just that minute left the house. Shells were bursting all round the place, a large piece going through the Officers' Mess at the Armoury, and another piece through the Quartermaster's Stores. It seems marvellous that our casualties were so small, only two men being wounded.

On Thursday, 17th December, Lieutenant General Sir Herbert Plumer, General Officer Commanding, Northern Command, assembled the garrison and read a telegram from Lord Kitchener, [the Secretary of State for War] complimenting the troops on their calmness, and the civil population on the absence of panic. General Plumer, addressing the troops, said that of course the incident should not be exaggerated, it being only a small part of a very large war; but this was the first time most of them had been under fire, and their calm behaviour throughout was splendid.

The enemy did not follow up his bombardment: but, had he done so and attempted to set foot on our shores, their behaviour was such as to assure everyone that they - the men of Durham and Yorkshire - were fully prepared, and would have been able to render an excellent account of themselves.

This account cannot be concluded without paying a tribute to the gallant behaviour of the civil population of the bombarded towns. A soldier expects, and indeed almost welcomes, such incidents as these; but it is very different for the worker in the city, whose courage is not fortified by discipline, by the presence of comrades in arms, and by the sustaining influence of 'esprit de corps'.

Men, women and children following their daily tasks do not expect to be blown to pieces in the streets or to have the roofs of their houses come crashing in over their heads. Yet the inhabitants of the Hartlepools behaved like soldiers. There was no panic - no wild rush for safety. An hour after the firing ceased normal life was resumed just as if nothing had happened. This seems to show that these northern people still possess those sterling qualities which we associated with their ancestors, yet which many feared that modern luxury and modern comforts had sapped.

This account was related by an officer of the Green Howards, writing in the Green Howards Gazette shortly after the event.

The 3rd Battalion Green Howards had been raised at the market town of Richmond, North Yorkshire, on the 4th August 1914 and had moved to West Hartlepool (where it remained throughout the war) on the 8th of August that year to become part of the Tees Garrison. The 3rd Battalion would be one of the few Green Howards battalions not to see active service abroad, but instead would remain at home in cadre form as a Reserve

Battalion to assist in raising recruits and training them for the other active service battalions of the Regiment. 1914.

There are two main reasons I will always remember Hartlepool. First, we were always told as recruits that we were the junior service and the senior service was the British Navy, and the Navy was marvellous. We were told no foreign ships could ever enter British waters and all that caper. Secondly it was the first time we were told in advance of what we were going to do. Usually we were never told anything, just fell in. You know, somebody yells at you and left turn, quick march and you find yourself doing something. But nobody told you about it in advance. Except at Hartlepool (and once at Passchendaele).

We weren't in Hartlepool actually, we were attached to the South Gare breakwater, a kind of peninsula at the mouth of the Tees. We were on this south breakwater, a company of us as part of coast command. The remainder went to Hartlepool and were billeted in the Town Hall. The breakwater was cut off with a ten-foot high barbed-wire fence, and it was ten-feet deep too. There was a railway line ran along this peninsula and at the end of the line there were two trucks, one with a portable searchlight and one with a fixed searchlight. The engineers worked the searchlight; we were just forming the guard, about a hundred of us. It was a nice cushy little billet as a matter of fact; there was a nice hut built on the wider side of the peninsula and we had 'biscuits' and a 'bed board' - the biscuits were like a square cushion two-and-a-half feet square; you had three of them, about as long as a man, and they were quite comfy.

Anyway on this particular night we were under barrack-room conditions with the bugler blowing all those calls. We hadn't got down to wartime when you abandoned things like that. Anyhow, he'd blown the Last Post and come to blow Lights Out, most of us were already in bed for there was nothing to stop up for once the Last Post had gone. Anyhow, instead of blowing Lights Out he blew another call, and we couldn't make out what it was. But we had a couple of reservists with us and they soon said, "This is a bloody alarm! What the hell's the matter? Get out! Get out!"

We got outside and lined up and out came the Commanding Officer.

"We've been told by the Admiralty that the German Fleet is at sea and they're making for our shores and they're expected to make a landing on the Northumbrian coast. You will all stand to. Don't take one iota of your equipment off and await orders. There's a train being shunted up the line with the engine steam up all night, and in the event that you're wanted you'll have to bundle into that quick and push off further north."

That was the first time I'd ever been told anything. Anyway we went to bed that night, using our haversacks for pillows.

In the morning we got up, had breakfast and then dispersed; some on guard duty at the gate, or at the top, while a few had nothing to do, except talk. Then we heard the first salvo.

"Get down!" cried the officers. We were on the breakwater and couldn't dig in so we simply lay down on the ground, while the officers stood up with their binoculars. Not that they could see anything because of the mist. But we could hear the shells coming over, though we didn't have the faintest idea what was going on. We thought our Navy was knocking the hell out of the German Fleet.

We'd been told the fleet was at sea and naturally assumed they were blowing the Germans out of the water. That's what we thought.

This went on until one of the officers commented, "I do believe there's something going on in Hartlepool across the way there." Hartlepool was four or five miles away. But we still thought it was a naval battle.

By the time the mist lifted the Germans had packed up and steamed off. A little later quite a few women came running down the line, the peninsula, outside the barbed-wire, calling out for someone, a son or husband, because they were local people and wanted to know everyone was okay. But of course nothing had happened to us, nothing at all. Then we had dinner, our midday meal, and were still wondering when some ships hove into sight from the south. When they came into view they were battleships, British Navy, all wonderful flags flying. There were two or three ships and the big one in front was the battle-cruiser Lion, Admiral Beatty's headquarters. You should have heard some of the comments from the older soldiers . . . "Bloody Navy!"

This edited account was related by Private William Henry Lunn. Born in Middlesbrough on 15th December 1896, William joined the 3rd Battalion Green Howards on 17th March 1914, aged 18. The battalion was at Richmond, North Yorkshire (home of the Regiment) at the outbreak of war and was moved, on 8th August to West Hartlepool, where it remained for the rest of the war. William was one of those on guard duty at South Gare during the bombardment. He was later drafted into the 6th Green Howards and served at Gallipoli. The 6th Battalion landed in the first wave of troops at Suvla Bay on 6th August. The assault by the Battalion was the first attack made by any unit of the New Army during the war. On 21st August the Battalion attacked Scimitar Hill and lost all its officers. Only 100 men, under a sergeant-major made it to the Turkish line. The Battalion, reduced to a strength of 285 (from 775) subsequently formed a composite battalion with the West Yorkshires. Following a spell in Egypt the Battalion moved to France and the Somme. It was here, now a Corporal, that William won the MM. At the Third Battle of Ypres William, then a Sergeant, served with the 32nd Light Trench Mortar Battery. He suffered an accident on 31st October 1917, whilst demonstrating the use of a Stokes Mortar and lost a leg. He survived the war and died on 2nd May 1998.

On the morning of the bombardment my mother, sister, five brothers and myself were sitting down to breakfast in William Street when shells began to fall. Soldiers were running down the street telling everyone to leave their homes as the street was in the direct line of fire. We all ran into the street and as we reached Church Close School a shell exploded killing many people including two of my brothers and my sister. Mother had her leg blown off and yet the baby she was carrying in her arms was unharmed. Although I didn't know it at the time, I think I was too dazed too realise, I was badly wounded in the legs and later had seventeen pieces of shrapnel removed. I was carrying my brother, aged three (I was twelve). He was also wounded and we later spent several weeks in hospital. However, I continued to run, still carrying my brother, and passed many people carrying all sorts of things. I particularly remember one old lady hurrying along with a birdcage in her hand. I ran on until I reached the gas works where many people had collected, only to be told to go back again. I turned back and finally

GENERAL DAMAGE

1,2&3: General street damage. 4: The 3rd Green Howards at West Hartlepool. 5: Rugby Terrace.

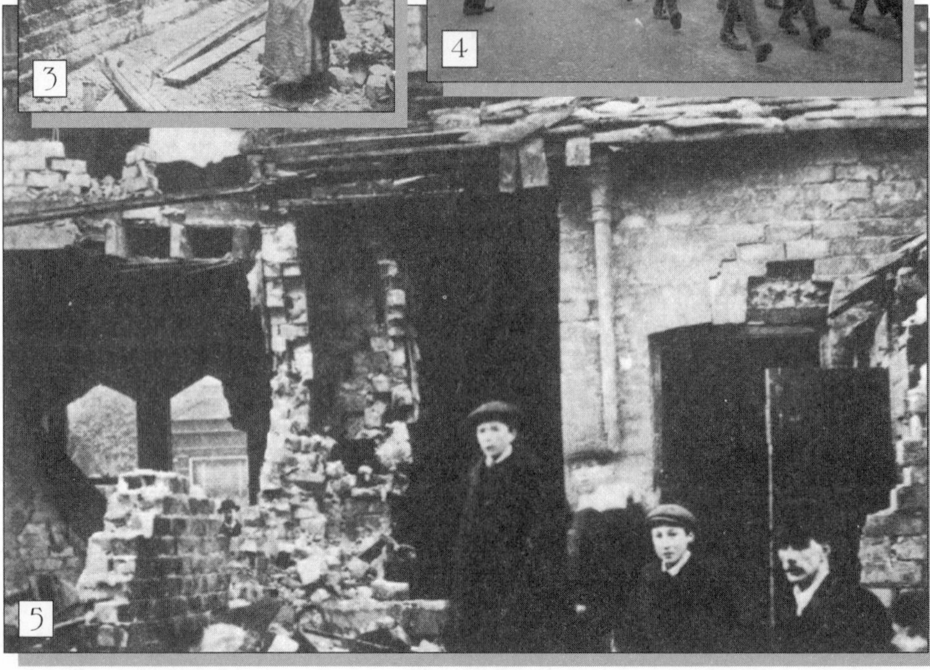

collapsed at Trinity Church. The next I remember was my brother and I being carried to hospital by two soldiers.

My father was serving in the army at the time but was given a compassionate discharge. As for the family of eight who sat down to breakfast that morning, three were dead, three wounded and only the baby and other younger brother escaped unhurt.

The above account was related by Joseph Dixon. Born in 1902 he was 12 at the time of the bombardment. The Dixons lived at 30 William Street. Fourteen-year-old George, eight-year-old Margaret and seven-year-old Albert all died. The baby son, John, that Mrs Dixon had been carrying when she was so seriously wounded survived unhurt. Joseph and three-year-old Billy, both wounded, spent many weeks in hospital after their ordeal, but eventually recovered, though their family was decimated.

We lived on Belk Street at the time of the bombardment. I was working at Gray's Central Shipyard and had just finished warming my can of tea, at about 8.20am, when the sound of gunfire could be heard. Everybody in the blacksmith's shop where I worked went out to see what was happening. In a few seconds a shell hit the offices and blew nearly all of it in the air. At the same time railway wagons were being blown sky high. The men who were running in that direction turned and made their way towards the back gate leading to Slag Island Quay. Nearing this gate I climbed one of the uprights at the ship's side which was on the stocks and in the course of construction, and saw that the gasometers were on fire. I shouted to the men who were running towards the gate to tell them what I could see.

"Get down you young fool!" they yelled back. By the time I reached Middleton Road the shells were coming over thick and fast. A lot fell in the timber ponds.

Reaching the junction of Middleton Road and Hartlepool Road I noticed a young boy stretched across the tram-lines face downwards and when I ran over to him I found out he was dead, with nearly half his chest blown away. His name was John McGuire. He lived on Cameron Road and had only recently started work at Gray's dockyard.

A few yards further on I saw Barney Hodgson of Water Street, pinned up against the Swedish Church wall bleeding very badly. I went to run towards him but he shouted, "Keep on running son, I'm done for." I think he was a brave man.

When I reached Belk Street and home, mother was propped up against the wall outside the house with blood running from her like water from a tap. In the road opposite her lay the body of a boy, Joseph Jacobs. I ran to the bottom of the street and took a barrow from a sculptor's yard and ran back with it to our house to put my mother on to take her to hospital. Then my brother Tom came up, and between us we got mother and the Jacobs boy onto the handcart. At the junction of Belk Street and Hart Road we stopped a coal cart and transferred mother and the boy onto it, asking the driver to take them to Cameron Hospital.

At the mortuary I had to identify my youngest brother, little Henry, who had been killed. Another brother was in hospital with leg injuries. Our family's casualties were mother who lost a leg and suffered multiple injuries, a brother killed, a brother with leg injuries and a nephew killed.

The above account was related by H. Bell. He and his family lived at 31 Belk Street at the time of the bombardment, and were greatly affected by the German attack.

The following account was related by Mrs E. M. Murray, the daughter of Barney Hodgson, in reply to the above account.

What Mr Bell said was quite correct. After my father (Barney Hodgson) had been home for breakfast he returned to the shipyard to see what was going on, but before he got there he stood sentry at the Swedish Church, sending children back home. He received two direct hits. I know he was very badly injured because I was the one who had to dispose of his clothes afterwards. I have never forgotten the sight of them. We didn't find out where he was until the following day, when my brother had to go to the Cameron Hospital to identify him.

COME!

Sons
Of the Islands, rise!
The German guns
Bellow to the skies
And rain their shell
Like hell
On England's coast.

~

This
To fulfil their boast,
Is but the first
And not the worst
Their hate will hiss
This German host.

~

They
Had sworn to come.
They had sworn to come.
They drank 'Unto the day,'
For years prepared the way.
Now hear the shrapnel hum
They will come, again!

~

Drum
And trumpet sound again:
Never before such need
For glorious deed.
Come up, come up, men!
You see your country bleed:
Come!

By George Weddell of Seaton Carew who witnessed the Hartlepool bombardment from his window that December morning. 1914.

My father was the Superintendent of the public market in Lynn Street. Our front door opened onto the market itself, and our back door opened on the market yard.

The market opened promptly at 8.00am and I was up getting my breakfast before setting off for Newburn School. It was then that the row began. There were explosions which gradually became so terrific that the concussion and vibration was severe enough to shatter some of the glass panels in the roof of the market and bring them down on the stalls beneath.

The danger from falling glass was so great that my father locked the front gates and the tenants of the open stalls took shelter in the small shops bordering the market. I well remember some of them coming into our kitchen and sitting round the fire discussing this unusual affair. It seemed to be generally agreed that there was a battle going on at sea. There they sat airing their knowledge whilst I listened open-mouthed, fidgeting in my seat and wanting to be off to school.

There was a public mortuary at the bottom of the market yard, and although the police were supposed to be in full control of the place, its maintenance and cleanliness were the responsibility of the market superintendent and for that reason he had a spare key. Human nature being what it is, when bodies were found on the beach or in the docks or on the railway, they were not carried all the way up to the police station to be reported and then brought back to the mortuary; the finders usually got the key at the market, put the body in and then carried on up to the police station to report it.

At 9.00am that morning there was a hammering at our back door and the driver of the Corporation coop cart demanded the key of the 'Dead House'. My father asked why he needed it and he said he had a body in the cart.

"What is it?" asked my father.

"A young lad," replied the driver.

"What happened to him?"

"He's been shot."

"Good heavens!" exclaimed my father, "Who did it?"

"Why man! Don't you know?" cried the astonished cart-man. "The Germans have been shelling us for the past hour. Do you mean to say I'm the first with a load? Get the place open quick because there'll soon be plenty more!"

Sure enough there were. Thirty-five bodies were brought into a place built to accommodate four, and the rest of the day was a nightmare that I was too young to remember. But I can remember the wails of distraught relatives who had wandered from place to place seeking loved ones who had gone out that morning as usual to work and had never returned, and whose fate was at last grimly verified in the 'Dead House' in the market yard.

I can still recall the eerie atmosphere as I had to sit in our familiar kitchen scarcely understanding why so many distressed strangers were coming in and out, having to peer in the gloom because all we had was the light of candles because all the gas was cut off because the gas holders had been hit. I too had my own small tragedy, for my mother took all my shirts to make decent the bodies of the children.

The above account was related by Robert Wood a well-known West Hartlepool historian.

I was 11 when the Hartlepools were bombarded. When we heard the gunfire and the crashing of houses, my brother-in-law, Corporal J. Lewis, who had arrived home from France on leave the night before, took us all, my mother, sister, young brother and me, out of the house to get away from the danger. We hadn't got far from Henry Street when a shell burst above us and wounded my mother whose arm was shattered near the shoulder. My brother-in-law was badly wounded in the leg and I was wounded in the knee. We got no further and were carried into a cellar at the back of Prissick Street School. We had to be lifted over the body of a workman who still had his can and Tommy tin in his hands. The cellar was full of wounded people. I remember one boy who had his leg blown off. He lived in the same street as me. The lady of the house ripped up all her sheets and linen to make bandages for us. It was all too tragic to forget.

The above account was related by Mrs E. Rickerby.

I was in charge of one gun during the action, which lasted about fifty minutes; quite the hottest fifty minutes I ever experienced, and we didn't half pepper them with lyddite shells.

The German ships, which were all battle-cruisers, appeared off our battery at 8.15am, and, spreading out like a fan, one on the right, one on the left and one in the centre, opened fire upon us at about 3,000 or 4,000 yards with the broadsides of their guns.

One shell dropped about two yards from me and ricocheted right over. Our chaps handing up ammunition said they saw it pass right over my head, and thought I had gone. However, it didn't burst. Nearly all my detachment were Territorials, and I had my eye upon them during the action, and must say they worked like heroes, every one.

The Germans got the range splendidly, but their shells kept falling to the left and right. We kept at it until two of them turned tail and cleared off. The other disappeared in a cloud of black smoke and flame. Whether she sank or not we cannot say.

Our casualties were very few. Three Territorials were killed and six Durham Light Infantrymen, standing just outside the battery, were blown to pieces. Our battery escaped with but little damage. The General commanding the district afterwards paraded us and expressed his thanks for the manner in which we stuck to our guns, and said he would commend our conduct to Lord Kitchener.

This account was related by Frederick Mallins to a friend at Penarth, Glamorganshire. Frederick had been a police constable before the war and was serving as a bombardier at Hartlepool at the time of the attack. He went on to earn the Military Medal with the Royal Garrison Artillery.

I saw three of our ships enter the docks on 15th December and saw five leave the next morning. I should have been on the Lighthouse Battery gun, but just prior to falling in to go on duty at 5.00am, Sergeant-Major Raw detailed me to go on Old Pier guard as there were two spare men on detachment.

At 5.00pm on Tuesday the 15th, the guard NCO and three gunners proceeded to take over. I did the first watch, 5.00pm to 7.00pm and then again at 11.00pm to

1.00am. At 11.30pm three destroyers approached the harbour. I asked who they were. They were the Doon, Test and Waveney. I directed the first one to the Victoria Dock entrance.

At 5.30am on the 16th, I was on the pierhead again when the three sailed. Another two ships, the submarine and the light cruiser Patrol, sailed after the bombardment started, the submarine first. The Patrol was put on course by two tugs and proceeded afterwards under her own steam. Just outside the ferries she put two long boats overboard preparing for action. At that time all our guard were at the head of the pier and we gave them a cheer as they passed. As for the Children's Friend, the motor fishing boat, it may have been she which sailed round inside of the New Pier looking for shelter.

We came off the pierhead and Mr McKenna fell on the sands wounded. We carried him up to the boathouse to await a stretcher. After that we just kept people up against the wall below St Andrew's Church, still keeping our eyes seawards to see that nothing approached.

The above account was related by an unnamed ex-gunner with the Durham Royal Garrison Artillery.

At the time of the bombardment I was employed as an office boy to Mr Warren, the Works Manager at the Central Marine Engine Works. I started work at 6.00am. Between 8.00am and 8.20am we heard gunfire which grew increasingly violent. At the same time the men became more and more apprehensive and once it was realised what was happening there was no holding them. All wanted to be home with their wives and children.

I have vivid recollections of the lads saying, "I wish I had a gun." What we would have done if we had I don't know. However, I found myself alone, not knowing where the others had gone, so I went to the store to see if anyone was about. There I saw Mr Tritschler, the chief storeman, giving first aid to a number of people and saying no one must touch them. He pointed to a railway shunter who I think died later. The question then arose about stretchers and two men volunteered to go to Hartlepool Hospital for some. As neither man knew where the hospital was I was asked to take them, which I did.

On the way we saw what to my young mind was a most pitiful sight. As men were carrying some of the dead on doors or planks the women, whose husbands had been out early or had not returned and who were only half-dressed, were crying out, "Is that Jack so and so?" or, "Is that Bill so and so?" Some of them fainted and men ran forward to catch them before they hit the ground.

At the hospital we managed, after a short delay, to get two stretchers. The nurses and doctors were busy attending to the wounded who were lying on the floor in the corridors. Dr Pearson dashed in, taking off his overcoat as he ran up the stairs. When we got back to work I went to see Mr Warren who was standing at his desk looking very grim and serious. I asked if there was anything else he wanted me to do.

"You'd better go home," he said.

On the way home I saw men carrying babies in blankets. Everyone seemed very grim and anxious. Women were sweeping up the glass from the shattered windows with tears running down their faces. At the top of Duke Street I met my

THE BAPTIST CHAPEL

The Chapel was at the end of
Baptist Street and Regent Street, Hartlepool.

father who was looking for me. He told me our house was slightly damaged. There was a small hole in the roof above the staircase. Some shrapnel had gone through the back bedroom door into the walls and had slit the bed to ribbons. My first job was to find my mother and younger brother who were missing. I found them at a friend's house near Grange Road having a cup of tea. Apparently mother had been outside in the yard hanging out some curtains she had just washed when the shelling started. As she went back into the house she heard a bang and ran inside only to get covered in a shower of dust and plaster at the bottom of the stairs. On examining herself she found her skirt slit all around in ribbons. The curtains were found to be in the same condition. On returning home we all set to to clear up the mess.

Before bedtime it started to rain and it came down in torrents, running down the stairs like a waterfall. Father went out and got some school slates and, together, he and Mr Beattie our next-door neighbour, managed to stop the water coming through the roof. Owing to the gasometer being hit the town was in total darkness. Fortunately we had a good oil lamp and father had the presence of mind to get some paraffin and candles. My brother and I slept on a 'shaky-down' in the kitchen and I have never slept so soundly before or since.

The above account was related by J. B. Tindale. He was born in 1900 and was 14 at the time of the bombardment. He and his family lived at 13 Duke Street and it was one of four in the street which was hit.

That Wednesday morning was a fine, but slightly foggy one. As my brother and I ate our breakfasts my mother remarked, "The wind is getting up, it'll be a fine day for washing."

The kitchen windows were rattling slightly. Soon the rattling became louder and we could hear dull thuds outside the house. The thuds grew louder and got faster and they soon became ear-splitting crashes.

As we ran out of the house the windows were blown in by the terrible concussion. Outside, people were gathering on an open patch of ground at the end of Turnbull Street. My mother decided to go down Middleton Road and find out what was happening. As she passed opposite the Swedish Church a friend, Barney Hodgson, told her that a naval battle was taking place outside the harbour. On reaching the gas works she turned back and was horrified to see Barney's bloodstained body. She ran home and told my brother and me that we would have to run to the country.

As we approached Dene Street there came a crash and I was knocked unconscious. On recovery I found that both my eyes had become so swollen I could hardly see and blood was pouring from a gash in my right cheek. Around me were several bodies, some half-covered by rubble. I staggered towards the Old Cemetery, calling out for my mother, but got no answer. Near the cemetery a school friend (Stuart Arnell) came to me and asked who I was - he didn't recognise me. On being told my name he took me by the arm and led me through the cemetery while shells were bursting all around us.

When we arrived at Thornville Road Stuart asked three women if they would allow me to bathe my face. They took one look at me and fled. Our next stop was on the main Elwick Road, where Stuart said he could see the gasometer burning.

Outside Elwick a motorcyclist told us to go back as the bombardment was over. When we reached the park I heard a neighbour's voice and asked if she had seen my mother. She called out to my father, who was a short distance in front and he ran and picked me up and carried me to the Cameron Hospital, where I soon received kind and efficient treatment.

I later learned that of the people gathered on that open space near Dene Street, thirteen were killed and twenty-two injured. I will never forget that 'fine washing day' as long as I live.

The above account was related by W. H. Larkin.

A year has rolled by since the inhabitants of the Hartlepools had the realities of war so vividly brought home to them. It was my privilege to be amongst the gallant officers and men who so pluckily held up the honour of Old England on that eventful morning. Such an experience leaves an indelible impression on the memory.

It was dark and cold when we turned out in the early morning and after partaking of a pot of hot coffee and a biscuit we quietly prepared the guns for action. About 6.30am a whisper went around that the Colonel was in the battery.

"There's something up," someone remarked, and, without any reason I must confess to a feeling of uneasiness and expectancy.

The morning was fine but, as is usual at that time of year, there was a haze over the sea. The dawn came slowly and at 8.00am when light was just becoming good, nothing had happened. Shortly afterward the naval lookout reported three warships coming in east by south-east.

At once we were all eyes and presently the majestic form of a large cruiser came into view past the lighthouse. Boom! Boom! went their guns, but the ships were firing out to sea and not at us. I had no doubt they were English cruisers and strained my eyes to see them, and if possible what they were firing at. My comrades were similarly employed and from the gun platforms and the top of mounds watched the incoming vessels and speculated as to the nature of the fight going on at sea. I noticed that all the time our guns, which were loaded, were kept trained on the ships.

At 8.05am the leading ship opened fire on us and we were suddenly disillusioned as to the character of our visitors. The first shot, an 11-inch shell I think, carried away the concrete wall on the right corner of the battery and killed the sentry and three other men of the 18th Durham Light Infantry. Another shell which came directly after killed two of our men who had gone to the assistance of the first men who fell.

It was the first time I had been under fire and the first time I had seen men killed in a fight. I have been asked if I felt nervous, well, I had no time to analyse my feelings. Immediately the first shot was fired the action became general and I think we were all glad to be employed. It kept us from thinking.

The Heugh Battery engaged the lead ship and the Lighthouse Battery the rear ship. I could not see the latter, but it was reported that the third round carried away her bridge. This was the Blücher. She came into view and the three ships appeared to be firing at the Heugh Battery for about fifteen or twenty minutes. At this time the noise was terrific and I have little more than a confused recollection of the din made by our guns and the enemy's bursting shells which were flying in fragments all around us.

I think those who gave any thought to the matter expected to see the Battery Command Post which contained the Battery Commander and staff demolished, it being the most prominent object, but singular to say it was not hit. The two leading ships steamed slowly towards the Old Cemetery and kept firing at the Battery, the shells mostly passing over Hartlepool Bay and Seaton Carew. The Battery then engaged the centre ship and finally got on to the last one which had remained at a distance of about 4,000 yards in front of us. She appeared to be on fire and at about 8.45am steamed away. The other two ships turned and gave us their starboard broadsides in passing out to sea and followed the Blücher.

The leading ship was said to be the Von der Tann and the middle ship the Moltke. I have since heard that the Von der Tann and Blücher were badly damaged by our fire and that many of their crew were killed or wounded. It is said their casualties numbered between 200 and 300. Be that as it may, they certainly did not have matters all their own way. Our men did their work well, for the contest was a most unequal one, and every man in the Battery ought to have been rendered 'hors de combat' [unfit to fight, or disabled].

It has been said the squadron's programme was to bombard the place for an hour, but that the effect of the batteries firing on them was to cause them to clear off after forty-two minutes.

The above account was related by a former member of the Durham Royal Garrison Artillery. The numbers given above for German dead and wounded were probably taken from unconfirmed reports in the Dutch press. As to the belief that one of the ships was the *Von der Tann* (which had been at Scarborough and Whitby) this was supposedly occasioned by ordnance being found in the Hartlepools which was of a calibre and weight, and which featured a certain pattern of rifling on the driving bands, that led people to believe it came from the ship. However, it was later reported that ammunition intended for the *Von der Tann* had also been issued to other ships in the group. 1915.

I was in a position to see all that was going on, whereas other people were shut in by houses except on the sea front, and those who lived on the high ground further inland. Those who lived on the sea front could see the shells, but not their effects. I believe a shell fell in Mary Street, which is behind the Marine Drive, but for the most part they went over the top and dropped in the harbour making huge splashes and throwing debris about.

I was an apprentice plater at the time and with my workmate, Stanley Westmoreland, was working on a keel in Gray's south yard. It was very quiet as the work was not very far advanced and we were the only ones down there.

Then we heard a noise like a shipful of hammering caulkers at it all at once. We looked at each other and as it slackened off we decided it was gunfire out at sea. If it was not too far off we would be able to see it from the boatdeck of the ship in the north yard which was nearing completion. Off we went right up to the captain's bridge. When we got there a few shipwrights who had been caulking the roof, and a few others who had heard the rattle of guns above the noise of the riveting hammers, were gazing out to sea over the headland, with the docks in

GENERAL DAMAGE

1&4: Street damage. 2: A local Police Constable and two Green Howards with unexploded shells. 3: A collection of shells. 5: The Green Howards try to retrieve a shell.

front of them, Middleton to the left and the coal dock and Harbour Terrace to the right.

It was misty and there was no horizon. We had just decided we were wasting our time when there was an almighty crash from the direction of Hartlepool and a column of black water, about two hundred feet high, stood up in the angle between the lighthouse (in full view at the end of Cliff Terrace) and the breakwater. I think that was the very first shell fired on the Hartlepools.

Other shells, fired too high, came over the headland and dropped in the channel and docks causing huge water spouts, all of them white now, not black as the first had been. Those that were fired too high fell on the houses in line with the batteries in William Street, Moor Terrace and Victoria Place. We could see the flashes from the bursting shells and the guns out at sea, yet we could not see the ships.

The guns from the rear battery opened up with a tremendous crash and the sky lit up with a brilliant orange flash. There were only three 6-inch guns, but there could have been thirty as far as the noise was concerned. Each time one of the guns fired there came that ear-splitting crack and the orange glow. There was no doubt the ships were trying to hit the batteries as the shells burst all around the area. Those that came over the top dropped in the channel and raised a column of water but if they hit anything solid they scattered splinters and debris from the centre of a cloud of smoke.

Once the shells started falling in the wrong place we thought what rotten shots the Germans were. But we thought too soon, for it was obviously deliberate. A stifling dust cloud started to appear among the sheds and stacked timber on the quayside. A shell dropped in Harbour Terrace and the roof lifted off and disintegrated high in the air, falling back down in splinters. Another fell among the pit props stacked about fifty yards from the side of the ship. We did not wait for that stack to come down, we went down as quickly as we could, over the side with no queuing for the ladders or gangways. Down the staging, about sixty feet, dropping from stage to stage all the way down.

I went straight to the blacksmith's shop near the bows of the ship and told those working at the fire nearest the door that the Germans were bombarding Hartlepool. With the clanging of the anvils and the thump of the steam hammers they had not heard anything out of the ordinary. The men there just laughed.

"What are you talking about?"

"Look at that!" I said pointing through the barred opening in the wall, which was used to let the smoke out, at the blazing gasometer. Flames were roaring high into the sky. The men threw down their hammers, left the hot iron on the anvil, snatched their coats and flew as if Old Nick himself was after them.

The back-gate man came running past, "Don't go out of the back gate," he warned, shouting, "Shells are dropping all over the place."

I followed the men out, but had got over my initial panic and began to think. It was nearly snack time, 8.30am, and I had left my parcel and can of tea on the furnace in the blacksmith's shop to keep the tea warm. So I went back into the empty shop for them. I had to pass the south-east flanging machine opposite the storekeeper's house. A shell had fallen there, but whether it was before I had passed earlier or after I can't recall. It could only have been a couple of minutes either way.

Anyway, parts of the shipyard always looked as if a shell had hit them!

The first person I caught up with was my father. He could not walk very quickly. "Will," he said, "Just listen to the seagulls screaming."

I could not see any seagulls and said so. We later learned the screaming was from the shells as they flew overhead. All the seagulls that usually lined the ridges of the warehouse had gone long since. When we got to the steps in front of the gate there was a crowd of men. In order to get out of the shipyard you had to come over the swing bridge, Racer's Bridge my grandfather used to call it, and along the road made through the corner of one of the huge warehouses which used to stand on the quaysides, built about a hundred years ago for storing grain.

We were all very nervous about crossing the bridge. There was an open view across the docks to the Headland and we felt as if we were being watched. Each time a group of men dashed over a shell seemed to drop in the dock followed by a huge white waterspout and other shells must have been bursting somewhere near because the surface of the docks was spouting little fountains of water of various heights as debris fell in. A shell came as the last group of us made for the shelter of the warehouse. It must have burst inside because afterwards when I saw the hole it seemed too small to make all the bricks, stones and dust that came through our side of the building. The building had huge shuttered openings for ventilation and loading or unloading purposes. I did not see anybody hurt, but if they were they did not stop.

We went out through the opening into Victoria Terrace where the people from Middleton and Harbour Terrace were streaming past. They had not even stopped to get dressed, but had come out as they were. One old dame, dressed only in her night-gown, held a cloth to her head which was streaming blood, but nobody seemed to be taking any notice, we were all just hurrying along. That was the only casualty I remember seeing.

I left my father when we got up to the tunnel in Church Street. He said he was going to the Royal Back Bar. He told me later that the barman had departed with the crowd so he had had to act as his own barman. What a treat for him! He did not get in until teatime. Of course it was dark by then, and there was not a single gaslight in the town.

Further up Church Street I met my foreman, Jim Kennedy. We had only taken a few paces when he saw dust rising from the Mail Office which also faced the open space of the docks. Orange glows still accompanied the shattering bangs of the guns so we decided to go by Ward Street and Thornton Street, but that was the last we heard.

I went up Grange Road as far as Grosvenor Street where I lived. A small crowd stood looking along the street. I thought number nine had been hit, but when I got nearer it turned out to be the house on the corner near the church. Actually it had been converted from a house into a shop by Mustard, the tailor. The shell had blown the shop away leaving the upstairs room overhanging a vacant space.

I went across the road to our back door and my goodness what a sight! Not a pane of glass was left, all the ceilings were cracked and one was down altogether. Everything was thick with soot and there was no gas to make a cup of tea. Mother was sitting crying, but there was nothing we could do. My grandmother lived across the road from Mustard's shop, so I went to see if she was alright. She did not seem very alarmed. The shell which had hit Mustard's had passed her front

GENERAL DAMAGE

1&3: Two views of Moor Terrace.
2: Victoria Place. 4: William Street.
5: Green Howards on Moor Terrace.

door, but she had not realised what was going on. Her house was in the same sad state as ours.

Once all the family were accounted for, I decided to go straight over to the Headland to see just what had been going on. The first damage I saw was at the hardware shop on the corner of Murray Street belonging to Donald Brown. I passed another badly wrecked house in Raby Terrace (now part of Raby Road, near Lowthian Road). Damage had been done to Sandringham Road and the corner of Middleton Road and Clarence Road. The gasometer on the other side of the bridge over the railway was riddled like a colander and the pavement close by was pitted and scarred. Further down Middleton Road a shell had pierced the 'L' of the German ship 'Denlbuah', lying at jetty 'A'. The letters were four feet high and painted along the ship's side.

There was no one standing about in Middleton. The casualties had all been cleared away and the people had gone. I don't remember any further damage until I passed St Hilda's Church. As yet there was no one guarding the damaged property.

A house in Victoria Place had been shattered and I had walked past the Rectory where half the tiles were missing. The nearer I got to Moor Terrace the worse the damage became until at the seaward end the terrace was devastated. A dead horse lay on the Friarage football ground. No attempt had yet been made to clear the road which was strewn with the glass and furniture which had been blown out of the houses. The window openings were draped with torn nets and daylight coming in where the roofs should have been.

The recess in front of the Heugh Battery was furrowed with deep trenches. The trajectory of the shells had been so low they had cut horizontal grooves in the ground right up to the walls of the batteries.

My younger brother, then fourteen, was delivering milk for Mr Owen of Middleton Grange. He pulled a milk barrow (a milk churn standing on an axle between two light cartwheels with handles like a barrow) and was on Cleveland Road (now Lancaster Road) heading towards the gasworks when a shell fell on that corner. When he saw the people laid in the street he turned and ran towards Brougham Terrace. He was terrified, and, seeing a clergyman coming out of a nearby house turned to him hoping for some comfort. But the man nudged him off like a rugby player, saying, "Get out of my way." That little act destroyed all the confidence my little brother ever had in the clergy.

I spent the rest of the afternoon writing to my older brother who was with the Royal Artillery. He was billeted at a house in Walnut Tree Close, Guildford, Surrey. There were several local lads in the battery and I wrote ten pages. It was read out to them and a newspaper offered my brother £5 for it. I don't know why he didn't take it. Years later the people at Walnut Tree Close wrote to tell me they still had the letter and would I like it back. I didn't.

There were several Germans who had made their homes in Hartlepool and hostile crowds broke their windows to make them the same as where the shells had done damage. The pork butchers, one in Alma Street and one in Lynn Street, also had their windows broken. One of the blocks of houses in Middleton Road was called Kaiser Terrace and it had its name chipped off.

People's nerves were all ragged, but more was to come. The biggest scare was on Friday, 18th December, when the word was passed around that the Germans were in the bay again and there was going to be another bombardment. The whole town was deserted in a few hours and everything with wheels was called up to help. My mother and sister went to Great Stainton and stopped there for a week.

Months afterwards everyone received cards telling them what to do and where to go in case of another bombardment - it was too late then.

The above account was related by William Boagey. He was born in 1895 and was 19 at the time of the bombardment. He lived on Grosvenor Street with his parents, two brothers and a sister.

We started with armour-piercing shells but for all the effect they had on the thick plating of the cruisers we might have been throwing marbles.

We were told to change to lyddite and fire onto the decks. Then we began to have some success.

Although the odds were so much against us I don't think there was any fear in the battery. You seemed to have no feelings. You just got on with the job. Duty was duty and that's all there was to it.

This account was related by John Waller, of 309 West View Road. John had been an ammunition man with the Lighthouse Battery and could remember how, just before the first shells whistled overhead on that bleak December morning, he was sitting on his hands (under orders) so that they would be kept warm and he nimble-fingered for the vital task of seeing to the gun. When the battery's gun had to disengage because the lighthouse was between it and the warships, John had made his way to the Heugh Battery. Near the gates he came across the body of one of the first victims covered by a blanket. He lifted the blanket to find it was Gunner Spence, aged 22, a long-standing friend who was to have been best man at his wedding a fortnight later. Throughout the area of the headland scores of people had been wounded by shrapnel and flying debris. John was put in charge of one of the parties of men sent to help in getting the casualties to hospital. And that is why his wife, Lydia, had one particularly vivid memory of her wedding day; it is of her bridegroom standing beside her in a uniform, the only one he had, stained with blood. John lived into retirement having been a shipwright.

I well remember the bombardment. We were called out of our billets before daylight. Gunner Jack Wilkinson and I were put on lookout duty, walking up and down between the guns on the Heugh Battery. At first we saw four destroyers going north, then out of the mist came three battle-cruisers and they started to fire at the destroyers. Jack thought we were going to witness a naval battle. Then, all of a sudden, the three ships gave us a broadside.

Captain Trechmann called, "Action!" He was the officer who directed the fire that morning.

I was doing No.2 on A1 gun and Jack was a loading number. A master gunner of the DRGA, a regular soldier, took over the gun-laying and was very good at it. We got a lot of hits. We started firing armour-piercing shells, but soon found our 6-inch shells no use on the armour-plating of the cruisers. So the order came to change to lyddite and to fire onto the decks of the cruisers, which we did with great success.

We started to fire at 4,500 yards and carried on until the ships put out to sea.

The Heugh Battery fired the last shells at 7,500 yards. We were the last to fire in the bombardment because the Lighthouse Battery was out of action owing to the lighthouse being in their line of fire. An 11-inch shell ricocheted off the apron on A2 gun and burst in the Rovers' field. If it had burst on the apron of the gun, the crew would have been killed.

Peace or war, there's nothing like a good, hot cup of tea. Our cooks, Billy Sanderson and Arthur Hall, must have been getting the tea ready all the time we were in action. As soon as we stopped firing out came the buckets-full of tea.

After the bombardment the gun crews formed the 41st Siege Battery (6-inch howitzer). We were sent to France and took part in all the great battles. The Battery lost many Hartlepool men on the Somme and at Plugstreet Wood near Ypres, and there were many more casualties on other parts of the front.

This account was related by former gunner Harry Tyson, of 17 Rowell Street, Hartlepool. Harry was a member of one of the gun teams at the Heugh Battery and long cherished his memory of the steaming buckets of tea which made such a welcome appearance immediately the firing ended. The 12-inch shell which ricocheted off the apron of the gun position and burst in the Rovers' Rugby field also killed a cow.

My father was a shipwright at W. Gray and Sons, and was therefore at work when the bombardment began. Mother was ill and had not been out for nearly three months. My sister and I were having breakfast before going to school when what we thought was a thunderstorm started. We soon found it was something more when the plates we were eating from crashed in two. As youngsters we were scared and brought mother downstairs . . . just in time, for the house was struck and the kitchen set on fire.

We started to try and put it out when the front of the house caught a shell and the bed mother had been sleeping in was hanging through the ceiling into the hall. We hadn't time to do anything more as the house was hit again and mother was fastened by her neck between the doors. I somehow got her free and thus saved her life. We managed to go to a friend's house and to stay there until mother felt stronger. My sister had strayed away and many were her experiences before we found her again.

The above account was related by Mary E. Dickinson, who, as a child had lived at 42 Belk Street.

Our house stood behind the Heugh Battery on Moor Terrace and I remember looking out of the bedroom window and seeing three warships that seemed to be so close to the shore I could have thrown a ball on to them. Then the first shells were fired and I gathered the children and headed for the cellar.

*

I was at my cabinet-making business when I heard the bombardment start. I dropped everything and dashed back to the house. I got there just as the bombardment was over. I came in through the back way and thought my wife must have left, but just then she came out of the cellar with the children.

We set about picking through what was left of our belongings. In one room stood a recessed altar, built by the original occupier of the house, and it was still intact, but the room had received a direct hit and was wrecked. The altar, with its statues, crucifix and flower vases wasn't even scratched. In another room a bureau I had made had been reduced to sawdust. I was able to pick up handfuls of it and run it through my fingers. The pans and cutlery in the kitchen had been welded together. Spoons, stamped with EPNS (Electro-plated nickel silver) had stamped the initials onto other spoons. The hall was split wide open, but a straw hat which had been hanging on a peg was still there. A wardrobe had been blown clean through a wall and into the next room. It looked like a smashed orange box.

I was able to stand at the back of the house and see right through the front. There was nothing left to block the view. The house became something of a showpiece and hundreds of people came to see it and take photographs. The fact that it was still standing after three hits shows it was pretty strongly built.

The first paragraph of the above account was related by Mrs Orde, the rest by Mr Orde. Their house, *Ocean House*, was situated on Moor Terrace and was badly damaged.

When the Hartlepools were bombarded I was with the Navy, having joined up in September. I was serving with the Tenth Cruiser Squadron along with another 'townee', Bob Hogan. As soon as we heard about the bombardment we obtained leave at once to return home.

When I arrived home my youngest brother, ten years old, and sister had just returned, at midnight, having run away into the country. They were both footsore, hungry and weary.

During the bombardment my brother and dozens of others were running past the gasholder when it received a direct hit. The holder collapsed and the gas was set alight. The force of the explosion blew the boys into the air and killed one boy. Another had his foot blown off, whilst a third was wounded in the arm by shell splinters. By some miracle my brother, who was in the middle of it all, remained unhurt.

A close friend lived next to the Baptist Chapel which received a direct hit. The blast from the explosion lifted the roof, blew in the front door and all of the windows.

My father, who had gone to work for the 8.00am start at Matson's at the bottom of the High Street, ran back home when the firing started. When he got back and saw the state of the house he was afraid to enter fearing they would all be dead, but instead found them all shell-shocked. He then went off to the local pub for some brandy and found it deserted, so he helped himself to a bottle.

A woman living opposite was in bed with a baby when a splinter went right through the house, wounding her in the arm. A social worker in Moor Terrace fled on hearing the guns and ran straight into a burst at her front door.

After the raiders departed soldiers from the Batteries came round calling out for any wounded or dead.

The after-effect in the local collieries was startling, but understandable. Many miners left the pits to join the colours and get at the Germans. They queued up at the recruiting offices and couldn't wait to be served with a rifle.

The above account was related by J. Cassidy.

I was coming out of the Richardsons Westgarth & Company offices after leaving the milk, shortly after 8.00am. Three shots were fired seawards and someone passed by saying they were practising. Then, in the twinkling of an eye, shells started falling all around - it was really frightening. One of the first salvos hit Richardsons Westgarth & Company's boiler shop, killing a number of men, and then the shells started coming thick and fast.

I was driving along Sea Terrace, Middleton, with my milk float when my pony was hit by a piece of shrapnel which tore a hole in its jaw one could put one's hand through. When I got out to see what had happened several women in their night-clothes got into the float. But with so much shrapnel flying around I told them the only sensible thing to do was to go and get their clothes on.

I hadn't gone much further when more people were hit and I was asked if it was possible for me to take some of the wounded to the hospital. I remember saying I did not think the pony was able to make the journey, she had weakened considerably and was bleeding heavily.

But I was willing to try and agreed to offload the milk and turn the float into a makeshift ambulance. I ferried three wounded men to the hospital in a laborious and terrifying journey. I was unable to get anything there to bind up the pony's jaw, but a woman gave me a pillow case and with that I managed to dress it.

I returned to Middleton to pick up my milk and then set off for home. At that time we lived at Middle Warren Farm and I decided to take a short cut by the gasworks at Greenland. When I was about ten yards away the gasometer was hit and I had to turn back. I unyoked the pony, and with the rein under my arm we took shelter in the timber props yards. But it was really no safer there either. I couldn't leave the pony and we ended up dodging from one stack of props to another. Eventually I reached home worn out by the ordeal.

It was all a nightmare. None of those who went through it could ever forget it. My pony survived, but the vet's fees cost me three times as much as I received in compensation.

This account was related by Alderman Charles Chambers (the 'father' of Hartlepool Council) who was delivering milk at the time of the raid.

I was six years old at the time of the attack on Hartlepool but can remember all the details. I lived with my parents and sister at 184 Hart Road. My mother and sister were already up and my father was just getting up.

I was halfway down the stairs when my mother picked me up in her arms and shouted to father to come quickly. Just as we got to the bottom of the stairs a shell came through the roof and we saw a big hole appear at the top of the stairs.

We couldn't get out of the house because of the slates coming down off the roofs. Mother sat me on the table and dressed me quickly and then stood with her arms around my sister and me, ready to throw herself on top of us if the bedroom floor caved in.

I remember there was a Salvation Army lass who calmed the crowds by singing hymns.

The above account was related by Mrs F. Whitton from Cottingham, Humberside. She was born in 1908, in Hartlepool, and was six at the time of the bombardment.

I was only five, but remember well the troubled morning of the bombardment. My mother was preparing breakfast before we went to school. My brother had been to Thompson's corner shop for a gill of milk and came hurrying in to tell mam that a fall pipe had fallen off the shop wall just in front of him. The next moment terrific bangs could be heard and my mother shepherded us into the bed-place sensing trouble.

We learned later of the tragedy in Dene Street, which was about four hundred yards from our street and of the Hart Road Methodist Church which had to be used as a mortuary.

I also remember the second scare, when most people fled through the Old Cemetery towards Elwick thinking the Germans had come back. We turned back, after going so far towards Elwick, on learning all was well and it was only a scare.

The above account was related by N. Tabley.

I was 10 at the time, and like most of the children I was not particularly frightened. I took it in fairly good part. Partly because when we first heard the terrific rumbling of the guns and so forth we felt it was just a naval practice.

We made breakfast at 8.00am, this was a rule so my father could get to the office, and I to school for 9.00am. As usual we were getting ready to sit down to breakfast when we heard this terrific rumbling of guns. Then mother came in from Mass at St Joseph's. I suppose it was about 7.55am, something like that. She came up Hutton Avenue and heard the rumbling. Someone walked up to her and said, "It's just a naval practice."

We sat down to breakfast, still thinking it was such, until there was a terrific bang next door and a shell went through into the next house, 34 Hutton Avenue where people called Hardy lived. We were fortunate because the shell, instead of being an exploding one, was time-fused, so what happened was it knocked a hole fifteen inches wide in the top corner of the house and went through into the billiard-room. It exploded there tearing umpteen holes in the billiard-table. It also blew all the glass out of the large window and sword-shaped pieces of glass came down and stuck in our lawn. The nose of the shell went right through the next house and the tail end, which we saw afterwards, apparently stayed in number 34.

By this time the shells were falling pretty heavily. One hit Mustard's tailor shop in Grosvenor Street which was within sight of St Paul's Church. It was practically demolished. One also landed in the middle of Hutton Avenue about halfway up the far side, before the bend. It made a considerable hole in the road.

The general hubbub was that shells were falling all over the place and we began to grow alarmed. We decided to stand in what we thought was the strongest part of the house, at the bottom of the stairs. We did not know about the safety of the underneath of the stairs in those days. There was no glass within a reasonable distance and we stood there a while until it got very bad.

Father wondered what was going on and went to see Councillor Boanson who lived opposite to ask what we were supposed to do. He said we all had to go to Elwick, so we immediately put on any clothes we had. I remember putting a loaf of bread under my arm as well, then we set off to walk to Elwick. We walked around the left hand side of the park, that is the top of Elwick Road, and continued straight on along what is now Egerton Road.

When going up Grange Road towards Elwick we saw a relatively small shell had fallen in the road and broken the tram wires. One of the officials was holding the wire with rubber gloves on, no doubt for reasons of safety. Perhaps someone was doing the same at the other end. There was a crater about a couple of feet deep and maybe three or four feet across near the tram track.

We passed the cricket field and continued on a rough road which went in the direction of Elwick. We were a little way down it when a chap came up on horseback.

"You can go back now, it's all over," he said.

"How is it?" people asked.

"Well," he replied, "The gasometer is in flames."

We trekked home and thought, as was natural at the time, that we would like a cup of tea. However, when we attempted to light the gas stove there was no gas. We made the fire up and put the kettle on the hob and that was that as far as we were concerned.

Later we looked around the damage and there was a considerable amount; Hartley Street, which was off Murray Street, was badly hit as was Gallen's Grocers Store which was caught by the blast coming up Hartley Street which it faced. Mother had a friend called Kilvington over in Hartlepool and wanted to go and see if she was alive or not. To get there she had to go along Cleveland Road and Lancaster Road where there was considerable damage and rubble. Officials tried to stop her, but she managed to get through. When she arrived at the house in Catherine Street she found her friend alive and well, but rather shaken, as was everyone. Sadly enough, some of her other friends, two sisters called Kay, were almost the first people killed as their house faced right onto the sea front. It was the gable-end of a terrace and received the full burst of the first few shells, killing them in their bedrooms.

Some of the damage I saw myself along Cleveland Road and Lancaster Road. One of the more poignant points was where a house had been almost entirely demolished, but the upstairs fireplace was still attached to the wall, even though there was no floor or anything around it. The teapot was still on the hob too, which was a reminder that people were going about their daily tasks when the disaster occurred.

The above account was related by an unnamed man.

I well remember the 16th December. It was just coming daylight when I left my home at 7.40am to go to work at Mrs Ibbitson's on Northgate. On my way I saw some of our soldiers going out on a route march, they were singing 'Tipperary'. It was a very grey morning.

I had not been at work very long when we heard rumbling noises which sounded a long way off, but gradually got louder and louder until they were deafening. We, that is the people in Northgate, did not really know what was happening, not until we saw people running down Middlegate half-clothed, screaming and shouting.

Another lady, Miss Florence Storm, also employed at Mrs Ibbitson's, and myself helped by giving hot drinks and clothes to those poor, helpless and frightened people, some attired only in their night-clothes and some of them maimed. It was a dreadful sight.

A few hours later I saw an ambulance taking the bodies of one of our soldiers who had been killed on the Battery, and some civilians who had also been killed, to the empty shop of Gray Peverell's in the lower part of the High Street which had opened as a mortuary.

The above account was related by Mrs Daisy Lupton.

I was six at the time of the Hartlepool bombardment. The morning had a typical mid-December outlook, cold, but not icy, with a sea mist drifting in. I had finished my breakfast and was getting my outdoor clothes ready to put on. The time was about five minutes past 8.00am. I had to leave home by 8.15am as I lived on Alma Street (near Mulgrave Road) and had to walk to Jesmond Road School, which was quite a distance for a little lad, especially if he didn't want a late mark against his name. I had put my clothes on and was just pulling on my top coat when there was a heavy rumbling sound, followed closely by a second and third. "It's thundering," I said to mother, but she was making her way to the front door and the bangs were growing louder. We reached the front door together. Mother opened it and looked out into the street just in time to see Mr Nielsen come round the corner from Mulgrave Road on his way to his picture-framing shop, as he did every morning.

"What are all the bangs, are they blasting?" mother asked.

"No, I think it may be something serious. You had better go inside," he answered.

Just then there was a strange whistling and whirring sound over our heads and we ran back into the hall and shut the door. There was a great big bang and the door blew open. It was all mother needed to make up her mind. Into the kitchen we went. The rest of the family was there, Sam, Jim and Edie, the baby. Father was away with the Royal Naval Reserve. Mother took hold of four-year-old Sam, put on his coat and cap and said to me, "You take hold of Sam, and take him down to your Aunt Edie's house and I'll bring Jim and the baby . . . and keep hold of his hand," she warned me. Aunt Edie's (mother's sister) was a big house on the corner of Alma Street and Tankerville Street (now Crowther's Corner).

Out of the house we went, and, half-running, made our way down Alma Street, listening to the constant noise of the shells as they passed overhead. Everywhere people kept close to the walls and could be seen dodging in and out of doorways. At last we reached Aunt Edie's house, kicked open the door and there was auntie with a look of amazement on her face.

"Have you come through this all on your own . . . and where's your mother?" Out she dashed to find mother, whom she met halfway down Alma Street with the baby under one arm and holding onto little two-year-old Jimmy with the other.

At Aunt Edie's plans had already been made and we were all to make our way into the country by way of Alma Street, Mulgrave Road, Grange Road and through the Park out on to the Elwick Road. My mother's other sister also lived there along with my sixty-eight-year-old grandfather. Edie's husband was away at sea, he was a Chief Steward in the Mercantile Marine.

GENERAL DAMAGE

1&3: Damaged railway trucks.
2: James Pearson, mortally wounded aboard the *SS Phoebe*. 4: Dene Street.
5: Cleveland Road.

By this time Alma Street was crowded from end to end with folk, some pushing prams loaded with bedding and food, some with cooking utensils hanging over the sides and handles, others were pushing handcarts loaded with bedding and little children on top, and yet others carried bundles on their backs. So out we went into the crowd. Grandfather decided at the last moment that he would stay put, and if the Germans landed at Middleton, as was being rumoured, they'd not enter his house unchallenged. He was only five feet two!

As we went up Alma Street we heard all kinds of explanations of what was happening, some were good guesses, some reasonable assumptions. But I remember one man who said he had been at the shipyard when he heard the first bang. He said he had seen a battleship firing at the battery and had seen the guns of the battery firing back. There were also complaints about how crowded Alma Street was. It was said that the folk from the east end of the town had been warned not to use Victoria Road or the bottom of Grange Road because the tram wires had been brought down and were writhing about on the ground, still live.

As we reached the top end of Alma Street, opposite Gordon Street, we noticed people passing on either side of a place in the middle of the road. When we got there we found out why. There before us was a stark instance of the terrible things that were happening all over town. In a small hole lay a boy's cap, covered in blood. I learned later that it belonged to a playmate of mine, Alfred Claude. He used to go every morning to the dairy in Mulgrave Road for his mother's daily bread and milk before he went to school. He had been doing just that on this fateful morning when he had been hit by a piece of shell which had fallen and exploded in Bright Street. On we went along Mulgrave Road and out into Grange Road and on up towards the park. By this time the gunfire did not seem so heavy, but the results were more evident, for we saw men pushing handcarts or driving ponies and flat carts on which were people who had been injured or killed and were being taken either to the Cameron Hospital or sadly to the mortuary. As we got to Wooler Road everyone remarked about the Red Cross flag flying from the mast of the Cameron Hospital. All eyes also turned to look back, over the fields, at the gasworks which had been hit and set on fire, but by this time was out. I heard someone remark that if it had not been for one brave man who had turned off the main outlet valve the consequences could have been far more serious.

We passed down the last part of Grange Road and round the park to Elwick Road, and it was here our turning point was reached, for we heard the sound of a motorcycle and above it the sound of the despatch rider's voice yelling, "Go back! Go back! It's safe. Go back."

I remember people looking at each other as if in doubt, before everyone turned back and went the way they had come. When we got back to our house the door was still open. My mother and aunts went in, got some of our clothes, came out again, shut the door and off we went to Aunt Edie's house, where we found grandfather sat reading in his chair, completely unruffled. The big kettle was put on the fire (because the gas was off), and meanwhile sandwiches and toast were got ready. That night we stayed at Tankerville Street. We three boys slept on a bed on the floor and we didn't need rocking to sleep I can tell you!

The above account was related by C. J. Watson. He was born in 1908 and was 6 at the time of the bombardment. His family lived at 174 Alma Street.

The Heugh and Lighthouse Batteries were situated within 150 yards of one another on this promontory

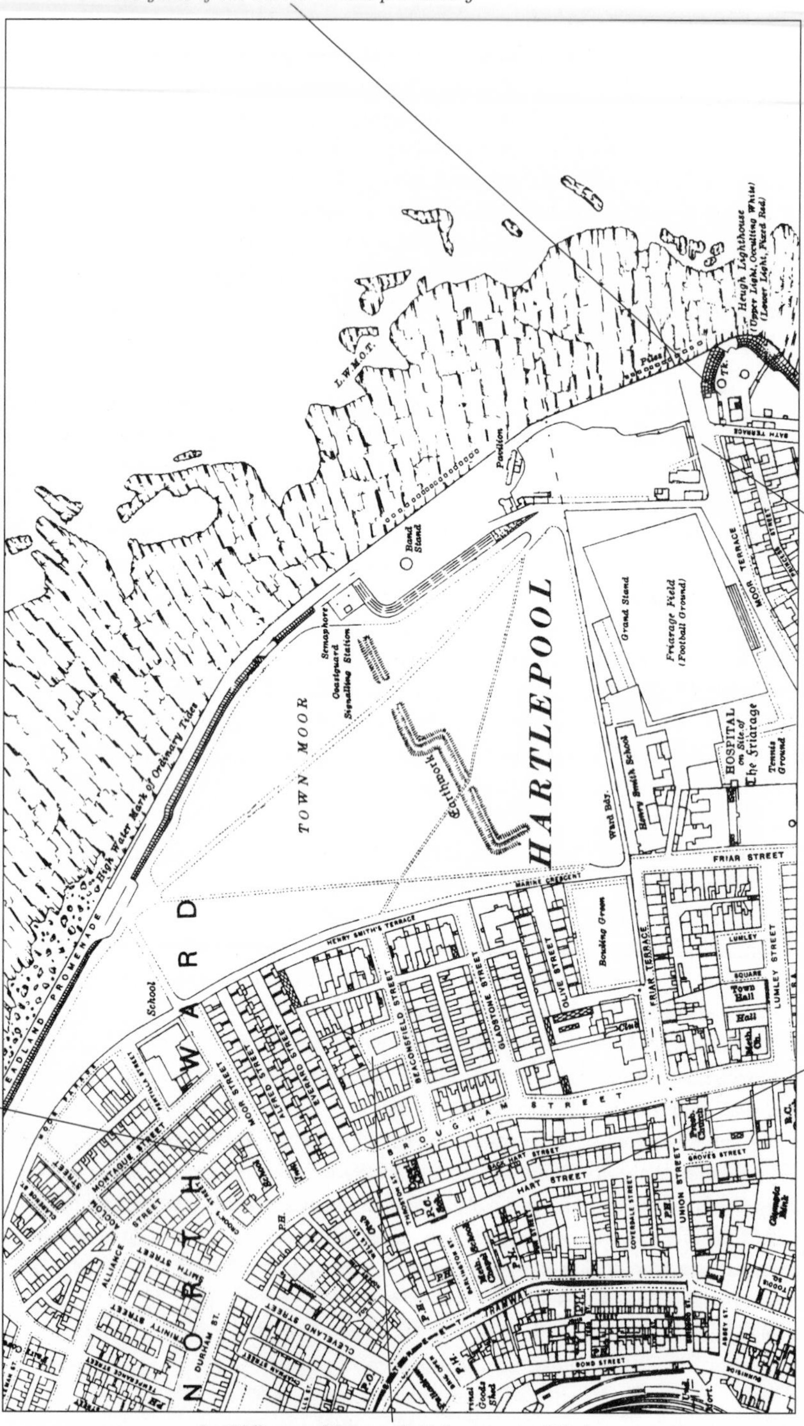

John Staunch, of 44 Alliance Street, was killed in Old Town, West Hartlepool

The home of Mr & Mrs Orde, at Moor Terrace, was very badly damaged and later attracted many sightseers

John Healy, of Hart Street, was killed by shrapnel while at work in one of the shipyards

Ivy Williams, of Beaconsfield Square, was killed when her house was demolished by a shell

I, John Horsley, of 21 Bedford Street, Hartlepool, state that on Wednesday morning the 16th December 1914, I proceeded to sea in the motor fishing boat Children's Friend at about twenty minutes to eight. When we got outside we saw three warships flying the Union Jack and English White Ensign. Just before that I saw the centre ship exchange signals with the lighthouse. They then hauled down the Union Jack and White Ensign and ran up the German flag. That was just before they opened fire on our destroyers about two or three miles east-north-east of the German warships.

There were four of our boats altogether. I turned about to come into Hartlepool, but the other three boats ran ashore on the sands north of Hartlepool. Shortly after, the leading ship fired on the batteries. Before they began firing at all, the centre ship showed a red light at the mast head which was answered by the other two with red lights. They fired on the batteries and the first shot from the Lighthouse Battery fell short; the second shot would have hit him but was a little to the north. The next smashed on board and appeared to do damage. I saw the shots from the battery hit the ships and as far as I could see very few of the battery shots missed. I saw some of the shots bounce off the ships' sides and go into the air.

At this time we were only half a mile from them. The crew had gone below and I called them out to see the way our guns were hitting the ships every time. When we were rounding the breakwater we saw the Patrol get hit. The submarine was alongside of her, a little to the north side.

We ran inside the breakwater for three or four minutes. The shells commenced to fall about and appeared to come over the battery.

When we got as far as the harbour opening, about three minutes before the firing ceased, we saw the Forward being towed out and cleared into West Hartlepool.

The above account was related by John Horsley, Skipper of the *Children's Friend.* 1914.

I was 13 at the time of the bombardment. I attended Henry Smith Grammar School and came into Hartlepool each day from Wellfield station where I lived. That morning the school train was packed with children from the colliery places, Thornley, Wingate, Wheatley Hill, Shotton, Castle Eden, Hesleden and Hart.

The guns were firing before we left Wellfield station, but we thought it was a heavy thunderstorm, nothing more. No instructions had been sent to the station-masters and my father who was the Station-Master allowed the train to leave. It was the same at Castle Eden, Hesleden and Hart, even though from Hart Station there was a very good view of the three warships firing. The train moved on, children leaning from all the windows watching what they thought was a naval battle.

About midway between Hart Station and Hartlepool the train came to a stop on an embankment where the sea came closer to the railway line. The ships were firing on one side and the gasometer was blazing on the other, but being children we didn't connect the two until the guard came running along the train saying that shells were passing over and we were all to get down on the floor.

The fact remained that a trainload of children was there on the railway embankment, stationary and a sitting target until the firing ceased and the ships departed. Then the train pulled slowly into West Hartlepool station, passing the burning gasometer on the way. We usually changed to an autocar, to be taken to Old Hartlepool, but we left the train to be met by two of our schoolmasters who had gone to a café on the sea front and had had the roof blown off over their heads. They were both half-dressed and dirty, but we were frightened and glad to see them. They showed us the shell hole through the station wall and told us there would be no trains running to take us home and telegraph communications were not possible either.

It was no use trying to get to school either as it was being used as a temporary hospital, being situated as it was very close to the real hospital. They said shells had fallen in our hockey field and killed our pet donkey. A shell had hit the headmaster's house too, though he and his family were safe. Our beloved Latin mistress [Etta Harris] was killed as she was getting ready for school. Our masters advised us to walk home and the long trek to the villages began.

Before getting out into the country we saw shops with broken glass, damaged houses, people being taken on stretchers to ambulances and the kind of devastation we came to know so well after a year in the Second World War.

During the late afternoon the little struggling groups of children began to crawl back into their villages, hungry and footsore. The older ones had been carrying the little ones on their backs, while pairs of them had made chairs with their hands to help the small ones along. I reached home after 4.00pm by train, as I had passed the home of a railwayman, a friend of my father, who had seen me and would not let me walk home. A train did run at 4.00pm and I was put on it.

I returned home to find my mother weeping, a thing I never forgot, as it was the first time in my young life I had known something make her weep so.

The above account was related by an anonymous lady.

I was 14 at the time of the bombardment and lived round the corner from the hospital. I had been waiting for the kettle to boil for breakfast when there was a terrific crash as the gun at the end of the street was fired.

I went to the door to see what was happening and as I put my hand on the doorknob it crashed to the wall and the hats from Thompson's shop flew past like a tornado.

We all went out into the street and had to step over the body of a boy called Crake. A solider passed by clutching a rifle and bayonet. In the middle of the road lay the body of Freda Wainwright.

We went on past the Baptist Chapel, hugging the wall round St Hilda's Church for protection as lumps of shrapnel flew over our heads. When we got to King Street we could see the smoke of the ships going down the channel. I dashed over to the Town Wall and saw the Patrol and Forward trying to put to sea.

I rejoined mother and we went on, passing Basil Ayre in Victoria Street; he was carrying a bag full of loaves with a Christmas cake perched on the top.

We hurried to the railway station in Northgate. A shell hit the ornamental top of the public library opposite, and another followed it which bounced off a pile of pit props. The props came down with a 'plomp' on the railway station forecourt and the crowds there beat a hasty retreat back along Northgate.

By this time mother's patience was exhausted and we sought refuge in a nearby house until the clamour had ceased.

The above account was related by Fred Jacques. Born in 1900, Fred was 14 at the time of the bombardment and lived with his family at 5 Prissick Street.

I was employed by Richardsons Westgarth & Company in the marine engineering side. On the morning of the bombardment we were just sitting down to have our breakfasts when the newsboy brought in our morning papers.

"The Germans are here!" he declared.

We treated it as a joke, but he had hardly finished speaking than we heard a rumbling noise which got gradually louder until we could hear the shells bursting overhead. With a tremendous crash one landed in the power station, bringing all the machinery to a standstill.

Realising the danger we decided to quit. As we passed through the gatehouse shells were still screaming overhead, yet in the midst of it all we were curious to see what was happening at sea. We rushed to the sea front and there beheld one of the German ships firing in our direction. Thinking better of it, we decided to seek cover and made for home.

As we rushed down Princes Street a shell wrecked the iron-dressing shop at Richardsons Westgarth and as we reached the corner of Sea Terrace another shell brought down the end of the office block. Pieces of shell and brickwork were flying all over the place. Five men lay dead and many others were wounded. Among those killed were James Leighton (whose house in Clifton Street was also hit), Charles Ramsey, Albert Cressy, James Cook and Edwin Ashcroft. Another man, Robert Ambrose, died later from his wounds.

With my home then being on the Heugh [the promontory] my way home was via the ferry or by Harbour Road. Both routes were inaccessible. Making our way to Middleton Road, still under fire, we got as far as the Railway Workshops where we sheltered by the wall, watching the shells dropping into the Coal Dock. One shell pierced the interned German ship the 'Denlbuah'.

Anxious now to get home we made a dash over the two dock gates for Harbour Terrace. This we were told by those passing was risky, as firing was still in progress.

Harbour Terrace presented a sorry spectacle. A shell had gone through an upper storey window, hurling the bedstead into the middle of the road with feathers and dust flying about everywhere. In their hurry to be away workmen had thrown away their tea cans and bait tins. Nearby a man and a young girl lay wounded. At the bottom of Church Street a man and a newsboy had been killed.

When firing ceased the Bank clock was showing 8.50am. The tram wires were down, so there were no trams for Hartlepool which meant we had to shank it. Opposite the Mail Offices a shell had cut through a telephone pole leaving the top half dangling from the overhead wires. This was probably the same shell which struck the Mail Office. In front of the Rink an 11-inch shell had made a crater big enough to hold a horse and cart. A man lay dead and the doctor was ordering his removal.

We were now coming face to face with crowds of people leaving Hartlepool, some only scantily clad. They told us of the havoc on the headland. Trudging for home we saw the Scandinavian Church was badly holed and the gas holder at Greenland was still blazing. The tram offices were damaged and two houses in Percy Terrace were wrecked and were still burning when we passed. There was now a flow of motors and all kinds of conveyances carrying the dead and dying to the hospitals. The damage was severest in the vicinity and in the line of the batteries.

The afternoon turned sunny, bringing with it crowds of sightseers.

The above account was related by John Davison.

I was working as a heater lad when the Hartlepools were bombarded. When the firing started everyone downed tools and ran to the bottom of the slag bank to have a look at the naval battle we thought was going on. The noise of the guns was terrific and as it was a foggy morning only the flashes could be seen. Thousands of sea birds were milling about in the sky.

After we had watched for a short time shells started hitting the slag bank and everyone ran for it. I decided to go to my home in Old Town and, along with a few others, took a short cut through the steelworks. At the main gate the steelwork's bobby stood warning men to keep away from a large shell lying near the gate. I think it had come through the blacksmith's shop. By the time I arrived at the Old Town gates the firing had died down a bit so I made a dash for home. When I got there the only one at home was the tiger-coloured cat. It had turned into a black cat when the kitchen had been covered in soot from the chimney, and some of the pictures had fallen off the walls.

Old Town was deserted and I went in search of my mother and sisters. I came to the house of the tinker, George Jobling. The side was blown in and three little girls lay dead in the road. A little further down the street a woman lay dead on the flagstones. I made my way round Knowles Street where a man had been killed when taking a short cut over the Old Town Mission wall. He had been working in Irvine's Harbour Yard and was identified by his belt as 'Tiger' Burgon, a shipyard holder-up. On the other side of the square an old man known as 'Watercress Bill' was shouting for help from the top floor. His staircase had been blown away and he had been blown out of his bed, but could not get down. I met George Burns, a hawker, collecting the dead on his flat cart.

When it was all over I went down the Sands Arch. The tide was out and the beach was pitted with shell holes. I heard my family were safe and were on their way home from the park. Afterwards visitors arrived from near and far to buy all the bits of shrapnel they could get hold of and some of the fly lads did a good business. For a long time afterwards soldiers were kept busy digging large unexploded shells out of the slag bank.

The above account was related by H. Dennis who worked at the steelworks.

Being on sick leave at the time of the bombardment from the Central Marine Engine Works, where I was apprenticed, I was running a milk round from Elwick that morning. When I neared the Park I heard what appeared to be gunfire practice at sea. When I got into the town there was chaos, the tram-wires in Grange Road were wrecked and lying on the ground. My journey was right where the shelling was taking place. Belk Street, Cameron Road and Dene Street all had people injured. The people were panicking and making an exodus to the country. When I got back to Elwick it was crowded like a feast day. The crippled children's home was full of casualties.

The above account was related by an unnamed resident of Elwick.

I was 15 at the time of the Hartlepool bombardment. There was no one at home in our house when the bombardment began. We had a newspaper shop in Exeter Street facing Alma Place and I was helping my mother to deliver morning papers. My father was at Gray's Shipyard where he worked.

We were in Lower Archer Street when the guns started firing and we did not take much notice at first. We thought it was a practice. Then we heard shells whining over our heads, so we went back home quickly. From the shop window we saw people streaming past in crowds, some in their night-dresses. Soon after, my father came from the dockyard. He said a shell had come through the roof of the shed where he was working. We packed a few things and set off up Grange Road towards the Park. People were carrying all kinds of things. We saw some-one carrying a new clipped hearthrug and others carrying Christmas cakes. When we got as far as the Park we were told it was safe to go back home, so we returned.

We had no light other than candles for some time because the gasometers had been hit, but our part of the town escaped serious damage. We had a severe shock on the Friday morning following the bombardment when there was a false alarm. People were most upset remembering that dreadful Wednesday.

The above account was related by J. Ballantine.

I was a nurse at Hartlepool Hospital and that day was supposed to be my day off; consequently I was in the nurses' home alone, all staff being on duty. On hearing the noise I looked through the bedroom window and saw through the morning mist the ships close by the shore firing their guns and shells were flying through the air. Realising what was happening I quickly got into my uniform and went to the hospital. Houses on the opposite side of the street had been hit and the street was a shambles.

My first instructions were to get the patients up, wrapped in blankets and their names and addresses attached to them. The wards were quickly filled with extra beds only a few inches between each. Patients were now in the entrance hall waiting to be allocated to their respective wards. Treatment was difficult as there was no gas or electricity, the gasometer having been hit. An extra operat-ing theatre was in use. Matron, doctors and senior nursing staff were there all day and well into the night.

At about 4.00pm, when it was getting dark, a man came to me and asked what had to be done, the mortuary being full. For a moment my heart seemed to stand still. I went up to matron, Miss Stevenson, a wonderful person, so cool and dignified. Her instructions were that all the bodies from the mortuary were to be put on flat carts and taken to Gray Peverell's shop, which was empty. As I was leaving she called me back, "You must stand by while this is being done, see that all are covered and leave the hospital reverently."

It was the most difficult thing I had had to do all day. For the first time I had time to think. As I stood there I offered up a prayer.

The above account was related by Nurse Simpson.

During the bombardment, and after it, I had the opportunity to see the ambulance societies at work. They went about giving first aid quietly and efficiently. I have no doubt they saved many lives. I think their work should be remembered.

The above account was related by F. M. Lavin.

A detachment of the 18th Durham Light Infantry, the Pals, of about 150 officers and NCOs and men were stationed in the Market (now the Borough Hall), for defence and guard duty at Hartlepool. On the morning of 16th December, at about 4.30am, we were awakened and given the order to parade. We were then issued with 250 rounds of ammunition each, which we had to put in our overcoat pockets as we had no other equipment. Our bayonets were fastened to our belts with string.

We were issued with a can of tea and were told by the officer that if nothing happened before 11.00am we could have the rest of the day off. We marched to the Spion Kop where we had some trenches.

At 6.00am my mate was placed on sentry duty on top of the trench. At 7.00am I relieved him. At about 8.00am I was talking to the Sergeant-Major and we looked towards the pier when we saw a flash and heard a loud explosion.

"What's that?" I asked. But he had already left me to go and report to the officers in the trench. I was on top all the time and saw the cruisers firing their broadsides into the town, the docks and sand banks by the Old Cemetery and also into the cove where the lifeboat was housed. They chased a motor fishing boat onto the sands and the fishermen jumped ashore, except one who was injured. He was creeping ashore, so two of our sergeants asked if they could bring him in. Under heavy shellfire they took him to the lifeboat house to be attended to. The sergeants should have been awarded a medal.

I saw the three cruisers steaming past the pier and the Old Cemetery. They turned east to go out of sight. Whilst on duty I saw the No.2 gasholder burning and the Cement Works chimney with a shell hole right through it.

At about 11.00am we were mustered to get something to eat. The cooks had made us some sausage sandwiches which we and the officers were glad to have. We were marched back to the town to help the rest of our detachment who were looking after the injured and the people whose homes had been damaged. At night eight of us were sent on guard duty to the lighthouse.

On the 17th three regiments were marched around the promenade to see the damage. In the afternoon I was at the bandstand when I saw Sir Edward Carson and Mr Churchill, who had been inspecting the damage.

The above account was related by T. M. Neill. The sergeants mentioned were Sergeant W. H. Heal (a Rovers footballer) and Sergeant M. Brewerton (from the Easington area).

7th (CYCLIST) BATTALION DEVONSHIRE REGIMENT

1: Frank Day (A) and two mates from the 2/7th at West Hartlepool October 1914. 2: 1003 Private Frank Day, 16th June 1914. 3: Devonshire Regimental cap badge. 4: Transport and motor cyclists at West Hartlepool, 1914.

I was 15 at the time and can still remember the terror and confusion on the 18th when the rumour went round that the Germans were back. It was worse then, because we knew what to expect. Whole families left the town with their goods piled high on prams or anything with wheels, even on their backs. I saw one woman with a Christmas cake in her arms. There can't have been many people left in Old Town or the areas near the sea.

The above account was related by L. Hewitson.

Wednesday, 16th December 1914.
Three German battleships sighted at 8.00am. Five minutes later commenced firing on Hartlepool. Flashes clearly seen and reports heard. Ships only three miles away. Told off for duty at Coastguards as despatch rider. Had exciting time while riding about with messages expecting shells to burst over us any minute.

The above account was entered in the diary of 1003 Private Frank Albert Day, 7th (Cyclist) Battalion Devonshire Regiment. Frank was born on 7th August 1897 and enlisted at Exeter on 16th June 1914. He was transferred to the newly raised 2/7th Battalion in October 1914. The 2/7th Devonshires were based at Redcar and formed part of the Northern Command's Coastal Defence. On 28th December 1916 Frank was sent to France and transferred to the 8th Devonshires on 20th January 1917. Wounded at the Battle of Bullecourt on 7th May 1917, Frank was discharged as 'no longer physically fit' on 18th February 1918. On 11th December 1933, Frank died, aged 36, as a result of the wounds he sustained at Bullecourt.

As fellow author John Ward did in his book *'Dawn Raid'* I leave the final comment on the bombardment of the Hartlepools to F. Collier:

I was 15 years old at the time of the bombardment and was employed as a telephone attendant at Greenland by the North Eastern Railway. During that week I was on the night shift (5.00pm to 6.00am). At about 2.15am on 16th December I received a telephone message from the district intelligence office in Mainsforth Terrace, asking the whereabouts of my traffic foreman, who was away from the office inspecting a goods train. When I gave this information I was instructed to turn all lights down low and refrain from using the telephone under any circumstances.

Surely if the public had been informed that there was a possibility of an attack, and there seemed to have been time to do this, some of those lives might have been saved.

SCARBOROUGH

AN ACCOUNT OF THE GERMAN SUBMARINE ATTACK ON SCARBOROUGH ON TUESDAY, 4TH SEPTEMBER 1917

Following the bombardments the three towns got back to something approaching normal. Within a week of the event cinema audiences up and down the country were being treated to the 'history' of the east coast raids, from which, it was said, 'a clear and moving impression of the extensive damage sustained at Scarborough, Whitby and Hartlepool could be obtained.' Only a couple of days after the raid York's cinemas were showing 'The Bombardment of Scarborough' and 'Havoc at Scarborough'. By Christmas the Palladium Picture Theatre on the Foreshore, which had escaped the worst of the shelling, was showing 'By the Kaiser's Orders'. It was probably a three-minute portion of one of these films which resurfaced in the mid 1970s, when it was featured on a Yorkshire Television programme on the 1914 bombardments produced by David Mould (now teaching in the USA) and presented by Austin Mitchell (now Labour MP for Grimsby). In one short clip a military funeral takes place, followed by a single volley salute of rifles; the funeral is that of Coastguard Frederick Randall of Whitby. Many of the scenes in the short pieces of film are recognisable as scenes captured by photographers and presented here.

As the war progressed and the high death tolls of the Somme and Passchendaele became a reality the losses at Scarborough, Whitby and Hartlepool would drift into insignificance, a mere footnote on the pages of history.

On the 25th December 1914 the *Von der Tann* was damaged during the first British naval air-raid on Cuxhaven. On the 24th January 1915, thirty-nine days after the bombardment, another attack on the east coast was foiled and a British battle-cruiser squadron under Beatty caught the Germans off Dogger Bank, sank the *Blücher* and damaged the *Seydlitz*. At a meeting of Scarborough Borough Council on 8th February 1915, it was resolved to send a message of congratulations to Admiral Beatty on *'an achievement which fully justifies this country's pride in its Navy'*.

In April 1915, the 5th Green Howards got their chance to revenge their families and homes. Alongside the valiant Canadians they stemmed the German advance after the first gas attack during the Second Battle of Ypres. From then on the people back home were treated to a steady flow of letters and cards, many of which appeared in the local newspapers, from the lads at the front.

In 1916, on the 25th April, the Norfolk towns of Lowestoft and Yarmouth were again attacked by German battleships. This time they were engaged by local naval forces and eventually made off. There were some 25 casualties reported. Between 31st May and 1st June 1916, at the Battle of Jutland the *Moltke*, *Von der Tann*, *Derfflinger* and *Seydlitz* were all damaged.

On the 1st July 1916 the Battles of the Somme opened and the roll of death mounted alarmingly, and at last, if anyone at home was left with any illusions about the glory and beauty of war and the noble sacrifice of the nation's youth, the war was seen for what it was, a war of attrition, where the only survivors, for there could be no winners, would be the last unit left standing or crawling in the mud of the Flanders battlefields. Indeed it is quoted that General Sir William Robertson (Chief of Staff to Sir John French in 1915 and Haig's only serious rival for succession to the command) once said that the war would only end when there were two British soldiers and one German left in the field. And the way the lifeblood of a generation was draining into the Flanders mud, that time was likely to come sooner rather than later.

The Submarine Attack

On Tuesday, 4th September 1917, a German U-boat surfaced off the Scarborough coast at approximately 6.45pm, and whilst surrounded by minesweepers, pleasure craft and small boats in the South Bay, subjected the town to a short barrage of some 30 shells. Three people were killed and several more were reported injured. On this occasion, however, it seemed like a mere scratch compared to the suppurating wound of the Western Front, where the nation had now gone through the absolute horror and carnage of the Somme (and was about to undergo the horror of Passchendaele - 12th October), and very little was written or said about the attack.

At the time the Illustrated War Record, which was produced weekly throughout the war, claimed the date to have been the 5th September and that 11 had been killed and 62 injured. Whether this was just inaccurate reporting, or for propaganda purposes is unclear, but it is a stark fact that the nation as a whole could hardly have cared less, for they had far more important matters on their minds.

Indeed even the local daily paper, the *Scarborough Evening News*, only gave the story page 3 priority in its edition of the 5th September, with barely more than four paragraphs. However, in the following day's edition, 6th September, the story warranted some eight full columns over pages 3 and 4.

The edition of the *Scarborough Pictorial* of Friday 7th, had had time to collate some of the information and reported on the deaths and inquests of the three victims. It began its account with a short editorial paragraph reminding people of the last bombardment in 1914:

> *Much life was compressed into the fifteen minutes which may be regarded approximately as the period of the visitation of a U-boat to Scarborough on Tuesday evening. For that brief spell the populace throbbed with tension. Many visitors to the town, who had never undergone a similar experience, will remember that quarter of an hour with vividness and in clear detail as long as they live. Townspeople will not of course forget it; but their recollections in the course of*

time may be clouded by the greater and even more dramatic experience that had undergone previously in this war, with its Hunnish side-issue of frightfulness.

That Tuesday late-summer evening was described as charming until the *'harsh shriek and whistle of shells and nerve-racking explosions'* had disturbed the peaceful tranquillity. A coastguard officer, on duty at the castle, stated later that he thought the submarine was some four miles south-east of the town, towards Cayton Bay.

As the small calibre shells fell the many small pleasure craft weaving in and out of the minesweepers in and off the South Bay dashed hurriedly for the presumed safe haven of the harbour. No ships were struck, though some reported close calls.

The roads along the Foreshore and Esplanade were thronged with locals and visitors alike, making the most of the late evening sunshine. Some turned and ran for shelter, others simply stood and watched the spectacle of the lone raider's guns spitting fire and raining shells on the undefended town. Children, playing in the sand on the beach, were snatched up by anxious parents and carried to safety. On this occasion there was no great exodus to the railway station of people eager to flee the town.

The angle of fire was much narrower and covered a much more confined area than had happened in 1914, as the battleships had steamed north to south and then traversed to rake the whole town with shellfire. On this occasion the submarine's shells fell in a general area encompassed on the west by Northway [then Albion Street] to the north by Columbus Ravine running through Woodall Avenue, on the east by the castle headland and to the south by the Foreshore Road. This corroborates the account given by the coastguard of the submarine being to the south-east of the town and almost stationary during the attack.

The damage, such as it was, occurred in the older parts of town and the Falsgrave, Manor Road and South Cliff areas all escaped any damage on this occasion.

Fanny Beswick was injured in the leg at her home at 109 Victoria Road when it was hit and the roof and bedroom were damaged. She was taken to the hospital for treatment.

On Hoxton Road a shell hit 107, the home of Mr Jackson, a labourer, and fragments of it flew off in all directions doing much damage. The blast and flying debris, mixed with shell fragments, injured Charles Bray of 110 Hoxton Road and fatally wounded thirty-nine-year-old Elizabeth Scott of number 108 who had been standing at her door listening to the thunder of the shells exploding. Her daughter Lilian rushed home from playing in the street to discover her mother crawling to a couch. The distraught girl helped her mother onto it before rushing off for help. Despite being taken to the hospital Elizabeth, the wife of PC John Scott, died from her injuries at 10.00pm.

At Mrs Wardman's confectionery shop at 1 James Street a shell entered the upper rear of the premises through the wall, struck an inner wall and spent itself against a wooden joist. In the shop below, a tin of biscuits was knocked from its shelf above Mrs Wardman and hit her on the head. Though she was relatively unscathed, the shop was badly damaged with the provisions scattered and mixed with broken glass from the shop's shattered windows. It was later revealed that Mrs Wardman's stock and shop were not insured and she suffered financially.

Mrs Coles, of 8 Eastborough, had a very narrow escape when a shell passed within inches of her as she stood beside her open shop door. The shell did some damage to the interior of the shop, but Mrs Coles suffered no more than shock and a splash or two of juice from some fruit which was thrown about by the blast. However, in the bakery, situated in the basement, a fire was started and a fire engine was called to deal with the blaze. On leaving the scene after dousing the blaze the engine backfired and a small panic ensued with people diving for cover and one little girl fainting with fright.

Meanwhile seventeen-year-old Alice Appleby of 8 Whitehead Hill, Sandside, was wounded in the leg whilst walking along Longwestgate. So serious was the wound it was feared for a time she might lose the leg, and according to the account given by Norman Hodgson (on page 450), it appears that this was, in fact, the case.

Waking from the lethargy caused by surprise, several of the minesweepers weighed anchor and made off to engage the submarine, firing as they went. As if unwilling to engage them the submarine loosed off a few more rounds and then dived for the depths to begin its run for safety.

Following the shelling visitors and locals alike wandered around the town to survey the damage of broken windows and damaged brickwork.

Three people had been mortally wounded during the shelling; Thomas Pickup, hit on Bland's Cliff, died on reaching the hospital, whilst Frederick Parry, struck whilst on the Foreshore, died half an hour later. The final death occurred at 10.00pm, when Elizabeth Scott expired despite the staff at the hospital having fought to save her for some three hours. Six more people were reported as having suffered wounds.

A coastguard officer later recounted that perhaps some thirty shells had fallen, of which he avowed that almost half had fallen short of the town and landed in the South Bay. Given the angle of attack, the relatively tight confined area, and the small damage done, it would appear that he was right and that perhaps some fifteen shells, at best, fell in the town.

There was a large crowd of visitors at the Post Office the following morning, all eager to wire their friends and relatives to tell them what they had lived through!

That evening (Wednesday, 5th September) a large 'war aims' meeting of almost a thousand people met on the West Pier and voted to pass the following message of sympathy to the victims via the Mayor:

> *This public meeting of visitors and townspeople of Scarborough expresses its deep sympathy with the relatives of the victims of German frightfulness in the recent U-boat outrage, and respectfully invites his worship the Mayor of Scarborough to convey the same to those interested.*

At the same time as the meeting the inquests into the deaths of two of the three victims were in progress at the Court House under the direction of the Borough Coroner, Mr Royle. The inquest opened with PC Scott being called to the stand. After identifying the body of his wife, Elizabeth, he gave an account of her demise. The constable had been on duty at the time of the incident and had been summoned to his home shortly after the raid began. On entering his house at 108 Hoxton Road, he had discovered his wife sprawled on a couch, barely conscious. She had moments earlier been standing in the doorway to the street when a fragment from a bursting shell had severed her femoral artery. The wound was fatal, and despite having been rushed to the hospital and treated, she had died at ten o'clock that night.

The constable, pale and close to tears, was allowed to leave the stand while his daughter, Lilian Scott gave her account of events to the inquest. Lilian had been outside, further along the street when the shell burst and had fled indoors to find her mother struggling to pull herself onto the couch from the floor. Unable to lift her stricken mother, the girl, almost beside herself, had rushed outside to find help. Once her mother was on the couch Lilian had rushed off again, this time to fetch a doctor. During all this her mother remained unconscious. In tears, her account over, Lilian was led from the stand.

Dr Godfrey, who was on duty at the hospital at the time Elizabeth Scott was admitted, then took the stand. He described her condition as 'extremely collapsed, very pale and evidently suffering from loss of blood'. He found a large perforating wound at the back of her right thigh and a smaller wound below her knee, on the upper calf, although on examination the wounds were found to be relatively clean of debris, the shell fragments having passed straight through the flesh and out the other side. The bleeding had all but stopped by the time she was admitted, but there was little they could do for her save make her comfortable and do their best to revive her. However, Dr Godfrey explained, she had gradually sunk further into unconsciousness and had subsequently died. He put her death down to haemorrhage and the shock from the perforating wound on her thigh.

Chief Officer Lawrence Reeve, the coastguard on duty at the station in the castle at the time - Reeve had been the second-in-command at the time of the 1914 bombardment - was then called to give a detailed account of the raid. From his vantage point on the Castle Hill Lawrence Reeve had been able to witness the entire event and recounted what he saw for the rapt inquest jury.

The Coroner decided, after hearing Lawrence Reeve's testimony, to hold the verdict in the case of Elizabeth Scott until the evidence in the next case, that of Thomas Temple Pickup, had been heard.

Mrs Pickup, of 2 Queen's Terrace (off Queen's Parade, above the North Bay), the wife of the deceased, was called as the first witness. She confirmed that her husband had been sat in the kitchen, quietly reading, when the shelling had begun. He had at once jumped up and rushed out into the street to see what was going on and there he met with the injuries which ended his life. She confirmed Thomas had worked for Tonks for 47 years and then resumed her place.

Next to the stand was an elderly gentleman named William Wimbush, who lived at Beech House on Bland's Cliff. William had been enjoying a pint in the Rose and Crown on Albert Row when the shelling started and, going to the door, he saw a man (he later found out was Thomas Pickup) stagger across the street and fall to the ground. Although he rushed to the man's aid, he was not strong enough to drag him back to the Rose and Crown. At this point another man had arrived and suggested they lift the wounded man onto his back.

However, a nurse, passing in haste to another urgent call, had stopped and loosened Thomas's clothing enough to uncover a bleeding wound in his side. The nurse re-covered the wound and hurried on her way. William then stated that one Miss Ellingham (the daughter of George Ellingham, landlord of the Rose and Crown) had then brought brandy to the wounded man and this had had the effect of temporarily reviving him. Some seven minutes later an ambulance arrived and took Thomas, who by this time had died, away.

William stated the wounded man had not spoken, though at first he had appeared to be conscious for he had attempted to cover his face with his arm.

William's place on the stand was taken by Inspector Mansfield, who stated that at about 7.15pm a man had rushed up to him at the corner of Queen Street and asked for the ambulance to be sent for a wounded man. The ambulance was despatched at once to collect the man, but he had been declared dead on arrival at the hospital and had been taken from there to the mortuary.

There the evidence ended.

Before the verdicts could be given the Coroner addressed the inquest:

> *The evidence is alphabetical in its simplicity and there is no doubt how these two persons came by their deaths. I have known PC Scott for a great number of years and have always known him as a most zealous officer and respectable man. And I am very grieved at the great loss he has suffered. As we have heard, the submarine fired about thirty shots and it is really quite wonderful that the results in the town were not more serious. I think no good can be done by dilating on the enormity of the offence committed by these ghastly and brutal attacks by the devil's spawn.*
>
> *However, there is one thing I would like to say, and that is there is no doubt that in philosophy, music and the arts Germany has stood in the forefront. Indeed, the greatest of philosophers, scientists, chemists and the mightiest fighting engines have been produced there since the world began. All that wonderful ability might have been a mighty blessing on the world, was it not the curse it was. And though these men have their wonderful brains and industry and extraordinary talents, yet there is this madness, this extraordinary and absurd idea that by murdering poor women, children and old men they can cause such terror in England that the people will rise, and with exceedingly bitter cries, call upon the government to make a disgraceful peace, actuated and influenced by this frightfulness.*
>
> *It simply shows that, as wonderful in intellect and as warriors they might be, they are so unutterably foolish as to even dream the English could be affected by such actions. These people, so clever in one way, are infantile and absurd in their judgement if they think to influence the English people this way. It is a huge mistake on their part, for the more this their monstrous cowardice is disclosed, the greater will be the grim determination of the English character to go to the utmost in crushing this militarism and this outcast among nations.*
>
> *Were it not for the sorrow we all feel at the distress occasioned, one would laugh at the absurdity, and the enemy's frightfulness would produce an effect directly opposed to that they had hoped to produce by these monstrous and wicked acts.*

The inquest jury brought the verdict that 'death was caused from a projectile fired from an enemy submarine' in both cases. The foreman joined with the Coroner, on behalf of the jury, in expressing sympathy with the relatives of the deceased.

The Chief Constable, on behalf of himself and the Borough Police Force, expressed his regret at the great sorrow which had fallen on their colleague PC Scott.

It is of interest to note that Thomas Pickup was the uncle of Albert Pickup, the custodian of the castle, whose family had had such a narrow escape in the bombardment of December 1914.

The inquest into the third victim was conducted the following evening.

The body of Frederick Parry was identified by his father, Benjamin Parry, and his occupation given as coachbuilder. Benjamin Parry stated he had last seen his son almost a fortnight ago.

It fell to Colour Sergeant Albert Bentley, of the Military Police, to give an account of Frederick's injuries. The Sergeant had been on duty on the Foreshore Road at the time of the enemy attack and had witnessed a shell burst some four yards from the unfortunate man, showering him with fragments of casing. One such hit him just above the left eye causing a severe wound. Sergeant Bentley had gone to his aid and tried to stem the bleeding. He had then helped carry the injured man to the nearby Royal Northern Sea Bathing Infirmary and Convalescent Home. There his wounds had been washed and dressed by a group of nurses and sisters.

The Sergeant had then sent for a doctor and Captain Murray of the Royal Army Medical Corps arrived shortly thereafter. The Captain examined Frederick's wounds, re-dressed them and then ordered his removal to the General Hospital on Friar's Entry. On arrival at the hospital Frederick had been examined by Dr Godfrey (who then took up the testimony), who found there to be a small wound over the left eye from which blood and brain fluid had been oozing freely. The doctor confirmed the track of the wound was through the brain toward the back of the throat. He also confirmed that Frederick never recovered consciousness, and was already dying and beyond help when admitted. On further examination there were found to be no other wounds save that mortal one to the head.

The inquest jury returned a verdict *'that death was due to injury from a shell fired by an enemy submarine engaged in the bombardment of Scarborough'* and an expression of sympathy with the man's relatives was made on behalf of the jury by its foreman.

Frederick Parry, a reservist with the 6th (Reserve) Battalion Lancashire Fusiliers was later laid to rest in his home town of Manchester; which is why, it is assumed, his name does not appear on the Scarborough War Memorial - though as I have previously pointed out, a number of men named on the memorial were not born in, or from Scarborough. It is more than likely that when the names for the memorial were being submitted in the early 1920s no one in the town remembered the young man from Manchester, killed whilst on holiday, and thus his name was never put forward for inclusion.

The Gentleman German ~ A Footnote

As I researched the submarine attack and the varying degrees of propaganda for the 1914 and 1917 raids I learned of another U-boat Captain, by the name of Carl Siegfried Ritter von Georg, who was in the habit, throughout the war, of actually ensuring the safety of the crews whose vessels he then went on to sink. His story is remarkable and merits a book in its own right.

On one single occasion on the night of 24th, and early morning of 25th September 1916, von Georg's *U57* actually rounded up the crews of thirteen Scarborough trawlers and sunk all their boats, bar one which was used as their prison until the following morning. Just after dawn von Georg stopped a neutral Norwegian cargo ship and arranged with her skipper to take the Scarborough fishermen to a British port. He then transferred his 126 prisoners from the fish-hold of the trawler *Fisher Prince* and bid them "Auf Wiedersehen," before sinking her with gunfire.

The fact that his whole career was littered with such incidents goes some way, perhaps, to putting into context the notion of the German Navy as both barbarous and murderous as promoted at the time in the press.

By early 1917 Scarborough had been closed as a fishing port due to the constant danger from mines and predatory U-boats plying their trade in coastal waters. All trawlers from the Scarborough fleet were ordered to Aberdeen and from there they fished in convoy for the remainder of the war.

As to the identity of the U-boat which attacked Scarborough on that sunny September evening in 1917, there appears to be no record of her in the surviving German naval records and it is quite possible she was one of the many vessels unaccounted for in the North Sea and probably sunk by mines - perhaps even one laid by the *Kolberg* in 1914!

Scarborough

In Their Own Write
Personal Accounts of the German Submarine Attack on Scarborough on Tuesday, 4th September 1917

The following extracts from letters and verse were written largely by the men and women of Scarborough. A number have been written up from interviews conducted during the 1970s by my friend, the author and journalist David Mould, and others from my own research among the survivors. Now, for the first time in 82 years they describe, in their own words, the day Scarborough underwent its second sea-borne attack, this time by a German submarine.

The author of the letter or verse always follows the piece. All accounts and verse date from, or relate to the 1917 attack on Scarborough.

I was there with my boyfriend on that day. We had just walked down along Westborough and had turned the corner onto the Foreshore when the shelling started. So we turned around and ran back up Westborough and into a house until it finished. A lady was killed in Hoxton Road, where we were staying.

This account was related by Mrs H. Brown of Ossett, West Yorkshire.

At the time of the 1917 shelling by a German U-boat my brother Leslie and I were playing on the castle. At the first shots my father bundled us swiftly into the Lady's Well for safety, fearing there would be shrapnel flying about and that we might be hurt, or worse.

This account was related by Aubrey Reeve, the youngest son of Chief Officer Lawrence Reeve. Lawrence gave evidence at the inquests. Whilst stationed in Scarborough the Reeve family lived in a house at the coastguard station, opposite St Mary's Church (at the castle end of Castle Road).

I was fishing off the middle pier with my two brothers when the shelling began in the daylight attack. The Harbour-Master ran out and shouted at us to get down behind a pile of wood.

On our return home, via Eastborough, we passed a basement baker's shop which a shell had entered - it was on fire. The fire engine was leaving by the time we got there and what with the steep slope it backfired causing a slight panic in which I promptly fainted!

I can still remember the whine of the shells going over our heads.

This account was related by Mrs Gladys Ness of Bootham, York.

The bakery mentioned belonged to Mr and Mrs Coles and was situated in the basement of 8 Eastborough.

It was late afternoon, early evening when the dickens of a noise started. I was on school holidays and staying with my granny at Neptune House on the Foreshore. The house was four storeys high and had a veranda which looked out to sea.

I saw a bright flash and then some smoke a great distance off out at sea. Then a noise like a terrific blast of escaping steam getting louder and louder occurred. Suddenly, fifty yards to the left and six feet from the Foreshore railings a shell exploded. The blast blew me over to the right and for a week I had a ricked back, but when I looked again a soldier, who had been all through the war in France so we heard, was lying on his back dead, with blood on his head.

A local girl lost a leg; she lived on Sandside and there were a few other deaths in the town. I ran downstairs and hid. I was getting a bit scared of shells by now as I knew what they could do.

This account was related by Scarborian Norman Hodgson from Hayes, Middlesex. Born in 1903 he was 14 at the time of the submarine attack. The man Norman saw was Frederick Parry, who was unconscious but not dead. In the very first report on the attack Frederick was said to be a soldier, but no subsequent reports or the report of the inquest mentioned this again. However, a search of 'Soldiers Died in the Great War' has revealed that indeed Frederick was with the 6th (Reserve) Battalion Lancashire Fusiliers. The girl who lost her leg was seventeen-year-old Alice Appleby.

THE SLAYERS

Oh, thrilling was your conquest, Supermen!
A mighty, doughty contest, Supermen!
The tortured victims' moans
And the splintered human bones
On the crimson paving stones,
Repaid your deed with interest, Supermen!

~

How well you chose your foe, Coward-men!
You knew just where to go, Coward-men!
If you heard the running feet
Of the children in the street
You would think it music sweet -
Hunting babies to and fro, Coward-men!

~

Oh, the target was so fair, Kaiser's men!
There were wives and children there, Kaiser's men!
You could send back to your bosses
And report 'colossal losses',
And receive your Iron Crosses
In the Potsdam limelight's glare, Kaiser's men!

~

Every dog must have its day, Brute-beast-men!
And there's vengeance on the way, Brute-beast-men!
You foul the seas just now,
With the devil at your prow,
But Britannia's made a vow
That she'll down you, come what may, Brute-beast-men!

Written by R. A. H. Goodyear. Taken from a souvenir postcard of the U-boat attack produced by local printers E. T. W. Dennis & Sons.

In 1917 I was down in the Valley with my father when we heard firing from the direction of the sea. A submarine had surfaced in the South Bay and lobbed a few shells into the town.

This account was related by Charles A. Pearson from Dewsbury. He was born in Scarborough in 1911 and was just 3 years old at the time of the 1914 bombardment and 6 at the time of the submarine attack.

Scarborough

The Armistice and Beyond, Epilogue and Author's Close

In 1914 the British Army at home was organised under the command of Headquarters Home Forces which was located at Horse Guards, Whitehall. The Home Forces comprised of seven area Commands; Aldershot Command (HQ Aldershot), Eastern Command (HQ 50 Pall Mall, London), Irish Command (HQ Dublin), Northern Command (HQ York), Scottish Command (HQ Edinburgh) Southern Command (HQ Salisbury), and Western Command (HQ Chester), and one District Command; London District (HQ Carlton House Terrace, London).

Superimposed on this structure was the Headquarters Central Force which commanded the First, Second and Third Armies. These in turn commanded all operational forces allocated for the defence of the British Isles, which largely tended to be those units still mobilising or training for overseas. However, in March 1916, this latter structure was disbanded and home defence came directly under the control of Headquarters Home Forces. To assist in this structure, the Headquarters of the Northern Army was situated at Norwich and the Headquarters of the Southern Army at Brentford.

As the war went on many of the units mentioned in the preceding narratives, having done their stint at home defence, eventually went abroad, or were used to fill gaps in units already serving overseas. Many of the same gunners who engaged the enemy at such places as Hartlepool, Ramsgate and Dover were eventually moved to France as the danger of enemy naval attacks receded and the greater need for gunners and heavy guns increased on the Western Front.

The bombardments of Scarborough, Whitby and Hartlepool greatly swelled the ranks of the British Army and many of those who rushed to enlist at the end of 1914 found themselves on the front line by mid-1915, there to seek some small revenge for the attacks on their homes. The 5th Green Howards were no exception, and indeed, such was the level of enlistment following the bombardment of Scarborough that the Battalion was able to raise a second full battalion, the 2nd/5th. This unit never saw

1

SCARBOROUGH REMEMBERS

1: Men of the 5th Green Howards who made it home. Most of their comrades lay buried beneath the Flanders mud. 2: The Scarborough War Memorial, unveiled in 1923. 3: The names of civilians killed in the 1914 and 1917 bombardments, with the omission of Margaret Briggs, killed at *Dunollie*, and the inclusion of Alice Painter who committed suicide on the 14th December. 4: The inscription on the Memorial.

2

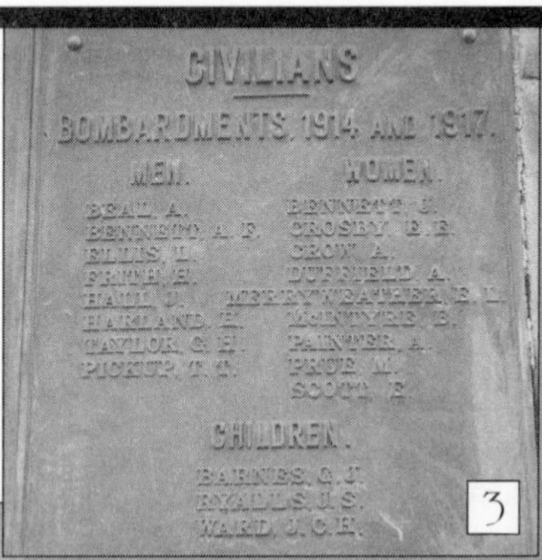
CIVILIANS
BOMBARDMENTS 1914 AND 1917.
MEN.
WOMEN.
CHILDREN.

3

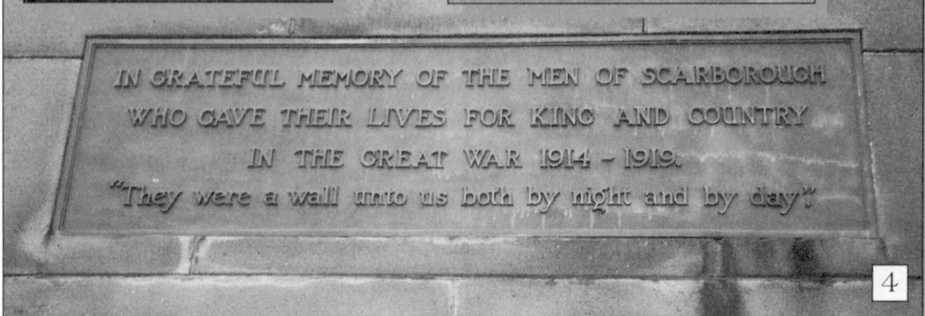
IN GRATEFUL MEMORY OF THE MEN OF SCARBOROUGH
WHO GAVE THEIR LIVES FOR KING AND COUNTRY
IN THE GREAT WAR 1914 - 1919.
"They were a wall unto us both by night and by day"

4

active service in its own right, but furnished men to make up losses in the 1st/5th Battalion. The 5th Green Howards landed in France on Sunday, 18th April 1915, and the full story of their first action, their 'Baptism of Fire', in which they held the line at St Julien alongside the courageous Canadians and earned the nickname the 'Yorkshire Gurkhas' for the ferocity of their fighting, is told in the first book of this series. The Battalion went on to take part in every major engagement on the Western Front until, decimated beyond repair, it was reduced to cadre status in late 1918, shortly before the Armistice, and the men who were left were drafted into the 4th Green Howards (also part of the 150th Brigade of the 50th (Northumbrian) Division). This book puts into perspective the Battalion's courageous behaviour and exemplary conduct in those first few days in France and provides the background to the rest of the series and the continuation of 'The War of the Yorkshire Gurkhas'.

By the time of the Armistice on the 11th hour of the 11th day of the 11th month of 1918 the country had been bled dry and the names of Ypres, the Somme and Passchendaele were names to chill one to the marrow, and the bombardments of Scarborough and the east coast towns had been put starkly into their true perspective. The horrendous casualty figures from the Somme and Passchendaele had now become a reality and with those huge losses the loss of life in the three north-east coastal towns became almost insignificant.

Ten days later, on 21st November 1918, the German High Seas Fleet surrendered and was interned at Scapa Flow, among it the *Seydlitz*, *Moltke*, *Derfflinger* and *Von der Tann* (the *Blücher* having already gone to the bottom at the Battle of Dogger Bank on 24th January 1915). With plans afoot for the allies to take the bulk of the German warships as prizes of war, Admiral Ludwig von Reuter gave the order for the ships to be scuttled. At 11.20am on 21st June 1919 the seacocks were opened and by 5.00pm all five German battle-cruisers, ten out of eleven battleships, four out of eight cruisers and thirty-two out of fifty destroyers had gone to the bottom. The raiders of the north-east coast had finally gone to their last resting place.

At home soldiers returned from the front, prisoners made it back, casualties left their hospital beds and everywhere men, changed for ever by their experiences of the war, endeavoured to come to terms with the horrors they had been through. It was not easy for any of them.

Gradually time passed, though many of the wounds refused to heal. The nation once more went about its business and memorials and monuments began to emerge across the land; in towns, cities and villages alike the dead were remembered.

On the 26th September 1923, following a sombre procession through the town, the route of which was thronged with thousands of local people, the Scarborough War Memorial was unveiled before local dignitaries and one of the largest crowds of townsfolk ever seen. After the main unveiling of the memorial by the Chairman of the War Memorial Committee, Councillor William Boyes, the four 'faces' bearing the twelve bronze plaques of names were unveiled by representatives of the Army, Navy, Royal Air Force and the Widows. The honour of representing the Army was given to Private Harold Merryweather of the 5th Green Howards, one of the original Battalion (the Yorkshire Gurkhas) who had landed in France in April 1915, and whose sister-in-law Emily had been killed in the bombardment of 1914.

The obelisk-style Memorial, designed by the very able Borough Engineer Harold W. Smith (the man largely considered responsible for much that Scarborians have taken civic pride in over the years) and paid for by public subscription to the tune of £5,000, was deliberately situated on the commanding promontory of Oliver's Mount, some five-hundred feet above sea-level, where it was, and remains today, visible from almost every part of the town. Built in hardy Yorkshire stone the memorial bears the names of the fallen, both military and civilian, with part of the main inscription reading:

> *In grateful memory of the men of Scarborough who gave their lives for King and Country in the Great War, 1914-1919. They were a wall unto us both by night and day.*

The date of 1919 referred not to the Armistice of 11th November 1918, which many regarded as the war's end, but to the 'official' end of the war on 19th July 1919.

Whitby's War Memorial is carved in wood and is housed in the parish church of St Mary's, high on the East Cliff, close to where the coastguard station and its attendant cottages stood, yet the names of her civilian victims are not listed. Whitby has no memorial to her dead of the bombardment.

In Hartlepool a War Memorial listing some of the dead of the bombardment is situated in the gardens at 'Red Heugh' on the lighthouse headland. There are also war memorials in the town centre of West Hartlepool and at Seaton Carew.

Epilogue and Author's Close

Over the intervening years there have been many bombardment 'specials' and much has been written about them. Ask anyone from Scarborough, Whitby or Hartlepool about it and the chances are, even today, that you will at least be given the odd snippet of information, or distantly remembered fact.

During the Second World War the towns again suffered as did very many more which were in reach of Hitler's planes and bombs. But the bombardments of 1914 are, and I suspect will always be, imprinted on each town's psyche. As each generation comes and goes it seems to pass on the very essence of the bombardment to the next, which then becomes the keeper of its town's collective bombardment memory. Now, eighty-five years on, that memory has finally been set down hard and fast, perhaps not in granite, but at least on paper, and with the deposit of this book in various archives across the country it is to be hoped that the 'collective memory' will survive another eighty-five years, at least.

Throughout the research and writing of this book I have all too often been at my wits' end in trying to decipher the conflicting information from the various sources available. However, one thing is abundantly clear, and that is that the people of Scarborough, Whitby and Hartlepool suffered the most terrible and terrifying ordeal they had, and perhaps ever will, face. It is clear to me, after completing this work that the incidents described herein should never be forgotten, either by the towns concerned or the nation as a whole.

After reading the narrative and the personal accounts I hope the reader is better able to see why, in the aftermath, so many young men joined the colours; why so many from Scarborough and Whitby joined the 5th Green Howards; and why they went to France in April 1915 and fought their first action with such ferocity - ferocity that earned them the nickname 'the Yorkshire Gurkhas'. In some small way, at the Battle of St Julien, those brave and eager lads had avenged the town, their homes and their families. It is perhaps also interesting to note that according to official records more people died in England from the German raids on the 16th December 1914 than British servicemen died on the same day on all the fronts we were engaged on. A sobering thought.

I hope too that the assumption I expressed in my introduction, with regard to the two distinct phases into which the bombardment of Scarborough fell, is now clearer.

During my research into this book I have had the privilege to meet and talk to a small handful of people who can justly claim to 'have been there' on that terrible day. Talking to each of them has helped me better understand just what an ordeal those minutes were for them and their families and friends. Each one could recall clearly, and with a vividness of memory which defies their many years, just where they were and what happened to them that morning. Each has enriched my life a little with their stories and certainly added greatly to this work. I am proud, and yet a little humbled, to number them now as friends. And I hope they are as proud of this work as I am proud of it and of them.

I hope this book stands as a small testament to the strength and courage of the men, women and children who lived through that terrible ordeal of Wednesday, 16th December 1914, and the subsequent days and weeks that followed; and that it stands as a suitable epitaph to those poor innocent souls, especially the children, who lost their lives on that infamous day; ***the day the east coast bled.***

May God grant them rest and may they now sleep peacefully in the knowledge that their story has at last been told in full, for at the going down of the sun, and in the morning, we shall remember them too.

Mark Marsay
Scarborough
December 1999

Bombardment Precautions

Common Sense Hints to the Public (Issued 1915)

In the absence of any official instructions on the subject of precautions to take during bombardment, the public must do a little hard thinking for itself, and out of this we may evolve a better plan than official advice could provide.

The risk of other bombardments is relatively small, but, nevertheless, it must not be ignored. The public must apply sensible precautions, and according to circumstances guide their actions. If this be done a good many lives may be saved.

Let us take the extreme case of an unfortified town suddenly bombarded in the morning when a sea mist obscures the outlook. The only warning may come from the sound of gunfire, and hence there is little time for elaborate measures of safety. At the first alarm people should leave the streets and avoid large public buildings such as railway stations and churches, and also keep well away from gasworks and power stations, factory chimneys and all prominent objects.

In hastening indoors the general rule should be to seek a cellar, a basement, or a ground floor room, and, where possible, these places should be at that side of the house which is furthest from the direction of the firing.

In each house within gun range of a hostile fleet a 'safety room' should be planned for emergency, and by a little forethought much can be done to minimise danger. Usually no more than one shell strikes the same dwelling house, unless it is very large, or prominent, or has some special significance for the bombarder.

If the basement of the dwelling house be selected for the shelter, it must be looked to as regards emergency exits, and if the number is limited, a pick, hammer and other implements should be stored there so that a way may be hacked out if necessary. Keep the garden tools there for instance.

With the non-basement and cellarless house the best must be done with a room on the ground floor most remote from the firing line. In this case rather more preparation is necessary. A shell may come through the roof and pierce the ceiling. Against this the best precaution is to lay mattresses and cloth on the floor of the room above. Of course, a big shell will not be stopped by a mattress, but it will give no small protection against the after-effects of an explosion. Whilst the family goes to the 'safety room' some one member should remain behind to make these preparations. He should draw all shutters in front of the house when the firing commences, lay mattresses on the floor above the shelter room, shut all doors, and if possible place a mattress against each window of the shelter room and against the door. Failing mattresses, take the bedclothes and other cloth articles and cover every weak spot, such as windows, doors and the wall nearest to the firing line.

We may now summarise the general precautions to be taken by each household in going into the shelter, whether cellar or ground floor:

1: Have candles, matches, food, water, clock and some tools in the room.

2: Gather the whole family there without delay.

3: Leave to one or two of the adults the work of clearing up as follows;

4: Draw all shutters, close all doors.

5: Turn off gas at the meter, turn off main electric switch.

6: Put out any oil lamps which may be burning.

7: Put water on the fires.

8: Pre-arrange with neighbours or police, what room you occupy. If houses adjoin try to establish some means of communication, as by knocking on the wall.

9: Place vessels filled with water in each room in case of fire.

10: If an explosion occurs let one member sally out to discover damage.

11: Await some public signal announcing that danger is over, or wait for half an hour after sound of firing has ceased.

If a bombardment breaks out at night it may not be feasible to take all these precautions, but by preparing a cellar or room beforehand much can be done in a few minutes. By allotting certain duties to each member of the family a vast amount of confusion will be avoided.

There remains the question of flight. During actual bombardment it is safer to stay indoors, especially if the simple precautions here outlined have been taken. People in dangerous buildings should however make for safer shelter at once. Should a shell fall near to a fugitive he should at once fling himself to the ground. Soldiers at the front become quite expert in dodging shells and they state that the force of the explosion is chiefly upwards. It also takes an outward or forward course from the direction fired. For example, if a shell comes from the east its lateral explosive force is principally directed westward.

Index A: Scarborough's Dead 1914

1: Index of those killed or died as a result of the bombardment.
2: Listed in alphabetical order, SURNAME, followed by available information.
3: All details relate to the bombardment of Wednesday, 16th December 1914, unless stated otherwise.
4: Where the hospital is mentioned it is the main hospital on Friar's Entry, unless stated otherwise.
5: Abbreviations used: B: Year/date of birth. D: Year/date of death.
6: Ages given are those at the time of the incident (i.e. December 1914) under which the entry is made.
7: Page numbers at the end of an entry indicate where the subject is mentioned in the text. The '(p)' indicates a picture.
8: Entries marked with an asterisk (*) contain their own explanatory notes.

Index B: Scarborough's Damage 1914 *(by name)*

1: Index of damage done and of those mentioned in the text.
2: Listed in alphabetical order, SURNAME, followed by available information.
3: All details relate to the bombardment of Wednesday, 16th December 1914, unless stated otherwise.
4: Where the hospital is mentioned it is the main hospital on Friar's Entry, unless stated otherwise.
5: Abbreviations used: B: Year/date of birth. D: Year/date of death.
6: Ages given are those at the time of the incident (i.e. December 1914) under which the entry is made.
7: Page numbers at the end of an entry indicate where the subject is mentioned in the text. The '(p)' indicates a picture.
8: Entries carrying the legend 'Gave account' indicate where an oral or written account has been provided.

ADDISON, John W. 5 Salisbury Street. Windows damaged.
AGAR, John Charles. 1 Wykeham Street. House damaged. Wife, Annie Elizabeth Watson, gave account. Son, Charles. *p61, p63.*
ALBEMARLE BAPTIST CHURCH, Albemarle Crescent. Reverend A. J. Burgoyne, Pastor. Built 1867. Seating for 750 people. West transept window struck, moulding chipped. *p69, p165.*
ALEXANDRA GARDENS, North Cliff. Gardens and bowling green. Opened 27.06.1908 by Mayor, Alderman Valentine Fowler. Gardens damaged. *p93.*
ALL SAINTS' CHURCH, Falsgrave Road. Roof and building damaged, west window broken. *p50(p), p51, p160(p) p225, p241.*
ALLAN, Mrs Ann. 23 Rosebery Avenue. Windows broken.
ALLISON, Mrs. 10 Spring Bank. Windows broken.
ALMA SQUARE BOARDING HOUSE, Alma Square. Damaged. *p69.*
ANDERSON, Alfred Ernest. Undertaker. Wife, Mary Elizabeth. 13 Granby Place, Queen Street. Gave account. *p208.*
ANDERSON, Frank. Fisherman. 3 Burr Bank, East Sandgate. Lost overboard from *Grace Darling*, 10.11.1914. *p141.*
ANDERSON, John. 2 Belgrave Terrace. Roof, upper storey and furniture badly damaged. *p51.*
ANDREWS, A. Member of Wireless Station Staff. *p54(p).*
ANDREWS, Mrs E. 40 Trafalgar Square. Half of house demolished. *p93.*
ARMSTRONG, Lawrence. Prep School Headmaster, Scarborough College, Filey Road. *p37, p204, p205, p206(p).*
ARMSTRONG, Percy. Headmaster, Scarborough College, Filey Road. *p37, p204, p205.*
ARNOLD, A. L. Music teacher. 118 Victoria Road. House severely damaged. *p71, p74(p).*
ARNOTT, F. 6 Prince of Wales Terrace. Windows broken. *p33.*
ASH, Mrs Rose. 57 Gladstone Road. House slightly damaged. Family fled town. Son, Ronald, age 10, gave account. *p81, p233.*
ASHLEY, T. A. P. Proprietor, Spa Boarding House, St Nicholas Parade. Seriously damaged. *p25, p262(p).*
ASKHAM, Mrs E. 40 Gladstone Street. Chimney, slates and guttering broken, fireplace demolished. *p83.*
ASTORIA BOARDING HOUSE, 51-56 Esplanade. Manageress: M. L. Constance. Damaged. *p35, p36(p).*
ASTROM, George. 14 York Place. Windows broken. *p70(p).*
ATKINSON, Byron. Bell Hotel, Bland's Cliff. Building severely damaged. *p21.*
ATKINSON, Charles. 1 Rothbury Street. Grocer at 45 Gladstone Road. Son, Harold Charles, age 23. D: 1980. Gave account. *p238, p239, p241.*
ATKINSON, H. Foreman at the Gas Works. 2 Gas House Cottages, Seamer Road. Missed by shell fragment. Gas holder holed. *p45.*
ATKINSON, Miss Mary. 39 & 41 Esplanade. Houses damaged. Visitors, Mrs Bell-Irving, from Scotland, and Bertha Lee, both wounded in legs, hospitalised, and both had one leg amputated. *p35.*
ATKINSON, V. 122 Falsgrave Road. Windows broken.

BAIN, Andrew. 51 St John's Road. Engineer's Manager. House badly damaged. Daughter, Lily, age 14, had narrow escape. *p52(p), p53.*
BAINBRIDGE, Misses. 8 York Place. Windows broken.
BAINES, Miss M. A. 8 Tindall Street. Windows broken.
BAKER, Frank. 7 York Place. Windows broken.
BAKER, Sarah E. 48 Esplanade. House badly damaged. *p35.*
BALMORAL HOTEL, 119 Westborough. Proprietor: Kirby. Building slightly damaged, windows broken. *p69.*
BANKS, Private R. 3rd King's Own Hussars. Wrote letter home. *p245.*
BARKER, Edythe. 129 North Marine Road. Wrote poem. *p249.*
BARKER, Miss E. 23 Esplanade. House damaged. *p33.*
BARLOW, Miss B. A. 26 Esplanade Gardens. Middle floor demolished. *p33.*
BARNES NURSING HOME, 47-49 Esplanade Road. Miss A. Greenwood, Matron. *p35.*
BARNES, Robert. 2 Coastguard Cottages, Paradise. Coastguard Leading Boatman. On duty at War Signal Station. *p17, p132(p).*
BARNETT, Edward. 5 Somerset Terrace. Roof damaged. *p29.*
BAYNES, Miss A. 85 Victoria Road. Windows broken, lower rooms damaged. *p71.*
BEAL, James William. Joiner. 28 Cambridge Street. Identified Alfred Beal at inquest. *p139.*
BEAN, Eugene. 21 Falsgrave Road. Windows broken.
BEAN, L. C. 42 Prospect Road. Manager for Thomas Laughton, Licensed Victualler. Building damaged. *p65.*
BEARDSLEY, Miss R. 17 Esplanade. House damaged. *p33.*
BEAUMONT, Robert. Manager, Grand Hotel, St Nicholas Cliff. Roof and rooms badly damaged. *p25, p27, p95, p105, p117, p199, p213, p230, p241 p269, p270(p), p284(p), p285.*
BEEFORTH, G. L. Justice of the Peace. 66 Esplanade. House damaged. Maid, Minnie Merrils had narrow escape. *p37.*
BELL, Alex. Builder. 61 Gladstone Street. Had near miss. *p79.*
BELL, Arthur. 1 Salisbury Street. Windows broken.
BELL, Edward. Asphalter. 2 Wrea Street. Works Foreman, doing street repairs on Burniston Road, was warned of attack by a stranger on 15.12.1914. *p121, p123.*
BELL, Mrs Mary M. 132 Falsgrave Road. Windows broken. *p53.*
BELL, Mrs. 9 Rosebery Avenue. Windows broken.
BELL, Sir Hugh. Lord Lieutenant of the North Riding of Yorkshire. Ironmaster and colliery owner. B: 10.02.1844, Walker-on-Tyne. Lord Lieutenant from 1906. D: 29.06.1931. *p144, p327, p328, p329, p330, p341.*
BELL-IRVING, Mrs. Visitor from Scotland wounded at Mary Atkinson's establishment, 39 & 41 Esplanade. Leg amputated. *p35.*
BENSON, Bentley. Wrote poem. *p215.*
BENTLEY, H. 3 Tindall Street. Slates damaged, windows broken. *p77.*
BERRYMAN, Henry. 17 West Square. Windows broken. *p69.*
BIELBY, J. Bielby & Company. 71 Victoria Road. Hay, straw and corn dealers. Premises damaged. *p71.*
BIELBY, Robert. 71 Victoria Road. Roof demolished, house damaged. *p71.*
BINNEY, E. Painter. 2 Brook Street. Roof, top bedroom, scullery and two doors damaged, windows broken. *p77.*
BINNS, Olive M. Age 16. Robin Hood's Bay. Gave account. *p208.*
BISSETT, Mrs A. 77 North Street. Bedrooms and sitting-room damaged. Family had narrow escape. *p87.*
BLACKBURN, Miss. 2 Belvedere Road. House damaged. *p41, p138(p).*
BOB. Guard dog and mascot at Wireless Station. Ran off when shelling started, found on the Racecourse. *p54(p), p55, p124(p), p243.*

BODDY, Miss. 6 Princess Royal Terrace. Headmistress, Queen Margaret's Girls School, Oliver's Mount Road. Building and grounds slightly damaged. *p41, p255.*

BODDY, W. H. 13 York Place. Windows broken.

BOLTON, Mrs E. Sheffield. Gave account. *p260.*

BOOTLAND, Edgar. 41 Gladstone Street. Room and interior wall damaged, windows broken. *p83.*

BOROUGH LAUNDRY, Beaconsfield Street. Elevator roof blown off, windows broken. *p47.*

BOROUGH POLICE FORCE, 5 Alga Terrace. South Cliff Station.

BOROUGH POLICE FORCE, Sandside. Foreshore Station.

BOROUGH POLICE FORCE, St Thomas Street, Central Police Station. PC Albert Oldroyd, Warrant Officer and Bailiff: Court of Record. Discovered body of Alice Painter on 14.12.1914. *p141.*

BOURNE, J. W. Gardener. 25 Harcourt Avenue. Windows broken.

BOWER, Albert. 36 Beechville Avenue. Windows broken. *p85.*

BOWMAN, Mrs Jane. 17 Spring Bank. Windows broken.

BOWMAN, Private. 5th Green Howards. Beaconsfield Street. Wounded, at the Electric Light Station, in ankles, thigh, wrist and head. Treated at Westborough Wesleyan Chapel hospital. *p47, p200(p), p210(p).*

BOYES, Miss A. 8 West Square. Windows broken. *p69.*

BOYNTON, George. Police Constable. North Riding Police Station. Sitwell Street. Expressed sympathy to relatives of John Hall. *p121.*

BRADLEY, Betsy. West Street. Wounds to head and abdomen. Taken to hospital. *p37.*

BRADLEY, John W. 39 Milton Avenue. Windows broken.

BRADLEY, Mrs Mary Ellen. 11 Asquith Avenue. Windows broken.

BRAMFITT, Miss. Sister of Alice Duffield, identified her at inquest. *p137.*

BRAND, Mrs. House badly damaged. 45 Seaton Terrace, Hibernia Street. *p83.*

BREX, Wells. Writer with the *Daily Mail* newspaper. *p149.*

BRIGGS, Mrs M. A. 39 Albemarle Crescent. Roof and upper storey damaged. *p69.*

BRIGGS, Thomas. Carter. Identified Margaret Briggs at inquest. *p139, p142.*

BRIGHAM, Mrs. Photographers. 20 Esplanade. Building damaged. *p33, p36(p).*

BRIGHTUM, Mrs Lucy. 19 Manor Road. Fled town. *p223.*

BROGDEN & WILSONS, Sussex Street. Scarborough Ironworks. Pattern chamber and models damaged. *p87.*

BROMET, Miss Elizabeth R. 21 Esplanade. House damaged. *p33.*

BROWN, Alfred E. 24 Rothbury Street. House badly damaged. *p83, p239.*

BROWN, J. W. Baker, Confectioner & Grocer. 110 Victoria Road. Windows broken.

BROWN, Mrs Georgina Eleanor. 34 Rothbury Street. Rear of house damaged. *p83.*

BROWN, Mrs Mary. 54 Ramsey Street. Rear of house and kitchen badly damaged. *p65, p217, p241.*

BROWN, Muriel (married name). Albion Road. Age 12. Gave account. *p247.*

BROWN, R. C. *Franklin Villa*, 6 St John's Avenue. Chemist. Hull Drug Stores, 3 Westborough. Roof and bathroom damaged, windows broken. *p55.*

BUCKETT, William. 26 Beaconsfield Street. Windows broken.

BUCKLE, Thomas E. 21 Kitchener Street, Haxby, York. Identified Mary Prew at inquest. *p139.*

BURGOYNE, Reverend A. J. Pastor. Albemarle Baptist Church, Albemarle Crescent. Built 1867. Seating for 750 people. West transept window struck, moulding chipped. *p69, p165.*

BURNETT, Misses. 17 York Place. Windows broken.

BURNISTON ROAD BARRACKS. Minor damage. *p95, p203.*

BURNS, George. 41 Harcourt Avenue. Windows broken.

BURNS, Iris. Daughter of Marion Outram, gave account. *p215.*

BURROWS, Henry Tate. 73 Eastborough. Wall, top storey, chimney stack and furniture damaged, windows broken. *p21.*

BURROWS, Mrs A. 7 West Square. Windows broken. *p69.*

BURTON, W. 11 Rosebery Avenue. Windows broken.

CAMERON, Mrs. 7 Spring Bank. House damaged. *p47.*

CAMMISH, Mary. Clarkson's Buildings, Longwestgate. Age 52. Wounded in neck. Taken to hospital. *p91.*

CAMMISH, Samuel. 14 Wykeham Street. Warehouseman for W. Morland, Sherwood Street. Narrow escape. *p77.*

CAMMISH, William. 54 Hoxton Road. Roof damaged. *p79.*

CAPPLEMAN, Johnson. Fisherman. 14 Ewart Street. Windows broken.

CARLTON HOTEL, 99 Westborough. Proprietor: John Charles Dickinson. Upper storey damaged. *p67.*

CARR, J. J. Painter & Decorator. 59 Victoria Road. Window broken.

CARTER, John W. 4 Albert Row. Outside walls and railings damaged, windows broken. *p89.*

CARTER, Mrs E. S. 12 York Place. Windows broken.

CARTER, Sidney. Businessman from Ravenscar. Travelled from Scarborough to Leeds. *p247.*

CASS, Fred. Linotype Operator. 17 Tindall Street. Windows broken.

CASTLEHOUSE BROTHERS. Motor Garage. 90-96 Victoria Road. Window broken.

CATLIN, W. Tenant, Olympia Picture Palace, Foreshore Road. Roof and café badly damaged. *p19, p21, p153(p), p272(p).*

CATLIN'S ARCADIA, South Foreshore Road. Roof damaged. *p21.*

CATTLEY, J. W. H. Manager, Palladium Picture Theatre, Foreshore Road. *p441.*

CAVE, John. 8 Church Street. Gave account. *p213.*

CENTRAL SCHOOL, Trafalgar Street West. Master: William T. Northorp. Mistress: Miss E. Craven. Infants' Mistress: Miss. M. Simpson. School built in 1873. Room for 1,800 pupils. Building hit and slightly damaged.

CHALMERS-PARK, J. Artist. Marine Parade. From Leeds. Flat and studio damaged. *p25.*

CHAMBERS, Miss Elizabeth. Milliner. 83a Victoria Road. Windows broken.

CHAPMAN, T. L. Joiner & Undertaker. 19 Auborough Street. Premises damaged. *p89.*

CHAPPELL, George N. Huddersfield, West Yorkshire. Wrote poem. *p267, p268.*

CHATWIN, E. W. *Oxenhope*, Stepney Road. Slates damaged, windows broken. *p51.*

CHRISTIAN, John. Fisherman. 21 Sandside. Wife, Maria, took in shipwrecked sailors. *p167, p169.*

CLARE & HUNT CHEMISTS, 2 South Street. *p28(p), p29, p30(p), p31, p139, p246(p), p247.*
CLARENCE GARDENS, Queen's Parade. Gardens damaged.
CLARKE, Miss. From Manchester. Housekeeper to Mrs J. S. Ingham, 26 Mayville Avenue. House destroyed. Buried under debris with owner. Both injured and hospitalised. *p85.*
CLARKE, Mrs Hannah. 6 Tindall Street. Windows broken.
CLARKE, Walter H. Clerk. 28 Beaconsfield Street. Windows broken.
CLARKSON, William. Baker & Confectioner. 13 Murchison Street. Employee, James Milnthorpe, found note left by Alice Painter on 14.12.1914. *p141.*
CLEVELAND FARMERS' DAIRY COMPANY, 81 Norwood Street. Windows broken. *p79.*
CLIFFE, Richard H. 43 Victoria Road. House badly damaged. *p71.*
CLUBLEY, William. 68 Commercial Street. House severely damaged. *p57.*
COATES, Alfred A. 69 Gordon Street. House damaged, windows broken. *p65, p244(p).*
COATES, Ida. Maid to Albert Prince Harrison, *Calthorpe House,* 141a Victoria Road. Harrison Brothers, Millers, Victoria Mills, Mill Street. *p249, p251, p253.*
COATES, Miss. 24 Westbourne Park. Windows broken. *p49.*
COATES, Mrs Hannah. 16 Avenue Road. House badly damaged. *p51.*
COCKERILL, Richard. 11 Spring Bank. Windows broken.
COE, George Frederick. 43 Norwood Street. Roof damaged, windows broken. *p73.*
COE, S. Shoe and Boot Repairer. 78 Victoria Road, on corner of Alma Parade. Employed Harry Harland who died of wounds on 26.12.1914. *p73.*
COLCLOUGH, Colin. 21 Asquith Avenue. Windows broken.
COLEMAN, Mrs. Employee of Tramway Company. Narrow escape on Falconer's Road. *p23.*
COLLINGS, Frederick Day. 31 Sherwood Street. Wife, Beatrice. Windows broken.
CONSTANCE, M. L. Manageress, Astoria Boarding House, 51-56 Esplanade. Damaged. *p35, p36(p).*
CONSTITUTIONAL CLUB, Huntriss Row. Steward: E. F. Nelson. Roof damaged, roof lights and reading-room window broken. *p23.*
COOK, FOWLER & OUTHET, 5 York Place. Windows broken.
COOK, Miss A. E. *Tower House,* 32 Esplanade. Windows broken. *p35.*
COOKE, Mrs A. 15 York Place. Joint tenants. Mitchell & Company, and Vernon Scarborough. Windows broken.
COOPER, Mrs Mary Ann. 24 Mayville Avenue. Walls damaged, windows broken. *p85.*
COOPER, Reverend Cecil. Vicar of St Mary's Parish Church, Castle Road. Vicarage at Belvoir Terrace badly damaged. *p29, p85, p158, p161.*
CO-OPERATIVE STORES BOOT SHOP, 176 Victoria Road, on corner of Belle Vue Street. Manager: Berthold Jenkinson. Premises badly damaged, windows broken. *p75, p76(p).*
CORDUKES, E. 2 Sherwood Street. Windows broken.
COTT, Frederick. 25 Sherwood Street. Windows broken.
COULTAS, David. Postman. Green Lane Farm, Scalby. Saw ships from Hayburn Wyke. *p11.*
COULTAS, Thomas. Stonemason. 27 Caledonia Street. Saw ships from Hayburn Wyke. *p11.*
CRABTREE, J. 56th Company, Army Service Corps. Wrote letter to Mayor. *p130.*
CRABTREE, Robert. 13 Asquith Avenue. Windows broken.
CRAVEN, Frederick. 8 Beaconsfield Street. Gave account. *p215.*
CRAVEN, J. H. Fishmonger. 150 Victoria Road. Windows broken.
CRAVEN, Miss E. Mistress, Central School, Trafalgar Street West. School built in 1873. Room for 1,800 pupils. Building hit and slightly damaged.
CRAVEN, William. 45 Albemarle Crescent. Rooms damaged. *p69.*
CRAWFORD, John. 24 Sherwood Street. Roof demolished, house damaged, windows broken. *p77.*
CRAWFORD. Caretaker, Gladstone Road School, Gladstone Road. Built 1890 for 1300 pupils. Main hall badly damaged, windows broken. Took children to cellar. *p79.*
CRITERION HOTEL, 49 Castle Road. Proprietor: Edward H. Newham. Roof damaged, windows broken. *p83.*
CROFT, John Francis. Town Farm, Gristhorpe. Gave account. *p201.*
CROFT, Mrs J. Draper. 82 Victoria Road. Windows broken.
CROFT, S. H. Joiner & Builder. 48 Castle Road. Windows broken.
CROOKS, John. 56 Wykeham Street. Copper damaged, windows broken. Daughter, Alice, taken to Scalby. *p63.*
CROSBY, John William. 61 St Thomas Street. Age 51. B: 16.12.1863. Tram Conductor. Shell cone in cradle of 16 month old son, Clifford. Roof and upper storey damaged. Wife, Margaret Jane. Daughter, Doris, age 7, gave account. Son, Bernard, age 3. *p87, p211.*
CROSBY, Lily. 10 Atlas Place. Age 22. Wounded in face and right shoulder. *p93.*
CROSSLAND. *Gresham House,* Queen's Parade. Rooms damaged, windows broken. *p93.*
CROW, William. 37 Harcourt Avenue. Windows broken. Wife, Mercy, gave evidence at inquest of daughter, Ada. *p135.*
CROWN GARAGE. John Smith, Garage Foreman. Crown Arcade, South Cliff. Crown Garage Yard. Roof damaged. *p39.*
CUNNINGHAM, 2565 Trooper Stanley Howard. Yorkshire Hussars. Age 16. B: 24.05.1898. Based at Scarborough. *p19, p168(p).*

DAGLISH, S. P. House Agent. 48 Londesborough Road. Rear of house badly damaged. *p50.*
DALTON'S BOOKSHOP, 69a Newborough. The book 'Imperial Germany' fell from shelves. *p127.*
DANIEL, A. M. 14 Royal Crescent. Assisted at the hospital.
DAVEY, Mrs L. 27 Westbourne Grove. Rear of house badly damaged. *p31.*
DAVIS, Trooper J. Yorkshire Hussars. Warned officers at Pavilion Hotel. *p17.*
DAVISON, F. Schoolmaster. 10 Harcourt Avenue. Windows broken.
DAVISON, Mrs. 8 Ewart Street. Windows broken.
DAVISON, Robert. Rulleyman. 99 Commercial Street. Daughter, Marjorie (later Hobson), age 12, fled to Scalby. Gave account. *p57, p259.*
DAWS, Captain E. J. 22 Raleigh Street. Commander of minesweeper/transport ship *John Sanderson.*
DEACON, George A. Toll Collector. 63 Tindall Street. Wrote poem. *p202.*

DEAN, Arthur. 8 Coastguard Cottages, Paradise. Chief Officer, Coastguard. On duty at War Signal Station. Gave evidence at inquests. *p54(p), p132(p), p133.*
DEARDEN, John. Builders' Merchant. Res: 21 Sherwood Street. Roof damaged, windows broken. Bus: 6-8 Sherwood Street. *p77.*
DEARLOVE, Mrs W. 17 Harcourt Avenue. Windows broken.
DELDAY, J. H. Draper. 50-52 Castle Road. Windows broken.
DENNIS, E.T.W. Printers. Westborough. Premises and stock damaged. *p67, p227.*
DENT, Thomas. Painter & Decorator. 15a North Street. Building damaged. *p87.*
DENT. Narrow escape. Westbourne Grove. House badly damaged. *p33.*
DERWENT, Norman. From Bradford, staying at 55 Holborn Terrace, Gladstone Road. House damaged. Jacket torn. *p80(p), p233, p238.*
DEVALL, Misses. 16 Raleigh Street. Front room and furniture damaged, windows broken. *p67.*
DEVLIN, John William. 76 North Street. Rear of house damaged. *p87.*
DICK, Dr James R. 6 West Street. On duty at hospital.
DICKINSON, John Charles. Proprietor, Carlton Hotel, 99 Westborough. Upper storey damaged. *p67.*
DIXON, John Thomas. Wife, Elizabeth. 7 Oxford Street. Chiffonier damaged, window broken. *p87, p256, p257.*
DIXON, Tyson. 24 Beaconsfield Street. Windows broken.
DOBSON, Joe. Whitesmith. 25a King Street. Rooms damaged. *p21.*
DOBSON, John W. 20 Ireton Street. Telegraph linesman. Father of George. House damaged. *p241, p243.*
DOBSON, Miss Constance. 35 Harley Street. Chimney damaged. *p57.*
DOBSON, Mrs. 15 Ireton Street. House damaged. *p241, p243.*
DOSDILL, Richard. 27 Beaconsfield Street. Windows broken.
DOUTHWAITE, George W. Baker. 58 Wykeham Street. Chimney, bedrooms, pantry and coalhouse damaged, windows broken. *p63.*
DOVE, Walter. Cabman. 39 Roscoe Street. Horse killed, stable and cab damaged. *p79, p125.*
DRAKE, Frank. Schoolteacher. 44 Ramsey Street. Wrote letter to family. *p65, p241, p243.*
DRAKE, Henry. Grocer. 22 Ireton Street. Windows broken. *p241.*
DRUMMOND, William. *Harlaxton,* 10 Alexandra Park. Boys' Master, Gladstone Road School, Gladstone Road. Built 1890 for 1300 pupils. Main hall badly damaged, windows broken. *p78(p), p79, p217, p223, p232(p), p233, p261, p265.*
DRYDALE, Richard. 2 Tindall's Lane.
DUFFIELD, John. 38 Esplanade. Wife Alice killed at Granville Private Hotel, 36-37 Esplanade. Gave evidence at inquest. *p35, p130, p137.*
DURANT, Wilfred. Royal Naval Volunteer Reserve. On duty at War Signal Station. *p132(p).*
DYDE, John. Master, Workhouse. 18 Dean Road. Building badly damaged. *p84(p), p85.*
DYER, Miss. 6 Spring Bank. Windows broken.

EAGLETON, Miss S. W. 113 Candler Street. Windows broken.
EAMAN, Miss. Eaman's Boot, Shoe & Hosiery Stores. 160 Victoria Road. Roof and furniture damaged, windows broken. *p71.*
EASTWOOD, Trooper James. Yorkshire Yeomanry. On duty at War Signal Station. *p132(p).*
EDEN, Frederick Paul. Joiner. 7 Brook Street. Age 33. Wounded in leg, neck and head at Co-operative stores new building. Given first aid by Lance-Corporal Bob Thompson. Hospitalised. *p75, p76(p), p88(p).*
EDMOND, Mrs. Age 90. Had narrow escape at 2 Wykeham Street. *p57, p58(p), p59, p60(p), p61, p125, p130, p131, p137, p223, p225, p226(p), p243, p250(p), p251.*
ELECTRIC SUPPLY WORKS, 6 York Place. Offices. Windows broken. *p200(p).*
ELECTRIC SUPPLY WORKS, Beaconsfield Street. Works premises at the top of Beaconsfield Street slightly damaged. Guard wounded. Resident Engineer, F. G. Holden. *p47, p200(p), p210(p).*
ELLIS, Reverend J. H. Curate of St Thomas's Church. Injured on Longwestgate. Treated by Dr Maingay. Recuperated at Nurse Robson's nursing home, Westborough. *p91, p229.*
ELLIS, William H. 46 Aberdeen Walk. House damaged. *p69.*
ELSDON, Christopher. Gardener. 17 Seamer Road. Greenhouses destroyed. *p47.*
EMERSON, Charles. Emerson's Boarding House. 5-6 Alfred Street. Windows broken. *p31.*
ENGLAND, R. J. Played organ at memorial service, St Mary's Parish Church, 19.12.1914. *p158, p161.*
EYRE, W. R. Chemist. 147 Falsgrave Road. House badly damaged, windows broken. *p53.*

FALSGRAVE FARM. Buildings damaged. Crater in field. *p57, p230(p).*
FALSGRAVE TEMPERANCE HALL, 143 Falsgrave Road. Windows broken. *p51.*
FAULDER, Miss C. 67 Gordon Street. Roof partly blown off. *p65.*
FAWCETT, Reverend G. T. Minister, St Sepulchre Street Primitive Methodist Chapel. 99 Castle Road. *p165.*
FAWCETT, T. M. Borough Accountant. 6 Park Avenue. Windows broken. *p50.*
FEETENBY, Mrs E. A. 52 Ramsey Street. Outhouse damaged, windows broken. *p65.*
FELL, Lily. 20 Hope Street. Gave account. *p256, p257.*
FINAN, J. Fireman. 35 Milton Avenue. Windows broken.
FINE ART SALOON, Marine Parade. Damaged. *p262(p).*
FISHER, C. 34 West Street. Roof and interior damaged. *p37.*
FISHER, George Edward. 11 Brinkburn Road. Rear of house and interior damaged.
FLEMING, William. 6 West Square. Windows broken. *p69.*
FLETCHER, George. Farmer. 16 Spring Bank. Furniture damaged, windows broken.
FLETCHER, John T. Plumber. 123 Victoria Road. Windows broken.
FLETCHER, William. 29 Esplanade. House damaged. *p33.*
FLETCHER. Worked for Leng, Milkman. Horse killed, Seamer Road, Scarborough.
FLETCHERS LIMITED, Meat Purveyors. 34 Victoria Road. Windows broken.
FLORAL HALL, North Cliff, Alexandra Gardens. Tenant: George Royle. Opened 1910. Re-opened after extensions, May 1912. Property of Corporation. Let during summer months for public entertainment and concerts. Building damaged. *p84(p), p93.*
FLOUNDERS, Marie E. (later Clifford). Gave account. *p285.*

FOREMAN, John. Baker & Confectioner. 98 Victoria Road. Roof, chimneys and top floor demolished, windows broken. Estimated damage £100. Appeared at inquest of Harry Frith. *p71, p139.*

FORSTER, R. H. Wrote poem. *p245.*

FOSTER, Mrs E. 20 West Square. House and bedroom damaged, windows broken. *p69.*

FOUND, T. Railway Porter. 10 Sherwood Street. Windows broken.

FOWLER, Miss. Mistress Queen Margaret's Girls School, Oliver's Mount Road. Building and grounds slightly damaged. *p41, p43, p279.*

GARTON, Ernest. Printer. 27 Stepney Avenue. Rear windows broken.

GARWOOD, Septimus. Butcher. 16 Tindall Street. Windows broken. Business: 32 Barwick Street.

GAWTHORPE, Lieutenant John. 8th Battalion, The West Yorkshire Regiment (Leeds Rifles) Territorials. *p285.*

GEER, B. Member of Wireless Station Staff. *p54(p).*

GELDARD, Miss A. E. *St Martin's Villa*, St Martin's Road. Interior damaged, windows broken. *p29.*

GENTLEMAN'S CLUB. Scarborough Gentleman's Club, 9 St Nicholas Cliff. Steward: James H. Rowden. Flat seriously damaged. *p23.*

GEORGE HOTEL, Newborough. Damaged. *p274(p).*

GIBSON, Ambrose Lord. 10 Park Avenue. Roof stripped and corner of house demolished. *p50.*

GIBSON, B. W. 19 Harley Street. South Bay bather. Gave evidence at inquests. *p13.*

GIBSON, J. M. 26 Westbourne Grove. Chimney and roof damaged. *p31.*

GIBSON, Mrs Jane E. 10 Tindall Street. Windows broken.

GILBANK, Albert. 18 Esplanade. House damaged. *p33.*

GILES, Dr Leonard. 4 Filey Road. On duty, with wife, at hospital.

GLADSTONE ROAD SCHOOL, Gladstone Road. Built 1890 for 1300 pupils. Boys' Master: William Drummond. Girls' Mistress: Gertrude Horsley. Infants' Mistress: Julia Pritchard. Caretaker: Mr Crawford, took children to cellar. Main hall badly damaged, windows broken. *p78(p), p79, p217, p223, p232(p), p233, p261, p265.*

GLAVES, Mrs. 17 Rosebery Avenue. Windows broken.

GOODS STATION. Signal box damaged.

GORBLE, Samuel. Tobacconist. 53 Castle Road. Windows broken.

GOUGH, David. 38 Albemarle Crescent. Roof damaged. Son, Stackwell, had narrow escape, coat and sovereign case damaged. *p69.*

GOULD, Reverend John. Minister of Westborough Wesleyan Chapel. 7 Avenue Road. Superintendent of Methodist Circuit and Chairman of York District. *p164.*

GOWAN, Alfred. 2 St Thomas Walk. Roof, wall and furniture damaged. *p87.*

GRAND HOTEL PICTURE HOUSE, Foreshore Road. Wall holed, interior damaged. *p21, p105, p117, p199, p213, p230, p241, p269, p270(p), p284(p), p285.*

GRAND HOTEL RESTAURANT, Foreshore Road. Severely damaged. *p105, p117, p199, p213, p230, p241, p269, p270(p), p284(p), p285.*

GRAND HOTEL, St Nicholas Cliff. Manager: Robert Beaumont. Roof and rooms badly damaged. *p24(p), p25, p27, p95, p105, p117, p199, p213, p230, p241, p269, p270(p), p284(p), p285.*

GRANVILLE PRIVATE HOTEL, 36-37 Esplanade. Proprietor: J. E. Truefitt. Alice Duffield killed on steps. Windows broken. *p35, p137.*

GRAY, G. 31 Harcourt Avenue. Windows broken.

GREEN, Frank. Ravenscar. Gave account. *p247, p249.*

GREENLAY, Henry. Vanman. 61 Murchison Street. Roof and chimney blown off, windows broken. *p65.*

GREENWOOD, Herbert. 1 Porrett's Lane. Age 29. Both legs broken by explosion at Kingscliffe Holiday Camp, 13 King Street. Premises severely damaged. *p21, p228(p), p266(p).*

GREENWOOD, Mrs A. Matron, Barnes Nursing Home, 47-49 Esplanade Road. *p35.*

GREGORY, Frank. Resident Manager, Londesborough Theatre & Picture House, 44 Westborough.

GREGORY, Miss Bertha. 4 Crown Crescent. Boarding house. Bedroom and furniture damaged. *p29.*

GRIERSON, W. T. Dentist. 74-78 Castle Road. House and laboratory damaged. *p83.*

GRIFFEN, Dr Walter. 1 Pavilion Terrace. On duty at the hospital.

HALLIDAY, George. Age 5. Asenby, near Thirsk. Wrote account. *p219.*

HALMPSHAW, William. Chemist. 44 Prospect Road. Wall damaged, front windows broken. *p65.*

HANDEL, Ernest. 12 Spring Bank. Windows broken.

HANSOM, Henry A. 6 Ewart Street. Windows broken.

HARAM, Thomas W. Clerk. 5 Candler Street. Wall and roof damaged. *p83.*

HARDGRAVE, Fred. Slater. 125 Victoria Road. Windows broken.

HARDGRAVE, Sydney. 3 Albert Row. Windows broken.

HARDGREAVES, Ernest. 15 Rosebery Avenue. Windows broken.

HARDING, Colin. Fisherman. Bridlington. Lost overboard from *Grace Darling*, 10.11.1914. *p141.*

HARDY, R. W. 166 Victoria Road. Windows broken.

HARLAND, George Charles. 52 Wykeham Street. Father of Henry 'Harry' Harland. *p73.*

HARLAND, John T. Postman. 47 Wykeham Street. Injured. *p63.*

HARLAND, John W. Coal Porter. 60 Wykeham Street. Windows broken. *p63.*

HARLAND, Walter. Wheelwright. 134 Falsgrave Road. Whipps Yard. Windows broken. *p53.*

HARPER, George. Furniture Remover. 81 St John's Road. Took refugees to Scalby. *p55, p259.*

HARRISON, Albert Prince. *Calthorpe House,* 141a Victoria Road. Harrison Brothers, Millers, Victoria Mills, Mill Street. Daughters: Audrey, Mabel, and Gertrude, age 27. Gertrude wrote letter to cousin in Canada. Training to be a nurse with St John Ambulance. Maid, Ida Coates. *p249, p251, p253.*

HARRISON, Mrs A. 97 North Marine Road. Chimney damaged, windows broken. *p93.*

HARRISON, Orderly Sergeant George M. 14th King's Hussars. Age 30. B: 12.09.1884. Gave account. *p202.*

HARRISON. St Nicholas Street. Roof damaged, windows broken.

HARROWBY, Misses. Cecil Boarding House. 34 Esplanade. House damaged. *p35, p225.*

HASTIE, Mrs Alice M. Grocer. 59 Eastborough. House badly damaged. *p21, p66(p).*

HAWKINS, G. H. Resident Manager, Opera House, St Thomas Street. Originally built as a circus. Altered and re-opened in July 1908.

HAWXWELL, Thomas. Jet Dealer. 2 Alma Parade. Business premises: Bland's Cliff. Stock damaged, windows broken. *p21.*
HEALD, Mrs. 8 Spring Bank. Age 74. Injured on head. Windows broken. *p47.*
HEALY, Mrs. 12 Sherwood Street. Windows broken.
HEELEY, F. 56th Company, Army Service Corps. Wrote letter to Mayor. *p130.*
HERBERT, Charles. 79 Commercial Street. Roof, walls and furniture severely damaged, windows broken. *p57, p212(p).*
HERBERT, Robert J. 25 Harley Street. Master, St Thomas's School, Longwestgate. Built 1896. Room for 371 children. Building slightly damaged, windows broken. *p91.*
HICK, Thomas. 14 Spring Bank. Windows broken.
HILL, Miss. *Kilburn House,* 40 Esplanade. Windows broken. *p35.*
HILL, Mrs. 1 Bath Terrace, Bland's Cliff. Damaged. *p20(p).*
HINCHEY, Mrs Elizabeth. Gladstone Road, 53 Holborn Terrace. Roof damaged. *p81, p238.*
HIRST, Captain John H. *Myrtle Bank,* Stepney Road. Windows broken. *p51.*
HIRST, George. 168 Victoria Road. Windows broken.
HIRST, Reginald V. 93 Falsgrave Road. Manager of Taylor's Drugstores, 91 Falsgrave Road. Roof damaged. *p53.*
HIRST, Thomas. Labourer. 43 Harcourt Avenue. Windows broken.
HOARE, Kate. 34 St Nicholas Cliff. Roof damaged. *p25.*
HOBSON, T. 3rd West Yorkshire Regiment. Wrote poem. *p255, p256.*
HODGSON, Marjorie. Age 10. Sister of Norman Hodgson. Granddaughter of Rose Jarvis. *p269, p271, p273, p275.*
HODGSON, Norman. Age 11. Witnessed 1914 & 1917 attacks. Grandson of Rose Jarvis. *p269, p271, p273, p275.*
HODGSON, W. G. 27 Sherwood Street. Windows broken.
HOLD, Benjamin. *West Leigh,* Stepney Road. Windows broken. *p51.*
HOLDEN, F. G. 4 Lonsdale Road. Resident Engineer, Electric Supply Works, Beaconsfield Street. Works premises at the top of Beaconsfield Street slightly damaged. Guard wounded. *p47, p200(p).*
HOLDEN, Harold. Royal Naval Volunteer Reserve. On duty War Signal Station. *p17, p132(p).*
HOLLINGS, Dr C. E. *Willow Dene,* Stepney Road. Windows broken. Attended John Hall. *p49, p51, p134.*
HOLLINS, H. H. Scarborough. Wrote poem. *p204.*
HOLMES, Mrs. *Albert House,* 1 Albion Road. House damaged. *p29.*
HOLTBY, Winifred. Pupil at Queen Margaret's Girls School, Oliver's Mount Road. Wrote account. *p41, p225, p275, p276(p), p277, p279, p281, p282(p), p283, p285.*
HOOKER, T. W. Fancy Dealer. Hooker's Fancy Warehouse. 7-11 Market Hall, Cross Street. Premises and stock damaged. Damage estimated at £20-£30. *p89.*
HOPPER, Albert E. Blacksmith. 2 Asquith Avenue. Windows broken.
HORD, John. Joiner. 19 Livingstone Road. Shell embedded in rear wall. *p67.*
HORLEY, Mrs E. 16 West Square. Windows broken. *p69.*
HORNBY, J. 56th Company, Army Service Corps. Wrote letter to Mayor. *p130.*
HORNBY, Robert. 11 Westwood. Wife, Constance. Son, William. Daughter, Lucy Ursula Surtees Hornby, aged 9, B: 20.12.1904, gave an account. *p257, p258(p).*
HORNSEY, John. 9 Elders Street. Chimney blown off. *p89.*
HORSLEY, Gertrude. Girls' Mistress, Gladstone Road School, Gladstone Road. Built 1890 for 1300 pupils. Main hall badly damaged, windows broken. *p79.*
HORSLEY, Thomas W. 10 Murchison Street. Corporation Employee. Daughter, Mary, age 21, wounded in leg and arm. *p65, p244(p).*
HOSPITAL, Friar's Entry. Roof damaged, slight interior damage. *p88(p), p447.*
HOWES, Mrs. 8 Harcourt Avenue. Windows broken.
HUBBARD, Thomas H. 16 Ewart Street. Windows broken.
HUDSON, Francis W. 7 Wrea Street. Roof damaged. *p83.*
HUGGAN, Halliday. *Crimbles Court,* Scalby. Took in refugees. *p57, p63, p259, p261.*
HUGHES, Llewelyn. 36 Ramsey Street. Chief Clerk for Birdsall, Cross & Black, Huntriss Row. Born North Wales. Wife: Elizabeth. Sons: Robert Llewelyn, age 5, B:31.03.1909, and Arthur. Daughters: Betty, Edith, and Irene. *p65, p214(p), p215, p216(p), p217, p218.*
HUNT & RUFF CHEMISTS, 81 Westborough. Windows broken. *p69.*
HUNTER, David. 76 Columbus Ravine. Cricket Coach.
HUNTER, Harry W. Police Constable. 72 Trafalgar Square. On duty War Signal Station. *p17, p19, p126(p), p132(p).*
HUNTER, J. H. Gas Stoker. 35 Stepney Avenue. Windows broken.
HUNTER, Robert. Builder. 14 Belle Vue Street. Roof and chimney blown off, windows broken. *p75.*
HUNTER, T. Flour & Corn Dealer. 7 Gladstone Road. House and shop damaged. *p81.*
HUTCHING, Miss. Mistress, Queen Margaret's Girls School, Oliver's Mount Road. Building and grounds slightly damaged. *p41.*
HUTTON, Dr James A. Borough Police Surgeon. 11 Albemarle Crescent. Examined body of Alice Painter on 14.12.1914. *p141.*
HYDE, Frederick. Reporter. 55 Holborn Terrace, Gladstone Road. House damaged. Also, Norman Derwent from Bradford, staying at home of Mr Hyde, jacket torn; and Miss M. White, escaped unharmed. *p80(p), p81, p233, p238.*

ILLINGWORTH, Harry Holden. Wydale Hall, Snainton. Took in wounded soldiers from Scarborough's hospitals to make room for bombardment wounded. *p91.*
INDUSTRIAL HOME FOR BLIND WOMEN, 13 Belgrave Crescent. Building damaged. *p51.*
INGHAM, Mrs J. S. 26 Mayville Avenue. House destroyed. Buried under debris with housekeeper, Miss Clarke, from Manchester. Both injured and hospitalised. *p85.*
INGLE, Robert. Coachman. 29 Tindall Street. Windows broken.
INSKIP, Mrs Maria. Antique Dealer. 19 Esplanade. House damaged. *p33.*
IRELAND, George. Waiter. 17 Church Stairs Street. Door damaged.
IRELAND, Henry. 64 Tindall Street. Wounded left shoulder. Taken to Westborough Wesleyan Chapel hospital.

JACKSON, C. H. Royal Crescent Lane. Roof blown off stables. *p31.*
JACKSON, Edwin. Farmer. Cliff Farm, Cayton Bay. *p237.*
JARAM, John. Builder & Contractor. 22 Esplanade. House damaged. *p33, p224(p).*

JARRETT, John R. 39 Tindall Street. Slates damaged, windows broken. *p77.*

JARVIS, Mrs Rose, and daughter Violet. *Neptune House,* 2 Neptune Terrace, 13 Foreshore Road. House badly damaged. *p20(p), p21, p271, p273, p275.*

JEFFERSON, Vasey. Milk Dealer. 20 Sherwood Street. Windows broken.

JENKINSON, Berthold. Manager, Co-operative Stores Boot Shop, 176 Victoria Road, on corner of Belle Vue Street. Premises badly damaged, windows broken. *p75, p76(p).*

JENNINGS, Driver John. RFA. Scarborough. Wrote letter home. *p204.*

JENNINGS, Sergeant William. RFA. Wrote letter home. *p6, p7.*

JENNINGS, Tyson. 15 Spring Bank. Windows broken.

JOHNSON, Mrs Ellen. 3 Harcourt Avenue. Windows broken. *p45.*

JOHNSON, Mrs S. A. 81 Victoria Road. Windows broken.

JOHNSON, Second-Lieutenant Stanley Morrell. Former pupil of Scarborough College. *p207.*

JOHNSTON, Robert Clarkson. Policeman (retired). 28 Rothbury Street. Father of Colour-Sergeant Johnston, King's Royal Rifle Corps, who gave an account. *p191, p192.*

JOHNSTONE, W. Member of Wireless Station Staff. *p54(p).*

KEAN, Miss. 23 Harcourt Avenue. Windows broken.

KEAST, C. Member of Wireless Station Staff. *p54(p).*

KEBLE, Mrs K. 6 Belvoir Terrace. House badly damaged. *p27, p110(p).*

KENT, Charles A. 12 Ewart Street. Windows broken.

KENT, Douglas W. 16 Beaconsfield Street. Windows broken.

KENT, Mary Ann. 10 Ewart Street. Windows broken.

KIDD, Matthew. Labourer. 22 Beaconsfield Street. Windows broken.

KIDD, W. M. Coal Dealer. 9 St John's Road. Windows broken.

KING, Martyn H. Printer. *Hope Cottage,* 32 Foreshore Road. Roof damaged. *p21.*

KINGSCLIFFE HOLIDAY CAMP, 13 King Street. Offices seriously damaged. *p21, p228(p), p266(p).*

KIRBY, Mrs Jane A. 3 Candler Street. Roof damaged, windows broken. *p83.*

KIRBY. Proprietor, Balmoral Hotel, 119 Westborough. Building slightly damaged, windows broken. *p69.*

KIRTLAN, Reverend E. J. B. Pastor, Queen Street Wesleyan Chapel. Built 1841. Renovated 1903. Seating for 1,400 people. Oldest Wesleyan Chapel in the town. Building damaged. *p89, p164.*

KITSON, J. 10 Grosvenor Crescent. House damaged. *p31.*

LAMB, Alfred. 170 Victoria Road. Windows broken.

LAND & COMPANY, William C. Grocers and Provision Merchants. 6-8 South Street. Premises damaged. *p29, p139.*

LANG. Archbishop of York, Memorial service, St Mary's Parish Church, Scarborough. 19.12.1914. *p158, p161, p316, p318.*

LARKIN, W. W. Borough Meteorologist. 9 Granby Place, Queen Street. Showed German visitors castle, 1913. *p174.*

LAUGHTON, Thomas. Licensed Victualler. Owner of 42 Prospect Road. Building damaged. *p65.*

LAWSON, J. 20 Beaconsfield Street. Windows broken.

LAYCOCK, Mrs. 67 Gladstone Road. Age 90. House badly damaged. Had to be helped away. *p81.*

LEE, Bertha. Visitor from Scotland wounded at Mary Atkinson's establishment, 39 & 41 Esplanade. Leg amputated. *p35.*

LEE, William. Tailor. Chairman of Burniston Parish Council. Watched ships sail towards Whitby. *p291.*

LENG, Edward. Milkman. 149 Victoria Road. Horse killed outside *Luxmount*, Seamer Road. *p49.*

LEWIS, Mrs A. 2 Harcourt Avenue. Windows broken.

LICKISS, Thomas. 4 Rosevale Terrace, Falsgrave Road. Warehouseman for W. Morland, Builders' & Plumbers' Merchant, Sherwood Street. Narrow escape at work. *p77.*

LIGHTFOOT, Mrs R. 40 Albemarle Crescent. Top storey badly damaged, windows broken. *p69.*

LIGHTFOOT, T. Joiner. 15 Tindall Street. Windows broken. Identified Edith Crosby at inquest. *p139.*

LINN, Fred. *Inkerman Villa,* 25 Seamer Road. House extensively damaged. *p44(p), p47.*

LINTON, Peter. 1 Beaconsfield Street. Windows broken.

LITTLE, Corporal Thomas. 1 Palace Hill. 5th Green Howards. Wrote letter to wife, Hannah. *p229.*

LITTLE, Dr. House surgeon. On duty at the hospital.

LONDESBOROUGH THEATRE & PICTURE HOUSE, 44 Westborough. Resident Manager: Frank Gregory.

LONDESBOROUGH, Lord William Francis Henry Denison. *Londesborough Lodge,* The Crescent. B: 30.12.1864. D: 30.10.1917. Lodge narrowly missed by shells. *p27, p147.*

LONDON & JOINT STOCK BANK LIMITED, 2 Alfred Street. Branch Manager: J. G. Martin. Windows broken. *p31, p36(p).*

LONSDALE, Thomas. Wrote poem. *p238.*

LORD, Mrs T. T. J. Tripe Dresser. 31 Albion Street. Roof damaged, windows broken. Niece and employee, Marion Outram, age 21, fled to Wombwell. Iris Burns, Marion's daughter, gave account. *p77, p215.*

LOUTH, J. 14 Friar's Gardens. Daughter, Nancy, age 15, helped at hospital, gave account. *p89.*

LUCCOCK, Thomas. 42 Gladstone Street. Greenhouse damaged, windows broken. *p83.*

LYSAGHT, S. R. Wrote poem. *p195.*

MAC'S CAFÉ, 36 St Nicholas Cliff. Proprietor: Mrs E. Whitaker. Roof holed, building damaged. *p25, p242(p).*

MACKARNESS, Venerable Archdeacon Charles Coleridge. St Martin's Road, Vicarage. Window broken. *p29, p163, p278(p).*

MACKWOOD, Fred. 14 Asquith Avenue. Windows broken.

MAINGAY, Dr Henry B. Surgeon. 33 Queen Street. On duty at hospital with wife, Kathleen. Son, Hugh, gave account. *p73, p91, p140, p229, p231.*

MAJOR, Arthur. Artist. 5 Harcourt Avenue. Windows broken.

MALTON, John. Secretary, Scarborough Brick & Tile Company Limited. *p44(p), p45.*

MARRINER, G. Fruiterer. Bow Street, 1 Columbus Ravine, opposite Merryweather's on Prospect Road, now Lower Prospect Road, Scarborough. Display window broken. *p63.*

MARSHALL & SNELGROVE, 4-11 St Nicholas Street. Drapers etc. Rear badly damaged. *p23, p242(p).*

MARSHALL, Miss M. E. 136 Falsgrave Road. Windows broken. *p53.*
MARSON, C. L. 56th Company, Army Service Corps. Wrote letter to Mayor. *p130.*
MASON, George. 6 Coastguard Cottages, Paradise. Coastguard Leading Boatman. On duty War Signal Station. *p19, p132(p).*
MASON, Richard. 19 Esplanade Gardens. Age 19. Wounded in both legs. Hospitalised. Leg amputated. *p33.*
MATSON'S TEMPERANCE HOTEL & BOARDING HOUSE, Westborough. Upper storey damaged. *p67.*
MAWMAN, J. W. 56a Hoxton Road. Roof damaged. *p79.*
MAWMAN, W. 3 Spring Bank. House damaged.
MCCALLOUGH, Mrs A. 153 Prospect Road. Owner of house in front of which Thomas Place, age 25, wounded left thigh Hospitalised at Westborough Wesleyan Chapel hospital. *p65, p244(p).*
MCCLOY, Sydney David. Scarborough College Prep School. Gave account. *p204, p205, p206(p), p207.*
MCGACHEN, G. S. *Luxmount*, Seamer Road. Horse killed outside (see Leng). House badly damaged. *p49.*
MCKINLEY, George. 94 Hampton Road. Wife, Alice, identified Leonard Ellis at inquest (sister-in-law). *p139.*
MCLAREN, Mrs. 45 Harcourt Avenue. Windows broken.
MEDLEY, J. Percival. Solicitor. 28 Westbourne Grove. Chimney and roof damaged. Appeared at inquest for relatives of Harry Frith. *p31.*
MERCER, Robert. 14 Sherwood Street. Windows broken.
MERRILS, Minnie. Maid at 66 Esplanade, for G. L. Beeforth, Justice of the Peace. House damaged, had narrow escape. *p37.*
MERRYWEATHER, George Hardwick. Shopkeeper. 43 Prospect Road. Wife, Emily, fatally wounded outside shop. *p63, p64(p), p130, p135, p136(p), p241, p455.*
MERRYWEATHER, Private Harold. Chapman Hotel, Blenheim Street. 5th Green Howards. Unveiled a portion of War Memorial in 1923. Brother-in-law of Emily Lois Merryweather. *p221, p455.*
METCALFE, Arthur. Painter. 3 Salisbury Street. House damaged. *p47.*
MICKLETHWAITE, J. L. 8 The Crescent. House damaged. *p27.*
MILBURN, W. Crossgates. Gave account. *p209.*
MILLIONS, John. 5 Spring Bank. House damaged.
MILNE, Mrs M. 14 Tindall Street. Windows broken.
MILNTHORPE, Henry E. 63 Murchison Street. House damaged, windows broken. *p67.*
MILNTHORPE, James. Employee of William Clarkson Baker & Confectioner, 13 Murchison Street. Found note left by Alice Painter on 14.12.1914. *p141.*
MILTHORP, Miss S. E. 130 Falsgrave Road. Windows broken.
MIRFIN, Mrs F. E. 3 West Square. Windows broken, *p69.*
MITCHELL & COMPANY, 15 York Place. Joint tenant. Windows broken.
MONCKTON-ARUNDELL, Honourable George. Captain. HQ Staff, 4th Cavalry Brigade. Wrote to Mayor. *p130.*
MONTPELLIER BOARDING HOUSE, Alfred Street. Upper storey badly damaged. *p31, p224(p).*
MOORE, Mrs A. M. 162 Victoria Road. Windows broken. *p75.*
MOORHOUSE, Mary Beatrice. 124 Falsgrave Road. House damaged, windows broken. Maid, Ada Crow, age 28, killed. *p53, p135.*
MORLAND, W. Builders' & Plumbers' Merchant. Sherwood Street. Warehouse and showrooms extensively damaged. *p77.*
MORLEY, Isaac. Plumber. 133 Victoria Road. Windows broken.
MOSEY, Captain William. Master Mariner & Bathing Inspector. 28 Falsgrave Road. Gave evidence at inquests. *p13, p51.*
MOTHERSDALE, Miss. 13 Tindall Street. Windows broken.
MULLETT, J. T. Wrote poem. *p263.*
MUNDY, Company Sergeant-Major T. 8th Green Howards. Wrote letter home. *p147.*
MUNICIPAL SCHOOL, Valley Road. Caretaker Francis W. Ogle took pupils to cellars. Roof and playground slightly damaged. *p31, p247, p297.*

NALTON, PC Harold. 6 Moorland Road. Gave first aid to John Wood. *p73.*
NAWTON, Detective Inspector George R. 42 Trafalgar Square. House badly damaged. *p93.*
NAYLOR & COMPANY, Coal Merchants. 129 Victoria Road. Windows broken. *p49.*
NAYLOR, Alfred. Coal Merchant. Naylor's Coal Yard. *Alice House*, Seamer Road. Windows broken. *p49.*
NELLIST, Thomas. Saw ships from Hayburn Wyke. *p11.*
NELSON, E. F. Steward, Constitutional Club, Huntriss Row. Roof damaged, roof lights and reading-room window broken. *p23.*
NELSON, Frank. 25 Beaconsfield Street. Windows broken.
NELSON, Jacob. 19 Harcourt Avenue. Windows broken.
NETTLETON, Henry. 53 Ramsey Street. Rear of house and furniture damaged, windows broken. *p65.*
NEWBY, C. W. North Eastern Stables. *Avondale,* 33 Sherwood Street. Wounded in eye. Windows broken. *p77.*
NEWHAM, Edward H. Proprietor, Criterion Hotel, 49 Castle Road. Roof damaged, windows broken. *p83.*
NEWHAM, Mark. Newham Brothers, Farmers. Scalby Hall. Gave account. *p219.*
NEWNES, James. 6 Harcourt Avenue. Windows broken.
NEWTON, John F. Publican, White Swan Inn, Main Street, East Ayton. Took in refugees. *p55, p122(p).*
NICHOLLS, Edwin R. 29 Beaconsfield Street. Windows broken.
NICOLL, Walter E. *Auchronie,* Manor Road. Secretary and Manager: Scarborough Tramways Company. Sheltered inside pile of tracks. *p123.*
NORMANDALE, James. Castle House garage, went to aid of George Harland Taylor on Albion Street. *p77, p137.*
NORMANTON, Fred. Hairdresser & Newsagent. 100 Victoria Road. House damaged, windows broken. *p71.*
NORTH CLIFF GOLF CLUB, Burniston Road. Course damaged. *p95.*
NORTH RIDING POLICE FORCE, Sitwell Street. Police Station, Major R. L. BOWER commanding.
NORTHORP, William T. Master, Central School, Trafalgar Street West. School built in 1873. Room for 1,800 pupils. Building hit and slightly damaged.
NORTON, Claude S. *Irton Manor,* Seamer. Shells destroyed 'planting'. *p45.*

O'CONNELL, Reverend Canon. Priest, St Peter's Roman Catholic Church, Castle Road. St Peter's Rectory. *p165.*

OATES, Miss A. M. C. Infants' Mistress, St Thomas's School, Longwestgate. Built 1896. Room for 371 children. Building slightly damaged, windows broken. *p91.*

OGDEN, F. Jobmaster. 32 Westbourne Park. Windows broken.

OGLE, Francis W. 110 Prospect Road. Windows broken. Caretaker of Municipal School. Took pupils to cellars. *p31.*

OLDROYD, PC Albert. Borough Police Force, Central Police Station, St Thomas Street. Warrant Officer and Bailiff: Court of Record. Discovered body of Alice Painter, 14.12.1914. *p141.*

OLYMPIA PICTURE PALACE, Foreshore Road. Tenant: W. Catlin. Roof and café badly damaged. *p19, p21, p153(p), p272(p).*

OPERA HOUSE, St Thomas Street. Originally built as a circus. Altered and re-opened in July 1908. Managing Director, Opera House Company: William Peacock. Resident Manager: G. H. Hawkins.

OUTRAM, Marion. Age 21. Niece and employee of Mrs T. T. J. Lord, Tripe Dresser, 31 Albion Street. Roof damaged, windows broken. Fled to Wombwell. Daughter, Iris Burns, gave account. *p77, p215.*

OVENDEN, H. Member of Wireless Station Staff. *p54(p).*

PAINTER, James Joseph. D: 22.08.1903. *p141.*

PALEY, George. 112 Prospect Road. Windows broken.

PALLADIUM PICTURE THEATRE, Foreshore Road. Manager: J. W. H. Cattley. *p441.*

PARKINSON, R. Y. 4 Spring Bank. Windows broken.

PAVILION HOTEL, Westborough. HQ for Yorkshire Hussars. Coping stones damaged. *p17.*

PAWSON, Reverend A. *Burleigh House*, 1 Highfield. Vicar of St James' Church. House badly damaged. *p49.*

PEACOCK, William. Managing Director, Opera House Company, Opera House, St Thomas Street. Originally built as a circus. Altered and re-opened in July 1908.

PEARCE, Dr. Throxenby Hall Convalescent Home. Throxenby Lane. Formerly part of the Londesborough Estates. House stood on site of the original Manor House, dating back to 1285. *p223.*

PEARCE, T. J. 10 Alma Square. Roof and walls damaged, windows broken. *p69.*

PEARSON, Alfred H. Joiner. 43 Stepney Avenue. Brickwork damaged, windows broken. Son, Charles, age 3, gave account. *p231.*

PENTICOST, A. Member of Wireless Station Staff. *p54(p).*

PEPPER, Mrs J. W. Sister of John Hall.

PERRY, J. Master Mariner. 126 Falsgrave Road. Windows broken.

PETCH, Arthur. 6 Belle Vue Street. Wife, Sarah Ann, injured in side. Wound stitched at home. *p73, p74(p).*

PETCH, W. T. Joiner, Contractor & Builder. 14 Belle Vue Parade. Business premises, Victoria Road, severely damaged. *p71, p274(p).*

PEXTON, W. H. 77 Falsgrave Road. Windows broken.

PHIPPS, Arthur. *Netley House*. 95 Victoria Road. Windows broken.

PICKERING, Mrs. 36 Gladstone Road. House severely damaged. *p81, p233.*

PICKERING, Taylor W. 2 Tindall Street. Windows broken.

PICKUP, Albert Edward. Scarborough Castle. Custodian. Age 53, B: 02.09.1861, D: 20.03.1946. Donkey, Topsy, fatally wounded. Wife, Emma Janine (née Handy), age 51, B: 23.09.1863, D: 19.04.1916; daughters, Doris Olga (later Waudby), age 15, B: 25.03.1899; Hilda Catherine, age 19, B: 18.05.1895, D: 03.02.1977; Madge Alberta (later Waudby), age 17, B: 27.09.1897, D: 06.08.1981; and Mildred Ena, age 13, B: 1901. *p19, p104(p), p446.*

PICKUP, J. F. Tinner. 3 Gladstone Road. Roof and upper rooms damaged. *p81.*

PLACE, John. Father of children at Westlands School. *p197.*

PLACE, Thomas. Age 25. Wounded left thigh, outside 153 Prospect Road. Hospitalised at Westborough Wesleyan Chapel hospital. *p65, p244(p).*

PORTEOUS, William. Joiner. 4 Asquith Avenue. Windows broken.

POST OFFICE, Aberdeen Walk. *p97, p99, p247.*

POSTILL, Edward. 6 Asquith Avenue. Windows broken.

POSTILL, Thomas. 3 Asquith Avenue. Windows broken.

POTTER, Private Herbert. 5th Green Howards. Age 17. Haxby, York. Gave account. *p99, p208.*

POWELL, Mrs V. 46 Albemarle Crescent. Windows broken. *p69.*

PRIMITIVE METHODIST CHAPEL, Gladstone Road. Roof badly damaged and minor interior damage. *p81.*

PRINCE OF WALES HOTEL, 30-31 Prince of Wales Terrace. Proprietor: Henry Furniss. Building damaged. *p32(p), p33, p199, p225, p281.*

PRITCHARD, Julia. Infants' Mistress, Gladstone Road School, Gladstone Road. Built 1890 for 1300 pupils. Main hall badly damaged, windows broken.

QUEEN MARGARET'S GIRLS SCHOOL, Oliver's Mount Road. Built 1859 as Princess Royal Hotel. Became Oliver's Mount School for Boys. Was opened by Archbishop of York on 23rd July 1901 as Queen Margaret's School for Girls. Winifred Holtby was a pupil during the war years. Miss Boddy, Headmistress. Miss Fowler, Mistress. Miss Hutching, Mistress. Building and grounds slightly damaged. *p41, p43, p225, p275, p276(p), p277, p279, p281, p282(p), p283, p285.*

QUEEN MARGARET'S HALL, 19 Filey Road. Miss Young. Halls of residence for Queen Margaret's Girls School. Building badly damaged. *p41, p225.*

QUEEN STREET WESLEYAN CHAPEL, Queen Street. Pastor: Reverend E. J. B. Kirtlan. Built 1841. Renovated 1903. Seating for 1,400 people. Oldest Wesleyan Chapel in the town. Building damaged. *p89, p164.*

RAILTON, E. Bond. Former Postmaster. 13 Lonsdale Road. Narrow escape. Age 79, B: 1836, D: 10.1915. *p41.*

RAILWAY STATION, Westborough. Damaged.

RAMM, William. 81 Commercial Street. House seriously damaged, windows broken. *p57.*

RANDALL, Mrs. *Wilton House*, 13a Bedford Street. House extensively damaged. *p69.*

RAW, Mr. Cayton. Reported shells. *p97.*

RAWDING, Thomas. Military Store Keeper. 3 Wykeham Street. Married, two children. *p63.*

REA, Walter Russell. MP. 7 The Crescent. House damaged. *p27, p110(p), p146, p328.*

REED, William. 52 Hoxton Road. Chimney and door damaged, windows broken. *p79.*

REEVE, Warrant Officer Lawrence Edward William. Coastguard Station, Castle Road. Age 49, B: 06.06.1865, D: 1919. On duty at War Signal Station, Castle Hill. Chief Officer in 1917. Gave evidence at inquests. 1918: in charge at Coastguard Station, Lundy Island. Wife, Martha Hazeldeen; daughter, Annie; sons Aubrey (gave account), Frank and Leslie. *p15, p17, p132(p), p445.*
REID, A. Member of Wireless Station Staff. *p54(p).*
REIXACH, José. 47 Esplanade. Windows broken. *p35.*
REVELEY, John T. Gasworks Labourer. 1 Asquith Avenue. Windows broken.
REYNARD, 22221 Private W. K. 8th West Yorkshires (Leeds Rifles). Gave account. *p285.*
REYNOLDS, William. 5 The Bolts, Sandside. Age 13. Two toes blown off, hospitalised. *p89.*
RICHARDSON, J. 25 St Thomas Street. Rear roof damaged, windows broken. *p87.*
RIDING, S. Fried Fish shop. 72 Castle Road. Roof and chimney damaged, windows broken. *p83.*
RIDLEY, Misses. Red Lea Boarding House. 1-5 Prince of Wales Terrace. House damaged. *p33, p225, p257, p278(p).*
RINES ARCADE, Castle Road. Plate glass window broken.
RINES, J. W. 56th Company, Army Service Corps. Wrote letter to Mayor. *p130.*
RINES, Mrs. *Normanhurst*, Valley Road. Roof damaged. *p31.*
RINGROSE, Hettie R. 71-72 Westborough. Nurse Robson. On duty at hospital. *p91.*
ROBERTS, A. W. Wrote poem. *p233.*
ROBINSON, Alfred Hind. Chairman of North Riding Police Court. *p120.*
ROBINSON, H. 65 Gordon Street. Roof, chimney, upper storey and furniture damaged, windows broken. *p65.*
ROBINSON, Miss A. 54 Castle Road. Bedroom damaged. *p83.*
ROBSON, Misses Alberta and Emily. 20 West Street. Third floor bedroom destroyed.
ROE, Thomas B. 9 York Place. Windows broken.
ROKEBY-HAILEN, J. C. Brighton. Wrote poem. *p259, p260.*
ROPER, PC Robert. 99 Queen's Parade, North Marine Road. Chimney blown off. *p93.*
ROWDEN, James H. 9 St Nicholas Cliff. Steward: Scarborough Gentleman's Club. Flat seriously damaged. *p23.*
ROWNTREE & SONS, 20-21 Westborough. Windows broken. *p67.*
ROWNTREE, Joshua. Solicitor. Justice of the Peace. 12 Ramshill Road. (3 Rawdon Villas). Wrote of John Hall. *p121, p221.*
ROWNTREE'S FURNITURE WAREHOUSE, Wooler Street. Building damaged, windows broken. *p83.*
ROYAL HOTEL, St Nicholas Street. Building damaged, windows broken. *p23, p148(p), p199, p241, p280(p).*
ROYAL NORTHERN SEA BATHING INFIRMARY & CONVALESCENT HOME, Foreshore Road. [Later, St Thomas's Hospital.] Patients moved. Building damaged. *p19, p167, p269, p271, p272(p) p273, p447.*
ROYLE, George. Tenant, Floral Hall, North Cliff, Alexandra Gardens. Opened 1910. Building damaged. *p84(p), p93.*
RUSSELL, John William. Grocer's Assistant. 38 Tindall Street. Gave evidence at inquests of Frith and Ellis. *p29, p139.*
RUSSELL, Mrs A. L. Wife of Chairman of Malton Urban Council. Organised help for refugees. *p123.*
RUTLAND ROOMS, North Place, off North Street. Mothers' Union Office chimney and room damaged. *p87.*
RYALLS, Jasper S. Engineer. 22 Westbourne Park. House damaged, windows broken. Grandson John Shields, age 14 months, son of George Ryalls, killed. Also killed, Miss Bertha McEntyre, age 42. George gave evidence at inquest. *p49, p52(p), p130, p131, p135, p137, p142.*

SALMON, J. Member of Wireless Station Staff. *p54(p).*
SANDERSON, Mrs. *Mount Lea*, 44 Filey Road. House badly damaged. Family fled to Pickering. Gave account. *p39, p211.*
SARGEANT, J. H. 108 Prospect Road. Windows broken.
SARONY and Company, 17 St Nicholas Street. Photographers. *p247.*
SAVILLE, Thomas. Traveller. 34 Lyell Street. Son, Cyril William, age 9, B: 17.05.1905, gave account. *p261.*
SAWDON, Charles. 1 Spring Bank. House damaged.
SAWDON, Marjorie. 14 Esplanade Gardens. Visitor, from Hull Road, Cottingham. Age 22. Wounded in neck and arm. Taken to hospital. *p33.*
SCALES, Mrs Alice. Boot & Shoe Dealer. 69 Victoria Road. Shop and house badly damaged. Mother of George, a Merchant seaman, slightly wounded, and of Robert. *p71.*
SCARBOROUGH COLLEGE, Filey Road. Windows broken, earth bank hit. *p37, p204, p205, p206(p).*
SCARBOROUGH CONVALESCENT HOME FOR CHILDREN, 84 Filey Road. Matron: Miss Stones. Garden shed blown to bits.
SCARBOROUGH TRAMWAYS COMPANY, Scalby Road. Secretary and Manager: Walter E. Nicoll. *p123.*
SCARBOROUGH WATERWORKS PUMPING STATION, Cayton Bay. Manager, George Sewell. *p43, p235, p237.*
SCARBOROUGH, Vernon. 15 York Place. Joint tenant. Windows broken.
SCARBROUGH BRICK & TILE COMPANY LIMITED, Seamer Road. Secretary: John Malton. Tower damaged. *p44(p), p45.*
SCOTT, Miss M. C. 38 Trafalgar Square. House badly damaged. *p93.*
SEABROOKE, Fred William. Chef. 19 Tindall Street. Windows broken.
SELLERS, Mrs Maggie. 26 The Bolts, Sandside. Wounded in thigh, taken to hospital. *p89.*
SEWELL, George. Manager, Scarborough Waterworks Pumping Station, Cayton Bay. *p43, p235, p237.*
SHARP, Mrs Bethel. 31 Norwood Street. Age 42. Wounded back and face. Taken to hospital. Mother of Millie, age 14. Wounded right arm. Taken to Westborough Wesleyan Chapel hospital. *p73, p274(p).*
SHAW, John. Grocer. 7 Carlton Terrace. Roof and upper rooms damaged, windows broken. *p33.*
SHAW, Mrs, of Retford, Nottinghamshire. Lived at Overton Terrace, Castle Hill. Age 5. Gave account. *p207.*
SHAW, Private H. Serving at No.2 Base Remount Depot, Le Havre, wrote letter home. *p208.*
SHEARING, Mrs. Acomb, York. Gave account. *p204.*
SHEPHERD, PC Robert. 6 Alga Terrace. Discovered body of Alfred Beal. Gave evidence at inquest. Found unexploded shell, Belvedere Road. *p39, p139, p140.*
SHEPHERDSON, Mrs M. A. 12 West Square. Windows broken, *p69.*
SHERWOOD, Miss E. 16 Sherwood Street. Windows broken.
SHIELDS, Frederick. 46 Prospect Road. Gateway, outer wall and sitting-room damaged. Windows broken. *p65.*
SHIELDS, William. Labourer. 13 Spring Bank. Windows broken.
SIDMAN, George. Jeweller. 1 Beulah Terrace. Injured forefinger.
SIDNEY, Mrs. Doncaster. Wrote letter. *p204.*

SIGSWORTH, Richard. Cab Proprietor. 8 Alfred Street. House damaged, windows broken. *p31.*
SIMPSON, Miss M. Infants' Mistress, Central School, Trafalgar Street West. School built in 1873. Room for 1,800 pupils. Building hit and slightly damaged.
SIMPSON, Mrs Hannah. 1 Albert Row. Windows broken.
SIMPSON, Mrs J. 10-11 St Thomas Walk. Roof and chimney damaged. *p87.*
SIMPSON, Mrs M. 33 Stepney Avenue. Windows broken.
SITWELL, Sir George and Lady Ida. *Wood End,* The Crescent. House damaged. Windows broken. *p27.*
SKELTON, J. W. Gardener. 19 St John's Road. House badly damaged. *p53.*
SLACK, William H. 16a St Nicholas Cliff. Brewer's Assistant. House damaged. *p25.*
SMAILES, Robert A. 33 Beaconsfield Street. Windows broken.
SMELT, T. Builder. 6 Clifton Street. Wounded head and wrist. *p83.*
SMITH, Captain Walter Cass. Harbour-Master. Vincent's Pier. Lighthouse and house damaged. *p94(p), p95, 96(p), p265, p269.*
SMITH, Charles. Antique & Silversmith. 4 South Street. Premises damaged. *p30(p), p31, p246(p), p247.*
SMITH, Charles. Butcher. 84 Victoria Road. Windows broken.
SMITH, Edwin. Greengrocer. 109 Prospect Road. Kitchen window broken. *p65.*
SMITH, Fred. Chauffeur to Dr Thornley. Assisted wounded chauffeur. Became Private Smith, Royal Flying Corps. *p127, p138(p).*
SMITH, John. Foreman, Crown Garage, Crown Arcade, South Cliff. Crown Garage Yard. Roof damaged. *p39.*
SMITH, Miss Czarena. Confectioner. 31 Raleigh Street. Door damaged, plate glass window broken. *p67.*
SMITH, Mrs Ellen. 41 Stepney Avenue. House and furniture severely damaged, windows broken. *p51.*
SMITH, Reverend E. Curate, St Saviour's Church, Gladstone Road. *p75.*
SMITH, Staff-Sergeant J. W. B. Army Service Corps (Mechanical Transport Section). Father of Fred Smith.
SMITH, T. J. 18 West Square. Roof severely damaged, windows broken. *p69.*
SMITH, Thomas. Fisherman. 24 Cook's Row. Father of Sydney, age 7, gave account. *p263, p265, p266(p), p267.*
SNOWDEN, Miss. 35 Rutland Terrace, Castle Road. House badly damaged. *p85.*
SOLLITT, A. G. 11 Tindall Street. Windows broken.
SOUTH CLIFF WESLEYAN CHURCH, Ramshill Road. Building damaged. *p29, p36(p).*
SOUTH STEEL BATTERY. *p102(p), p265, p267, p271.*
SOUTHWICK, J. H. Postman. 164 Queen's Parade, North Marine Road. Damage to lower rooms. *p84(p), p93.*
SPA BOARDING HOUSE, St Nicholas Parade. Proprietor: T. A. P. Ashley. Damaged. *p25.*
SPINK, H. Boot & Shoe Dealer. 142 Victoria Road. Windows broken.
ST COLUMBA'S CHURCH, Columbus Ravine. Building damaged. *p85.*
ST MARTIN'S ON THE HILL, South Cliff. Consecrated 1863. Damaged. *p29, p163, p225.*
ST MARY'S PARISH CHURCH, Castle Road. Vicar: Reverend Cecil Cooper. Curate: Reverend W. Owen Thomas. Roof damaged. *p17, p29, p85, p158, p161.*
ST PETER'S ROMAN CATHOLIC CHURCH, Castle Road. Priest, Reverend Canon O'Connell, St Peter's Rectory. *p165.*
ST SAVIOUR'S CHURCH, Gladstone Road. Curate: Reverend E. Smith. Badly damaged. *p75.*
ST SEPULCHRE STREET PRIMITIVE METHODIST CHAPEL, 99 Castle Road. Minister: Reverend G. T. Fawcett. Built 1866, on original site of first chapel of the denomination in Scarborough.
ST THOMAS'S SCHOOL, Longwestgate. Built 1896. Room for 371 children. Master: Robert J. Herbert, 25 Harley Street. Infants' Mistress: Miss A. M. C. Oates. Building slightly damaged, windows broken. *p91.*
STEAD, Robert. 7 Rosebery Avenue. House badly damaged, windows broken. *p47.*
STEELE, Mrs E. A. 4 Wykeham Street. Windows broken. *p61.*
STELLINGS, Fred. 2a Ewart Street. Windows broken.
STEPHENSON, Ambrose. 2 Spring Bank. Windows broken.
STEPHENSON, Mrs G. H. Railway Station-Master's wife, Malton. *p123.*
STEPHENSON, Mrs M. J. 47 Albemarle Crescent. Windows broken. *p69.*
STEVENS, Mrs Mary. 37 Stepney Avenue. Windows broken.
STEVENSON, Alfred. Coachman. 2 Salisbury Street. Windows broken. Wife: Diana Cecilia. Son: 2234 Private James Richard, 5th Green Howards. *pV(p), p23, p120.*
STEVENSON, George. Chauffeur. 1 Taylor's Yard, Friar's Entry. Wife, Sarah. Rear windows broken. *p89, p120, p231.*
STEWART, Mrs M. 120 Falsgrave Road. Windows broken.
STOBART, Mrs. 6 West Bank. Windows broken. *p47.*
STONES, Miss. Matron, Scarborough Convalescent Home for Children, 84 Filey Road. Garden shed blown to bits.
STOREY, Samuel. Commission Agent. 38 Londesborough Road. *p109.*
STORRY, Robert. 41 Seamer Road. Windows broken. *p47.*
STRANGE, Albert. 29 Westbourne Grove. Headmaster of School of Art, Municipal School. House damaged. *p31.*
STRINGER, Mrs A. Grocer. 74 Murchison Street. Fanlight and interior damage, windows broken. *p67.*
STUNNELL, Victor. Boy Scout attached to the Wireless Station. *p54(p).*
STURDY, Sergeant G. R. 16 Commercial Street. Meirut Division, Indian Army. Fiancé to Ada Crow. *p53, p135.*
SUMMERS BROTHERS, 15 North Street. Furniture Dealers. Building and stock damaged. *p87.*
SUTCLIFFE, Albert. 18 Sherwood Street. Windows broken.
SWIFT, Arthur. Tailor. 31 Beaconsfield Street. Windows broken.
SWIFT, Thomas. 4 St Thomas Walk. Tailor. Roof and chimneys damaged, windows broken. *p87.*

TATE, W. Plumber. 39 Harcourt Avenue. Windows broken.
TATHAM, Colonel C. J. W. *The Priory,* Valley Road. Windows broken. *p31.*
TAYLOR, Charles E. 36 Norwood Street. House severely damaged, landing and staircase blown away. *p73, p239.*
TAYLOR, Dr William Charles Everley. Surgeon. 34 Queen Street. Dr and Mrs Taylor on duty at hospital.
TAYLOR, George. Solicitor. Registrar of Court of Record and Borough Coroner. Clerk of the Peace. 2 Grosvenor Road. Office: 37 Queen Street. Conducted inquests. *p130, p131, p133, p134, p135, p137, p139, p140.*
TAYLOR, Jack. *Moss Dene,* Manor Road. Grocer, 20 Westborough. *p144, p244(p).*
TAYLOR, John. 45 North Street. Publican of Staffordshire Arms. Son, George Harold, age 15, killed.

TAYLOR, Mrs. *Rothsay House,* 32 Prince of Wales Terrace. Roof damaged. *p33.*
TEANBY, Walter. 30 Westbourne Park. Windows broken.
TEMPEST, Lieutenant-Commander Alec S. Signal boy on *HMS Lion.* Wrote account. *p287.*
TEMPLE, Mrs Mary A. 5 Albert Row. Outside walls and railings damaged, windows broken. *p89.*
TEMPLE, William. Fisherman. 43 Castle Road. Ex PC. Son, John, age 10, wounded in arm, taken to hospital. *p83.*
TENISON, Dr Adolf. Station Road, Scalby. Treated George Warley's baby girl. *p57, p261.*
THACKWRAY, Charles. 149 Falsgrave Road. Windows broken.
THACKWRAY, G. B. Teacher of Music. 52 Westborough. Windows broken.
THE RED HOUSE, Sitwell Street. Home for fallen girls founded by Lady Sitwell. Windows broken. *p55.*
THOMAS, Reverend W. Owen. Curate, St Mary's Parish Church, Castle Road. *p85, p158, p161.*
THOMPSON, Lance-Corporal Bob. Gave first aid to Fred Eden.
THOMPSON, Oliver. 10 Mount Pleasant. Scalby. Telephone Exchange. Served Royal Flying Corps. Wife, May. Son, Arthur, age 6. Daughter, May, age 4, gave account. *p241.*
THOMSON, Mrs. 5 Asquith Avenue. Windows broken.
THORNLEY, Dr J. H. Surgeon. 35 Esplanade Road. On duty at the hospital. *p127.*
THORNTON & WATERFALL. Owners: Waverley Temperance Hotel, 9 Westfield Terrace. Windows broken. *p69.*
THORNTON, Mrs E. 5 Belvoir Terrace. Windows broken.
THRUSTLE, John T. 65 Murchison Street. House damaged, windows broken. *p67.*
TINDALL, G. W. Limited. Clothiers. 89 Victoria Road. Windows broken.
TINDALL, Richard. 25 Prospect Road. Roof badly damaged. *p63.*
TINDALL, Robert L. 29 Sherwood Street. Windows broken.
TINDALL, Selina J. 1 Belvedere Road. House damaged. Maid, Edith Crosby killed. *p41.*
TINDALL, Thomas. Gardener. 103 Seamer Road. Windows broken.
TODD, Private Arthur H. 5th Green Howards.
TONKS, Miss Marie. *Belgrave Lodge,* 14 Belgrave Crescent. Windows broken. *p51.*
TOWER HOUSE, 32 Esplanade. Miss A. E. Cook. Windows broken, *p35.*
TOWN HALL, St Nicholas Street. Formerly St Nicholas House and Estate. Purchased by Borough in 1898. Borough Engineer's plans for alteration approved 1899. Town Hall opened July 1903. Building damaged. *p25, p148(p), p233, p241.*
TROUSDALE, Francis. 6 Gladstone Lane. House severely damaged. *p80(p), p81.*
TRUEFITT, J. E. Granville Private Hotel. 36-37 Esplanade. Windows broken. Alice Duffield killed. *p35, p137.*
TUGWELL, A. J. Hairdresser. Justice of the Peace. *Cheam House,* Cromwell Terrace. Roof of business premises at 35 St Nicholas Cliff damaged. *p25.*
TURNER, Charles S. 35 Tindall Street. Slates damaged, windows broken. *p77.*
TURNER, E. Joiner & Wood Carver. 26 Sherwood Street. Windows broken.
TURNER, G. F. 56th Company, Army Service Corps. Wrote letter to Mayor. *p130.*
TURNER, John Henry. Solicitor. *Dunollie,* 31 Filey Road. Gave evidence at inquest of maid, Margaret Briggs, age 30 (B: Huddersfield 1884), killed. *p37, p38(p), p39, p139, p140, p201, p205, p207, p213, p225, p239, p252, p253, p260.*
TURNER, Robert. 28 Sherwood Street. House, workshop and tools badly damaged, windows broken. *p77.*
TYMON, S. Fruiterer. 3 Brook Street. Windows broken.

USHER, George E. Grocer. 39 Gladstone Street. Wounded; piece of shell embedded in lip. House and interior damaged, windows broken. *p81.*

VARLEY, David. Fish Merchant. 21 Tindall Street. Windows broken.
VASEY, R. O. 56th Company, Army Service Corps. Wrote letter to Mayor. *p130.*
VASEY, Thomas E. Printer & Stationer. 83 Victoria Road. Windows broken.
VIOLETTA, Madame. Milliner. 87 Victoria Road. Windows broken.
VOSE & COMPANY, 13a Foreshore Road. Premises damaged. *p19, p20(p), p21, p273.*

WALKER, Mrs Kathleen. 14 Lonsdale Road. House badly damaged. *p41, p234(p), p257, p264(p).*
WALKER, Mrs M. A. *Ribblesdale,* Seamer Road. Windows broken.
WALKER, Thomas Baden. Age 14 (B: 14.05.1900).
WALLER, Henry S. Fish Dealer. *Ebor Villa,* 8 St John's Road. House badly damaged. *p53.*
WALLIS, John. 166 Queen's Parade, North Marine Road. Damage to lower rooms, windows broken. *p93.*
WALSH, James. 4 Coastguard Cottages, Paradise. Coastguard Boatman. On duty at War Signal Station. *p17, p132(p).*
WALTON, Victor. *Prospect House,* 24 Foreshore Road. Claimed shell that went through Vose's. *p21, p273.*
WARD, Arthur M. 25 Tindall Street. Windows broken.
WARD, Frank. 22 Sherwood Street. Windows broken.
WARD, George. *Coneysthorpe,* 11 Park Avenue. Lady in bed escaped unhurt. Wall damaged, windows broken. *p50.*
WARD, Miss M. 151 Falsgrave Road. Doors damaged, windows broken.
WARLEY, George. 71 Hampton Road. Baby daughter injured. Son, A. N. Warley, of Tunbridge Wells, gave account. *p57, p261.*
WARRINER, Robert. Special Constable. 23 Elmville Avenue. *p19.*
WATKINSON, Robert. 11 York Place. Windows broken.
WATSON, Catherine. Early arrival at Gladstone Road School. *p79.*
WATSON, Fred. 27 Prospect Road. Roof damaged, chimney knocked off. *p63.*
WATSON, Henry. 53 Westborough. House damaged. *p67.*
WATSON, Mrs. 6 Albion Road. Windows broken. *p29.*
WAVERLEY TEMPERANCE HOTEL, Thornton & Waterfall. 9 Westfield Terrace. Windows broken. *p69.*
WEBB, Albert. Age 28. Wounded thigh, leg and wrist. Taken to Westborough Wesleyan Chapel hospital. *p73.*
WEBSTER, Mrs Harriet. 163 Falsgrave Road. Wounded on hand. *p53.*
WEBSTER, Reginald. Gave account. *p286(p), p287, p289.*
WEBSTER, William. 77 Commercial Street. House damaged, windows broken. *p57.*

WEIGHILL, Lieutenant E. Hilary. 5th Green Howards. On guard at Wireless Station and Electric Supply Works. *p54(p), p210(p).*
WELBURN, PC W. 56 Falsgrave Road. Borough Police Force and Fire Station, Falsgrave Station. *p209.*
WELLS, Robert. Confectioner. 182 Victoria Road. House badly damaged. *p71.*
WESTBOROUGH WESLEYAN CHAPEL, Westborough. Minister: Reverend John Gould. Built 1862, seats for 1,260 people. Chapel basement used as hospital. *p47, p164, p253.*
WESTLANDS SCHOOL, 1-5 Westbourne Grove, and Trinity Road. Headmistress: Miss E. H. Wood. *p31, p197.*
WEYDALE HOUSE. Shell fell close by.
WHERRITT, G. Tobacconist. 2 Royal Hotel Shops, St Nicholas Street. Stock damaged, windows broken. *p25.*
WHITAKER, Mrs E. Proprietor, Mac's Café, 36 St Nicholas Cliff. Roof holed, building damaged. *p25, p242(p).*
WHITE SWAN INN, Main Street, East Ayton. Publican: John F. Newton. Took in refugees. *p55, p122(p).*
WHITE, E. T. 56th Company, Army Service Corps. Wrote letter to Mayor. *p130.*
WHITE, Frank A. Councillor. Esplanade Boarding Establishment. Belmont Road. Building and interior damaged, windows broken. *p33, p240(p), p278(p).*
WHITE, Jane. Age 55. Wounded in back. Taken to Westborough Wesleyan Chapel hospital. *p57.*
WHITE, John William. Age 77. Wounded head, nose and side. *p44(p), p49.*
WHITE, Miss M. Staying at 55 Holborn Terrace, Gladstone Road. House damaged. Unharmed. *p80(p), p233, p238.*
WHITE, Mrs M. 23 Beaconsfield Street. Windows broken.
WHITEHOUSE. Electrician. Workhouse, 18 Dean Road. Pieced together shell fragments. *p84(p), p85.*
WHITFIELD & Son. Chemist's. 6 Filey Road. Windows broken.
WHITFIELD, J. Solicitor. *Adelphi Chambers,* Westborough. Acted for Land & Company at inquest of Harry Frith. *p139.*
WHITWORTH, Mrs H. 39 Stepney Avenue. Windows broken.
WILCOX, R. J. 86 Victoria Road. Windows broken.
WILKINSON, Dr C. A. Surgeon. Acting Medical Officer of Health. 56 Gladstone Street. On duty at hospital. *p135.*
WILLIAMS, J. Member of Wireless Station Staff. *p54(p).*
WILLIAMS, John. Gardener. 18 Milton Avenue. Windows broken.
WILSON, F. C. 9 Spring Bank. Windows broken.
WILSON, J. W. Butcher. 102 Victoria Road. Front windows broken. *p71.*
WILSON, John F. Builder. 1 Belle Vue Street. Gave evidence at inquest of Mary Prew. *p75, p131, p139.*
WILSON, Mrs. 4 Harcourt Avenue. Windows broken.
WINN, Mrs J. R. 71 Eastborough. Roof damaged, windows facing sea broken. *p21.*
WINTERINGHAM, Mrs. 10 York Place. Windows broken.
WIRELESS STATION, Falsgrave Park. *p54(p), p55, p243.*
WITTUP, J. 19 Norwood Street. Roof and bedroom damaged, windows broken. *p71.*
WOOD, Arthur. 7 Hanover Road. Head book-keeper, Scarborough Electric Supply Company. Wounded in head. Fled town with wife and son, Clifford, age 12, also wounded in head. Gave account. *p69.*
WOOD, John. 4 Belle Vue Street. Age 11. Wounded in head, given up for dead three times, survived. Attended by PC Nalton. Taken to hospital. Son of John Wood. *p73.*
WOOD, Miss E. H. Headmistress, Westlands School, 1-5 Westbourne Grove and Trinity Road. *p31, p197.*
WOOD, R. D. 1 Candler Street. Roof damaged, windows broken. *p83.*
WOODALL, W. O. 11 The Crescent. Windows broken.
WOODHOUSE, George H. *Grasmere,* Seamer Road. Manager of North Eastern Window Cleaning Company. Windows broken.
WORKHOUSE, 18 Dean Road. John Dyde, Master. Building badly damaged. *p84(p), p85.*
WORSLEY, Sir William Arthington, Bart. Hovingham Hall. Gave account. *p123.*
WORSLEY, Sir William Arthington. 2nd Green Howards. Son of Sir William Arthington Worsley, Bart. *p123.*
WRAY, David. Grocer. 80 Victoria Road. Windows broken.
WRAY, Mrs A. 21 York Place. Windows broken.
WRIGHTSON, Alfred. Ironmonger. 140 Victoria Road. Windows broken.
WRIGHTSON, C. H. *Rosevear,* Seamer Road. House Agent. House extensively damaged. *p47.*
WROE, Violet. Girlfriend then wife (married 22.09.1920) of Harold C. Atkinson. *p239, p241.*
WYDALE HALL, Snainton. Harry Holden Illingworth. Took in wounded soldiers from Scarborough's hospitals to make room for bombardment wounded. *p91.*

YEOMAN, S. F. 34 Westbourne Park. Windows broken. Foreman of inquest jury. *p134, p140.*
YOUNG, E. Labourer. 22 Tindall Street. Windows broken.
YOUNG, Miss. Mistress of Queen Margaret's Hall, 19 Filey Road. Halls of residence for Queen Margaret's Girls School. Building badly damaged. *p41.*

Index C: Scarborough's Damage 1914 *(by street)*

1: Index of damage done and of those mentioned in the text.
2: Listed in alphabetical order, STREET, followed by name of owner or occupier and available information.
3: All details relate to the bombardment of Wednesday, 16th December 1914, unless stated otherwise.
4: Where the hospital is mentioned it is the main hospital on Friar's Entry, unless stated otherwise.
5: Abbreviations used: B: Year/date of birth. D: Year/date of death.
6: Ages given are those at the time of the incident (i.e. December 1914) under which the entry is made.
7: Page numbers at the end of an entry indicate where the subject is mentioned in the text. The '(p)' indicates a picture.
8: Entries carrying the legend 'Gave account' indicate where an oral or written account has been provided.

Aberdeen Walk, 46. ELLIS, William H. House damaged. *p69.*
Aberdeen Walk. POST OFFICE. *p97, p99, p247.*
Albemarle Crescent, 11. HUTTON, Dr James A. Borough Police Surgeon. Examined Alice Painter. *p141.*
Albemarle Crescent, 38. GOUGH, David. Roof damaged. Son, Stackwell, narrow escape, coat and sovereign case damaged. *p69.*

Albemarle Crescent, 39. BRIGGS, Mrs M. A. Roof and upper storey damaged. *p69.*
Albemarle Crescent, 40. LIGHTFOOT, Mrs R. Top storey badly damaged, windows broken. *p69.*
Albemarle Crescent, 45. CRAVEN, William. Rooms damaged. *p69.*
Albemarle Crescent, 46. POWELL, Mrs V. Windows broken. *p69.*
Albemarle Crescent, 47. STEPHENSON, Mrs M. J. Windows broken. *p69.*
Albemarle Crescent. ALBEMARLE BAPTIST CHURCH. Reverend A. J. Burgoyne, Pastor. Built 1867. Seating for 750 people. West transept window struck, moulding chipped. *p69, p165.*
Albert Row, 1. SIMPSON, Mrs Hannah. Windows broken.
Albert Row, 3. HARDGRAVE, Sydney. Windows broken.
Albert Row, 4. CARTER, John W. Outside walls and railings damaged, windows broken. *p89.*
Albert Row, 5. TEMPLE, Mrs Mary A. Outside walls and railings damaged, windows broken. *p89.*
Albion Road, 1. *Albert House.* HOLMES, Mrs. House damaged. *p29.*
Albion Road, 6. WATSON, Mrs. Windows broken. *p29.*
Albion Road. BROWN, Muriel (married name). Age 12. Gave account. *p247.*
Albion Street, 31. LORD, Mrs T. T. J. Tripe Dresser. Roof damaged, windows broken. Niece and employee, Marion Outram, age 21, fled to Wombwell. Iris Burns, Marion's daughter, gave account. *p77, p215.*
Alexander Park. Newly built house damaged.
Alexandra Park, 10. *Harlaxton.* DRUMMOND, William. Boys' Master, Gladstone Road School. *p78(p), p217, p223, p232(p), p233, p261, p265.*
Alfred Street, 2. LONDON & JOINT STOCK BANK LIMITED. Branch Manager: J. G. Martin. Windows broken. *p31, p36(p).*
Alfred Street, 5-6. EMERSON, Charles. Emerson's Boarding House. Windows broken. *p31.*
Alfred Street, 8. SIGSWORTH, Richard. Cab Proprietor. House damaged, windows broken. *p31.*
Alfred Street. MONTPELLIER BOARDING HOUSE. Upper storey badly damaged. *p31, p224(p).*
Alga Terrace, 5. South Cliff Station, BOROUGH POLICE FORCE.
Alga Terrace, 6. SHEPHERD, PC Robert. Discovered body of Alfred Beal. Gave evidence at inquest. Found unexploded shell, Belvedere Road. *p39, p139, p140.*
Alma Parade, 2. HAWXWELL, Thomas. Jet Dealer. Business premises: Bland's Cliff. Stock damaged, windows broken. *p21.*
Alma Square, 10. PEARCE, T. J. Roof and walls damaged, windows broken. *p29.*
Alma Square. ALMA SQUARE BOARDING HOUSE. Damaged. *p29.*
Asquith Avenue. *p45.*
Asquith Avenue, 1. REVELEY, John T. Gasworks Labourer. Windows broken.
Asquith Avenue, 2. HOPPER, Albert E. Blacksmith. Windows broken.
Asquith Avenue, 3. POSTILL, Thomas. Windows broken.
Asquith Avenue, 4. PORTEOUS, William. Joiner. Windows broken.
Asquith Avenue, 5. THOMSON, Mrs. Windows broken.
Asquith Avenue, 6. POSTILL, Edward. Windows broken.
Asquith Avenue, 11. BRADLEY, Mrs Mary Ellen. Windows broken.
Asquith Avenue, 13. CRABTREE, Robert. Windows broken.
Asquith Avenue, 14. MACKWOOD, Fred. Windows broken.
Asquith Avenue, 21. COLCLOUGH, Colin. Windows broken.
Atlas Place, 10. CROSBY, Lily. Age 22. Wounded in face and right shoulder. *p93.*
Auborough Street, 19. CHAPMAN, T. L. Joiner & Undertaker. Premises damaged. *p89.*
Avenue Road, 7. GOULD, Reverend John. Minister of Westborough Wesleyan Chapel. Superintendent of Methodist Circuit and Chairman of York District. *p164.*
Avenue Road, 16. COATES, Mrs Hannah. House badly damaged. *p51.*

Beaconsfield Street. *p47.*
Beaconsfield Street, 1. LINTON, Peter. Windows broken.
Beaconsfield Street, 8. CRAVEN, Frederick. Gave account. *p215.*
Beaconsfield Street, 16. KENT, Douglas W. Windows broken.
Beaconsfield Street, 20. LAWSON, J. Windows broken.
Beaconsfield Street, 22. KIDD, Matthew. Labourer. Windows broken.
Beaconsfield Street, 23. WHITE, Mrs M. Windows broken.
Beaconsfield Street, 24. DIXON, Tyson. Windows broken.
Beaconsfield Street, 25. NELSON, Frank. Windows broken.
Beaconsfield Street, 26. BUCKETT, William. Windows broken.
Beaconsfield Street, 27. DOSDILL, Richard. Windows broken.
Beaconsfield Street, 28. CLARKE, Walter H. Clerk. Windows broken.
Beaconsfield Street, 29. NICHOLLS, Edwin R. Windows broken.
Beaconsfield Street, 31. SWIFT, Arthur. Tailor. Windows broken.
Beaconsfield Street, 33. SMAILES, Robert A. Windows broken.
Beaconsfield Street. BOROUGH LAUNDRY. Elevator roof blown, windows broken. *p47.*
Beaconsfield Street. BOWMAN, Private. 5th Green Howards. Wounded at Electric Supply Works in ankles, thigh, wrist and head. Treated at Westborough Wesleyan Chapel hospital. *p47, p200(p), p210(p).*
Beaconsfield Street. ELECTRIC SUPPLY WORKS. Works premises at the top of Beaconsfield Street slightly damaged. Guard wounded. Resident Engineer, F. G. Holden. *p47, p200(p), p210(p).*
Bedford Street, 1. FRITH, Harry. Driver with W. C. Land & Company. Age 45. Killed on South Street. *p28(p), p29, p131, p139, p165.*
Bedford Street, 13a. *Wilton House.* RANDALL, Mrs. House extensively damaged. *p69.*
Beechville Avenue, 36. BOWER, Albert. Windows broken. *p85.*
Belgrave Crescent, 13. Industrial Home for Blind Women. Building damaged. *p51.*
Belgrave Crescent, 14. *Belgrave Lodge.* TONKS, Miss Marie. Windows broken. *p51.*
Belgrave Terrace, 2. ANDERSON, John. Roof, upper storey and furniture badly damaged. *p51.*
Belle Vue Parade, 14. PETCH, W. T. Joiner, Contractor & Builder. Business premises, Victoria Road, severely damaged. *p71, p274(p).*
Belle Vue Street, 1. WILSON, John F. Builder. Gave evidence at inquest of Mary Prew. *p75, p139.*
Belle Vue Street, 4. WOOD, John. Age 11. Wounded in head, given up for dead three times, survived. Attended by PC Nalton. Taken to hospital. Son of John Wood. *p73.*
Belle Vue Street, 6. PETCH, Arthur. Wife, Sarah Ann, injured in side. Wound stitched at home. *p73, p74(p).*
Belle Vue Street, 14. HUNTER, Robert. Builder. Roof and chimney blown off, windows broken. *p75.*
Belmont Road. WHITE, Frank A. Councillor. Esplanade Boarding Establishment. Building and interior damaged, windows broken. *p33, p240(p), p278(p).*

Belvedere Road, 2. BLACKBURN, Miss. House damaged. *p41, p138(p).*
Belvoir Terrace, 5. THORNTON, Mrs E. Windows broken.
Belvoir Terrace, 6. KEBLE, Mrs K. House badly damaged. *p27, p110(p).*
Belvoir Terrace. COOPER, Reverend Cecil. Vicar of St Mary's Parish Church. Vicarage badly damaged. *p29, p85, p158, p161.*
Beulah Terrace, 1. SIDMAN, George. Jeweller. Injured forefinger.
Bland's Cliff. ATKINSON, Byron. Bell Hotel. Building severely damaged. *p21.*
Bland's Cliff, 1 Bath Terrace. HILL, Mrs. House damaged. *p20(p).*
Blenheim Street, Chapman Hotel. MERRYWEATHER, Private Harold. 5th Green Howards. Unveiled a portion of War Memorial in 1923. Brother-in-law of Emily Lois Merryweather. *p221, p455.*
Bow Street, 1 Columbus Ravine. MARRINER, G. Fruiterer. Opposite Merryweather's on Prospect Road - now Lower Prospect Road. Display window broken. *p63.*
Brinkburn Road, 11. FISHER, George Edward. Rear of house and interior damaged.
Brook Street, 2. BINNEY, E. Painter. Roof, top bedroom, scullery and two doors damaged, windows broken. *p77.*
Brook Street, 3. TYMON, S. Fruiterer. Windows broken.
Brook Street, 7. EDEN, Frederick Paul. Joiner. Age 33. Wounded in leg, neck and head at Co-operative stores new building. Given first aid by Lance-Corporal Bob Thompson. Hospitalised. *p75, p76(p), p88(p).*
Burniston Road, Barracks. Minor damage. *p95, p203.*
Burniston Road. NORTH CLIFF GOLF CLUB. Course damaged. *p95.*
Burr Bank, 3. (East Sandgate). ANDERSON, Frank. Fisherman. Lost overboard from *Grace Darling*, 10.11.1914. *p141.*

Caledonia Street, 27. COULTAS, Thomas. Stonemason. Saw ships from Hayburn Wyke. *p11.*
Cambridge Street, 28. BEAL, James William. Joiner. Identified Alfred Beal at inquest. *p139.*
Candler Street, 1. WOOD, R. D. Roof damaged, windows broken. *p83.*
Candler Street, 3. KIRBY, Mrs Jane A. Roof damaged, windows broken. *p83.*
Candler Street, 5. HARAM, Thomas W. Clerk. Wall and roof damaged. *p83.*
Candler Street, 113. EAGLETON, Miss S. W. Windows broken.
Carlton Terrace, 7. SHAW, John. Grocer. Roof and upper rooms damaged, windows broken. *p33.*
Castle Road, 35 Rutland Terrace. SNOWDEN, Miss. House badly damaged. *p85.*
Castle Road, 43. TEMPLE, William. Fisherman. Ex PC. Son, John, age 10, wounded in arm, taken to hospital. *p83.*
Castle Road, 48. CROFT, S. H. Joiner & Builder. Windows broken.
Castle Road, 49. CRITERION HOTEL. Proprietor: Edward H. Newham. Roof damaged, windows broken. *p83.*
Castle Road, 50-52. DELDAY, J. H. Draper. Windows broken.
Castle Road, 53. GORBLE, Samuel. Tobacconist. Windows broken.
Castle Road, 54. ROBINSON, Miss A. Bedroom damaged. *p83.*
Castle Road, 72. RIDING, S. Fried Fish shop. Roof and chimney damaged, windows broken. *p83.*
Castle Road, 74-78. GRIERSON, W. T. Dentist. House and laboratory damaged. *p83.*
Castle Road, 99. ST SEPULCHRE STREET PRIMITIVE METHODIST CHAPEL. Minister: Reverend G. T. FAWCETT. Built 1866, on original site of first chapel of the denomination in Scarborough.
Castle Road, Coastguard Station. REEVE, Warrant Officer Lawrence Edward William. Age 49, B: 06.06.1865, D: 1919. On duty at War Signal Station, Castle Hill. Chief Officer in 1917. Gave evidence at inquests. 1918: in charge at Coastguard Station, Lundy Island. Wife, Martha Hazeldeen; daughter, Annie; sons Aubrey (gave account), Frank and Leslie. *p15, p17, p132(p).*
Castle Road. RINES ARCADE. Plate glass window broken.
Castle Road. ST MARY'S PARISH CHURCH. Vicar: Reverend Cecil Cooper. Curate: Reverend W. Owen Thomas. Roof damaged. *p29, p85, p158, p161.*
Castle Road. ST PETER'S ROMAN CATHOLIC CHURCH. Priest, Reverend Canon O'Connell, St Peter's Rectory. *p165.*
Cayton Bay, Cliff Farm. JACKSON, Edwin. Farmer. *p237.*
Church Stairs Street, 17. IRELAND, George. Waiter. Door damaged.
Church Street, 8. CAVE, John. Gave account. *p213.*
Clifton Street, 6. SMELT, T. Builder. Wounded head and wrist. *p83.*
Columbus Ravine, 76. HUNTER, David. Cricket Coach.
Columbus Ravine. ST COLUMBA'S CHURCH. Building damaged. *p85.*
Commercial Street, 16. STURDY, Sergeant G. R. Meirut Division, Indian Army. Fiancé to Ada Crow. *p53, p135.*
Commercial Street, 68. CLUBLEY, William. House severely damaged. *p57.*
Commercial Street, 77. WEBSTER, William. House damaged, windows broken. *p57.*
Commercial Street, 79. HERBERT, Charles. Roof, walls and furniture severely damaged, windows broken. *p57, p212(p).*
Commercial Street, 81. RAMM, William. House seriously damaged, windows broken. *p57.*
Commercial Street, 99. DAVISON, Robert. Rulleyman. Daughter, Marjorie (later Hobson), age 12, fled to Scalby. Gave account. *p57, p259.*
Cook's Row, 24. SMITH, Thomas. Fisherman. Father of Sydney, age 7, who gave account. *p263, p265, p266(p), p267.*
Cromwell Terrace, *Cheam House*. TUGWELL, A. J. Hairdresser. Justice of the Peace. Roof of business premises at 35 St Nicholas Cliff damaged. *p25.*
Cross Street, 7-11 Market Hall. HOOKER, T. W. Fancy Dealer. Hooker's Fancy Warehouse. Premises and stock damaged. Damage estimated at £20-£30. *p89.*
Crown Arcade, South Cliff. CROWN GARAGE. John Smith, Garage Foreman. Crown Garage Yard. Roof damaged. *p39.*
Crown Crescent, 4. GREGORY, Miss Bertha. Boarding house. Bedroom and furniture damaged. *p29.*

Dean Road, 18. WORKHOUSE. John Dyde, Master. Building badly damaged. Whitehouse, an electrician, pieced together shell fragments. *p84(p), p85.*

Eastborough. *p66(p), p68(p).*
Eastborough, 59. HASTIE, Mrs Alice M. Grocer. House badly damaged. *p21, p66(p).*
Eastborough, 71. WINN, Mrs J. R. Roof damaged, windows facing sea broken. *p21.*
Eastborough, 73. BURROWS, Henry Tate. Wall, top storey, chimney stack and furniture damaged, windows broken. *p21.*
Elders Street, 9. HORNSEY, John. Chimney blown off. *p89.*
Elmville Avenue, 23. WARRINER, Robert. Special Constable. *p19.*
Esplanade Gardens, 14. SAWDON, Marjorie. Visitor, from Hull Road, Cottingham. Age 22. Wounded in neck and arm. Taken to hospital. *p33.*
Esplanade Gardens, 19. MASON, Richard. Age 19. Wounded in both legs. Hospitalised. Leg amputated. *p33.*
Esplanade Gardens, 26. BARLOW, Miss B. A. Middle floor demolished. *p33.*
Esplanade Road, 35. THORNLEY, Dr J. H. Surgeon. On duty at the hospital. *p127.*

Esplanade Road, 47-49. BARNES NURSING HOME. Miss A. Greenwood, Matron. *p35.*
Esplanade, 17. BEARDSLEY, Miss R. House damaged. *p33.*
Esplanade, 18. GILBANK, Albert. House damaged. *p33.*
Esplanade, 19. INSKIP, Mrs Maria. Antique Dealer. House damaged. *p33.*
Esplanade, 20. BRIGHAM, Mrs. Photographers. Building damaged. *p33, p36(p).*
Esplanade, 21. BROMET, Miss Elizabeth R. House damaged. *p33.*
Esplanade, 22. JARAM, John. Builder & Contractor. House damaged. *p33, p224(p).*
Esplanade, 23. BARKER, Miss E. House damaged. *p33.*
Esplanade, 29. FLETCHER, William. House damaged. *p33.*
Esplanade, 32. COOK, Miss A. E. *Tower House.* Windows broken. *p35.*
Esplanade, 34. HARROWBY, Misses. Cecil Boarding House. House damaged. *p35, p225.*
Esplanade, 36-37. TRUEFITT, J. E. Granville Private Hotel. Windows broken. *p35, p137.*
Esplanade, 39 & 41. ATKINSON, Miss Mary. Houses damaged. Visitors, Mrs BELL-IRVING, from Scotland, and Bertha LEE, both wounded in legs, hospitalised, and both had one leg amputated. *p35.*
Esplanade, 40. *Kilburn House.* HILL, Miss. Windows broken. *p35.*
Esplanade, 47. REIXACH, José. Windows broken. *p35.*
Esplanade, 48. BAKER, Sarah E. House badly damaged. *p35.*
Esplanade, 51-56. ASTORIA BOARDING HOUSE. Manageress: M. L. Constance. Damaged. *p35, p36(p).*
Esplanade, 66. BEEFORTH, G. L. Justice of the Peace. House damaged. Maid, Minnie Merrils had a narrow escape. *p37.*
Ewart Street. *p47.*
Ewart Street, 2a. STELLINGS, Fred. Windows broken.
Ewart Street, 6. HANSOM, Henry A. Windows broken.
Ewart Street, 8. DAVISON, Mrs. Windows broken.
Ewart Street, 10. KENT, Mary Ann. Windows broken.
Ewart Street, 12. KENT, Charles A. Windows broken.
Ewart Street, 14. CAPPLEMAN, Johnson. Fisherman. Windows broken.
Ewart Street, 16. HUBBARD, Thomas H. Windows broken.

Falsgrave Farm. Buildings damaged. Crater in field. *p57, p230(p).*
Falsgrave Road, 4 Rosevale Terrace. LICKISS, Thomas. Warehouseman for W. Morland, Builders' & Plumbers' Merchant, Sherwood Street. Narrow escape at work. *p77.*
Falsgrave Road, 21. BEAN, Eugene. Windows broken.
Falsgrave Road, 28. MOSEY, Captain William. Master Mariner & Bathing Inspector. Gave evidence at inquests. *p13, p51.*
Falsgrave Road, 56. Falsgrave Station, BOROUGH POLICE FORCE and Fire Station. PC W. Welburn. *p209.*
Falsgrave Road, 77. PEXTON, W. H.Windows broken.
Falsgrave Road, 93. HIRST, Reginald V. Manager of Taylor's Drugstores, 91 Falsgrave Road. Roof damaged. *p53.*
Falsgrave Road, 120. STEWART, Mrs M. Windows broken.
Falsgrave Road, 122. ATKINSON, V. Windows broken.
Falsgrave Road, 124. MOORHOUSE, Mary Beatrice. House damaged, windows broken. Maid, Ada Crow, age 28, killed. Daughter of William Crow. *p53 , p135.*
Falsgrave Road, 126. PERRY, J. Master Mariner. Windows broken.
Falsgrave Road, 130. MILTHORP, Miss S. E. Windows broken.
Falsgrave Road, 132. BELL, Mrs Mary M. Windows broken. *p53.*
Falsgrave Road, 134. Whipps Yard. HARLAND, Walter. Wheelwright. Windows broken. *p53.*
Falsgrave Road, 136. MARSHALL, Miss M. E. Windows broken. *p53.*
Falsgrave Road, 143. FALSGRAVE TEMPERANCE HALL. Windows broken. *p51.*
Falsgrave Road, 147. EYRE, W. R. Chemist. House badly damaged, windows broken. *p53.*
Falsgrave Road, 149. THACKWRAY, Charles. Windows broken.
Falsgrave Road, 151. WARD, Miss M. Doors damaged, windows broken.
Falsgrave Road, 163. WEBSTER, Mrs Harriet. Wounded on hand. *p53.*
Falsgrave Road. ALL SAINTS' CHURCH. Roof and building damaged, west window broken. *p50(p), p51, p160(p), p225, p241.*
Falsgrave Road. Overhead tram lines brought down.
Filey Road, 4. GILES, Dr Leonard, (and wife) on duty at hospital.
Filey Road, 6. WHITFIELD & Son. Chemist's. Windows broken.
Filey Road, 19. QUEEN MARGARET'S HALL. Miss YOUNG. Halls of residence for Queen Margaret's Girls School. Building badly damaged. *p41.*
Filey Road, 31. *Dunollie.* TURNER, John Henry. Solicitor. Gave evidence at inquest of maid, Margaret Briggs, age 30 (B: Huddersfield 1884), killed. *p37, p38(p), p39, p139, p140, p201, p205, p207, p213, p225, p239, p252, p253, p260.*
Filey Road, 44. *Mount Lea.* SANDERSON, Mrs. House badly damaged. Family fled to Pickering. *p39, p211.*
Filey Road, 84. SCARBOROUGH CONVALESCENT HOME FOR CHILDREN. Matron: Miss Stones. Garden shed blown to bits.
Filey Road. SCARBOROUGH COLLEGE. Windows broken, earth bank hit. *p37, p204, p205, p206(p).*
Foreshore Road, 13. *Neptune House,* 2 Neptune Terrace. JARVIS, Mrs Rose, and daughter Violet. House badly damaged. *p20(p), p21, p271, p273, p275.*
Foreshore Road, 13a. VOSE & COMPANY. Premises damaged. *p19, p20(p), p21, p273.*
Foreshore Road, 24. *Prospect House.* WALTON, Victor. Claimed shell that went through Vose's. *p20, p273.*
Foreshore Road, 32. *Hope Cottage.* KING, Martyn H. Printer. Roof damaged. *p21.*
Foreshore Road. GRAND HOTEL PICTURE HOUSE. Wall holed, interior damaged. *p21, p105, p117, p199, p213, p230, p241, p269, p270(p), p284(p), p285.*
Foreshore Road. GRAND HOTEL RESTAURANT. Severely damaged. *p105, p117, p199, p213, p230, p241, p269, p270(p), p284(p), p285.*
Foreshore Road. OLYMPIA PICTURE PALACE. Tenant: W. Catlin. Roof and café badly damaged. *p19, p21, p153(p), p272(p).*
Foreshore Road. PALLADIUM PICTURE THEATRE. Manager: J. W. H. Cattley. *p441.*
Foreshore Road. ROYAL NORTHERN SEA BATHING INFIRMARY AND CONVALESCENT HOME. [Later St Thomas's Hospital.] Patients moved. Building damaged. *p19, p167, p271, p271, p272(p), p273.*
Friar's Entry. HOSPITAL. Roof damaged, slight interior damage. *p87.*
Friar's Gardens, 14. LOUTH, J. Daughter, Nancy, age 15, helped at hospital. *p89.*

Gladstone Lane, 6. TROUSDALE, Francis. House severely damaged. *p80 (p), p81.*
Gladstone Road, 3. PICKUP, J. F. Tinner. Roof and upper rooms damaged. *p81.*
Gladstone Road, 7. HUNTER, T. Flour & Corn Dealer. House and shop damaged. *p81.*
Gladstone Road, 36. PICKERING, Mrs. House severely damaged. *p81, p233.*

Gladstone Road, 53 Holborn Terrace. HINCHEY, Mrs Elizabeth. Roof damaged. *p81, p233, p238.*
Gladstone Road, 55 Holborn Terrace. HYDE, Frederick. Reporter. House damaged. Also, Norman Derwent from Bradford, staying at home of Mr Hyde, jacket torn; and Miss M. White, escaped unharmed. *p80(p), p81, p233, p238.*
Gladstone Road, 57. ASH, Mrs Rose. House slightly damaged. Family fled town. Son, Ronald, age 10, gave account. *p81, p233.*
Gladstone Road, 67. LAYCOCK, Mrs. Age 90. House badly damaged. Had to be helped away. *p81.*
Gladstone Road. GLADSTONE ROAD SCHOOL. Built 1890 for 1300 pupils. Boys' Master: William Drummond. Girls' Mistress: Gertrude Horsley. Infants' Mistress: Julia Pritchard. Caretaker: Mr Crawford, took children to cellar. Main hall badly damaged, windows broken. *p78(p), p79, p217, p223, p232(p), p233, p261, p265.*
Gladstone Road. PRIMITIVE METHODIST CHAPEL. Roof badly damaged and minor interior damage. *p81.*
Gladstone Road. ST SAVIOUR'S CHURCH. Curate: Reverend E. Smith. Badly damaged. *p75.*
Gladstone Street, 39. USHER, George E. Grocer. Wounded; piece of shell embedded in lip. House and interior damaged, windows broken. *p81.*
Gladstone Street, 40. ASKHAM, Mrs E. Chimney, slates and guttering broken, fireplace demolished. *p83.*
Gladstone Street, 41. BOOTLAND, Edgar. Room and interior wall damaged, windows broken. *p83.*
Gladstone Street, 42. LUCCOCK, Thomas. Greenhouse damaged, windows broken. *p83.*
Gladstone Street, 56. WILKINSON, Dr C. A. Surgeon. Acting Medical Officer of Health. On duty at hospital. *p135.*
Gladstone Street, 61. BELL, Alex. Builder. Near miss. *p79.*
Gordon Street, 65. ROBINSON, H. Roof, chimney, upper storey and furniture damaged, windows broken. *p65.*
Gordon Street, 67. FAULDER, Miss C. Roof partly blown off. *p65.*
Gordon Street, 69. COATES, Alfred A. House damaged, windows broken. *p65, p244(p).*
Gristhorpe, Town Farm. CROFT, John Francis. Gave account. *p201.*
Grosvenor Crescent, 10. KITSON, J. House damaged. *p31.*
Grosvenor Road, 2. TAYLOR, George. Solicitor. Registrar of Court of Record and Borough Coroner. Clerk of the Peace. Office: 37 Queen Street. Conducted inquests. *p130, p131, p133, p134, p135, p137, p139, p140.*

Hampton Road, 71. WARLEY, George. Baby daughter injured. Son, A. N. Warley, of Tunbridge Wells, gave account. *p57, p261.*
Hampton Road, 94. MCKINLEY, George. Wife, Alice, identified Leonard Ellis at inquest (sister-in-law). *p139.*
Hanover Road, 7. WOOD, Arthur. Head book-keeper, Scarborough Electric Supply Company. Wounded in head. Fled town with wife and son, Clifford, age 12, also wounded in head. Gave account. *p69.*
Harcourt Avenue, 2. LEWIS, Mrs A. Windows broken.
Harcourt Avenue, 3. JOHNSON, Mrs Ellen. Windows broken. *p45.*
Harcourt Avenue, 4. WILSON, Mrs. Windows broken.
Harcourt Avenue, 5. MAJOR, Arthur. Artist. Windows broken.
Harcourt Avenue, 6. NEWNES, James. Windows broken.
Harcourt Avenue, 8. HOWES, Mrs. Windows broken.
Harcourt Avenue, 10. DAVISON, F. Schoolmaster. Windows broken.
Harcourt Avenue, 17. DEARLOVE, Mrs W. Windows broken.
Harcourt Avenue, 19. NELSON, Jacob. Windows broken.
Harcourt Avenue, 23. KEAN, Miss. Windows broken.
Harcourt Avenue, 25. BOURNE, J. W. Gardener. Windows broken.
Harcourt Avenue, 31. GRAY, G. Windows broken.
Harcourt Avenue, 37. CROW, William. Windows broken. Wife, Mercy, gave evidence at inquest of daughter, Ada. *p135.*
Harcourt Avenue, 39. TATE, W. Plumber. Windows broken.
Harcourt Avenue, 41. BURNS, George. Windows broken.
Harcourt Avenue, 43. HIRST, Thomas. Labourer. Windows broken.
Harcourt Avenue, 45. MCLAREN, Mrs. Windows broken.
Harcout Avenue. *p45.*
Harley Street, 19. GIBSON, B. W. South Bay bather. Gave evidence at inquests.
Harley Street, 25. HERBERT, Robert J. Master: St Thomas's School, Longwestgate. *p91.*
Harley Street, 35. DOBSON, Miss Constance. Chimney damaged. *p57.*
Hibernia Street, 45 Seaton Terrace. BRAND, Mrs. House badly damaged. *p83.*
Highfield, 1. *Burleigh House.* PAWSON, Reverend A. House badly damaged. *p49.*
Hope Street, 20. FELL, Lily. Gave account. *p256, p257.*
Hoxton Road, 52. REED, William. Chimney and door damaged, windows broken. *p79.*
Hoxton Road, 54. CAMMISH, William. Roof damaged. *p79.*
Hoxton Road, 56a. MAWMAN, J. W. Roof damaged. *p79.*
Huntriss Row. CONSTITUTIONAL CLUB. Steward: E. F. Nelson. Roof damaged, roof lights and reading-room window broken. *p23.*

Ireton Street, 15. DOBSON, Mrs. House damaged. *p241, p243.*
Ireton Street, 20. DOBSON, John W. Telegraph linesman. Father of George. House damaged. *p241, p243.*
Ireton Street, 22. DRAKE, Henry. Grocer. Windows broken. *p241.*

King Street, 13. KINGSCLIFFE HOLIDAY CAMP. Offices seriously damaged. *p21, p228(p), p266(p).*
King Street, 25a. DOBSON, Joe. Whitesmith. Rooms damaged. *p21.*
King Street. HEALTH OFFICE. Premises damaged. *p21.*
King Street. RED CROSS HQ. Roof and upper storey seriously damaged. *p23, p70(p).*
King Street. WATERWORKS OFFICE. Shell embedded in wall. *p23.*
Kitchener Street, 21. Haxby, York. BUCKLE, Thomas E. Identified Mary Prew at inquest. *p139.*

Livingstone Road, 19. HORD, John. Joiner. Shell embedded in rear wall. *p67.*
Londesborough Road, 38. STOREY, Samuel. Commission Agent. *p109.*
Londesborough Road, 48. DAGLISH, S. P. House Agent. Rear of house badly damaged. *p50.*
Londesborough Road, Back. ELLIS, Leonard. Porter at Clare & Hunt's Chemists. Age 49. Killed on South Street. *p29, p131, p139, p246(p), p247.*
Longwestgate, Clarkson's Buildings. CAMMISH, Mary. Age 52. Wounded in neck. Taken to hospital. *p91.*
Longwestgate. ST THOMAS'S SCHOOL. Built 1896. Room for 371 children. Master: Robert J. Herbert, 25 Harley Street. Infants' Mistress: Miss A. M. C. Oates. Building slightly damaged, windows broken. *p91.*
Lonsdale Road, 4. HOLDEN, F. G. Resident Engineer, Electric Supply Works.
Lonsdale Road, 13. *Lawnside.* RAILTON, E. Bond. Former Postmaster. Narrow escape. Age 79. D: 10.1915. *p41.*
Lonsdale Road, 14. WALKER, Mrs Kathleen. House badly damaged. *p41, p234(p), p257, p264(p).*

Lyell Street, 34. SAVILLE, Thomas. Traveller. Son, Cyril William, age 9 (B: 17.05.1905) gave account. *p261.*

Main Street, East Ayton. WHITE SWAN INN. Publican: John F. Newton. Took in refugees. *p55, p122(p).*
Manor Road, 19. BRIGHTUM, Mrs Lucy. Fled town. *p223.*
Manor Road, *Auchronie*. NICOLL, Walter E. Secretary and Manager: Scarborough Tramways Company. Sheltered inside pile of tracks. *p123.*
Manor Road, *Moss Dene*. TAYLOR, Jack. Grocer, Westborough, 20. *p144, p244(p).*
Marine Parade. CHALMERS-PARK, J. Artist. From Leeds. Flat and studio damaged. *p25.*
Mayville Avenue, 24. COOPER, Mrs Mary Ann. Walls damaged, windows broken. *p85.*
Mayville Avenue, 26. INGHAM, Mrs J. S. House destroyed. Buried under debris with housekeeper, Miss Clarke, from Manchester. Both injured and hospitalised. *p85.*
Milton Avenue. *p45.*
Milton Avenue, 18. WILLIAMS, John. Gardener. Windows broken.
Milton Avenue, 35. FINAN, J. Fireman. Windows broken.
Milton Avenue, 39. BRADLEY, John W. Windows broken.
Moorland Road, 6. NALTON, PC Harold. Gave first aid to John Wood. *p73.*
Mount Pleasant, 10. Scalby. THOMPSON, Oliver. Telephone Exchange. Served Royal Flying Corps. Wife, May. Son, Arthur, age 6. Daughter, May, age 4, gave account. *p241.*
Murchison Street, 10. HORSLEY, Thomas W. Corporation Employee. Daughter, Mary, age 21, wounded in leg and arm. *p65, p244(p).*
Murchison Street, 13. CLARKSON, William. Baker & Confectioner. Employee, James Milnthorpe, found note left by Alice Painter on 14.12.1914. *p141.*
Murchison Street, 61. GREENLAY, Henry. Vanman. Roof and chimney blown off, windows broken. *p65.*
Murchison Street, 63. MILNTHORPE, Henry E. House damaged, windows broken. *p67.*
Murchison Street, 65. THRUSTLE, John T. House damaged, windows broken. *p67.*
Murchison Street, 74. STRINGER, Mrs A. Grocer. Fanlight and interior damage, windows broken. *p67.*

Newborough, 69a. DALTON'S BOOKSHOP. 'Imperial Germany' fell from shelves. *p127.*
North Cliff, Alexandra Gardens. FLORAL HALL. Tenant: George Royle. Opened 1910. Re-opened after extensions, May 1912. Property of Corporation. Let during summer months for public entertainment and concerts. Building damaged. *p84(p), p93.*
North Cliff. ALEXANDRA GARDENS. Gardens and bowling green. Opened 27.06.1908 by Mayor, Alderman Valentine Fowler. Gardens damaged. *p93.*
North Marine Road, 97. HARRISON, Mrs A. Chimney damaged, windows broken. *p93.*
North Marine Road, 99 Queen's Parade. ROPER, PC Robert. Chimney blown off. *p93.*
North Marine Road, 129. BARKER, Edythe. Wrote poem. *p249.*
North Marine Road, 164 Queen's Parade. SOUTHWICK, J. H. Postman. Damage to lower rooms. *p84(p), p93.*
North Marine Road, 166 Queen's Parade. WALLIS, John. Damage to lower rooms, windows broken. *p93.*
North Place, off North Street. RUTLAND ROOMS. Mothers' Union Office chimney and room damaged. *p87.*
North Street, 15. SUMMERS BROTHERS. Furniture Dealers. Building and stock damaged. *p87.*
North Street, 15a. DENT, Thomas. Painter & Decorator. Building damaged. *p87.*
North Street, 45. TAYLOR, John. Publican of Staffordshire Arms. Son, George Harold, age 15, killed. *p77.*
North Street, 76. DEVLIN, John William. Rear of house damaged. *p87.*
North Street, 77. BISSETT, Mrs A. Bedrooms and sitting-room damaged. Family had narrow escape. *p87.*
Norwood Street, 19. WITTUP, J. Roof and bedroom damaged, windows broken. *p71.*
Norwood Street, 31. SHARP, Mrs Bethel. Age 42. Wounded back and face. Taken to hospital. Mother of Millie, age 14, wounded right arm. Taken to Westborough Wesleyan Chapel hospital. *p73, p270(p).*
Norwood Street, 36. TAYLOR, Charles E. House severely damaged, landing and staircase blown away. *p73, p239.*
Norwood Street, 43. COE, George Frederick. Roof damaged, windows broken. *p73.*
Norwood Street, 81. CLEVELAND FARMERS' DAIRY COMPANY. Windows broken. *p79.*

Oliver's Mount Road. QUEEN MARGARET'S GIRLS SCHOOL. Built 1859 as Princess Royal Hotel. Became Oliver's Mount School for Boys. Was opened by Archbishop of York on 23rd July 1901 as Queen Margaret's School for Girls. Winifred Holtby was a pupil during the war years. Miss Boddy, Headmistress. Miss Fowler, Mistress. Miss Hutching, Mistress. Building and grounds slightly damaged. *p41, p43, p225, p275, p276(p), p277, p279, p281, p282(p), p283, p285.*
Oxford Street, 7. DIXON, John Thomas and Elizabeth (wife). Chiffonier damaged, window broken. *p87, p256, p257.*

Palace Hill, 1. LITTLE, Corporal Thomas. 5th Green Howards. Wrote letter to wife, Hannah. *p229.*
Paradise, 2 Coastguard Cottages. BARNES, Robert. Coastguard Leading Boatman. On duty at War Signal Station. *p17, p132(p).*
Paradise, 4 Coastguard Cottages. WALSH, James. Coastguard Boatman. On duty at War Signal Station. *p17, p132(p).*
Paradise, 6 Coastguard Cottages. MASON, George. Coastguard Leading Boatman. On duty at War Signal Station. *p19, p132(p).*
Paradise, 8 Coastguard Cottages. DEAN, Arthur. Chief Officer, Coastguard. On duty at War Signal Station. Gave evidence at inquests. *p54(p), p132(p), p133.*
Park Avenue, 6. FAWCETT, T. M. Borough Accountant. Windows broken. *p50.*
Park Avenue, 10. GIBSON, Ambrose Lord. Roof stripped and corner of house demolished. *p50.*
Park Avenue, 11. *Coneysthorpe*. WARD, George. Lady in bed escaped unhurt. Wall damaged, windows broken. *p50.*
Pavilion Terrace, 1. GRIFFEN, Dr Walter. On duty at the hospital.
Peasholm Park. Shell fell in boating lake, blew up ducks.
Porrett's Lane, 1. GREENWOOD, Herbert. Age 29. Both legs broken by explosion at Kingscliffe Holiday Camp, 13 King Street. Premises severely damaged. *p21, p228(p), p266(p).*
Prince of Wales Terrace, 1-5. RIDLEY, Misses. Red Lea Boarding House. House damaged. *p33, p225, p257, p278(p).*
Prince of Wales Terrace, 6. ARNOTT, F. Windows broken. *p33.*
Prince of Wales Terrace, 30-31. PRINCE OF WALES HOTEL. Proprietor: Henry Furniss. Building damaged. *p32(p), p33, p199, p225, p281.*
Prince of Wales Terrace, 32. *Rothsay House*. TAYLOR, Mrs. Roof damaged. *p33.*
Princess Royal Terrace, 6. BODDY, Miss. Headmistress, Queen Margaret's School for Girls, Oliver's Mount Road. *p41, p225.*
Prospect Road, 25. TINDALL, Richard. Roof badly damaged. *p63.*
Prospect Road, 27. WATSON, Fred. Roof damaged, chimney knocked off. *p63.*
Prospect Road, 42. BEAN, L. C. Manager for Thomas LAUGHTON, Licensed Victualler. Building damaged. *p65.*
Prospect Road, 44. HALMPSHAW, William. Chemist. Wall damaged, front windows broken. *p65.*
Prospect Road, 46. SHIELDS, Frederick. Gateway, outer wall and sitting-room damaged. Windows broken. *p65.*
Prospect Road, 108. SARGEANT, J. H. Windows broken.

Prospect Road, 109. SMITH, Edwin. Greengrocer. Kitchen window broken.
Prospect Road, 110. OGLE, Francis W. Caretaker of Municipal School. Windows broken. Took pupils to cellars. *p31.*
Prospect Road, 112. PALEY, George. Windows broken.
Prospect Road, 153. MCCALLOUGH, Mrs A. Owner of house in front of which Thomas Place, age 25, wounded left thigh. Hospitalised at Westborough Wesleyan Chapel hospital. *p65, p244(p).*

Queen Street, 9 Granby Place. LARKIN, W. W. Borough Meteorologist. Showed German visitors castle, 1913. *p174.*
Queen Street, 13 Granby Place. ANDERSON, Alfred Ernest. Wife, Mary Elizabeth. Undertaker. Gave account. *p208.*
Queen Street, 33. MAINGAY, Dr Henry B. Surgeon. On duty at hospital with wife, Kathleen. Son, Hugh, gave account. *p73, p91, p140, p229, p231.*
Queen Street, 34. TAYLOR, Dr William Charles Everley. Surgeon. Dr and Mrs Taylor on duty at hospital.
Queen Street. QUEEN STREET WESLEYAN CHAPEL. Pastor: Reverend E. J. B. Kirtlan. Built 1841. Renovated 1903. Seating for 1,400 people. Oldest Wesleyan Chapel in the town. Building damaged. *p89, p164.*
Queen's Parade. CLARENCE GARDENS. Gardens damaged.
Queen's Parade. *Gresham House.* CROSSLAND. Rooms damaged, windows broken. *p93.*

Raleigh Street, 16. DEVALL, Misses. Front room and furniture damaged, windows broken. *p67.*
Raleigh Street, 22. DAWS, Captain E. J. Commander of minesweeper/transport ship *John Sanderson. p122(p).*
Raleigh Street, 31. SMITH, Miss Czarena. Confectioner. Door damaged, plate glass window broken. *p67.*
Ramsey Street, 36. HUGHES, Llewelyn. Chief Clerk for Birdsall, Cross & Black, Huntriss Row. Born North Wales. Wife: Elizabeth. Sons: Robert Llewelyn, age 5, B:31.03.1909, and Arthur. Daughters: Betty, Edith, and Irene. *p65, p214(p), p215, p216(p), p217, p218.*
Ramsey Street, 44. DRAKE, Frank. Schoolteacher. Wrote account to family. *p65, p241, p243.*
Ramsey Street, 52. FEETENBY, Mrs E. A. Outhouse damaged, windows broken. *p65.*
Ramsey Street, 53. NETTLETON, Henry. Rear of house and furniture damaged, windows broken. *p65.*
Ramsey Street, 54. BROWN, Mrs Mary. Rear of house and kitchen badly damaged. *p65, p217, p241.*
Ramshill Road, 12. (3 Rawdon Villas). ROWNTREE, Joshua. Solicitor. Justice of the Peace. Wrote of John Hall. *p121.*
Ramshill Road. SOUTH CLIFF WESLEYAN CHURCH. Building damaged. *p29, p36(p).*
Roscoe Street, 39. DOVE, Walter. Cabman. Horse killed, stable and cab damaged. *p79, p125.*
Rosebery Avenue. *p47.*
Rosebery Avenue, 7. STEAD, Robert. House badly damaged, windows broken. *p47.*
Rosebery Avenue, 9. BELL, Mrs. Windows broken.
Rosebery Avenue, 11. BURTON, W. Windows broken.
Rosebery Avenue, 15. HARDGREAVES, Ernest. Windows broken.
Rosebery Avenue, 17. GLAVES, Mrs. Windows broken.
Rosebery Avenue, 23. ALLAN, Mrs Ann. Windows broken.
Rothbury Street, 1. ATKINSON, Charles. Grocer at 45 Gladstone Road. Son, Harold Charles, age 23, D: 1980 (Age 89), gave account. *p238, p239, p241.*
Rothbury Street, 24. BROWN, Alfred E. House badly damaged. *p83, p239.*
Rothbury Street, 28. JOHNSTON, Robert Clarkson. Policeman (retired). Father of Colour-Sergeant Johnston, King's Royal Rifle Corps, who gave an account.
Rothbury Street, 34. BROWN, Mrs Georgina Eleanor. Rear of house damaged. *p83.*
Royal Crescent Lane. JACKSON, C. H. Roof blown off stables. *p31.*
Royal Crescent, 14. DANIEL, A. M. Assisted at the hospital.

Salisbury Street. *p47.*
Salisbury Street, 1. BELL, Arthur. Windows broken.
Salisbury Street, 2. STEVENSON, Alfred. Coachman. Windows broken. Wife: Diana Cecilia. Son: 2234 Private James Richard, 5th Green Howards. *pV(p), p23, p120.*
Salisbury Street, 3. METCALFE, Arthur. Painter. House damaged. *p47.*
Salisbury Street, 5. ADDISON, John W. Windows damaged.
Sandside, 21. CHRISTIAN, John. Fisherman. Wife, Maria, took in shipwrecked sailors. *p167.*
Sandside, 5 The Bolts. REYNOLDS, William. Age 13 (B: 1901). Two toes blown off, hospitalised. *p89.*
Sandside, 26 The Bolts. SELLERS, Mrs Maggie. Wounded in thigh, taken to hospital. *p89.*
Sandside. Foreshore Station, BOROUGH POLICE FORCE.
Scalby Hall. NEWHAM, Mark. Newham Brothers, Farmers. Gave account. *p219.*
Scalby Road. SCARBOROUGH TRAMWAYS COMPANY. Secretary and Manager: Walter E. Nicoll. *p123.*
Scalby, *Crimbles Court.* HUGGAN, Halliday. Took in refugees. *p57, p63, p259, p261.*
Scalby, Green Lane Farm. COULTAS, David. Postman. Saw ships from Hayburn Wyke. *p11.*
Scarborough Castle. PICKUP, Albert Edward. Custodian. Age 53, B: 02.09.1861, D: 20.03.1946. Donkey, Topsy, fatally wounded. Wife, Emma Janine (née Handy), age 51, B: 23.09.1863, D: 19.04.1916; daughters, Doris Olga (later Waudby), age 15, B: 25.03.1899; Hilda Catherine, age 19, B: 18.05.1895, D: 03.02.1977; Madge Alberta (later Waudby), age 17, B: 27.09.1897, D: 06.08.1981; and Mildred Ena, age 13, B: 1901. *p19, p104(p), p446.*
Seamer Road. *p47.*
Seamer Road, 2 Gas House Cottages. ATKINSON, H. Foreman at Gas Works. Missed by shell fragment. Gas holder holed. *p45.*
Seamer Road, 17. ELSDON, Christopher. Gardener. Greenhouses destroyed. *p47.*
Seamer Road, 25. *Inkerman Villa.* LINN, Fred. House extensively damaged. *p44(p), p47.*
Seamer Road, 41. STORRY, Robert. Windows broken. *p47.*
Seamer Road, 103. TINDALL, Thomas. Gardener. Windows broken.
Seamer Road, *Alice House.* NAYLOR, Alfred. Coal Merchant. Naylor's Coal Yard. Windows broken. *p49.*
Seamer Road, *Grasmere.* WOODHOUSE, George H. Manager of North Eastern Window Cleaning Company. Windows broken.
Seamer Road, *Luxmount.* MCGACHEN, G. S. Horse killed outside (see Leng). House badly damaged. *p49.*
Seamer Road, *Ribblesdale.* WALKER, Mrs M. A. Windows broken.
Seamer Road, *Rosevear.* WRIGHTSON, C. H. House Agent. House extensively damaged. *p47.*
Seamer Road. SCARBROUGH BRICK & TILE COMPANY LIMITED. Secretary: John Malton. Tower damaged. *p44(p), p45.*
Seamer, *Irton Manor.* NORTON, Claude S. Shells destroyed 'planting'. *p45.*
Sherwood Street, 2. CORDUKES, E. Windows broken.
Sherwood Street, 10. FOUND, T. Railway Porter. Windows broken.
Sherwood Street, 12. HEALY, Mrs. Windows broken.
Sherwood Street, 14. MERCER, Robert. Windows broken.
Sherwood Street, 16. SHERWOOD, Miss E. Windows broken.

Sherwood Street, 18. SUTCLIFFE, Albert. Windows broken.
Sherwood Street, 20. JEFFERSON, Vasey. Milk Dealer. Windows broken.
Sherwood Street, 21. DEARDEN, John. Builders' Merchant. Res: Roof damaged, windows broken. Bus: 6-8 Sherwood Street. *p77.*
Sherwood Street, 22. WARD, Frank. Windows broken.
Sherwood Street, 24. CRAWFORD, John. Roof demolished, house damaged, windows broken. *p77.*
Sherwood Street, 25. COTT, Frederick. Windows broken.
Sherwood Street, 26. TURNER, E. Joiner & Wood Carver. Windows broken.
Sherwood Street, 27. HODGSON, W. G. Windows broken.
Sherwood Street, 28. TURNER, Robert. House, workshop and tools badly damaged, windows broken. *p77.*
Sherwood Street, 29. TINDALL, Robert L. Windows broken.
Sherwood Street, 31. COLLINGS, Frederick Day, and Beatrice (wife). Windows broken.
Sherwood Street, 33. *Avondale.* NEWBY, C. W. North Eastern Stables. Wounded in eye. Windows broken. *p77.*
Sherwood Street. MORLAND, W. Builders' & Plumbers' Merchant. Warehouse and showrooms extensively damaged. *p77.*
Sitwell Street. BOYNTON, George. Police Constable. North Riding Police Station. Expressed sympathy to relatives of John Hall. *p121.*
Sitwell Street. Police Station, NORTH RIDING POLICE FORCE. Major R. L. Bower commanding.
Sitwell Street. THE RED HOUSE. Home for fallen girls founded by Lady Sitwell. Windows broken. *p55.*
Snainton. WYDALE HALL. Harry Holden Illingworth. Took in wounded soldiers from Scarborough's hospitals to make room for bombardment wounded.
Somerset Terrace, 5. BARNETT, Edward. Roof damaged. *p29.*
South Cliff. ST MARTIN'S ON THE HILL. Consecrated 1863. Damaged. *p29, p163, p225.*
South Foreshore Road. CATLIN'S ARCADIA. Roof damaged. *p21.*
South Street, 2. CLARE & HUNT CHEMISTS. *p28(p), p29, p30(p), p31, p139, p246(p), p247.*
South Street, 4. SMITH, Charles. Antique & Silversmith. Premises damaged. *p30(p), p31, p246(p), p247.*
South Street, 6-8. LAND & COMPANY, William C. Grocers and Provision Merchants. Premises damaged. *p29, p139.*
Spring Bank. *p47.*
Spring Bank, 1. SAWDON, Charles. House damaged.
Spring Bank, 2. STEPHENSON, Ambrose. Windows broken.
Spring Bank, 3. MAWMAN, W. House damaged. *p79.*
Spring Bank, 4. PARKINSON, R. Y. Windows broken.
Spring Bank, 5. MILLIONS, John. House damaged.
Spring Bank, 6. DYER, Miss. Windows broken.
Spring Bank, 7. CAMERON, Mrs. House damaged. *p47.*
Spring Bank, 8. HEALD, Mrs. Age 74 (B: 1840). Injured on head. Windows broken. *p47.*
Spring Bank, 9. WILSON, F. C. Windows broken.
Spring Bank, 10. ALLISON, Mrs. Windows broken.
Spring Bank, 11. COCKERILL, Richard. Windows broken.
Spring Bank, 12. HANDEL, Ernest. Windows broken.
Spring Bank, 13. SHIELDS, William. Labourer. Windows broken.
Spring Bank, 14. HICK, Thomas. Windows broken.
Spring Bank, 15. JENNINGS, Tyson. Windows broken.
Spring Bank, 16. FLETCHER, George. Farmer. Furniture damaged, windows broken.
Spring Bank, 17. BOWMAN, Mrs Jane. Windows broken.
St John's Avenue, 6. *Franklin Villa.* BROWN, R. C. Chemist. (Hull Drug Stores, 3 Westborough.) Roof and bathroom damaged, windows broken. *p55.*
St John's Road, 8. *Ebor Villa.* WALLER, Henry S. Fish Dealer. House badly damaged. *p53.*
St John's Road, 9. KIDD, W. M. Coal Dealer. Windows broken.
St John's Road, 19. SKELTON, J. W. Gardener. House badly damaged. *p53.*
St John's Road, 51. BAIN, Andrew. Engineer's Manager. House badly damaged. Daughter, Lily, age 14, had narrow escape. *p52(p), p53.*
St John's Road, 81. HARPER, George. Furniture Remover. Took refugees to Scalby. *p55, p259.*
St Martin's Road, Vicarage. MACKARNESS, Venerable Archdeacon Charles Coleridge. Window broken. *p29, p163, p278(p).* .
St Martin's Road. *St Martin's Villa.* GELDARD, Miss A. E. Interior damaged, windows broken. *p29.*
St Nicholas Cliff, 9. Scarborough Gentleman's Club. Steward: James H. Rowden. Flat seriously damaged. *p29.*
St Nicholas Cliff, 16a. SLACK, William H. Brewer's Assistant. House damaged. *p25.*
St Nicholas Cliff, 34. HOARE, Kate. Roof damaged. *p25.*
St Nicholas Cliff, 36. MAC'S CAFÉ. Proprietor: Mrs E. Whitaker. Roof holed, building damaged. *p25, p242(p).*
St Nicholas Cliff. GRAND HOTEL, Manager: Robert BEAUMONT. Roof and rooms badly damaged. *p24(p), p25, p27, p95, p105, p117, p199, p213, p230, p241, p269, p270(p), p284(p), p285.*
St Nicholas Parade. Spa Boarding House. T. A. P. ASHLEY, Proprietor. Damaged. *p25, p262(p).*
St Nicholas Street, 2 Royal Hotel Shops. WHERRITT, G. Tobacconist. Stock damaged, windows broken. *p25.*
St Nicholas Street, 4-11. MARSHALL & SNELGROVE. Drapers etc. Rear badly damaged. *p23, p242(p).*
St Nicholas Street, 17. SARONY and Company. Photographers. *p247.*
St Nicholas Street. HARRISON. Roof damaged, windows broken.
St Nicholas Street. ROYAL HOTEL. Building damaged, windows broken. *p23, p148(p), p199, p241, p280(p).*
St Nicholas Street. TOWN HALL. Formerly St Nicholas House and Estate. Purchased by Borough in 1898. Borough Engineer's plans for alteration approved 1899. Town Hall opened July 1903. Building damaged. *p25, p148(p), p233, p241.*
St Thomas Street, 25. RICHARDSON, J. Rear roof damaged, windows broken. *p87.*
St Thomas Street, 61. CROSBY, John William. Age 51 (B: 16.12.1863). Tram Conductor. Shell cone in cradle of 16 month old son, Clifford. Roof and upper storey damaged. Wife: Margaret Jane. Daughter: Doris, age 7, gave account. Son: Bernard, age 3. *p87, p211.*
St Thomas Street, Central Police Station, BOROUGH POLICE FORCE. PC Albert Oldroyd, Warrant Officer and Bailiff: Court of Record. Discovered body of Alice Painter 14.12.1914. *p141.*
St Thomas Street. OPERA HOUSE. Originally built as a circus. Altered and re-opened in July 1908. Managing Director, Opera House Company: William Peacock. Resident Manager: G. H. Hawkins.
St Thomas Walk, 2. GOWAN, Alfred. Roof, wall and furniture damaged. *p87.*
St Thomas Walk, 4. SWIFT, Thomas. Tailor. Roof and chimneys damaged, windows broken. *p87.*
Station Road, Scalby. TENISON, Dr Adolf. Treated George Warley's baby girl. *p57, p261.*
St Thomas Walk, 10-11. SIMPSON, Mrs J. Roof and chimney damaged. *p87.*
Stepney Avenue, 27. GARTON, Ernest. Printer. Rear windows broken.
Stepney Avenue, 33. SIMPSON, Mrs M. Windows broken.
Stepney Avenue, 35. HUNTER, J. H. Gas Stoker. Windows broken.

Stepney Avenue, 37. STEVENS, Mrs Mary. Windows broken.
Stepney Avenue, 39. WHITWORTH, Mrs H. Windows broken.
Stepney Avenue, 41. SMITH, Mrs Ellen. House and furniture severely damaged, windows broken. *p51.*
Stepney Avenue, 43. PEARSON, Alfred H. Joiner. Brickwork damaged, windows broken. Son, Charles, age 3, gave account. *p231.*
Stepney Road, *Myrtle Bank.* HIRST, Captain John H. Windows broken. *p51.*
Stepney Road, *Oxenhope.* CHATWIN, E. W. Slates damaged, windows broken. *p51.*
Stepney Road, *West Leigh.* HOLD, Benjamin. Windows broken. *p51.*
Stepney Road, *Willow Dene.* HOLLINGS, Dr C. E. Windows broken. Attended John Hall. *p49, p51, p134.*
Stepney Road. Shell made hole in field.
Sussex Street. BROGDEN & WILSONS. Scarborough Ironworks. Pattern chamber and models damaged. *p87.*

Taylor's Yard, 1. (Friar's Entry). STEVENSON, George. Chauffeur. Wife, Sarah. Rear windows broken. *p89, p120, p231.*
The Crescent, 7. REA, Walter Russell. MP. House damaged. *p27, p110(p), p146, p328.*
The Crescent, 8. MICKLETHWAITE, J. L. House damaged. *p27.*
The Crescent, 11. WOODALL, W. O. Windows broken.
The Crescent, *Londesborough Lodge.* LONDESBOROUGH, Lord William Francis Henry Denison. B: 30.12.1864. D: 30.10.1917. Narrowly missed by shells. *p27.*
The Crescent, *Wood End.* SITWELL, Sir George and Lady Ida. House damaged. Windows broken. *p27, p55.*
Throxenby Lane. PEARCE, Dr. Throxenby Hall Convalescent Home. Formerly part of the Londesborough Estates. House stood on site of the original Manor House, dating back to 1285. *p223.*
Tindall Street, 2. PICKERING, Taylor W. Windows broken.
Tindall Street, 3. BENTLEY, H. Slates damaged, windows broken. *p77.*
Tindall Street, 6. CLARKE, Mrs Hannah. Windows broken.
Tindall Street, 8. BAINES, Miss M. A. Windows broken.
Tindall Street, 10. GIBSON, Mrs Jane E. Windows broken.
Tindall Street, 11. SOLLITT, A. G. Windows broken.
Tindall Street, 13. MOTHERSDALE, Miss. Windows broken.
Tindall Street, 14. MILNE, Mrs M. Windows broken.
Tindall Street, 15. LIGHTFOOT, T. Joiner. Windows broken. Identified Edith Crosby at inquest. *p139.*
Tindall Street, 16. GARWOOD, Septimus. Butcher. Windows broken. Business: 32 Barwick Street.
Tindall Street, 17. CASS, Fred. Linotype Operator. Windows broken.
Tindall Street, 19. SEABROOKE, Fred William. Chef. Windows broken.
Tindall Street, 21. VARLEY, David. Fish Merchant. Windows broken.
Tindall Street, 22. YOUNG, E. Labourer. Windows broken.
Tindall Street, 25. WARD, Arthur M. Windows broken.
Tindall Street, 29. INGLE, Robert. Coachman. Windows broken.
Tindall Street, 35. TURNER, Charles S. Slates damaged, windows broken. *p77.*
Tindall Street, 38. RUSSELL, John William. Grocer's Assistant. Gave evidence at inquests of Frith and Ellis. *p29, p139.*
Tindall Street, 39. JARRETT, John R. Slates damaged, windows broken. *p77.*
Tindall Street, 63. DEACON, George A. Toll Collector. Wrote poem. *p202.*
Tindall Street, 64. IRELAND, Henry. Wounded left shoulder. Taken to Westborough Wesleyan Chapel hospital.
Tindall's Lane, 2. DRYDALE, Richard.
Trafalgar Square, 38. SCOTT, Miss M. C. House badly damaged. *p93.*
Trafalgar Square, 40. ANDREWS, Mrs E. Half of house demolished. *p93.*
Trafalgar Square, 42. NAWTON, Detective Inspector George R. House badly damaged. *p93.*
Trafalgar Square, 72. HUNTER, Harry W. Police Constable. On duty War Signal Station. *p17, p19, p126(p), p132(p).*
Trafalgar Street West. CENTRAL SCHOOL. Master: William T. Northorp. Mistress: Miss E. Craven. Infants' Mistress: Miss. M. Simpson. School built in 1873. Room for 1,800 pupils. Building hit and slightly damaged.

Valley Road, *Normanhurst.* RINES, Mrs. Roof damaged. *p31.*
Valley Road, *The Priory.* TATHAM, Colonel C. J. W. Windows broken. *p31.*
Valley Road. MUNICIPAL SCHOOL. Caretaker Francis W. Ogle took pupils to cellars. Roof and playground damaged. *p31, p247.*
Victoria Road, 34. FLETCHERS LIMITED. Meat Purveyors. Windows broken.
Victoria Road, 43. CLIFFE, Richard H. House badly damaged. *p71.*
Victoria Road, 59. CARR, J. J. Painter & Decorator. Window broken.
Victoria Road, 69. SCALES, Mrs Alice. Boot & Shoe Dealer. Shop and house badly damaged. Mother of George, a Merchant seaman, slightly wounded, and of Robert. *p71.*
Victoria Road, 71. BIELBY, J. Bielby & Company. Hay, straw and corn dealers. Premises damaged. *p71.*
Victoria Road, 71. BIELBY, Robert. Roof demolished, house damaged. *p71.*
Victoria Road, 78. COE, S. Shoe and Boot Repairer. On corner of Alma Parade. Employed Harry Harland who died of wounds.
Victoria Road, 80. WRAY, David. Grocer. Windows broken.
Victoria Road, 81. JOHNSON, Mrs S. A. Windows broken.
Victoria Road, 82. CROFT, Mrs J. Draper. Windows broken.
Victoria Road, 83. VASEY, Thomas E. Printer & Stationer. Windows broken.
Victoria Road, 83a. CHAMBERS, Miss Elizabeth. Milliner. Windows broken.
Victoria Road, 84. SMITH, Charles. Butcher. Windows broken.
Victoria Road, 85. BAYNES, Miss A. Windows broken, lower rooms damaged. *p71.*
Victoria Road, 86. WILCOX, R. J. Windows broken.
Victoria Road, 87. VIOLETTA, Madame. Milliner. Windows broken.
Victoria Road, 89. TINDALL, G. W. Limited. Clothiers. Windows broken.
Victoria Road, 90-96. CASTLEHOUSE BROTHERS. Motor Garage. Window broken.
Victoria Road, 95. *Netley House.* PHIPPS, Arthur. Windows broken.
Victoria Road, 98. FOREMAN, John. Baker & Confectioner. Roof, chimneys and top floor demolished, windows broken. Estimated damage £100. Appeared at inquest of Harry Frith. *p71, p139.*
Victoria Road, 100. NORMANTON, Fred. Hairdresser & Newsagent. House damaged, windows broken. *p71.*
Victoria Road, 102. WILSON, J. W. Butcher. Front windows broken. *p71.*
Victoria Road, 104. ABBEY, Frank. Fruiterer. Front windows broken. *p71.*
Victoria Road, 110. BROWN, J. W. Baker, Confectioner & Grocer. Windows broken.
Victoria Road, 118. ARNOLD, A. L. Music teacher. House severely damaged. *p71, p74(p).*
Victoria Road, 123. FLETCHER, John T. Plumber. Windows broken.

Victoria Road, 125. HARDGRAVE, Fred. Slater. Windows broken.
Victoria Road, 129. NAYLOR & COMPANY. Coal Merchants. Windows broken. *p49.*
Victoria Road, 133. MORLEY, Isaac. Plumber. Windows broken.
Victoria Road, 140. WRIGHTSON, Alfred. Ironmonger. Windows broken.
Victoria Road, 141a. *Calthorpe House.* HARRISON, Albert Prince. Harrison Brothers, Millers, Victoria Mills, Mill Street. Daughters: Audrey, Mabel, and Gertrude, age 27. Maid, Ida Coates. Gertrude wrote letter to cousin in Canada. Training to be a nurse with St John Ambulance. *p249, p251, p253.*
Victoria Road, 142. SPINK, H. Boot & Shoe Dealer. Windows broken.
Victoria Road, 149. LENG, Edward. Milkman. Horse killed outside *Luxmount*, Seamer Road. *p49.*
Victoria Road, 150. CRAVEN, J. H. Fishmonger. Windows broken.
Victoria Road, 160. EAMAN, Miss. Eaman's Boot, Shoe & Hosiery Stores, Roof and furniture damaged, windows broken. *p71.*
Victoria Road, 162. MOORE, Mrs A. M. Windows broken. *p75.*
Victoria Road, 166. HARDY, R. W. Windows broken.
Victoria Road, 168. HIRST, George. Windows broken.
Victoria Road, 170. LAMB, Alfred. Windows broken.
Victoria Road, 176. CO-OPERATIVE STORES BOOT SHOP. On corner of Belle Vue Street. Manager: Berthold Jenkinson. Premises badly damaged, windows broken. *p75, p76(p).*
Victoria Road, 182. WELLS, Robert. Confectioner. House badly damaged. *p71.*
Vincent's Pier. SMITH, Captain Walter Cass. Harbour-Master. The Lighthouse. Lighthouse severely damaged, house damaged. *p94(p), p95, p96(p), p265, p269.*

West Bank. *p47.*
West Bank, 6. STOBART, Mrs. Windows broken. *p47.*
West Square, 3. MIRFIN, Mrs F. E. Windows broken. *p69.*
West Square, 6. FLEMING, William. Windows broken. *p69.*
West Square, 7. BURROWS, Mrs A. Windows broken. *p69.*
West Square, 8. BOYES, Miss A. Windows broken. *p69.*
West Square, 12. SHEPHERDSON, Mrs M. A. Windows broken. *p69.*
West Square, 16. HORLEY, Mrs E. Windows broken. *p69.*
West Square, 17. BERRYMAN, Henry. Windows broken. *p69.*
West Square, 18. SMITH, T. J. Roof severely damaged, windows broken. *p69.*
West Square, 20. FOSTER, Mrs E. Third floor bedroom destroyed, windows broken. *p69.*
West Street, 6. DICK, Dr James R. On duty at hospital. *p37.*
West Street, 34. FISHER, C. Roof and interior damaged. *p37.*
West Street. BRADLEY, Betsy. Wounded to head and abdomen. Taken to hospital. *p37.*
Westborough, 20-21. ROWNTREE & SONS. Windows broken. *p67.*
Westborough, 44. LONDESBOROUGH THEATRE & PICTURE HOUSE. Resident Manager: Frank Gregory.
Westborough, 52. THACKWRAY, G. B. Teacher of Music. Windows broken.
Westborough, 53. WATSON, Henry. House damaged. *p67.*
Westborough, 71-72. RINGROSE, Hettie R. Nurse ROBSON. On duty at hospital. *p91.*
Westborough, 81. HUNT & RUFF CHEMISTS. Windows broken. *p69.*
Westborough, 99. CARLTON HOTEL. Proprietor: John Charles DICKINSON. Upper storey damaged. *p67.*
Westborough, 119. BALMORAL HOTEL. Proprietor: Kirby. Building slightly damaged, windows broken. *p69.*
Westborough, *Adelphi Chambers.* WHITFIELD, J. Solicitor. Acted for Land & Company at inquest of Harry Frith. *p139.*
Westborough. DENNIS, E.T.W. Printers. Premises and stock damaged. *p67, p227.*
Westborough. MATSON'S TEMPERANCE HOTEL & BOARDING HOUSE. Upper storey damaged. *p67.*
Westborough. PAVILION HOTEL. HQ for Yorkshire Hussars. Coping stones damaged. *p17.*
Westborough. RAILWAY STATION. Damaged.
Westborough. WESTBOROUGH WESLEYAN CHAPEL. Minister: Reverend John GOULD. Built 1862, seats for 1,260 people. Chapel basement used as hospital. *p47, p164, p253.*
Westbourne Grove, 26. GIBSON, J. M. Chimney and roof damaged. *p31.*
Westbourne Grove, 27. DAVEY, Mrs L. Rear of house badly damaged. *p31.*
Westbourne Grove, 28. MEDLEY, J. Percival. Solicitor. Chimney and roof damaged. Appeared at inquest for relatives of Harry Frith. *p31.*
Westbourne Grove, 29. STRANGE, Albert. Headmaster of School of Art, Municipal School. House damaged. *p31.*
Westbourne Grove, and 1-5 Trinity Road. WESTLANDS SCHOOL. Headmistress: Miss E. H. Wood. *p31, p197.*
Westbourne Grove. DENT. Narrow escape. House badly damaged. *p33.*
Westbourne Park, 22. RYALLS, Jasper S. Engineer. House damaged, windows broken. Grandson John Shields, age 14 months, son of George Ryalls, killed. Also killed, Miss Bertha McEntyre, age 42. George gave evidence at inquest. *p49, p52(p), p130, p131, p135, p137, p142.*
Westbourne Park, 24. COATES, Miss. Windows broken. *p49.*
Westbourne Park, 30. TEANBY, Walter. Windows broken.
Westbourne Park, 32. OGDEN, F. Jobmaster. Windows broken.
Westbourne Park, 34. YEOMAN, S. F. Windows broken. Foreman of inquest jury. *p134, p140.*
Westfield Terrace, 9. WAVERLEY TEMPERANCE HOTEL. Thornton & Waterfall. Windows broken. *p69.*
Westwood, 11. HORNBY, Robert. Wife, Constance. Son, William. Daughter, Lucy Ursula Surtees Hornby, aged 9, B: 20.12.1904, who gave an account. *p257, p258(p).*
Wireless Station. Falsgrave Park area. Shells fell short, premises evacuated. Guard dog 'Bob' ran off. *p124(p).*
Wooler Street. ROWNTREE'S FURNITURE WAREHOUSE. Building damaged, windows broken. *p83.*
Wrea Street, 2. BELL, Edward. Asphalter. Works Foreman, street repairs, Burniston Road. Warned of attack by stranger (15.12.1914). *p121, p123.*
Wrea Street, 7. HUDSON, Francis W. Roof damaged. *p83.*
Wykeham Street, 1. AGAR, John Charles. House damaged. Wife, Annie Elizabeth Watson, gave account. Son: Charles. *p61, p63.*
Wykeham Street, 2. BENNETT. House severely damaged. Four people killed: Mrs Johanna Bennett, Albert Featherstone Bennett, George Barnes and John Wood. *p57, p58(p), p59, p60(p), p61, p125, p130, p131, p137, p225, p226(p), p243, p250(p), p252.*
Wykeham Street, 3. RAWDING, Thomas. Military Store Keeper. Married, two children. *p63.*
Wykeham Street, 4. STEELE, Mrs E. A. Windows broken. *p61.*
Wykeham Street, 14. CAMMISH, Samuel. Warehouseman for W. Morland, Sherwood Street. Narrow escape. *p77.*
Wykeham Street, 47. HARLAND, John T. Postman. Injured. *p63.*
Wykeham Street, 52. HARLAND, George Charles. Father of Henry 'Harry' Harland. *p73.*

Wykeham Street, 56. CROOKS, John. Copper damaged, windows broken. Daughter, Alice, taken to Scalby. *p63*.
Wykeham Street, 58. DOUTHWAITE, George W. Baker. Chimney, bedrooms, pantry and coalhouse damaged, windows broken. *p63*.
Wykeham Street, 60. HARLAND, John W. Coal Porter. Windows broken. *p63*.

York Place, 5. COOK, FOWLER & OUTHET. Windows broken.
York Place, 6. ELECTRIC SUPPLY WORKS. Offices. Windows broken.
York Place, 7. BAKER, Frank. Windows broken.
York Place, 8. BAINBRIDGE, Misses. Windows broken.
York Place, 9. ROE, Thomas B. Windows broken.
York Place, 10. WINTERINGHAM, Mrs. Windows broken.
York Place, 11. WATKINSON, Robert. Windows broken.
York Place, 12. CARTER, Mrs E. S. Windows broken.
York Place, 13. BODDY, W. H. Windows broken. COLEMAN, Mrs. Employee of Tramway Company. Narrow escape on Falconer's Road. *p13*.
York Place, 14. ASTROM, George. Windows broken. *p70(p)*.
York Place, 15. COOKE, Mrs A. , MITCHELL & COMPANY, and Vernon SCARBOROUGH. All joint tenants. Windows broken.
York Place, 17. BURNETT, Misses. Windows broken.
York Place, 21. WRAY, Mrs A. Windows broken.

Index D: Scarborough's Official Damage 1914 *(by area)*

1: Taken from Scarborough Borough Council's 'official' map of AREAS - compiled in December 1914 - which indicated where shells landed (but not where peripheral damage was done). At least one shell, often more, fell in the following streets or places (the list does not give details of damage to individual properties, such as *Dunollie* which comes under Filey Road). General area covered by shelling - from Burniston Barracks (north of town) out to Hackness (west of town) to Irton (south-east of town) to Cayton (south of town).
2: All details relate to the bombardment of Wednesday, 16th December 1914, unless stated otherwise.
3: Official figures:

Properties struck - 209	Shells recorded - 489	Killed - 18
Churches - 7	Additional shells reported - 30	Injured - 84
Public buildings - 10	Hotels - 5	Duration - 25 minutes

4: At least one shell, often more, fell in the vicinity of the following places (areas marked with an asterisk (*) have their current names for reader reference).

ATHLETIC GROUND
BETTON QUARRIES
BURNISTON ROAD
CARR HOUSE LANE
CASTLE
CLARENCE GARDENS
CORNELIAN AVENUE
DEEPDALE AVENUE
ESPLANADE GARDENS
FALSGRAVE MOOR
FALSGRAVE MOOR HOUSE
FILEY ROAD
FLORAL HALL GARDENS
GAS WORKS
GREEN CROFT GARDENS
*HARVEST WAY
*HAVER'S HILL
HIGH DEEPDALE
HOLBECK GARDENS
IRTON
IRTON MOOR
ITALIAN GARDENS
JACKSON'S LANE
KNIPE POINT
MARINE DRIVE
MIDDLE DEEPDALE
MOORHOUSE FARM
NORTH CLIFF GOLF COURSE
*NORTHSTEAD MANOR DRIVE
*NORTHSTEAD MANOR GARDENS
OLIVER'S MOUNT
OLIVER'S MOUNT PLANTATION
OSGODBY
PEASHOLM BOATING LAKE
PROSPECT HOUSE FARM
QUEEN MARGARET'S ROAD
*RYNDLE CRESCENT
*RYNDLE WALK
SEAMER MOOR HILL
SEAMER MOOR LANE
SOUTH CLIFF GARDENS
*SOUTH CLIFF GOLF COURSE
SPRINGHILL BRICKWORKS
SPRINGHILL WOODS
WEAPONNESS PARK
*WEST GARTH GARDENS
*WEYDALE AVENUE
WEYDALE HOUSE
WHEATCROFT CLIFFS

Index E: Scarborough's Official Damage 1914 *(by street)*

1: Taken from Scarborough Borough Council's 'official' map of STREETS - compiled in December 1914 - which indicated where shells landed (but not where peripheral damage was done). At least one shell, often more, fell in the following streets or places (the list does not give details of damage to individual properties, such as *Dunollie* which comes under Filey Road).
2: All details relate to the bombardment of Wednesday, 16th December 1914, unless stated otherwise.

ABERDEEN WALK
ALBEMARLE CRESCENT
ALBION ROAD
ALEXANDER PARK
ALFRED STREET
ASQUITH AVENUE
AUBOROUGH STREET
AVENUE VICTORIA
BATH TERRACE
BEACONSFIELD STREET
BEDFORD STREET
BELLE VUE STRET
BELMONT ROAD
BELVEDERE PLACE
BELVOIR TERRACE
BLAND'S CLIFF
CAMBRIDGE STREET
CANDLER STREET
CASTLE ROAD
COLUMBUS RAVINE
COMMERCIAL STREET
CROMWELL ROAD
CROMWELL STREET
CROWN CRESCENT
DEAN ROAD
EASTBOROUGH
ELDERS STREET
ESPLANADE
ESPLANADE ROAD
FALSGRAVE ROAD
FORESHORE ROAD
FRIAR'S ENTRY
FRIARAGE SCHOOL
FULFORD ROAD
GLADSTONE ROAD
GLADSTONE STREET
GOODS STATION
GORDON STREET
GROSVENOR CRESCENT
GROSVENOR ROAD
HANOVER ROAD
HARCOURT AVENUE
HIBERNIA STREET
KING STREET
LIGHTHOUSE
LONSDALE ROAD
MANOR ROAD
MANOR ROAD GARDENS
MAYVILLE AVENUE
MURCHISON STREET
NEWBOROUGH
NORTH MARINE ROAD
NORTH STREET
NORWOOD STREET
OLIVER'S MOUNT ROAD
PARK AVENUE
PRINCE OF WALES TERRACE
PROSPECT ROAD
RALEIGH STREET
RAMSEY STREET

RAMSHILL
ROSCOE STREET
ROSEBERY AVENUE
ROTHBURY STREET
SALISBURY STREET
SEAMER ROAD
SEAMER ROAD BRICKWORKS
SHERWOOD STREET
SIGNAL STATION
SOMERSET TERRACE
SOUTH STREET
SPA GARDENS
SPA WALLS
SPRING BANK
ST HELEN'S SQUARE
ST JAMES ROAD
ST MARY'S CHURCH
ST NICHOLAS CLIFF
ST NICHOLAS STREET
ST THOMAS STREET
ST THOMAS WALK
STEPNEY AVENUE
THE CRESCENT
TRAFALGAR SQUARE
TRINITY ROAD
VALLEY BRIDGE ROAD
VICTORIA ROAD
WEST BANK
WEST SQUARE
WEST STREET
WESTBOROUGH
WESTBOURNE GROVE
WESTBOURNE PARK
WESTWOOD ROAD
WREA STREET
WYKEHAM STREET
YORK PLACE

Index F: Scarborough's Memorial Service 1914

1: Index of those who attended the Memorial Service at St Mary's Parish Church, Scarborough, on Saturday, 19th December 1914.
2: Listed in alphabetical order, SURNAME, followed by available information.
3: All details relate to the bombardment of Wednesday, 16th December 1914, unless stated otherwise.
4: Abbreviations used: Res: Home address. Bus: Business address.
5: Ages given are those at the time of the incident (i.e. December 1914) under which the entry is made.
6: Page numbers at the end of an entry indicate where the subject is mentioned in the text. The '(p)' indicates a picture.

ADAMSON, G. P. Assistant Secretary of the Hospital, Friar's Entry. Res: 34 Nansen Street. Assisted at the hospital.
ASCOUGH, William. Alderman. 21 Grange Avenue.

BARKER, Thomas Christopher. Councillor. Architect. Bus: Grosvenor Chambers, Westborough.
BIELBY, John. Councillor.
BLACK. G. B. Solicitor. Justice of the Peace. Clerk to Borough Magistrates. *North Holm.* 173 Columbus Ravine. *p121.*
BRIGGS, Arthur. Councillor.

CARR, R. H. 9 West Square.
CHAMBERS, H. T. Secretary, Cliff Bridge Company. Res: 111 Murchison Street.
COLE, Robert. Chief Collector of Rates. 9 Seamer Road.
CUFF, Dr Robert. Justice of the Peace. Res: *Bryercliffe,* 40 Filey Road. Bus: St Nicholas Parade.

DIPPIE, James. Justice of the Peace. *Harrietfield,* 33 Filey Road.
DONNER, H. E. Clerk to North Riding Magistrates. *p120.*
DUXBURY, T. 125 Columbus Ravine.
DYDE, John. Master, Workhouse. 18 Dean Road. *p84(p), p85.*

EDEN, T.

FAWCETT, T. M. Borough Accountant. 6 Park Avenue. *p51.*
FENBY. J.
FERGUSON, Reverend A. Curate of St Paul's. 19 St Nicholas Cliff.
FIRTH, Major. 10 Victoria Avenue.
FLETCHER, Frank. Councillor. Insurance Inspector. 48 Westborough.
FOWLER, Valentine. Alderman (Deputy Mayor). *p257.*
FOWLER, William Hastings. Alderman. Solicitor. *Langford House,* Westwood.

GAWNE, Eden H. Justice of the Peace.
GIBSON, George Fawcett. Councillor. 59-67 North Marine Road.
GIBSON, W. W. Draper. 47 Westborough.
GOODRICKE, Francis. 5 Pavilion Square.
GRAHAM, Christopher Colborne. Mayor. Alderman. *Oriel House,* Oriel Crescent. *p99, p117, p118(p), p121, p144, p146, p158, p233.*
GRAHAM, Miss Maisie. (Daughter of Christopher Colborne Graham.) Mayoress.
GRANGER, Reverend T. Superintendent of Primitive Methodist Chapel. Res: 37 Garfield Road. *p81.*

HALL, George. Scarborough. Brother of John Hall.
HALL, Henry. Leeds. Brother of John Hall.
HALL, William. Leeds. Brother of John Hall.
HART, Tasker. Solicitor. 29 Trinity Road.
HEBDEN, J.
HEYS, R. G. *Ellerburn,* Stepney Road.
HOPWOOD, J. L. Councillor.

JONES, Sydney. Town Clerk. 1 Filey Road.

KING, Herbert. Chemist. Borough Analyst. 8 Avenue Road.
KIRTLAN, Reverend E. J. B. 104 North Marine Road. Pastor, Queen Street Wesleyan Chapel. *p164.*

LAND, Lieutenant-Colonel.
LILLEY, W. 53 Falsgrave Road.
LOCKLEY, Reverend W. H. United Methodist Chapel, Claremont Chapel, Castle Road. *p163.*

MALTON, John. Councillor. *Croyle Villa,* Manor Road.
MARKS, Henry. Musical Instrument Dealer & Tuner. Secretary, Scarborough Free Church Council. 11Queen Street.
MERRYWEATHER, Reverend H.

MIDDLETON, Reverend J. A. Pastor of Bar Congregational Church. *p165.*
MILLHOUSE, William. Water Engineer. 7 Cromwell Road.
MOORE, Abraham. Builder. Councillor. *Rockville,* Stepney Road.
MORGAN, Fred Percival. Accountant. Councillor. 6 Grange Avenue.

PEPPER, B. W. Nephew of John Hall (killed).
PEPPER, R. J. Nephew of John Hall (killed).
PIRIE, James. Alderman. 105 Castle Road.
POOLE, Timothy. Coast Agent, Port of Hull Society. 34 Barwick Street.

REA, Mrs. Wife of Walter Rea MP. *p27.*
REA, Walter Russell. MP. 7 The Crescent. *p27, p146.*
RICHARDSON, Russell. Solicitor. 7 Queen Street.
RICKETT, Sir J. Compton. MP.
ROSE, George William. Confectioner. Councillor. 9 South Street & 9 Ramshill Road.
ROWNTREE, Allan. Draper. 33-39 Westborough.
ROWNTREE, G. Justice of the Peace. *Riseborough,* Weaponness Avenue. *p225, p227.*
ROWNTREE, John Watson. Grocer. Alderman. *The Rowans,* Westover Road.
ROWNTREE, Joshua. Solicitor. Justice of the Peace. 3 Rawdon Villas, 12 Ramshill Road. *p121, p221.*
ROWNTREE, W. S. Justice of the Peace. *Endcliffe,* Granville Road.

SAYNER, William. Borough Treasurer. *Rokeby,* 19 Holbeck Road.
SINFIELD, J. Confectioner & Tobacconist. Justice of the Peace.
SMITH, Edwin. Greengrocer. 109 Prospect Road. *p65.*
SMITH, H. W. Borough Engineer. 7 Seamer Road. *p455.*
SMITH, Lieutenant W. Riley. Yorkshire Hussars Reserves.
STANNERS, T. Grocer. 36 & 41 Aberdeen Walk.

TASKER, J. Plumber. 46 Ramshill Road.
TAYLOR, Dr William Charles Everley. Surgeon. 34 Queen Street.
TAYLOR, E. M. Deputy Town Clerk. 97 Murchison Street.
TAYLOR, George. Solicitor. Registrar of Court of Record and Borough Coroner. Clerk of the Peace. Res: 2 Grosvenor Road. Bus: 37 Queen Street. *p130, p131, p133, p134, p135, p137, p139, p140.*
TETLEY, A. S. Headmaster of Municipal School. 22 Avenue Road.
THOMAS, Reverend W. O. 36 Trafalgar Square.
THOMPSON, Miss Alice. 3 St Martin's Square.
TINDALL, George William. Councillor. *Menethorpe,* Stepney Road.
TINDALL, Miss Augusta.
TUGWELL, A. J. Hairdresser. Justice of the Peace. Res: *Cheam House,* Cromwell Terrace. Bus: 35 St Nicholas Cliff. *p25.*
TURNBULL, S. P. Justice of the Peace. *Norbury,* Weaponness Park.
TYRELL, Reverend C. F. Curate of St John's. 3 Brunswick Terrace.

UNDERWOOD, Robert. Secretary of Education Committee. *Linthorpe,* 73 Scalby Road.

WAIN, George. 12 Granby Place, Queen Street.
WALKER, Reverend P. C. *Ramsdale Bank,* Belmont Road.
WALLIS, Edward. Grocer. 4 West Parade Road.
WESTWOOD, Joseph B. 11 Granby Place, Queen Street.
WHITE, Frank A. Councillor. Esplanade Boarding Establishment, Belmont Road. *p33, p240(p), p278(p).*
WHITTAKER, M. T. Alderman. 1Weaponness Park.
WILKINSON, Dr C. A. Surgeon. Acting Medical Officer of Health. Head of St John Voluntary Ambulance Brigade (HQ YMCA). Res: 56 Gladstone Street. *p135.*
WRIGHT, W. M. Drapers & Hosiers. 31-32 Newborough.
WYRILL, Captain John. Master Mariner. 28 Grange Avenue.

YORKE, Regimental Sergeant Major. Yorkshire Hussars Reserves.

Index G: Scarborough's Dead 1917

1: Index of those killed or who died as a result of the attack.
2: Listed in alphabetical order, SURNAME, followed by available information.
3: All details relate to the submarine attack of Tuesday, 4th September 1917, unless stated otherwise.
4: Where the hospital is mentioned it is the main hospital on Friar's Entry, unless stated otherwise.
5: Abbreviations used: B: Place of birth.
6: Ages given are those at the time of the incident (i.e. September 1917) under which the entry is made.
7: Page numbers at the end of an entry indicate where the subject is mentioned in the text and/or relevant photographs.

PARRY, 240541 Lance-Corporal Frederick William. 6th (Reserve) Battalion Lancashire Fusiliers. Age 22. B: Moston, Manchester. Coachbuilder. Of Moston, Manchester. Wounded on Foreshore Road. Died of wounds. *p444, p446, p447, p450.*
PICKUP, Thomas Temple. Age 64. Cabinet maker with Tonks. Of and killed at 2 Queen's Terrace. *p444, p445, p446.*

SCOTT, Mrs Elizabeth. Age 39. Of 108 Hoxton Road. Mortally wounded, died in hospital. *p443, p444, p445, p446.*

Author's Appeal For Information

Further information is still sought about the people mentioned in this book. If you have any information, or photographs, please contact the author (via the offices of the publisher).

Index H: Scarborough's Damage 1917 *(by name)*

1: Index of damage done and those mentioned in the text.
2: Listed in alphabetical order, SURNAME, followed by available information.
3: All details relate to the submarine attack of Tuesday, 4th September 1917, unless stated otherwise.
4: Where the hospital is mentioned it is the main hospital on Friar's Entry, unless stated otherwise.
5: Abbreviations used: B: Year/date of birth. D: Year/date of death.
6: Ages given are those at the time of the incident (i.e. September 1917) under which the entry is made.
7: Page numbers at the end of an entry indicate where the subject is mentioned in the text. The '(p)' indicates a picture.
8: Entries carrying the legend 'Gave account' indicate where an oral or written account has been provided.

APPLEBY, Albert Edward. Sandside, 8 Whitehead Hill. Wife: Alice Ann. Daughter: Alice. Age 17. Leg wound. Hospitalised. *p444, p450.*

BENTLEY. Colour Sergeant Albert Bentley. Military Police. Gave evidence at inquest of Frederick Parry. *p446, p447.*
BESWICK, Fanny. 109 Victoria Road. Roof and bedroom damaged, windows broken. Injured leg. Hospitalised. *p443.*
BINNS, F. B. Hartley. 47 Eastborough. Visitor, from 10 Walker Street, Cleckheaton. Injured.
BRAY, Charles. 110 Hoxton Road. Injured. Walls and doors damaged, windows broken. *p443.*
BROWN. Mrs H. Brown. Ossett, West Yorkshire. Gave account. *p449.*

COLES, A. Baker & Confectioner. 8 Eastborough. Bakery damaged, windows broken. *p443, p450.*
COLLINSON, Miss Alice. 64 St Thomas Street. Roof and walls damaged, windows broken.

DICKINSON'S GARAGE. Somerset Terrace. Roof damaged, windows broken.

GIBSON, George W. 117 Hoxton Road. Windows broken.
GODFREY, Dr F. 5 Montpellier Terrace. On duty at hospital, attended Elizabeth Scott, examined Frederick Parry. *p445.*
GOODYEAR, R. A. H. Wrote poem which appeared on a postcard by E. T. W. Dennis & Sons. *p450, p451.*

HODGSON, Norman. Aged 14. Hayes, Middlesex. Gave account. *p450.*
HOSPITAL. Friar's Entry. Roof damaged, slight interior damage. *p88(p), p447.*

JACKSON, W. H. Labourer. 107 Hoxton Road. Interior damage, windows broken. *p443.*
JOHNSON, John. F. 111 Hoxton Road. Windows broken.

KELL, John. 4 Cambridge Street. Windows broken.

LEWIS & COMPANY. 64a St Thomas Street. Roof and walls damaged, windows broken.
LICKISS, Arthur. 111 Victoria Road. House damaged, windows broken.

MANSFIELD, Inspector. Gave evidence at the inquest of Thomas Pickup. *p445.*
MILNER. Henry. 6 Eastborough. Wall, cellar damaged, windows broken.
MURRAY. Captain Murray. Royal Army Medical Corps. On duty at the Royal Northern Sea Bathing Infirmary. Examined Frederick Parry. *p447.*

NESS. Gladys Ness. Bootham, York. Gave account. *p450.*

PARRY. Benjamin Parry. From Manchester. Gave evidence at inquest of son, Frederick Parry. *p446.*
PAVILION HOTEL. Westborough. Coping stones damaged. *p17.*
PEARSON, Charles A. Dewsbury. Aged 6. Gave account. *p451.*
PICKERING, Ada. 37 James Street. Injured.
PICKUP, Mrs. 2 Queen's Terrace. Wife of Thomas Temple. Gave evidence at inquest. *p445.*
POST OFFICE TAVERN. Eastborough, Merchant's Row. Landlord: George Renwick. Windows broken.

RAILWAY STATION. Roof damaged, windows broken.
REA, Mrs. 145 Longwestgate. Injured.
REEVE, Chief Officer Lawrence Edward William. Castle Road, Coastguard Station. Age 52, B: 06.06.1865, D: 1919. On duty at War Signal Station, Castle Hill. Gave evidence at inquests. 1918: in charge at Coastguard Station, Lundy Island. Wife, Martha Hazeldeen; daughter, Annie; sons Aubrey (gave account), Frank and Leslie. *p15, p17, p132(p), p445, p449.*
ROSE AND CROWN HOTEL. Albert Row. Proprietor: George Ellingham. Windows broken. *p199, p445.*
ROYAL NORTHERN SEA BATHING INFIRMARY & CONVALESCENT HOME. Foreshore Road. [Later St Thomas's Hospital.] Patients moved. Building damaged. *p19, p167, p271, p271, p272(p), p273, p447.*
ROYLE, G. E. Scarborough Borough Coroner. Solicitor. 16 Queen Street. Conducted inquests. *p444, p445, p446.*
RUMFORD, Mrs. 19 South Foreshore Road. Windows broken.

SMITH, James. 41 Eastborough. Windows broken.
ST HILDA'S. Queen Street. Windows broken.

WALTON, Victor. 23 South Foreshore Road. Windows broken.
WARDMAN, Mrs H. Confectioner. 1 James Street. House, interior and stock damaged, windows broken. *p443.*
WIMBUSH, William. *Beech House*, Bland's Cliff. Gave evidence at the inquest of Thomas Pickup. *p445.*

Author's Appeal For Information

Further information is still sought on all aspects of the bombardments and the various military and naval units mentioned in this book. If you have any information, or photographs, you are asked to contact the author (via the offices of the publisher).

Index I: Scarborough's Damage 1917 *(by street)*

1: Index of damage done and those mentioned in the text.
2: Listed in alphabetical order, STREET, followed by available information.
3: All details relate to the submarine attack of Tuesday, 4th September 1917, unless stated otherwise.
4: Where the hospital is mentioned it is the main hospital on Friar's Entry, unless stated otherwise.
5: Abbreviations used: B: Year/date of birth. D: Year/date of death.
6: Ages given are those at the time of the incident (i.e. September 1917) under which the entry is made.
7: Page numbers at the end of an entry indicate where the subject is mentioned in the text and/or relevant photographs.
8: Entries carrying the legend 'Gave account' indicate where an oral or written account has been provided.

Index J: Whitby's Dead 1914

1: Index of those killed or died as a result of the bombardment.
2: Listed in alphabetical order, SURNAME, followed by available information.
3: All details relate to the bombardment of Wednesday, 16th December 1914, unless stated otherwise.
4: Entries marked with an asterisk (*) contain their own explanatory notes.
5: Abbreviations used: B: Year/date of birth. D: Year/date of death.
6: Ages given are those at the time of the incident (i.e. December 1914) under which the entry is made.
7: Page numbers at the end of an entry indicate where the subject is mentioned in the text and/or relevant photographs.

MILLER, Mrs Winefride. Age 50. Invalid. Of *Springfield House*, 3 Spring Hill Terrace. Mortally wounded. Died in nursing home, 3.00pm, 25.12.1914. *p299, p303, p305, p309, p326, p333, p335, p346, p364(p).*

RANDALL, Frederick. Age 30. D: 16.12.1914. Coastguard Boatman. Killed at coastguard signal station cottages. *p297, p303, p305, p314, p316, p319, p326, p345, p346, p355, p363, p441.*

TUNMORE, William Edward. Age 61. D: 16.12.1914. Railway 'rulleyman'. Killed at Boghall Cabin. *p301, p305, p307, p314, p316, p322, p323, p326, p346, p351.*

*STEPHENSON, Annie Margaret. Age 48. D: 16.12.1914. Of Thorpe. Not 'officially' listed as died in or because of the bombardment. *p305.*

*WARTERS, Mary Elizabeth. Age 55. D: 16.12.1914. Of Ridgewood. Not 'officially' listed as died in or because of the bombardment. *p305.*

Index K: Whitby's Damage 1914 *(by name)*

1: Index of damage done and those mentioned in the text.
2: Listed in alphabetical order, SURNAME, followed by available information.
3: All details relate to the bombardment of Wednesday, 16th December 1914, unless stated otherwise.
4: Abbreviations used: B: Year/date of birth. D: Year/date of death.
5: Ages given are those at the time of the incident (i.e. December 1914) under which the entry is made.
6: Page numbers at the end of an entry indicate where the subject is mentioned in the text. The '(p)' indicates a picture.
7: Entries carrying the legend 'Gave account' indicate where an oral or written account has been provided.

CLOUGH, Fred. Councillor. Butcher. 9 Sandgate. Attended special compensation meeting of Whitby Urban District Council. *p319, p320, p321, p322.*
COGHLAN, Mr & Mrs. Attended funeral of William Tunmore. *p322.*
COLLIER, Raymund. Ironmonger. 2 Baxtergate. Also 4 Flowergate. Brother of Winefride Miller. Gave evidence at inquest. *p335.*
COLLIER, William George. 12 Esk Terrace. Apartments. General damage, windows broken.
CONSERVATIVE CLUB. Silver Street. Dome broken, billiard-tables damaged.
CONVENT CONVALESCENT HOME. Chubb Hill Road. Convent of the Sisters of Mercy. Lady Superior: Sister T. F. Dobson. Cared for Winefride Miller. *p299, p303, p333.*
COOK, R. C. Councillor. Boot Dealer. 5 Flowergate. At special compensation meeting of Whitby Urban District Council. *p319, p320, p321, p322.*
CORNER, J. 5 East Terrace. Upper room damaged, windows broken.
COTTAGE HOSPITAL. Grape Lane. Dr Edward BAINES attended Winefride Miller.
CRAWTHER. Foreman of inquest jury. *p314.*
CROSS, Mr & Mrs Charles George. Upgang Lane. Attended funeral of William Tunmore. *p322.*
CURTIS, Sergeant. Inmate of Red Cross Hospital, Sleights. Assisted Major-General Trotter to bury unexploded shell. *p303.*

DAVIE, Charles Southerdon. Chief Officer of Coastguard. Gave evidence at inquests of Randall and Miller. Represented coastguard at funeral of Frederick Randall. *p314, p316, p319, p335.*
DAWSON, W. Attended funeral of William Tunmore. *p322.*
DEAN, Mr & Mrs. Sent flowers to funeral of William Tunmore. *p322.*
DITCHBURN, Mrs. Blown over by blast in fields.
DOBSON. Mr. 22 Silver Street. Unexploded shrapnel shell dug out of Ruswarp Rifle Range field. Wife and daughter attended funeral of William Tunmore. *p303, p322.*
DOUGHTY HOUSE. 1 Royal Crescent. Slightly damaged. *p317(p).*
DOWELL, Mrs Ann. 29 Flowergate. Fruiterer. Sent flowers to funeral of William Tunmore. *p322.*
DUCK, John & Sons. Butchers. 1 Sandgate. Wife attended funeral of William Tunmore. *p322.*

ELECTRIC POWER STATION. Church Street. Unscathed. *p307, p354.*
ENDLE, Captain T. O. Commanding 'F' Company, 7th (Cyclist) Battalion Devonshire Regiment, based at Whitby. *p346.*

FARQUAHAR. Coastguard. Pall bearer at funeral of Frederick Randall. *p319.*
FAVIS, 918 Private. 'F' Company, 7th (Cyclist) Battalion Devonshire Regiment, based at Whitby. Slightly wounded at War Signal Station, suffered shock, taken to hospital. *p297, p326, p345, p346.*
FILBURN, Mrs. Albion Place. Injured by falling masonry. Upper rooms demolished, windows broken. *p299.*
FISHER, Henrietta, 1 Falcon Terrace. Daughter of Isaac Fisher. Trapped by window when bombardment began. *p299, p301, p355.*
FISHER, Isaac. Greengrocer. 1 Falcon Terrace. *p307, p355.*
FORTH, Frederick Douglas. 13 Windsor Terrace. Roof blown off, upper rooms wrecked, windows broken.
FOXWORTHY, Sergeant Louis Henry. 'F' Company, 7th (Cyclist) Battalion Devonshire Regiment, based at Whitby. Born in Dartmouth and enlisted there. Although a Sergeant whilst serving with the 7th Devonshires at Whitby, he was killed in action on the Western Front on 8th October 1918 as 290034 Corporal Foxworthy, whilst serving with the 9th (Service) Battalion Devonshire Regiment. *p297, p326, p345.*
FRALER. 2 Grove Street. Roof, chimney and upper rooms damaged.

GALE. W. Boy Scout. 2 Normanby Terrace. Bugler, sounded last post at funeral of Frederick Randall. Son of John C. Gale. *p319.*
GALLOWAY, William M. *Corra Lynn*, Stakesby Vale. Attended funeral of William Tunmore. *p322.*
GAS WORKS. Unscathed. *p357, p359.*
GASKIN, John. Solicitor's clerk. *West Lea.* Roof and upper rooms damaged. Building damage £74/1s/7d. Furniture damage £34/4s/0d. Wife attended funeral of William Tunmore. *p314(p), p317(p), p322, p348(p), p352.*
GIBBIN, W. Attended funeral of William Tunmore. *p322.*
GIBSON, C. Attended funeral of William Tunmore. *p322.*
GIBSON, Laura. Fancy Repository. 12 Marine Parade. Stock damaged, window broken. *p301.*
GOODRIDGE, Captain Alan. Commanding 'F' Company, 7th (Cyclist) Battalion Devonshire Regiment, based at Whitby. Attended funeral of Frederick Randall. *p307, p319, p323, p326, p345.*
GRAHAM, Oscar E. Sanitary Inspector. Falcon Terrace. House damaged, fire started, but extinguished. Windows broken. *p299.*
GRAY, William Seaton. 16 St Hilda's Terrace. Clerk to Whitby Urban District Council. Attended special compensation meeting of Whitby Urban District Council. Attended funeral of William Tunmore. *p319, p320, p321, p322.*
GRIFFIN, Edward 'Teddy'. 52, The Cragg. Steps damaged. Seventh son, George Shrapnel, born, 9.05am, 16.12.1914. *p295, p307, p309, p340(p).*

HALEY, Miss. Sent flowers to the funeral of William Tunmore. *p322.*
HALL, Thomas. 38 Commercial Street, Norton. Railway Guardsman, North Eastern Railway. Gave account. *p351.*
HAMILTON, William Henry. 3 Belle Vue Terrace. Headmaster of St John's Church of England School, Windsor Terrace. School undamaged. Children uninjured. *p301, p346.*
HARKER, William, and daughter, Miss I. Harker, 7 Crescent Avenue, sent flowers to funeral of William Tunmore. *p322.*
HARLAND, Captain. Attended funeral of William Tunmore. *p322.*
HARMER, Mrs. And staff of office, warehouse and yard of Whitby Goods Station, the Station-Master and Whitby Passenger Station staff, sent flowers to the funeral of William Tunmore. *p322.*
HARMSTON, James Egan. *Westgrove,* Prospect Hill. Mayor. Justice of the Peace. Presided at special compensation meeting of Whitby Urban District Council. *p319, p320, p321, p322, p327, p328, p329, p331.*
HARRISON, Captain John. 3 Cleveland Terrace. Master Mariner. House damaged, windows broken.
HARROWING, John Henry. Low Stakesby. Justice of the Peace. Member of the Emergency Committee. Offered assistance in streets shortly after shelling ceased.
HASLOP, I. Attended funeral of William Tunmore. *p322.*
HAWKINS, Coastguard. Pall bearer at funeral of Frederick Randall. *p319.*
HEADLAM, Aaron. Stakesby Road. Daughter, Miss G. Headlam, attended funeral of William Tunmore. *p322.*
HEARN, Colour Sergeant. 'F' Company, 7th (Cyclist) Battalion Devonshire Regiment, based at Whitby. *p295, p324(p), p325.*
HESELTON, Mrs Jane. 13 Normanby Terrace. Windows broken. Fled with four daughters to Romanby, Northallerton. *p351, p352.*
HILL, Albert Ernest. Music Teacher. 3 Spring Hill Terrace. Windows broken. *p299.*
HODGSON, Richard. Fruiterer. 96 Church Street. Roof slightly damaged.
HOGG, Christpher. Haxby, York. Gave account. *p355.*

HOGGARTH, Mrs. Attended funeral of brother-in-law William Tunmore. *p322.*
HOLEY, J. S. Attended funeral of William Tunmore. *p322.*
HOOD. Secretary, Red Cross. *p303.*
HORNE & SON. Printers and Stationers. 17-18 Bridge Street. Publishers of *Whitby Gazette*. *p307.*
HOWE, Mrs C. Bingley, West Yorkshire. Gave account. *p355.*
HUME, David. *Rivington,* Prospect Hill. Draper at 5 Baxtergate. House severely damaged.
HUSTLER, Polly. Church Street. *p354.*
HUTCHINGS, Corporal. 'F' Company, 7th (Cyclist) Battalion Devonshire Regiment, based at Ness Point, Robin Hood's Bay. *p297, p345.*

JACKSON, John. *Bandora House,* 4 Windsor Terrace. Roof and chimney damaged.
JACKSON, Mrs D. L. Formerly of Kiln Yard, 16. Gave account. *p365, p366.*
JEFFERS, Albert James. Coastguard. B: coastguard station, Bear Island, Bantry Bay, County Cork, 16.10.1883. Aged 31. Pall bearer at funeral of Frederick Randall, *p293, p319, p354, p355.*
JEFFERS, John. Son of Coastguard Jeffers. Gave account. *p354, p355.*
JEFFERS, Nellie (née Corner). Born Whitby, 23.11.1890. Aged 24. Wife of Coastguard Jeffers. *p354, p355.*
JEFFERSON, Private L. Army Service Corps. Attended funeral of William Tunmore. *p322.*

KELLY, John 'Jack', age 9, B: 17.12.1907, son of Thomas McGarry Kelly. Gave account. *p358(p), p359, pp361, p362(p), p363.*
KELLY, Thomas McGarry. Licensee, Monkshaven Public House, Church Street. Fisherman. 1863-1950. Wife, Sarah Elizabeth (née Redmond). 1866-1931. Children: Catherine; Ada; Minnie; Hilda; Betty; Ethel; and John ('Jack'). *p358(p), p359, p361, p362(p), p363.*
KIPLING, John Stephen. Draper. Hilton's Yard, 5. Age 23, B: Whitby, 25.10.1891. Sent postcard to sister. Enlisted Royal Army Medical Corps, 08.03.1915 (married Florence Mary Fowler same day). D: 08.06.1917, Whitby, kidney failure as result of being gassed. Buried Whitby cemetery. *p353(p), p356(p), p357, p358(p).*
KIPLING, William. Younger brother of John Stephen Kipling. Gave account. *p357, p358(p).*
KNAGGS. Sergeant, Red Cross. *p303.*

LANG. Archbishop of York. *p158, p161, p316, p318.*
LAWRENCE, Sergeant. 'F' Company, 7th (Cyclist) Battalion Devonshire Regiment, based at Runswick Bay. *p326.*
LAWS, John. 22 Gray Street. Roof damaged. *p299.*
LEE, William. Tailor. Chairman of Burniston Parish Council. Watched ships sail towards Whitby. *p291.*
LIBERAL CLUB. Spring Hill. Secretary: Joseph SEWELL. Windows broken.
LICKLEY, Mrs. Sent flowers to funeral of William Tunmore. *p322.*
LIGHT, Private. 'F' Company, 7th (Cyclist) Battalion Devonshire Regiment, based at Ness Point, Robin Hood's Bay. *p297, p345.*
LORAINS, Ernest. Goods Porter, North Eastern Railway Company. Gave evidence at inquest of William Tunmore. *p316, p322.*

MANNING, Private. 'F' Company, 7th (Cyclist) Battalion Devonshire Regiment, based at Ness Point, Robin Hood's Bay. *p297, p345.*
MARINE INN, Marine Parade. Proprietor: Thomas TAYLOR. Brickwork damaged, windows broken.
MARSAY, Elizabeth Welbury. 23 Pier Road. Age 5, B: 15.03.1909. Twin sister of Benjamin Garminsway Marsay. Gave account. *p363, p365.*
MARSHALL, John. 3 Gray Street. Wife wounded in leg. House severely damaged. *p299.*
MARWOOD, Christopher. *Stone House,* 21 St Hilda's Terrace. Justice of the Peace. House severely damaged, and demolished.
MCGREGOR, Captain Charles. Chubb Hill Road. Master Mariner. Foreman of jury at Winefride Miller's inquest. *p333.*
MEAD, Mrs T. Attended funeral of cousin William Tunmore. *p322.*
MEADOWFIELD HALL BOYS' SCHOOL. Downdinner Hill. Headmaster: D. Currie. School badly damaged, no one hurt. *p301, p302(p).*
MELTON, Arthur. Manager of the Scarborough & Whitby Brewery offices. St Ann's Staith. Age 25. B: 1889. Gave account. *p357, p359.*
MILLER, Roy. Boy Scout. 9 Victoria Square. Son of Captain William Miller, Master Mariner. On duty at Signal Station, wounded in leg, amputated. Became manager of a bank. *p297, p303, p318, p322, p326, p345, p346, p347, p361.*
MITCHELL, James. Delivery Lad. Scoresby Terrace. Age 16. Member of Youths' Drill Company. Awarded RSPCA Silver Medal. *p305, p348(p).*
MORFOOT, E. Attended funeral of William Tunmore. *p322.*
MORFOOT, H. Attended funeral of William Tunmore. *p322.*
MORRIS. Attended funeral of cousin William Tunmore. *p322.*
MOYSEY, Private. Despatch Rider. 'F' Company, 7th (Cyclist) Battalion Devonshire Regiment, based at Whitby. Near miss on Royal Crescent. *p307, p325.*
MUMBY, A. Policeman. Attended funeral of Frederick Randall. *p319.*

NORTON, Captain George. Master Mariner. 3 Park Terrace. Roof and upper storey damaged, windows broken.

PALFRAMAN, Albert. Councillor. 13 Wellclose Terrace. Attended special compensation meeting of Whitby Urban District Council. *p319, p320, p321, p322.*
PALMER, Margaret. Cliff Street, 41. Daughter, Edith M. (later Rochester). Age 7. Pupil at Cliff Street School. Gave account. *p347.*
PARKIN, Harold. Age 10. Pupil at St Hilda's Roman Catholic School. Gave account. *p347, p349.*
PARKINSON, Robert. Telegraphist at the Coastguard Station, wounded in hand and leg. *p297.*
PARRATT, Miss Emily. Headmistress at Cholmley School, Church Street. Daughter of Thomas William Parratt. *p365.*
PARRATT, R. Thornton-le-Dale. Attended funeral of William Tunmore. *p322.*
PARRATT, Thomas William. *Falcon House,* Spring Hill Terrace. Mrs Parratt was a teacher at St John's Church of England School. Roof damaged, windows broken. Attended funeral of William Tunmore. *p299, p322, p346.*
PARRY-OKEDEN, Reverend G. E. C. Attended funeral of William Tunmore. *p322.*
PEARSON, James William. *Mayville,* Robin Hood's Bay. Age 25. Fatally wounded aboard *SS Phoebe*, Hartlepool. D: 3.15pm. Buried 19.12.1914. Son of Captain Richardson Pearson. *p387.*
PEART, George. Saved lives in the *Rohilla* disaster. *p295.*
PERN, Dr Lionel. 27 Skinner Street. Physician & Surgeon at the Dispensary, Church Street. Attended birth of George Shrapnel Griffin. Attended Winefride Miller. Gave evidence at the inquest. *p309, p333, p335.*
PHILLPOT, Mrs J. 12 Gray Street. Turned up at relations with Christmas cake under her arm. *p346.*
PINKNEY, G. P. Attended funeral of William Tunmore. *p322.*
POLICE STATION. Spring Hill. Unscathed. *p307.*
PRENTICE, William. George Street. School Attendance Officer. Attended funeral of William Tunmore. *p322.*
PROSPECT HILL FARM, Prospect Hill. Fields ploughed up.
PURNELL, Private. 'F' Company, 7th (Cyclist) Battalion Devonshire Regiment. Based at Robin Hood's Bay (Ness Point). *p345.*

PURVIS, Private W. Royal Army Medical Corps, BEF, France. Wrote letter to Mr Todd of *Westoo House*, Church Lane. *p352.*
PYMAN. Chairman, local Emergency Committee. *p328.*

RAW, Dr Herbert Harland. *Spring Hill House,* Spring Hill. Physician & Surgeon. Medical Officer & Public Vaccinator for East Whitby District. Garden wall damaged, windows broken. *p317(p).*
REID, John. 9 Cleveland Terrace. Councillor. Attended special compensation meeting of Whitby Urban District Council. *p319, p320, p321, p322.*
RHODES, Mrs W. A. Ruswarp Bank. Near miss. *p307.*
RIPPON, Arthur. Spring Hill Terrace. Master Mariner. Windows broken.
ROBINSON, Frederick. 2 Gray Street. House and interior severely damaged. *p299, p346.*

SAMPLE, Mr & Mrs. Sent flowers to funeral of William Tunmore. *p322.*
SAMUEL, Herbert. President, Local Government Board.
SCOTT, Thomas Keat. 3 Albion Terrace. Town Surveyor, Council Chambers, Flowergate. Windows broken.
SEWELL, Joseph. Secretary: Liberal Club, Spring Hill. Windows broken.
SHEATH, Captain Charles. 13 Esk Terrace. Windows broken.
SHEPHARD, Courtenay. *Elford Villa,* Prospect Hill. House severely damaged.
SHORT, A. Attended funeral of William Tunmore. *p322.*
SIMPSON, Miss. 24 Bagdale. Sent flowers to funeral of William Tunmore. *p322.*
SMITHSON, John. 14 Esk Terrace. Plumber. Exterior gas main and garden wall damaged, windows broken.
ST HILDA'S ROMAN CATHOLIC SCHOOL. Spring Hill. Mixed school under the administration of the Sisters of Mercy. *p347, p349.*
ST JOHN'S CHURCH, Baxtergate. Curate: Rev. C. Snushall. Officiated at funerals of Frederick Randall and William Tunmore. *p319, p322, p323.*
ST MARY'S PARISH CHURCH. East Cliff. Windows broken. Curate, Rev. Walter Bancroft officiated at the funeral of Frederick Randall. Attended funeral of William Tunmore. *p299 p319. p322, p335.*
ST MICHAEL'S CHURCH. Church Street. *p357.*
ST MICHAEL'S SCHOOL. Church Street. *p354, p359, p363.*
STEELE, T. Attended funeral of William Tunmore. *p322.*
STONEHOUSE, Frank. Child at St Michael's School. *p363.*

TANFIELD, George. 15 Gray Street. Apartments. Attended funeral of William Tunmore. *p322.*
TANFIELD, W. Attended funeral of William Tunmore. *p322.*
TATE, William. 16 Esk Terrace. Coal & Coke Merchant. General damage, windows broken.
TESSEYMAN, John Robert. 24 Silver Street. Plumber & Gasfitter. Attended funeral of William Tunmore. *p322.*
THEAKER, George William. 17 Esk Terrace. Master Mariner. General damage, windows broken.
THISTLE, Miss. 6 Belle Vue Terrace. Attended funeral of William Tunmore. *p322.*
TODD, T. E. *Westoo House*, Church Street. Received letter from Private Purvis, RAMC. *p352.*
TOMLINSON, Mr & Mrs. Sent flowers to funeral of William Tunmore. *p322.*
TRACEY, Commandant Louis. *Fairlawn.* Represented Whitby District Volunteer Training Corps at funeral of Frederick Randall. Sent flowers to the funeral of William Tunmore. *p309, p322.*
TRATTLES, Thomas. *Westholme,* Upgang Lane. Jet ornament worker. Footpath damaged.
TROTTER, Major-General Sir J. K. Inspected and buried unexploded shell, Sleights. *p303.*
TRUEMAN, G. W. *Harbour View*, 1 Esk Place. House severely damaged.
TUNMORE, Elizabeth. 14 Gray Street. Wife of William Tunmore. *p322.*
TURNBULL, Thomas. Airy Hill. House damaged.
TURNER, E. L. Councillor. At special compensation meeting of Whitby Urban District Council. *p319, p320, p321, p322.*
TURNERDALE HALL. Ruswarp. Shell in field.

URMSTON, W. Attended funeral of William Tunmore. *p322.*

VIVIAN. Scout Master. *p318.*

WARD, Mrs. Teacher, Cholmley School, Church Street. *p365.*
WATTS, William. 28 Esk Terrace. Postmaster. Injured leg. *p299.*
WEATHERILL, J. B. Councillor. At special compensation meeting of Whitby Urban District Council. *p319, p320, p321, p322.*
WEIR, William. 11 Esk Terrace. Apartments. General damage, windows broken.
WELBURY, Thomas. *Fair Isle Cottage*, Tin Ghaut, off Grape Lane. Master Mariner. Grandfather of Elizabeth and Benjamin Marsay. *p363, p365.*
WELLBURN, George Simpson. 3 Hanover Terrace. Tailor. 13 Bridge Street (business).
WELLBURN, Mrs G. S. Wellburn. 3 Hanover Terrace. Attended funeral of William Tunmore. *p322.*
WHALEY, Coastguard. Pall bearer at funeral of Frederick Randall. *p319.*
WHITE, Robert William. *Adderstone*, Crescent Avenue. Attended funeral of William Tunmore. *p322.*
WHITEHEAD, Second-Lieutenant B. 'F' Company, 7th (Cyclist) Battalion Devonshire Regiment, based at Ness Point, Robin Hood's Bay. *p326, p345.*
WILKINSON. River Gardens, Sleights. Shell in field.
WILSON, M. Councillor. At special compensation meeting of Whitby Urban District Council. *p319, p320, p321, p322.*
WINSPEAR, J. Signal man. Unhurt. Signal box windows broken.
WOOD, Alexander. 7 Horner's Terrace. Worked for *Whitby Gazette*. Wife, Jane Elizabeth. Daughter Eva, aged 8, B: 13.06.1906, gave account. *p353(p), p354.*
WOOD, Mr & Mrs. Doncaster. Sent flowers to funeral of William Tunmore. *p322.*
WOODWARK, Thomas H. Councillor. Solicitor. 16 Bagdale. At special compensation meeting of Whitby Urban District Council. Attended funeral of William Tunmore. *p319, p320, p321, p322.*

Author's Appeal For Information

Further information is still sought on all aspects of the bombardments and the various military and naval units mentioned in the book. If you have any information, or photographs, you are requested to contact the author (via the offices of the publisher).

Index L: Whitby's Damage 1914 *(by street)*

1: Index of damage done and those mentioned in the text.
2: Listed in alphabetical order, STREET, followed by available information.
3: All details relate to the bombardment of Wednesday, 16th December 1914, unless stated otherwise.
4: Abbreviations used: B: Year/date of birth. D: Year/date of death.
5: Ages given are those at the time of the incident (i.e. December 1914) under which the entry is made.
6: Page numbers at the end of an entry indicate where the subject is mentioned in the text. The '(p)' indicates a picture.
7: Entries carrying the legend 'Gave account' indicate where an oral or written account has been provided.

Airy Hill Farm. BURNETT, John Hassell. Son, Ernest. Aged 7. Gave account. *p346, p347.*
Airy Hill. Fields ploughed up.
Airy Hill. TURNBULL, Thomas. House damaged.
Albion Place. FILBURN, Mrs. Injured by falling masonry. Upper rooms demolished, windows broken. *p299.*
Albion Terrace, 3. SCOTT, Thomas Keat. Town Surveyor, Council Chambers, Flowergate. Windows broken.

Bagdale, 16. WOODWARK, Thomas H. Councillor. Solicitor. At special compensation meeting of Whitby Urban District Council. Attended funeral of William Tunmore. *p319, p320, p321, p322.*
Bagdale, 24. SIMPSON, Miss. Sent flowers to funeral of William Tunmore. *p322.*
Baxtergate, 2. COLLIER, Raymund. Ironmonger. Also 4 Flowergate. Brother of Winefride Miller. Gave evidence at inquest. *p335.*
Baxtergate, ST JOHN'S CHURCH. Curate: Rev. C. Snushall. Officiated at funerals of Frederick Randall and William Tunmore. *p319, p322, p323.*
Baxtergate. BUCHANNAN, George. Whitby Coroner. Officiated at inquests. *p314, p316, p333.*
Belle Vue Terrace, 3. HAMILTON, William Henry. Headmaster of St John's Church of England School, Windsor Terrace. School undamaged. Children uninjured. *p346.*
Belle Vue Terrace, 6. THISTLE, Miss. Attended funeral of William Tunmore. *p322.*
Bobby's Bank. Telegraph wires brought down.

Chubb Hill Road. CONVENT CONVALESCENT HOME. Convent of the Sisters of Mercy. Lady Superior: Sister T. F. Dobson. Cared for Winefride Miller. *p299, p303, p333.*
Chubb Hill Road. MCGREGOR, Captain Charles. Master Mariner. Foreman of jury at Winefride Miller's inquest. *p333.*
Church Street, 96. HODGSON, Richard. Fruiterer. Roof slightly damaged.
Church Street, Monkshaven Public House. KELLY, Thomas McGarry. Licensee. Fisherman. 1863-1950. Wife, Sarah Elizabeth (née Redmond). 1866-1931. Children: Catherine; Ada; Minnie; Hilda; Betty; Ethel; and John ('Jack'), age 9, B: 17.12.1907. Gave account. *p358(p), p359, p361, p362(p), p363.*
Church Street, *Westoo House.* TODD, T. E. Received letter from Private Purvis, RAMC. *p352.*
Church Street. CHOLMLEY SCHOOL. *p365, p366.*
Church Street. ST MICHAEL'S SCHOOL. *p354, p359, p363.*
Cleveland Terrace, 3. HARRISON, Captain John. Master Mariner. House damaged, windows broken.
Cleveland Terrace, 9. REID, John. Councillor. Attended special compensation meeting of Whitby Urban District Council. *p319, p320, p321, p322.*
Cliff Street, 41. PALMER, Margaret. Daughter, Edith M. (later Rochester). Age 7. Pupil at Cliff Street School. Gave account. *p347.*
Cliff Street. CLIFF STREET SCHOOL. Opened 1894. *p347.*
Commercial Street, 38. Norton. HALL, Thomas. Railway Guardsman, North Eastern Railway. Gave account. *p351.*
Cragg, The, 52. GRIFFIN, Edward 'Teddy'. Steps damaged. Seventh son, George Shrapnel, born 9.05am, 16.12 1914. *p307, p309, p340(p).*
Crescent Avenue, 7. HARKER, William, and daughter, Miss I. Harker, sent flowers to funeral of William Tunmore. *p322.*
Crescent Avenue, *Adderstone.* WHITE, Robert William. Attended funeral of William Tunmore. *p322.*
Crescent Avenue, *Highfield.* BRECKON, Mrs. Attended funeral of cousin William Tunmore. *p322.*

Downdinner Hill. MEADOWFIELD HALL BOYS' SCHOOL. Headmaster: D. Currie. School badly damaged. No one hurt. *p301, p302(p).*

East Cliff. ABBEY HOUSE. Barn/stable. Roof holed. *p299, p303, p344(p), p355, p357, p361.*
East Cliff. ABBEY. St Hilda's Abbey and Lodge. Damaged. *p292(p), p296(p), p297, p307, p322, p347, p350(p), p351, p352, p357, p361.*
East Cliff. ST MARY'S PARISH CHURCH. Windows broken. Curate, Rev. Walter Bancroft officiated at the funeral of Frederick Randall. Attended funeral of William Tunmore. *p299, p319, p322, p335.*
East Terrace, 5. CORNER, J. Upper room damaged, windows broken.
Esk Place, 1. *Harbour View.* TRUEMAN, G. W. House severely damaged.
Esk Terrace, 11. WEIR, William. Apartments. General damage, windows broken.
Esk Terrace, 12. COLLIER, William George. Apartments. General damage, windows broken.
Esk Terrace, 13. SHEATH, Captain Charles. Windows broken.
Esk Terrace, 14. SMITHSON, John. Plumber. Exterior gas main and garden wall damaged, windows broken.
Esk Terrace, 15. BARTON, Captain William. Master Mariner. Front of house and garden wall damaged, windows broken. *p300(p).*
Esk Terrace, 16. TATE, William. Coal & Coke Merchant. General damage, windows broken.
Esk Terrace, 17. THEAKER, George William. Master Mariner. General damage, windows broken.
Esk Terrace, 24. BEECROFT, Mrs Charles. Attended funeral of William Tunmore. *p322.*
Esk Terrace, 28. WATTS, William. Postmaster. Injured leg. *p299.*
Esk Terrace. CAWTHORNE, John George. Councillor. Attended special compensation meeting of Whitby Urban District Council. *p319, p320, p321, p322.*

Fairlawn. TRACEY, Commandant Louis. Represented Whitby District Volunteer Training Corps at funeral of Frederick Randall. Sent flowers to funeral of William Tunmore. *p309, p319, p322.*
Falcon Terrace, 1. FISHER, Isaac. Greengrocer. Daughter, Henrietta, trapped by window when bombardment began. *p299, p307, p355.*
Falcon Terrace. GRAHAM, Oscar E. Sanitary Inspector. House damaged, fire started, but extinguished. Windows broken. *p299.*
Flowergate, 5. COOK, R. C. Councillor. Boot Dealer. At special compensation meeting of Whitby Urban District Council. *p319, p320, p321, p322.*
Flowergate, 29. DOWELL, Mrs Ann. Fruiterer. Sent flowers to funeral of William Tunmore. *p322.*

George Street. PRENTICE, William. School Attendance Officer. Attended funeral of William Tunmore. *p322.*
Grape Lane. COTTAGE HOSPITAL. Dr Edward Baines attended Winefride Miller.
Gray Street, 1. BURNETT, Robert. Butcher. House received a direct hit. *p346.*
Gray Street, 2. ROBINSON, Frederick. House and interior severely damaged. *p299, p346.*
Gray Street, 3. MARSHALL, John. Wife wounded in leg. House severely damaged. *p299.*
Gray Street, 12. PHILLPOT, Mrs J. Turned up at relations with Christmas cake under her arm. *p346.*
Gray Street, 15. TANFIELD, George. Apartments. Attended funeral of William Tunmore. *p322.*
Gray Street, 22. LAWS, John. Roof damaged. *p299.*
Grove Street, 1. BLEWETT, T. H. Secretary, Whitby Football Club. Roof, chimney, upper walls and rooms damaged, windows broken. *p300(p).*
Grove Street, 2. FRALER. Roof, chimney and upper rooms damaged.

Hanover Terrace, 3. WELLBURN, George Simpson. Tailor at 13 Bridge Street. Wife attended funeral of William Tunmore. *p322.*
Horner's Terrace, 7. WOOD, Alexander. Worked for *Whitby Gazette*. Wife, Jane Elizabeth. Daughter Eva, aged 8, B: 13.06.1906, gave account. *p353(p), p354.*

Low Stakesby. HARROWING, John Henry. Justice of the Peace. Member of the Emergency Committee. Offered assistance in streets shortly after shelling ceased.
Lower George Street. General damage.
Lower Gray Street. General damage.

Marine Parade, 12. GIBSON, Laura. Fancy Repository. Stock damaged, window broken. *p301.*
Marine Parade, MARINE INN. Proprietor: Thomas Taylor. Brickwork damaged, windows broken.

Normanby Terrace, 2. GALE. W. Boy Scout. Bugler, sounded last post at funeral of Frederick Randall. Son of John C. Gale. *p319.*
Normanby Terrace, 13. HESELTON, Mrs Jane. Windows broken. Fled with four daughters to Romanby, Northallerton. *p351, p352.*
North Road, *Sandal Villa.* Windows broken.

Park Terrace, 3. NORTON, Captain George. Master Mariner. Roof and upper storey damaged, windows broken.
Pier Road, 23. MARSAY, Elizabeth Welbury. Age 5, B: 15.03.1909. Twin sister of Benjamin Garminsway Marsay. Gave account. *p363, p365.*
Pier. DAVIE, Charles Southerdon. Chief Officer of Coastguard. Gave evidence at inquests of Randall and Miller. Represented coastguard at funeral of Frederick Randall. *p314, p316, p319, p335.*
Prospect Hill, *Elford Villa.* SHEPHARD, Courtenay. House severely damaged.
Prospect Hill, *Elford.* BUCKLE, Major E. J. Bentley. Whitby representative of the RSPCA. *p307.*
Prospect Hill, *Hill Crest.* BRUCE, J. House damaged, dinner-table holed, windows broken. Attended funeral of William Tunmore. *p307, p322.*
Prospect Hill, *Rivington.* HUME, David. Draper at 5 Baxtergate. House severely damaged.
Prospect Hill, *Westgrove.* HARMSTON, James Egan. Mayor. Justice of the Peace. Presided at special compensation meeting of Whitby Urban District Council. *p319, p320, p321, p322, p327, p328, p329, p331.*
Prospect Hill. PROSPECT HILL FARM. Fields ploughed up.

Rocky Bed Lane. Stable loft roof damaged.
Royal Crescent. MOYSEY, Private. Despatch Rider. 'F' Company, 7th (Cyclist) Battalion Devonshire Regiment, based at Whitby. Near miss. *p307, p325.*
Royal Crescent. Road damaged.
Ruswarp Bank. RHODES, Mrs W. A. Near miss. *p307.*
Ruswarp. TURNERDALE HALL. Shell in field.

Sandgate, 1. DUCK, John & Sons. Butchers. Wife attended funeral of William Tunmore. *p322.*
Sandgate, 9. CLOUGH, Fred. Councillor. Butcher. Attended special compensation meeting of Whitby Urban District Council. *p319, p320, p321, p322.*
Scoresby Terrace. MITCHELL, James. Delivery Lad. Age 16, B: 1898. Member of Youths' Drill Company. Awarded RSPCA Silver Medal. *p305, p348(p).*
Silver Street, 22. DOBSON. Mr. Unexploded shrapnel shell dug out of Ruswarp Rifle Range field. Wife and daughter attended funeral of William Tunmore. *p303 p322.*
Silver Street, 24. TESSEYMAN, John Robert. Plumber & Gasfitter. Attended funeral of William Tunmore. *p322.*
Silver Street. CONSERVATIVE CLUB. Dome broken, billiard-tables damaged.
Skinner Street, 18-22. BARRY, William Ernest. Music Seller. Attended funeral of William Tunmore. *p322.*
Skinner Street, 27. PERN, Dr Lionel. Physician & Surgeon at the Dispensary, Church Street. Attended birth of George Shrapnel Griffin. Attended Winefride Miller. Gave evidence at the inquest. *p309, p333, p335.*
Sleights. CURTIS, Sergeant. Inmate of Red Cross Hospital. Assisted Major-General Trotter to bury unexploded shell. *p303.*
Sleights. River Gardens. WILKINSON. Shell in field.
Sleights. TROTTER, Major-General Sir J. K. Inspected and buried unexploded shell. *p303.*
Sneaton. BEEFORTH, Henry. Shells in fields.
Spring Hill Road, *West Hill House.* BULMER, A. T. House severely damaged. Took refuge in cellar, unhurt. *p299, p300(p), p310(p).*
Spring Hill Terrace, 2. RIPPON, Arthur. Master Mariner. Windows broken.
Spring Hill Terrace, 3. HILL, Albert Ernest. Music Teacher. Windows broken. *p299.*
Spring Hill Terrace, *Falcon House.* PARRATT, Thomas William. Mrs Parratt was a teacher at St John's Church of England School. Roof damaged, windows broken. Attended funeral of William Tunmore. *p299 p322, p346.*
Spring Hill Terrace. General damage.
Spring Hill. General damage.
Spring Hill. LIBERAL CLUB. Secretary: Joseph Sewell. Windows broken.
Spring Hill. *Spring Hill House.* RAW, Dr Herbert Harland. Physician & Surgeon. Medical Officer & Public Vaccinator for East Whitby District. Garden wall damaged, windows broken. *p317(p).*
Spring Hill. ST HILDA'S ROMAN CATHOLIC SCHOOL. Mixed school under the administration of the Sisters of Mercy. *p347, p349.*
St Ann's Staith. MELTON, Arthur. Manager of the Scarborough & Whitby Brewery offices. Age 25. Gave account. *p357, p359.*
St Hilda's Terrace, 16. GRAY, William Seaton. Clerk to Whitby Urban District Council. Attended special compensation meeting of Whitby Urban District Council. Attended funeral of William Tunmore. *p319, p320, p321, p322.*
St Hilda's Terrace, 21. *Stone House.* MARWOOD, Christopher. Justice of the Peace. House severely damaged, and demolished.

Stakesby Road. HEADLAM, Aaron. Daughter, Miss G. Headlam, attended funeral of William Tunmore. *p322.*
Stakesby Vale, *Corra Lynn.* GALLOWAY, William M. Attended funeral of William Tunmore. *p322.*
Stakesby Vale, *The Hut.* BROWN, W. Councillor. Attended special compensation meeting of Whitby Urban District Council. Attended funeral of William Tunmore. *p319, p320, p321, p322.*

Tin Ghaut, off Grape Lane. *Fair Isle Cottage.* WELBURY, Thomas. Master Mariner. Grandfather of Elizabeth and Benjamin Marsay. *p363, p365.*

Upgang Lane, *Westholme.* TRATTLES, Thomas. Jet ornament worker. Footpath damaged.
Upgang Lane. CROSS, Mr & Mrs Charles George. Attended funeral of William Tunmore. *p322.*
Upper George Street. General damage.
Upper Gray Street. General damage.

Victoria Square, 9. MILLER, Roy. Boy Scout. Son of Captain William Miller, Master Mariner. On duty at Signal Station, wounded in leg, amputated. Became manager of a bank. *p297, p303, p318, p322, p326, p345, p346, p347, p361.*

Wellclose Terrace, 13. PALFRAMAN, Albert. Councillor. Attended special compensation meeting of Whitby Urban District Council. *p319, p320, p321, p322.*
West Lea. GASKIN, John. Solicitor's clerk. Roof and upper rooms damaged. Building damage £74/1s/7d. Furniture damage £34/4s/0d. Wife attended funeral of William Tunmore. *p314(p), p317(p), p322, p348(p), p352.*
Windsor Terrace, 4. *Bandora House.* JACKSON, John. Roof and chimney damaged.
Windsor Terrace, 12. AGAR, Joseph. Roof, upper storey damaged, windows broken.
Windsor Terrace, 13. FORTH, Frederick Douglas. Roof blown off, upper rooms wrecked, windows broken.
Windsor Terrace. ST JOHN'S CHURCH OF ENGLAND SCHOOL. Headmaster: William Henry Hamilton. School undamaged. Children uninjured. *p301, p346.*

Index M: SS Rohilla Dead

The hospital ship '*SS Rohilla*' was wrecked off Whitby on 30th October 1914. She lost 90 officers and men, only 14 of whom were identified. A monument to their memory was erected by the British India Steam Navigation Company Limited (owners of the *Rohilla*) in Whitby Cemetery.

Ambrose, A.
Anderson, W. E.

Barron, W. *(identified)*
Barter, H. J.
Birtwhistle, M.
Blakeley, J.
Brain, G.
Brown, John. 3rd Engineer
Burney, A. H.
Burns, J. J.

Cain, J.
Cameron, D.
Cowie, J. C.
Cribb, H. J.
Currell, J.
Cwydir, Very Reverend Canon *(Roman Catholic Priest)*

Daly, W. J.
Dawson, F.
Dawson, W.
Duffy, M. J.
Dunkley, F.

Elsworth, A. C.

Foggarty, J. J.

Gibson, C. B.
Gibson, W.
Gillies, A.
Gover, G. *(identified)*
Graham, J.

Hare, J. *(identified)*
Harrison, F. W.
Henderson, S.
Hodkinson, H.
Horsburgh, J.
Horsfield, T.
Horsfield, W.

Kelly, J.
Kerr, J.
Kirk, G.

Mackenzie, J.
Mardell, G. H.
McBride, H. T.
McCallum, A.
McDonald, D.
McDonald, W.
McGlasham, A.
McLeod, N.
McMillan, A.
McNaughtan, J.
Milner, G. W. M.
Moor, P. C. 3rd Officer
Morgan, F. W.
Morris, S. *(identified)*
Muir, W.
Murphy, J.

Neville, M. A.
Nicholson, L. *(identified)*
Nicol, J.
Nisbet, D. *(identified)*

Ogilvie, W.

Page, A. *(identified)*
Parsons, G. E.
Paton, D. *(identified)*
Paton, J. *(identified)*
Perrin, William. Electrician
Petty, A.
Petty, T.
Pickles, J. T.

Queenan, J.

Rafferty, P.
Randell, F.
Reid, A.
Reid, J.
Robins, H.
Rose, E. *(identified)*
Ross, J. G. *(identified)*

Scott, A.
Scott, R. D.
Sellars, J.
Shute, A. E.
Smith, B.
Smith, J. *(identified)*
Stewart, A.
Stewart, J.

Tarbet, M. *(identified)*
Tinney, J.
Torrance, D.

Watson, R.
Watts, H.
Weatherstone, H. W. *(identified)*
White, W.

Index N: The Hartlepools' Dead 1914 *(military and naval)*

1: Index of military and naval personnel killed or who died as a result of the bombardment.
2: Listed in alphabetical order, SURNAME, followed by available information.
3: All details relate to the bombardment of Wednesday, 16th December 1914, unless stated otherwise.
4: Abbreviations used: B: Year/date of birth. D: Year/date of death.
5: Ages given are those at the time of the incident (i.e. December 1914 etc.) under which the entry is made.
6: Page numbers at the end of an entry indicate where the subject is mentioned in the text. The '(p)' indicates a picture.
7: Entries marked with an asterisk (*) contain their own explanatory notes.

CLARK, 18/707 Private Charles Stephen. 18th Battalion, Durham Light Infantry. Born West Hartlepool. Enlisted West Hartlepool. Killed in action. *p373.*
CREDLAND, 177695 Harold. Able Seaman. Age 37. HMS *Doon.* Died of wounds. 17.12.1914. Buried Harton Cemetery, South Shields.
CUMMINGS, J/8662 Ernest Charles. Able Seaman. Age 20. HMS *Patrol.* Lost overboard, died. 16.12.1914. Commemorated in Holy Trinity Churchyard, Seaton Carew. County Durham.

FRASER, SS/109383 James. Stoker 1st Class. Age 23. HMS *Doon*. Lost overboard, died. 16.12.1914. Commemorated on the Chatham Naval Memorial, Kent. *p371*.

HOOK, 224557 Ralph Weston. Leading Seaman. Age 28. HMS *Patrol*. Killed in action. 16.12.1914. Buried Linthorpe Cemetery, Middlesbrough.

HOUSTON, 5693 Gunner William Stephen. Durham Royal Garrison Artillery. Born Middlesbrough. Enlisted West Hartlepool. Killed in action. *p373*.

JONES, 18/295 Private Theophilis Jones. 18th Battalion, Durham Light Infantry. Born Darlington. Enlisted West Hartlepool. Killed in action. *p373, p377*.

LIDDLE, 18/107 Private Alex Olliffe. 18th Battalion, Durham Light Infantry. Born Darlington. Enlisted Darlington. Killed in action. *p373*.

*LITTLE, Sapper Samuel. Durham Royal Engineers. I could not find any contemporary accounts which listed this man as killed on 16.12.1914. He is listed as died on 07.12.1914. Having studied a number of official military accounts none of them list a Royal Engineer as killed during the bombardment. The only time an unnamed Royal Engineer does crop up in a tally of the dead is in an account by Major F. A. Yorke of the Royal Artillery, written in April 1930 (sixteen years after the event); he also stated that only 1 member of the 18th Durham Light Infantry was killed, when in actual fact 6 were killed, and he further states that 4 members of the Durham Royal Garrison Artillery were killed, when in fact only 2 were killed. It is this account I believe to be in error and which has led to Sapper Little being erroneously added to the list in more recent accounts. Yorke's error was later corrected in a thorough account of the bombardment of Hartlepool written by Captain W. A. Murley of the Royal Artillery.

*MARTIN, George Charlton. Armourers Crew. HMS *Patrol*. Reported killed (unconfirmed).

MAY, K/3590 Frederick George. Stoker 1st Class. Age 24. HMS *Doon*. Died of wounds. 22.01.1915. Buried Deal Cemetery, Kent.

MINKS, 18/328 Private Thomas. 18th Battalion, Durham Light Infantry. Born Medomsley, County Durham. Enlisted Newcastle upon Tyne. Wounded, died of wounds, Hartlepool, 17.12.1914. *p373*.

RIGSBY, Leading Seaman H. H. Killed on HMS *Hardy*. *p391*.

ROGERS, 18/369 Private William. 18th Battalion, Durham Light Infantry. Born Bishop Auckland. Enlisted Spennymoor. Killed in action. *p373*.

SHERIDAN, 280091 Patrick Joseph. Engine Room Artificer 1st Class. HMS *Patrol*. Died of wounds. 16.12.1914. Buried at St Joseph's Roman Catholic Cemetery, North Ormesby, Yorkshire.

SPENCE, 15428 Gunner Robert. Durham Royal Garrison Artillery. Born Hartlepool. Enlisted West Hartlepool. Killed in action. *p373, p423*.

TURNER, 18/398 Private Leslie Dobson. 18th Battalion, Durham Light Infantry. Born Heaton. Enlisted Newcastle upon Tyne. Killed in action. *p373*.

WOOLGAR, Able Seaman G. W. Killed on HMS *Hardy*. *p391*.

Index O: The Hartlepools' Dead 1914 *(civilians by name)*

Civilians - 112 (114 including Thomas Jeffrey and Charles Tate).

1: Index of those killed or who died as a result of the bombardment.
2: Listed in alphabetical order, SURNAME, followed by available information.
3: All details relate to the bombardment of Wednesday, 16th December 1914, unless stated otherwise.
4: Abbreviations used: B: Year/date of birth. D: Year/date of death.
5: Ages given are those at the time of the incident (i.e. December 1914 etc.) under which the entry is made.
6: Page numbers at the end of an entry indicate where the subject is mentioned in the text. The '(p)' indicates a picture.
7: Entries marked with an asterisk (*) appear on the 'Hartlepool War Memorial' situated in Red Heugh Gardens.

*ALLEN, Annie. Age 25. 14 Victoria Place.
ALLEN, Robert Alfred. Age 10. 52 Crimdon Street.
*AMBROSE, Robert L. Age 33. 65 Everard Street. *p383, p434*.
ARNOLD, Hannah. Age 33. 48 Gas Street.
*ASHCROFT, Edwin. Age 29. 19 Penrith Street. *p383, p434*.
*ASQUITH. William. Age 51. 22 Town Wall.
AUSTRIN, Beart Beaumont. Age 33. 3 Mary Street.
*AVERY. William Gordon. Age 49. 7 Victoria Place. Salvation Army Adjutant. *p385, p396(p)*.

*BACKHAM. Cuthbert John. Age 42. 5 Church Street.
BELL, Henry Stephen. Age 11. 31 Belk Street. *p379*.
BINNS, Samuel. Age 68. 21 Ramsey Street.
BRENNAN, Margaret. Age 52. 53 Belk Street.
BROOKBANKS, Charles Abraham. Age 35. 4 Fawcett Street.
*BUNTER, James. Age 32. 13 Commercial Street, Middleton.
BURGON, Robert. Age 31. 7 Mill Street, Old Town. *p387, p435*.

*CAPELING, Nicholas. Age 25. 4 Darlington Street. Coming out of shipyards was struck on face by shrapnel, managed to walk to an ambulance but died in hospital. *p385*.
CAWS, Dorothy. Age 25. 57 Grosvenor Street. *p379*.
*CHAPPLE, William. Age 15. 18 Slake Terrace, Middleton.
CHURCHER, William H. Age 26. 29 Clarendon Road.
*CLARK, John. Age 54. 5 Kinburn Street.
CLAUDE, Alfred Camille Bernard. Age 12. 11 Gordon Street. *p383, p431*.
COOK, Harold. Age 10. 40 Turnbull Street.
*COOK, James. Age 37. 28 Rokeby Street. *p383, p434*.

COOK, Robert Wilfred. Age 8. 40 Turnbull Street.
COOPER, Edward. Age 16. 2 Exeter Street. *p381*.
*CORNER, Annie. Age 37. 1 Dock Street.
CORNER, Bridget. Age 39. 4 Dock Street, Old Town.
*CORNFORTH, Charles. Age 63. 3 Lilly Street. *p383*.
*CORNFORTH, Jane Ann. Age 17. 3 Lilly Street. *p383*.
*CORNFORTH, Polly. Age 23. 3 Lilly Street. *p383*.
*COX, Thomas Garbutt. Age 26. 2 Durham Street.
*CRAKE, John William. Age 15. 19 Wood Street. *p387*.
CRESSY, Albert Edwin. Age 29. 48 Turnbull Street. *p383, p434*.

*DIXON, Albert. Age 7. 30 William Street. *p385, p407, p409*.
*DIXON, George Edward. Age 14. 30 William Street. *p385, p407, p409*.
*DIXON, Margaret Ellen. Age 8. 30 William Street. *p385, p407, p409*.
DRING, George. Age 47. 30 Elliott Street. *p381*.

EVANS, John. Age 32. 30 Charlotte Street.

FRANKLAND, Catherine. Age 4. 3 Leeds Street, Old Town. *p379*.

*GEIPEL, Ethel Mary. Age 36. 17 Cliff Terrace.
GRAY, William. Age 23. 3 Ballast Hill, Blyth. Engineer's steward. *p387*.

*HAMILTON, Jessie. Age 21. 50 Malton Street.
*HARPER, Elizabeth Agnes. Age 49. 4 Moor Terrace. *p381*.
*HARRIS, Etta. Age 30. *Ivyholm*, South Crescent. Teacher at the Henry Smith Grammar School. *p381, p432*.
HARRISON, Mary Ann. Age 60. 24 Dene Street.
*HEALEY, John. Age 63. 18 Hart Street. *p385*.
HENDERSON, Joseph. Age 47. 45 Turnbull Street.
HENIGHAN, Margaret. Age 8. 18 Dock Street, Old Town. *p381*.
*HERBERT, Selina. Age 3. 5 William Street.
HESLOP, Thomas. Age 7. 19 Brafferton Street.
*HIGHAN, Thomas. Age 11. 9 Henry Street. *p379*.
*HODGSON, John. Age 62. 58 Stephenson Street.
HODGSON, Sarah. Age 56. 32 Thirlmere Street.
HODGSON, William 'Barney'. Age 43. 9 Water Street. *p387, p403, p409, p410, p415*.
*HORSLEY, Hilda. Age 17. 9 Wood Street. Tailoress. *p381*.
*HUDSON, Charles William. Age 21. 43 Mary Street. Apprentice engineer. *p383*.
HUNTER, Margaret Ann. Age 47. 11 Bridge Street, Old Town. *p387*.
HUNTER, Samuel Hall. Age 16. 1 Alexander Terrace. *p381*.

JACKSON, Edith. Age 39. 49 Perth Street.
JACOBS, Joseph. Age 13. 32 Belk Street. *p381, p409*.
*JEFFREY, Thomas. Recorded on Hartlepool War Memorial as having been killed in the bombardment.
JOBLING, Hannah. Age 4. 22 South Street, Old Town. *p379, p435*.
JOBLING, Sarah. Age 6. 22 South Street, Old Town. *p379, p435*.

*KAY, Annie M. Age 34. *Rockside*, Cliff Terrace. *p373 , p379, p396(p), p428*.
*KAY, Florence J. Age 32. *Rockside*, Cliff Terrace. *p373, p379, p396(p), p428*.

*LEE, Clementina. Age 25. 6 Victoria Place.
*LEIGHTON, James S. Age 56. 16 Clifton Street. *p383, p434*.
LOFTHOUSE, Benjamin. Age 7 months. 25 Belk Street. *p379*.
LYNETT, James. Age 42. 11 Staindrop Street. *p389*.

*MARSHALL, Catherine. Age 86. 41 Mary Street.
MCGUIRE, John. Age 15. 58 Cameron Road. *p387, p409*.
*MEASOR, Christopher. Age 10. 11 Well's Yard. *p385*.
MOON, Julia. Age 68. 11 Dover Street. *p379*.
MOSSOM, Thomas. Age 55. 2 John Street.

NECY, Eleanor. Age 6 months. 2 Pilot Street, Old Town. *p379*.

OLIVER, Joseph. Age 44. 6 Carlisle Place.
OWEN, Mary Ellen. Age 17. 1a Pilot Street, Old Town. *p379*.
OWEN, Rose. Age 43. 1a Pilot Street, Old Town. *p379*.

PEARSON, James William. Age 25. *Mayville House*, Robin Hood's Bay. Mortally wounded aboard *SS Phoebe*. *p387, p420(p)*.
PEART, Charles. Age 2. 30 Turnbull Street. *p381*.
PEART, William. Age 5. 30 Turnbull Street. *p381*.
PHILLIPS, Thomas. Age 16. 2 Leeds Street, Old Town.

RAMSEY, Charles L. C. Age 37. 24 Osborne Road. *p383, p434*.
RAYBOULD, Hannah. Age 36. 37 Darlington Terrace.
*REDSHAW, Margaret A. Age 47. 50 Watson Street. Shopkeeper. *p385*.

SARGINSON, William. Age 22. 67 Beechwood Road.
SCARR, Thomasina. Age 44. 1 Richardson Street. Father was a gunner with the Royal Field Artillery.
SIMMONS, Stanley. Age 5. 22 Campion Street. *p385*.
SKELTON, Matthew. Age 54. 82 Studley Road.

*STAUNCH, John. Age 41. 44 Alliance Street. *p381.*
*STEWART, Stanley. Age 6. 20 William Street.
STOKER, Jane. Age 41. Cook to William Ropner at *Ambleside*. *p379.*
*STRINGER, Ethel. Age 12. 10 William Street.
SULLIVAN, Daniel. Age 47. 3 Harrison Street. Plater's helper. *p385.*
*SWALES, Matthew Hastings. Age 36. 21 Croft Terrace.

TATE, Charles. Reported at the inquests as having died of abdominal wounds. *p389.*
THEAKER, Richard. Age 23. 63 Turnbull Street. Platelayer. *p383.*

*UNTHANK, Frank. Age 14. 24 Wood Street. *p385.*

*WAINWRIGHT, Freda. Age 19. 10 Henry Street. *p389, p433.*
WALKER, Albert. Age 9. 14 Turnbull Street.
WALKER, Stanley. Age 6. 14 Turnbull Street.
*WATSON, Mary E. Age 40. 164 Hart Road. *p383.*
*WATT, Amy. Age 22. 2 Marine Crescent.
WHEELWRIGHT, Bewick. Age 14. 15 South Street, Old Town.
*WHITECROSS, John M. Age 6. 34 William Street.
*WHITECROSS, Peter. Age 8. 34 William Street.
WILKINSON, Laura Annie Harrison. Age 12. 20 Dene Street.
*WILLIAMS, Ivy. Age 31. 8 Beaconsfield Square. *p383.*
WITTY, Stanley W. Age 10. 27 Belk Street.
WOODS, Josiah. Age 36. 6 Harbour Terrace.
WOODS, Martha Jane. Age 6. 6 Harbour Terrace.
*WOODS, Samuel N. Age 19. 18 Lumley Street.
*WRIGHT, William. Age 51. 4 Crook Street.

*YOUNG, Bertie. Age 13. 7 Princes Street, Middleton. *p387.*

Index P: The Hartlepools' Dead 1914 *(civilians by street)*

Civilians - 112 (not including Thomas Jeffrey and Charles Tate for whom there are no addresses).
1: Index of those killed or who died as a result of the bombardment.
2: Listed in alphabetical order, STREET, followed by available information.
3: All details relate to the bombardment of Wednesday, 16th December 1914, unless stated otherwise.
4: Abbreviations used: B: Year/date of birth. D: Year/date of death.
5: Ages given are those at the time of the incident (i.e. December 1914 etc.) under which the entry is made.
6: Page numbers at the end of an entry indicate where the subject is mentioned in the text and/or relevant photographs.
7: Entries marked with an asterisk (*) appear on the 'Hartlepool War Memorial' situated in Red Heugh Gardens.
8: Some street names, e.g. Mary Street, Mill Street and Dock Street, appear in both Hartlepool and West Hartlepool.

Alexander Terrace, 1. HUNTER, Samuel Hall. Age 16. *p381.*
*Alliance Street, 44. STAUNCH, John. Age 41. *p381.*
Ambleside. STOKER, Jane. Age 41. Cook to William Ropner. *p379.*

Ballast Hill, 3. Blyth. GRAY, William. Age 23. Engineer's steward. *p387.*
*Beaconsfield Square, 8. WILLIAMS, Ivy. Age 31. *p383.*
Beechwood Road, 67. SARGINSON, William. Age 22.
Belk Street, 25. LOFTHOUSE, Benjamin. Age 7 months. *p379.*
Belk Street, 27. WITTY, Stanley W. Age 10.
Belk Street, 31. BELL, Henry Stephen. Age 11. *p379.*
Belk Street, 32. JACOBS, Joseph. Age 13. *p381, p409.*
Belk Street, 53. BRENNAN, Margaret. Age 52.
Brafferton Street, 19. HESLOP, Thomas. Age 7.
Bridge Street, 11. Old Town. HUNTER, Margaret Ann. Age 47. *p387.*

Cameron Road, 58. MCGUIRE, John. Age 15. *p387, p409.*
Campion Street, 22. SIMMONS, Stanley. Age 5. *p385.*
Carlisle Place, 6. OLIVER, Joseph. Age 44.
Charlotte Street, 30. EVANS, John. Age 32.
Church Street, 5. BACKHAM, Cuthbert John. Age 42.
Clarendon Road, 29. CHURCHER, William H. Age 26.
*Cliff Terrace, 17. GEIPEL, Ethel Mary. Age 36.
*Cliff Terrace, *Rockside*. KAY, Annie M. Age 34. *p373 , p379, p396(p), p428.*
*Cliff Terrace, *Rockside*. KAY, Florence J. Age 32. *p373 , p379, p396(p), p428.*
*Clifton Street, 16. LEIGHTON, James S. Age 56. *p383, p434.*
*Commercial Street, 13. Middleton. BUNTER, James. Age 32.
Crimdon Street, 52. ALLEN, Robert Alfred. Age 10.
*Croft Terrace, 21. SWALES, Matthew Hastings. Age 36.
*Crook Street, 4. WRIGHT, William. Age 51.

*Darlington Street, 4.CAPELING, Nicholas. Age 25. Struck by shrapnel, walked to an ambulance but died in hospital. *p385.*
Darlington Terrace, 37. RAYBOULD, Hannah. Age 36.
Dene Street, 20. WILKINSON, Laura Annie Harrison. Age 12.
Dene Street, 24. HARRISON, Mary Ann. Age 60.
*Dock Street, 1. CORNER, Annie. Age 37.
Dock Street, 4. Old Town. CORNER, Bridget. Age 39.
Dock Street, 18. Old Town. HENIGHAN, Margaret. Age 8. *p381.*

Dover Street, 11. MOON, Julia. Age 68. *p379.*
*Durham Street, 2. COX, Thomas Garbutt. Age 26.

Elliott Street, 30. DRING, George. Age 47. *p381.*
*Everard Street, 65. AMBROSE, Robert L. Age 33. *p383, p434.*
Exeter Street, 2. COOPER, Edward. Age 16. *p381.*

Fawcett Street, 4. BROOKBANKS, Charles Abraham. Age 35.

Gas Street, 48. ARNOLD, Hannah. Age 33.
Gordon Street, 11. CLAUDE, Alfred Camille Bernard. Age 12. *p383, p431.*
Grosvenor Street, 57. CAWS, Dorothy. Age 25. *p379.*

Harbour Terrace, 6. WOODS, Josiah. Age 36.
Harbour Terrace, 6. WOODS, Martha Jane. Age 6.
Harrison Street, 3. SULLIVAN, Daniel. Age 47. Plater's helper. *p385.*
*Hart Road, 164. WATSON, Mary E. Age 40. *p383.*
*Hart Street, 18. HEALEY, John. Age 63. *p385.*
*Henry Street, 10. WAINWRIGHT, Freda. Age 19. *p389, p433.*
*Henry Street, 9. HIGHAN, Thomas. Age 11. *p379.*

John Street, 2. MOSSOM, Thomas. Age 55.

*Kinburn Street, 5. CLARK, John. Age 54.

Leeds Street, 2. Old Town. PHILLIPS, Thomas. Age 16.
Leeds Street, 3. Old Town. FRANKLAND, Catherine. Age 4. *p379.*
*Lilly Street, 3. CORNFORTH, Jane Ann. Age 17. *p383.*
*Lilly Street, 3. CORNFORTH, Charles. Age 63. *p383.*
*Lilly Street, 3. CORNFORTH, Polly. Age 23. *p383.*
*Lumley Street, 18. WOODS, Samuel N. Age 19.

*Malton Street, 50. HAMILTON, Jessie. Age 21.
*Marine Crescent, 2. WATT, Amy. Age 22.
*Mary Street, 41. MARSHALL, Catherine. Age 86.
*Mary Street, 43. HUDSON, Charles William. Age 21. Apprentice engineer. *p383.*
Mary Street, 3. AUSTRIN, Beart Beaumont. Age 33.
Mill Street, 7. Old Town. BURGON, Robert. Age 31. *p387, p435.*
*Moor Terrace, 4. HARPER, Elizabeth Agnes. Age 49. *p381.*

Osborne Road, 24. RAMSEY, Charles L. C. Age 37. *p383, p434.*

*Penrith Street, 19. ASHCROFT, Edwin. Age 29. *p383, p434.*
Perth Street, 49. JACKSON, Edith. Age 39.
Pilot Street, 1a. Old Town. OWEN, Mary Ellen. Age 17. *p379.*
Pilot Street, 1a. Old Town. OWEN, Rose. Age 43. *p379.*
Pilot Street, 2. Old Town. NECY, Eleanor. Age 6 months. *p379.*
*Princes Street, 7. Middleton. YOUNG, Bertie. Age 13. *p387.*

Ramsey Street, 21. BINNS, Samuel. Age 68.
Richardson Street, 1. SCARR, Thomasina. Age 44. Father was a gunner with the Royal Field Artillery.
Robin Hood's Bay, *Mayville House.* PEARSON, James William. Age 25. Mortally wounded aboard *SS Phoebe*. *p387, p430.*
*Rokeby Street, 28. COOK, James. Age 37. *p383, p434.*

*Slake Terrace, 18. Middleton. CHAPPLE, William. Age 15.
*South Crescent, *Ivyholm*. HARRIS, Etta. Age 30. Teacher at the Henry Smith Grammar School. *p381, p432.*
South Street, 15. Old Town. WHEELWRIGHT, Bewick. Age 14.
South Street, 22. Old Town. JOBLING, Hannah. Age 4. *p379, p435.*
South Street, 22. Old Town. JOBLING, Sarah. Age 6. *p379, p435.*
Staindrop Street, 11. LYNETT, James. Age 42. *p389.*
*Stephenson Street, 58. HODGSON, John. Age 62.
Studley Road, 82. SKELTON, Matthew. Age 54.

Thirlmere Street, 32. HODGSON, Sarah. Age 56.
*Town Wall, 22. ASQUITH. William. Age 51.
Turnbull Street, 14. WALKER, Albert. Age 9.
Turnbull Street, 14. WALKER, Stanley. Age 6.
Turnbull Street, 30. PEART, Charles. Age 2. *p381.*
Turnbull Street, 30. PEART, William. Age 5. *p381.*
Turnbull Street, 40. COOK, Harold. Age 10.
Turnbull Street, 40. COOK, Robert Wilfred. Age 8.
Turnbull Street, 45. HENDERSON, Joseph. Age 47.
Turnbull Street, 48. CRESSY, Albert Edwin. Age 29. *p383, p434.*
Turnbull Street, 63. THEAKER, Richard. Age 23. Platelayer. *p383.*

*Victoria Place, 14. ALLEN, Annie. Age 25.
*Victoria Place, 6. LEE, Clementina. Age 25.
*Victoria Place, 7. AVERY, William Gordon. Age 49. Salvation Army Adjutant. *p385, p396(p).*

Water Street, 9. HODGSON, William 'Barney'. Age 43. *p387, p403, p409, p410, p415.*

*Watson Street, 50. REDSHAW, Margaret A. Age 47. Shopkeeper. *p385.*
*Well's Yard, 11. MEASOR, Christopher. Age 10. *p385.*
*William Street, 10. STRINGER, Ethel. Age 12.
*William Street, 20. STEWART, Stanley. Age 6.
*William Street, 30. DIXON, Albert. Age 7. *p385, p407, p409.*
*William Street, 30. DIXON, George Edward. Age 14. *p385, p407, p409.*
*William Street, 30. DIXON, Margaret Ellen. Age 8. *p385, p407, p409.*
*William Street, 34. WHITECROSS, John M. Age 6.
*William Street, 34. WHITECROSS, Peter. Age 8.
*William Street, 5. HERBERT, Selina. Age 3.
*Wood Street, 19. CRAKE, John William. Age 15. *p387.*
*Wood Street, 24. UNTHANK, Frank. Age 14. *p385.*
*Wood Street, 9. HORSLEY, Hilda. Age 17. Tailoress. *p381.*

Index Q: The Hartlepools ~ General 1914

1: General index of those mentioned in the text and not included elsewhere.
2: Listed in alphabetical order, SURNAME, followed by available information.
3: All details relate to the bombardment of Wednesday, 16th December 1914, unless stated otherwise.
4: Abbreviations used: B: Year/date of birth. D: Year/date of death.
5: Ages given are those at the time of the incident (i.e. December 1914 etc.) under which the entry is made.
6: Page numbers at the end of an entry indicate where the subject is mentioned in the text. The '(p)' indicates a picture.
7: Entries carrying the legend 'Gave account' indicate where an oral or written account has been provided.

ARNELL, Stuart. *p415.*

BALLANTINE, J. Gave account. *p436.*
BEATTIE. Duke Street. *p413.*
BEDLINGTON, Margaret. Had a narrow escape when friend Margaret Hunter was killed. *p387.*
BEDLINGTON, Thomas. Had a narrow escape when friend Robert Burgon was killed. *p387, p435.*
BELL, H. 31 Belk Street. Found the body of John McGuire at the junction of Middleton and Hartlepool Roads. Gave account. *p387, p409, p410.*
BELL. Coroner. *p379.*
BISHOP OF DURHAM. *p377.*
BOAGEY, William. Grosvenor Street. Aged 19. Gave account. *p417, p419, p420, p422, p423.*
BOANSON. Councillor. Hutton Avenue. *p427.*
BODIAM, Albert Victor. Leading Seaman. HMS *Doon*. Wounded.
BREWERTON, Sergeant M. 18th (Service) Battalion Durham Light Infantry. *p437.*
BROWN, Donald. Hardware shop, Murray Street. *p422.*
BROWN, Private R. B. 18th Battalion, Durham Light Infantry. Wounded.
BRUCE, Captain Alan C. Royal Navy, Senior Naval Commander at Hartlepool and Commander of HMS *Patrol*. Appointed 27.01.1914. *p369, p371, p377, p432, p433.*
BURNS, George. Hawker. *p435.*

C9, HM Submarine. Involved in defence of Hartlepool. Lieutenant-Commander C. L. M. Dering. *p369, p371.*
CAMERON HOSPITAL. *p415, p431.*
CARR, Cissie. Watson Street. Ailing friend of Margaret Redshaw who was killed. *p385.*
CASSIDY, J. Royal Navy. 10th Cruiser Squadron. Gave account. *p425.*
CASSIDY, T. S. Gave account. *p401.*
CAWS, William. Grosvenor Street, 57. Father of Dorothy (aged 27) who died. *p379.*
CEMETERY BATTERY. On the coast of Hartlepool. *p392, p393.*
CENTRAL MARINE ENGINE WORKS. *p383, p413.*
CHAMBERS, Charles. Milkman, Middle Warren Farm, Hartlepool. Became Alderman and 'father' of Hartlepool Council. Gave account. *p426.*
CHILDREN'S FRIEND. Fishing vessel. Skipper, John Horsley. 21 Bedford Street. Gave account. *p413, p432.*
CLAYTON, Mrs S. Gave account. *p403.*
COLLIER, F. Telephone attendant, North Eastern Railway. Gave account. *p439.*
CONSTANCE. Fishing vessel, reported sunk. *p377.*

DAVISON, John. Gave account. *p434, p435.*
DAY, 1003 Private Frank. 7th (Cyclist) Battalion Devonshire Regiment (TF). Gave account. *p438(p), p439.*
DEES, Private T. W. 18th Battalion, Durham Light Infantry. Wounded.
DENLBUAH. German ship damaged at Hartlepool in docks. *p422, p434.*
DENNIS, H. Gave account. *p435.*
DERING, Lieutenant-Commander C. L. M. *C9*, HM Submarine. Involved in defence of Hartlepool. *p369, p371.*
DICKINSON, Mary E. 42 Belk Street. Gave account. *p424.*
DIXON, Joseph. 30 William Street. Aged 12. Lost three members of his family. Gave account. *p407, p409.*
DOON, HMS. Light cruiser involved in defence of Hartlepool. Lieutenant-Commander Harry M. Fraser. Appointed August 1914. *p369, p371, p377, p413.*
DOUTHWAITE, Sergeant, Durham Royal Garrison Artillery (TF). Awarded Distinguished Conduct Medal - first won on British soil - for 'extracting live cartridge from the breech of a gun which had misfired'. *p393.*
DURHAM LIGHT INFANTRY, 18th Service Battalion, Durham Pals. *p105, p369, p373, p377, p398, p416, p437.*
DURHAM ROYAL GARRISON ARTILERY (TF). *p367, p369, p373, p377, p393, p403.*

FAIRY COVE. *p369.*
FARMER, Captain Jack. Lighthouse Battery. *p399.*
FISH, Captain 'Frank' Francis Edward. 3rd Green Howards garrisoning Hartlepool on 16th December 1914. Captain Fish was later attached to the 2nd Green Howards, a regular battalion, and survived until killed in action on 17th May 1915. He is buried at the Guards Cemetery, Windy Corner, Cuinchy, France.

FORWARD, HMS. Light cruiser involved in defence of Hartlepool. Commander Frederick P. Lodger-Symonds. Appointed April 1914. *p369, p371, p432, p433.*
FRASER, Lieutenant-Commander Harry M. Appointed August 1914 to HMS *Doon,* Light cruiser involved in defence of Hartlepool. *p369, p371, p377, p413.*

GALE, Clifford Alfred. Stoker 1st Class. HMS *Doon.* Wounded.
GARRETT, Private William. 18th Battalion, Durham Light Infantry. Wounded.
GILBERT, Charles. Stoker 1st Class. HMS *Patrol.* Wounded.
GRAINGER, Julia. Daughter of Julia Moon (aged 68), 11 Dover Street, who died.
GRAND HOTEL. *p403.*
GRAY'S SHIPYARD. *p407, p417, p424.*

HALL, Arthur. Cook, Durham Royal Garrison Artillery (TF), Heugh Battery, Hartlepool. *p424.*
HARDY. 34 Hutton Avenue. House seriously damaged. *p427.*
HARTLEPOOL GAS & WATER COMPANY. *p377, p396(p).*
HARTLEPOOL ROVERS FOOTBALL CLUB. *p369, p424.*
HAWRIDGE, Frederick William. Mate. HMS *Doon.* Wounded.
HEAL, Sergeant W. H. 18th (Service) Battalion, Durham Light Infantry. *p437.*
HENRY SMITH GRAMMAR SCHOOL. *p432.*
HEUGH BATTERY, The. Involved in the defence of Hartlepool. *p367, p369, p373, p375, p393, p397, p398, p399, p400, p401, p416, p422, p423, p424, p434.*
HEWITSON, L. Gave account. *p439.*
HILL, Major Richard. 3rd Green Howards. Hartlepool Garrison. D: 17.02.1915. Buried at All Saints' Churchyard, Thornton le Dale, North Yorkshire. *p403.*
HOGAN, Bob. Royal Navy. 10th Cruiser Squadron. *p425.*
HOPE, Acting Bombardier J. J. Durham Royal Garrison Artillery (TF), Heugh Battery, Hartlepool. Awarded Military Medal (MM). *p393.*
HORNE, William Frederick. Able Seaman. HMS *Doon.* Wounded.
HORSLEY, William. 9 Wood Street. Father of Hilda (aged 17), identified her for the inquest. *p381.*

IBBOTSON, Mrs. Northgate. *p428.*
Ivyholm, South Crescent. Mrs Jackson. Where Etta Harris was killed. *p381.*

JACOB, Edward Charles. Leading Seaman. HMS *Doon.* Wounded.
JACQUES, Fred. 5 Prissick Street. Aged 14, Family had to climb over body of John Crake and Freda Wainwright to get out of their home. Gave account. *p387, p389, p433, p434.*
JACKSON, Mrs. *Ivyholm,* South Crescent. Where Etta Harris was killed. *p381.*
JESMOND ROAD SCHOOL. *p429.*
JOBLING, George. Grandfather of Sarah (aged 6) and Hannah (aged 4) of 22 South Street, gave account of their deaths at the inquest. *p379, p381, p435.*
JOBLING, Lily. Aunt of Sarah (aged 6) and Hannah (aged 4) of 22 South Street, identified bodies for inquest. *p379, p435.*

KENNEDY, James. Foreman, Gray's Shipyard. *p420.*
KNOX-LITTLE, Lieutenant-Commander Charles H. Appointed 24th August 1912 to HMS *Test,* light cruiser involved in defence of Hartlepool. *p369, p371, p413.*

LAMB, Private D. 18th Battalion, Durham Light Infantry. Wounded.
LANGDALE, George. Pattern maker. Belk Street. Gave evidence at the inquest of Charles Ramsey. *p383.*
LARKIN, W. H. Gave account. *p415, p416.*
LAVIN, F. M. Gave account. *p437.*
LIGHTHOUSE BATTERY, The. Involved in the defence of Hartlepool. *p367, p369, p373, p375, p379, p393, p397, p398, p399, p400, p401, p412, p416, p424, p432.*
LODGER-SYMONDS, Commander Frederick P. Appointed April 1914 to HMS *Forward,* light cruiser involved in defence of Hartlepool. *p369, p371, p432, p433.*
LUNN, Private William Henry. 3rd Green Howards. Gave account. *p406, p407.*
LUPTON, Daisy. Gave account. *p428, p429.*

MALLIN, Acting Bombardier F. W. Durham Royal Garrison Artillery (TF), Heugh Battery, Hartlepool. Awarded Military Medal. His was first medal to be struck at Royal Mint and to be presented. *p393.*
MALLINS, Bombardier Frederick. Durham Royal Garrison Artillery. Gave account. *p412.*
MAVER, Renwick Graham. Able Seaman. HMS *Doon.* Wounded.
MCDONALD, John. Gave evidence at the inquest of Joseph Jacobs. *p381.*
MCKENNA. Durham Royal Garrison Artillery. Wounded. *p413.*
MCLURE, Robert. Shipwright 2nd Class. HMS *Patrol.* Wounded.
MEASOR, Martha. 11 Well's Yard. Son, Christopher (age 10) was killed. *p385.*
MILNE, James. Stoker 1st Class. HMS *Doon.* Wounded.
MOY, HMS. Light cruiser involved in defence of Hartlepool. Lieutenant-Commander Charles G. Naylor. Appointed 24.10.1914. *p369.*
MOYNIHAN, John. Stoker 1st Class. HMS *Doon.* Wounded.
MURRAY, M. E. Daughter of William 'Barney' Hodgson. Gave account. *p410.*
MUSTARD. Tailor. *p420, p427.*

NAYLOR, Lieutenant-Commander Charles G. Appointed 24th October 1914 to HMS *Moy,* light cruiser involved in defence of Hartlepool. *p369.*
NEILL, T. M. Former member of 18th (Service) Battalion, Durham Light Infantry. Gave an account. *p437.*
NEILSON. Picture framer. *p429.*

ORCHARD HOUSE. *p405.*
ORDE, Mr & Mrs. *Ocean House,* Moor Terrace. Badly damaged. Both gave accounts. *p424, p425.*
OWEN, Charles. 1a Pilot Street. Wife, Rose (aged 43) and daughter, Mary Ellen (aged 17) both killed. *p379.*

PACE. William James. Leading Seaman. HMS *Patrol*. Wounded.
PAILOR, Thomas. Sergeant-Major, Lighthouse Battery. Gave account. *p399, p400, p401.*
PATROL, HMS. Light cruiser involved in defence of Hartlepool. Captain Alan C. Bruce. Royal Navy, Senior Naval Commander at Hartlepool. Appointed 27.01.1914. *p369, p371, p377, p432, p433.*
PEARSON, Dr. Hartlepool Hospital. *p413.*
PHILIPS, Sarah. Dessmaker. Gave evidence at the inquest of Hilda Horsley. *p381.*
PORT WAR SIGNAL STATION. *p369, p371, p373.*
POWELL, Private G. H. 18th Battalion, Durham Light Infantry. Wounded.

RAW, Sergeant Major. Durham Royal Garrison Artillery. *p412.*
RICHARDSON, Captain Evan John. 3rd Green Howards. Hartlepool garrison. Killed in action 25.09.1915, serving with 2nd Green Howards. Commemorated on Loos Memorial, France. *p405.*
RICHARDSONS WESTGARTH & COMPANY. *p383, p401, p426, p434.*
RICHMOND, Robert Henry. ERA 3rd Class. HMS *Patrol*. Wounded.
RICKERBY, Mrs E. Gave account. *p412.*
ROBERTS, Lieutenant-Commander Ralph W. H. Appointed 26.06.1914, to HMS *Waveney*, light cruiser involved in defence of Hartlepool. *p369, p371, p377, p392, p413.*
ROBINSON, Private L. H. 18th Battalion, Durham Light Infantry. Wounded.
ROBSON, Lieutenant-Colonel Lancelot. Commanding Officer Durham Royal Garrison Artillery and Fire Commander at Hartlepool. Received Distinguished Service Order. Also, Most Distinguished Order of St Michael and St George in June 1917, presented by King and Queen at Hartlepool. Born Sunderland 01.03.1855. Civilian: Journeyman plumber. Elected to town council 1897 (member for Park Ward). Mayor 1907-1908. Alderman 1908. Resigned Council 1923 after 26 years' service. Military: Bugler, aged 15, 3rd Durham Rifles. Rose through the ranks. Commissioned 1890. Promoted full Colonel 05.08.1918. Died 30.08.1936. *p369, p371, p373, p375, p393, p395, p397, p398, p399, p416.*
ROLLO, Captain. 3rd Green Howards. Hartlepool garrison. Not listed as died. *p403.*
ROPNER, William. *Ambleside*. Employer of Jane Stoker, age 41, cook, killed. *p379.*
ROYAL ENGINEERS. Durham Fortress Territorial Force. *p369, p377.*
RUTHERFORD, Private Thomas. 18th Battalion, Durham Light Infantry. Wounded.

SANDERSON, William. Cook, Durham Royal Garrison Artillery (TF), Heugh Battery, Hartlepool. *p424.*
SCOTT, Lance-Corporal H. A. 18th Battalion, Durham Light Infantry. Wounded.
SIMPSON, Nurse. Gave account. *p436, p437.*
SIMPSON, Private J. A. 18th Battalion, Durham Light Infantry. Wounded.
SOUTH GARE BATTERY. *p369, p371, p397, p403, p406, p407.*
STAMP, Richard. Discovered body of Rose Owen and Eleanor Necy on Dock Street. *p379.*
STEVENSON, Miss. Matron, Hartlepool Hospital. *p436.*
STORM, Florence. *p428.*
STRAIN, Dr. Acting house surgeon at the mortuary. Gave evidence at the inquest of Joseph Jacobs. *p381.*

TABLEY, N. Aged 5. Gave account. *p427.*
TEMPLE, T. M. Aged 16. Gave account. *p401, p403.*
TEST, HMS. Light cruiser involved in defence of Hartlepool. Lieutenant-Commander Charles H. Knox-Little. Appointed 24.08.1912. *p369, p371, p413.*
TINDALL, J. B. Office boy at Central Marine Engine Works. 13 Duke Street. Aged 14. Gave account. *p413, p415.*
TOWN HALL. *p405, p406.*
TRECHMANN, Captain O. L. Commander Heugh Battery, Hartlepool. Durham Royal Garrison Artillery. Cousin of Captain R. W. Trechmann.
TRECHMANN, Captain R. W. Commander Lighthouse Battery, Hartlepool. Durham Royal Garrison Artillery. Cousin of O. L. Trechmann. *p399, p423.*
TRISTRAM, Major. Commanding Officer 18th (Service) Battalion, Durham Light Infantry (Durham Pals), two companies, Hartlepool.
TRITSCHLER. Chief Storeman. Central Marine Engine Works. *p413.*
TYSON, Harry. Durham Royal Garrison Artillery (TF), Heugh Battery, Hartlepool. 17 Rowell Street. Gave account. *p423, p424.*

WALLER, John Durham. Ammunition man, Royal Garrison Artillery (TF), Lighthouse Battery, Hartlepool.
WALLER, John. Formerly of Durham Royal Garrison Artillery. 309 West View Road. Gave account. *p423.*
WANLESS, Private G. J. 18th Battalion, Durham Light Infantry. Wounded.
WARREN. Works Manager, Central Marine Engine Works. *p413.*
WATSON, C. J. 174 Alma Street. Aged 6. Gave account. *p429, p431.*
WATSON. Mayor. *p392.*
WATTS, William. Stoker 1st Class. HMS *Doon*. Wounded.
WAVENEY, HMS. Light cruiser involved in defence of Hartlepool. Lieutenant-Commander Ralph W. H. Roberts, appointed 26.06.1914. *p369, p371, p377, p392, p413.*
WAYSIDE FLOWER. Fishing vessel, reported sunk. *p377.*
WEDDELL, George. Seaton Carew. Wrote poem. *p410.*
WESTMORELAND, Stanley. Apprentice at Gray's Shipyard. *p417.*
WHITTON, Mrs F. Cottingham, Humberside. Born in Hartlepool in 1908, Aged 6 . Gave account. *p426.*
WILKINSON, Gunner Jack. Durham Royal Garrison Artillery. Sentry duty at Heugh Battery. *p423.*
WILLIAMS, Captain. Commanding Officer of the Royal Engineers (Durham Fortress TF), detachment, Hartlepool.
WILSON, Samuel. Gave evidence at the inquest of John Staunch. *p381.*
WOOD, Robert. Hartlepool historian. Son of J. Wood, Market Keeper. Gave account. *p411.*
WORKHOUSE. *p377.*

Author's Appeal For Information

Further information is still sought about the bombardments and the people and places mentioned in this book. If you have any information, or photographs, you are requested to contact the author (via the offices of the publisher).

Index R: The General Index

1: General index of people, places etc. not mentioned in the preceding indexes.
2: Listed in alphabetical order, SURNAME/NAME/TITLE etc., followed by available information.
3: All details relate to the bombardment of Wednesday, 16th December 1914, unless stated otherwise.
4: Abbreviations used: B: Year/date of birth. D: Year/date of death.
5: Ages given are those at the time of the incident (i.e. December 1914 etc.) under which the entry is made.
6: Page numbers at the end of an entry indicate where the subject is mentioned in the text. The '(p)' indicates a picture.
7: Entries for Scarborough, Whitby and Hartlepool are only given where the name of the town appears in a section other than its own (i.e. the entries listed below for Scarborough have not included any mention of the town in the Scarborough 1914 or 1917 sections of the book, but only where the town is mentioned in the Whitby and Hartlepool sections).
8: If the item or subject you are looking for is not listed below, please see the index for the specific place/ incident/date.

Aberdeen. Scotland. *p166, p447.*
Aboukir. British cruiser sunk by German submarine *U9*. *p9, p322.*
Ahlefeld, Lieutenant. See *U27*.
Aisne. *p5.*
Ajax. British battle-cruiser, under Vice-Admiral Sir George John Scott Warrender. *p113.*
Alastair. Coasting vessel out of Montrose bound for London. Towed lifeboats of Norwegian steamship *Eli* to Scarborough, 25.12.1914. *p169.*
Aldersgate. London. Sent message to Whitby. *p335.*
Ambuscade. British cruiser (3rd Cruiser Squadron) involved in the defence of Hartlepool. *p391.*
Ariadne. German cruiser lost at Heligoland 28.08.1914. *p9.*
Armentières. *p5.*
Asquith, Herbert Henry. (1852-1928). Liberal Prime Minister 1908-1916. After the outbreak of war Asquith headed a Liberal-Conservative coalition 1915-1916. *p101, p114(p), p146, p328.*
Atholl Palace Hotel. Pitlochry, Scotland. Queen Margaret's School evacuated to the hotel. *p281.*
Audacious. British dreadnought. *p9.*
Australia. *p318.*
Ayton. Near Scarborough. *p97, p243.*

Baden Powell, General. *p318, p319.*
Balfour, Arthur James. (1848-1930). Conservative Prime Minister 1902-1905. Foreign Secretary 1916-1919. *p101.*
Banyers. Hired trawler. 448 tons. Struck mine. Sunk 06.01.1915 off Scarborough. *p169.*
Barnardo's Homes, Dr. The council sent message to Whitby. *p321.*
Battle-cruiser. Hybrid warship; speed of a cruiser, striking power of a battleship. Resembling battleships, they had one less turret, less armour, more powerful engines and longer hulls and were fast enough to escape from any warship they could not destroy. The first British battle-cruisers performed well at the Battle of the Falklands (November and December 1914), but by late 1916 their effectiveness was being questioned. The first battle-cruiser was the *Invincible*.
Battleship. The most powerful of modern warships, considered the ultimate naval weapon. Floating fortresses built to house the largest naval guns available. However, the all-steel, heavily armoured ships of the early 1900s were considered obsolete with the introduction of the 'Dreadnought' class in 1906. Battleships before this became known as 'Pre-Dreadnoughts'.
Beatty, Admiral Sir David. (1871 to 1936). Appointed to command of Grand Fleet's Battle-Cruiser Squadron 1913. Succeeded Jellicoe as Commander-in-Chief, 1916, promoted over eight senior admirals. Took surrender of German High Seas Fleet at Rosyth, 1918. First Sea Lord 1919-1927. *p113, p115, p116(p), p117, p441.*
Belper Spiritualist Society. Sent message to Whitby. *p335.*
Berliner Neusten Nachrichten. German newspaper. *p119.*
Berliner Tageblatt. German newspaper. *p119, p155.*
Berwick Guardians. Sent message to Whitby. *p335.*
Birmingham. British cruiser. *p115.*
Black Legion. *p99.*
Blücher. German heavy cruiser. Completed 1909. Inaccurate imitation of British battle-cruiser *Invincible*. Due to British misinformation *Blücher* was built with smaller main guns, and lacked the speed or firepower of a battle-cruiser. Part of Admiral Hipper's North Sea Scouting Group. Part of Hartlepool raiding party 16.12.1914 under the command of Fregattenkapitän (Commander) Erdmann. Outgunned and sunk at Dogger Bank, 24.01.1915. *p11, p105, p109, p113, p287, p295, p326, p371, p376(p), p373, p375, p392, p393, p397, p400, p416, p441, p455.*
Bolton, M. Cambridge. Sent message to Whitby. *p339.*
Bombardment Precautions. Appeared in local press January 1915. *p440.*
Bootle. Liverpool. *p331.*
Boston. Norwegian cargo ship. Bound Bremen to London. Struck mine 3 miles east of Scarborough, 22.12.1914. Captain and crew of 16 escaped without serious injury in lifeboats. Ship drifted onto Filey Brigg. Built 1905 at Nylands, Vackstad, Christiania. Owner Fred Olsen. Length 225'. Breadth 33'7". Captain, A. J. Olsen. *p167.*
Boyes, Councillor William. Chairman of the Scarborough War Memorial Committee. *p455.*
Bridlington Chronicle. Newspaper. *p281.*
Bridlington Corporation. Sent message to Whitby. *p320.*
Bridlington. East Yorkshire. *p123, p127, p129, p283.*
Brighton. *p149.*
British Expeditionary Force (BEF). *p3, p5.*
Brittain, Vera. (1893-1970). Writer. *p275, p283.*
Bubb, Miss. Mistress at Queen Margaret's School, Scarborough. *p275, p277.*
Burniston. Near Scarborough. *p121.*
Bushel. Inspector of the Local Government Board. Inspected damage at Whitby. *p321.*

Cardiff Chamber of Commerce. Sent messages. *p129, p320.*
Castle Eden. *p432.*
Cayton Bay. Near Scarborough. *p43, p167, p235, p237, p443.*
Cayton. Near Scarborough. *p97.*
Centurion. British battle-cruiser, under Vice-Admiral Sir George John Scott Warrender. *p113.*

Cholmley, Sir Hugh. Governor of Whitby, 1636. *p291.*
Chrichton, Miss. Mistress at Queen Margaret's School, Scarborough. *p275.*
Church, Councillor. Cambridge. Sent message to Roy Miller, Whitby. *p319.*
Churchill, Winston Leonard Spencer. (1874-1965). Served army, Boer War. Conservative MP 1900. Joined Liberals 1904. First Lord of the Admiralty 1911-1915. Rejoined army 1915, served France. Minister of Munitions 1917. Prime Minister of coalition 1940-1945. Prime Minister 1951-1955. Nobel Prize for Literature 1951. *p101, p113, p114(p), p117, p145, p437.*
City. Steamer picked up crew of the *Elterwater*, 16.12.1914. *p166.*
Clark, Lieutenant-Colonel Edward C. Kitson. Commanding Officer, 8th Battalion, West Yorkshire Regiment (Leeds Rifles) Territorials. *p103, p285.*
Cologne Gazette. German newspaper. *p156.*
Conqueror, William the. *p99.*
Conqueror. British battle-cruiser, under Vice-Admiral Sir George John Scott. *p113.*
Coronel. South America. *p9.*
Craddock, Admiral. *p9.*
Cressy. British cruiser sunk by German submarine *U9*. *p9, p322.*
Crew, Marquess of. Secretary of State for India. *p101.*
Cromer. *p149.*
Cruiser. Originally a British concept. Planned as smaller and faster than a battleship. There were two distinct types of cruiser, each designed for different operations. Heavily armoured cruisers, with powerful main armament and strong side armour were used as fast scouts alongside battleships in engagements with other fleets. Protected cruisers, with deck armour but no side armour, were used to protect trade routes, troop-ships and outposts. Built in large numbers by both Britain and Germany during the war, used extensively in the North Sea area of operations.
Cuxhaven. First naval air-raid by seaplanes, 25.12.1914. The attack on the Zeppelin base at Nordholz, was intended to provoke German warships out of Wilhelmshaven into battle. The raid was considered a failure. The battle-cruiser *Von der Tann* collided with a cruiser whilst manoeuvring to avoid bombs. *p113, p441.*

D5. British submarine damaged by mines off Yarmouth. *p109.*
Daily Express. British newspaper. *p311.*
Daily Mail. British newspaper. *p149.*
Daily Mirror. British newspaper. *p142, p150.*
Daily Sketch. British newspaper. *p97, p142, p150.*
Daily Telegraph. British newspaper. *p147.*
Dardanelles. *p3, p151.*
Day, 1003 Private Frank. 7th (Cyclist) Battalion Devonshire Regiment (TF). *p438(p).*
Deptford. Merchant vessel. 1,208 tons. Struck mine. Sunk 24.02.1915 off Scarborough. 1 dead. *p169.*
Derfflinger. German class of battle-cruiser. Slightly enlarged version of *Seydlitz*, with bigger guns. Both *Derfflinger* (after which the class was named) and *Lützow* were completed in July 1914. Launched from Blohm & Voss shipyard, Hamburg. For statistics see page 10. Part of Hipper's Scouting Group. Part of Scarborough & Whitby raiding group, 16.12.1914. Kapitän (Captain) zur See von Reuter. Took part in Battle of Dogger Bank and suffered heavy damage at Jutland, 1916. Despite British press reports that the ship had been sunk, *Derfflinger* limped back to base. Scuttled Scapa Flow, June 1919. *p10(p), p11, p13, p43, p113, p140, p265, p326, p442, p455.*
Deutsche Tageszeitung. German newspaper. *p155.*
Devonshire Regiment. 7th (Cyclist) Battalion, Territorials. *p293, p294(p), p295, p297, p307, p311, p313(p), p322, p323, p324(p), p325, p326, p341, p343, p345, p346, p438(p).*
Dogger Bank. The Battle of Dogger Bank took place on 24.01.1915 following the German raids on the north-east coast. The British had had advance warning of another raid by Hipper's Scouting Group (minus the *Von der Tann* which had been damaged at Cuxhaven). Admiral Beatty steamed from Rosyth to meet Hipper's group with five battle-cruisers and six fast light cruisers. They were also joined by other cruisers and destroyers from Harwich. The British made contact with Hipper's force at 7.20am on 24th January, and though the Germans made a run for it, believing they could outpace the British, Beatty's force caught up by 9.30am and the parallel lines of battleships confronted each other. Damage was done to the *Seydlitz* and the *Blücher*, while the Germans hit the *Lion*, Beatty's flagship, and forced it out of the battle at about 11.00am. Despite an almost certain British victory, the fear of mines and a doubtful submarine sighting persuaded Beatty to break off from the engagement. British signalling confusion prevented Beatty's order for his best ships to chase and engage Hipper being relayed and instead an order for the destruction of the *Blücher* was given and subsequently took place. *p113, p287, p441, p455.*
Dover. *p453.*
Dunkirk. *p291.*
Durham, Lord. Lord Lieutenant of the County of Durham. *p392.*
Durham. *p405.*

Eastbourne Gazette. Newspaper. *p151.*
Eastbourne. *p149.*
Eastbourne. Sent message. *p129.*
Eastfield. Near Scarborough. *p99.*
Egidy, Captain. See *Seydlitz* (Flagship of Admiral Hipper).
Egypt. *p3, p407.*
Elfrida. Merchant vessel. 2,624 tons. Struck mine and sank 07.01.1915 off Scarborough. *p169.*
Eli. Norwegian steamship struck mine off Scarborough and sank 25.12.1914. The Captain and his 14 man crew took to the lifeboats and were towed to Scarborough by the coasting vessel *Alastair*. The ship, out of Blyth, had been bound for Rouen with a cargo of coal. Master, Captain Sveen. *p169.*
Elterwater. Merchant vessel. 1,228 tons. Struck mine and sank 16.12.1914 off Scarborough. *p166.*
Emden. German light cruiser. Built 1908. Formed part of Admiral von Spee's East Asiatic squadron in August 1914. Detached to prey on Allied trade and troop transport routes in the Indian Ocean. Sank 17 merchant ships and captured a Russian auxiliary cruiser. Sank the Russian cruiser *Zemcug* in Penang harbour 28.10.1914. Destroyed by Australian cruiser *Sydney* at the Cocos Islands 09.11.1914. *p146.*
Erdmann, Commander. See *Blücher*.
Evening Mail. Newspaper. *p154.*

Falkland Islands. South Atlantic. *p9, p101, p155, p158.*
Fane. Of Bergen. Bound South Shields to Rouen with coal. Came ashore off Whitby, 24.12.1914, towed to Tyne by tug.
Farne Islands. *p9.*

New Zealand. British battle-cruiser, under Admiral Sir David Beatty. *p113*.
Newcastle. Board of Guardians. Sent message to Whitby. *p335*.
Newcastle. *p23, p169, p201, p243*.
Nicholls, Second-Lieutenant. Royal Engineers, Aldershot. Sent message to Roy Miller, Whitby. *p319*.
Night Hawk. Hired trawler. 287 tons. Struck mine and sank 25.12.1914 off Scarborough. *p167, p452*.
Nimmo, D. Hamilton. Scotland. Sent message to Whitby. *p337*.
Nonne Bosschen. *p5*.
Northern Daily Mail. Newspaper. *p389*.
Norton. Near Malton, North Yorkshire. *p351*.
Nürnberg Kurier. German newspaper. *p156, p157*.
Nürnberg. German light cruiser. *p9*.
Nürnberger Zeitung. German newspaper. *p119, p157*.

Oak. British destroyer. *p287*.
Orianda. Hired trawler. 273 tons. Struck mine and sank 19.12.1914 off Scarborough. *p166*.
Orion. British battle-cruiser, under Vice-Admiral Sir George John Scott Warrender. *p113*.
Orsett Urban District Council, Kent. Sent message to Whitby. *p320*.
Orsett Rural District Council. Sent message to Scarborough. *p129*.
Osgodby. Near Scarborough. *p97*.
Otranto. *p9*.

Palace Hotel. Pitlochry, Perthshire. Queen Margaret's School evacuated to the hotel after bombardment. *p41, p225*.
Park Hotel. Keswick. Scarborough College removed to the hotel after bombardment. *p37, p204, p205, p206(p)*.
Passchendaele. *p3, p151, p335, p406, p441, p442, p455*.
Passing. Minesweeper 58. Struck mine and holed. *p166, p254(p)*.
Perseus, Captain. *p155*.
Philips. Sent message to Whitby. *p321*.
Pickering. North Yorkshire. *p41, p97, p349*.
Pitlochry. Perthshire. *p43, p281*.
Plumer, General Sir Herbert. Commanding Officer Northern Command in 1914/15. Went on to command 2nd Army Corps on the Western Front. Considered one of the more able and popular commanders. *p389, p405*.
Pohl, Admiral von. *p158*.
Prince of Wales' National Relief Fund. *p321*.
Princess Olga. Merchant vessel. 998 tons. Struck mine and sank 16.12.1914 off Scarborough. *p166*.
Princess Royal. British battleship. *p287*.
Prosser, Lance-Corporal. Yorkshire Hussars. *p235*.

Queen Mary. British battle-cruiser, under Admiral Sir David Beatty. *p113, p287*.
Queensbury. Scarborough lifeboat. *p166, p169*.

Rameses. Trawler damaged in Scarborough harbour. *p97*.
Ramillies. British battleship. *p286(p), p287, p288(p), p289*.
Ramsgate. *p453*.
Ravenscar. North Yorkshire. *p249, p295, p326, p345*.
Red Cross. *p19, p70(p), p253, p281, p303*.
Redcar Urban District Council. Sent message to Whitby. *p335*.
Redcar. *p293, p335*.
Reuter, Admiral Ludwig von. *p455*.
Reuter, Captain von. See *Derfflinger*.
Reventlow, Count. *p155, p156*.
Rheims. *p316*.
Richmond. North Yorkshire. *p405, p407*.
Rillington. Near Malton, North Yorkshire. *p123*.
Roberts, Mrs. Stewardess aboard the *Rohilla*. Survivor of the *Titanic*. *p293*.
Robertson, General Sir William. Chief of Staff to Sir John French 1915. *p442*.
Robin Hood's Bay. North Yorkshire. *p208, p295, p297, p325, p326, p345, p387*.
Rohilla. Master, Captain Neilson. *p290 (list of the dead), p291, p292(p), p293, p295, p309*.
Rook, Sergeant. Yorkshire Hussars. *p235*.
Rosyth. Scotland. *p115, p117, p287*.
Rowntree's. York. *p103*.
Royal Oak. British battleship. *p288(p)*.
Rudston. East Yorkshire. Birthplace of Winifred Holtby. *p283, p285*.
Runciman, Sir Walter. MP for Hartlepool. *p109*.
Runswick Bay. *p295, p325, p326*.
Russell, Mrs C. M. Stoke Newington. Sent message to Whitby. *p321*.
Ruswarp. *p301, p303, p352, p359*.

S119. German torpedo-boat sunk on 17.10.1914 from which VB codes were retrieved. *p111*.
Saltwick. Whitby. *p291, p293*.
Sandsend. *p295, p325*.
Sapphire. Fishing vessel. 289 tons. Struck mine and sank 01.03.1915 off Filey. 1 dead. *p169*.
Scalby. Near Scarborough. *p121, p243*.
Scapa Flow. *p455*.
Scarborough Evening News. Newspaper. *p442*.
Scarborough Pictorial. Newspaper. *p150, p442*.
Scarborough War Memorial. *p140, p141, p142, p447, p454(p), p455, p456*.
Scarborough. *p293, p295, p297, p305, p311, p320, p325, p327, p330, p333, p335, p336, p337, p341, p347, p352, p355, p371, p389, p391, p392, p416*.
Scharnhorst. German cruiser. *p9*.
Scheer, Admiral von. *p392*.

Schlieper, Rear-Admiral. *p154.*
Scotland Yard. London. *p331.*
Seamer. Near Scarborough. *p31, p45, p243, p279.*
Seaton Carew. *p403, p416, p455.*
Seaton Delaval. *p295.*
Selby. *p103, p316.*
Seydlitz. Flagship of Admiral Hipper. German battle-cruiser. Completed 1913, similar to *Moltke* and *Goeben*. Part of Hartlepool raiding group. Kapitän (Captain) zur See von Egidy. Survived Battle of Dogger Bank and Jutland. Surrendered at Armistice. Scuttled at Scapa Flow, June 1919. Raised for scrap, 1930. Specifications page 372. *p11, p105, p109, p113, p287, p295, p325, p326, p371, p372(p), p373, p375, p392, p397, p400, p441, p442, p455.*
Sharp, Captain George. Master of the SS *Hydro*. 134 Cromwell Road, Grimsby. *p326.*
Sheffield. *p354.*
Shipping Lost to Mines1914-1916 (list). *p507.*
Ships Engaged. December 1914 (list). *p508.*
Shotton. *p432.*
Sitwell, Lady Louisa. Widow of Sir George Sitwell 3rd Baronet. Bought *Wood End* in 1870 when son George, 4th Baronet, was 10 years old. Lady Louisa was a generous benefactor to Scarborough and was also keen on improving the morals of the townsfolk. Her son George married Lady Ida Denison, the third daughter of the 1st Earl of Londesborough in 1886. The couple had three children, all of whom were writers: Edith was born at *Wood End* on 07.09.1887 and died 09.12.1964; Osbert was born in London on 06.12.1892 and died 04.05.1969; Sacherverell was born at *Belvoir House*, the Crescent, on 15.11.1897. Sir George Sitwell was elected Member of Parliament for Scarborough in 1885 and again in 1892. He and his family lived at *Belvoir House* on the Crescent until 1904, when they moved into *Wood End*, where they stayed until 1929. Lady Ida Sitwell died in 1934 and Sir George Sitwell died in 1943. Scarborough Corporation bought *Wood End* in 1934 for £4,500. *p27, p55.*
Skegness. Wesleyan Sunday School. Sent message to Whitby. *p337.*
Sleights Institute. *p303, p349.*
Sleights. Near Whitby. *p303.*
Smith-Dorien, General Sir. *p5.*
Somme. *p3, p151, p332, p335, p441, p442, p455.*
South Africa. *p3.*
South Gare. *p293, p397, p403, p406, p407.*
South Shields. *p166.*
Southampton. British cruiser. *p115.*
Southwold. *p99.*
Spee, Vice-Admiral von. *p9.*
St Albans Corporation. Sent message to Whitby. *p320.*
St Julien. *p455, p456.*
Stafford. Town Council. Sent message to Whitby. *p337.*
Staithes. *p295, p325, p326, p343.*
Stamfordham. Private Secretary to George V. *p309.*
Stapleton. Vicar of Seamer. *p279.*
Strensall. *p103.*
Sunday Chronicle. Newspaper. *p147.*
Suvla Bay. *p3.*

Tägliche Rundschau. German newspaper. *p156.*
Tapken, Vice-Admiral. Hipper's second-in-command, aboard the *Von der Tann*. *p11, p113.*
Tate, William. Irish-American commanding 'Black Legion' at Fishguard. *p99.*
Tees. *p9, p325.*
Temple Newsam. Leeds. *p285.*
Terschelling. One of the West Frisian islands, in the North Sea, off the coast of the Netherlands. *p101, p111.*
Thames. *p155.*
Thirsk. North Yorkshire. *p322.*
Thornley. *p432.*
Tiger. British battle-cruiser, under Admiral Sir David Beatty. *p113, p287.*
Times, The. British newspaper. *p109, p149, p341.*
Tipperary. Ireland. *p241.*
Tirpitz, Admiral Alfred Friedrich von. (1849-1930). Born in Prussia. Joined Prussian Navy in 1865. He was ennobled in 1900 and rose to Lord High Admiral in 1911. As Secretary of State for the Imperial Navy (1897-1916) he raised a fleet to challenge British supremacy of the seas and acted as its commander between 1914 and 1916. Tirpitz advocated unrestricted submarine warfare and resigned when this policy was opposed. He was later to take a seat in the Reichstag. *p6(p), p142, p164, p311.*
Titanic. *p293.*
Torquay. Sent message. *p129.*
Trethowan, Miss. Mistress at Queen Margaret's School, Scarborough. *p277.*
Tunstall. Wesley Place Sunday School. Sent message to Whitby. *p337.*
Turner, Corporal. Yorkshire Hussars. *p235.*
Tussaud. *p307.*
Tyne. *p115, p371, p393.*
Tyrwhitt, Commodore. Commander of Harwich Force. *p101, p112, p115.*

U9. German submarine. *p9.*
U17. German submarine. *p9.*
U27. German submarine which guided raiders through to east coast. Kapitän (Captain) zur See Wegener. Oberleutnant (Lieutenant) Ahlefeld. *p9.*
U57. German submarine. See Captain Ritter von Georg.
U94. German submarine. *p394.*
Unity. British cruiser (3rd Cruiser Squadron) involved in the defence of Hartlepool. *p391.*

Vienna Extrablatt. German newspaper. *p157.*
Volta. Trawler damaged in Scarborough harbour. *p97.*

Von der Tann. Flagship of Rear Admiral Tapken. Germany's first large warship driven by modern turbine engines, country's first battle-cruiser. Completed 1910. Launched from Blohm & Voss shipyard, Hamburg. Part of Scarborough raiding group. Kapitän (Captain) zur See Hahn. Suffered damage during the British air-raid on Cuxhaven. Despite severe damage at Jutland remained afloat and escaped. Scuttled Scapa Flow, 1919. Raised for scrap, 1930. Specifications page 8. *p7, p8(p), p11, p13, p43, p109, p113, p140, p265, p287, p289, p326, p346, p416, p441, p442, p455.*

Waberthwaite. Cumberland. *p352.*

Warrender, Vice-Admiral Sir George John Scott. 7th Baronet of Lochend, East Lothian. Commanded the British force in pursuit of the German Scouting Group. *p113, p115, p117.*
Watson, Mrs H. Ramsgate. Sent message to Whitby. *p337.*
Weekly Despatch. Periodical. *p341.*
Wegener, Captain. See *U27.*
Weighill, Lieutenant E. Hilary. 5th Green Howards. On guard duty Wireless Sation and Electric Supply Works, Scarborough. *p54(p), 210(p).*
Welburn. Surveyor/Engineer. Employed to survey damage at Whitby. *p322.*
Wellfield. *p432.*
Western Front. *p3, p7, p9, p333, p453, p455.*
Wheatley Hall. *p432.*
Whitby Gazette. Newspaper. *p309, p311, p332, p339, p341, p354, p366.*
Whitby Museum. *p326.*
Whitby. *p105, p112, p115, p119, p120, p144, p145, p147, p149, p161, p269, p391, p392, p416, p441, p455.*
White Nab. Near Scarborough. *p43.*
Widenmann, Commander. See *Kolberg.*
Wingate. *p432.*
Withernsea Urban District Council. Sent message to Whitby. *p335.*

Yarmouth. Norfolk. *p109, p111, p442.*
York. *p31, p97, p103, p129, p203, p233, p243, p285, p325, p328.*
Yorkshire Hussars. *p43, p128(p), p228(p), p235, p237, p280(p).*
Yorkshire Post. Newspaper. *p327.*
Yorkshire Televison. *p441.*
Yorkshire. *p5, p405.*
Ypres. *p5, p442, p455.*
Yser Canal. *p245.*

Index S: Shipping Losses ~ North Sea 1914~1916

List of shipping lost to mines and causes unknown (most probable cause, mines) in the North Sea between 1914 and 1916.

Torpedo Boat 11. 263 tons.
Sunk 7th March 1916.
Amphion. Light Cruiser. 3,440 tons.
Sunk 6th August 1914.
Arethusa. Light Cruiser. 3,500 tons.
Sunk 11th February 1916.
Banyers. Hired trawler. 448 tons.
Sunk 6th January 1915. Off Scarborough.
C29. Submarine. 321 tons.
Sunk 29th August 1915.
C33. Submarine. 321 tons.
Sunk 4th August 1915. Cause unknown.
Charity. Hired drifter. 102 tons.
Sunk 24th October 1915. Cause unknown.
Copious. Fishing vessel. 100 tons.
Sunk 3rd November 1914. Off Yarmouth.
9 dead (including Skipper).
Coquette. Destroyer. 355 tons.
Sunk 7th March 1916.
Crathie. Hired trawler. 210 tons.
Sunk 27th August 1914. Off River Tyne.
D2. Submarine. 600 tons.
Sunk 25th November 1914.
Cause unknown.
D5. Submarine. 620 tons.
Sunk 3rd October 1914.
Deptford. Merchant vessel. 1,208 tons.
Sunk 24th February 1915.
Off Scarborough. 1 dead.
E3. Submarine. 791 tons.
Sunk 18th October 1914. Cause unknown.
E5. Submarine. 791 tons.
Sunk 7th March 1916. Cause unknown.
E6. Submarine. 791 tons.
Sunk 26th December 1915.
E16. Submarine. 805 tons.
Sunk 22nd August 1916. Cause unknown.
E24. Submarine. 807 tons.
Sunk 24th March 1916. Cause unknown.
E26. Submarine. 807 tons.
Sunk 6th July 1916. Cause unknown.
E30. Submarine. 807 tons.
Sunk 22nd November 1916.
Cause unknown.
E37. Submarine. 807 tons.
Sunk 1st December 1916. Cause unknown.
Earl Howard. Fishing vessel. 226 tons.
Sunk 11th December 1914.
Off Spurn Point. Cause unknown.
9 dead (including Skipper).
Elfrida. Merchant vessel. 2,624 tons.
Sunk 7th January 1915. Off Scarborough.
Elterwater. Merchant vessel. 1,228 tons.
Sunk 16th December 1914.
Off Scarborough. 6 dead.
Fauvette. Armed boarding steamer.
2,544 tons. Sunk 9th March 1916.
Garmo. Hired trawler. 203 tons.
Sunk 20th December 1914.
Off Scarborough.
Gem. Merchant vessel. 461 tons.
Sunk 25th December 1914.
Off Scarborough.
10 dead (including Master).
Golden Oriole. Fishing vessel. 50 tons.
Sunk 22nd January 1915. Off Lowestoft.
Khartoum. Merchant vessel. 3,020 tons.
Sunk 27th November 1914.
Off Spurn Point.
Lassoo. Destroyer. 1,010 tons.
Sunk 13th August 1916.
Lightning. Destroyer. 320 tons.
Sunk 30th June 1915.
Linaria. Merchant vessel. 3,081 tons.
Sunk 26th December 1914. Off Filey.
Lord Carnarvon. Fishing vessel. 50 tons.
Sunk 20th November 1914. Off Yarmouth.
10 dead (including Skipper).

Maori. Destroyer. 1,035 tons.
Sunk 7th May 1915.
Mary. Hired trawler. 256 tons.
Sunk 5th November 1914. Off Yarmouth.
Membland. Merchant vessel. 3,027 tons.
Sunk 15th February 1915.
Cause unknown.
20 dead (including Master).
Miura. Hired trawler. 257 tons.
Sunk 23rd August 1915. Off Yarmouth.
Night Hawk. Hired trawler. 287 tons.
Sunk 25th December 1914.
Off Scarborough.

Ocana. Fishing vessel. 260 tons.
Sunk 23rd December 1914.
Off Flamborough Head. 9 dead.
Orianda. Hired trawler. 273 tons.
Sunk 19th December 1914.
Off Scarborough.
Princess Beatrice. Hired trawler. 214 tons.
Sunk 5th October 1914. Off River Tyne.
Princess Olga. Merchant vessel. 998 tons.
Sunk 16th December 1914.
Off Scarborough.
Recolo. Fishing vessel. 170 tons.
Sunk off Spurn Point. 2 dead.
Sapphire. Fishing vessel. 289 tons.
Sunk 1st March 1915. Off Filey. 1 dead.
Speedy. Torpedo gunboat. 810 tons.
Sunk 3rd September 1914.
Off the Humber.
Speeton. Hired trawler. 205 tons.
Sunk 31st December 1915. Off Lowestoft.
Thomas W. Irvin. Hired trawler. 201 tons.
Sunk 27th August 1915. Off River Tyne.
Windsor. Fishing vessel. 172 tons.
Sunk 22nd January 1915.
Off Spurn Point.

Total: ***48 vessels***

Tonnage: ***41,165 tons***

Index T: Night Hawk

The survivors of minesweeper No.57, *Night Hawk*, which was sunk three and a half miles east of Scarborough, on Christmas Day, Friday 25th December 1914, by a mine. Five men drowned, one man died of injuries, seven survived.

ALSTON, John J. Grimsby.
BEE, Felix. Grimsby.
BROWN, Frederick. Grimsby.
BURNETT, J. Grimsby.
CROSMAN, W. H. Grimsby.
EVANS, Harry. Captain. Grimsby.
SENIOR, W. E. Sub-Lieutenant. Grimsby.

Note: CHAPPELL, Alfred. Chief Engineer. Cleethorpes. Age 28 (B: 1886). Died of injuries before being brought ashore.

Index U: Main Ships Engaged 1914

The main German and British ships engaged at Scarborough, Whitby and the Hartlepools on Wednesday, 16th December 1914.

GERMAN

Blücher - Fregattenkapitän Erdmann - Commander Erdmann - bombarded Hartlepool.
Derfflinger - Kapitän zur See von Reuter - Captain von Reuter - bombarded Scarborough & Whitby.
Kolberg - Fregattenkapitän Widenmann - Commander Widenmann - laid mine screen in North Sea off Filey & Flamborough Head.
Moltke - Kapitän zur See von Levetzow - Captain von Levetzow - bombarded Hartlepool.
Seydlitz - Kapitän zur See von Egidy - Captain von Egidy - (Flagship of Admiral Hipper) - bombarded Hartlepool.
U27 - Kapitän zur See Wegener - Captain Wegener - submarine which reconnoitered and guided German battle group through minefields.
U27 - Oberleutnant Ahlefeld - Lieutenant Ahlefeld - Wegener's second-in-command, acted as guide aboard Hipper's Flagship *Seydlitz*.
Von der Tann - Kapitän zur See Hahn - Captain Hahn - (Flagship of Rear Admiral Tapken) - bombarded Scarborough & Whitby.

BRITISH

C9 - Lieutenant-Commander C. L. M. Dering - part of Hartlepool Flotilla, dived and grounded whilst attempting to leave harbour.
Doon - Lieutenant-Commander Harry M. Fraser (appointed August 1914) - part of Hartlepool Flotilla, engaged enemy ships, hit and damaged, withdrew.
Forward - Commander Frederick P. Lodger-Symonds (appointed April 1914) - part of Hartlepool Flotilla, was not engaged.
Moy - Lieutenant-Commander Charles G. Naylor (appointed 24th October 1914) - part of Hartlepool Flotilla, engaged enemy ships 8.10am, withdrew.
Patrol - Captain Alan C. Bruce (appointed 27th January 1914) - part of Hartlepool Flotilla, hit twice while attempting to leave harbour, not engaged.
Test - Lieutenant-Commander Charles H. Knox-Little (appointed 24th August 1912) - part of Hartlepool Flotilla, engaged enemy ships, was hit, withdrew.
Waveney - Lieutenant-Commander Ralph W. H. Roberts (appointed 26th June 1914) - part of Hartlepool Flotilla, engaged enemy ships, withdrew.

Author's Appeal For Information

Information is sought on the incidents listed in the following 'Diary of Attacks'. If you have any information on any of them please contact the author (via the offices of the publisher).

Index V: German Attacks 1914~1918

DIARY OF RECORDED ATTACKS MADE AGAINST THE BRITISH MAINLAND

1914

3rd November
Battle-cruisers bombarded Yarmouth. Raiders attacked *HMS Halcyon* and scattered mines, one of which destroyed British submarine *D5*.

10th December
U-boats raided Dover - *U11* was lost.

16th December
Battle-cruisers *Moltke*, *Seydlitz* and *Blücher* bombarded the Hartlepools (8.10am). Engaged by Hartlepool's naval flotilla of light cruisers and two shore batteries. Battle-cruisers *Derfflinger* and *Von der Tann*, accompanied by light cruiser *Kolberg* (which laid mines off Flamborough Head), bombarded Scarborough at 8.00am, and Whitby at 9.00am.

24th December
Plane dropped bomb on Dover. Hole in a garden - no casualties. First raid on England.

25th December
Plane, over Sheerness, driven off before it could do any damage.

1915

19th January
Airship *L3* out of Cuxhaven attacked Yarmouth, King's Lynn, Snettisham and other Norfolk towns and villages; 4 killed, 15 wounded, 1 soldier wounded. First airship raid on England.

30th January
Submarine *U21* shelled Vickers works on Walney Island and sank three British steamers off Fleetwood, Lancashire.

21st February
Planes dropped bombs on Colchester, Coggeshall and Braintree, Essex, at night.

23rd February
Submarine attacked Folkestone.

14th April
Airship *L9* attacked the Tyne area.

16th April
Planes attacked Faversham and Sittingbourne. Airship dropped bombs in both Essex and Suffolk.

30th April
Airship *LZ38* attacked Ipswich and Bury St Edmunds.

10th May
Two airships, *LZ38* and *LZ39*, attacked Southend, Leigh-on-Sea and Westcliff in the early hours. 100 bombs dropped. 1 killed, 2 wounded. Damage £20,000.

17th May
Airship *LZ38* attacked Ramsgate.

26th May
Airship *LZ38* attacked Southend.

31st May
Airship *LZ38* attacked London, bombed East End; 7 killed, 35 wounded.

4th June
Zeppelin raid on Kent, Essex and Yorkshire.

6th June
Zeppelin raid on Hull, Grimsby and East Riding; 24 killed, 40 wounded. Airship *LZ39* sighted over Harwich.

12th June
Airship *LZ39* again sighted over Harwich.

15th June
Zeppelin raid on Durham and Northumberland; 18 killed, 72 wounded.

3rd July
Plane sighted over East Suffolk.

9th August
Zeppelin raid on Yorkshire, Suffolk and Dover; 17 killed, 21 wounded. Airship *L12* damaged by gunfire, destroyed near Ostend by aircraft.

12th August
Zeppelin raid on Suffolk and Essex; 6 killed, 25 wounded. One airship reached east coast, three turned back due to engine trouble.

16th August
U-boat shelled Parton, Harrington and Whitehaven on the Cumberland coast.

17th August
Zeppelin raid on London by naval airships *L10*, *L11* and *L14*. Also attacked Kent and Essex. Bombs dropped on Leyton and Leytonstone; 10 killed, 48 injured.

7th September
Zeppelin raid on London. Raiders included *L10*, *L11*, *L13*, *L14*, *L15*, *L16* and *LZ74*. Group also attacked Suffolk; 18 killed, 38 wounded.

8th September
Zeppelin raid on London. Raiders included *LZ77*. Group also attacked Norfolk and North Riding; 26 killed, 94 wounded. Damage £2,000,000.

11th September
Airship *LZ77* attacked Essex. No casualties reported.

12th September
Airship *LZ74* attacked Essex and Suffolk. No casualties reported.

13th September
Airship *LZ77* attacked Suffolk. No casualties reported. Planes attacked and bombed Margate; 2 killed, 6 wounded.

13th October
Zeppelin raid on London. All naval airships involved. Also attacked Norfolk, Suffolk and Home Counties; 71 killed, 128 wounded.

1916

23rd January
Planes attacked Dover and East Kent.

31st January
Zeppelin raid by *L11*, *L13*, *L14*, *L15*, *L16*, *L17*, *L19*, *L20* and *L21*, over Suffolk, Midlands and Yorkshire. Targets included Walsall, Dewsbury, Tipton, Burton-on-Trent, Ilkeston, Derby and Loughborough; 70 killed, 113 wounded.

9th February
Seaplanes attacked Margate and Broadstairs.

20th February
Four seaplanes attacked and bombed Lowestoft and Walmer.

29th February
Seaplane attacked Broadstairs and Margate. Crashed into sea, picked up by French.

5th March
Airships *L11*, *L13* and *L14* attacked Hull, East Riding, Lincoln, Leicester, Rutland and Kent; 18 killed, 53 wounded.
19th March
Four seaplanes attacked Deal, Dover, Margate and Ramsgate; 14 killed, 26 wounded. One raider destroyed by Flight-Commander Bone.
30th March
Airships *LZ81* and *LZ88* sighted over east coast.
31st March
Five Zeppelins, including *L15*, *LZ87*, *LZ90* and *LZ93*, attacked and bombed Lincoln, Essex and Suffolk. 90 bombs dropped; 48 killed, 64 wounded. One raider engaged at 9,000 feet and bombed by Lieutenant Brandon, RFC. *L15* hit by gunfire and fell into sea off Kentish Knock; crew of 17 captured.
1st April
Airships *L11* and *L17* out of Nordholz attacked Durham and the North Riding; 22 killed, 130 wounded.
2nd April
Six Zeppelins, including *LZ88* and *LZ90*, attacked London, East Suffolk, Northumberland and Scotland (bombs fell on Edinburgh and Leith); 13 killed, 24 wounded.
4th April
Airships *L11* and *L17* sighted over Norfolk.
5th April
Three airships, *L11*, *L13* and *L16* attacked Durham and Yorkshire; 1 killed, 9 wounded.
24th April
Three Zeppelins attacked Norfolk, Lincoln, Cambridge and Suffolk. Plane driven off from attack on Dover.
25th April
Ten airships, including *LZ87*, *LZ88*, *LZ93* and *LZ97*, attacked London, East Suffolk, Essex and Kent. Battle-cruiser squadron off Lowestoft for 30 minutes, engaged by local forces; 25 wounded. Jellicoe informed Admiralty at 4.20am 'enemy shelling Lowestoft'. Beatty, with Battle-cruiser Fleet, sailed towards Terschelling and narrowly missed cutting the ships off.
26th April
Airship *LZ87* attacked Margate.
2nd May
Five Zeppelins, including *L20* and *LZ98*, attacked Yorkshire, Northumberland and Scotland, 100 bombs dropped; 9 killed, 30 wounded.
3rd May
Plane attack on Deal; 4 wounded.
19th May
Seaplanes attacked Kent coast, Dover bombed. One raider brought down by British naval patrol off Belgian coast.
9th July
Plane raid over North Foreland and Dover.
11th July
U-boat shelled Seaham Harbour.
28th July
Zeppelin attack on Lincoln and Norfolk.
31st July
Zeppelin raid on Norfolk, Suffolk, Cambridge, Lincoln, Nottingham and Kent.
2nd August
Zeppelin raid on Norfolk, East Suffolk and Kent.
9th August
Zeppelin raid on Northumberland, Durham, Yorkshire, Hull and Norfolk; 10 killed, 16 wounded.
12th August
Seaplanes attacked Dover; 7 wounded.
23rd August
Airships *LZ97* and *LZ98* sighted over East Suffolk.
25th August
Zeppelin raid on London, East Suffolk, Essex and Kent; 9 killed, 40 injured.
2nd September
Zeppelin *SLXI* attempted to attack London.
3rd September
Thirteen Zeppelins, including *LZ90*, *LZ97*, *LZ98* and *SLXI*, attacked London, the East Riding, Lincolnshire, Nottingham, Norfolk, Suffolk, Cambridge, Huntingdonshire, Essex, Hertfordshire, Bedfordshire and Kent. One airship destroyed at Cuffley, Enfield, by Lieutenant Robinson, RFC; awarded VC. 4 killed, 12 wounded.
22nd September
Seaplane sighted over Dover.
23rd September
Twelve Zeppelins attacked London, Lincolnshire, Nottinghamshire, Norfolk and Kent. *L32* and *L33* brought down over Essex; one shot down in flames by British plane at Great Bursted, other brought down by gunfire near Mersea Island, crew surrendered. 40 killed, 130 wounded.
25th September
Seven Zeppelins attacked Lancashire, Yorkshire and Lincolnshire; 43 killed, 31 injured (16 casualties, Bolton, Lancashire).
1st October
Zeppelin raid on London, Lincolnshire, Norfolk, Cambridgeshire, Northamptonshire and Hertfordshire. Zeppelin brought down in flames at Potter's Bar by RFC. Lieutenant Brandon and Lieutenant Tempest awarded DSO. 1 killed, 1 wounded.
22nd October
Plane sighted over Sheerness.
23rd October
Plane attacked and bombed Margate; 2 wounded.
23rd November
Six torpedo-boat destroyers shelled the northern end of Downs, driven off by Ramsgate drifter night patrol.
26th November
Naval attack on Lowestoft. British armed trawler *Narval* sunk.
27th November
Zeppelin attack on Durham, Yorkshire, Staffordshire and Cheshire. 100 bombs dropped. One Zeppelin brought down over Durham coast by RFC, one damaged by gunfire and brought down off Norfolk coast by RFC. 4 killed, 37 wounded.
28th November
Plane raid on London. One plane brought down in France. 10 wounded.

1917

25th January
Torpedo-boat destroyer shelled Southwold.
25th February
Torpedo-boat destroyer raid on Broadstairs and Margate. British torpedo-boat destroyer engaged boats in English Channel. 2 killed.

1st March
Torpedo-boat destroyer raid, out of Zeebrugge, on Broadstairs.
16th March
Plane attack on Kent and Margate. Five Zeppelins attacked Kent and Sussex. Return flight, overtaken by fresh winds. Only *L40* and *L41* reached Ahlhorn. *L35* down at Dresden, *L42* at Jüterbog, *L39* destroyed by French gunfire over Compiègne following morning.
17th March
Plane raid over Kent.
18th March
Torpedo-boat destroyer raid on Kent coast. Ramsgate shelled. *HMS Paragon* torpedoed, British torpedo-boat destroyer *Llewellyn* damaged, but reached Dover.
5th April
Plane bombed Ramsgate.
21st April
Six torpedo-boat destroyers attempted a raid on Dover. *HMS Broke* rammed and sank *G85*, *HMS Swift* sank *G42*.
27th April
Torpedo-boat destroyers shelled Ramsgate. Raiders engaged by British monitor *Marshal Ney* and by 6-inch shore batteries.
7th May
Plane dropped four bombs in north-east London; 1 killed, 2 wounded.
23rd May
Five airships, *L40*, *L42*, *L43*, *L44* (Flag of Airship Commodore Captain Strasser) and *L45*, attacked Harwich and East Anglia: 3 killed, 16 wounded. *L43* struck by lightning on return flight to Nordholz but was undamaged.
25th May
Attack by 17 planes on Folkestone. Three planes brought down by Royal Naval Air Service out of Dover. 95 killed, 193 wounded.
5th June
Plane attack over Essex and Kent. Raiders intercepted off Ostend by British patrols out of Dunkirk. Two of sixteen destroyed, two more sent down out of control. 13 killed, 34 wounded.
13th June
Daylight attack by 15 Gothas on London, Margate and Essex. One raider brought down. 162 killed, 432 wounded.
17th June
Airship *L42* bombed Dover. London intended target, bad weather prevented it. Airships *L44*, *L45* and *L48*, unable to attack London, attacked Suffolk. *L48* brought down in flames by RFC.
4th July
Fourteen planes attacked Suffolk and Essex (Harwich). Two planes brought down in flames, a third damaged south-east of Ostend by British naval aircraft out of Dunkirk. 17 killed, 30 wounded.
7th July
Largest plane raid against British mainland to date. Twenty-four planes (including 3rd Air Squadron) attacked London and Margate in daylight. General Post Office bombed. 57 killed, 193 wounded. Four raiders brought down on return flight, one at the mouth of Thames, two 40 miles from east coast and fourth off River Scheldt. Two British pilots and one observer killed, another observer wounded. Two British planes destroyed, two more crashed. Combined casualties; 60 killed, 194 wounded.
22nd July
Approximately 21 planes of 3rd Air Squadron attacked Essex and Suffolk (Harwich and Felixstowe). Formation broken up and driven off. One raider brought down near Belgian coast by patrol of RFC. 13 killed, 26 wounded.
12th August
Twenty planes of 3rd Air Squadron attacked Essex and Kent (Southend and Margate). Gotha destroyed over Belgian coast. 32 killed, 46 wounded.
18th August
3rd Air Squadron attempted to reach east coast.
21st August
Two Zeppelins driven off Yorkshire coast.
22nd August
Ten planes from 3rd Air Squadron attacked Margate, Ramsgate and Dover. Three raiders brought down, five of supporting squadron lost. 12 killed, 25 wounded.
2nd September
Planes sighted over East Kent. Dover bombed; 1 killed, 6 wounded.
3rd September
3rd Air Squadron attacked Kent (Sheerness and Chatham). 132 killed, 96 wounded.
4th September
U-boat shelled Scarborough; 3 killed, several wounded. Twenty planes from 3rd Air Squadron attacked London and Home Counties at night. One plane brought down off Sheerness. 19 killed, 71 wounded.
24th September
Zeppelin attack on Yorkshire and Lincolnshire; 3 wounded. 3rd Air Squadron attacked London, Kent and Essex. 21 killed, 70 wounded.
25th September
3rd Air Squadron attacked London and Kent. 9 killed, 23 wounded.
28th September
Twenty planes from 3rd Air Squadron attacked Home Counties, driven off from London. One plane reported downed in Thames Estuary, a second off coast.
29th September
Attack on London by three groups of planes from 3rd Air Squadron, broken up by anti-aircraft fire. Three planes got through. 14 killed, 87 wounded.
30th September
3rd Air Squadron attacked London, Kent and Essex. Ten planes penetrated London's outer defences, five reached London. 14 killed, 38 wounded.
1st October
Attack on London by four groups of planes from 3rd Air Squadron. Small number got through and bombed south-west area. Kent and Essex also attacked. 11 killed, 41 wounded.
19th October
Attack by 11 airships on London, Midlands and eastern counties. One airship drifted over London with engines off and dropped three bombs. On return flight, strong wind pushed many over France, three brought down at Saint Clément,

Serquex and Sisteron. Two lost over the sea. Only six returned. 36 killed, 55 wounded.

29th October
Plane attack on Essex.

30th October
3rd Air Squadron attacked Calais and Sheerness.

31st October
3rd Air Squadron, comprising 30 planes in 7 groups, attacked London, Kent and Essex at night. Three planes penetrated London's defences. 10 killed, 22 wounded. Plane sighted over Dover.

6th December
Early morning attack by 25 planes of 3rd Bomber Squadron. Six planes reached London. Kent and Essex also attacked. Two planes brought down. 8 killed, 28 wounded.

18th December
3rd Bomber Squadron attacked east coast. Five planes reached London. Kent and Essex also attacked. One raider brought down by gunfire off Kent coast, another thought destroyed in the English Channel. 14 killed, 85 wounded.

22nd December
3rd Bomber Squadron attacked Kent coast. One plane forced down over land, crew captured.

1918

14th January
Torpedo-boat destroyers attacked Yarmouth. *SS Horsham* damaged. 4 killed, 8 wounded.

28th January
Fifteen planes from 3rd Bomber Squadron, in three groups, attacked London. Five planes penetrated London's defences. Later another one reached London. Some 70 British aircraft sent up. Raider brought down in flames over Essex. 67 killed, 166 wounded.

29th January
Plane attack on London, Kent and Essex; 10 killed, 10 wounded.

15th February
Dover shelled by U-boat; 1 killed, 7 wounded.

16th February
Six planes attacked London. One penetrated defences. 12 killed, 6 wounded.

17th February
Seven planes attacked London. One penetrated defences. 21 killed, 32 wounded.

18th February
Planes attacked London.

7th March
Eight planes attacked London. Two penetrated defences. 23 killed, 39 wounded.

12th March
Three Zeppelins attacked Yorkshire and Hull; 1 killed.

13th March
Zeppelin attack on Durham and Hartlepool; 8 killed, 39 wounded.

12th April
Zeppelin attack on Lincolnshire, Lancashire and Warwick; 7 killed, 20 wounded.

19th May
3rd Bomber Squadron attacked London. Five raiders destroyed, two others ditched in flames into sea. 49 killed, 177 wounded.

17th June
Planes attacked Kent.

5th August
Five airships off East Anglia. *L70*, Germany's most modern airship with Commodore Captain Strasser aboard, brought down in flames 40 miles from land. Last attempt of the war to attack British mainland.

AIR AND SEA RAIDS ON GREAT BRITAIN

Military Personnel:

Killed: *310*
Wounded: *551*

Civilians:

Killed : *1,260*
(554 men, 411 women, 295 children)
Wounded: *3,490*
(1,508 men, 1,210 women, 772 children)

Total casualties: 5,611

Index W: Citation

Leeds Rifles ~ *Croix de Guerre*

The Leeds Rifles, 8th Battalion West Yorkshire Regiment were awarded the French *Croix de Guerre* (mentioned on page 117) the citation for which was contained in General Order no.430 of 10th December 1918 and signed by the French General Guillaumat, the General Officer Commanding the Fifth Army. The citation read:

> *A most distinguished battalion. Under the energetic command of Lieutenant-Colonel Norman Ayrton England, it took a brilliant part in the hard fighting between the 20th and the 30th July which resulted in the capture of the valley of the Ardre. On the 23rd July 1918, after forcing a way through the thick undergrowth of the Bois de Petit Champs, it carried an important position in the face of sustained fire of enemy forces, and held it in spite of heavy losses and the determined efforts of the enemy to recapture it.*

The French only conferred this honour on two other British regiments - the Devonshires and the Shropshire Light Infantry - and a battery of the Royal Field Artillery.

Photograph Acknowledgements

Note: a proportion of the photographs used have had their captions altered where information has been available to correctly identify a subject or person. In some cases this was impossible and the original captions have been attached. If there are errors I apologise for this.

Cover Illustration: The painting *'Remember Scarborough'* by Edith M. Kemp-Welch, showing Britannia exhorting the populace to avenge the town which is seen burning in the background, was painted following the bombardments in 1914 and was presented to the town on 13th December 1915. It was used by the Parliamentary Recruitment Committee in poster form to aid recruitment. The painting now hangs in Scarborough's Town Hall. Edith Kemp-Welch, who exhibited between 1898 and 1939, was from Bushey, Hertfordshire and was best known for her miniatures. She was the sister of Lucy E. Kemp-Welch.

Author's Portrait: Mike Morrell, Top Hat Photography: p457.
Author's Collection: v, 3, 28 (1), 30, 32 (1), 36 (1), 64 (1), 74 (2&4), 76 (1&2), 78 (2), 80 (2), 84 (5), 88 (2), 94 (1), 104 (4), 110 (1), 128 (2), 143 (2), 183 (3), 188 (2&3), 192 (1), 195 (1), 198 (1&4), 212 (3&5), 234 (2), 246 (3), 250 (2&4), 252, 254 (5), 270 (2&3), 274 (5), 278 (1&4), 284 (1,3&4), 292 (2), 296 (3), 340 (2), 364 (1), 396 (4), 402 (2), 408 (2&5), 418 (4), 454 (2,3&4).
Amalgamated Press: 6 (2&3), 128 (3,4,5,6&8), 183 (1&2), 402 (3&4), 414 (1), 418 (1).
Lucy Askew: 258.
Raoul Cunningham: 168, 180.
E. T. W. Dennis & Son: 176 (4), 178 (1), 183 (5).
Devon & Dorset Regimental Archive: 294 (2), 324 (3&4), 438 (4).
Eva Emmett: 353 (1).
Green Howards Regimental Museum: 2, 4 (2&3), 98 (1).
Greenhill Books: 8, 10, 12, 372, 374, 376.
Peter Helmore: 324 (1&2).
Robert Hughes: 18 (1,2&4), 36 (2,3,4&5), 44 (4), 50 (1), 52 (5), 80 (3&4), 84 (1,3&4), 94 (2), 102, 138 (1), 148 (3), 153 (2&3), 214, 216, 228 (2), 230 (2,3&4), 236 (1,2,3,4&5), 240 (4&5), 242 (1&5), 278 (1,2,3,4&6), 280 (2&3).
Hull Central Library: 276, 282.
'I Was There': 6 (1), 408 (3), 418 (2).
'Illustrated War Record': 114 (2&4), 116 (1&4), 118 (1).
Trevor Land: 126 (2), 270 (1), 266 (1).
Shirley Langdale: 454 (1).
Dick Martin: 24 (2), 38 (2), 50 (2), 153 (1), 188 (1), 234 (1), 296 (1&4), 302 (1,2&7), 317 (3), 340 (4), 350, 396 (1,2&3), 402 (1&5), 414 (2&3), 418 (3), 421, 430 (1,3,4&5).
Sydney McCloy: 206.
Jack Middleton: 358 (1), 362.
David Mould: 178 (2).
Jessie Muncer: 353 (2), 356, 358 (2).
Anne Pilling: 294 (1), 438 (1,2&3).
Aubrey Reeve: 190.
Betty Rose: 210 (A).
Scarborough Pictorial (& Scarborough Mercury Company): 4 (1&4), 20, 28 (2&3), 32 (2), 38 (1), 44 (3), 52 (1,2,3,4&6), 54, 58 (3), 60 (2), 64 (2), 66 (2), 74 (3), 78 (3), 84 (2), 98 (2,3&4), 122, 124, 128 (7), 132, 136 (1), 138 (2), 148 (2), 173, 176 (1,2 &3), 178 (2,4&5), 194 (3), 196 (3), 198 (2&3), 200, 210, 212 (4), 220 (3), 224 (1&2), 226, 232 (1), 240 (1,2,3&6), 258 (4), 244 (2&5), 246 (1&2), 272, 274 (1,3&4), 278 (5), 284 (2).
Simon Smith: 24 (1&3), 44 (1&2), 60 (3&4), 74 (1), 80 (1), 96, 104 (1), 110 (2), 126 (1), 128 (1), 148 (1&4), 160 (2&3), 188 (4), 194 (4), 196 (1&4), 212 (2), 220 (1&4), 224 (3), 228 (3), 234 (3), 248, 250 (1&3), 264 (1&3), 270 (4), 274 (2).
Sydney Smith: 266 (2&3).
W. H. Smith Directory: 118 (2).
Susan Stobart: 408 (4), 418 (5).
Jack Taylor: 32 (3), 36 (6), 38 (3), 58 (1,2&4), 60 (1), 64 (3), 66 (1&3), 68, 70, 76 (3), 78 (1), 88 (1&3), 94 (3), 104 (2&3), 110 (3&4), 136 (2), 138 (3), 143 (1&3), 160 (1), 171, 176 (5), 185, 192 (2&3), 194 (2), 196 (2), 212 (1), 220 (2), 228 (1), 230 (1), 232 (2), 236 (6), 242 (2,3&6), 244 (1,3&4), 254 (1,2,3&4), 262, 264 (2&4).
Twenty Years After: 114 (1&3), 116 (2&3).
War Illustrated: 408 (1).
Janet Webster: 183 (4), 286, 288.
Peter Wharton: 344.
Whitby Museum: 300 (1,2&3), 302 (3,4,5&6), 310 (1,3&4), 313, 315, 317 (1,2&4), 338, 340 (1&3), 348 (2,3&4), 364 (2&3).
Eva & Tom Wood: 292 (1&3), 296 (2), 300 94), 310 (2), 340 (5), 348 (1), 430 (2).

I would like to sincerely thank all of the above for the use of their photographs which have greatly enhanced this work.

General Acknowledgements

I would like to thank the following (listed in alphabetical order) for their generous help with the research and production of this work. This is my 'Roll of Honour' and I hope all those named feel as proud of this book as I do.

ANDERSON, Ron, for providing an account and family information.
ASKEW, Lucy, for providing an account, family information and photographs.
BARTHOLEMEW, Tony, for taking the photo of the painting for the cover.
BELFITT, Marie, for uncovering the truth about Alice Painter.
BURKE, Dorothy, for providing family information.
COUNTY RECORD OFFICE, NORTHALLERTON, for permission to reproduce the Frank Drake letter.
CUNNINGHAM, Adrian and Raoul, for providing an account, family information and photographs.
DENNIS, E.T.W. & Sons, for permission to reproduce material from the 1915 souvenir booklet *'The German Raid on Scarborough'*.
DEVON & DORSET REGIMENT. Lieutenant-Colonel N. Parmley, Curator of the Keep Military Museum, for assistance with the 7th (Cyclist) Battalion Devonshire Regiment, and the Regimental Headquarters (Mr L. Murphy) for permission to reproduce material from the Devonshire Regiment's archives.
DICKINSON, Kenneth, for the loan of material.
EMMETT, Eva, for providing an account, family information and photographs.
FOSTER, John, for providing an account and family information.
FRISKNEY, Len, for providing information on *U57* and its Captain, Carl Siegfried Ritter von Georg.
GRAND HOTEL. Michael Prendergast, for providing information.
GREEN HOWARDS REGIMENTAL MUSEUM. Lieutenant-Colonel Neil McIntosh, for permission to reproduce material from Regimental and Battalion records. Major Roger Chapman and Steve Rarity, for their assistance in tracking down archive material.
GREENHILL BOOKS. Lionel Leventhal, for permission to reproduce material from 'German Warships of World War One'.
HALL, Ian, for assistance with the 8th West Yorkshire Regiment (medals).
HALL, Monika, for German newspaper translations undertaken for David Mould.
HALLIDAY, James, for family information.
HARRISON, Michael, for providing an account and family information.
HARTLEPOOL MUSEUMS SERVICE. Elizabeth Law, Collections Manager, for material and assistance on the Hartlepools.
HELMORE, Peter, for providing information and photographs on the 7th Devonshires.
HOLTBY COLLECTION. Jo Edge & J. A. Wilkinson, Hull Central Library, for permission to reproduce material from the collection. The majority of the collection was donated by Winifred's friend and Literary Executor, Vera Brittain. Donations continue from people who knew or worked with her. The collection holds thousands of items from her life and work. At the time of writing the collection was undergoing a two-year programme of conservation and cataloguing. The aim is to preserve it and allow greater public access to anyone interested in the life and work of one of Yorkshire's most remarkable 20th century writers.
HOPKINSON, Lily, for providing an account and family information.
HUGHES, David, for providing information on the Hartlepool War Memorials.
HUGHES, Robert, for providing an account, family information and photographs.
HUNTER, Derek, for providing family information.
IMPERIAL WAR MUSEUM. Dr John Bullen, Department of Exhibits & Firearms, for making available his research and published material. Colin Bruce, Department of Printed Books, for providing the names of the German warship captains.
LAND, Trevor, for the loan of material.
LIDDLE COLLETION. Peter Liddle, (Founder and former Keeper), for allowing me access to the collection.
MARTIN, Dick, for the loan of material.
MCCLOY, David and Patricia, for providing an account, family information and photographs.
MIDDLETON, Mr & Mrs, for providing an account, family information and photographs.
MITCHELL, Austin, MP, for his support, the video tape of the 1977 'Calendar' broadcast, and for writing the Preface.
MOULD, David, for putting his correspondence at my disposal, for permission to reproduce from his book *'Remember Scarborough 1914!'*, and for writing the Foreword.
MUNCER, Jessie, for providing an account, family information and photographs.
NATIONAL ARMY MUSEUM. Alastair Massie, for providing the account (ref: 9409-14) of William Lunn MM of the Green Howards.
ORDNANCE SURVEY, for providing contemporary street maps of Scarborough, Whitby and Hartlepool.
PICKUP, Alan Wales, for providing family information.
PICKUP, Colin and Nina, for providing family information and photographs.
PILLING, Anne M., for providing information and photographs on the 7th Devonshires.
PLUNTON, Bob, for additional information on *Dunollie*.
PODMORE, Tony, for assistance with the history of the Green Howards Territorials.
PUBLIC RECORD OFFICE, for permission to use material.
REEVE, Aubrey, for providing an account, family information and photographs.
ROYAL ARTILLERY HISTORICAL TRUST. J. M. Phillips, Historical Secretary, for providing information on the Hartlepools.
ROYAL NATIONAL LIFEBOAT INSTITUTION. Barry Cox, Librarian, for providing extensive information on the work of the east coast lifeboats during the 1914/15 period.
ROYAL NAVAL MUSEUM. Allison Wareham, Head Librarian, for providing information on shipping losses in the North Sea.
SAVILE, Sir Jimmy, for his personal message and support.
SAVILLE, Cyril, for providing an account and family information.

SCARBOROUGH BOROUGH COUNCIL. Mike Stevenson and Chris Hall, Planning Department, for assistance with the maps. Dr Jane Mee, for assistance with obtaining the cover illustration which is reproduced by permission of Scarborough Museums & Gallery, Department of Tourism and Leisure Services, Scarborough Borough Council.

SCARBOROUGH LIBRARY. David Fay, Group Librarian, for permission to reproduce material from the 'Scarborough Room' archive.

SEWELL, Stanley, for providing an account and family information.

SHAW, Marion, author of 'The Clear Stream: A Life of Winifred Holtby' and literary executor of the Winifred Holtby Estate, for permission to reproduce material.

SHILETTO, Carl, for donating his own research and collection of memorabilia.

SLY, John, Editor of Coin & Medal News, for his research on my behalf at the Public Record Office.

SMITH, Captain Sydney, and Liz Costello, for providing an account, family information and photographs.

SMITH, Simon, for providing photographs from his extensive postcard collection.

STEFFANSON, Carl, from Create Publishing Services (part of the Redwood Group), for valuable assistance over a number of technical matters concerned with pre-production.

WEBSTER, Janet, for providing family information and photographs.

WHARTON, Peter, for the loan of material.

WHITBY LIBRARY. The reference section, for helping with research into the bombardment and the *Rohilla* disaster.

WHITBY MUSEUM, and the Whitby Literary & Philosophical Society, for unprecedented access to, and permission to reproduce from their archives. I would especially like to thank SYD BARNETT, who spent a considerable amount of time assisting my research.

WHITEHEAD, Dorothy, for providing an account and family information.

WOOD, Tom, for assistance with research.

YORKSHIRE REGIONAL NEWSPAPERS. The Editors of the *Scarborough Evening News* and the *Whitby Gazette*, for permission to reproduce material from the titles of 1914-1918.

Thanks for continued and sustained moral support also go to:

Shirley and Mike Marsay, Margaret and Andrew Pettener, Ray, Joan and Steve Flint of Santona Publications, Joy and James Pickup, Margaret Mayes, Ray Westlake and Tonie Holt.

If there is anyone I have forgotten to mention I apologise most profusely.

Special thanks go to:

WARD, John, for kind and very generous permission to use material from his book 'Dawn Raid' (see sources).

Also the following people who assisted John and whose material he put at my disposal;

D. Anderson, J. Anderson, J. Ballantine, H. Bell, W. Bennison, G. N. Benson, W. Boagey, D. P. Brosch, M. Burke, S. Burton, D. Bygott, J. Cassidy, T. S. Cassidy, C. Chambers, T. C. Charman, S. Claydon, J. J. Colledge, F. Collier, J. Davison, W. Davison, H. Dennis, J. Dixon, W. Dixon, A. E. Duffield, D. Ellmers, J. Forbes, T. Forbes, W. Frankland, O. Groos, K. Haberman, E. Hall, R. Harrison, L. Hewitson, M. Hoban, R. Horsley, E. Hunter, F. Hutchinson, F. Jacques, T. Kennedy, A. Lacey, W. H. Larkin, C. Leslett, F. M. Lavin, E. Law, A. Lee, D. Lupton, J. Major, H. Middleton, F. Miller, E. M. Murray, C. McBean, T. M. Neill, E. A. Noble, T. Pailor, E. Rickerby, S. B. Roberts, L. U. Scholl, S. H. Shannon, F. Sutton, M. Smith, N. Tabley, T. M. Temple, J. B. Tindale, H. Tyson, R. Tyson, J. Waller, M. Waller, C. J. Watson, I. M. Ward, R. Wood; also the following: Gray Art Gallery and Museum; Stiftung Deutches Schiffahrtsmuseum; World Ship Society; National Maritime Museum; 'Deutches Museum Munich; Northern Daily Mail; Mail Hartlepool.

Extra special thanks go to:

CROWTHER, Diane, Senior Editor at Great Northern Publishing, for her care with the numerous drafts of the manuscript and her invaluable help in creating and verifying the various indexes contained herein.

. . . and finally, but above all else, I acknowledge my debt to

GORDON RICHARD CROWTHER (1939-1997)

and his generosity which has made all of this possible.

His warmth of spirit and appetite for life are sorely missed.

Main Reference Materials

Adelson, R., *Mark Sykes - Portrait of an Amateur*, J. Cape, 1975.
Ayton Women's Institute, *The History of Ayton* (Privately Printed), Ayton Women's Institute.
Bailey, Staff Sergeant B., *The Artillery Defence of Hartlepool*, The Journal of the Royal Artillery, 1975.
Banbury, Major P., *The Sledmere Cross* (unpublished), 1996.
Churchill, Winston S., *The World Crisis 1911-1918 - Abridged and Revised*, Thornton Butterworth, 1931.
Dupey and Dupey, *The Collins Encyclopedia of Military History*, HarperCollins, 1993.
Goldrick, James, *The King's Ships were at Sea,* Tri-Service Press Limited.
Hammerton, Sir John, Editor, *'I was There!', Volume 1, British Pluck and Luck at the Hartlepools,* The Waverley Book Co. Ltd., London.
Haythornthwaite, Philip J., *The World War One Source Book*, Arms and Armour Press, 1994.
Holt, Tonie and Valmai, *In Search of the Better 'Ole*, Milestone, 1985.
James, Brigadier E. A., *British Regiments 1914-1918*, Naval and Military Press, 1993.
Jarvis, S. D. & D. B, *The Cross of Sacrifice Volume 1, Officers who died in the service of British, Indian and East African Regiments and Corps 1914-1919*, Roberts Medals, 1993.
Laffin, John, *A Western Front Companion*, Alan Sutton Publishing, 1994.
Latham, Brigadier H. B., *The Bombardment of the Hartlepools*, The Journal of the Royal Artillery.
Martin, Sydney, *The Rohilla*, unpublished.
Mould, David H., *Remember Scarborough 1914!*, Hendon Publishing, 1978.
Murley, Captain W. A., *The Bombardment of the Hartlepools*, The Journal of the Royal Artillery.
Pope & Wheal, S. and E. A., *The Macmillan Dictionary of the First World War*, Macmillan, 1995.
Powell, Colonel G., *The History of the Green Howards - 300 Years of Service*, Arms & Armour, 1992.
Robson, Lieutenant-Colonel L., *Bombardment of the Hartlepools*, The Journal of the Royal Artillery, 1922.
Stevenson, J. R., *Accumulated diaries and papers* (unpublished).
Swinton, Major General Sir Ernest, *Twenty Years After*, Newnes, 1938.
Thompson, B., *The Great War Dead of Ayton* (unpublished), 1986.
Tovey & Podmore, Colonel W. J. and Major A. J., *Once a Howard - Twice a Citizen*, Volunteers Press, 1995.
Ward, J. M., *Dawn Raid*, Printability Publishing, 1989/92.
Wylly, Colonel H. C., *The Green Howards in the Great War*, Privately Printed, 1926.
Wyrall, E., *The History of the 50th Division*, Lund Humphries, 1939.
Yorke, Major F. A., *The Bombardment of the Hartlepools*, The Journal of the Royal Artillery, 1930.

The Times Diary & Index of the Great War 1914-1918, Hayward 1985.
The Macmillan Encyclopaedia, Macmillan London Limited, 1988.
Kelly's Directory of the North and East Ridings of Yorkshire, Kelly's Directories Limited London, 1913.
The Scarborough, Filey, Scalby & District Directory 1914, W. H. Smith & Son, Scarborough, 1914.
The Scarborough, Filey, Scalby & District Directory 1915, W. H. Smith & Son, Scarborough, 1915.
German Warships of World War One - Royal Navy's Official Guide to Capital Ships, Cruisers, Destroyers, Submarines and Small Craft, Greenhill Books, Lionel Leventhal Limited, 1992.
Jane's Fighting Ships of World War One, Studio Editions, 1990.
A German Crime - Bombardment of Scarborough, December 16th 1914, Scarborough Mercury Company Limited, 1915.
Leeds and the Amateur Military Tradition - The Leeds Rifles, Patricia Mary Morris, 1983, thesis unpublished.
Memorial of the German East Coast Raids and Bombardment by Sea and Air, Hood & Co. Ltd., 1915.
Scarborough Pictorial for the period 1914-1918.
Scarborough Evening News for the period 1914-1918.
Whitby Gazette for the period 1914-1918.
Bridlington Chronicle, 1915.
The German Raid on Scarborough, E. T. W. Dennis and Sons, 1915.
The German Raid on Whitby, Abbey Press, 1915.
The German Raid on Scarborough, Charles John Taylor, unpublished, 1915.
Living in the Danger Zone, Major A. B. Brockwell, unpublished.
Scarborough Municipal School Magazine, 1914.
Scarborough Fair, A. S. Taylor, unpublished, 1976.
Battle Honours Awarded for the Great War, Ray Westlake, 1992.
Officers died in the Great War, 1914-1919, Hayward & Son, 1988.
Soldiers died in the Great War, 1914-1919, Hayward & Son, 1989.
The Official History of the Great War, France and Belgium 1914, Volumes 1&2, Imperial War Museum/Battery Press, 1995.
The Official History of the Great War, France and Belgium 1915, Volume 1, Imperial War Museum/Battery Press, 1995.

Contemporary street maps of the three towns dating from 1912 and 1919 provided by the Ordnance Survey.

Available Now . . .

PART ONE OF THE
WAR OF THE YORKSHIRE GURKHAS

BAPTISM OF FIRE

The 5th Green Howards
at the Battle of St Julien,
during the Second Battle of Ypres,
April 1915

This unique book tells the story of the young men, volunteers from Yorkshire and the north-east, away from home for the first time, who stepped into the breach in the allied line in April 1915 and, alongside the lion-hearted Canadians, brought to a halt the advancing might of the German Army.

Despite poison gas, a withering bombardment, lack of supplies and fresh water the Territorials of the 5th Green Howards stood their ground and did all that was asked of them in this, their first action of the Great War.

Indeed, such was their fighting ferocity that it earned them the nickname 'The Yorkshire Gurkhas'; a reputation they would live up to time and again as they fought in all the major engagements on the Western Front.

Here, together for the first time, is a sterling narrative account of that battle and the thoughts and feelings of the men who fought it. Here too is their poetry, evocative of both their innocence and their courage. Alongside the text are their photographs, many published for the first time in over eighty years, and with them the biographical details of the men the Green Howards are proud to call 'The Yorkshire Gurkhas', the men who underwent their 'Baptism Of Fire' at St Julien in April 1915.

Available direct from the publisher for just £7.99 (postage and packing free).
Add your name to our mailing list and get substantial discounts on all our titles.

DETAILS:

Title:	**BAPTISM OF FIRE**
ISBN:	0-9535204-0-4
Author:	Mark Marsay
Genre:	Non-Fiction/Military History
Length:	224 pages - black and white
Size:	130mm x 197mm (portrait)
Cover:	paperback - full colour
Cover Price:	**£7.99**

Great Northern Publishing
PO Box 202
Scarborough
North Yorkshire
YO11 3GE

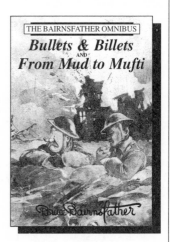

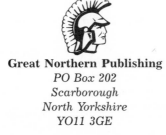